THE SELECTED LETTERS OF

TENNESSEE WILLIAMS

VOLUME II • 1945–1957

BY TENNESSEE WILLIAMS

PLAYS

Baby Doll & Tiger Tail
Camino Real
Candles to the Sun
Cat on a Hot Tin Roof
Clothes for a Summer Hotel
Fugitive Kind
The Glass Menagerie
A Lovely Sunday for Creve Coeur
Mister Paradise and Other One-Act Plays
Not About Nightingales
The Notebook of Trigorin
Something Cloudy, Something Clear
Spring Storm
Stairs to the Roof
Stopped Rocking and Other Screen Plays
A Streetcar Named Desire
Sweet Bird of Youth

THE THEATRE OF TENNESSEE WILLIAMS, VOLUME I
Battle of Angels, A Streetcar Named Desire, The Glass Menagerie
THE THEATRE OF TENNESSEE WILLIAMS, VOLUME II
The Eccentricities of a Nightingale, Summer and Smoke, The Rose Tattoo, Camino Real
THE THEATRE OF TENNESSEE WILLIAMS, VOLUME III
Cat on a Hot Tin Roof, Orpheus Descending, Suddenly Last Summer
THE THEATRE OF TENNESSEE WILLIAMS, VOLUME IV
Sweet Bird of Youth, Period of Adjustment, The Night of the Iguana
THE THEATRE OF TENNESSEE WILLIAMS, VOLUME V
The Milk Train Doesn't Stop Here Anymore, Kingdom of Earth (The Seven Descents of Myrtle), Small Craft Warnings, The Two-Character Play
THE THEATRE OF TENNESSEE WILLIAMS, VOLUME VI
27 Wagons Full of Cotton and Other Short Plays
THE THEATRE OF TENNESSEE WILLIAMS, VOLUME VII
In the Bar of a Tokyo Hotel and Other Plays
THE THEATRE OF TENNESSEE WILLIAMS, VOLUME VIII
Vieux Carré, A Lovely Sunday for Creve Coeur, Clothes for a Summer Hotel, The Red Devil Battery Sign

27 Wagons Full of Cotton and Other Plays
The Two-Character Play
Vieux Carré

POETRY

Collected Poems
In the Winter of Cities

PROSE

Collected Stories
Hard Candy and Other Stories
One Arm and Other Stories
The Roman Spring of Mrs. Stone
The Selected Letters of Tennessee Williams, Volume I
The Selected Letters of Tennessee Williams, Volume II
Where I Live: Selected Essays

Tennessee Williams, ca. 1956

THE SELECTED LETTERS OF

TENNESSEE WILLIAMS

VOLUME II • 1945–1957

EDITED BY ALBERT J. DEVLIN

CO-EDITED BY NANCY M. TISCHLER

A NEW DIRECTIONS BOOK

In memory of
Lyle Leverich, Dick Leavitt, and Jordan Massee
friends of Tennessee

The Selected Letters of Tennessee Williams, Volume II, is published by arrangement with The University of the South, Sewanee, Tennessee.

Design by Sylvia Frezzolini Severance
Manufactured in the United States of America
New Directions Books are printed on acid-free paper.
First published clothbound by New Directions in 2004
Published simultaneously in Canada by Penguin Books Canada Limited

Library of Congress Cataloging-in-Publication Data

Williams, Tennessee, 1911-1983.
[Correspondence. Selections]
The selected letters of Tennessee Williams / edited by Albert J. Devlin
co-edited by Nancy M. Tischler.
p. cm.
Includes index.
Contents: v. 2. 1945-1957
ISBN 0-8112-1600-4 (alk. paper)
1. Williams, Tennessee, 1911-1983—Correspondence. 2. Dramatists, American—20th century—Correspondence. I. Devlin, Albert J. II. Tischler, Nancy Marie Patterson. III. Title.
PS3545.I5365 Z48 2000
812'.54—dc21
[B] 99-087398

New Directions books are published for James Laughlin
by New Directions Publishing Corporation,
80 Eighth Avenue, New York, NY 10011

CONTENTS

LIST OF ILLUSTRATIONS

Page iv, frontispiece: By permission of the Harry Ransom Humanities Research Center, University of Texas at Austin (hereafter HRC).

Page 1: Tennessee Williams, Dallas, 1945. From the collections of the Texas/Dallas History and Archives Division, Dallas Public Library, used by permission.

Page 8: Tennessee Williams with Bill Liebling and Audrey Wood. Courtesy of the Jordan Massee Collection.

Page 27: James Laughlin, founder of New Directions Publishing Corporation. From the New Directions Archive.

Page 52: Tennessee Williams and Pancho Rodriquez, New Orleans. Courtesy of the Richard F. Leavitt Collection, University of Tennessee (hereafter Leavitt Collection).

Page 90: Pancho Rodriguez, Margo Jones, and Walter Dakin, New Orleans, 1947. By permission of the HRC.

Page 91: Tennessee Williams and Irene Selznick. Leavitt Collection.

Page 121: Thomas Hart Benton, *The Poker Night*. By permission of T.H. Benton and R.P. Benton Testamentary Trusts/Licensed by VAGA, New York, NY.

Page 135: The principal Broadway cast of *A Streetcar Named Desire*, 1947. Leavitt Collection.

Page 156: Tennessee Williams and Gore Vidal, Rome, 1948. Courtesy of Gore Vidal.

Page 182: Jo Mielziner, full set design for *Summer and Smoke*, 1948. From the New Directions Archive.

Page 209: Rehearsal of *Summer and Smoke* (1948). Tennessee Williams, Margaret Phillips, Margo Jones, and Tod Andrews. Leavitt Collection.

Page 214: Thomas Hart Benton, *The Poker Night*. By permission of T.H. Benton and R.P. Benton Testamentary Trusts/Licensed by VAGA, New York, NY.

Page 223: Tennessee Williams and Frank Merlo. Leavitt Collection.

Page 227: Tennessee Williams and Luchino Visconti. Leavitt Collection.

Page 257: Carson McCullers and director Harold Clurman examining the script of *The Member of the Wedding* (1950). Copyright Eileen Darby Images, Inc.

Page 276: Tennessee Williams and Grandfather Dakin, Key West. Leavitt Collection.

Page 304: Tennessee Williams, Irene Selznick, and the "clown," Oliver Evans. Leavitt Collection.

Page 340: Tennessee Williams and the "legendary" Paul Bigelow. Courtesy of the Jordan Massee Collection.

Page 347: Tennessee Williams and mannequin. Photograph by Sanford Roth. From the Sanford Roth Collection, courtesy of the Academy of Motion Picture Arts and Sciences.

Page 350: Elia Kazan directing Vivien Leigh and Kim Hunter in *A Streetcar Named Desire* (1951). By permission of the Wesleyan University Cinema Archives.
Page 360: Boris Aronson, *The Rose Tattoo* (1951). By permission of the HRC.
Page 367: Christopher Isherwood. Photograph by Caskey; from the New Directions Archive.
Page 373: Cheryl Crawford, founding member of The Group Theatre and The Actors Studio. Photograph by Carl Van Vechten, used by permission of the Van Vechten Trust. From the Beinecke Library, Yale University.
Page 409: postcard, "CALLED." Courtesy of the Jordan Massee Collection.
Page 418: Edwina and Tennessee Williams, Key West. Leavitt Collection.
Page 428: Davis Patty, Walter Dakin, and Tennessee Williams, Columbus, Mississippi, 1952. Leavitt Collection.
Page 431: Elia Kazan examining the script of *Camino Real* (1953). Leavitt Collection.
Page 465: Lemuel Ayers, full set design for *Camino Real* (1953). From the New Directions Archive.
Page 471: Margo Jones and Brooks Atkinson, Dallas. From the collection of the Texas/Dallas History and Archives Division, Dallas Public Library.
Page 478: Tennessee Williams and Donald Windham, Houston, 1953. Photocolor, Houston, Texas.
Page 485: Paul Bowles, Tangier. Photographer unknown. Courtesy of Virginia Spencer Carr.
Page 495: Tennessee Williams and Maria Britneva on the Lido, 1953. From the New Directions Archive.
Page 496: postcard (front and back), "Harry's Bar, Venezia." Courtesy of Special Collections and Archives, University of Houston Libraries.
Page 529: Tennessee Williams and Anna Magnani. Leavitt Collection.
Page 559: Ben Gazzara and Burl Ives, *Cat on a Hot Tin Roof* (1955). From the New Directions Archive.
Page 568: Jo Mielziner, full set design *for Cat on a Hot Tin Roof* (1955). From the New Directions Archive.
Page 579: Eli Wallach and Carroll Baker, *Baby Doll* (1956). From the New Directions Archive.
Page 583: postcard, "Waitin' to Hear from You." By permission of the Wesleyan University Cinema Archives.
Page 596: Elia Kazan and Tennessee Williams on the *Baby Doll* set in Benoit, Mississippi, 1955. Warner Bros. photograph from the Billy Rose Theatre Collection, The New York Public Library for the Performing Arts, Astor, Lenox and Tilden Foundations.
Page 614: Lilla Van Saher, Jane Bowles, and Tennessee Williams aboard the *Queen Frederica*, 1956. Leavitt Collection.
Page 635: Boris Aronson, full set design *for Orpheus Descending* (1957). Courtesy of Lisa Aronson.

INTRODUCTION

Of the 800 collected letters, notes, and telegrams that fall into the years of Volume II, nearly 350 appear in *The Selected Letters of Tennessee Williams*. They begin in May 1945 as a restless playwright, beset by fame, prepares to leave for Mexico City. They end a dozen years later as a dejected playwright, still mulling the hazards of Broadway, prepares to sail for the Far East after the failure of *Orpheus Descending* (1957). If Volume I of *The Selected Letters* was "a manual of survival," of timely escape from "'two-by-four situations,'" Volume II is an account of the rising odds against escape in the years of Tennessee Williams's maturity. In both cases, escape was intended to refresh the imagination and to keep the threat of being "peddled" at bay, but the deft, intuitive maneuvers of youth have become ponderous and deliberate and aided by addictions. Nothing better evokes the altered mood of Volume II than the beleaguered closing of a letter to Audrey Wood: "This is the end of a long, hard day, and the end of a long, hard summer, and I suppose it is the beginning of a long, hard Fall, but what the hell, we are still with it!" (September 28, 1951).

Six major Broadway shows—each preceded by tedious, nerve-wracking negotiations and followed by tour, film, and revival—fill the calendar of Volume II. They confirm Williams's view of playwriting as the most "exhausting" of art forms: "It literally takes the strength of an ox . . . to carry a play from conception all the way through to its opening night on Broadway." Policing the regime were the "hard-boiled critics" (March 21, 1951) who demanded instant and repeated success, especially from Tennessee Williams, whose aura of self-interest and sexual difference did little to soften his critical reception. These and other pressures form the refrain of Volume II: one of exhaustion, of being written out, used up, dismissed from the theatre, whose economic order Williams had failed to uphold. "It's awful," he warned Carson McCullers, "how quickly a theatrical reputation declines on the market. A few years ago and I could have anything I wanted in the theatre, now I have to go begging. Two plays that didn't make money and, brother, you're on the skids!" (August 1952).

As the letters indicate, the "recessive periods" of Volume II were painful and prolonged and not easily separated from the fame of *Streetcar* (1947), whose daunting effect Williams described to Elia Kazan: "I have been floundering around most of the time since Streetcar, flapping my arms in the air as if they were wings" (July 29, 1952). But the "flapping," however futile it may have seemed at the time, was not without point or direction, nor would the plays that initially failed to "make money"—*Summer and Smoke* (1948) and *The Rose Tattoo* (1951)—lack successful revival. Williams absorbed their sharp lessons and went on to challenge the realistic tenets of Broadway with *Camino Real* (1953), an imaginative farrago whose brief run further greased the "skids" of his career. Underlying the frantic pace of production, and the acute addiction to writing, was a challenge to Broadway that Williams issued in 1949 and then repeated following mixed notices for *The Rose Tattoo*. He claimed for dramatists the same latitude given to painters and poets, arguing that it usually "takes ten years of a man's life to grow into a new major attitude toward . . . the world he exists in" (March 21, 1951). However quixotic the calculation, Williams gradually developed a new "attitude" in the years of Volume II, one shaped by the "world" as he came to know it and brilliantly deployed in *Cat on a Hot Roof* (1955).

Volume I bristled with international disorder, but for Williams the parochial tenor of St. Louis and the conventional ties of family and home were far more disturbing. Their unhappy influence he moderated by taking brief sanctuary in such bohemian quarters as New Orleans, Laguna Beach, and Key West. In Volume II Williams no longer traveled on a budget, nor were the post-war years so overtly beset with danger; but as an artist of achievement and accrued sensitivity, he felt, and annually fled, the pressures of living in America. Its repressive culture, epitomized by Senator Joseph McCarthy, remanded political dissidents and homosexuals to the margins of national life. Williams was publicly accused of Communist leanings and covertly investigated by Naval Intelligence as a sexual deviant. *Time* magazine considered him a dissolute writer, as did Francis Cardinal Spellman, who enjoined the faithful from seeing *Baby Doll* (1956) "under pain of sin." Paris, Rome, Barcelona, and Tangier replaced the American enclaves in Williams's ceaseless travel, adding materially to the distant, broken rhythms of Volume II. These and other public pressures formed a new "attitude" which is first evident in *Cat on a Hot Tin Roof*. The intense inwardness of Williams's earlier theatre—nostalgia, retrospection, resignation, idealism, despair—would not suffice in *Cat*, which is driven instead by prophecy: "Mendacity is a system that we live in."

Elia Kazan understood this truth, both as a subject of congressional investigation in 1952 and as Williams's friend and favored director. Volume II contains twenty letters addressed to Kazan and as such it represents the first major infusion of this correspondence into the record. (Some eighty additional letters, notes, and telegrams written by Tennessee Williams are held by the Wesleyan University Cinema Archives. The Kazan side of the exchange is less well represented.) To read the extensive Williams correspondence is to appreciate the complexity of the relationship and to withhold categorical judgment. During the years of Volume II, Williams depended heavily upon the magic of Kazan's staging to bring out the latent drama of his plays. Kazan often resisted such importuning by delay, demand for revision, and reluctant refusal. His creative will no doubt blurred the distinction between authorship and direction, but the initial drafts submitted to Kazan—which are documented in the annotations—were often so rushed or fragmentary as to invite elaborate notes for revision. Especially intriguing is the way that each checked the other's lapses in taste or judgment. Kazan declined to film Williams's "cornball" additions to *Streetcar*, while Williams lectured his northern friend on the logic of race in the Mississippi Delta. Most importantly, the selected letters follow the controversial production of *Cat*, revealing Williams's critique of the play in the tryout stage and his efforts to supply motivation for Brick without violating the mysterious origins of his passivity.

The Audrey Wood letters, the largest gathering in Volume II, mark the busy intersection of art and commerce that followed the production of *Streetcar*. Wood astutely managed this enterprise and remained the playwright's first and most trusted reader. But the perils of management are evident in Williams's oddly conjoined fears of being "peddled" unduly and mismanaged financially, perhaps with excessive self-interest on the part of his agent and her husband, Bill Liebling. Their repeated attempts to draw Williams into a production partnership, if only to avoid such abrasive managers as Irene Selznick, stimulated the client's penchant for suspicion and led to the abrupt dissolution of a company formed to produce *Orpheus Descending*. Perhaps the most tender moment in Volume II is to be found in Wood's reassurance of Williams as he painfully tried new themes following *Streetcar*: "Know that I love you dearly as a man and admire you as much as always as a writer" (March 5, 1950).

Williams's identity as a writer was formed among his "own kind of vague, indefinite folks" (Volume I, October 21, 1939) in the dreaded "City of St. Pollution." Family correspondence in Volume I accounts for one-third of the collection and as such it preserves both the lyrical core of memory and the domestic base upon which Tennessee Williams's theatre was founded. Family letters are greatly reduced in the sequel, a reflection of events which ended any semblance of shared living in St. Louis: the mental illness and hospitalization of Rose, the death of "Grand," Dakin's military service, the final separation of Cornelius and Edwina, and especially the older son's liberating success in *The Glass Menagerie* (1945). Never were the ties of family broken, but they are significantly loosened in Volume II and replaced in part by alternative bonds. By Maria Britneva, the Lady St. Just, a new friend and traveling companion, whose protective gestures both served and irritated the playwright; by Carson McCullers, another new friend and correspondent, with whom Williams briefly considered a scheme to live and work together, which Audrey Wood deemed "pure madness"; especially by intimate relationships with Pancho Rodriguez and Frank Merlo. The latter began in the fall of 1948 and persisted until Merlo's death in 1963. From the beginning the union was volatile, troubling, and marked by strategic separation and sexual leeway. The stock view of the relationship, which casts Tennessee Williams as the restless, promiscuous partner and Merlo as the staunch *bourgeois*, requires second thought in light of the letters and journal entries published in Volume II. At the same time, Merlo adjusted more smoothly to Williams's public-professional life than did Rodriguez, and he was undoubtedly more reliable in crises which affected the playwright. In special moments of physical need and emotional intensity, Williams acknowledged that "my 'Horse' is my little world" (*Journal*, December 30, 1953).

It is fitting that Volume II end with Tennessee Williams and Elia Kazan in conversation. Of their friendship, Kazan wrote many years later that he and Williams were quite similar: "We both felt vulnerable to the depredations of an unsympathetic world, distrustful of the success we'd had, suspicious of those in favor, anticipating put-downs, expecting insufficient appreciation and reward." Kazan's "most loyal and understanding friend" following the debacle in Washington "was Tennessee Williams" (Kazan, *A*

Life, p. 495). So annealing was their sympathy that they collaborated on four major productions in less than a decade. Each derived fame and a measure of wealth from their legendary collaboration, whose seesaw rhythm—volatility and patience, candor and reserve, trust and suspicion—is happily preserved in letters of uncommon length, detail, and self-revelation. In closing, Williams adds a grace note to the collection, as it were, lamenting the failure of *Orpheus Descending*, whose proper "'key'" Kazan would surely have found, and expressing guarded optimism for the future, which is the story of Volume III. What has changed from Williams's earlier proclamations is not the sacred nature of art—its redemptive effect—but the exceedingly high cost of its service.

Albert J. Devlin
Columbia, Missouri
September 2004

EDITORIAL NOTE

Volume II of *The Selected Letters of Tennessee Williams* is intended to provide complete, accurate texts and to preserve as many authorial conventions as publication will allow. Each heading begins with a reference number followed by the correspondent's name, the letter's place of origin and date of composition, and a bibliographical description of the original source, including its present location.

Marked SH (Stationery Headed) is the stationery of hotels, clubs, ships, railways, and other organizations—evidence of Tennessee Williams's relentless travel and incessant composition. Williams's own notations of address and date have also been preserved, but they are often supplemented with data placed in brackets. Bracketed too is the editorial dating of correspondence which is undated in part or whole. When available, postmarked envelopes (PM) are cited to approximate the time of composition. Dating evidence is also drawn from concurrent and recipient letters and especially from the journal, which begins in 1936 and continues, with lapses, through the years of Volume II. Information pertinent to composition, dating, or manuscript provenance may often be found in the final paragraph of the annotations.

The selected letters are transcribed from original sources held by institutions and individual cited in the Key to Collections. The few exceptions to this rule are noted in the heading. The great majority of letters is also published here for the first time. Those few printed in *Remember Me to Tom* (1963), Edwina Dakin Williams's memoir, have been transcribed from original manuscript sources. Williams typed most of his correspondence in block form with double spacing used to mark paragraph breaks. Economy requires that the indented form of his autograph letters be used in Volume II. Closings and signatures are also printed on one line and their punctuation regularized. Salutations remain unedited.

Tennessee Williams's erratic spelling has not been corrected, save in the case of mechanical or inadvertent error, nor has capitalization or punctuation been standardized. The intrusive convention [*sic*] is not used. Rough syntax has occasionally been smoothed with the insertion, in brackets, of elements needed to create a readable text. In no case has an addition been made where the author's intention is not reasonably clear. Brackets are also used to enclose a description of the state of the manuscript: [*end of letter missing*]. Strikeovers are retained when they are decipherable and significant. Ellipsis is Williams's own practice and is used primarily for emphasis or punctuation rather than to indicate omission.

Bracketed annotations follow nearly every letter and are not keyed to a footnote or other visual system of identification. The intent, as in Volume I, is to discourage the usual discontinuous practice of letter reading, one which occasions undue editorial intrusion into the text and invites the reader to break its pace and mood to consult a language of explication. The annotations are not, however, without design. Some few, especially those which open a unit of letters or summarize a phase of travel, begin with a statement of orientation before taking up specific items mentioned in the letter. Items selected for annotation are paragraphed to follow the letter's internal order of composition. Occasionally an annotation will be delayed until the item of interest has been developed in successive or closely related letters. Sources used in drafting the annotations include material drawn from letters of Williams not chosen for publication (usually because of their repetitive and/or perfunctory nature), from the unpublished journal, and related correspondence. These and many other documentary sources are identified and may be consulted by readers who wish to supplement the annotations. Dates for Williams's extensive works are given parenthetically in the annotations, according to the following practice: Non-dramatic texts are dated by their first appearance in print or, if unpublished, by their manuscript date and provenance. Dramatic texts are dated by their first major performance unless otherwise noted. To keep the reader apprized of Williams's complex body of writing, the dating of texts is repeated with the first mention of each in the six parts of Volume II.

The great majority of persons, events, and texts mentioned in the letters has been identified to the extent warranted by importance. A brief biographical statement, including life dates, usually accompanies the first appearance of each of TW's correspondents.

ACKNOWLEDGMENTS

Grateful acknowledgment is made to leading scholar-critics for their basic research on Tennessee Williams: the late Lyle Leverich, Williams's authorized biographer, and Donald Spoto, an earlier writer; Andreas "Andy" Brown, who was instrumental in forming the Williams collection at the Humanities Research Center, Austin, Texas; Drewey Wayne Gunn, who published the first major description of the Williams canon, and George W. Crandell, who gave it definitive bibliographical form. Acknowledgment is also due Brian Parker and Sarah Boyd Johns for pioneering genetic study of the plays; Brenda Murphy for incisive performance history; and Allean Hale, Kenneth Holditch, and Philip Kolin for long devotion to Williams scholarship.

Valuable information, as well as engaging correspondence, may be found in two earlier collections: *Tennessee Williams' Letters to Donald Windham, 1940-1965*, and *Five O'Clock Angel: Letters of Tennessee Williams to Maria St. Just, 1948-1982*. Edited, respectively, by Donald Windham and Maria St. Just, the volumes often provide a revealing counterpoint to letters included in the present collection. The unpublished journal of Tennessee Williams, forthcoming under the editorship of Margaret Thornton, is quoted by special arrangement with Yale University Press. Special thanks are due Margaret Thornton for generous support of the "Letters" project.

The preponderance of letters in Volume II is drawn from the seminal Williams collection at the Harry Ransom Humanities Research Center, University of Texas at Austin. *The Selected Letters* could not have been undertaken in the present form without the support of this exemplary institution. Very special thanks and admiration are reserved for Tara Wenger, Pat Fox, and Elizabeth L. Garver. Their competence, friendliness, and timely assistance ably represent the cultural and intellectual virtues of the HRC.

Thanks are also due for the support and courtesy of other major collectors of Williams correspondence: Billy Rose Theatre Collection, New York Public Library for the Performing Arts (Robert Taylor); Butler

Library, Columbia University (Bernard R. Crystal); Harvard Theatre Collection (Fredric Woodbridge Wilson); Houghton Library, Harvard University (Leslie Morris); Wesleyan University Cinema Archives (Leith Johnson and Joan Miller). The many other collectors, institutional and private, who kindly supplied letters or research material are listed in the Key to Collections.

Four years of preparation have revealed special friends and benefactors of *The Selected Letters*. None is more appreciated than the estate of Elia Kazan, which gave permission to examine the Kazan archive at Wesleyan University (Middletown, Connecticut) and to publish a selection of Williams's correspondence with his close friend and collaborator. Dakin Williams, the only surviving member of the playwright's immediate family, has also given access to important papers and answered questions which no one else could presume to address. Jordan Massee, recently deceased, also gave valuable papers and photographs and astutely answered questions about his friendship with Williams and Paul Bigelow. Before his death, Richard F. Leavitt, compiler of *The World of Tennessee Williams*, offered valuable advice on the selection of photographs. The biographers of Williams's correspondents and friends—especially Virginia Spencer Carr (Carson McCullers), Gerald Clarke (Truman Capote), Fred Kaplan (Gore Vidal), Helen Sheehy (Margo Jones), and Ralph Voss (William Inge)—have greatly facilitated research for Volume II. So have Stephanie Womack and Sean Battles, who joined the "Letters" project through the Undergraduate Mentorship Program at the University of Missouri. Thanks are due Stephanie Womack for research on the production and reception history of *A Streetcar Named Desire*. Sean Battles has served with uncommon energy and intelligence as the primary research assistant for Volume II. No doubt his talents, and good nature, will grace journalism as noticeably as they have literary scholarship. Matthew Alofs, who first joined the project though the MU Mentorship Program, has prepared the main indexes of Volume II with typical efficiency and skill. Richard Kramer, a Williams scholar in his own right, has provided valuable liaison with libraries and collectors in New York, while Travis Pittman has provided the same service in Austin. Finally, to a diverse group of readers—Elizabeth Garver, Heather Moulaison, Joan Smith, Nicholas Moschovakis, and Steve Lawson—who gave valuable advice on the manuscript sincere thanks are given.

Professor Devlin's research was supported by several grants and a research leave funded by the University of Missouri Research Board and Research Council. Generous assistance was supplied by reference and special collections librarians at the University of Missouri: Anne Barker, Anne Edwards, Margaret Howell, Hunter Kevil, and Michael Muchow, as well as an Interlibrary Loan staff headed by Marilyn Voegele. To the University of the South, copyright holder of the works of Tennessee Williams, grateful acknowledgment is made for permission to edit and publish the playwright's correspondence. Peggy Fox, president of New Directions, Thomas Keith, editor, and Sylvia Frezzolini Severance, book designer, deserve praise for their good care and perseverance. Finally, Jennifer Zarrelli transcribed the letters with her typical competence and good cheer.

The following librarians, research assistants, and other friends and informants have provided valuable help in preparing Volume II: Hilary Aid, Columbia, Missouri, Beth Alvarez, University of Maryland; Pamela Arceneaux, Williams Research Center, New Orleans; Annie Armour, University of the South; Lisa Aronson, New York; Fred Bauman, Library of Congress; Andrea Beauchamp, University of Michigan; Robert Bray, Middle Tennessee SU; Linda Briscoe, Humanities Research Center; Jackson Bryer, University of Maryland; Alison Carrick, Washington University; Ruth Carruth, Yale University; Kay Cattarulla, Dallas Museum of Art; Mark Cave, Williams Research Center, New Orleans; Erin Chase, Huntington Library; Cathy Cherbosque, Huntington Library; William Bedford Clark, Texas A&M University; Lynda Claassen, University of California, San Diego; Robert Collins, University of Missouri; April Cunningham, Huntington Library; Sharon DeLano, *The New Yorker*; Luke Dennis, Harvard Theatre Collection; Mitch Douglas, International Creative Management, New York; Elizabeth Dunn, Duke University; William Eigelsback, University of Tennessee; Pamela Evans, Mission, Texas; Annette Fern, Harvard Theatre Collection; Jack Frick, Canton, North Carolina; Michelle Gachette, Harvard University; Kim Gallon, University of Pennsylvania; Cara Gilgenbach, Kent State University; Julie Grob, University of Houston; Barbara Hall, Margaret Herrick Library; Susan Halpert, Houghton Library, Harvard University; Christopher Harter, Indiana University; Cathy Henderson, Humanities Research Center; Noah Heringman, University of Missouri; Robert Hines, Canton, North Carolina; Howard Hinkel, University of Missouri; Sue Hodson, Huntington Library; Tom Hyry, Yale University; Dan Isaac, New York;

Russell James, Columbus-Lowndes Public Library, Columbus, Mississippi; Kirsten Jensen, University of Arizona; J.C. Johnson, Boston University; Fred Kaplan, New York; Nathaniel Keller, Columbia, Missouri; David Kessler, University of California, Berkeley; John Kirkpatrick; Humanities Research Center; Suzanne Marrs, Millsaps College; Edwin Matthias, Library of Congress; Rebecca Melvin, University of Delaware; Janie Morris, Duke University; Timothy Murray, University of Delaware; Sean Noel, Boston University; Carol Meszaros, University of Michigan; Nita Murphy, Taos Historic Museums; Nathaniel Parks, Boston University; Margaret Sayers Peden, University of Missouri; Bridget Pieschel, Mississippi University for Women; Sue Presnell, University of Indiana; Thomas Richardson, Mississippi University for Women; Carol Roark, Dallas Public Library; Jenny Romero, Margaret Herrick Library; Myrtle Rosen, Taos, New Mexico; Donald Share, Harvard University; Nancy Shawcross, University of Pennsylvania; Ellen Shea, Radcliffe Institute; Kathy Smith, Indiana University; Fred Todd, San Antonio; Carol Turley, UCLA; James and Catherine Wallace, Columbia, Missouri; Rick Watson, Humanities Research Center; Raymond Wemmlinger, Hampden-Booth Theatre Library, New York; Shawn Wilson, Kinsey Institute, Indiana University.

ABBREVIATIONS

ALS	Autograph letter signed
APCS	Autograph postcard signed
ca.	about
Carr	Virginia Spencer Carr, *The Lonely Hunter: A Biography of Carson McCullers*. New York: Doubleday & Company, 1975.
Collected Stories	Tennessee Williams, *Collected Stories*. New York: New Directions, 1985.
Conversations	*Conversations with Tennessee Williams*. Ed. Albert J. Devlin. Jackson, MS: University Press of Mississippi, 1986.
Journal	The unpublished journal of Tennessee Williams. Forthcoming from Yale University Press. Ed. Margaret Thornton.
Kazan	Elia Kazan, *Elia Kazan: A Life*. New York: Alfred A. Knopf, 1988.
Leverich	Lyle Leverich, *Tom: The Unknown Tennessee Williams*. New York: Crown Publishers, 1995.
Memoirs	Tennessee Williams, *Memoirs*. New York: Doubleday & Company, 1975.
n.d.	no date of publication
PM	Postmarked
qtd.	quoted
rpt.	reprinted
SH	Stationery headed
Spoto	Donald Spoto, *The Kindness of Strangers: The Life of Tennessee Williams*. Boston: Little, Brown and Company, 1985.

St. Just	*Five O'Clock Angel: Letters of Tennessee Williams to Maria St. Just, 1948-1982*. Ed. Maria St. Just. New York: Alfred A. Knopf, 1990.
TL	Typewritten letter unsigned
TLS	Typewritten letter signed
TLSx	Typewritten letter signed copy
TLx	Typewritten letter unsigned copy
TW	Tennessee Williams
Where I Live	Tennessee Williams, *Where I Live: Selected Essays*. Ed. Christine R. Day and Bob Woods. New York: New Directions, 1978.
Windham	*Tennessee Williams' Letters to Donald Windham, 1940-1965*. Ed. Donald Windham. New York: Holt, Rinehart and Winston, 1977.

KEY TO COLLECTIONS

Beinecke	Beinecke Rare Book and Manuscript Library, Yale University
Boston U	Howard Gotlieb Archival Research Center, Mugar Memorial Library, Boston University
BRTC	Billy Rose Theatre Collection, The New York Public Library for the Performing Arts, Lincoln Center
Columbia U	Rare Book and Manuscript Library, Columbia University
Dallas Public Library	Texas/Dallas History and Archives Library Division, Dallas Public Library
Duke U	Special Collections Library, Duke University
Herrick	Margaret Herrick Library, Center for Motion Picture Study, Academy of Motion Picture Arts and Sciences, Beverly Hills, California
Houghton	Houghton Library, Harvard University
HRC	Harry Ransom Humanities Research Center, University of Texas at Austin
HTC	Harvard Theatre Collection, Houghton Library, Harvard University
Huntington	Manuscripts Department, Huntington Library, San Marino, California
Kent State U	Department of Special Collections and Archives, Kent State University Libraries
Kinsey Institute	Kinsey Institute Library and Special Collections, Indiana University
Leavitt	*The World of Tennessee Williams*. Ed. Richard F. Leavitt. New York: G.P. Putnam's Sons, 1978.
Library of Congress	Manuscript Division, The Library of Congress, Washington, D.C.

Massee Collection	Private collection of Jordan Massee, Macon, Georgia
Northwestern U	McCormick Library of Special Collections, Northwestern University
Princeton U	Department of Rare Books and Special Collections, Princeton University
Rendell	Kenneth W. Rendell Gallery, New York
SHS of Wisconsin	State Historical Society of Wisconsin, Madison, Wisconsin
Smith Collection	Private collection of Jane Lawrence Smith, New York
Southern Illinois U	Special Collections, Morris Library, Southern Illinois University
St. Just	*Five O'Clock Angel: Letters of Tennessee Williams to Maria St. Just, 1948-1982*. Ed. Maria St. Just. New York: Alfred A. Knopf, 1990.
Todd Collection	Fred W. Todd Collection, Williams Research Center, Historic New Orleans Collection, New Orleans
UCLA	Department of Special Collections, Research Library, University of California, Los Angeles
U of Chicago	Department of Special Collections, University of Chicago Library
U of Delaware	Special Collections, Hugh H. Morris Library, University of Delaware
U of Houston	Special Collections and Archives, University of Houston Libraries
U of Pennsylvania	Annenberg Rare Book & Manuscript Library, University of Pennsylvania Library
Windham	*Tennessee Williams' Letters to Donald Windham, 1940-1965*. Ed. Donald Windham. New York: Holt, Rinehart and Winston, 1977.
WUCA	Wesleyan University Cinema Archives, Middletown, Connecticut

PART I

1945-1947

Overleaf. Tennessee Williams, Dallas, 1945:
"It was terribly hot and I had to run around as much as N.Y."

1. To Eddie Dowling

[Dallas, Texas]
[May 30, 1945]
[TLx, 2 pp. HRC]

Dear Eddie:

I am very grateful for your letter and the understanding in it. What a delicate operation we performed together, all of us, and what a strong bond it should be and I think is - now that it's worked out so well! Artists are peculiar creatures - no one is more guiltily aware of this than I! - the strain we work under, so much greater than that of all the mundane occupations - makes us touchy, difficult even for each other always to understand - but we have such a great community of interest that the differences are relatively slight and unimportant, at least they should be.

I am leaving early tomorrow morning for Mexico after a week here with Margo - catching a plane, which always makes me nervous - I am not a good flyer. I hope to settle down at some quiet place and devote myself to work - much neglected since last Fall - for the next two months.

I have met nearly everyone connected with Margo's Dallas Theatre and I feel that the outlook is really wonderful. I attended a meeting of the executive board. They are a very capable, serious and progressive bunch, completely earnest about what they're doing, and determined to push it through. Margo has dedicated herself to this thing heart and soul and, knowing her, and having met her co-workers, I'm fairly certain that something very important to all of us is going to happen down here. I think it will be valuable to theatre all over the country.

For me personally, it means a place to experiment and clarify. I have no interest at this time in more Broadway productions, for I feel that my problem is getting work done, not produced, - which takes so much time from the other and more important struggle. This is not really selfish, since I can make no important contribution without a great deal of solitary labor. But a theatre like Margo's is an excellent place to remain in touch with stage while at the same time escaping the exhausting responsibilities of Broadway - a proving ground for things I'm not sure of. "Battle" is a case in point. I still have no script that is really definitive of that play but feel that one might come out of a production down here, so it is tentatively our plan to do it here sometime next season. Naturally I hope this trial will interest you, if it comes off. I can think of no one in the theatre to whom a theatre like Margo's would offer more interest than to you, because of your peculiar devotion to theatrical frontiers, so we both are hoping you will watch what goes on here.

Now that a road-company of "Menagerie" is being organized I think the matter of its direction ought to be taken up. I have talked with Margo about this and know that she is eager to undertake it. Of course it should be as close a duplication of what was done with the original company as possible, and so it seems to me that Margo would be the only right person. You are busy as an actor and producer so I am sure you would need another's assistance on this job. There will be just as many problems with this company as there were with the original production - possibly even more - and we don't want it to fall short, in any respect, of the best that could be offered. I don't think this is anything that I have [to] "sell" you on, for you know how faithful Margo is to whatever she undertakes, and her deep "family" interest in the "Menagerie" which no one else could match.

Please let me hear from you while I am in Mexico. My love to Laurette, Julie, Tony - Randy, Bill, Jean and all of the company.

Ever,

[Eddie Dowling (1894-1976) produced and directed *The Glass Menagerie* (1945) and played Tom Wingfield to Laurette Taylor's incomparable Amanda. He recently answered TW's conciliatory letter of May 17 with thanks for having written "a beautiful play" and regret that the "shoddy" (May 19, 1945, HRC) tactics of his co-producer and backer, Louis J. Singer, had added to the "strain" of production. TW deferred an offer to restage *Battle of Angels* (1940), a notorious failure in Boston, with a tribute to Dowling's innovative presence on Broadway.

From Mexico City TW informed his family that Dallas had been "terribly hot" (June 6, 1945, HTC) and gregarious and that he had disappointed his host, Margo Jones, by remaining only a week. He did, however, join the "board" of Theatre '45 and began to revise *Battle of Angels* for the relaxed "proving ground" of Dallas. Conceived as an antidote to Broadway, Jones's experiment in decentralized theatre would shun recent hits, revive a few classics each season, and develop the talent of such gifted new playwrights as TW.

Jones, Dowling's co-director in the "original company" of *The Glass Menagerie*, would not direct the tour production.]

2. *To Guthrie McClintic*

SH: Hotel Geneve
7a. De Londres 130
Mexico City, Mexico
Friday [June 1, 1945]
[TLS, 2 pp. HRC]

Dear Guthrie:

I flew down here yesterday from Dallas. I have never liked flying and did not spend a comfortable moment in the plane, but was so exhausted by Dallas that the quickest way of getting furthest seemed best.

I'm sorry I missed your call but the long wire was very heartening and I am happy over Katharine Willard being Emmie. I have not yet had a chance to pick up my mail at Wells-Fargo, will do that this morning, and I hope you've thought of some people for me to meet. I have loads of names given me in Dallas by various sweet old ladies, which would only bring me in contact with more sweet old ladies. My seclusion in the Dallas hotel room was enjoyed very briefly and the stay turned into a social whirl-wind. I met Ida Camp and all her crowd, which correspond roughly to the 'horsey set on Long Island', although one or two of the women are fabulously and crazily amusing - if only you could have a concealed dictaphone when they are talking! All the energy and color seems to have gone into the Dallas females and the poor husbands look as if they had donated entirely too much blood and to the wrong cause. They just sit around holding glasses with a look which is far away but not dreamy, while the women rock and roar in one continual effusion.

One thing I didn't count on - in reference to Margo's project - is the vitality of these women. It is really out of the world, and if Margo can get them on her side - miracles may happen! Of course they don't have any real discrimination, these women, but they are snobs and in my opinion you can do almost anything with snobs if you handle them carefully. I suspect they will embrace almost anything if it is presented to them as having "smartness". They suck up all the "new books" like vacuum cleaners, in fact I don't see how it is possible to read that much and that fast. Of course they are still gabbing about 'Forever Amber'. But some of them have even been reading Richard Wright. When they get a few drinks under their girdles, their talk becomes right down lascivious, and that is another good sign for "The Project". All it needs to have is something phallic about it.

And as a matter of fact that something may be the title! At any rate, they are all very interested in it, though Ida Camp said she wasn't sure that she was "behind it".

Margo wants to open her season with "Battle of Angels" and I think it might be a good thing. There is a lot of material in that play that is worth salvaging, and I have never prepared a definitive script of it, and this would be a good chance to. She wants to get Bobby Jones down here to design it and music by Bowles.

This hotel I am in is impossible so will not be my address. Must find a place where there is swimming and a balcony or patio where I can work in the sun and privacy. As usual I feel a terrible desolation in Mexico, but I must grit my teeth for a week or so until it wears off. The electric signs here are lovely! They are the color of soft drinks and much livelier than the ones on Broadway.

I will go, now, and pick up the letters you mention and let you know where I am when I settle.

Tenn.

[Guthrie McClintic (1893-1961) was the producer/director of more than fifty original Broadway plays and revivals, many starring his wife, the distinguished Katharine Cornell. He rejected *You Touched Me!* in 1943, but the work had gained stature following the success of *The Glass Menagerie* and was now being cast for a late-September opening on Broadway. Katherine Willard, as indicated, would play one of the leads.

The women of Dallas were "still gabbing about" *Forever Amber* (1944), Kathleen Winsor's *succès de scandale* set in Restoration England. Richard Wright's autobiography, *Black Boy* (1945), was number two on national bestseller lists when TW visited Dallas in May.]

3. To Audrey Wood

[Mexico City]
6/20/45
[TLS, 1 p. HRC]

Dear Child of God:

I wrote you a very gloomy letter the last time for I had swallowed one of those Mexican bugs that prey on American tourists and I was feeling very low indeed. But I found a little Mexican doctor who gave me shots and pills, enough to kill a horse with - but I survived the treatment and have been feeling exceptionally well ever since.

Disregard the instructions affecting prize money in last Memo. Won't need it as I have wired Chase Natl. to let me draw $500. through Banco de Commercio in Mexico. This will, I hope, see me through the Mexican junket and perhaps even back to the wilds of Texas and New York.

I have met the following here: Leonard Bernstein, Dolores Del Rio, Rosa Covarrubias, Norman Foster (Now directing Mexican films), Romney Brent's sister, Balanchine, Chavez, and many lesser notables of the International Set (!) all of whom have invited me places. But it is not like Chicago and New York, that is, the society is not at all exhausting and I have plenty of time to work. And I love Mexico, I think it is really and truly my native land! I will stay here till it is almost time to go back for "YTM".

Guthrie has sent me several wires about casting and I also got a wire from Katharine Cornell (Signed Kit) saying she had seen "Menagerie" and wanted me to write her one. And today - having pinched myself, I know I am wide awake! - I received a letter from Lawrence Stanislavsky Langner, the one who operates that famous Art Theatre on E. 56th Street - saying that he still has the scenery of "Battle" stored at Westport and has a new director in mind for it! This was profoundly touching, but also a little funny I thought - so I am mentioning it to you and Liebling!

One cannot help loving people who make you laugh! And I think the Guild has been favored by the Gods because their serious antics have even gotten a chuckle out of Cothurnus! - Imagine enticing us with the news that that horrible old brown set, probably all webbed and molded, was waiting for us in a store-room at Westport! Of course my instinct is to wire Lawrence, "You should have stood in Miami!" But instead I shall write him one of my nicest testimonials of affection, for this last communication has completed the cycle, often observed in life, from deepest tragedy to lightest farce!

Love - 10.

[Audrey Wood (1905-1985) represented TW from 1939 until their parting thirty-two years later.

"Prize money" of $1,500 accompanied the Sidney Howard Award announced on June 5. The citation lauded TW as "a vigorous new talent" who "has the sense

*Tennessee Williams with Bill Liebling and Audrey Wood: "A very small and dainty woman with . . . a look of cool perspicacity in her eyes" (*Memoirs*).*

of poetry and of character of which great drama is made." Earlier selection of *The Glass Menagerie* by the Drama Critics' Circle gave TW two of three major awards for the past season. Mary Chase won the Pulitzer for *Harvey* (1944).

Leonard Bernstein seemed harsh and egotistical, although TW later described him as a "true" (*Memoirs*, p. 94) revolutionary in social expression. The ballet master George Balanchine disliked Mexico City and feared that his "girls," as TW mocked, were "sick with sumzings" (qtd. in Windham, p. 173) in New York. Dolores Del Rio, a veteran of silent films and Hollywood musicals of the 1930s, had returned to her native Mexico to restore a fading career in the cinema. TW met her at the home of Rosa Covarrubias, an American-born dancer married to the painter and writer Miguel Covarrubias.

Guthrie McClintic's "wires" brought a terse reply from TW: "Clift has more experience and charm Brown has more foxy upstart quality I have dysentery You decide" (telegram, June 9, 1945, HRC). Montgomery Clift played the role of Hadrian in *You Touched Me!*

Ever cautious, Wood instructed TW to "be quiet" (July 5, 1945, HRC) about writing a play for Katharine Cornell, lest he restrict her ability to sell it.

Lawrence Langner and Theresa Helburn, co-directors of the Theatre Guild, supervised the first professional staging of a TW play, *Battle of Angels*. Langner wrote earlier to congratulate TW on the success of *The Glass Menagerie* and to propose that the Guild offer *Battle* once again. Even "Cothurnus," stern image of tragedy, would be amused, TW thought, by the "antics" of the venerable Theatre Guild.]

4. To Lawrence Langner

[Mexico City]
6/20/45
[TLS, 1 p. Beinecke]

Dear Lawrence:

A whole pile of my mail, tied up somewhere on the trail between New York, Dallas and Mexico City, finally overtook me this morning, including the particularly welcome letter from you.

The statement in PM was sincerely meant. There are times, especially in the theatre, when it is only fair to judge by intentions and not by results, and God knows you and Terry had every intention of making "Battle" a good show. It was not quite in the book, nor in the stars, and our plans "ganged aft agley". As for the re-write, I was in no condition at the time to straighten things out, for I had gone through the most disturbing experience of my life. I solved a few dramaturgic problems by augmenting the physical action in the last half, but the more serious problem of expressing a violent theme in terms that were acceptably controlled and measured, of clarifying my ideas and characters - my state of mind at the time was by no means equal to!

But there are bolts of lightning in the script which may still be harnessed and put to work for the theatre, so it may interest you and Terry to know that Margo Jones is planning to try it out at her Dallas Theatre, perhaps as an opening production and perhaps designed by Robert Edmond Jones. With this in mind, I have prepared another version of the script with the use of whatever new restraint and technical knowledge I may have picked up along the years since Boston, 1940. The prologue and epilogue have been eliminated, also the fire phobia and the rather pompous stuff about the boy's book. My stake in this is a purely abstract one. I don't want another Broadway production, perhaps not for four or five years, for it is too nervously exhausting and takes too much time from my essential business, for I have done such a microscopic part of what I wanted to do in everything I've undertaken, and life is a tiny peep-hole at this big show!

You and Terry are so closely bound up with my first years in the theatre, and in a way that was finally so helpful, that I feel you are definitely a part of my professional family and I part of yours.

Cordially, Tennessee.

[Audrey Wood may have prompted the "statement in PM" to counter recent charges by TW that the Theatre Guild had "messed up" *Battle of Angels*. Lawrence Langner (1890-1962) could not "agree" that the Boston production had been "'superb'" (June 6, 1945, HRC), as TW now maintained, but he thanked him nonetheless and allowed the earlier criticism to pass.

Although factually flawed, the interview in *PM Magazine* (rpt. in *Conversations*, pp. 12-19) is notable for TW's guarded reference to his sister Rose, whose charm and beauty are cited but not her chronic mental illness or hospitalization in Missouri.

The latest revision of *Battle of Angels* concerns Val Xavier's mortal fear of fire and the portentous book which he is writing.

This letter bears a reception date of July 3, 1945.]

5. To Margaret "Margo" Jones

SH: Hotel Lincoln
Revillagigedo 24, Mexico. D.F.
[Mexico City]
June 25, 1945.
[TLS, 2 pp. HRC]

Dear Margo:

It must be three or four in the morning but I am not a bit sleepy so will try writing a letter which is a usually effective narcotic.

The correspondance got here after about ten days - God knows why it takes so long to get my mail across the border, I think they must be making a special study of it. I always try to put in something I think will be interesting for the censor, which is perhaps a mistaken policy.

I am dying to know how you came out on the new building deal. And just why it was necessary. And all about Milzener's plans. Was it a serious crisis? I do hope you got it all straightened out by now.

My nerves always get tied up in knots about the middle of the summer, due to heavy work or some emotional cycle that moves with the seasons - whatever it is - this summer is no worse than usual, perhaps somewhat better - but the last few days I've been about to jump out of my skin, and though I've finally made loads of acquaintances, I don't feel like seeing anybody. Society here is nice, though. I am dancing a lot for the first time since I left college and there are two or three little Indians who take me around sight-seeing, Etc. And I am crazy about the bull-fights and have joined a Y which has a lovely out-door pool, only two blocks from my hotel. Mexico is full of accidental beauty, like passing an archway, right in a city block and seeing a big white rooster staring imperially back at you, blind beggars led along the street by tiny, tiny, dirty, dirty white dogs, things like that. I am trying to work some of them into a fantasy of several scenes, on which I alternate with the long play begun in Chicago. - I have met Dolores Del Rio and Norman Foster, and perhaps if I come back here next year, I may try to do some work on a Mexican film. Not having the Hayes office, their art films can be very exciting. Photographically, plastically - they are far superior to nearly all American pictures. I am picking up bits of the language constantly, though I havn't tried to. - Love it!

I'm glad I have that lovely picture of you, you look so strong and idealistic in it! Not that you ain't, Baby! But everybody notices it and says, 'Muy bonita!'

Just gotten and immediately lost a letter from little Bob Carter, the kid you met in Chicago. I hadn't let him know I'd left New York and he is now there and doesn't know a soul and of course is utterly wretched. I can't think of a soul to tell him to see. As a matter of fact I don't have one N.Y. associate - Don being on Nantuckett island - that I think would be a safe and advantageous contact for such a youngster - Do you? And besides I have lost the letter, now, and don't have his address. Must write by way of Chicago. The very young really break my heart, though God knows youth's an advantage! But, oh - ! The years, the years - !

That rooster I saw in the archway is lifting his voice - Me Voy! A Duerme! Is that correct?

If anything important comes up, call me long-distance. - I haven't heard one note out of Mother since I left New York. Do you suppose she is angry I didn't stop in St. Louis - or what? McClintic is trying to get Robert Fleming out of the British army for Hadrian, but Clift and Phil Brown are still in the running.

With love, 10.

[Margo Jones (1911-1955) met a shy, impoverished TW in New York in 1942 and became enamored of the man and his work. Her staging of *You Touched Me!* (1943) and "The Purification" (1944) in regional theatres sealed their friendship and led TW to recommend that she assist Eddie Dowling in directing *The Glass Menagerie*.

Jo Mielziner, acclaimed set designer of *The Glass Menagerie*, was asked by Jones to evaluate a theatre building in Dallas, which he found "impractical" (qtd. in Windham, p. 175).

Work on *A Streetcar Named Desire* (1947) and *Camino Real* (1953)—the "long play" and the "fantasy"—would occupy TW through the following winter in New Orleans.

Hollywood producers established the "Hayes office" in 1921 to forestall external censorship of the film industry. The first director, Will H. Hays, was followed by Joseph Breen, whose hand was strengthened by the censorship crusades of the 1930s and fell heavily upon the filming of TW's theatre, beginning with *The Glass Menagerie*.

"Little Bob Carter," one of the "university kids" (qtd. in Windham, p. 159) whom TW met during tryouts of *The Glass Menagerie*, later thanked TW for the gift of a sweater and added that it "fits perfectly. I can't imagine how you ever found out my size so well" (March 28, 1945, Private Collection). TW inscribed an early draft of *Streetcar* to Carter "in return for the Key to Chicago" ("Electric Avenue," n.d., HRC).]

6. *To Margaret "Margo" Jones*

[Guadalajara, Mexico]
[early-July 1945]
[TLS w/ autograph marginalia
and enclosure, 2 pp. HRC]

Dear Margo:

The original of this article, which was probably somewhat better put together, was lost in the departure from Mexico [City]. I had to reproduce it here in Guadalajara from memory. I had meant to mail it the same evening I wrote it, in accordance to my wire, as I know you want it quickly, but your wire came in the middle of my pulling up stakes which as you know is always a soul-shaking experience for me. There has only been a delay, however, of about 24 hours and I hope they get it through the censors quickly. I am crazy about this part of Mexico. The air and the scenery are like around Taos, and Guadalajara is clean and lovely. The plaza at night is really like a dream. White lamp-posts all along the walks with fivebranch lamps on them. In the middle a band-stand, octagonal, with graceful loops and Victorian flourishes, all traced with lights and a big chandelier in the middle. The cathedral and old government buildings around it. My hotel has a big out-door spring-water swimming pool and the view from my room, (the bed has inner-spring mattress and 4 pillows) is across a wide pale green plain to a range of green and purple mountains. It is only eight pesos a day (about $1.50 American money), yellow tile and cream-colored walls, everything immaculate. Visiting Chapala for a few days tomorrow: it is the big lake where Lawrence wrote 'The Plumed Serpent'. I am writing a play about a were-wolf - Cabeza de Lobo - inspired by a Mexican painting of one. It will be a bit longer than Purification and I hope it may finally be good enough to use on a program with it. It is full of horror, so after working on it I have to sleep with my light on.

Will see you around the fifteenth in Dallas. Wire you exact time of arrival so you can do something about a place for me.

Has the Project blown up yet?

Love, Tennessee.

[TW joined the select company of Katharine Cornell and Robert Edmond Jones in publicizing Theatre '45. He praised Margo Jones's vision and drive and renewed his criticism of Broadway for ignoring "the real theatrical needs" of the country. That "a true art theatre" had now emerged in the South did not surprise TW, endowed as the region was with the "emotional richness and vitality" of its heritage. In a patriotic closing he urged local patrons to support the "vast cargo of heart-hungry youth" returning from war: "You've got to give them a richer life than they went away from" (*Dallas Morning News*, July 22, 1945, sec. 4, pp. 1-2).

TW later drafted a preface for the "fantasy" begun in Mexico City and given strong new impetus by his trip to Guadalajara. From this "dream-like" journey arose the principal characters of *Camino Real:* Marguerite Gautier, the ill-fated Dame aux Camélias, and Kilroy, the "poor man's Don Quixote." Their "juxtaposition" formed a "new congruity of incongruities," which required a text "less written than painted" ("Foreword," May 1946, HRC).

In Cabeza de Lobo the Gypsy describes a legendary werewolf which takes "the form of a beautiful virgin" at each full moon and "descends to the village" to claim a lover, who is allowed "to lift" (n.d., HRC) her veil. The roles of the Gypsy and her daughter, Esmeralda, as well as a major scene with Kilroy, are evident in this early source for *Camino Real*. TW later used "Cabeza de Lobo" as fictional shield for the Barcelona scenes in *Suddenly Last Summer* (1958).

Penned in the left-hand margin of page 1 is the notation "billiard & ping pong tables on veranda - noiseless at night." Enclosed was "A Playwright's Statement" (July 1945, HRC), which appeared in the *Dallas Morning News*.]

7. To Robert Penn Warren

SH: "Gran Hotel"
Guadalajara, Jal., Mex.
July 16, 1945.
[TLS, 2 pp. Beinecke]

Dear Mr. Warren:

I was confined to the hospital for an eye operation the two weeks before I left the States and nearly all the events of that period are somewhat shadowy, but I believe that among them was the especially dream-like reading to me of a letter of invitation to record some of my verse for the collection at the library of Congress. It seems like a paranoiac fantasy invented to compensate for critical reactions to my verse, but as I am not ordinarily subject to these, I am recklessly assuming that it has some basis in fact. - I am going to be in Washington early in September when a play of mine will be tried out in that city. If the invitation is actual and still holds good, I will be happy and proud to say a piece for you at that time. I have heard the recordings of poets at Harvard, including the one of Joyce which is really a treasure. But what a pity it seems to me that nobody ever got Hart Crane's voice, when so many of the canaries, finches, and sparrows have been shrilling their pipes off - there is not one peep from the nightingale!

I hope you feel the same way about him, for otherwise this comment will be mistakenly construed as impolite to the others - all I mean is I could not like them half so well if I didn't love Crane more!

Cordially, Tenn. Williams

[Robert Penn Warren (1905-1989) succeeded his friend and former Fugitive-Agrarian confederate Allen Tate as Consultant in Poetry of the Library of Congress (1944-1945). His "invitation" to TW was part of an ambitious plan to record both older and younger poets reading from their selected work. The Library of Congress holds no such recording by TW—some in the series have not survived—nor have the editors found any evidence that he followed through on his promise to read.

TW once cast himself as a "frail ghost-brother" of Hart Crane and asked that the poet "guide" (*Journal*, August 23, 1942) his uncertain career. TW found inspiration, sources, and titles for his own work in *The Collected Poems of Hart Crane* (1933), a volume which he "appropriated" from Washington University in St. Louis and often packed for travel.

The eye operation performed in New York in early-May was TW's fourth since 1941, the result of "a childhood game of considerable violence" (*Memoirs*, p. 74). TW would describe the "shadowy" period of the latest surgery as one which gave peace and protection to a writer disillusioned by the success of *The Glass Menagerie* (see "On a Streetcar Named Success," 1947; rpt. in *Where I Live*, pp. 15-22).]

8. To Audrey Wood

SH: Western Union
Laredo Tex
1945 Jul 28 AM 4 50
[Telegram, 1 p. HRC]

AUDREY WOOD=

MANUSCRIPTS HELD FOR INSPECTION AT BORDER REMAINING TILL CLEARED PLEASE WIRE HUNDRED DOLLARS HOTEL HAMILTON LAREDO=

TENNESSEE WILLIAMS.

["Certainly feel your manuscripts worth hundred dollars of anybodys money," Audrey Wood replied, and cabled the "vast amount" (July 28, 1945, HRC) to her stranded client. Donald Windham learned the outcome of TW's conflict with U.S. Customs following the apparent seizure of "One Arm" (1948). The missing script had not been confiscated but typically mislaid by TW "beneath a pile of dirty shirts" (qtd. in Windham, p. 176). He concealed the discovery from Customs, allowing the story of a mutilated gay prostitute to enter the States unexamined. TW quickly passed through Dallas and returned to New York in time for rehearsals of *You Touched Me!*]

9. To Burton Rascoe

SH: Shelton Hotel
Lexington Avenue
48th to 49th Streets
New York
August 11, 1945
[TLS, 4 pp. U of Pennsylvania]

Dear Burton Rascoe:

During my peaceful retreat into Mexico I received a letter from a New York friend that contained the news that you had attacked the printed versions of my plays in your column. And so I was very agreeably surprised when I returned to town this week to discover these articles, which I read for the first time, were not attacks at all but really quite fair and reasonable and in some respects more charitable than I myself would be inclined to speak of them. You have a command of irony and a wit that could make the object squirm, as Mr. Nathan has frequently done, but there is a distinct difference in that your motives are obviously more humanitarian. You don't feel that an effective attack is necessarily a savage one. You made several excellent points against me in these columns, and they are made so fairly or cleanly that I must say - <u>Touché</u>! I have worked very hard with nerves that are usually ragged and now and then I have let myself explode into ill-considered and sophomoric bursts of rhetoric. It is quite possible that some of the things I said in the preface to 'Battle' were in that category, certainly they were put in a way that was over-emphatic. It is always darkest just before daybreak, and even as recently as those remarks came off my feverish portable - (the present red ink is just because the ribbon is upside down!) - I was right behind the 8-ball, my most familiar location! I was outwardly calm but inwardly boiling and I suppose it was inevitable that some of this should escape in angry writing.

However I would like to clarify my feelings about the commercial theatre.

It is not that I am <u>against</u> something as much as that I am intensely <u>for</u> something else. - For the past two years I have been terribly concerned, with Margo Jones, in the establishment all over the States of professional theatres [which] are not of a strictly commercial kind. I've just come back from the scene of such an enterprise which is THEATRE '45 now being organized in Dallas, Texas. And so when the chance is offered, I try to point out the advantages such a plan has for creative workers in theatre, the advantage it has over theatres run primarily for profit. When you are for something you have to make negative comments on whatever it is you would like to see revised or improved on.

As you point out, the commercial theatre has always and will always exist. And why not? All I feel is that it is inadequate and unsuitable to the entire needs of artists working in the theatre. Only recently one of the greatest of these, Alla Nazimova, died in California after being off the stage - how many years? - at least ten, I believe. It is the possibility of such talent as hers having no place to hang its hat that makes me feel so passionately that there must be these other kinds of theatre in America than the kind which must look to its pocket before its heart.

I have been luckier than I deserve but that ought not to blind a person to privations and disappointments elsewhere. I know of fine actors who are so devoted to the theatre that they are willing to serve it in backstage obscurity if they are lucky enough to serve it at all, and I know of at least one playwright with considerably more talent than some of us who are successful ones - who at last reports was working in the kitchen of a Hollywood night-club. If there were theatre capitals such as the one now being formed in Dallas all over the States - theatres that are subsidized and ardently supported by their own communities - not little or amateur theatres but full-fledged professional ones that employ theatre-workers as a permanent family group - giving them security in place of the gradually wearing-out process of fear and privation, attention in place of neglect, action and release in place of repression and dissipating idleness, fellowship in place of embittering loneliness and isolation - If there were such theatres as commonly as there are state universities and civic orchestras, wherever the community is large enough to support them - Think what a happy difference it would make for all of us and what we might be inspired to do and be!

Then you may feel like beating the drum with more influence and eloquence than any of us now beating it! I can't think of anyone associated with the stage - even the down-right gold-prospectors - who don't have more to gain than to lose by the catching on of such an idea, for all it means is that the theatre will be a thousand times as great and powerful as it now is in this country! If it starts out well in Dallas - and God grant that it may!

- it will spread like a grass-fire and multiply like rabbits! - There will be a tremendously increased demand for all of these items - plays, actors, designers, stage-hands, producers, directors, singers, dancers, clowns, acrobats - and even the circulation of Mr. Nathan's books will undoubtedly increase!

I don't think that art is a weapon but I think it is certainly an instrument and was there ever a time when a new and powerful instrument was needed to work on human society more than the present? Millions of home-coming young men are bringing keyed-up nerves and pentup emotions and new ideas and - most of all! - a terrific restless urge to create and express instead of merely to defend and struggle and destroy! They deserve these new avenues of self-realization that a resurgent nation-wide professional theatre can give them! Deserve them and truly need them.

Long live Broadway, and all the brave individuals in it who have held it valiantly above the level of mere profit-making - the national theatres we dream of might well be dedicated to the Eddie Dowlings of this Broadway, the Guthrie McClintics, Theatre Guilds and Group Theatres, that have striven usually against the tide to keep truth and poetry flowing through the wings and across the footlights. It is these islands that I have hopped across to my present footing and it is to them that my devoir is due. You may call them the commercial theatre if you want to be technical about it - but I call them The Theatre! And the seeds of a so much greater Theatre to come.

This is a long, long letter but I know you have been a good friend of the Wingfields and I feel that I can talk to you without constraint.

I will be in town here for about a month and if you would like to have a drink with me - and maybe Audrey - I wish you would call me sometime.

Cordially, Tennessee Williams

[Burton Rascoe (1892-1957), drama critic for the *New York World-Telegram*, qualified his initial praise of *The Glass Menagerie* by implying that superb production values had obscured the play's faulty structure (June 11)—a slighting strategy devised by George Jean Nathan, whom TW considered a nemesis. Publication of the book in July revealed the incompatible roles of author and director and led to a further qualification of praise. The written defense of Tom's survival had been converted by Eddie Dowling's "Catholic" conscience into "another evasion" of duty. The "humanitarian feelings" (July 30) of the audience were aptly served and the character of Tom given the sympathy which it lacked.

Rascoe's column of June 16 drew TW's closest attention and reply. Quoting the author's preface to *Battle of Angels*, Rascoe chastised TW for having bitten the hand which was feeding him royalties of $1,500 per week. (He probably did not know that TW had given half of the profits of *The Glass Menagerie* to his mother, Edwina.) Most offensive was TW's comparison of entrusting the theatre arts to "business men and gamblers" and "the conduct of worship" to "a herd of water-buffalos" ("The History of a Play," *Pharos*, 1945, p. 113). Rascoe concluded that TW "owes much" to the "'commercial' genius" of Dowling and to the "gambling chance" of the backer, Louis J. Singer, for having "turned a faulty play into a smash hit."]

10. To the Williams Family

SH: Shelton Hotel
Lexington Ave. & 49th St.
New York 17, N.Y.
[August 15, 1945]
[TLS, 2 pp. HRC]

Dear Folks:

I plan to write each of you individually but at present am lucky to sandwich in one letter to all, what with "You Touched Me" in rehearsal and Aunt Ella in town and the phone ringing just about every three minutes. I am disappointed, too, that I couldn't get through Saint Louis. It looked as if I was going to be stranded in Dallas for another week, as there were no train reservations to be had on account of the transfer of troops going on. Then I wangled a plane reservation through the Braniffs who own one of the big air-lines and managed to get back just in time for the start of rehearsals. Everything looks very favorable. We have one of the finest casts ever assembled, particularly Edmund Gwenn, the English character actor, in the role of the old Captain. We are going to open in Boston in about three weeks.

Aunt Ella seems to be fine. I took her and Lucy Pearce out to dinner at a lovely Penthouse restaurant a few nights ago and today am taking them to lunch in the garden restaurant at the Ritz-Carlton. Lucy took us all, including two of her sons to dinner and the theatre - to see Harvey - and a little excitement was added when she lost her diamond watch-bracelet. Then found it still lying under the table at the restaurant where we had dinner - several hours later. Cousin Lucy is very peculiar, really a character, she admits that she gets everything she wants from the black market regardless of cost. But I like her a lot now that I have seen her several times.

Mary Hunter is rehearsing a show, too. Hers opens in Boston the same time ours does. Hers is an all-negro musical show starring Katharine Dunham. I'm afraid Mary is pretty hard up now so I am praying that it will be a hit. I had brought a lovely silver compact back from Mexico with me which I was intending to give you, Mother - but I didn't get through Saint Louis. When I saw poor Mary, she was so nervous and depressed that I decided to give her the compact because I thought you would prefer her to have it. It seemed to cheer her up considerably.

I have not seen 'Menagerie' since I came back but I visited the cast backstage. Laurette is behaving herself marvellously and the show is still the biggest hit in town. They are now planning a London company, as announced in this morning's paper. Guthrie is also intending to have a London company of "You Touched Me" so I may have two shows in England before long. When that happens I think we should go there!

The book has come out of 'Menagerie' and Audrey has several copies at her office. I told her to send them to you all. Laughlin is in town and is preparing to bring out a book of my one-act plays.

I hope Congress revises the tax situation soon enough to help us preserve some funds.

We open in New York September 17th - Mother, if you are coming up for the opening - and I think you should - you had better make your reservations now. Why don't you fly up this time?

Give me Dakin's address. I want to congratulate him on his commission.

With much love to you all, Tom.

[Not scarcity of "reservations" but fear of his father, Cornelius, kept TW from visiting St. Louis at this time. Such estrangement did not, however, prevent his contributing to the support of "Aunt Ella," Cornelius's sister, who was visiting from Knoxville.

The parallel fortunes of Mary Hunter and TW may have seemed poignant to each and were perhaps the underlying reason for the latter's impulsive gift. Hunter, a founder of the American Actors Company (1938-1944), was TW's first choice to produce *You Touched Me!*, but the sounder financial management of Guthrie McClintic had prevailed. Hunter's new play, *Carib Song* (1945), closed after thirty-six performances on Broadway.

Plans for "a London company" of *The Glass Menagerie* were announced in the *New York Times* on August 15, 1945, the source for dating this letter.]

11. To Margaret "Margo" Jones

[Shelton Hotel, New York]
[early-September 1945]
[TLS w/ autograph postscript, 1 p. HRC]

Look, baby, I haven't time to write much right now. Not only rehearsals, incessant phone calls and pleasures and pains too innumerable to mention - but an old maid Aunt is in town, and though on my father's side, she is such a sweet old thing that I cannot neglect her!

I had lunch yesterday with a friend and emissary of Bill Inge and I gave him a good talking to. I think I have sold them on the absolute necessity of having an off-Broadway production of Bill's play. I will take an option on it myself - if necessary - provided some arrangement is made by which the advances are repaid to me in the usual fashion out of the play's royalties. That is between you and Bill and the Dramatist Guild - except that I will advance the money provided Dallas has not yet come through with it.

I have discussed with Audrey the question of making this gift to the Project and she is not at all in favor of it - I mean the $1500. It is the only money I have which is tax-exempt and I believe I have told you that she and my lawyer have calculated that I will have about one thousand left at the end of the year when taxes and living-expenses are deducted. Also, confidentially, 'Menagerie' advance sales at this point are only $30,000. which is hardly congruous with the idea that we will run for years! Until I know where I stand financially it would be rather foolish to make any large disbursals, even to anything so important. I may seem stingy to you and the girls in the little pink stucco cottage - but surely you can imagine how I feel, that it is necessary to protect myself and my work - primarily the latter - from what would be the final blow of finding myself broke again. - The volume of money coming into my hands at the present time means nothing except to the government. And I don't even <u>like</u> the <u>Truman</u> administration! - The Mirror says in its editorial page that we 'are making giant strides toward Traditional Americanism with Truman!' - URP! (If we can work out any way of making contribution - will do.)

I cannot materially affect the success of your undertaking except by such means as I have already used. Give unto Caesar the things which are Caesar's may be a somewhat misfit quotation but it contains the germ of an idea relative to my feelings. Your problem is Dallas, I wish I could help you with it, - you know that! But I have tilted at wind-mills, too, and sometimes thrown them over. It can be done. You will do it. But in the meantime let us be understanding and realistic!

We have a swell cast for "YTM" - Gwenn, Clift, and Willard are doing great jobs but I think the real surprise is going to be our ingenue, Marianne Stewart, who played the Annabella role in "Jacobowsky" in her only previous Broadway appearance. She has the shape of a pin-up girl and the talent of a first-rate emotional actress. If she plays as she is developing now, she will be a sensation! - And Guthrie has a very sound instinct as a director, particularly of this script.

The London Menagerie is Dowling bull. As far as I can make out.

Love - 10.

P.S. We go to Boston Sunday. Open here 25th - hope you come up.

[*You Touched Me!* was put into rehearsal on August 14, with tryouts set for Boston in September.

William Inge met and interviewed TW shortly before *The Glass Menagerie* opened in Chicago (rpt. in *Conversations*, pp. 6-8). Inge's own domestic comedy, *Farther Off from Heaven* (1947), would not be immediately staged on Broadway—the apparent mission of the "emissary"—but produced as the initial offering of Margo Jones's Theatre '47. Revised and renamed, it became the Broadway hit *The Dark at the Top of the Stairs* (1957). TW introduced Inge to Audrey Wood, who became his agent and who guided the friends through sharp competition in the 1950s.

Jones apparently asked TW to contribute $1,500 to "the Project" as he passed through Dallas en route to New York. The "girls" were assistants Joanna Albus, Rebecca Hargis, and June Moll, who worked in a guesthouse on the Burford estate which served as temporary headquarters. The original Burford home is now a fashionable restaurant known as The Mansion.

Marianne Stewart played the "ingenue," Matilda Rockley, in *You Touched Me!* She was last seen on Broadway in S.N. Behrman's comedy *Jacobowsky and the Colonel* (1944), with direction by Elia Kazan and music by Paul Bowles, close friends and collaborators of TW.

"Dowling bull" refers to Eddie Dowling's announcement in the *New York Times* (August 15, 1945) of plans for a London production of *The Glass Menagerie*.

TW probably wrote this letter in the week of September 2, 1945, before traveling to Boston for the opening of *You Touched Me!* The two-week tryout

(September 11-22) produced solid reviews for the play and excellent notices for Edmund Gwenn as the rollicking Captain Rockley.]

12. To Walter Edwin Dakin

SH: Hotel Algonquin
West 44th Street
New York 18, N.Y.
Sept. 28, 1945
[ALS, 4 pp. Columbia U]

Dear Grandfather -

I am happy that you have gotten away from home and the unpleasant situation there. I am sure it must be a relief to you, as it always was to me, to be removed from a certain party's vicinity. His behavior has always been shocking and incomprehensible - I can only suppose, charitably as possible, that he is not quite sane.

The play opened Tuesday night. The notices were "mixed" - that is, they ranged from excellent to poor. Not as good reviews as "The Menagerie" received but nevertheless business at the box-office is lively and the audiences seem to love it. We are hopeful of having a good run.

I am planning to spend the winter in the South, probably New Orleans. So I thought I might join you in Memphis and we could go to Columbus together for a visit. I expect I'll leave here in about a month as I can work better out of New York.

I am sending a checque which I hope you will use to have a good time. Mother is going around very socially. And to the theatre nearly every night. She is flying back to Saint Louis Tuesday.

Everyone who met you here last Spring regrets that you didn't come back this time. You seem to have made a vivid and favorable impression on all of them!

Much love, Tom.

[Cornelius Williams caused the "unpleasantness" by heavy drinking and rude treatment of his father-in-law, Walter Dakin (1857-1954), long retired from the active Episcopal ministry and living periodically at his daughter Edwina's home in Clayton, Missouri, a well-to-do suburb of St. Louis.

You Touched Me! opened on September 25 to mixed reviews and unfavorable comparisons with *The Glass Menagerie*, to which it bears a passing resemblance. TW and his collaborator Donald Windham had transformed D.H. Lawrence's ruthless wartime story (1922) into a quaint romantic comedy with an updated World War II setting. The action transpires in a "shut-down" pottery plant in rural England to which the bibulous Cornelius Rockley, a former sea captain, has retired after grounding his last commission. He flouts the strict decorum of his old-maid sister, Emmie, vigilant guardian of his delicate daughter Matilda's virginity. Into this sterile world comes Hadrian, once a foster child who lived with this family, now a Royal Canadian Air Force bombardier, who seeks to awaken Matilda's sexuality and take her back with him to Canada. The battle lines are drawn between the sexes, with a prissy Anglican priest joining Miss Emmie's campaign for celibacy.

Audrey Wood read the mood of the critics on opening night, as TW related in *Memoirs*: "As I filed out of the theatre with crestfallen Windham, my collaborator, she said in a sort of crooked-mouth whisper, 'Mixed notices, dear'" (p. 96). *You Touched Me!* closed on January 5, 1946, after 109 performances.]

13. To Kenneth Thorpe Rowe

SH: Shelton Hotel
Lexington Ave. & 49th St.
New York 17, N.Y.
November 4, 1945
[TLS, 1 p. Beinecke]

Dear Mr. Rowe:

The Theatre Guild is now in such a pre-eminent position, with such a distinguished record behind it and with so much continuing force and vitality still evident through its successful venture into the new field of light opera, that I would not be surprised to see it undertake now and then a production that would correspond to what the major film studios occasionally turn out called a 'prestige film'. As you know, that is one in which more than the usual or routine degree of artistry is invested, a film which is aimed not simply at success but to show the world how much can be accomplished in the amateur spirit and with the professional and highest professional facilities. It is perhaps too rarely that the single artist working alone is possessed by this ideal of perfection, to do not only what is successful and expedient but what is the fullest and highest realization. But it is ever so much more rarely that this impulse really takes hold of a company, and when a company has a set number of things to do in a limited time and only so much alloted to each, the ideal of perfection when it occurs cannot be very freely or easily indulged. Nevertheless it should be, just for the pure joy and catharsis of doing it.

I wrote Mr. Langner last summer that I was in no haste to have "Battle" done again. The reason is that I am waiting until some producer is moved to approach this script in the amateur spirit (with the highest professional skill) that I have mentioned above, to make a 'prestige' production out of it of the highest order. Maybe that is what Lawrence has in mind, for certainly no managers in New York are in a position more favorable to such an undertaking, and of course I would be very happy to talk to him about it any time he wishes.

Cordially - Tenn. Williams

[Kenneth Rowe (1900-1988) was on leave from the University of Michigan to direct the annual playwriting seminar of the Theatre Guild. Apparently he revived the past summer's discussion of *Battle of Angels*. Apropos of such interest, Audrey Wood had regaled TW with news of Theresa Helburn's blithe proposal to do a "season of plays formerly ruined by the Theatre Guild," adding that "on such a list your play would get their very best second-rate attention" (July 5, 1945, HRC).

The light operas to which TW refers are *Oklahoma!* (1943) and *Carousel* (1945). Massive hits by Richard Rodgers and Oscar Hammerstein II, they helped to modernize the musical stage and to make the Theatre Guild "resoundingly rich."

The "amateur spirit" was a constant ideal in TW's lifelong critique of Broadway. In "Something Wild" (1948), TW recalls the innocence and dynamism of the St. Louis Mummers, a community theatre group which staged two of his apprentice plays in the late 1930s. Theirs was a "kind of excessive romanticism" (*Where I Live*, p. 9) which he seldom found in theatres run for profit.]

14. To James "Jay" Laughlin

SH: Hotel Touraine, Boston
Wed. A.M. (3:30) [November 14, 1945]
[ALS, 3 pp. Houghton]

Dear Jay -

I'd hoped we'd have more time and less company last night. There was a lot I wanted to talk over with you, mainly my work. I have a childish need, right now, for reassurance about it - more than usual - and that is why I started reading things to you. It was not out of vanity but out of self-distrust. I have become suspicious of myself and what I've been doing - perhaps because of the vast alteration (improvement???) in my manner of living.

You are my literary conscience - the only one outside of myself - so I am over-awed by you and it isn't easy to talk to you.

I am disturbed by your apparently real dissatisfaction with your own life. I would be glad to have you tell me more about it if you think I am able to advise or help in any way.

We should have had 2 or 3 bottles of champagne last night and talked a lot more. So let me know when you have another evening in New York.

Ever, Tennessee.

(The reading has not yet occured. I have a room. Oliver is prowling the streets.)

[As TW's "literary conscience," James Laughlin (1914-1997) cared less for profit than for quality and most of all for writing that was adventurous and new. His bold venture in publishing, New Directions, would issue some forty separate titles by TW during the next six decades.

Oliver Evans, a friend who joined TW for the "reading" at Harvard, is cast here, and later in fiction, as a tireless gay cruiser.]

15. To James "Jay" Laughlin

[Shelton Hotel, New York]
Monday - [November/December 1945]
[TLS w/ autograph marginalia
and postscript, 2 pp. Houghton]

Dear Jay:

Your letter meant a lot to me! Immediately I felt a resurgence of vitality and went back to work on the play with such vigor that I worked out a brand new climax and ending which I think makes it definitely a solid thing in my hands.

The work on ONE ARM was so long-drawn-out and tormented by my inability to fuse matter with style and the sensational with the valid, that I was unable to read it myself with a clear perception, but what you say about it - if you are not just being kind - indicates that I have done the second thing

James Laughlin, founder of New Directions Publishing Corporation: "You are my literary conscience."

at least acceptably. That gives me a wonderful feeling! All of my good things, the few of them, have emerged through this sort of tortured going over and over - "Battle", "Menagerie", the few good stories. "YTM" is an example of one that didn't work out, not with any amount of struggle, though it was (the labor) pretty terrific. But always when I look back on the incredible messiness of original trials I am amazed that it comes out as clean as it does.

In one way the Boston reading went off pretty well. I was not scared of the audience as I thought I would be and they all said that I read so everybody could hear me. But I made the terrible mistake of trying to read "Dos Ranchos". It went all to pieces while I was reading it. It began to sound like shit. My voice became loud and expressionless and I kept going on, hoping to find a passage suitable to close with. I really murdered it! As I did not give them a synopsis to begin with or select in advance the parts that could be offered out of context. However I closed with a couple of very bawdy folk-poems which at least put them back in a fairly pleasant humor. I kept looking at poor Mr. Mathieson on the front row. He was squirming in his seat the whole time and looked much more unhappy than I was, like a school-boy about to suffer some awful punishment. However he was wonderfully nice about it and I liked him best of anyone there. Oliver says that he is the most erudite man in America! There was an English faculty tea preceding the reading. I had told Mr. Spencer that it would be necessary for me to have a stiff drink on the platform just to give me moral support, even if I didn't drink it. But he demurred over this, said he didn't think there was any opaque glasses and if I drank anything on the platform it would have to be something that looked like water, such as straight gin or vodka. All I had with me was a pint of yellow brandy, so I poured a stiff shot of it in my tea at the faculty thing, and I think they were all shocked and apprehensive over it, though very polite. All except a professor named Sterling Lanier. I told him that my middle name was Lanier and that we must be related and he raised his eyebrows and said 'The ramifications of the Lanier family are immense and appalling!' I was just drunk enough (I was cold sober soon as I got on the platform) to be just as saucy as he was and we engaged in a verbal tilt over our tea, in which I, having the stronger tea, did not come out unimpressively.

The next day I made some recordings. They said the records could be offered for public distribution provided they were subsidized so I gave them a cheque for $142. to subsidize them. If they are all sold I will get back royalties amounting almost to that sum. Anyway it seemed to please them a great deal, as it was the first time a poet had done such a thing. Ought to make them suspicious of the poetry!

See you Wednesday.

Tenn.

Would you like to see "5 folders of Crane material, including penny arcade photo of him" - ? A Mr. Jack Birss in Brooklyn has invited me to inspect them any evening.

[Drafting of *Summer and Smoke* (1948), the play in progress, began in New York in the preceding spring. Its "climax and ending" never ceased to plague TW and led to multiple experiments.

James Laughlin recently encouraged TW to "write another story as good as One Arm" (Saturday {November, 17, 1945} Houghton). Drafts dated May 1942 and August 1945 (HRC) reveal that the story had doubled in length during its "tortured" composition, perhaps with some blurring of the pure, instinctive morality of Oliver Winemiller, the one-armed gay hustler. TW worked on the later script in Mexico and completed it in Dallas after the harrowing passage through Customs.

TW's reading at Harvard on November 14 was arranged by Theodore Spencer, a kindly scholar-poet whom Laughlin and many other Harvard students considered their favorite professor. F.O. Matthiessen is the "squirming" author of *American Renaissance: Art and Expression in the Age of Emerson and Whitman* (1941). Sterling Lanier, the Harvard "professor" with whom TW jousted, was actually a teaching fellow at work on a doctorate in American literature. He died in 1974.

TW read the verse play "Dos Ranchos or, The Purification," a meditation on incest written in the dark poetic style of Lorca and published in *New Directions Eight* (1944). TW's recording of seven briefer poems is preserved in the Woodberry Poetry Room, Harvard College Library.

TW wrote this letter between November 19 and December 3, 1945, and probably mailed it later in December from New Orleans, as a notation penned in the upper margin of page 1 suggests: "Dear Jay - wrote this in N.Y. - just found it among my papers."]

16. To Donald Windham

SH: The Pontchartrain Apartment Hotel
New Orleans 12, La.
[December 26, 1945]
[TLS, 2 pp. HTC]

Dear Don:

The lovely wind-instrument just reached me and I want to tell you at once how enchanted I am by it, as you must have known I would be. In spite of its extreme fragility it arrived altogether intact, not a bit displaced or broken, and I have been wandering around my room with it, unable to set it down, as it tinkles and jingles. It will go in the brightest spot of my new Apartment which I move into tonight or tomorrow and which is a dream, all the windows being shuttered doors twelve feet high and with a balcony looking out on the negro convent and the back of St. Louis cathedral, easy sanctuary in times of duress. I also loved your card, "The Peaceable Kingdom", although Miss Lion looks as if she were about to start something.

I was going home for Xmas but fortunately all north-bound planes were grounded, which heaven-sent dispensation kept me here. Christmas day was one of those exquisitely soft balmy days that occur here between the rains in winter, felt like an angel's kiss. I spent it in the Quarter in the apartment I am going to occupy as the present tenant, moving out this week, was almost as fortuitious a discovery as the apartment itself. It was so warm that we had dinner in a patio and wore skivvy shirts and dungarees. This present tenant has an aged grandmother who is the all-time high in southern ladies innocense. She entered our room this morning at a very early and most inopportune moment and as she strolled by the bed she remarked, "You boys must be cold, I am going to shut these doors."

I would like to know if Jane got a job in the Hamilton show. Received a little hand-painted picture from Neil Fitzgerald with a cross note about hating to go on tour, so it must mean that "YTM" is taking to the road. I don't imagine any of them are very happy about it as they do not seem like the sort of little group that would find each other terribly stimulating on long train-rides. Just imagine Mr. Fitzgerald and Miss Whozit who plays Matilda at breakfast in a diner! One can sometimes be happier thinking of the things one has missed than those one has had. But they were all rather sweet, especially when you consider the rather disheartening circumstances at the Booth.

Audrey sent me a clipping from Montreal that contained a withering attack on Miss Hopkins and Louis J. Singer. The latter delighted me, but I was sorry for Miriam.

My coffee has come up and I must get to work, though it is hard to take my eyes off the wind-instrument.

I have ordered you a copy of "Goodbye to Berlin" when it comes from New Directions press. I know you've read it but I thought you'd like one to keep.

Best wishes for the New Year, and love,

Tennessee

[TW's arrival in New Orleans in 1938 was antidote to the stagnant, "dangerously cornered" feeling of life in St. Louis: "Here surely is the place that I was made for if any place on this funny old world" (*Journal*, October 16 and December 28, 1938). The present return (ca. December 12) followed a similar period of exile in

New York: "Broadway seems like some revolting sickness, that involves vomiting and eating and shitting all at once" (qtd. in Windham, p. 178). TW "put up" at the Pontchartrain, a "plush hotel" (*Memoirs*, p. 99) near the Garden District which bespoke his new affluence. By late-December he was living in the "heterogeneous" Vieux Carré once again.

TW met Donald Windham (b. 1920) in New York in 1940. Their friendship would be strained by collaboration on *You Touched Me!* and further tested by myriad slights and wrongs, real or imagined, as TW's fame grew in the 1940s. Nonetheless TW wrote some of his finest letters to Windham, who published a collection in 1977.

Earlier in December TW prepared the "Folks" for his own fervently desired absence at Christmas: "It is impossible to get a train reservation at this time but I have my name at several plane companies and they are going to call me if any cancellation comes in" (Tuesday {December 18, 1945} HTC).

Jane Smith has informed the editors that she is not familiar with the "Hamilton show"—probably *Angel Street* (1941)—nor does she know to which theatrical "job" her friend TW may have been referring.

TW imagined a tense scene on tour between Neil Fitzgerald, the effete Reverend Guildford Melton, and Marianne Stewart, the decorative Matilda, in *You Touched Me!*

In 1946 New Directions issued the *Berlin Stories*, a reprint of Christopher Isherwood's autobiographical tales (1935/1939) of pre-war Germany. TW ranked them with Chekhov.

TW later informed Windham that this letter was lost in moving and not mailed.]

17. To Audrey Wood

710 Orleans St.
[New Orleans, Louisiana]
Jan. 3, 1946.
[TLS w/ autograph postscript, 1 p. HRC]

Dear Audrey:

If you can imagine how a cat would feel in a cream-puff factory you can imagine my joy at being back in the Quarter. It was always my particular milieu but I was never here before with money! Now I can afford a place where the windows are all doors twelve feet-high with shutters, and a balcony looking out on the negro convent and the back of the cathedral. I never put on a shirt, just a leather jacket, I go unshaven for days and nobody says, Look at that bum, they say, That is the fellow who wrote The

Glass Menagerie! Droit de Seigneur, Noblesse Oblige and Honi Soit Qui Mal Y Pense, all rolled into one! I make my own coffee, have breakfast cream you have to dip out with a spoon, no telephone to ring, three friends who are all Mexicans and no more, a swimming club in the neighborhood, and long unbroken days to work in.

So far I have no servant to clean the place but I have been promised a negro girl to come in. She had better hurry!

I was very happy over the cigarette case, it being one of the only two gifts I received, more than I deserved for I didn't even send cards to my friends and I broke my promise to come home for Xmas on the thin excuse of planes being grounded. Conditions at home must be worse than terrible, for my father has retired from business, is at home all the time so poor grandfather has to stay in his room all the time. They can't stand the sight of each other! I will have to do something for Grandfather, but I don't know what. Perhaps bring him down here.

Please call the Shelton and give them my forwarding address, 710 Orleans. I have a short script for you and a more exciting longer one may come on soon.

Love to you and Liebling, Tenn.

Send me Story, please. Unobtainable here.

[A draft version of this letter found TW mulling his estate with little "joy." The simpler life of New Orleans had occasioned "a bad spell of self-examination and castigation," whose only "refuge is work." "Poets," however, "cannot forget time. A certain amount is in you and you have got to use it as well and as prudently as you can so that when the iceman cometh there will be some stuff worth keeping in the ice-box" (n.d., Private Collection).

The forthcoming production of *The Iceman Cometh* (O'Neill, 1946) was well known at this time and may have influenced TW's imagery. The same colloquial expression appears in a draft of *Streetcar,* which is partially typed on stationery of the Pontchartrain Hotel: "Who's been getting it all this summer? The ice man?" (n.d., HRC), asks a frustrated George (Mitch) of Blanche DuBois in a study of Scene Nine.

TW recalls that he could "see in the garden behind the cathedral the great stone statue of Christ, his arms outstretched as if to invite the suffering world to come to Him" (*Memoirs*, p. 99). The "convent" of the Sisters of the Holy Family, a religious order of "negro" nuns, was a place of charitable and educational work from 1881 to 1964. The building now houses the Bourbon Orleans Hotel.

The "short script" is "The Unsatisfactory Supper" (1946), a somber companion of the one-act play "27 Wagons Full of Cotton" (1945). The "more exciting" work in progress is *Streetcar*.

"The Important Thing," an early story of sexual discovery, appeared in the current number of *Story* magazine (November-December 1945). The editor, Whit Burnett, first published TW in 1939 and was probably mindful of his recent success.

Partially canceled in the letterhead is the imprint of the Pontchartrain Hotel in New Orleans.]

18. To William Carlos Williams

710 Orleans
[New Orleans, Louisiana]
[January 1946]
[TLS w/ autograph marginalia, 1 p. Beinecke]

Dear W.C. Williams:

I don't know why you should have felt any hesitation whatsoever about writing me about your play. My God, if there is no willingness among poets to be of any help they can to each other - what in hell have we! (Alas, we know!) But so far I have always enjoyed being helpful when I can be at all.

Audrey is peculiar little girl (of 40). My suggestion is that you <u>talk</u> to her, for she will do so much more out of personal interest and she is a soft enough person, in spite of years in the hardest racket, to want to do more for those whom she genuinely likes and she is still capable of genuine liking. So go and talk to her and in the meantime I will explain to her your position in the world of letters, that side of it which she has little opportunity to know. The chances are that she has heard of your name, at least, and I think you are the honest type of person she goes for.

Don't send me the play. I want to read it but I am entirely too negligent about mailing things back and this is especially true when I am working hard as I am now. I rarely mail the letters I write - I trust this will be an exception. Besides you will know better than anyone else can tell you whether or not you have done with this play what you wanted, and Audrey is the one to judge its saleability - no agent is infallible in this respect, however.

Best of luck to you, Tenn.

[William Carlos Williams (1883-1963) was advised by his friend and publisher James Laughlin to ask if TW's "hot shot agent" might represent his new play, *A Dream of Love* (1949). He later paid special tribute to poems by TW appearing in *New Directions Nine* (1946): "Camino Real," "Recuerdo," and "Lady, Anemone" (see *William Carlos Williams and James Laughlin: Selected Letters*, ed. Witemeyer, 1989, pp. 124-125).

Penned in the lower margin and keyed to the second paragraph is the notation "as your play is probably highly eclectic by her standards explain about it to her."

TW wrote this letter between January 3 and 15, 1946, as related correspondence indicates. Partially canceled in the letterhead is the imprint of the Pontchartrain Hotel in New Orleans.]

19. To the Williams Family

710 Orleans
[New Orleans, Louisiana]
[mid-January 1946]
[ALS, 3 pp. HTC]

Dear folks -

I got a wire from Laurette asking me to call her long distance as she had something to tell me "very important". I called her yesterday - it seems that "Menagerie" is going to give a "command performance" for the President and Washington dignitaries in Washington on Jan 27th. Laurette insists that I must come up for it. If Audrey approves, I shall - as it is unquestionably a big occasion. I will arrange either to go or return by way of Saint Louis so I can combine the two trips. If Grandfather feels able to go I would be happy to give him the trip as a Xmas present. I suppose we would meet the President and there may be a White House dinner, according to Laurette. She was very thrilled over it, but sorry it was Truman instead of Roosevelt.

I am busy as can be, working on a long script and hate to leave off even for a short trip.

It is ideal conditions here. Though I still haven't secured a maid to clean up my apt. and it is beginning to look it.

Much love - Tom.

[The "'command performance'" of *The Glass Menagerie* was scheduled for January 27 to inaugurate the "Roosevelt Birthday Celebration." TW and Laurette Taylor were ardent admirers of the deceased president, if not of Truman, his successor from Missouri.

Partially canceled in the letterhead is the imprint of the New Orleans Athletic Club.]

20. To Audrey Wood

710 Orleans.
[New Orleans, Louisiana]
Jan. 15, 1946.
[TLS, 2 pp. HRC]

Dear Audrey:

I don't know what to do about Washington. Have you any advice to give me? Laurette wired me to call her and I did. She informed me of the honor and seems to expect me to come up for it. Do you think it justifies the trip? As you know I am not very much excited by social occasions but at the same time I want to do what is expected of me. What would go on there? Would there be a dinner at the White House? That might be too important to pass up.

I am afraid I will have to do something immediately about Grandfather. Got the most awful letter this morning from Mother. Dad retired from business at New Years and subsequently retired to his bedroom with the bottle. Does nothing but stay home and drink. When sufficiently drunk I think he is dangerous. Mother says that he talks threateningly and abusively to my grandfather, and I have received a letter from grandfather virtually imploring me to take him to New Orleans with me. I don't think I could have grandfather in this small apartment with me and get much work done, but I am hoping that I can find a suitable boardinghouse for him here, am working on that. These are the last few years of his life and he should not be allowed to spend them in such hellish circumstances as those now prevailing at home. As for Mother, she embodies all the errors and mistakes and misunderstandings that her time and background could produce, she is so full of them that she is virtually a monument of them, nor has she out-grown a single one of them - her mental horizon has apparently never expanded one inch - I'm sure I could never live with her again! - but I respect her endurance, a sort of tragic magnitude she does seem to have! - <u>society</u> should be <u>scourged</u> for producing such

"Christian martyrs"! - such monuments of misapprehension! - undoubtedly she once had the makings of an awfully fine woman.

I am switching back and forth between two long plays, the one about the sisters started in Chicago and one about a Spinster begun in New York. Right now I am doing more with the sisters, it is now set in New Orleans and is called "A Street-car Named Desire" - there is one by that title that runs close by my apartment, and proceding in the other direction down the next street is one called "Cemetaries". In spite of this I am not really in a very morbid state of mind, as this might suggest.

Were you disappointed in the one-act? Your silence about it offers that impression. It was the first one-act I've done in quite a while. Perhaps it lacks something that I used to have in my earlier one-act plays. The tragic intensity in a small sphere, such as 'This Property', was partly out of my own desperation at the time it was done and now that I am on better terms with existence - some of that may be lost. I hope not too much of it and I hope I can go on drawing new perceptions out of experience, but all that I can actively do is to go on working and hoping that my wish to do something new will not take me outside of what is communicable to a large enough audience.

Have you heard of William Carlos Williams? Laughlin wants me to read one of his plays and recommend it to you for marketing. I wrote Williams not to send me the play but to give it to you directly, as I always forget to send things back to people. He is one of the top three or four American poets [and] has immense prestige in his field, but his work in drama may not be anything for Broadway. You can tell. His address is Dr. W. C. Williams, 9 Ridge Road, Rutherford, New Jersey. He is a fine fellow, and I am flattered that Laughlin thought of us both in this connection.

Ever, Tenn.

[Audrey Wood advised TW that the command performance of *The Glass Menagerie* could not "be treated too lightly" from "a good business standpoint." She also urged that he "do something about" his grandfather, bullied as he was by Cornelius, and promised to be as "helpful" (January 19, 1946, HRC) as possible.

The "long plays" in progress are *A Streetcar Named Desire* and *Summer and Smoke*. TW experimented with Chicago and Atlanta as settings for *Streetcar* before deciding upon New Orleans. He also arrived at the famous title after testing at least eight alternatives.

Wood informed TW that she was "tremendously" moved by the "very frailty" of his new one-act, "The Unsatisfactory Supper" (January 19, 1946, HRC). It shares with "27 Wagons Full of Cotton" a Mississippi Delta setting and much the same cast of characters, if with variant names and roles. Their antics, rife with venality, pathos, and humor, would be recast in *Baby Doll* (1956).

A Dream of Love was not "Broadway material," Wood advised William Carlos Williams, and urged that he "clarify the story in dramatic terms" (May 7, 1946, HRC). The play was published by New Directions in 1948 and performed the following year by an off-Broadway company. It was not Williams's first or last foray into theatre.]

21. To Oliver Evans

[710 Orleans Street
New Orleans, Louisiana]
[mid-January 1946]
[TLS, 1 p. HRC]

My dear Daughter:

I have been turning things over in my mind, which is where I also turn things over sometimes, and have come to the conclusion that it is time for you to be brought out in society. Your term with the Sisters has taught you many useful things, such as your needle-work, your dancing and your singing of those charming French songs. You have acquired many graces for the drawing-room, but it is time that you learned there are rooms to a house, besides the music room, the drawing room, the library and the kitchen. In short I think it is time that you were brought into association with a select number of your mother's friends' children, so that you may experience a little of the harmless gaiety which is suitable to one of your years and station in society. As a matter of fact, I am writing the Sisters at once in regard to this view and suggesting that you be prepared and equipped for emergence from the convent. I have suggested a few purchases for your wardrobe, six or seven changes of light-weight underwear, one taffeta with a train and one without a train, a small, girlish hat with some discreet kind of paper flower on it - no plumes are worn by the younger girls this season, though matrons of your mother's standing sometimes display them in the afternoons. I do not know if your figure requires a corset, for I have not seen you lately and a girl's figure undergoes rapid changes at your time of life, but it would be good to have one just in case! I am sorry it will be necessary for you to travel alone - that is, if a suitable duenna cannot be provided from the convent. However the Sisters will surely instruct the conductor to look out for you and see that you are [not] engaged in conversation by strangers, for that is something your mother knows only too well may lead to serious misapprehensions if not real compromise.

I have a delightful small furnished apartment at 710 Orleans, half a block from the cathedral. Three big rooms, a small study and a balcony that faces the negro convent. The streets are teeming with ambulatory vistas, the small dark kind that are barely contained by their buttons and while I know that you will grieve for the Sisters left behind you, I have no doubt that certain errands of piety and mercy may draw you occasionally out upon the streets.

I did like the poem, though it is perhaps more like a collection of sharp and vivid notes for an essay than a lyric. But that is your particular style. I hope to hear of you writing more prose also.

Ever, Tenn.

[Oliver Evans (1915-1981) and TW met in the early 1940s and became close friends and traveling companions. The New Orleans-born poet and critic taught at several universities after taking a master's degree at the University of Tennessee in 1941.

TW's satire was inspired no doubt by the propinquity of his apartment to the "negro convent," once a festive ballroom and reportedly the site of the famous quadroon balls of antebellum New Orleans. TW's allusion to a delicate, cloistered sexuality led Evans to recall a much coarser trade at the Shelton Hotel in New York, where TW lived during the staging of *You Touched Me!* Writing as "Olivia," Evans wishes her "sainted Mother" a "safe and speedy return" to services at the "Shelton Cathedral": "I have even gone so far as to make a special offering at the shrine of Our Lady of the Steam Room." Olivia herself planned to "linger yet awhile" in New York, "surrounded by the pious Sisters of our beloved Order of St. Vaseline" (n.d., HRC).

This letter is tentatively dated on the basis of stationery and typography which resemble TW's correspondence of January 15, 1946, to Audrey Wood.]

22. *To James "Jay" Laughlin*

["enroute to Washington D.C."]
Jan. 25, 1946.
[TLS w/ autograph postscript, 2 pp. Houghton]

Dear Jay:

We are passing through Hattiesburg Mississippi enroute to Washington D.C. for the "command performance" of "Menagerie". I had decided not to go up for it as I have so fallen in love with N.O. LA that I was unwilling to part with it for even a week-end, but a young lady friend of mine thought differently and bought my ticket and poured me on the train more or less forcibly. She is along too and that may be why she was firm about it. In fact I am going through quite an experience with this young lady. She is one of these people with a passion for lost causes, is beautiful enough to have anybody she wanted but is apparently attracted only by the line of most resistance. So she came down here from New York and so far the most complete and graphic candor on my part has not convinced her that propinquity will not conquer all. I have always been more or less overlooked by goodlooking women and once upon a time I sometimes suffered acutely from the fact, so the novelty of the situation makes it all the more impossible to cope with. I dare say you have had infinitely more experience in the matter and at any rate are infinitely more resourceful, so let us exchange fatherly advices. No, I don't want to be "saved", I don't think anyone has ever been happier with his external circumstances than I have learned how to be, and as for my internal circumstances, only I can affect them. So is there anything to be gained from the complicating entrance of a lady? I would like to arrange for you to meet her, for she is a delectable article for anyone on the market. Or are you still engaged by the dark lady of the sonnets in New York? I do hope you will come to New Orleans with her, and if Sylvia - yes, that is her name - is still down here - she threatens to get a job here - something very interesting might develop for you. At any rate you will love New Orleans and it is a grand place to take anybody you are in love with as it rains so much but always clears up after while. - Your poem about the girl and her lost husband - like the one about Baudelaire - has a richness of texture ~~and feeling~~ that you don't always indulge in. Incidentally I received a letter of lavish praise from Bigelow about your book of poems. I hope I have saved it for you. Bigelow is my brightest friend, too. He is a fascinating personality that

I hope you may get to know. A bit like Isherwood's Mr. Norris, - that is, in the mysteries of his origin Etc. - but much deeper and warmer I think. I think he is a bit supernatural, a sort of very wonderful 'witch!'

I got all the books and am delighted with "27 Wagons", it is perfectly gotten out. Bob's jacket is a dream! I hope the critics don't make you suffer for it. Some of the characters are a bit peculiar and the author does not come thru as a terribly wholesome individual. I wrote Audrey at once about W.C.W'S play - I hope she will feel inclined to do something about it. She will if it appears at all marketable.

In spite of what you say about my prose I think it is pretty awkward and I think I can get my best effects, with good directors and actors, on the stage when there is so much besides verbal values to work with - except when there is a subject like "One Arm" that you can't put on the stage as it now exists. - If you have a chance to - see a picture with the awful name of "Fallen Angel". I think it's extraordinary in some respects. It could almost be happening, the characters come as close to life as any the screen has ever touched and some of the scenes - the psychological suggestions, perhaps undeliberate - are really haunting.

I hope that this new girl will continue to give you interest if not happiness in New York. Or Vermont.

Ever, Tenn.

P.S. I am so shy with this girl Sylvia that I suffer acutely when alone in a room with her. Have you ever felt that way with anyone? I have told her I feel that way - she makes it worse by enquiring every few minutes, 'Am I making you uncomfortable? Do you want me to go out now? Is it all right if I sit here? Don't talk to me unless you want to, Etc.' Then she sits there with her brilliant eyes taking in every embarassed change of expression as if she were conducting some marvelous experiment in a lab so that I don't know where to look, let alone what to say. Exactly like Lillian Gish or at best Harold Lloyd in an old silent film. What are women made of?!

In a week or so I am going to send you a 30 or 35 p. Ms. of a "work for the Plastic Theatre" with Mexican backgrd. & characters that include Oliver Winemiller, Baron de Charlus, and Don Quixote! I want it produced on a program with Dos Ranchos.

["Sylvia" has not been identified, but TW apparently told his mother of her presence in New Orleans, and of her encumbered condition. "I can't imagine," Edwina replied, that "you are doing much work with a distracting lady on hand. How come she has 'nothing to do' when she has two children?" (February 16, 1946, Private Collection).

His friend Paul Bigelow, TW thought, resembled the title character of Christopher Isherwood's novella *The Last of Mr. Norris* (1935; rpt. by New Directions, 1946). Norris is a charming voluptuary of mysterious origin and illicit means of support who epitomizes the disordered life of pre-war Berlin.

New Directions published *27 Wagons Full of Cotton and Other One-Act Plays* on December 27, 1945. The cover art, which derives from the title play, shows a long thin plume of smoke rising from a burning gin. The *New York Times* reviewer was typical of others in finding TW's characters so peculiar as to be outside "the boundaries of credibility and unfeigned sympathy" (February 24, 1946).

The melodramatic plot of *Fallen Angel* (1945) turns upon the murder of Stella (Linda Darnell), a small-town waitress, whose dark, alluring beauty haunts the drifter, Eric Stanton (Dana Andrews). *Fallen Angel* was considered a disappointing sequel to Otto Preminger's direction of *Laura* in 1944.

TW intended the latest draft of *Camino Real*, subtitled "A Work for the Plastic Theatre" (n.d., HRC), to be performed with "Dos Ranchos" ("The Purification"). Oliver Winemiller, the vagrant hustler of "One Arm," would soon be renamed Kilroy. TW advocated "a new, plastic theatre which must take the place of the exhausted theatre of realistic conventions" ("Production Notes," *The Glass Menagerie*, 1945). The emphasis would fall upon visual and aural rather than literary effects and would require innovative "subtleties" of direction and stage design.]

23. To Neil Fitzgerald

[710 Orleans Street
New Orleans, Louisiana]
[February 1946]
[TLS, 2 pp. HRC]

Dear Neil:

You see I am faithful to the Shelton, at least to their stationary!

Of course I was inexpressibly sad about what happened to our play. I also feel that it needn't have happened, and that's what makes it hurt so. I am now in a position to write a play about a mother's sorrow for the death of an invalid child, for I felt exactly that way about it. I so wanted it to live!

Nobody writes me from New York except Donnie and poor Windham lives in such a world of his own that I don't get much news out of him. When you have time I would appreciate some account of things there. How did Antigone fare with the press? I have only read one notice, THE SUN, which corresponds to what I felt about the play when I read it. I can't understand how Cornell or even McClintic could be so obtuse about a silly script.

I have a lovely apartment here in the French Quarter. Ceilings about 12-feet high and a balcony that looks out on the back-yard of the Cathedral. The atmosphere and life is tranquil and I have been working continually. Two long scripts are in progress and a short-long play Mexican fantasy with music and dancing is finished: it is only about 55 pages long, however, and I won't know how good it is till I've let it set for a while. The speeches are frighteningly long!

Neil, your work in "YTM" and our association is one of my very happiest memories in the theatre: not just a memory but a lasting experience I am sure. I hope it will be your fortune to find an excellent part.

Any change in the Shelton management must be an improvement! When I'm coming back I will wire you in the hope you can get me another suite there, however. I had a good time in spite of the bitches at the desk! - and that old white-headed bull-dog - is he still patroling the lobby?

Love, Tenn

[Neil Fitzgerald (1893-1982)—the Rev. Guildford Melton in *You Touched Me!*—apparently lived at the Shelton Hotel in New York, whose stationery TW playfully used for this letter. News of a "change" in hotel management may have reminded TW of the former manager's warning note: "It has been called to our attention you have been in the habit of doing considerable entertaining in your room 1832" (November 23, 1945, Private Collection). TW's "chicken run" and Oliver Evans's "raids on the steam room and the bar" (qtd. in Windham, p. 179) were observed no doubt by the "white-headed bull-dog" who patrolled the lobby.

The Cornell-McClintic production of *Antigone* opened to mixed reviews on February 18. Ward Morehouse, writing in the *New York Sun*, granted the boldness of the experiment—based upon Anouilh's wartime adaptation (1943)—but he and other reviewers found the updated Sophocles to be jarring in effect and not "very stimulating theater" (February 19, 1946).]

24. To Audrey Wood

SH: Western Union
New Orleans La
1946 FEB 26 PM 1 18
[Telegram, 1 p. HRC]

AUDREY WOOD=

IF USE OF UNDERSTUDY IS DAMAGING PLAY PLEASE INVOKE ANY LEGAL RIGHTS I MAY HAVE TO CLOSE TILL TAYLOR RESUMES PART OR STAR REPLACEMENT IF SHE DOES NOT. LOVE=

TENNESSEE.

[Audrey Wood cabled TW and later wrote in detail about Laurette Taylor's severe laryngitis and absence from the cast of *The Glass Menagerie*. To Wood's dismay—and Taylor's also—the play continued to run with the understudy taking the role of Amanda. Wood viewed this decision as yet another skirmish in the "Dowling-Taylor Civil War" and confirmation that the backer, Louis J. Singer, "loves money more than art" (to TW, February 26, 1946, HRC). She urged TW to "send very strong wires" stating his "concern for Taylor's health" and instructing that the play be closed during her illness to avert "possible damage" (telegram, February 25, 1946, HRC) to the property itself.

Taylor, nearing sixty-two, had been continuously in rehearsal or performance of *The Glass Menagerie* for fifteen months. Because she recovered from similar throat problems during the Chicago run, there probably seemed little cause for alarm. In retrospect her declining health can be dated from this episode.]

25. To Paul Bigelow

710 Orleans.
[New Orleans, Louisiana]
PM: New Orleans, February 27, 1946
[ALS, 4 pp. Columbia U]

Dear Paul -

If only you had sent me that "Bundle of letters" a little earlier in my career. It is much too late for me to learn the efficacy of the sponge bath and the advisability of bathing my "sacred inner organs" - and when I think of the times that I have been "drugged and stupefied by unscrupulous men" I could scream!

I have been having quite a hectic time of it - living with a little Mexican full of tricks, for about two months. I didn't mind her bringing in trade as long as she saved a little of her energy for my own entertainment but recently she started falling asleep as soon as her trade departed. So I kicked her out of bed and sent her out on the streets. She is a pretty thing - She took refuge with a Creole belle who had wanted her badly while she was staying with me but was considerably disconcerted to have her altogether on his hands. I wrote her a mildly affectionate note of farewell which she mistakenly interpreted as a plea to return. So back she came tonight with her 2 shirts, alarm clock and perfume. When I left the apartment she was singing gaily in the bathtub and no doubt I will return to find her coiled snake-like around at least 2 more sailors. These Mexicans are charming little things - if you can live through them! I wonder how Miss Maxwell would handle the situation! Alas, I have never been able to scream very convincingly about my beautiful body!

I have been hard at work in spite of distracting circumstances - completed a Mexican fantasy and am plowing through a New Orleans play - more gradually.

Don't plan to leave here till it's finished - maybe not for three or four months.

I love it here, though society isn't much. I have been going out to some of the debutante parties but no balls - I don't have a tux and don't want to bother with one.

Let me hear from you. Love to you both!

Tenn.

[Paul Bigelow (1905-1988) was variously a journalist, raconteur, aspiring playwright, and production assistant to the Theatre Guild and Cheryl Crawford. In 1939 he and his friend Jordan Massee moved from Georgia to New York, where they met TW.

Pancho Rodriguez, the new companion, "occupied the center" of TW's life "from the late fall of {1945} till at least half a year later" (*Memoirs*, p. 99). "Miss Maxwell" is Gilbert Maxwell, poet, friend, and informal biographer of TW.]

26. To Audrey Wood

[710 Orleans Street
New Orleans, Louisiana]
March 12, 1946
[TLS, 1 p. HRC]

Dear Audrey:

I have read over Camino Real and I don't think it ought to be typed up in its present form. In this version the only good scene is the one at the Gypsy's. I don't see anything objectionably coarse in that. Kilroy is the name that you see written in public places nowadays. "Kilroy was here", "Kilroy is here", Etc. is the favorite inscription on walls of bars, stations, cheap hotel rooms, fences. So in writing about him I wanted to catch the atmosphere of the world he lived in, bars, stations, cheap hotel-rooms. An atmosphere of the American comic-strip transposed into a sort of rough, colloquial poetry. Comic-strip bar-room idyll, the common young transient's affair with longing and disappointment, a very rough sort of tenderness mixed with cynicism. Touches of coarseness were necessary to get that effect. Of course the veil-lifting was symbolic of something more intimate, but since visually it [is] only a veillifting, I don't see why it should be offensive. It was a mistake to identify the couple as ~~Jacques~~ Casanova and Camille. Better to call them "Actor & Actress" or "He and She". And their long scene together should be cut down to include only the street-cleaners and the long monologue commencing "This dusty plaza with its dried up fountain." The Baron should be eliminated and the play begin with Kilroy's entrance. That will make it a lot shorter but clearer and stronger. I will prepare this version when I can take the time off my longer script. I think it is worth doing as the Kilroy sections and the ending have charm. And if I make a good script of it, it will go nicely with "Dos Ranchos".

I am getting back on "The Street-car Named Desire". I hope reading it over will not be as shocking as "Camino". I sometimes wonder if any professional (?) writer can write as badly as I.

I want to buy an inexpensive second-hand car to knock about in, the weather is becoming so nice here. Do you think I can afford to? Taylor and movie-sale are both so uncertain that I cannot feel any economic security.

With love, Tenn.

[A call from Audrey Wood instructing TW to "'put it away, don't let anybody see it'" (qtd. in *Memoirs*, p. 101), was reportedly her first acknowledgment of *Camino Real*. The "only good scene" refers to Block Seven, where Kilroy unveils Esmeralda in a coy simulation of sex that Wood apparently found "coarse." Much later TW observed that agents "are sometimes very obtuse in their recognition of an original and striking piece of work in its early stages" (*Memoirs*, p. 101).

Casanova and Camille were listed in the Broadway credits of *Camino Real* as "Gentleman of Fortune" and "Lady of Legend." TW retained the Baron de Charlus, Proust's aging homosexual, but as initially staged in New York, the play began with the entrance of the Survivor, rather than Kilroy.

Later in March TW learned that Cary Grant was considering an independent film production of *The Glass Menagerie*, in which he would take the "star role" and "an effort" would be made "to secure Laurette Taylor" (telegram, Vincent to Wood, March 22, 1946, HRC). In reply Wood stated "that Tennessee Williams has evolved a way of avoiding an unhappy ending" (telegram, to Vincent, April 5, 1946, HRC), should this be a commercial consideration.]

27. To Audrey Wood

SH: Adler Hotel
75 Linden near Main
Memphis, Tenn.
April 21, 1946.
[TLS, 2 pp. HRC]

Dear Audrey:

I would like to have this story typed up and one copy sent to <u>Laughlin</u> (500 5th Ave.). I know that you may not like it and so I am not suggesting that you send it to anyone else. If you should like it, you may use your own discretion, which is always best, about sending it other places. But send one copy to me as I want sometime to make a short (maybe two act) play out of it, in which case the title might be changed to "Some of God's Creatures". That might make a good over-all title for a group of my short plays. (will send address later)

I have bought a super-jalopy (a 1937 model convertible Packard roadster) and am proceding gradually toward home. The car is still beautiful in spite of its age, all black and shiny silver, and very gracefully designed with leather seats that smell wonderful in the sun, although the stuffing is beginning to come out of them. However the radiator is cracked so that it has to be filled with water about every ten miles and the tires have blown out with the regularity of percussion instruments in a Shostakovitch symphony. I have had to buy a complete set of new ones, including tubes, between here and Baton Rouge. But I have learned how to use an hydraulic jack and a lug-wrench, which is really a milestone in my life! The car has unlimited speed, eight cylinders! I intend to have it over-hauled in Saint Louis, and then procede West, probably to Taos, N.M. It will be wonderful for the desert!

I have not gotten as far along with either of the long plays as I intended. The last few weeks in New Orleans were awfully hectic. I had disagreements with the owner of the apartment-building and was put out of my nice apartment and could not find another that was at all agreeable. When I get to another stopping place (Taos?) I hope to surround myself with acres of uninhabited terrain and concentrate on an active singular existence. Let come of it what may!

Somebody named Perlmutter has written me a couple of times asking that I endorse a drive against cancer. I've lost his letter so don't know where to answer. If you can get in touch with him, please tell him that I am completely against it, the disease.

I am going to leave here this afternoon for Saint Louis.

With love, Tennessee.

P.S. I have stored a trunk containing papers and other belongings at a warehouse called Gallagher's in New Orleans.

[Audrey Wood may have surprised TW by cabling that she liked his new story, "The Night of the Iguana," a "great deal" (May 17, 1946, HRC). It shares with the later play (1961) a setting at the Hotel Costa Verde near Acapulco and scenes between Miss Jelkes and a male protagonist who, like the tethered creature of the title, is "helpless." The first draft of the story, however, is openly gay in design. An older and a younger writer reveal their sexual tension in caustic discussions of the prying Miss Jelkes and of "homolectuals" who must either turn "vicious" or "crack" (April 1946, HRC).

TW withheld a more provocative story from Wood entitled "Desire and the Black Masseur" (1948). He knew that this tale of a bi-racial sado-masochistic affair ending in cannibalism would have given her "fits!" (to Laughlin, April 23, 1946, Houghton).

TW's abrupt departure from New Orleans continued his perennial battle with landlords, usually a result of such colorful guests as Oliver Evans, who had joined the ménage at 710 Orleans. For Evans's "amazingly frequent convenience" (qtd. in Windham, p. 184), TW placed a mattress on the floor.

Herbert Perlmutter asked many prominent Americans, including TW, to lobby Congress on behalf of a massive government program aimed at finding a cure for cancer.

TW last visited his family in March 1945, before *The Glass Menagerie* was transferred to New York.]

28. To Amado "Pancho" Rodriguez y Gonzalez

[53 Arundel Place
Clayton, Missouri]
[late-April 1946]
[TLS, 1 p. HRC]

Dear Pancho:

I am sorry I couldn't talk to you much on the phone. We have two phones, one upstairs and one down and Mother usually listens at the other phone. I was terrified that you would say something. She had already opened and read your telegram and they are full of conjecture and suspicion occasioned by that. It will be a little embarassing to tell them now that I am going to Taos. I should have warned you more about my home situation. But don't worry about it.

I wanted to ask you all kinds of things but had to cut the conversation as short as possible because of the eavesdropping. Why did you leave N.O. so suddenly? I hoped you would wait till I had finished my stay here - I have to stay here about a week - and then I might have picked you up somewhere on the road. It is unfortunate that you have to arrive there not knowing anybody. Though I am sure Spud will be nice to you. Had you met him in New Orleans? Oh, yes, in the Bourbon house. I've just gotten here and am not functioning mentally after the terrific grind on the road.

I will wire you some money tonight. Can't send much at the present as my funds were badly depleted by tire-purchases and unexpected costs on the road. Have to draw on my N.Y. bank this week. When that comes in can wire you some more. I wish you would write me immediately but please be extremely careful what you put in any communication addressed here. Make the letter very casual but tell me where you are staying in Taos, how you like it - do you think you'll be happy there? Is there anything you can do? Staying with me you would not need much money but knowing you, I am afraid you will be restless without something in the way of an occupation. I shall be writing awfully hard during the days and there is not society of the sort in New Orleans - although I consider that to be an advantage.

However the important thing is that I shall see you very soon! I plan to leave here in exactly a week. It ought not to take me more than four days on the road, as I shall get the car in good condition while here. We can talk about everything when I arrive.

Stay out in the sun, rest, relax! Don't worry about anything. You may not like the desert at first but it will grow on you if you give it a chance. I hope you will look up Dorothy Brett and also Mrs. Lawrence if she is around Taos. Give them all my regards and particularly Spud. I am glad you have met him and I appreciate any help he's giving you - I'm sure you must have felt pretty lost when you first hit there.

Will you look around for a small (2 or three room) house, if any such thing is available around Taos. Spud might know. Mrs. Rendall mentioned some apartments in the Haworth foundation. Love -

Tennessee.

[A report that TW met Pancho Rodriguez (1921-1995) at Taos—presumably when he last visited the city in 1943—is not documented, nor is it supported by correspondence (see Spoto, pp. 121-122). TW later placed their meeting in New York in June 1946, discreetly removing the principals from New Orleans, where they probably met in late 1945 (see *Memoirs*, p. 99). Pancho's family roots were in southwest Texas (Eagle Pass) near the Mexican border.

By March 1946 TW found New Orleans and the "Mexican affair" a "bit miasmic" (qtd. in Windham, p. 184) and availed himself of travel once again. Probably sensing evasion, Pancho quit his job and preceded TW to Taos. His telegram and repeated calls for money raised suspicions at home and led TW to surmise that "the cat is all but out of the bag." Dakin, "home from India," was grinning "foxily" (qtd. in Windham, p. 188) at his brother's sexual proclivity.

TW met "Spud" Johnson, writer, publisher, and secretary to Mabel Dodge Luhan, and Dorothy Brett, painter and devotee of D.H. Lawrence, during his first visit to Taos in 1939. He and Brett became sympathetic friends after a meeting in her rented room, which was reached by an Indian ladder: "One day a young man came climbing up my ladder, he had been told to come and see me, I think about Lawrence. He said he wanted to be a playwrite, that he was determined to be one.

That he was called Tennessee Williams, the Tennessee a nickname given him at school because he came from Tennessee. He was so young and ambitious, and sure of himself. He certainly carried out his ambitions" (Brett, unpublished autobiography, n.d., Northwestern U).]

29. To the Williams Family

[Holy Cross Hospital
Taos, New Mexico]
May 23, 1946
[TLS, 2 pp. HTC]

Dear Folks:

I am leaving the hospital today and considering that I have had a major operation I am feeling remarkably well. I shall have to take it easy for about three weeks and am going up to Frieda Lawrence's place to rest and recuperate. I shall spend most of the time lying out-doors in a hammock.

The experiences since I left Saint Louis have been so unpleasant that I don't even like to write about them. I took sick the first day on the road, started having sharp pains. I was immediately afraid of appendicitis and [so] I called in a doctor that evening when I arrived at Springfield, Mo. He said it was just cramps from nervousness, so I went on the next day. Fortunately the bearings burnt-out which compelled me to stop in Alva, Okla. I saw another doctor who thought I had a kidney stone and advised me to take the train up to Wichita to see a specialist there, which I did. He put me in a hospital for a couple of days. I had X-rays and while nothing seemed to be revealed the doctor there diagnosed it as low-grade appendix but dismissed me from the hospital thinking an operation was not necessary. I had to leave the car as it would not be ready for several weeks, parts being difficult to replace. So I went on to Taos by bus, continuing to suffer. When I got here I had a fever and a blood-count of 18,000 which indicated a serious infection. The doctors here put me right in the hospital. The pains had suddenly stopped so they suspected the appendix had burst. Naturally I was quite alarmed at this news. They decided they had better operate immediately, and did that evening. According to the doctors (there were two of them) the appendicitis was a lucky accident, for when they made the incision they discovered another acute condition which might not otherwise have been suspected. Something called "Meccles diverticulum" (phonetic spelling) which is attached to the small intestine was seriously infected and at the point of rupture which would have caused peritonitis. Had to be removed. Also appendix. I was on the table about two hours as they had to talk things over. They are very young doctors, the surgeon being just 31, and recently out of the army, but they seem to be quite modern and capable. They told me there was nothing malignant in the condition. I don't suppose they would tell me if it was, so I thought it might be a good idea for Dr. Alexander to call or write them for a fuller account of their findings. If it was anything more serious than they represented to me, it might be better for me to go to New York where the best treatment is available. Up till the day I left Saint Louis I had had no pain or sickness whatsoever, had been unusually well all winter in New Orleans, not a sign of any intestinal trouble and putting on weight. Well, life is full of surprises! I must have an excellent constitution for I was sitting up the second day after the operation and walking around the fifth. I feel a bit weak and shaky now but otherwise pretty good. Have started working again on my plays. Everyone here has been wonderful, I am never alone, my room is full of flowers. Mabel Dodge Luhan, the local social dictator, paid me a call, Frieda and Brett have called nearly every day and my Mexican friend Pancho has served as Secretary and kept me with books and a radio. The people around here are the kindest I have met, and the country is indescribably beautiful. Frieda's ranch is the nicest part of it!

Audrey writes that she has sold a couple of my stories, one to Madamoiselle for four hundred dollars, and one to Town & Country which is also one of the highest paying mags. I hope these will cover my sickness expenses. I should have had hospital insurance!

I hope you have not been worried. These things happen to all of us now and then and you have to take them philosophically.

I will write you again in a short time.

With love, Tom.

[TW was attended at Holy Cross Hospital by Drs. Albert Rosen and Ashley Pond. The aftermath of the operation (ca. May 15) was probably more complicated than the procedure itself, which the surgeon's widow, Myrtle Rosen, has described as "fairly simple." Legend has it that Pancho Rodriguez caused a post-operative row by scaling a balcony and making his way into TW's bed. The nuns who found them together had "a fit," as Mrs. Rosen recalled with a grin. Polish nuns of the order of the Holy Family of Nazareth arrived in 1937 to staff the new hospital, unprepared as they were for ministry to TW.

TW planned to convalesce at Kiowa Ranch, the "place" in the mountains where Frieda Lawrence and her husband had briefly lived in the 1920s. TW thought it "the dreamiest spot on earth" and hoped that D.H. Lawrence's lingering "spirit" would "animate" (to Wood, n.d., HRC) his own. The ascent on May 23 was marked by liberal toasting of wine, sudden "breathlessness," and a "wild" return to the hospital with Frieda driving her car like "a firetruck" (*Memoirs*, p. 104). Her friendship with TW led to the present invitation, as it had to her support for earlier literary projects related to Lawrence.

On June 2 TW wired Audrey Wood from Albuquerque that he and Pancho were "driving East" (June 2, 1946, HRC) and planned to spend the summer at Woodstock, New York, with Oliver Evans. Neither health related fears nor an early departure from Taos had deterred TW from preparing "a revised and abridged version of 'Camino Real'" (to Wood, n.d., HRC).]

Tennessee Williams and Pancho Rodriquez, New Orleans: "My Mexican friend Pancho."

30. To Audrey Wood

[31 Pine Street
Nantucket, Massachusetts]
[June 1946]
[TLS, 2 pp. HRC]

Dear Audrey:

I meant to see you again before I left New York but the visit there tired me so I wasn't fit to see anyone. I decided on Nantucket and here I am. Have engaged a little house for the season. Pancho is with me, doing the cooking and housework while I resume work on a play. I detest the "Olde Antique Shoppe" atmosphere of the island and the old ladies on it, but the swimming is good and I shall make every effort to tie myself down. Perhaps I am all right now, as the doctors tell me, but I feel very unsettled inside, as if hung together by a few loose strings, so I want to get as much work done as quickly as I can.

I don't believe I told you about my car. It is still at the Ford garage in Alva, Okla. The owner of the garage was a perfect bastard about it. He wired me to call for it but when we arrived in Alva it still wasn't ready. We hung around that horrid place for a week waiting for it. It had been there for over a month. But they kept stalling and finally told me that one of the new parts, something called an "insert", didn't fit and it would take ten more days to get a new one. Then I said I would have to leave the car as I couldn't wait around any longer. The manager was extremely snotty. Said he would just stop work entirely on the car if I left town. Now I have about a thousand dollars invested in the car - the motor having been almost completely rebuilt - so I don't want to throw it away. I wonder if Eddie Cohen could not write the man, assuring him that I will pay for the repairs if and when completed and that I have a friend who will call for the car and drive it East for me. (Jane Lawrence's husband, Tony, has offered to do this.) In any case, I don't think it is legal for the garage owner to refuse to complete a job and thus make it impossible to remove a car that he has agreed to repair. I don't know what legal action could be taken if he persists in that attitude, but since he is agent for the Ford Motor company, perhaps some pressure could be exerted through the Detroit headquarters. The car is a '37 Packard convertible - the bearings had burnt out and the bill for labor and replacements (which I have not yet paid but will when work is completed) was $137.85. There were two people in Alva interested in buying the car if the repairs were completed. And I would like to have it myself. Could Eddie do anything about this? Garage owner is Mr. Davis, Ford Garage Alva, Oklahoma. - Sorry to worry you with it.

I saw Wycherly. All but first three scenes - I got in a bit late. I thought she was doing a reasonably good job but it seemed just a substitution. She does not have Taylor's humor. That was the big deficiency. And Taylor's little insertions which only she could put over sounded pretty incongrous coming from Wycherly. I don't think she is really right for the part. Hope you'll find someone better, if a road company is organized. Of course this opinion is only based on her performance in the last three scenes the night I was there.

I wish Taylor and Wycherly both would get a certain line right: It's the one about Tom taking a service-car home from the office. Taylor and Wycherly both say "Station-wagon" which is of course fantastic! The wonderful thing about Taylor is that she can get away with anything, even that!

I didn't see her or call her - or Dowling either - while I was in New York, so perhaps it is better not to let either know I was there.

My address here is 31 Pine Street, Nantucket, Mass.

With love, 10.

[A fragment of TW's journal, apparently the first preserved entry since late 1943, records a depressing trip to Alva, Oklahoma, to reclaim the Packard, abandoned a month earlier and still not repaired. "Been here three days with Pancho - we have both descended into a nearly speechless gloom and apathy. . . . I wonder how much more I can take. If the operation had not knocked me out nervously I would bear up better. As it is I'm a quivering mass of anxieties" (June 5, 1946). TW later confirmed the decisive effect of his illness: it had made a "zombie" of him, "a man infected with creeping death," who "felt himself excused from emotional participation with anything but the people he could create in his work" (qtd. in Windham, pp. 298-299).

TW and Pancho visited New York before settling on Nantucket Island, rather than Woodstock, for the remainder of the summer. On June 24 TW approved a request from Gilmor Brown that *Stairs to the Roof* (1945) be restaged at the Pasadena Playhouse in 1947. He also wanted Brown, the supervising director, "to see" *Camino Real* after he had "brooded over it a while longer" (June 24, 1946, Huntington). TW probably resumed work on *Summer and Smoke*.

Margaret Wycherly replaced Laurette Taylor during her vacation in June.

Transfer of *The Glass Menagerie* to a new theatre and a cut in the top from $4.20 to $3.60 were planned to coincide with Taylor's return to the cast on July 1—in hopes of reversing a decline in business.

The anachronism cited by TW occurs in Scene Six of *The Glass Menagerie*, where Amanda says to Laura, "I gave your brother a little extra change so he and Mr. O'Connor could take the service car home." A former resident of St. Louis has described the service car as "a cross between the streetcar and a taxi. It made regular stops, cost a quarter (more than streetcar fare), and reached a destination quicker and perhaps more safely."

Penned in the upper margin of page 1 is a probable filing date of July 1946. A retyped excerpt (paragraph #2) held by the HRC bears a reception date of June 24, 1946, indicating that the letter was probably written in the week of June 16.]

31. To Frieda Lawrence

31 Pine St.
Nantucket Mass!
June 25, 1946.
[TLS, 1 p. HRC]

Dear Frieda:

We have finally come to rest, after weeks of exhausting travel, here on Nantucket Island. It is nothing like as nice as Taos and Pancho and I both are sad about being unable to stay there. It would have been heavenly. I am a bit disgusted with myself for the cowardly retreat, for after all it would be better to die at a place like your ranch than to live on Nantucket Island. Everything here is very Antique Shoppe in atmosphere, full of aggresive propriety. We went to a tea-party yesterday that cured me of all such social occasions. The old ladies and gentlemen all sat around in a circle and stared at me and Pancho till I became so nervous that my tea-cup rattled like castanets. Fortunately the swimming is good. That is the only good thing. I spend half the day writing, furiously to make up for lost time, and the rest on the beach. And I am still full of uneasiness and apprehension of a vague, continual sort. I am afraid those doctors and nervous nuns must have cut out a large piece of my guts! How I would like to talk to you and Lawrence for an evening in front of the ranch stove. (When I talked to you I always seemed to be talking to Lawrence also.)

Do you know our car is still in Oklahoma? They kept us waiting around in that awful dust-bowl town for a week while they fooled around, doing practically nothing. Then told us some of the new parts didn't fit and we'd have to wait another ten days. So we gave up and left the car there and came East by train. It is still there and I don't think they have any intention of repairing it. Horrible people!

Thank you so much for sending the book I left there. We have the picture of you and the cartoon of Lawrence on the mantal of our little house here which we have taken for the season. Did I tell you that I have acquired an original letter of Lawrence's? Thornton Wilder presented it to me last fall at the Boston opening of You Touched Me. It was nicely mounted by Wilder and inscribed underneath. Wilder was crazy about "Y.T.M." - saw it three times. He is here on Nantucket but I haven't seen him yet as his mother is very sick right now.

Pancho is cooking and getting better at it all the time. I am writing. That seems to be the whole story.

Please give Brett our affectionate greetings, and the same to the Vanderbilts and Mrs. Luhan and Spud. And Angelino!

With God's permission a reverdici!

Ever, Tennessee.

[Vivid and endearing memories of Frieda Lawrence (1879-1956) date from TW's first visit to Taos in 1939, when she befriended the young writer and approved his plan to write a play about her husband's life in New Mexico. During a second visit in 1943, TW described Frieda to James Laughlin as a lusty "Valkyrie," the "only exciting woman I've known!"

Mabel Dodge Luhan, patron of artists and writers, urged the Lawrences to settle at Taos in the early 1920s. Contrary to reports, the present meeting with Luhan was TW's first.

"Angelino" is Frieda's companion, Angelo Ravagli, an officer whom she met in Italy in 1925 and married many years later.

The address and date of this letter appear to be in Pancho Rodriquez's hand.]

32. To James "Jay" Laughlin

[31 Pine Street
Nantucket, Massachusetts]
[mid-July 1946]
[TLS w/ enclosures, 2 pp. Houghton]

Dear Jay:

It is good to know that you still think of me. I have been having a bad time of it and have felt dissociated from almost everything else. The physical machine in a state of collapse and what may politely be called the spiritual element, crouching in the corner with both hands clapped to its eyes.

I was on my way to New Mexico in an ancient Packard convertible which I bought in New Orleans when I took suddenly and without any warning quite ill. Had to have an emergency operation in Taos, performed by an almost amateur doctor and some nervous Nuns. They thought it was acute appendix but it turned out to be an acute 'Meccles diverticulum' which they say is a section of the small intestine. It was cut out and I have been in a prolonged state of shock ever since. The day after the operation one of the good Sisters of the Holy Cross came into my room and advised me to make my peace with the Lord as whatever improvement I showed would only be temporary. Ever since then, and despite the assurances of the doctors, I have been expecting to die, which is something I have never really looked forward to at all. So I gave up my plan of remaining in Taos for the summer and rushed East and took a house on Nantucket - and tried to forget my apprehensions in hard work on a long play. But it is not so easy. I had x-ray pictures taken last week which they told me did not show anything wrong but even if this is quite true, I will probably remain in a state of morbid alertness for a long time. Consequence of having nerves! - "Oh, for a robust conscience and the Viking spirit in life!"

I am interested to hear you are going to Europe. I am planning (if I don't die!) to go to Spain next year. And Constantinople, Greece, and Russia. My Mexican friend, Pancho, is still with me and wants to go to Europe, too. Perhaps we can make a party of it.

I got the typed story. The Masseur does <u>not</u> eat the bones. It is clearly stated that he puts them in a sack which he drops in the lake at the end of the car-line. So the story is all right on the realistic level.

I am sending two more. Have the "Saint" one typed for me, it's the original only copy. The long one gets a bit too preachy toward the end as I started thinking of it as a one-act or two-act play. It would be good theatre if one could get it produced, I think.

Audrey read this long one and showed it to my kid brother, just out of the CBI air-force, when he visited New York while I was out West. She asked him if she ought to show it to anybody and he said 'Yes'. But right afterwards wrote me a letter saying I was going to come to an end like Edgar Allan Poe, if not worse. On the whole, a sympathetic letter, however. He is a bright kid, though not at all like me. Has a law-degree. I want him to practise law in New York so he could take a hand in my affairs (theatrical). I think they have been bungled. "The Menagerie" has not been sold to the movies and it is slowly dying at the box-office - should have been sold in the very beginning when it was hot! But I am kept in the dark about such matters and never really know how things stand. Not even what I have in the bank!

Have you read Carson McCuller's new book? I think it's superb.

Ever, Tenn.

P.S. I wrote this some time ago. Just discovered I hadn't mailed it. Damned gloomy letter! Ought to tear it up as I am feeling more cheerful now. Carson McCullers is here, visiting me as the result of a brief correspondance. The minute I met her she seemed like one of my oldest and best friends! We are planning to collaborate on a dramatization of her last book soon as I get my present play finished. I think this play will be last effort to write for Broadway. From now on I shall write for a nonexistant art-theatre.

I am enclosing the two 'myths' which belong with the one about the 'Masseur'. Will you have these typed for me, as you did with the other? Either send me a bill for them or deduct the typing cost from royalties. And send me copies. I read them to Carson and she seemed very pleased with them. - Tell Lowry I think his story in ND #9 is magnificent!

[TW spent the week of July 7 in New York hoping to relieve a mind "full of hypochondriacal anxieties." He informed his mother that Elizabeth Curtis, a wealthy socialite whom he met through Oliver Evans, had provided lodging "just off Park avenue" and made the "arrangements" (n.d., HTC) for his medical testing.

Apropos of "morbid alertness" and "nerves," TW quotes a favorite passage from *The Master Builder* (Ibsen, 1892): "Oh, for a robust conscience and the Viking spirit in life!" (Act Three).

Stories cited by TW are "Desire and the Black Masseur," which James Laughlin has apparently misconstrued, and two other recent works, "Chronicle of a Demise" (1948) and "The Night of the Iguana." At least seven "quality" magazines would reject "Iguana" before it first appeared in TW's collection, *One Arm* (1948).

TW wrote this letter in the week of July 14, while the postscript was written, and the letter presumably mailed, later in the month—after Carson McCullers had reached Nantucket. Accounts which place her on the island before mid-July are not confirmed by TW's summer correspondence or itinerary. McCullers's "new book," *The Member of the Wedding*, was published on March 19, 1946, and was generally well received. TW read and admired her first novel, *The Heart Is a Lonely Hunter*, when it was published in 1940.

The "'myths'" probably belong to an unpublished gathering of stories entitled "Three Myths and A Malediction" (n.d., HRC). Listed on the title page are "Blue Roses and the Polar Star," "Desire and the Black Masseur," "The Myth," and "The Malediction" (1945)—a forerunner of *One Arm*.

Robert Lowry's story "Layover in El Paso" (*New Directions Nine*, 1946) concerns a young soldier on leave who forsakes visiting his family to court an aging floozy whom he meets on the train. The story may have reminded TW of his own "layover" in El Paso, where he was stranded in 1939 amid "choking" dust and "sterile" mountain scenery.]

33. To Katharine "Kit" Cornell

[31 Pine Street
Nantucket, Massachusetts]
July 31, 1946.
[TLS, 1 p. HRC]

Dear Kit:

Forgive me for not answering your wire sooner. I have been in a quandary about the play. Almost immediately after I wrote you about it, I really read it through for the first time and as always happens at a first reading, I was profoundly depressed to find it was so different from what I thought I was writing. My impulse was to throw it into the ocean, but instead I went back to work on it. I conceived a new ending, much lighter than the one before and yet not at all violating the play's quality. However it made a lot of the earlier material unsuitable and reduced the play's length to about 60 pages. Out of eight scenes there are now about four that are reasonably readable. I will bring it over to Martha's Vineyard and read you, or let you read, as much as I dare, however embarassing it may be to us both.

Right now Carson McCullers - you probably know of her novels - is visiting me here in Nantucket. She is planning to dramatize her wonderful book, "The Member of the Wedding", and we are sort of working together. I advising her, and she me.

She'll be leaving here in about a week. She is terrified of journeys and I may accompany her to the mainland and I thought perhaps we could stop off at Martha's Vineyard and spend an evening with you, at which time you could look at what I've done on the play. "Portrait With A Parasol". That's the new title. The heroine carries a yellow silk parasol. Eventually it should be good, but you must not expect anything now.

You will love Carson! Probably the sweetest person in the literary world! I felt immediately that you should know each other.

Ever, Tennessee.

[TW assured "Kit" Cornell (1893-1974) that he was "feverishly" writing a play for her and would send a copy "in a week or two." The "plot is slight," he added: "A Mississippi spinster tells the story of her luckless romance with 'the wild boy of the town.'" The present ending apparently replaced a "tragic" conclusion in which Alma's suicide was relieved by a "fantasy" (to Cornell, July 10, 1946, HRC) of life everlasting in a good-time house. This early draft stage of *Summer and Smoke* appears to exist only in fragmentary scenes and passages of dialogue.

TW mentioned to Paul Bigelow his delight in reading *The Member of the Wedding*, only to discover—or recall—that Bigelow's friend, Jordan Massee, was Carson McCullers's third cousin. TW presumably used this contact to invite McCullers to visit Nantucket, where she worked on a dramatic version of her novel, and he continued to revise *Summer and Smoke*. To Audrey Wood he described McCullers as "a strange girl" with "a phobia that she is going to faint in public and be put in jail!" ({July 29, 1946} HRC). She planned to leave the island in early-August, after a visit of nearly three weeks. (TW's letter to Wood is misdated August 29, 1946; the editors have assigned a date of composition one month earlier.)

Virginia Spencer Carr, McCullers's biographer, remarks that a tipsy Carson introduced herself to Miss Cornell by asking for a sanitary napkin.]

34. To Amado "Pancho" Rodriguez y Gonzalez

[31 Pine Street
Nantucket, Massachusetts]
[July/August 1946]
[TLS, 1 p. HRC]

Dear Pancho:

Perhaps I have not made certain things clear to you, and just in that case I will put them down in black and white.

1. As you ought to know, I have no one else in my emotional life and have no desire for anyone else.

2. I have never thought of you as being <u>employed</u> by me. That is all an invention of your own. If we were man and woman, it would be very clear and simple, we would be married and simply sharing our lives and whatever we have with each other. That is what I had thought we were actually doing. When I say 'Pancho is doing the cooking and house-work' I am only saying that Pancho is being kind enough to help me, and knowing me as you do, you should realize that that is the only way in which I could possibly mean it.

3. This is a dark, uncertain period that we are passing through and a time when we ought to stand beside each other with faith and courage and the belief that we have the power in us to come back out in the light.

4. I love you as I have never loved anyone else in my life.

5. You are not only my love but also my luck. For 3 months I have lived in a dark world of anxiety, inexpressible even to you, which has made me seem different - You may not have guessed this, but you are about the only thing that has kept me above the water.

10.

[Pancho Rodriguez kept house for TW and Carson McCullers, but by late-July he was in "a mysterious Mexican rage" and had "packed his trunk" (to Wood, {July 29, 1946} HRC) to leave the island—resentful, TW surmised, of his and Carson's friendship and his own subservient role. Pancho remained on Nantucket, reconciled perhaps by TW's appeal.]

35. To Audrey Wood

31 Pine Street,
Nantucket. [Massachusetts]
August 29, 1946.
[TLS w/ autograph postscript, 1 p. HRC]

Dear Audrey:

I had gone down to W.U. to wire you to hold the scripts for revision when they handed me your wire. I think you are probably right about witholding them for a while. I made the mistake of promising them too early to Cornell and I hated to let her down as she seemed so eager to get an idea of what I was doing. Also I've felt so insecure about the play that I needed strongly someone else's interest and advice. Sometimes the solitary struggle of writing is almost too solitary for endurance! I am sure I would work better and easier if I could feel more casually about it but I get so tied up in the things emotionally that it hinders me. I hope that you were able to feel in the play a sort of Gothic quality - spiritually romantic - which I wanted to create. It is hard for you to use such stuff in a modern play for a modern audience, but I feel it is valid. But requires awfully careful treatment. It would be infinitely easier to do it on the screen. I am going to send you the silent film sequences which I think should accompany the script whether or not they are to be incorporated in a stage production. Incidentally, if you could interest a movie producer in the play as a screen story I would be eager to work on a screen adaptation of it prior to a stage production. (If a stage production isn't possible now). I also hope you will feel that it might be practicable to actually combine the silent film sequences (perhaps 16 MM.) with the stage scenes. I will send you at the same time a rewrite of Scene V, which is the most incomplete scene in the script you now have. The best place I can think of for an entirely additional scene is between scenes three and four - leading up to Alma's first visit to John's office. Of course if the film sequences are admissible, no more material will be necessary as they round out the story quite completely. - Of course Cornell is not the only ultimate possibility. If it is worked out well enough it might be a vehicle for a star team like Hepburn and Tracy.

I dread making another trip - it takes all day to get from here to New York except by air, and I don't think I can afford air-travel under the present indefinite circumstances. However I will wire you or call you about the

Pittsburgh trip a few days in advance. - Will you please ask Eddie Colton to send my brother (Officer's Mail Section, Lowry Field, Denver) all the titles, Etc. that I sent him for my Packard? Dakin is going to take possession of the car. - With love.

Tennessee

P.S. Please mail me a copy of typed script.

[TW's "solitary struggle" produced the "first reading version" of *Summer and Smoke*. The epigraph from Rilke—"Who, if I were to cry out, would hear me among the angelic orders?"—bespeaks the frustration of Alma Winemiller, a young woman who has been placed in the conservative culture of the Delta and tempted by the sexual freedom afforded to the men whom she knows. The "Gothic quality" to which TW refers is conveyed by the Episcopal manse, Alma's spiritual setting, which reinforces both her moral idealism and cloistered condition. A stone fountain in the form of an angel, one of four staging areas, marks the perennial conflict of spirit and flesh. "Her name," Alma explains, "is Eternity and her body is stone and her blood is - mineral water . . ." ("Summer and Smoke," August 1946, HRC).

A typical film sequence begins with "Alma lying sleepless in bed," dissolves to the notorious Moon Lake Casino, and ends with her "knocking" ("Silent Screen Interludes," n.d., HRC) on the door of John Richardson's (later Buchanan) office. Audrey Wood claimed that she was open to the use of "motion picture techniques" (to TW, September 6, 1946, HRC) in *Summer and Smoke* and awaited further information. TW later described his plan to use "stage and screen in combo" as a "lunatic notion."

The closing of *The Glass Menagerie* (August 3, 1946) and the delayed sale of film rights made TW's finances seem "indefinite." TW confided to Edwina that "the play could have run another year if Laurette and Dowling had stayed on good terms and the show had been properly managed" (n.d., HRC). Taylor's declining health, seemingly overlooked by TW, may have hastened the play's closing after 561 performances.

The tour of *The Glass Menagerie* was set to open in Pittsburgh on September 2, 1946, with Pauline Lord playing Amanda and Eddie Dowling directing the new company. None of the original players entered the cast.]

36. To Katharine "Kit" Cornell

31 Pine Street
Nantucket [Massachusetts]
September 5, 1946
[TLS, 1 p. HRC]

Dear Kit:

I haven't known what to say to you about the play so I have put off writing. I took it into New York to have it typed up about two weeks ago. I had the copies delivered to Audrey as she naturally insists on reading my work first. Then I received, after returning to the island, a long wire from her in which she said she thought it would be unwise to show it in the present form. She thought you and Guthrie might be "sufficiently disappointed to make other plans". To tell you the truth, this only confirmed my own feeling, or suspicion. I felt terribly insecure about it, as you probably understood when I visited you. I don't think Audrey is altogether gloomy about it. At least she said it "had many things to recommend it" but needed a good deal of building. The typed manuscript turned out to be only about 80 pages. It would have been full length if I had not scrapped two original ideas, one being narration and the other silent film sequences. I still think the silent film sequences was a good idea, if at all practicable. Some of the best material in the story could only be shown on the screen. And I think the combination of screen and stage has an exciting value as something new in the American theatre. (It has been tried in Europe). I will include the film sequences in the next typed version. (As something tentative).

I'm leaving the island about Sept. 15th and I hope by that time Audrey may feel that I have done enough to show you. It is a hard play to write and of course the important thing for all concerned (if any beside myself) is to do the best possible job regardless of time. If it takes unreasonably long, I naturally won't expect you to wait for it but I'll do all I can to urge it along rapidly. Illness and anxiety were a great impediment in the early stages.

I visited Carson McCullers in Nyack to see how she was coming along with her dramatization. That is taking longer than expected, too. It's her first attempt at theatre and it's a bit hard for her to think in theatrical terms. She has the delicate novelist's suspicion of dramatic effects. Meeting you was good for her. Made a deep impression and greatly increased her respect for theatre.

With love and best wishes, Tennessee

["Narration" and "film sequences" were attractive devices for a playwright who struggled with exposition, as did TW. Alma's opening lines in an early draft of *Summer and Smoke*—"I was twenty-nine the summer that I met him, and I felt this to be the last summer of my youth" ("The Water Is Cool," n.d., HRC)—are sharply reminiscent of Tom's prologue in *The Glass Menagerie*.

TW's interest in "film sequences" recalls a similar plan to use "magic-lantern slides" in *The Glass Menagerie*. Both projects reveal a playwright's fascination with film, perhaps stimulated by TW's early relation with the director Erwin Piscator, who often used documentary footage (and narrators) to historicize his "epic theatre."

TW visited Carson McCullers in late-August, when he returned to New York to deliver the latest draft of *Summer and Smoke*.]

37. To Walter Edwin Dakin

SH: Nantucket Island, Massachusetts
Sept. 9, 1946
[TLS, 2 pp. HRC]

Dear Grandfather:

I just now heard through Audrey that you had been ill. Mother hadn't mentioned it to me. In fact I haven't heard from her in about a month and I haven't known exactly where you were, although I knew it was in Ohio. I have wanted to write to you all summer but have been uncertain of the address. I hope you realize that I have been thinking of you and am very unhappy over the fact we couldn't be together somewhere. As you know I was very sick last Spring and for quite a while after the operation. I just had to throw myself down on the beach here for a couple of months and forget everything else. I got so behind with my work that when I was able to resume it I had to devote myself to it all the time, trying to finish a long play for Katharine Cornell in time for her to read it and make her plans for the Fall. It still isn't finished and she hasn't seen it yet but the worst is over. It has a Mississippi delta background like most of my other plays. I shall really have to go back South pretty soon and renew my acquaintance with some of our old home-towns such as Columbus if I am going to continue to write about them. Do you remember Marion Wise who lived near us in Columbus and played with Rose? He was here in Nantucket this summer and we met each other. Of course I didn't remember him but he did me. He is living in New York and has an excellent job with an advertising firm. If I return South this Fall or winter, as I am planning to do, I hope I can spend a little while in Columbus. It would probably help me to add some authentic background to the new play.

Audrey says you are better now. I know how you love to be up and around but you must take your time about it. I suspect that you have not paid enough deference to your years and have tried to go out too much in society this summer.

The road company of "The Glass Menagerie" has opened in Pittsburgh and got very good notices. Audrey went over to see it. She reported the road company to be quite good so the royalty checks will start rolling in again I trust.

I am going back to New York city the sixteenth of this month. It is difficult for me to work there so I probably won't remain more than a week. Then will return somewhere in the South to finish up the new play. Let me know if there is anything I can do for you. And take the best care of yourself!

With much love, Tom

[Edwina and Audrey Wood apparently conspired to shield TW from news that his grandfather had suffered a "severe heart attack" at the Friends Boarding Home in Waynesville, Ohio. "He is much better now," Wood later informed TW, explaining that just as Edwina was preparing to go to her father, she received a letter "saying, 'Don't come. Will send for you when I need you'" (September 6, 1946, HRC). The Friends Home in Waynesville—Walter Dakin's birthplace—was founded by local Quakers to provide "rooms for the elderly, retired teachers, and transients."

Wood saw *The Glass Menagerie* in Pittsburgh and reported that Pauline Lord "will be quite good when she finally has conquered the part," although "she will never be as good as Taylor" (to TW, September 6, 1946, HRC). The part of Tom (Richard Jones) was well played, she thought, but the Gentleman Caller (Edward Andrews) and Laura (Jeanne Shepherd) were disappointing. Nonetheless the Pittsburgh critics wrote of the play's "soaring beauty" and business was good.]

38. To Audrey Wood

SH: Nantucket Island, Massachusetts
[ca. September 9, 1946]
[TLS, 2 pp. HRC]

Dear Audrey:

Thank you for your long and helpful letter. I am sorry I couldn't get to Pittsburgh. I had hoped to but my digestion got out of order again. I haven't been able to eat a regular meal in about a week. I am disgusted with myself thoroughly, and thoroughly baffled, for it is not like me to be so pusillanimous. This play is something I should be able to handle with perfect ease for it is the sort of material I've always handled best but either nervous or physical fatigue is making it absurdly difficult for me. I have been making some progress on a second draft but the real flowering must wait for a better psychological period than I am in at the moment or simply till I am feeling a bit better.

Carson phoned me that she is coming up here tomorrow with her husband, bringing the finished first draft of her dramatization. I suspect it will need a good deal more work, too. Her theatrical eye is not yet fully developed, of course. I'll suggest that she have you read what she's done.

The fiction editor of the New Yorker, William Maxwell, was on the island and wrote me a note. I asked him over - he says they'd be happy to use some of my short stories if I have any suitable. You or Laughlin may have something, though I can't think what it would be. Laughlin is talking about bringing out a book of them, perhaps privately, at $5 a copy.

Pancho and I are leaving the Island the 16th or 17th, and I will be in New York for a few days before continuing South. If you happen to know of procurable hotel space (a double room) I wish you'd reserve it for the night of the 16th. The Lawrences are getting thrown out of their apartment - Squatters rights don't work in the U.S.A. - so we can't stay with them.

The International outlook is becoming quite fearful. Don't you think there ought to be an organized movement in the Theatre to insist upon a clarification of U.S. foreign policy? It appears to me that Byrnes and the administration have formulated a policy of their own in line with the most reactionary elements in the country and they are taking the shortest cut to world destruction through their inflammatory meddling in Europe. This is without the understanding or sanction of the vast body of Americans who, like everybody else, will go down the drain if we're drawn into war with Russia. I think there ought to be popular demonstrations of all kinds in protest against it. The theatre could start such a program.

The news of Grandfather's illness is horribly upsetting. I wired mother and she answered that he was much improved and I have written him. The human situation - God!

With love, Tenn

[Audrey Wood's "helpful letter" bore advice but no statement of enthusiasm for *Summer and Smoke*. Wood suggested that TW expand the roles of Alma's mother and aunt and that he treat small-town rituals of courtship and marriage with greater authenticity. The death of John Richardson's father revealed a more serious and finally intractable flaw. The climactic event not only lacked detail but its redemptive effect upon the son, whom Alma silently loves, had been stated rather than dramatized: "There is no indication what happens to father except Alma's speech, 'Your father's dying in order for you to redeem yourself' etc." (September 6, 1946, HRC).

The New Yorker published only one story by TW: "Three Players of a Summer Game" (1952).

One Arm and Other Stories, the collection planned by James Laughlin, would require a limited edition as well as selective distribution and review. "Tenn's Broadway reputation should not be compromised" (September 5, 1946, Houghton), Laughlin assured Wood, in earlier remarks meant to disarm her.

Discussion of Cold War politics may have been provoked by *Time* magazine, where TW often found his news. The report that Secretary of State Byrnes had made "the great American decision" (September 9, 1946) to keep Germany from entering the Soviet Union is perhaps the "inflammatory meddling" to which TW refers.

This letter bears an incomplete reception date of "9/ /46."]

39. To Guthrie McClintic

[New York]
[September 1946]
[TLS, 1 p. HRC]

Dear Guthrie:

I can't tell you what it means to me to have the continuing interest of yourself and Kit in the play that I have promised and delayed so often. The trouble is entirely in myself: it is ailing because I am. It is the sort of material that I use best but there is simply a lack of physical energy, which with me is creative energy, to get it over the hurdles except by slow stages. Progress <u>is</u> being made, though. I hope that Audrey will agree that enough has been done to show you before I leave town. I am going South, at my doctor's advice. He says the rat-race of New York is too much for me. I had gotten so I simply could not eat anything. After a few days in the hospital that condition has passed but I must be careful to avoid a recurrence.

My love to both you and Kit, and be assured of my best efforts to make you a play.

Ever, Tennessee

["Am I dying?" TW wrote, as he prepared to leave Nantucket by ferry on September 14. By noon he felt "a bit better" and described his progress to the mainland: "I have a little private state room, procured from a kind lady by Pancho. I do not think much. Brain really seems sort of anesthetized. Carson is with me {McCullers had returned to Nantucket for a brief second visit} and she has been an angel. Though I have only really felt like seeing Pancho. He has <u>not</u> been an angel . . . but I think we love one another" (*Journal*, September 14, 1946).

An undated journal entry reveals the cause of TW's persistent illness: "Today I have entered St. Luke's hospital for purgation of a tape worm. A rugged ordeal tomorrow salts and medicines all day." Donald Windham found TW "regally withdrawn" when he visited St. Luke's and concluded that their "lives had gone different directions" (Windham, p. 192).

TW was hospitalized in the week of September 15, 1946. Precisely when he was released and left with Pancho for New Orleans is unclear.]

40. To Audrey Wood

[632½ St. Peter Street
New Orleans, Louisiana]
[early-October 1946]
[TLS, 2 pp. HRC]

Dear Audrey:

I am very well situated here in a furnished apartment on the nicest street in the Quarter, only $75. a month. It has a huge front room with a grand piano and furniture that belongs to an antique dealer!

I have been feeling well since I got here and Miss Alma is making progress. In fact I now think the play may run over the usual playing length. I am developing several new ideas which means more time but the result will be worth it. For one thing I am building up Mrs. Winemiller, as you suggested. I have a new comedy idea. Her sister Albertine eloped with a fraudulent promotor, a man who built something called a Mechanical Museum and got all the Winemillers friends to invest in it. It was a collection of mechanical marvels and "a big snake", sort of a side-show that travelled about the country. Albertine was deserted and died, Mr. Forsythe

the promoter, landed in jail. At every opportunity Mrs. Winemiller, who is obsessed with clearing her sister's and Mr. Forsythe's name of connection with the scandal, refers to the Musee Mecanique and describes the marvels as if it were still going on under prosperous circumstances. Perhaps if it is built up sufficiently it would make a part for Laurette! - Tell Guthrie that I am expanding the play in this way and ask him to be patient about it.

I received a heart-breaking letter from Grandfather. He is just waiting to die in that Quaker home in Ohio! Speaks of it with resignation and beautiful courage but I can't think of it without wanting to bat my head against a brick wall. I am going to send him a checque. Of course there is nothing that money or anything else could do. It seems such a pity he had to wait for it, that it couldn't just have come quietly, without any warning as nobody who ever lived deserved an easy way out as much as he does!

Pancho returned here with me and is resuming his old job at the best department store.

I hope MGM offers a good price for the one-act. I had never thought of expanding it and don't think I ever would. But I think we should retain the right to produce it in its present form in a program of one-acts.

With love, Tennessee.

I hope you have sent "The Angel in the Alcove" to the typist. A copy should go to Laughlin. Carson says that she thinks Madamoiselle would take it. I am sending you another little story I found in the Bigelow box - to be typed up.

[Once settled in the Quarter, TW reverted to old rites of authorship: "I would rise early, have my black coffee and go straight to work" (*Memoirs*, p. 109). Further revision produced a second draft of *Summer and Smoke* dated November 1946 and entitled "A Chart of Anatomy" (HRC). The variant title refers to a "lecture" in Scene Eleven in which young Dr. John Buchanan affirms only the appetites and the finality of death and corruption.

TW developed Mrs. Winemiller in relation to her sister Albertine and the whimsical "Musee Mecanique." Mrs. Winemiller's "breakdown," a consequence of her sister's death "in a good-time house" in New Orleans, created a burden of care for Alma and her clerical father as well as the town's polite disapproval. TW no doubt saw and perhaps visited the Musée Méchanique which operated at 523

Royal Street during his visit to New Orleans in early 1939. Kenneth Holditch has identified the curious landmark and noted that it was moved to San Francisco for the Golden Gate Exposition, which TW visited in July 1939.

MGM's interest in "This Property is Condemned" (1941) led Audrey Wood to set film rights at "fifty thousand dollars" and to add deceptively that TW "had always considered possibility making three act play" (telegram, to Freed, October 12, 1946, HRC).

Rejected by *Mademoiselle* and *Town and Country*, "The Angel in the Alcove" first appeared in *One Arm and Other Stories* in 1948. The "Angel" refers to TW's maternal grandmother, Rosina Otte Dakin ("Grand"), whose ghostly figure casts "a gentle, unquestioning look" upon her grandson's sexual difference. TW later wrote that "'Grand' was all that we knew of God in our lives!" ("Grand," 1964).

This letter, which is written on stationery of the Shelton Hotel in New York, bears a reception date of October 8, 1946.]

41. To Walter Edwin Dakin

632½ St. Peter Street
New Orleans, La.
PM: New Orleans, October 10, 1946
[TLS, 2 pp. HTC]

Dear Grandfather:

I have returned to my winter quarters in New Orleans and was lucky enough to get an apartment almost as soon as I arrived, a very lovely one, furnished by an antique dealer with his own things. A huge living room with four double windows, the size of two large rooms. Two bedrooms, one of which I am using for a study, a kitchen and a bath with automatic heater. I was planning to stay in New York for a while but it is so crowded there that it was not possible for anybody to get me even a hotel room for more than one night. I was sick when I arrived in New York, so I went straight into the hospital and stayed there till I could get space on a plane to New Orleans. I had been over-working and it had affected my stomach. I couldn't eat anything solid for about a week. That condition has now cleared up and I am feeling well again. I am still working on the play for Miss Cornell. Have been working on it for about a year now and it is just getting into shape. But I still haven't shown it to her. I wanted it to be as good as possible before she sees it. I think it will eventually be an excellent play for her. Or somebody else.

I am glad that you are taking a calm and philosophical attitude toward your present illness. That always helps you to recover. I have had heart-trouble for ten years now and I am not afraid of it anymore. By the calendar I am somewhat younger than you, but only by the calendar which is an unimportant thing. You are one of the youngest people I have ever known, and incidentally one of the two people I have most loved and admired in this world. You know who the other one was and still is.

The Menagerie seems to be doing well on the road. It made over $24,000. one week in Saint Louis. So Mother and I are getting our royalty checks again. I am enclosing a check for you in case there is a little extra something you may want or need. When you are able to come South I want you to remember that I have a room for you here and that I would love having you with me for the winter.

All of the seasons debutantes are coming to my apartment a week from this Saturday. One of them is the niece of a friend of mine and he is using my apartment to entertain them. The social life down here is always very pleasant and I have more nice friends here than anywhere else.

Don't worry! Take care of yourself!

With much love to you, Tom

[TW's authorized biographer, the late Lyle Leverich, states that "Tennessee believed all his life, despite repeated diagnoses to the contrary, that his 'defective heart' was an organic condition" rather than one subject to passing "emotional and physical stress" (Leverich, p. 148).

The tour of *The Glass Menagerie* in St. Louis "was completely sold out for all performances" and "very well" received, as Dakin Williams, on military leave at the time, informed his brother. Eddie Dowling's "absence" from the cast he thought "a tremendous improvement" (October 6, 1946, HRC).

In the preceding winter TW and Pancho entertained "society beaux" following a debutante party, but their "whirl in high society" ended abruptly with gossip about the homosexual ménage at 710 Orleans. "I am told that my name is now mentioned only in whispers in mixed company" (qtd. in Windham, pp. 181-182). This event or another like it was embellished in *Memoirs* and given a salacious finale (pp. 100-101).

Partially canceled in the letterhead is the imprint of the New Orleans Athletic Club. Penned on back of the envelope in Walter Dakin's hand is the notation "A dear precious letter I value it highly."]

42. To Walter Dakin Williams

632½ St. Peter St.
N.O., LA.
Oct. 11, 1946
[TLS, 1 p. HTC]

Dear Dakin:

Awfully sorry you've had all this trouble with the car. About the title: Louisiana is one of the few states where a bill of sale is equivalent to a title. They didn't give me anything but the papers Colton sent you. Nothing was lost. I found out in Alva, Okla. that these papers were inadequate outside of La. I will go to the place where I bought the car and see if I can get a title or something that will satisfy a Denver buyer. Perhaps it would be simpler for me to just transfer the car to your legal ownership. Would it? - If the car is now in good running condition and you have any use for it, why don't you just keep it? But do whatever you think best. I would like to have a car but think I'll wait till I can get a new one. I hope that you will take some steps against the bastard Davis in Alva. At least write the Ford headquarters in Detroit about his chicanery. I think he is already in their bad graces and he should have his dealer's license revoked. He did everything possible to take advantage of us both.

I have given up all thought of a musical career and will be happy to surrender my title to the guitar without compensation.

I had planned to stay in New York for a while, till my new play is finished but it was impossible to get even a hotel room there, so I flew South almost immediately and have now gotten a lovely apartment in New Orleans. It is a better place for me to work. I'm afraid Miss Cornell is getting pretty impatient for the play. She still hasn't read any version of it. The more I do on it, the more there seems yet to be done, but the final result should be gratifying.

I'm awfully distressed over Grandfather's condition. He wrote me a pretty blue letter. I sent him a checque for a hundred dollars and have been writing him. I really think Mother ought to go up there. It's awful to think of him being without any close relatives and apparently likely to die at any time.

Audrey just wired me that she has received an offer of $150,000. and ten percent of Picture gross over one million and something for the screen rights to "Menagerie". I wired her back the terms were okay. Of course they are considerably less than the original prospects but since the show has closed on Broadway one cannot expect much. When you get out of the army I think you should try to connect with a law-firm in the East. Then you could protect my financial interests. The Menagerie was badly handled all the way around. I am sure Audrey did what she thought was best but it was a mistake not to accept a moderately good price in the beginning. I am including a movie scenario in the script of my new play and I hope that I can sell the screen rights simultaneous with the play when it is finally finished.

Love - Tom.

[The saga of the Packard continued with Dakin Williams (b. 1919) seeking title clearance to sell the car, which TW provided.

On October 16 Audrey Wood cabled TW that Charles Feldman had "officially" bought film rights of *The Glass Menagerie*. She added that the columnist Louella Parsons reported an initial payment of $500,000, "which I wish were true," Wood lamented, and went on to explain that "bad business" (October 16, 1946, HRC) in San Francisco had convinced her to sell rights at this time. TW replied that he was "very happy over deal" (October 18, 1946, HRC). Laurette Taylor's prolonged illness and inability to tour nationally or to star in a London production may have helped to depress the value of film rights.

Charles Abramson, Feldman's astute assistant, reported that dealing with Wood and her attorney had been "a very difficult business." Their proposal for an initial payment of $350,000 and a predetermined release agreement bespoke fears, he thought, that the "gossamer" play may fail as a film, or that TW, a lucky novice, "may never write another successful property" (to Feldman, February 4, 1946, HRC).]

43. To Margaret "Margo" Jones

[632 ½ St. Peter Street
New Orleans, Louisiana]
Oct. 17, 1946
[TLS, 1 p. HRC]

Dear Margo:

I have been extraordinarily lucky here. Got a lovely furnished apartment my second day, owned and furnished by an antique dealer with real good taste. A huge living room with the sort of work-table in it I've always wanted, about half a block long! With a sky-light directly over it. Also a Grand piano and some old Italian pieces. (You can have them, baby!) And I have been feeling well and getting a lot of work done. Miss Alma and her wild young doctor are coming to life in their native climate. For a while the silent film sequences were only tentative and I was careful to keep the main body of the play independant of them, but now I'm going whole hog and making them an integral part of the script. I know it can be done, the question is - Will anybody do it? (Don't mention this to anyone till the play is finished). Working is life, the only real true life, the rest is incidental. People are shadows except when I am trying to put them on paper. So I am a bastard, and have been ever since I started writing.

I sent Pancho home to visit his folks as he had not seen them since he got in the army. He served two and a half years in the South Pacific, right in the thick of it, and then was let out of the army without an honorable discharge simply because he had a spell of confusion and talked too trustingly to an officer about it. So he has nothing to show for what he went through, and none of the G.I. compensations, which I think is an outrage. I think something should be done about it in Washington. He is coming back here to resume his old job at a department store.

I am afraid the 29th is too early for me to make another trip. But if I find that I can, I'll wire you. Of course I could not get too clear an impression of the script from that scattered reading in your hotel room, but I can see you have a tough job on your hands. However that has never dismayed you.

I certainly want to work with you again on something. You feel about work as I do, though it doesn't traumatize your social character so badly. I would like to start on the West coast with a play and bring it all the way across the country for two or three months before going into New York. (Wouldn't it really be easier to cast and just as easy to stage a production out there?)

With love to you and Joanna and wishes for your success!

Tenn.

[Pancho Rodriguez may have received a Section VIII discharge for "undesirable habits or traits of character." During World War II the majority of such legal separations from military service were "honorable," the discharge without honor reserved for aggravated cases involving "psychopathic behavior, chronic alcoholism, or sexual perversion."

Margo Jones was currently on leave from Theatre '46 to direct *Joan of Lorraine* (1946), the new Maxwell Anderson play starring Ingrid Bergman. "Tough job" would not adequately describe her experience.]

44. To Margaret "Margo" Jones

632 ½ St. Peter Street
[New Orleans, Louisiana]
Tuesday Morning. [November 19, 1946]
[TLS, 1 p. HRC]

Dearest Margo:

I've just heard a flash over my radio about the brilliant success of your opening. If the news reaches New Orleans before noon the next day you know it must be something! This puts you publicly in the top rank of New York directors and I'm more happy about it than I can say. I could tell from the brief glance I took that it was an extremely tricky play to put on and I'm sure more than usual credit will go to the direction. Mil felicidades!

I am working on a final draft of "A Chart of Anatomy" and it looks like the commitment with Cornell is out. Guthrie and Audrey got together over the second draft and decided it was not right for her. Guthrie wired me enthusiastically about the play and Audrey says they are "thinking in terms of a younger Helen Hayes" and he took the script to England. But I would not make any commitment with Guthrie as I don't think the play is the sort of thing for him, as I told you. I want you to see the final draft first. The second ran to 174 pages and the remaining work is mostly weeding out inessential material and I think I can eliminate the silent film sequences, all but maybe one. I'm afraid they would break the poetic unity. The part I meant for Cornell is a terrifically demanding role. It is a young part, about 27, but I can't think of any younger actress who could handle it except perhaps Hepburn. The male part is almost as big but much more easily cast.

Are you coming South now?

With much love, Tenn.

P.S. The Lorca play was thrilling to me, and also to Pancho whose Spanish background gave it special appeal. Our thanks and affectionate greetings to Joanna.

[Maxwell Anderson and Ingrid Bergman reportedly lost confidence in Margo Jones's relaxed style of direction and doubted her ability to bring *Joan of Lorraine* to New York. Apparently unbeknown to TW, she had been fired during tryouts in Washington and replaced by Sam Wanamaker. The "tricky" play reached Broadway on November 18, 1946, won positive reviews, and ran for nearly 200 performances. Jones was fully credited as director and paid all of her contractual fees, as her agent, Audrey Wood, had doubtless arranged.

Kit Cornell's withdrawal from *Summer and Smoke* surprised and disappointed TW. Wood, however, thought it inevitable that the commanding actress, last seen on Broadway as Antigone, would balk at the role of a woman dominated by parents, church, and "a man she loves but who doesn't love her" (to TW, November 18, 1946, HRC).

Lorca's play *La Casa de Bernarda Alba* (1945) was "the best thing" which TW had read "lately" (n.d., Houghton), as he observed to James Laughlin in the new year.

Partially canceled in the letterhead is the imprint of the Pontchartrain Hotel in New Orleans.]

45. To Audrey Wood

[632 ½ St. Peter Street
New Orleans, Louisiana]
Nov. 22, 1946.
[TLS w/ enclosure, 2 pp. HRC]

Dear Audrey:

Your long letter about the play was gratefully received. I am so anxious for this play to turn out right, almost absurdly so!

I feel that the relationship between John and Alma is entirely valid, even her offering herself to him in their last scene together as it is continually stressed that she is going through a profound change, having lived up till then by standards which were not natural to her, but this offer can be played and directed delicately enough to avoid a shock.

I am taking all the film sequences out. But they should be kept as the basis for a film scenario.

You are entirely right about the phony effect of the epidemic. I think if it is established that his father was engaged in that work immediately prior to his death (was in the fever district rather than attending medical convention) it will seem believable that John, after his father's death, continued the father's work and developed the serum which redeems him in the public eye.

As for Nellie, her infatuation with John is established in the first ~~two~~ scenes of the play. I felt that a brief scene between her and John - post-redemption - would be enough to prepare for their ultimate marriage. He remarks that he had told her to keep their plans secret and it should be established that the ceremony is to be simple, semi-private one. My mother's marriage in Columbus, Miss. came as an almost complete surprise to nearly all her friends in the town: it was performed in the church but privately and was a shocking surprise to the congregation as my father was considered "too fast" for a minister's daughter.

You are also entirely right about the original last scene being better. I always thought that was the best scene in the play but that it continued the play's action too long after what was its actual culmination in Alma's final loss of John. I think I have worked out a good solution in the pages enclosed, which brings John and Nellie back into the play through a dual scene at the very end and also makes clearer John's feeling for Alma. A rather complicated feeling but one that is totally understandable to me and I think with proper handling can be made so to even a Broadway audience. John is sincere when he says "he felt a hunger for her which wasn't a physical hunger". She represented certain ideals - principles - ineffable qualities - which he was running away from and even after assuming adult responsibility, he was still repelled (as much as attracted) by her kind of intensity.

My objection to the casino set is mainly for physical reasons. I think this play has to move with the same fluidity as Menagerie in order to hold attention. There should be no curtain except at intermission and a shifting of light should move it smoothly and swiftly from scene to scene. Also I like to keep the poetic unity of the three permanent sets, the two interiors and the elevated out-door fountain-set. The only value in the casino set I mind sacrificing is that of Serio's appearance which somewhat prepared for his use in the old doctor's death. I dislike all the talk about "honor" and "plumes" and I think that can be dispensed with. Having a long last scene there is plenty of cutting which I can now afford to do. In a play of such romantic intensity, you are continually stepping on eggs and have to make sure that you step lightly. Some are bound to be broken here and there, no matter how lightly you step on them!

I am glad to hear that Margo has made good with the Bergman show as I feel that Margo and I, working together, could do more on this play than any other director. Margo likes intensely romantic material and I think she knows how to handle it, and she believes in fidelity to the author's intention. Also she spares no effort in giving a thing the best physical support, while Guthrie is inclined to "cut corners" financially as well as artistically. I don't think a typical, hard-boiled Broadway director could feel sincerely enough about this script to direct it sincerely. - How do you feel about The Playwrights' Company? Do you think they might consider a play by a non-member? I have had some correspondance with Robert Sherwood. He wired me about the Washington race-discrimination deal and I added my name to the protest and he has since written a very friendly letter of thanks, enclosing clippings. - I think their set-up is ideal for a playwright. His own choice in all matters. - After them, I would consider the Theatre Guild providing it is understood they will give sufficient license and control to author. I am not afraid of them anymore.

As for my health, that has been ever since the operation a disturbing problem, in fact a constant shadow. I don't have the severe attacks of pain that I had just before the operation, but keep on having discomfiting symptoms and a general weakness which continually remind me of it. The doctor here, like the ones in New York, tell me that I do not have a malignant condition but there is a certain ambiguity in their attitude which does not reassure me and I don't know what to make of it. And my nature is not bold enough to be sure that I want to. I have never had a particle of physical courage about anything!

Has Laughlin misplaced or lost the stories? I trust not. I have an idea for a lovely long story about a sad little Mexican who repairs watches - called 'Joy Rio'. I hope I can write it when I've finished this play. There are so many things I want to do, no end of them!

Love - Tenn.

P.S. I <u>can</u> get this last version ready, at least roughly, in about a week.

If I feel well enough, I might venture to New York with it for a week, provided I could be assured of a hotel room. Do you approve of this idea?

[Audrey Wood cited a second major flaw after reading the latest version of *Summer and Smoke*. Women might accept the relationship of Alma and John, but she feared that "most men won't quite understand why John, who has all the freedom in the world sexually, should remain so fascinated by a woman like Alma for such a long period of time" (to TW, November 18, 1946, HRC).

The "original" ending of *Summer and Smoke* is set in the rectory, a house of ill repute since the death of Alma's father, and consists mainly of verbal foreplay between Alma and Floyd Kramer, a "slightly paunchy" salesman whom she has met at the train station. As the play ends he kisses Alma "with clumsy, middle-aged passion" ("Summer and Smoke," August 1946, HRC).

TW realized the seriousness of Wood's criticism and enclosed "a dual scene" written to validate John's attraction to Alma. John and Nellie play their marital discord, and John his longing for Alma, against Alma's interlude with Kramer, in houses adjacent to each other. "How pitiful for you both that you made the mistake of taking me instead," Nellie says, to which John replies, "She had - too much of something . . ." (Revision of Original Ending, n.d., HRC).

The Playwrights' Company which produced *Joan of Lorraine* did not publicly announce the firing of Margo Jones, nor perhaps did Wood broach the subject to TW at this time.

The story about "a sad little Mexican who repairs watches" is entitled "The Mysteries of the Joy Rio" (1954).

This letter bears a reception date of November 23, 1946.]

46. To Edwina Dakin Williams

SH: New Orleans Athletic Club
New Orleans 16, La.
Dec. 3, 1946
[ALS, 4 pp. HTC]

Dear Mother -

Surprised and happy to get the box of gifts, presumably for Xmas, though there was only a Santa Claus seal to indicate it.

Haven't heard from you in so long was afraid you might be ill.

I have been absorbed in work, as usual. Had to rewrite my latest play a couple of times and am still applying some final touches.

Audrey is peculiarly taciturn about the picture sale of "Menagerie".

She wired me about it a month ago but I have received no further confirmation.

Margo passes through here this week for a short visit on her way to Dallas after directing Ingrid Bergman in the hit play "Joan of Lorraine."

I know you're happy to have Dakin home. The check he sent me was incorrectly made out for two dollars instead of $200. I hope this was a slip of the pen. I think he should take a commission for the sale, so deduct about $25. when you make out another check.

Tell Grandfather I am looking forward to his visit and I think I can put him up comfortably - there is a long flight of stairs to my apartment which is on third floor. Otherwise it should suit him perfectly - I hope he is feeling well.

Love to you all, Tom.

[Correspondence between TW and Edwina (1884-1980) is sharply reduced in volume 2 of *The Selected Letters*. Disagreement over Rose's care and Edwina's apparent coolness toward Pancho Rodriguez (see letter #52) may have contributed to the "sad distance" (*Journal*, June 6, 1954) which came to separate them.

The contract for film rights of *The Glass Menagerie* had been refined in the preceding month and was "ready" (HRC) for signing, as Audrey Wood informed TW on December 13. She had shielded her suspicious client from a tedious legal process that would have baffled and distracted him.

Margo Jones's visit to New Orleans occasioned a reading of "Paper Lantern," a variant title of *Streetcar*, and "Chart of Anatomy." Blanche DuBois was impressive, Jones thought, but she was "completely obsessed" by "Chart." Her letter of thanks ends with familiar praise for TW: "There is nobody living who can write like you do" (January 7, 1947, HRC). Jones may have informed TW at this time of her embarrassing experience with *Joan of Lorraine*.

Walter Dakin was "most unhappy" living with Edwina "because of the unfriendly attitude of Dad" (December 3, 1946, HRC), TW reported to Wood.]

47. To Audrey Wood

SH: Western Union
New Orleans La
1946 Dec 10 AM 11 11
[Telegram, 1 p. HRC]

AUDREY WOOD=

INEXPRESSIBLY SHOCKED AND GRIEVED WIRED YOU SUNDAY BUT WIRE RETURNED. WILL TRY TO WRITE ARTICLE. LOVE=

TENNESSEE.

[Laurette Taylor suffered a heart attack and died on December 7, 1946, at the age of sixty-two. TW did not attend the service in New York but wrote a poignant "appreciation" of Taylor's career: "In this unfathomable experience of ours there are sometimes hints of something that lies outside the flesh and its mortality. I suppose these intuitions come to many people in their religious vocations, but I have sensed them more clearly in the work of artists and most clearly of all in the art of Laurette Taylor. There was a radiance about her art which I can compare only to the greatest lines of poetry, and which gave me the same shock of revelation as if the air about us had been momentarily broken through by light from some clear space beyond us" ("An Appreciation," *New York Times*, December 15, 1946, sec. 2, p. 4).

John Buchanan's admission that "a vaporous something" may give "value" to "this unfathomable experience of ours" ("A Chart of Anatomy") became in effect the final line which TW wrote for Laurette Taylor.]

48. To Audrey Wood

SH: New Orleans Athletic Club
New Orleans 16, La.
1/9/47
[TLS, 2 pp. HRC]

Dear Audrey:

Grandfather just arrived today and I have been extremely busy preparing for him. I thought it would be better to get him a room close to my apartment as I don't have much space, but no rooms were available so I had to make a place for him here. Luckily we had a small extra room but it was practically unfurnished. The only nice room in the house, the big front room with the skylight, is the one in which I work. As Grandfather is now unable to read his only diversion is listening to the radio. I do hope that I can settle him comfortably and happily somewhere in Florida. We are driving down there soon as the weather clears up, perhaps in a day or two.

Concerning "Chart": I agree with you that the remaining movie sequence should be left out. As for the ending, I deliberated a great deal about that and finally I felt that the shorter and simpler ending was preferable. The long one is more theatrical and better in itself but it is like the beginning of another play and is not as true to the play as a whole. The short ending by the fountain contains all the implications of the longer one and I feel there is poetic rightness in returning to the stone angel in the last scene. I think we should keep that other ending in reserve but have the Ms. typed up with this one. I do think the script should be typed up now, in its present form, as I do not feel it would be wise for me to continue work on it now. My interest has shifted to the other long play which I hope will turn out stronger. Somehow or other, for a complex of psychological reasons, I did not do as well with "Chart" as I should have. I shall have to read it over when it has been typed up and a little time has elapsed before I can form a clear impression of it myself. I do know there is too much material, particularly in the beginning. It needs a tighter development, perhaps the complete elimination of one or two early scenes. I hate tedium above all else and I am afraid there is a tedium in that part of the play. As for actresses, I have wondered if it would interest the English actress Celia Johnson who was so remarkable in Coward's film "Brief Encounter". Perhaps it could be done first in England.

The problems of the other play are totally different. It is relatively short, 94 pages, structurally very compact, one set, about six characters and rather harsh, violent and melodramatic with some pretty rough characters: a relief after the rectory.

Here is a brief account of my living expenses. As the play has a New Orleans background it can be said that my residence here is for professional purposes. Apartment: $150 a month. Food and incidental living expenses about the same amount a week. Then I have regular medical expenses which you are acquainted with. Garage: $20 a month. During the Spring and summer, Pancho travelled with me as my secretary-companion and general assistant, due to my ill health. As you know we travelled extensively, to New Mexico, back from there to New York, then to Nantucket where we maintained a house for the season. Then back to New York where I was a week in a hospital. Then South to New Orleans where I resumed work on my New Orleans play. I now have my grandfather as a dependant and have been helping him financially for some time. I bought a car here for $1400. The maintenance of this car should also be included and the cost of my operation in Taos which you can check on. I do not remember figures very clearly: I am afraid you will have to approximate the travelling expenses for the two of us and let us allow Pancho a monthly salary of $200, which he is easily worth. If this is not detailed enough, wire me. In other details why not follow last year's?

Happiness and good fortune! With love,

Tenn.

[Walter Dakin arrived in New Orleans three months shy of his ninetieth birthday.

The preferred ending of "'Chart'" is set in the park and cast with a younger, slimmer version of the original traveling salesman. Archie Kramer accepts a "merciful" tablet from Alma and obeys her invitation to "sit down beside me, stranger." She then "inclines her head" to his shoulder and asks wearily, "Do you - mind?" (November 1946, HRC). The brief scene was intended to confirm Alma's loss of John Buchanan and to end the play on a note of tender resignation. In later revision TW roused the players and supplied the upbeat ending used on Broadway and published thereafter: Alma and Archie hail a taxi and depart for the pleasures of Moon Lake Casino.

In the preceding December TW returned to *Streetcar*, whose prospects for a "harsh" ending had also led to experiments with uplift. Eddie Zawadzki—an early version of Mitch named for a St. Louis friend of TW—forgives Blanche her lies and promiscuity at the urging of his sick mother, who has "suffered" herself and "wants to know" ("Electric Avenue") this vulnerable woman. The play ends with a near promise of marriage. A tougher, more cynical Blanche who secretly desires Ralph (Stanley) radically changed the ground of experimentation. By dismissing her rape in a hard-boiled morning-after scene—"I am really surprised the walls are still standing"—Blanche confirms her sensuality and resilience and earns the faint respect of her antagonist. The scene ends with Blanche preparing to go "away somewhere" in search of "life" (n.d., HRC). TW was still "experimenting with different endings" in the new year, as he informed Audrey Wood, but "otherwise" the play was "complete" (January 3, 1947, HRC).

TW closes the letter, which bears a reception date of January 10, 1947, with a hopeful list of income tax deductions.]

49. To Amado "Pancho" Rodriguez y Gonzalez

SH: Hotel La Concha
Key West, Florida
[ca. January 31, 1947]
[TLS w/ autograph postscript, 2 pp. HRC]

Dear Pancho:

We got here 2 days after I left New Orleans, made the entire trip from outskirts of Tampa to Miami in about eight hours, came on to Key West the next morning. Trip was swell except for the last ten miles when the water boiled out of the radiator and a tire blew out at the same time. I had no tools for changing the tire and was scared to put sea-water in the radiator so we were stranded quite a while till a negro truck-driver came along and put us together again. They had a couple of nice rooms for us here with connecting bath. Grandfather made friends with the Episcopal minister and has had a nice time socially. We spend the afternoons on the beach and I have been doing a lot of work in the mornings. The Poker Night is developing into a strong play, I believe, and I am hopeful about it. I think the change was good for me, physically, but I miss being with you all the time. We must take the next trip together. From my sixth floor window I can see the ocean almost all around the island and a breeze comes through all the time. It would be an excellent place to live permanently, that is, to have a small home - and a boat! Grandfather has bought a pith helmet and a pair of swimming trunks covered with palm-trees - you cannot imagine what a fantastic sight he is! Everyone smiles at us on the street, we are such an odd-looking couple, I suppose. Yesterday he walked in a fruit-store and said, "I want a dozen California oranges!" And it takes him half an hour to order a meal because he really wants everything on the menu. I have to read it to him all the way through several times shouting like a circus-barker. But he is enjoying himself and that is really the object of the trip. I dread having to drive all the way back over the same road. Maybe we'll make it a bit longer and go up the East coast instead. I think we'll leave here not later than Feb. 5th.

I have just noticed that "Menagerie" is supposed to open in Washington for two weeks Feb. 3rd. As you know, I signed a pledge, with practically all other important playwrights, not to have a show in Washington while negros are being kept out of Washington theatres. This creates a most embarassing situation. I had no idea they were bringing the show into Washington and now I must wire Audrey to do what she can to stop it. Heaven knows what! Will probably also wire Dramatist Guild for advice about legal steps to prevent opening. Very upsetting!

Have you gone back to work? How are things? You promised to write me!

With love, Tennessee.

Please give this check to real estate co. Also one for Catharine.

[TW replaced the Packard with a "snow-white secondhand Pontiac convertible" (*Memoirs*, p. 112) which also gave trouble on the road. Nonetheless the trip to Key West was a bracing, productive experience: "Not till Grandfather came and you escaped with him to Florida did you really seem to catch hold of life again - and wrote 'Streetcar' all in about 6 weeks. . . . You recovered your lost manhood!" (*Journal*, October 27, 1947).

Walter Dakin enjoyed meeting Miriam Hopkins and her husband at Ernest Hemingway's former house on Whitehead Street. They "are stopping at the finest hotel in Key West," he informed Edwina, "we are not" (February 10, 1947, Columbia U). Hopkins starred in *Battle of Angels* and had endeared herself to TW by staunchly defending the play against the Boston censors.

"The Poker Night," a variant title of *Streetcar*, remained in strong contention through the spring. Audrey Wood thought it "suggested a Western action novel" and urged that the now famous title be used instead.

TW's report of progress on *Streetcar* led to a prescient thought, as Pancho Rodriguez awaited TW's return to New Orleans: "I have sometimes felt that I was hampering him and that he could not write with me around. I will hate leaving him but it is the best way out" (Rodriguez to Jones and Albus, February 13, 1947, HRC).

To his friend Donald Windham TW recommended room #602 in the Hotel La Concha for its "clean sweep of the sea that covers the bones of Crane" (qtd. in Windham, p. 193).]

50. To Audrey Wood

Western Union
Key West Flo
1947 Jan 31 PM 3 19
[Telegram, 1 p. HRC]

AUDREY WOOD=

JUST NOTIFIED PLAY BOOKED INTO WASHINGTON NEXT WEEK. CONTRARY TO MY PLEDGE WITH ALL OTHER PLAYWRIGHTS TO BOYCOTT

WASHINGTON THEATRES WHICH BAR NEGROES. THINK IT DISGRACEFUL TO VIOLATE PLEDGE WILL WIRE DRAMATISTS GUILD UNLESS YOU ADVISE OTHER ACTION TODAY. LOVE=

TENNESSEE.

[TW's apology appeared in the *New York Times* on February 3, 1947, opening night of *The Glass Menagerie* at Washington's National Theatre: "I want to state that I have protested bringing 'The Glass Menagerie' into Washington, but have no legal power to prevent it. I can only express my humiliation that a play of mine should be denied to Negroes in the nation's capital. Any future contract I make will contain a clause to keep the show out of Washington while this undemocratic practice continues" (p. 23). The *Menagerie's* co-producer, Louis J. Singer, was quoted in the same article as feeling "badly" himself but holding that "the contracts were signed nine months ago and there is nothing one can do now."

The National, the only legitimate theatre in Washington at the time, was the focus of racial protest which grew in 1947 to include the support of Actors Equity, the Dramatists' Guild, and some forty-odd active playwrights. TW had been contacted in 1946 by Robert Sherwood, a protest leader, and joined the first group of writers to support the "boycott." Marcus Heiman, lessee of the National, was not unsympathetic, but he resented "the guinea pig aspect of the case" and claimed that he was following the social customs of Washington and, implicitly, of the theatre itself.]

51. To Audrey Wood

Western Union
Jacksonville Flo
1947 Feb 19 PM 12 41
[Telegram, 1 p. HRC]

AUDREY WOOD=

THANKS FOR YOUR GOOD OFFICES. CAR AND I RELEASED. PLEASE WIRE GRANDFATHER FIFTY DOLLARS AT NEW ORLEANS ADDRESS. HE IS NOW THERE AND MAY BE DESTITUTE. LOVE=

TENNESSEE.

[The Highway Patrol stopped TW near Jacksonville, Florida, as he returned to New Orleans. Dakin Williams recounts the episode in *Tennessee Williams: An Intimate Biography* (1983): "He had no taillights, something he hadn't thought to check. They asked him for his driver's license, and he didn't have that either. The police were convinced he must be either criminal or crazy, and handcuffed his wrist to his ankle. He was thrown into jail, spent a night with a crowd of whores, dope addicts and drunks, put up $300 bail and finally had to study for and pass a driving test before he was allowed to move on." The foregoing report is based upon *Memoirs*, where TW includes the piquant detail of "a redheaded youth" (p. 112) picked up while hitchhiking.

Audrey Wood's "good offices" consisted of wiring the Florida Highway Patrol that TW "is a very reputable citizen" and "one of the country's best playwrights" (February 18, 1947, HRC). Walter Dakin had returned to New Orleans by plane.]

52. To Audrey Wood

[632 ½ St. Peter Street
New Orleans, Louisiana]
[late-March 1947]
[TLS, 2 pp. HRC]

Dear Audrey:

You are so much closer to the whole situation than I am that I think it would [be] foolish and presumptuous of me to tell you what to do about the English rights. I always prefer to follow my heart - or my instinct - in matters wherever that is at all practical, and my heart and my instinct prefer to work with Randy and Bill simply because they are young, struggling, and definitely in the class of "right guys". We know what Dowling is like and personally I have never wanted any part of Singer (except his millions, which I can't get). Also I am deeply indignant over their - particularly Dowling's - cynical attitude toward the road-company. It is really a travesty of the play, mainly because of the glaring, stupefying incompetence of one member of the cast, Eddie Andrews. I think if they had really respected the play, even just as a commodity, they would not have allowed it to drag about the country in this disgraceful condition when all they had to do was fire or buy out one intolerable actor to make a creditable company of it. Of course I realize that Singer probably does not know a bad from a good actor but Dowling certainly does and he should have paid some attention. For these reasons I feel an instinctive reluctance to continue with them. On the other hand I am sure that you have considered the situation from all angles and are in a much better position to make a decision in the matter, and therefore I would rather you made up your own mind about it.

My dislike of Singer is premised, that is - originates - from his attempt to make me sabotage the play in Chicago with fantastic "happy" endings and other tripe, and his arrogant, bullying attitude up till the time the play was proven a commercial success. Perhaps he has redeemed himself since then. I am still afraid of him, though. Finally, I don't particularly care, at this point, whether there is a London production or not. You decide!

(I hope all this does not sound ill-humored, as I am in a very reasonable humor tonight).

Grandfather suddenly insisted on leaving. I think Mother gave him the idea that I was not altogether fitting company for a clergyman to keep. I doubt if he subscribes to her ideas in the matter, he is much too liberal for that, but evidently she talked him into going, which was a real sorrow to me as I had grown so attached to him and it was such a joy having him with me. He broke down and cried as I left him at the train. I felt heartsick about the old man venturing forth again by himself, for he is really more dependant (visually, Etc.) than he appears. However he has many friends in Memphis who will look out for him to a great extent, and I have told him to rejoin me for the summer if he wants to. I don't know <u>where</u> I shall go. Do you think anything will be done about "Poker Night" this summer? I hope the production can be arranged for early Fall. I want to take a very active part in it, particularly casting, and I am wondering whether that would be done more likely on the East or West Coast. This sounds as though I were quite certain it <u>will</u> be produced. Actually I am only hoping so, very strongly. Would appreciate your advice as to which Coast I should go to. I don't want to move around more than necessary. To my mind the play should open a long way from Broadway, and any contract should stipulate a minimum of six weeks on the road. - Do you think Blanche at all right for Bankhead? My fear is that Bankhead would not be sympathetic enough in the softer aspects of the character. But she would certainly be thrilling in the big scenes.

Windham has sent me a bunch of his stories. One long one is truly superb and I want you to see it. I am writing a foreword.

With love, Tenn

Please do advise me about where to go!

Pancho Rodriguez, Margo Jones, and Walter Dakin, New Orleans, 1947: "I wish Tom would marry her" (letter, Walter Dakin to Edwina, March 19, 1947).

[TW's failure to consult Audrey Wood on "English rights" of *The Glass Menagerie* put her in a "difficult situation" (to TW, March 26, 1947, HRC) once again. The contract which she reluctantly drew gave Will Gould and Randy Echols, stage managers in the original company, one week to form a partnership with Eddie Dowling and Louis J. Singer. The American managers had no legal rights, Wood informed TW, but at this time she favored their inclusion as ballast to an inexperienced production team.

Harsh criticism of Eddie Andrews, the touring Gentleman Caller, was a byproduct of TW's recent trip to Boston to evaluate Pauline Lord for the London production of *The Glass Menagerie.*

Walter Dakin's departure for Memphis was well planned and probably not—as TW suspected—the result of Edwina's moralistic prompting. There was, however, an undercurrent of family criticism regarding Pancho Rodriguez. Dakin Williams wrote earlier in March to assure TW of Edwina's safe return following her visit to New Orleans. He noted that "Mother knows nothing of my reasons for disliking P. Though she shares my opinion of him in general." Pancho, he advised, is not "an asset to you socially" and "has all the attributes of . . . well . . . you know what" (March 8, 1947, HRC). When Dakin visited New Orleans in April, he was apparently propositioned by Pancho, an episode which he reported to TW with further advice and indignation regarding his brother's indiscreet life (see *Tennessee Williams: An Intimate Biography*, pp. 141-142).

This letter bears a reception date of April 1, 1947.]

53. *To Audrey Wood*

Western Union
New Orleans La
1947 Apr 8 PM 3 02
[Telegram, 1 p. HRC]

AUDREY WOOD=

MY TRAIN LEAVES 5:30 WEDNESDAY EVENING ARRIVES 8:15 THURSDAY EVENING. THIS WOMAN HAD BETTER BE GOOD=

TENNESSEE.

[Irene Selznick, Audrey Wood's choice to produce *A Streetcar Named Desire*, awaited TW's arrival and inspection in Charleston, South Carolina: "She is supposed to have 16 million dollars *and* good taste. I am dubious" (qtd. in Windham, p. 198). Selznick recalls meeting a shy, taciturn author with a cast in his "cloudy" left eye who oddly turned away whenever she spoke to him. TW quickly accepted her as

Tennessee Williams and Irene Selznick: "This woman had better be good."

producer and signed the contracts with little sentiment or ceremony. Selznick wired her assistant, Irving Schneider, with a coded report of success: "'Blanche has come to live with us. Hooray and love'" (qtd. in Selznick, *A Private View*, 1983, p. 297).]

54. To James "Jay" Laughlin

632 ½ St. Peter,
New Orleans, La.
April 9, 1947
[TLS w/ enclosure, 2 pp. Houghton]

Dear Jay:

I was afraid you had decided that I was "Derriere garde" and crossed me off your list.

The heat and dampness are descending on New Orleans and it is like a Turkish bath only not as socially inspiring. So I am wondering whether to go East or West. From the looks of things generally, one would do well to get clear out of the country and stay out for at least the opening stages of "The American Century". I have a feeling that if we survive the next ten years, there will be a great purgation, and this country will once more have the cleanest air on earth, but right now there seems to be an unspeakable foulness. All the people at the controls are opportunists or gangsters. The sweetness of reason died out of our public life with FDR. There doesn't even seem to be a normal intelligence at work in the affairs of the nation. Aren't you frightened by it?!

I have done a lot of work, finished two long plays. One of them, laid in New Orleans, A STREETCAR CALLED DESIRE, turned out quite well. It is a strong play, closer to "Battle of Angels" than any of my other work, but is not what critics call "pleasant". In fact, it is pretty <u>un</u>pleasant. But Audrey is enthusiastic about it and we already have a producer "in the bag". A lady named Irene Selznick (estranged wife of David Selznick and a daughter of Louis B. Mayer). Her chief apparent advantage is that she seems to have millions. Audrey says that she also has good taste. Of course I am skeptical. But I am going half-way to meet her. She is flying down to Charleston and I up and we are to have a meeting-conference tomorrow evening at the Hotel Fort Sumter. This is all Audrey's idea. I recognize the danger of working with a Female Moneybags from Hollywood but Audrey claims the woman is "safe" and will give an "all-out" production, which is what the play requires to put it over. Unfortunately we have fallen out with Dowling and the main problem is to find a really strong but fastidious director. (And a good female star).

The other play, which I worked on all last summer, intended for Miss Cornell, was a disappointment and a pretty bad one. In fact, I was so depressed over it that I am surprised that I was able to go on working. Margo does not feel that way about it and she is planning to try it out this summer in Dallas. Eventually something might work out of it. The basic conception was very pure and different from anything else I have tried. It was built around an argument over the existence of a "human soul" but that got pretty thoroughly lost in a narrative that somehow slipped to the level of magazine fiction, or worse.

Donnie (Windham) sent me a group of his short-stories and I am happy to report that they are excellent, especially a long one called "The Starless Air" which I want you to read. I think it is the finest portrait I have seen of middle-class southern society. It makes KAP seem "cute". I am to write a foreword before Donnie submits them to publishers. It is a difficult job as the qualities I like in the stories are so difficult to define. Except in such vague and cliche terms as "organic" "pure" "honest" Etc. But then I could never write criticism anyhow.

I am becoming infected with your passion for Kafka, since reading "The Burrow". It is so like our State Department, or any neurotic personality. Except that of course the little animal in the burrow devoured the "smaller fry" for much more sympathetic motives, and his apprehension was more sensible.

Audrey says she sent you a bunch of stories. Which ones do you lack? Check with the enclosed list and let me know or notify Audrey. I am glad you still want to do the volume, and I hope you still want to do it privately so we can include the best ones.

Ever, Tennessee

[Henry Luce, influential founder of *Time* and *Life* magazines, foresaw an American "powerhouse" defeating Nazi Germany and spreading its unique democratic ideals around the world, creating in effect "the 20th Century—our Century" ("The American Century," *Life*, February 17, 1941). Luce's jingoism, it seemed to TW, had hardened into a risky Cold War policy of containing Communism, as recently formulated by the Truman Doctrine. Intertwined with this aggressive foreign policy were signs of growing intolerance and repression at home.

Donald Windham's family reminiscence, "The Starless Air," was dramatized and produced in 1953, with direction by TW. The story was later collected in *The Warm Country* (1962), with a brief introduction by E.M. Forster.

Fear of a great unknown "enemy" assails the rodent-speaker in Franz Kafka's late story "The Burrow" (1931).

Of sixteen stories on "the enclosed list," eleven appeared in the collection *One Arm*.]

55. To Amado "Pancho" Rodriguez y Gonzalez

[The Royalton, New York]
Tuesday - [April 15, 1947]
[ALS, 4 pp. HRC]

Dear Pancho -

It looks like I may either be tied up here several days longer or <u>else</u> have to make another trip up here before going west. I think it is definitely better to get everything ironed out now as I see no point in taking the trip twice.

I signed contract with Irene in Charleston but they insisted I come up to see the designer and select a director. We are now engaged in these problems which are very involved. I still may get away tomorrow (Wednesday) night. Otherwise may have to stay through Thursday or Friday. I sent you a money-order last night.

Irene thinks my presence in California would be more valuable as she expects most of the casting will be done at that end. So we can get started out there soon as I return from New York.

All my time here is taken up with interviews and conferences. Irene is nice but overwhelmingly energetic and a real slave-driver - But I think she is determined to give the show the best of everything that money can buy. She will be in California this summer, too.

This is a tough job, baby, but a great deal - in fact, everything - depends on it. I just hope the old Toro will stand up under pressure!

In Calif. we must get in a quiet, restful place so I can reserve some energy. You can help me a lot if you want to.

Will see you in a few days - sorry it took this long.

Yours - 10.

P. S. Planning to leave Thursday night. (tomorrow)

[The "old Toro" remained in New Orleans while TW traveled to Charleston and New York. Audrey Wood sternly enforced this rule, stating "twice on the phone" that he "should come '*alone!*'" The "Princess was inconsolable" (qtd. in Windham, p. 198), TW reported to Donald Windham.]

56. To Elia "Gadge" Kazan

[632 ½ St. Peter Street
New Orleans, Louisiana]
April 19, 1947
[TLS, 2 pp. WUCA]

Dear Gadge:

I am bitterly disappointed that you and Mrs. Selznick did not come to an agreement. I am wondering what was the primary trouble - the script itself or your unwillingness to tie up with another producer. Frankly I did not know that you were now in the producing field. Working outside of New York has many advantages but a disadvantage is that you lack information about such things. I have known you only in the capacity of actor and director.

I am sure that you must also have had reservations about the script. I will try to clarify my intentions in this play. I think its best quality is its authenticity or its fidelity to life. There are no "good" or "bad" people. Some are a little better or a little worse but all are activated more by misunderstanding than malice. A blindness to what is going on in each other's hearts. Stanley sees Blanche not as a desperate, driven creature backed into a last corner to make a last desperate stand - but as a calculating bitch with "round heels". Mitch accepts first her own false projection of herself as a refined young virgin, saving herself for the one eventual mate - then jumps way over to Stanley's conception of her. Nobody sees anybody <u>truly</u>, but all through the flaws of their own ego. That is the way we all see each other in life. Vanity, fear, desire, competition - all such distortions within our own egos - condition our vision of those in relation to us. Add to those distortions in our <u>own</u> egos, the corresponding distortions in the egos of the <u>others</u> - and you see how cloudy the glass must become through which we look at each other. That's how it is in all living relationships except when there is that rare case of two people who love intensely enough to burn through all those layers of opacity and see each others naked hearts. Such a case seems purely theoretical to me.

However in creative fiction and drama, if the aim is fidelity, people are shown as we never see them in life but as they are. Quite impartially, without any ego-flaws in the eye of the beholder. We see from outside what could not be seen within, and the truth of the tragic dilemma becomes apparent. It was not that one person was bad or good, one right or wrong, but that all judged falsely concerning each other, what seemed black to one and white to the other is actually grey - a perception that could occur only through the detached eye of art. (As if a ghost sat over the affairs of men and made a true record of them) Naturally a play of this kind does not exactly present a theme or score a point, unless it be the point or theme of human misunderstanding. When you begin to arrange the action of a play to score a certain point the fidelity to life may suffer. I don't say it always does. Things may be selected to score a point clearly without any contrivance toward that end, but I am afraid it happens rarely.

Finding a director aside from yourself who can bring this play to life exactly as if it were happening in life is going to be a problem. But that is the kind of direction it has to have. (I don't necessarily mean "realism": sometimes a living quality is caught better by expressionism than what is supposed to be realistic treatment.)

I remember you asked me what should an audience feel for Blanche. Certainly pity. It is a tragedy with the classic aim of producing a katharsis of pity and terror, and in order to do that Blanche must finally have the understanding and compassion of the audience. This without creating a black-dyed villain in Stanley. It is a thing (misunderstanding) not a person (Stanley) that destroys her in the end. In the end you should feel - "If only they all had known about each other!" - But there was always the paper lantern or the naked bulb!

(Incidentally, at the close of the play, I think Stanley should remove the paper lantern from the bulb - after Blanche is carried out and as he goes to resume the game.)

I have written all this out in case you were primarily troubled over my intention in the play. Please don't regard this as "pressure". A wire from Irene and a letter from Audrey indicate that both of them feel you have definitely withdrawn yourself from association with us and that we must find someone else. I don't want to accept this necessity without exploring the nature and degree of the differences between us. (Especially as they are now talking about someone I have never heard of, an Englishman named Tyrone Guthrie - sounds like some frightening kind of hybrid! - don't, please, mention any of this to anybody but Molly!)

Sincerely, Tennessee.

P.S. And also because I would want to be certain that we were in full accord and understanding about the play's intention.

[TW saw *All My Sons* (1947) while in New York and immediately opened a correspondence with Elia Kazan (1909-2003). He wrote that the play "'tops any direction I have seen on Broadway,'" adding that he would send "'congratulations'" to Arthur Miller and a copy of his own work to Kazan. "'It may not be the sort of play that interests you but I hope so'" (qtd. in Kazan, pp. 326-327). Kazan recalled that he did not "rush to read" *Streetcar* and wondered if he and TW "were the same kind of theatre animal—Miller seemed more my kind" (Kazan, p. 327).

The present letter follows a breakdown in early negotiations with Kazan as TW returned to New Orleans on April 17. Audrey Wood informed him of Kazan's abrupt withdrawal of interest and surmised that it was meant "either to unnerve us, frighten us, or make him seem harder to get and therefore increase his bargaining power later on" (April 18, 1947, HRC). TW urged her "to keep Irene partly immobilized" until he could return to New York and added that he had "not given up on Kazan" (April 21, 1947, HRC). Restored negotiations with Kazan would identify artistic control and billing, rather than script, as the chief obstacles to his direction of *Streetcar*.

Tyrone Guthrie's stage credits were numerous but almost exclusively English. His only recent direction on Broadway was a Theatre Guild revival of *He Who Gets Slapped* (1946), which was not well received.

Typed in the upper margin of p. 1 is TW's return address "C/o Audrey Wood, 551 Fifth Ave., N.Y."]

57. To Irene Mayer Selznick

[632 ½ St. Peter Street
New Orleans, Louisiana]
April 21, 1947
[TLS, 1 p. Private Collection]

Dear Irene:

I am shocked by Kazan's behavior. As for myself, I don't care how a director or actor treats me as long as he does a good job. He could spit in my face every morning and if he was the right man for the job, I'd wipe it off and say, Thank you! But I do not at all like his discourtesy to you and I find it particularly baffling after our conversations at dinner and on the phone, as on both occasions I had the distinct impression that he felt a genuine interest and even enthusiasm. This would not be worth bothering over except for the fact that it leaves us with so few names we can dare to consider.

John Huston comes next on my list. He is the only one mentioned who has a record that would indicate he would know how to handle such a "special" and "difficult" assignment as this one. As for Tyrone Guthrie, he is English. This is an American play with a peculiarly local or provincial color. And I remember "Piccadilly Peg's" bewilderment over Mississippi. We flew down there so she could absorb it in 48 hours.

Logan? Well, he belongs with Kauffman and Kanin in a group of directors who function brilliantly with a certain type of very slick Broadway product. "On Borrowed Time" comes closest to being a similar type of play, but even that is not really similar. It would be sheer speculation, as far as I can see. These men know Broadway, but the rest of the world is a fog. And I am not articulate enough to help them. I have a feeling that Huston knows more than Broadway and Hollywood. At least he has a literary acquaintance with the outside world and is sensitive to poetic values which unfortunately anyone who directs my work has to deal with if the work is to survive at all. - That is what makes the problem so difficult. - I will not mention Margo Jones to you, now, for you have already expressed your feeling about a woman-director. But the hour may come when the word is torn from my lips! (Margo and I together did the only good production of "You Touched Me" at Pasadena. Her advantage is that she and I have a hand-in-glove understanding of each other as persons and workers.)

I leave here tomorrow or Wednesday. I am driving and am a liesurely driver so I cannot say the definite day I'll get in New York but I will wire you and Audrey along the road of my progress. I want to get a place on the water near enough to New York so that we can be easily accessible to each other and yet I can have "tranquillity". I hope you and Audrey will get together a complete list of directors who are available so we can go through them exhaustively when I get to New York.

Ever, Tennessee.

[Irene Selznick (1907-1990) was seldom at a loss for words, but Audrey Wood's invitation to produce *Streetcar* had left her nearly speechless: "All I could say was, why? I reminded her that I was not only a novice, I had just had a failure," which closed in Philadelphia. Wood's reply, "'Find me someone else'" (qtd. in *A Private View*, pp. 294-295), bespoke a theatre establishment which lacked fresh production talent and respect for the author's intention. These qualities Wood foresaw in Selznick, as well as a sizeable bankroll and extensive Hollywood connections. "I truly felt," she later explained, "that after what Williams had been through in the past, he had to have complete protection, artistically as well as financially" (*Represented by Audrey Wood*, 1981, p. 151).

TW considered John Huston's screenplay for *The Maltese Falcon* (1941) "one of the finest pieces of dramatic writing ever produced." Huston's recent staging of *No Exit* (1946) received sharply mixed reviews and closed after thirty-one performances on Broadway. Paul Bowles adapted the original Sartre play.

Annie Get Your Gun (1946) was the latest of several hit musicals directed by Joshua Logan, who was Selznick's early choice to stage *Streetcar*. He made his directorial debut on Broadway in Paul Osborn's bittersweet comedy *On Borrowed Time* (1938).]

58. To Elia "Gadge" Kazan

SH: The Park Central
Seventh Avenue · 55 to 56 Street
New York City 19, N.Y.
May 1, 1947
[TLS, 4 pp. WUCA]

Dear Gadge:

I was immensely pleased to find your letter waiting for me here and to learn that there is no real impasse in the situation. I only got here last night after a full week on the road driving up from New Orleans. I talked immediately to Audrey and Bill. They are 100% in agreement with me in feeling that you are the man we want, the only one that we would feel really secure with. This afternoon I saw Irene. "Saw" is putting it mildly. "Heard" is closer but not by any means an adequate statement! It was one of those three-or-four-hour audiences that you have already experienced. It is funny. No matter how intelligent these people are, one thing they can't understand and that is how downright brutal it is to make anyone who is doing creative work go through these awful, interminable "consultations". They wear you down, debilitate you, finally suck you dry - if you let them! I cannot tell you how fully I sympathize with your allergy to all the peripheral involvements, complications, arguments and discussions that go with the usual play production. We have only so much energy to give, even to our most cherished work - it is all too quickly depleted - so it is certainly a sad thing that so much of it must be dissipated in all the incidental "fuss" that goes with a production. It almost makes you wish you'd never shown the play to anybody! - This is not directed at Irene but at producers in general. The freshness of vision and energy of attack are wastefully spent in arguments over things that should be simply and immediately decided by one or two people. - I am glad you use the word <u>fusion</u>. It is diffusion that seems to be the basic fault in so many productions. The various elements simply don't form a congruous whole. It is certainly not deprecating the plastic elements of the theatre (I think that exciting theatre is half a plastic art) to insist that they be dominated by the unifying influence of the script-and-director. If those two elements are in accord at the outset, so closely that they really constitute a single unit of two complementary parts, everything in the production should take shape under them and in that way fuse all the elements into a single artistic conception. I am getting all wound up in words, but you understand me. - Then something is created, whether it be a success or failure, something is brought to <u>be</u>. A living thing not just a hunk of formless matter. That is what we are interested in doing, making something <u>live</u>, - <u>Basta</u>!

I am going to put things as clearly and frankly as possible. - Irene still considers you the best director but she is now somewhat afraid of you. She thinks you are likely to be tyrannical or autocratic. I believe she visualizes herself being bodily ejected from the theatre and me writing new scenes with a bayonet at my ribs! (That's over-stating it a bit.) But I think what is needed to straighten things out, if you want to direct this show half as much as I want you to - is to give her a bit of reassurance along that line. After all she is primarily in this for fun, and her fun - I suppose - will come from feeling that she is somehow participating. If this could be managed without exposing yourself to undue interference - I feel it could be.

Irene says you think the play needs considerable re-writing. As you never said this, or intimated it, in our talk or your letter, I don't take this seriously, but I think it is only fair to tell you that I don't expect to do any more important work on the script. I spent a long time on it and the present script is a distillation of many earlier trials. It certainly isn't as good as it could be but it's as good as I am now able to make it. - I have never been at all difficult about cuts and incidental line-changes but I'm not going to do anything to alter the basic structure - with one exception. For the last scene, where Blanche is forcibly removed from the stage - I have an alternative ending, physically quieter, which could be substituted if the present ending proves too difficult to stage. That's about all the important change I could promise any director, and only that if the director finds the other unworkable.

If you are content with this understanding about the script - then I can just say - "Irene, I want Gadge and won't take anyone else." AUDREY and Bill would back me up, and I think could run interference for you all the way down the field.

I guess that's about all. Except I think we are anticipating more trouble with Irene than is really likely. I think we are dealing with a woman of sincerity and ethical principles, as well as considerable sense and taste, who is right now over-compensating nervously for some emotional shock. I suspect this producing adventure is partly a kind of occupational therapy for her, and once we show her a certain warmth and deference she will have the good sense to stay in her own corner except when called for.

I think it will work out, in fact I'm sure it will, if we are firm but gentle!

Ever, Tennessee.

Write me c/o Audrey Wood, 551 Fifth Ave., as I will retreat to the country soon as I find a place. All I really want to know is your willingness to accept the script as it now stands.

[TW returned to New York in late-April to monitor negotiations between Irene Selznick and Elia Kazan, the latter now at work in California. Kazan reportedly told TW during his earlier visit that he would direct *Streetcar* only if Selznick were fired as producer. As further incentive he framed an alarming picture of her father, Louis B. Mayer, and her estranged husband, David O. Selznick, "sitting in the front row during rehearsals" (*A Private View*, p. 299). Selznick apparently had similar fears that Kazan would be "tyrannical or autocratic" and usurp her authority as producer.

Kazan wired TW that he had not "put bayonet in an author's ribs for a heck of a time" and promised to accept *Streetcar* "exactly as is." He also suggested that Selznick check his references. "There are an awful lot of people I've worked with whom I didn't terrify" (May 5, 1947, HRC).]

59. To Irene Mayer Selznick

SH: The Park Central
Seventh Avenue · 55 to 56 Street
New York City 19, N.Y.
Friday Night [May 1947]
[TLS, 2 pp. Private Collection]

Dear Irene:

Just had a talk over phone with Audrey. I am leaving early tomorrow morning for the Cape.

Audrey told me Gadge's terms and I must admit - though I have no idea what directors ordinarily receive - that these seem pretty stiff.

Irene, I don't think you have yet given sufficient consideration to the idea of direction by <u>myself</u> <u>and</u> Margo Jones. I know and appreciate your aversion to direction by a woman. However this would actually be direction by the author <u>through</u> a woman who is the only one who has a thorough interpretative understanding of his work. Also I think you must have observed how much direction is actually incorporated in the script itself. In writing a play I see each scene, in fact every movement and inflection, as vividly as if it were occuring right in front of me. However I could not direct by myself as I am insufficiently articulate. However with Margo I <u>could</u>. We have a sort of mental short-hand or Morse code, we are so used to each other and each other's work, and with Margo it would be a labor of love. Love cannot be discounted, even in a hardboiled profession, as one of the magic factors in success. I have a profound conviction that the two of us, working on this script, with you and Audrey and Liebling as a supporting team - could do something a little better with the play than any other single director, including Gadge. I felt that all along but pressed for Gadge because I felt at the outset that you were irrevocably prejudiced against another woman-director. Well, there is only one woman director and that's Margo. Regardless of what anyone says, I know she has the stuff - and her shortcomings are exactly what I am able to supply. With her I could also continue to function as a writer, during the rehearsals, but with any other - perhaps even Gadge - I don't think I would be able to achieve much more. I mean we have a way of stimulating each other.

Irene, this is not to be construed as pressure. I just thought - in view of the stiff terms offered by Kazan - that you should know that there is an alternative and it is in fact an alternative which I think is even preferable. Needless to say my direction would be gratuitous and Margo's terms would be negligible compared to the others.

I hope you will think about this. See you next week.

Love, Tennessee.

[Elia Kazan's "stiff" terms for directing *Streetcar* stipulated his billing as co-producer and a twenty-percent share of the profits, in addition to the "usual fee and top percentage of the gross." Irene Selznick threatened "to step aside" rather than "knuckle under" to such "an ultimatum" (*A Private View*, pp. 299-300).

TW informed Margo Jones at this time that he had originally recommended three directors to Selznick: Jones, Kazan, and John Huston. Selznick, he claimed, was still smarting over the failed "woman-director" of "Heartsong," the Laurents play which closed in Philadelphia, and "swore that she would take another 'over her dead body.'" Presumably Kazan was the beneficiary of Selznick's "aversion to direction by a woman" (n.d., HRC).

Related correspondence indicates that TW wrote this letter on May 9, 1947, shortly before he and Pancho Rodriguez left for Provincetown.]

60. To Elia "Gadge" Kazan

[Peter Nyholm House
Provincetown, Massachusetts]
[May 1947]
[TLS, 2 pp. WUCA]

Dear Gadge:

I sincerely hope by the time you get this everything will be straightened out among the lawyers. When I pulled out of town they were still in a huddle and the fur was flying. There was nothing I could do except stand pat, so I did - and removed myself to the Cape. I have taken a little house right on the water and about a mile out of town and my friend Pancho and I are now busy painting everything red, white, yellow and green to counteract the grey weather. When you get back to this Coast, I hope you will come up here for a week-end. It might be the best place to go over the script. Needless to say, I am eager for your ideas. I think this play has some excellent playing scenes but there are also some weak passages and some corny touches. I am determined to weed these out as much as possible before we go into rehearsal. You and I may not agree about exactly which and where these are but I am sure a lot of good will come out of consultation between us. The cloudy dreamer type which I must admit to being needs the complementary eye of the more objective and dynamic worker. I believe you are also a dreamer. There are dreamy touches in your direction which are vastly provocative, but you have a dynamism that my work needs to be translated into exciting theatre. I don't think "Pulling the punches" will benefit this show. It should be controlled but violent. - I went to see "All My Sons" again. I was more impressed than ever, the way lightning was infused into all the relationships, everything charged with feeling, nothing, even the trivial exchanges, allowed to sag into passivity. Yes, I think you can try new things in my play. In that sense it might be good for you, and it will certainly be good for me. It is a <u>working</u> script. I think we can learn and grow with it and possibly we can make something beautiful and alive whether everyone understands it or not. People are willing to live and die without understanding exactly what life is about but they must sometimes know exactly what a play is about. I hope we can show them what it is about but since I cannot say exactly what it is about, that is just a hope. But maybe if we succeed in our first objective of making it alive on the stage, the meaning will be apparent.

On second visit to "Sons", I decided that Malden was right for Mitch. I hope you agree. The face is comical but the man has a dignified simplicity and he is a great actor. I also met Burt Lancaster. Was favorably impressed. He has more force and quickness than I expected from the rather plegmatic type he portrayed in The Killers. He also seemed like a man who would work well under good direction.

Let me know if you can come down here or would rather work with me in New York. We have a guest room here and it would be a pleasure to have you with us. - I want to absorb your ideas as early as possible so that I will have plenty of time to chew them over by myself and extract what is helpful.

Ever, Tennessee

[TW hoped to find "tranquillity" at Provincetown as the "working script" of *Streetcar* was revised and the production assembled. He had summered there in the early 1940s with some of the same friends who now reappeared on the Cape: Fritz Bultman and family, David Gregory, a New York friend and aspiring writer, Donald Windham and Sandy Campbell, the artist Buffie Johnson, and Jane Lawrence and Tony Smith.

Karl Malden played the supporting role of George Deever in *All My Sons*. His character attempts to restore a father's honor following an unfair wartime conviction. Malden would play Mitch in *Streetcar*. Burt Lancaster appeared as Alvaro in the film version of *The Rose Tattoo* (1955).]

61. To Margaret "Margo" Jones

[The Royalton, New York]
Friday, May 23, 1947.
[ALS, 3 pp. HRC]

Dearest Margo -

I have taken a little house in Provincetown for the summer but immediately after moving in, I had to return to N.Y. and thrash out the director-problem with Mrs. Selznick. Well, she has finally signed Kazan, virtually on her own terms. He wanted to be co-producer but she beat him down on that. You know how I hate fighting, uncertainty, Etc. It has been hell, and has made me sick again. This morning I had a very disquieting experience.

My mouth suddenly filled with blood. Pancho called the doctor and he has put me to bed for a couple of days. I hope I will be able to go back to Provincetown early this week (next) as I cannot - obviously - take the strenuous life anymore. Honey, I pray to God I can come to Dallas in July. Somehow I am more eager to see your production [of] "S. & S." ~~even~~ than "Streetcar." If I don't make it - and I am planning to make it - you must know it is simply a matter of impossibility that prevents me. But I shall do everything I can to make it possible for me to make the trip.

Of course you will have first option on this script - as director-producer. That is a promise.

I don't want it brought into N.Y., however, too soon after "Streetcar". It would not be fair to either play. Nor would I be in any condition to go - immediately - through another production. It is something that takes so much out of you. I would prefer to hold it at least until after Christmas. And perhaps I will be able to make some good changes before it is produced up here. The conception is so much better than the script as it now stands. Eventually - perhaps soon - a lot could be done to strengthen it.

I am delighted with your report (and brochure) of the company. How I would love to see all the plays, especially the beautiful Inge play. I know Carol will be thrilling in it.

See Chaplin's new film. It is a brilliant piece, in its unity of style and delicacy. Real Cinematic art.

I look forward to seeing you and Joanna. Incidentally, if you have extra copies of those lovely photographs in the brochure, I would love a copy of you both, to put up in the summer cottage, until I see you again.

Sorry to write such a dull letter but I have taken a seconal tablet and am nearly asleep.

Love, love, love! Tennessee.

[Irene Selznick refused to share authority as producer, but she agreed to a compromise billing: "Irene M. Selznick presents Elia Kazan's Production of *A Streetcar Named Desire*." She also gave Kazan twenty percent of the show, reducing her own share and that of the investors accordingly.

Pancho Rodriguez added to "the strenuous life" of New York by shredding TW's clothes and books, although not his manuscripts, and publicly denouncing two of his friends as the "'biggest whores on Broadway'" (qtd. in *Memoirs*, p. 106). TW apologized to Donald Windham, a victim of Pancho's misplaced jealousy, and admitted that he foresaw no "happy ending" to the "impossible situation" (qtd. in Windham, p. 200).

TW's view of *Summer and Smoke* had not changed appreciably since the preceding December, when he termed the play "an unhappy cross between Dr. Faustus and a radio soap-opera!" (to Wood, December 3, 1946, HRC). He now repeated a promise to Margo Jones that she would bring the show to New York, if it proved to be "Broadway material" (n.d., HRC). *Summer and Smoke* was set for a July 8 premiere at Theatre '47 in Dallas.

Charlie Chaplin played a witty bluebeard in his "new film," *Monsieur Verdoux* (1947).

The "seconal tablet" is TW's first reference in letters to this particular drug, a barbiturate prescribed as a sedative and hypnotic.]

62. *To Audrey Wood*

[Peter Nyholm House
Provincetown, Massachusetts]
[mid-June 1947]
[TLS w/ autograph postscript, 1 p. HRC]

Dear Audrey:

Margo is already yelping for me to show in Dallas but I shall remain here through June. I expect I'll pass through New York, say, about June 30th, and spend that day there, proceding the next to Dallas. May have to make it a couple days earlier, depending on length of trip. You'll know definitely early next week. I don't think much publicity about <u>me</u> is wise until the play has opened successfully. Neither my political sentiments nor my unconventional mode of living would make a favorable impression from what I can observe of public opinion. Of course a profile in "LIFE", which Irene mentioned, would be difficult to resist if obtainable: usually their treatment is more impersonal.

As for Mother investing: if the show costs about $100,000. I don't suppose there would be any return on investment until that amount has been paid off. Is this right? There are several things to consider. Coming recession, prissy moral attitudes of the N.Y. press, but mostly the casting of Blanche. I would not recommend investment in this show to any friend until that part has been satisfactorily cast. By satisfactorily I mean with a really powerful dramatic actress in the part. Sullavan is strictly compromise on that score. She is the sort of actress that would get "excellent personal notices" but do the play no good: unless she has more on the ball than we derived from her readings. Right now Tandy is the only one who looks good to me and I am waiting till I see her and hear her. Could you leave a piece ($5000.) open until Blanche is cast? Then I'll know whether or not Mother ought to invest.

Another question: will Tandy be in New York this summer? Could she come East for inspection here? If she was the Blanche we dream of, then I could dispense with the Coast trip which I dread making, as I would probably have to travel alone, and when I got there, would probably be subjected to intense pressure for script changes: the best I can do for this production is to stay in good shape for rehearsals. There isn't much in the script that should be altered until we know the exact limitations of the Blanche selected and hear the lines spoken. I will do a lot of cutting then. The rewrite on Scene V does not read as well as original but I think it will play better and is more sympathetic for Blanche. (Makes Mitch more important to her). - Francine Larrimore wants to read for Blanche!

Love, Tenn.

Expect me in N.Y. about June 27.

[A "profile" of TW appeared in *Life* magazine on February 16, 1948.

Audrey Wood suggested that Edwina invest in *Streetcar* as a "way of setting up a trust fund" (to TW, June 11, 1947, HRC) for Rose.

Margaret Sullavan, a veteran actor who had won major awards in theatre and film, was apparently Irene Selznick's choice to play Blanche. TW could not, however, "see her purging the emotions with anything stronger than pathos" (to Selznick, June 13, 1947, Private Collection). His judgment may have been shaded by the many popular films in which Sullavan played ingenue or leading lady to Jimmy Stewart, Fredric March, and Charles Boyer.

In the preceding January Hume Cronyn directed Jessica Tandy in "Portrait of a Madonna" (1945), a one-act play with strong intimations of *Streetcar*. He advised Wood of his wife's "fine" performance and now claimed that "Tandy is the only person in the world who can play Blanche" (Wood to TW, June 6, 1947, HRC). Wood informed TW that film work—ironically, *Forever Amber* (1947)—would keep Tandy on the Coast and that his own presence there was unavoidable (June 19, 1947, HRC).

As Scene Five of *Streetcar* evolved, TW replaced Blanche's disdainful criticism of Mitch with a more subtle analysis of their social and intellectual differences. Her strong antipathy to marrying Mitch was also softened, both to gain sympathy for Blanche and to prepare for her discovery that his protection is needed.

This letter bears a reception date of June 16, 1947.]

63. To Margaret "Margo" Jones

SH: Santa Fe Super Chief
[early-July 1947]
[TLS, 2 pp. HRC]

Dearest Margo:

It breaks my heart to miss the rehearsal period in Dallas. I know you don't need me but I would have so loved being there. However I had an imperative summons from Mme. Selznick. She said Tandy and others could not wait any longer for a decision about casting as they had other offers and commitments. I could not approve casting without seeing them so there was nothing to do but go out there immediately. I do hope Tandy is right. We heard two actresses in N.Y., Pamela Brown and Margaret Sullavan, both disappointing. Sullavan would do but she lacked any of the fragility Blanche should have and Pamela was cold. I did not realize it was going to be so terrifically hard to cast. If the right one doesn't turn up I will not go on with the production. With the wrong actress this would repeat the experience with "Battle". I am still working on the last scene as I think that is the weak point in the script.

I shall leave the Coast the moment it is possible, that is, when some decision is reached about Blanche. It should not take more than a week to explore everything there and I shall then come back through Dallas. I feel very hopeful about "Summer & Smoke". I would not if anyone else were doing it. It is such a romantic play that I think it really expresses you more than it does me. When it is done in a real theatre, design will add a great deal. See the picture of "Stairs to the Roof" in Theatre Arts. I think Summer should be performed against a sky like that. Practically no walls.

Jo's designs for Streetcar are almost the best I've ever seen. The back wall of the interior is translucent with a stylized panorama showing through it of the railroad yards and the city (when lighted behind). It will add immensely to the poetic quality. He must also do Summer.

I hope Balfour is working out. You must work mostly against

monotony in that part, the same as on Blanche. If an interpretation is too exageratted it becomes monotonous.

Liebling sent someone over to see me whom he said would make a perfect John in Summer. He looked like Mickey Rooney, only a little taller.

David Gregory is on the train with me as he is also called West on business. Pancho is along, too. I felt he would make the trip easier for me, and I dreaded making it alone. We are going to stay in a guest-house on the estate of George Cukor. - I will call or wire you in a few days. My address is c/o Irene Selznick, 1050 Summit Drive, Beverly Hills. (at present). - David is finishing a straight play! - Haven't read it yet but the idea sounds great. - Will you come East after the summer work-out? Or do you intend to enter a sanitarium with Blanche?

Ever with love, 10.

[TW wired Audrey Wood to arrange for his and Pancho's trip to the West Coast on June 30. Margo Jones held out hope that he would attend the premiere of *Summer and Smoke*, but "Mme. Selznick" proved a greater force of nature than the "Texas Tornado."

The English actor Pamela Brown made her Broadway debut in recent Theatre Guild productions of *The Importance of Being Earnest* (Wilde, 1895) and *Love for Love* (Congreve, 1695).

Reprinted in *Theatre Arts* (July 1947) was a still from the recent Pasadena Playhouse production of *Stairs to the Roof* (February 26-March 9, 1947).

Irene Selznick accepted Jo Mielziner's "high terms" for designing *Streetcar* because he claimed that it would be "the best job he's ever done!" (April 18, 1947, HRC). At the time, Wood may have shared this information with TW to soften Kazan's apparent withdrawal and to calm a nervous author by touting Selznick's production.

Katharine Balfour rather than Margaret Phillips played Alma in the Dallas production of *Summer and Smoke*. In the preceding spring TW advised Jones "to eliminate the play" from her repertory if Phillips were unavailable. Only she "would justify a summer production" (April 17, 1947, HRC). In effect TW repeated Wood's advice that he could no longer afford to "have a play casually tried out" (to TW, April 2, 1947, HRC).]

64. To Helen Hayes

[c/o Irene Selznick
1050 Summit Drive
Beverly Hills, California]
July 23, 1947
[TLS, 1 p. Private Collection]

Dear Miss Hayes:

Charlie Feldman who owns the picture rights to "Menagerie" has told me that there is a chance you might be induced to play in the film when it is made. I do hope there is reason to entertain such a hope, as I cannot think of any actress now living who would portray Amanda more beautifully on the screen. Charlie showed me the screen treatment of the play and I was genuinely enthusiastic over the work done on it. It is in very good taste and structurally it shows an improvement over the original. He has asked me to do a little additional work on it, and I am taking the script back East for that purpose. I feel that if it is properly cast it will be a picture of distinction and I am most eager to know how you feel about it.

Cordially, Tenn. Williams

[Helen Hayes would play Amanda in the London stage production of *The Glass Menagerie* (1948) but not in the 1950 film version.]

65. To George Cukor

SH: The Stoneleigh
Dallas, Texas
August 3, 1947.
[TLS w/ autograph marginalia, 2 pp. Herrick]

Dear George:

I don't know what awful thing we did in L.A. to be sent to Dallas! You cannot conceive of how hot it is. If you could just lie still it would be endurable but there is a great deal of entertainment going on.

I suppose seeing the play was worth it, as Margo had done a remarkably good job under the limitations of her tiny theatre. The play has a living quality which Margo always gets in her productions and to my surprise it seems to have a strong popular appeal. Two hundred people were turned away from last night's performance and it has been like that right along. We have been talking about doing it in New York. I think a better plan would be to open on the West Coast and do L.A. and Frisco and Chicago for as long as possible and then come into New York in the early Spring, as I don't want to follow "Streetcar" too close. How do you feel about opening a play on the West Coast? I would like rehearsing out there. The life agrees with me, and now I feel at home there, having made so many friends. I don't think I have ever felt so close to anybody in such a short time as I did to you, George. You have a wonderful gift for dissolving the walls between people which I have always suffered from, being usually unable to do anything about it. You were kindness itself, taking us in so cordially and giving us the hospitality of your heavenly place. I have never been treated like that before, anywhere, and I will not soon forget it. Irene had praised you lavishly but for once I feel the lady was guilty of understatement.

Perhaps more than anything else, even the play, a letter waiting for me here gave me happiness. It was from the one friend to whom I was afraid to show "Streetcar". Donald Windham, who worked with me on "You Touched Me." He is occupying the house during my absence. He found a copy of the play lying around and read it and pronounced it superior to "Menagerie". I had been so afraid of his judgement! He is a merciless critic. (And I think he is going to be one of the literary landmarks some day - for his stories which are extraordinary.) I also found a letter from Carson McCullers who is now in Paris. Do you know her work? I think all of her books, especially the last one, "Member of the Wedding", would make great films.

You promised to give me G.G'S phone number or address in N.Y. Will you send it to me care of Audrey?

Affectionately, Tennessee.

[Many gay celebrities found a haven at George Cuckor's lavish estate in Hollywood, including TW, whose week-long stay was arranged by Irene Selznick. It was probably through Cukor (1899-1983), who directed Greta Garbo in *Camille* (1937), that TW met the reclusive star, writing to Donald Windham that she goes by the name of Harriet Brown and "is really hermaphroditic, almost as flat as a boy" (qtd. in Windham, p. 201).

Margo Jones opened Theatre '47 in June with a repertory of five plays, including *Farther Off from Heaven*, by William Inge, and *Summer and Smoke*, as it was now firmly entitled. The building which she selected in cramped, post-war Dallas sat only 200 and required the expedient of staging in the round. The *Times* critic Brooks Atkinson admired TW's "rueful idyll" of the South, but he warned that its transfer to New York would involve "a calculated risk": "For the magic of the informal staging in Theatre '47 has completely unpacked the heart of Mr. Williams' poignant narrative. The Broadway style is seldom that sensitive" (*New York Times*, August 10, 1947).

TW wrote to Atkinson from Provincetown, beginning a long and friendly correspondence. Atkinson briefly replied how "very much interested" he and his wife were in the playwright's "experience" (August 25, 1947, Private Collection) with *Summer and Smoke*.

Penned in the upper margin of page 1 is the notation "Provincetown, Mass. Gen. Del."]

66. To Margaret "Margo" Jones

[Peter Nyholm House
Provincetown, Massachusetts]
August 15, 1947
[TLS, 1 p. HRC]

Dearest Margo:

The day I left New York Audrey told me she was having our lawyer make out a contract for "Summer and Smoke". Please let me hear from you about this contract when you receive it, your complete reaction. I do not know what the terms in it will be as I did not discuss it with Audrey. If it is unsatisfactory in any respect contact me directly before you do Audrey. I know that Liebling (and probably Audrey) thinks you should have a co-producer. What is your feeling about this? Would a co-producer relieve you of some business details and simplify the production? Audrey seemed to feel that it would. My own feeling is that I want to avoid any and all complications: in other words, a total autonomy between the two of us with no outside pressure and interference. I don't know if you are ready to assume that much responsibility so I would like to have your own direct and explicit reaction. Speak as freely as possible as anything you have to say will be just between the two of us. I feel that this play should be financed fully before "Streetcar" comes in, to provide against the possibility "Streetcar" might fail and it would then be more difficult to raise backing. Also I think it would strengthen my bargaining position if we kept as quiet as possible about our agreements until after "Streetcar" has opened in N.Y. I mean if Selznick Etc. know that my next play is sewed up they will be less anxious to stay in my good graces. It is nasty but sometimes necessary to think in such terms. (That is one of the things I want to avoid in the future).

We are back at Provincetown. Buffie Johnson is also in town. Otherwise nothing interesting. I started working on another long play today: just the opening shot. But I shall not push it hard until after "Streetcar" is in. I call it Quebrada, meaning The Cliff. The scene is a hotel at Acapulco built on a cliff over the Pacific which will be used symbolically as the social and moral precipice of our times, the characters some intellectual derelicts: will be able to use Mexican music!

When are you coming East? Our phone number is Provincetown 973 M if you want to call me. Address General delivery.

Love from myself and Pancho, Tennessee.

[TW and Pancho Rodriguez planned to return to Provincetown ca. August 8.

Margo Jones rejected the "idea of a co-producer" (to TW, August 20, 1947, Private Collection) for the Broadway production of *Summer and Smoke*. The "autonomy" which TW preferred is a near restatement of Elia Kazan's formula for directing *Streetcar*: "'I work best in single collaboration with the author. I'll never go back to working for a producer when it means consulting with him (her) on every point as well as with administrators, executives, production committees, agents, backers and various and sundry personal associates'" (to TW, qtd. in Kazan, p. 329).

"Quebrada" appears to be a dramatic adaptation of the story "The Night of the Iguana."]

67. To Audrey Wood

[Peter Nyholm House
Provincetown, Massachusetts]
August 25, 1947
[TLS, 3 pp. HRC]

Dear Audrey:

A good many things have happened to upset and disturb me in connection with the management of "Streetcar" and I am sure you would want me to tell you frankly about them. In the first place, the new last scene of the play, the crucial scene upon which the success or failure of the play may very well depend, has either been lost or deliberately withheld for it is not in the new scripts, one of which Irving has just now delivered to me. I worked on various versions of this scene the whole time I was on the Coast and in Dallas and on the train coming to New York. I delivered it to a typist at the Selznick office together with the other (less important) revisions with the clearly stated and unmistakable direction that all of these revisions were to be incorporated in a new script. I did this so that Gadge would have the new script, and particularly the new last scene, to read and consider when he went into his Connecticutt retreat. It now turns out that Gadge has never seen my revision of the last scene. He told me this on the phone. Weeks are passing at a period when every day counts, without any exchange of views on this all-important last scene. A mystery is made about it. Nobody even seems to know where my original copy of it is? Now this is the sort of high-handed, officious and arbitrary treatment that seems to characterize the Selznick company. My work is too important to me, in fact it has always been and is now even more so - for me to accept this sort of treatment from a company that has only produced one failure which closed out of town. I suppose this sounds as if I were gnashing my teeth with rage. I admit that is true. I am. I am willing to accept the bungling of the Garfield deal and the nerve-wracking battle that was waged to secure the right director, but when arbitrary action is taken interfering with my irreductible rights as an author, I'm not going to take it. This is not a sudden display of peevishness on my part. I entered the agreement with Selznick because we were led to believe that we would have what we wanted in every respect and that there were great advantages to be derived from her management in casting due to her Hollywood connections. These advantages have not materialized. In fact the casting has been just about the biggest headache I've had in my theatrical experience - outside of Boston. I am not alone in this opinion, as you must know if you have talked to Kazan. It was bad management that announced Garfield in the papers before he was signed and I strongly suspect that good management would have signed him. The play has already been damaged and compromised before it has even gone into rehearsals.

I am getting this off my chest now in order to clear the atmosphere and so you will understand that if it is necessary for me to take a strong independant stand at any point in my future dealings with the Selznick company that you will see I am not doing it capriciously but with a feeling of justification. I am not going to lose this play because of poor management and I am going to see to it that it is protected in every possible and reasonable way because that is what I have a right to expect as the one who has given most and who has the most at stake. A play is my life's blood.

I also want you to know that my personal feelings toward everyone involved are sincerely and perfectly friendly. I like Irene as a person. I just feel that I am being asked to gamble, to take more of a risk, than is equitable for a playwright who is now in a position, after much effort and travail, to make choices and decisions for himself and to give his work the maximum protection.

So much for my state of being, at this point.

The actor George Beban was flown out here from the Coast and read for me this morning. This actor has had summer stock experience and has chased a stage coach in a Grade B Western. It was his first time on a horse. He is more adventuresome than I. I don't want to put my play under him. He gave a fair reading. He is of medium height with a rather tough and virile quality but he was monotonous, there was no gradation to his reading, no apparent humor or dexterity which comes from experience and from natural acting ability. He read one scene on his feet and his body movements were stiff and self-conscious with none of the animal grace and vitality (When I say grace I mean a virile grace) which the part calls for and it made me more bitterly conscious than ever of how good Garfield would have been. I think it was a brutal experience for this actor, and I do regard actors as being human beings some of them just as sensitive and capable of disappointment and suffering as I am. I don't understand why he was put through this ordeal with no more apparent attributes than he showed this morning. Of course it was a great strategic error, if the Selznick office hoped to interest me in this actor, to accompany him with the new scripts, for when I saw that my final scene had been left out I was somewhat distracted from anything else. I am sure, however, that I gave the actor a pretty fair appraisal, notwithstanding this factor. None of us, Gadge, Irene or I, were at all impressed by the screen-tests we saw of him on the Coast.

That leaves us with Marlon Brando, of the ones that have been mentioned to date. I am very anxious to see and hear him as soon as I can. He is going to read for Gadge and if Gadge likes him I would like to have a look at him. I also think it would be a good idea for someone outside the Selznick office to explore the Garfield situation. I should like to know if there are terms he would accept, at this point. And precisely what those terms are so that I myself can judge whether or not they were reasonable and practicable for this production. I don't think it would be wise, now, to let him sign for less than a full season - that is, till May - but I think he should be sounded out for his financial terms under that consideration. Gadge thinks any other management would have signed him and I am inclined to go along with Gadge's opinion as he knows Garfield better than the rest of us.

I think at this point we must avoid all unnecessary friction with the Selznick office but be prepared to take decisive action. Irene should not know that I have talked things over with Gadge and that he has expressed these opinions, for it would only make trouble between them which would further complicate our position.

I am aware of the possibility that Gadge and I both may perhaps have judged Irene mistakenly in her conduct of the Garfield affair.

Please tell Colton, for me - I'll write him myself a bit later - that I want a contract drawn up with Margo that will leave the date of production to our joint discretion, and that whether or not we have an associate producer should also be at our joint discretion, to be discussed and decided when we are ready to put that play in production. I now regard Margo with absolute reverence, because I know that in any dealings with her I would know exactly what was going on all the time and there would be a real autonomy of management and artistic control.

Affectionately yours, Tennessee

[Audrey Wood answered TW on August 27, typing the letter herself to insure confidentiality. The latest revisions of *Streetcar* had not been "lost" or "withheld" but sent first to Irene Selznick's office in California, as per usual practice. They were now on their way to Elia Kazan (August 27, 1947, HRC).

Selznick recalls that revision of the last scene of *Streetcar* was "confined to Blanche's departure, which was not only over-long but too harrowing" (*A Private View*, p. 301). TW attempted to soften the original "Poker Night" sequence by removing Blanche's more extreme symptoms—catatonic and hallucinatory—as well as her sedation with a hypodermic needle and departure in a straitjacket.

In July Hume Cronyn re-staged "Portrait of a Madonna" at the Actors' Lab to coincide with TW's visit to the West Coast. Tandy's portrayal of the delusional Miss Collins made it "instantly apparent" that "Jessica was Blanche" (*Memoirs*, p. 132), and she was signed.

John Garfield and Elia Kazan were friends and former members of the Group Theatre (1931-1941), but Garfield's loyalty, protests aside, was to a flourishing career in Hollywood. His "signing" to play Stanley was announced on August 1 but by the 18th plans had begun to unravel, as reported in the *New York Times*. A "very disturbed" TW cabled Wood for "complete details on Garfield situation and advance notice of any new terms offered him" (August 18, 1847, HRC). Garfield reportedly sought a limited run of four months and a guarantee of the film role, which Selznick rejected.]

68. To Audrey Wood

[Peter Nyholm House
Provincetown, Massachusetts]
August 29, 1947.
[TLS, 2 pp. HRC]

Dear Audrey:

I am grateful for your hand-made letter which was eloquent and moving, all the more so because of the technical difficulties. My rage is pacified and in spite of all the gnashing my teeth including the new bridge-work are still in place. The last scene arrived from the Coast. I do not know why it went there (exclusively) but since it has returned in good shape I am willing to surrender all suspicion of caballistic intentions. There is perhaps a touch of paranoia in my mind lately: I am like Mother Wingfield, I am not paranoiac but my life is paranoia.

I can't tell you what a relief it is that we have found such a God-sent Stanley in the person of Brando. It had not occured to me before what an excellent value would come through casting a very young actor in this part. It humanizes the character of Stanley in that it becomes the brutality or callousness of youth rather than a vicious older man. I don't want to focus guilt or blame particularly on any one character but to have it a tragedy of misunderstandings and insensitivity to others. A new value came out of Brando's reading which was by far the best reading I have ever heard. He seemed to have already created a dimensional character, of the sort that the war has produced among young veterans. This is a value beyond any that

Garfield could have contributed, and in addition to his gifts as an actor he has great physical appeal and sensuality, at least as much as Burt Lancaster. When Brando is signed I think we will have a really remarkable 4-star cast, as exciting as any that could possibly be assembled and worth all the trouble that we have gone through. Having him instead of a Hollywood star will create a highly favorable impression as it will remove the Hollywood stigma that seemed to be attached to the production. Please use all your influence to oppose any move on the part of Irene's office to reconsider or delay signing the boy, in case she doesn't take to him. I hope he will be signed before she shows in New York.

We had a full house this week, Joanna, Margo and Marlon in addition to Pancho and I. Things were so badly arranged that Margo and Brando had to sleep in the same room - on twin cots. I believe they behaved themselves - the fools! We had fixed a double-decker bunk for Margo and Joanna to occupy but when Margo climbed into her upper bunk several of the slats refused to support her. Also the plumbing went bad so we had to go out in the bushes. I had a violent quarrel with the plumber over the phone so he would not come out. Also the electric wiring broke down and "plunged us into everlasting darkness" like the Wingfields at supper. All this at once! Oh, and the kitchen was flooded! Marlon arrived in the middle of this domestic cataclysm and set everything straight. That, however, is not what determined me to give him the part. It was all too much for Pancho. He packed up and said he was going back to Eagle Pass. However he changed his mind, as usual. I am hoping that he will go home, at least to New Orleans, while the play is in rehearsal, until December. He is not a calm person. In spite of his temperamental difficulties he is very lovable and I have grown to depend on his affection and companionship but he is too capricious and excitable for New York especially when I have a play in rehearsal. I hope it can be worked out to keep him in the South for that period or at least occupied with a job. That would make things easier for me. I think it would also help a lot if I could find a small furnished apartment. Hotels are never restful enough. Are you having any luck with that problem? Perhaps some real estate agent would find one for me. I will stay on here until needed for casting.

Wherever it is possible I want to have my professional connections with persons I know, understand and am fond of, reciprocally, so I know you will understand my wish to publish through Laughlin and produce "Summer & Smoke" through Margo. I think such action gives a meaning to life: that is, sharing faith and keeping loyalties. Sometimes there is a conflict with professional interests, but unless that conflict is really important, I think it is better to sacrifice a little of the material advantage. I am not delivering a sermon to you on this subject as it is one on which we have no difference of opinion whatsoever, I am only putting this down to clarify my reasons for sometimes asking you to disregard what you, as my representative, feel always obliged to protect. I would not make commitments with any friend that would <u>seriously</u> imperil my work, as that always comes first, and in both these instances I feel there is actually no material <u>dis</u>advantage and very likely an advantage. So this is not being terribly noble, after all . . .

With love, Tennessee.

["Finding a Stanley," Elia Kazan recalls, "proved almost as simple—once we forgot about movie stars (the natural place for Irene to look)—as finding Blanche" (Kazan, p. 341). Marlon Brando's reading so impressed a visiting Margo Jones that she "jumped up and let out a 'Texas Tornado' shout." It was "'the greatest reading'" that she had "'ever heard—in or outside of Texas!'" (qtd. in *Memoirs*, p. 131). The twenty-three-year-old Brando had two promising Broadway seasons to his credit and was well known to Kazan for his supporting role in *Truckline Café* (1946), a play of little merit by Maxwell Anderson which Harold Clurman and Kazan had co-produced.

"Not a calm person" refers to another violent episode with Pancho, who reportedly tried to run down TW with the Pontiac and then subjected Margo Jones and Joanna Albus to "a night of horror" (*Memoirs*, p. 134). His apparent provocation was TW's meeting of a young man at the Atlantic House and their subsequent idyll in the sand dunes. Frank Merlo, "a youth of Sicilian extraction," would become TW's "closest, most long-lasting companion" (*Memoirs*, p. 132), when they met again in New York.]

PART II

1947-1948

Overleaf: Thomas Hart Benton, The Poker Night *(from* A Streetcar Named Desire*).*

69. To Irene Mayer Selznick

SH: Provincetown, Massachusetts
Sept. 8, 1947
[TLS, 3 pp. Private Collection]

Dear Irene:

I hope you will forgive me for stealing another week on the Cape. The Indian summer here is too glorious to miss altogether: a mellow golden light suffuses everything and the lingering warmth is much sweeter. Now that the tourists have gone the real salty character of the fishing community emerges. - I talked to Gadge and he said he wouldnt need me till the fifteenth. I plan to return to New York by then. As the four principals have been cast (and very happily), I don't think there is anything very urgent or immediate for me to do in New York right now. I do want to check with Lehmann on the music. I have not heard from him since our meeting last month. I would like to have a hand in the selection of Eunice. But I am sure that you all can weed out the field and let me look over the final contestants. As for the poker players: I am sure Gadge will do a good job on them. ~~I don't think it will hurt to cast the Mexican for comedy. A plump~~ There is the Mexican and Steve Hubbs in addition to Mitch and Stanley. Steve should be a big beefy guy. The Mexican is called a "Greaseball". Might be cast accordingly. I would say all men around Stanley's age, or a bit older. Eunice is a coarse and healthy character. The nurse is a bit sinister: a large and masculine type. I don't know whether or not you want to use the Mexican woman selling the tin flowers. Check with Gadge on that. If not her speeches can be easily deleted from the script.

As for the last scene, I will give it another work-out. I feel that my last revision on it is the best to date. It has not as much "plus-quality" in the writing as I would like. However I think it will play well. Where it lacks most is the dialogue between Stella and Eunice: there is still something too cut-and-dried in the necessary exposition between them. I will try (but can't promise) to improve on that. I would like your opinion about the relative sympathetic treatment of the doctor. It may soften too much. We mustn't lose the effect of terror: everybody agrees about that.

I have talked to Irving and Audrey about getting Joanna into the company. I don't believe you have met her, which is unfortunate as she is a very rare person. She is not quite right for any part in the play but could understudy Eunice and the nurse, not that she is their type but is an excellent actress who could play anything in a pinch. However her real value would be in backstage relations. She would take an intense personal interest in everything connected with the play and would serve in countless ways in addition to "holding the book". She is one of those miracles of general competence! Every show needs somebody like that to hold things together behind the scenes. My idea was that she could be engaged as promptress and understudy for a couple of the women. It would mean a great deal to her for personal reasons. She was not at all happy last summer at Dallas. Margo wants her back there but Joanna definitely wants to stay with a New York show and particularly this one which she is crazy about.

It seems that I will have an Apartment when I arrive in N.Y. Expect me on the 15th.

With love, Tennessee.

[Selection of Kim Hunter and Karl Malden completed the principal cast of *A Streetcar Named Desire* (1947). Finding a Stella was uncertain and prolonged. Only by chance did Irene Selznick "spot three lines in *Variety* mentioning that Kim was touring in a small stock company upstate. . . . I dared to propose her." Hunter would make a difficult adjustment to the role in her first appearance on Broadway. Malden, by contrast, was "the first and last" to read for the part of Mitch and "was wonderful" (Selznick, *A Private View*, 1983, p. 303).

Elements of jazz and the blues in Alex North's score were intended to "fit," as Elia Kazan put it, the respective violence and desperation of Stanley and Blanche. Lehman Engle, musical director, supervised the four-piece band tucked away in the Ethel Barrymore Theatre.

The "exposition" between Stella and Eunice in Scene Eleven of *Streetcar* reveals that Stella has settled for the self-preserving lie, denying that Stanley raped her sister.

Joanna Albus served as an uncredited staff assistant in the *Streetcar* company.]

70. To Walter Dakin Williams

[Hotel Algonquin, New York]
PM: New York, September 20, 1947
[TLS, 1 p. HRC]

Dear Dakin:

I am sorry we didn't get together on your trip East. You came a little too late to visit me in Provincetown as I was leaving the day after I got your wire.

Is it true that you are entering a law-firm in St. Louis? Audrey got that impression. Are you sure this will suit you better? I wish you had made some legal connection in New York, for I would then be able to put you in charge of my financial and legal affairs. I am not happy over having them entirely under one control as they now are, as my lawyer is also the Lieblings lawyer. I think it is best to separate the two. Perhaps after "Streetcar" opens I can make some different arrangement, for then my business affairs will be too complicated for me to watch over carefully. I don't feel that I have realized as much, financially, from the last play as I should have and I want to be more careful about the new ones. If you come to New York for the opening of "Streetcar", we can talk that over.

I am moving into a small apartment the first of October. It is just one room with a kitchenette and bath but it's the best available. It is right off Park avenue on 36th street, one of the few blocks in New York that have real trees. Living at the Algonquin is a strain as the place is infested with actors looking for jobs. It is impossible to get from the door to the elevator, a fairly short distance, without being snagged by one.

Have they found anyone to take Rose around? And where is Grandfather planning to go after Sewanee?

With love, Tom.

[Discharged from the Army Air Corps as a captain, Dakin Williams briefly taught law at St. Louis University before joining the local firm of Martin, Peper & Martin.

Rose Williams was beginning her eleventh year as a patient at Farmington State Hospital in southeastern Missouri. Visits by TW were rare, and painful, and perhaps discouraged by Edwina, who feared that they would unnerve her son. TW had recommended to the superintendent that a companion be found to accompany Rose on brief trips away from the hospital.]

71. To Amado "Pancho" Rodriguez y Gonzalez

108 E. 36th Street [New York]
Oct. 1947.
[TLS w/ autograph marginalia
and postscript, 2 pp. HRC]

Dear Pancho:

I was awfully happy to get your letter this morning with the account of your day with the nephews. They seem to take after their uncle in some respects.

This is the first I have heard from you about the garage's offer for the car. Perhaps you wrote about it before and the letter didn't reach me. It seems like a good offer. I will look through my papers for the registration card you want. Is that all that will be necessary to make the transaction?

I wish I could write you an equally amusing letter but I don't have any little nephews to supply me with comic material. I feel very sober and dull. And when I get home at night, after a day at the disposal of the Selznick company and the Liebling-Wood Corporation, I barely have the strength to hit the typewriter keys. You must try and forgive me for being so stupid and do write me whenever you can. It does me good to hear about your peaceful family life in New Orleans where I would much prefer to be. However I have now moved into my apartment. It can hardly be called that as it is really just one room with little kitchenette and bathroom. No one has learned the phone number so I have a feeling of privacy which is a comfort after the Algonquin. Jo Healy has been taking me to all the openings. She gets tickets through the agency she works for. There has only been one hit so far this season and it is a war-play which the public may not support long. We start rehearsals Monday. Gadge is full of vitality and optimism. Miss Tandy has arrived in town looking very pretty with her new blond hair and all the script changes have been approved and finally typed up.

Today I got a notice to call the Athletic Club so perhaps it has been arranged for me to join there. I have been swimming daily at the "Y", walking a good deal, and have managed to lose seven pounds. I also had to give up potatoes - which I love. But when I saw my new photographs - with a face like a full moon only not nearly so bright - I knew that something must be done about it. I had other pictures taken after I lost the 7 pounds and the new ones are quite nice. I'll send you one.

Grandfather wrote me a long letter from the Wm. Len hotel in Memphis. He says he is waiting for me to come South again. Dear old man, he is so brave and wonderful, going along by himself at the age of ninety! I sent him a nice check, for I doubt that Mother had provided for him sufficiently.

I also got a note from Oliver who has gone to teach at Nebraska. No news in it.

Buffie is furious with me because I stood her up at a cocktail party. When I last saw her she was entertaining a woman whom she introduced to me as "The Countess Hamilton". A plain-looking woman with bulging blue eyes and seedy looking out-fit - but anyhow she was a countess so Buffie was nearly bursting with pride. She told me that I was not fit to associate with well-mannered people! I agreed with her and left. She is now in her house but only one room is reasonably finished. And Irene is about to have kittens.

Jane Lawrence is back in town. Her hair is light golden red but she looked awfully tired the day I saw her. She helped me pack my things and move over here and I am going to do what I can to help her find a singing job in a show. However the chances are not good as the theatrical season seems to be unusually bad. Few shows opening and those of doubtful quality.

I took Celeste Holm (musical star) to hear your niece, Carmen, sing. She liked her and may interest other people. Jo Healy invited Carmen to lunch but Carmen did not even acknowledge the invitation. I can't imagine why. Jo lives with Gypsy Rose Lee and has many theatrical contacts. She took quite a friendly interest in Carmen because of me.

Take care of yourself. Be good, be good, be good! And take your nephews to the zoo. I expect to see you in a couple of months. You might enquire at the Pontalba if the lady Mrs. Vacarro knows could get me an apartment there. That is, if, if, if!

Your loving friend, Tenn.

P.S. Will mail papers this week-end. Please wire collect name of buyer and garage.

[Pancho Rodriguez was persuaded—perhaps by Irene Selznick—to rejoin his family in New Orleans shortly after he and TW arrived in New York on September 14. In seeking title clearance, he was following TW's advice to sell the Pontiac should repairs prove costly.

Rehearsals of *Streetcar* afforded TW no relief from dullness: "This was a lost day. I went to bed at 9 a.m. and got up when it was getting dark and did nothing but attend rehearsals. Tonight I made the mistake of drinking coffee. My belly aches a bit in a dull way and my mind seems to imitate that feeling." The journal passage ends with the admission that "today I was particularly aware of missing Pancho" (Monday {October 1947}).

The "war-play" *Command Decision* (1947), by William W. Haines, closed after 408 performances on Broadway. TW's escort appears to have been Jo Healy, a Theatre Guild friend from the early 1940s who would serve at times as a companion for Rose.

TW closes with a litany of family, friends, and celebrities, including Celeste Holm, the original Ado Annie of *Oklahoma!* (1943) fame. He would be joined by Pancho much sooner than expected or seemingly desired.

TW wrote this letter before rehearsals of *Streetcar* began on October 6, 1947. Keyed to the fifth paragraph is a marginal reference to Walter Dakin, "Send him a card!"]

72. To Margaret "Margo" Jones

[108 East 36th Street, New York]
[October 1947]
[TLS, 2 pp. HRC]

Dearest Margo:

I am commencing the Sabbath at three P.M. with a stiff slug of Scotch, about three fingers, with a little faucet water, being too nervous to get out the ice-cubes. This sounds like things are going badly. Actually I believe they are going pretty good. I cannot find words to tell you how wonderful Jessica and Gadge are, and what a superb combination their talents appear to be. I have never seen two people, except maybe you, work as hard on anything. Or have as much respect for each other, which is so important. Gadge's method is to stage one new scene each day and to go over all the preceding scenes in sequence. Tomorrow, Monday, he will stage the final, eleventh scene, which I think is the crucial one. We have not come into conflict on any point. Occasionally I have to suggest a little less realistic treatment of things, to which he always accedes. His great gift is infusing everything with vitality. Sometimes in his desire to do this he neglects to dwell sufficiently upon a lyric moment. However this is not through failure to comprehend them, and he is always eager for my advice. Everybody is working out fine with the possible exception of Kim Hunter. She was very bad at first, is now improving but will, I am afraid, always be the lame duck in the line-up. She too is working like a fire-horse but is not a very gifted actress, and shows up badly in contrast to one as emotionally and technically rich as Jessica. You should see Joanna! She is everybody's darling! The Selznick office possesses her body and soul and they consider her the pearl beyond price! (Which she undoubtedly is). I have not had a chance to talk to her since the production started.

Honey, you don't know what a wonderful gift that pressed wood was!

My fire is my big comfort here. And that pressed wood is miraculous, the way it starts blazing right up and keeps at it! Every time I light a fire with it, I think about Margo whose gift to the world is fire, the fire of belief and devotion in comparison to which everything else in this universe is a heap of dead ashes.

Here is a bit of news for you. The Mexican problem returned to Manhattan a couple of days ago, quite unexpectedly, and is now sharing the one-room apartment with me. Manana he will look for a job. (Always Manana). I don't know what has happened but something has flown out the window, maybe never to return. Sympathy is not enough. There must be respect and understanding on both sides. I wish I could talk to you about this. I am terribly troubled. I don't think I am acting kindly, and that is what I hate above all else.

Please send me a little bulletin, just a few lines, on the Project.

With love, 10.

[Kim Hunter recalls that TW would silently advise Elia Kazan by tucking a note into his "coat pocket." Kazan, TW confirms, "was one of those rare directors who wanted the playwright around at all rehearsals. . . . Once in a while he would call me up on stage to demonstrate how I felt a certain bit should be played. I suspect he did this only to flatter me for he never had the least uncertainty in his work" (*Memoirs*, p. 135). Uncertainty was the lot of Irene Selznick, who feared that Marlon Brando's Stanley would never overcome his legendary mumbling.

TW ambivalently recorded Pancho's return to New York: "My feeling for P. has more or less definitely fallen from desire to custom though my affection is not lost. I don't think it was time or repetition. It was partly that but other things, a spiritual disappointment was the more important factor. He is incapable of reason. Violence belongs to his nature as completely as it is abhorrent to mine. Most of all, I want and now must have - simple peace. The problem is to act kindly and still strongly, for now I know that my manhood is sacrificed in submitting to such a relationship. Oh, well - it will work out somehow" (*Journal*, October 27, 1947).

Margo Jones assured TW that he was "incapable of acting unkindly" toward Pancho and urged that he not allow his "huge responsibility to the world" to be affected by this "dangerous" relationship. She advised that he "take a definite stand once and for all" (Tuesday night {October 1947} HRC).

TW may have written this letter on Sunday, October 19, 1947, after Pancho's return to New York.]

73. *To Amado "Pancho" Rodriguez y Gonzalez*

SH: The Ritz-Carlton, Boston
[November 1947]
[TLS, 3 pp. HRC]

Dear Pancho:

I expect I'll see you in New York early this week, and I sincerely hope that I'll find you in a pleasant and reasonable state of mind. I myself am so tired that it is impossible for me right now to cope with unreasonable moods. In my life there has been so much real tragedy, things that I cannot speak about and hardly dare to remember, from the time of my childhood and all the way through the years in between that I lack patience with people who are spoiled and think that they are entitled to go through life without effort and without sacrifice and without disappointment. Life is hard. As Amanda said, "It calls for Spartan endurance." But more than that, it calls for understanding, one person understanding another person, and for some measure of sacrifice, too. Very few people learn until late in life how much courage it takes to live, but if you learn it in the beginning, it will be easier for you. Excuse me for preaching. I am not a good preacher and perhaps I have no right to. But I feel concerned for you, worried over your lack of purpose. You have so much more than I have in so many ways. Your youth, your health and energy, your many social graces which I do not have. Life can hold a great deal for you, it can be very rich and abundant if you are willing to make some effort and to stop thinking and acting altogether selfishly. In this world the key to happiness is through giving, more than getting. For instance when you see that someone needs peace more than anything else, needs quietness and a sense of security, you cannot expect to involve that person in continual turmoil and tension and anxiety and still have him cherishing your companionship all the time. No, for his own protection if he wishes to go on living and working, he must withdraw sometime from these exhausting conditions. One does not suffer alone. It is nearly always two who suffer, but sometimes one places all the blame on the other.

Of all the people I have known you have the greatest and warmest heart but you also unfortunately have a devil in you that is constantly working against you, filling you with insane suspicions and jealousies and ideas that are so preposterous that one does not know how to answer them.

It is a terrifying thing. You must face it and make a determined effort to master it now before it becomes too well-established. Try to understand all those whom you get these foolish prejudices against. If you know them you'll see how wrong you are and laugh at yourself. Most of all - get busy at something. Then you will regain your self-confidence and independance and you will take a man's place in the world.

You know that my affection for you and my loyalty to you as a friend remains unalterable and that while I am alive you will have my true friendship always with you.

Ever, Tennessee.

[Notices for the Boston tryout of *Streetcar* (November 3-15, 1947) were generally positive, if qualified by moral concerns and "second thoughts" regarding the play's stature as tragedy. Especially flattering were reviews of Jessica Tandy's performance, which was deemed "superb, imaginative and illuminating." Notices for Marlon Brando, while strong, did not justify the fear that he would dominate Tandy and make the play his own. The Boston censor tried, without success, to have the rape scene struck.

TW probably wrote this letter before Pancho Rodriguez made a "surprise visit" to Boston and burst into his room at the Ritz-Carlton. He was pacified and removed by Irene Selznick, whose suite was nearby. TW wrote in *Memoirs* that "it was years" (p. 137) before he saw Pancho again.]

74. To Amado "Pancho" Rodriguez y Gonzalez

[108 East 36th Street, New York]
[ca. late-November 1947]
[TLS, 1 p. HRC]

Dear Pancho:

There are some things I feel I ought to try to say to you and since you don't apparently want me to talk to you I will try to write them. If I had not cared for you deeply you would not have hurt me and if you had not hurt me I would not have "blown my top" as I did. I spoke and acted in a blind rage. Maybe you don't know what provoked it and maybe I don't either. It just happened, as I told you it might happen at lunch that day, when I said I thought it would be safer for us to live separately. There was a tight coil of emotion in me as a result of the two preceding incidents -

which any little thing could set off. And it did. If you search your heart you will understand these things. I have never said an untrue thing to you all the times that I have been with you except in those few blind panicky moments when it seemed, perhaps unreasonably, that you had never cared for me at all and that I had been just a matter of convenience for whom you held contempt. To explain those things you have to go back through the entire history of a life, all its loneliness, its disappointments, its hunger for understanding and love. ~~And perhaps even you get only a~~ No, there is no point in talking about it any further. I don't ask anything of you, Pancho, this is not to ask anything, not even your pardon. I only want to tell you that I am your friend and will remain so regardless of how you may feel toward me. I offered you more of my heart than I have anybody in the last five years, which you may not have wanted and may now despise but believe me it is still full of the truest affection for you. Wherever you are I want you to have happiness - salud, amor y pesados!

10.

[The dating of this letter is speculative in light of the ceaseless turmoil and periodic ruptures of TW's relationship with Pancho Rodriguez. Nonetheless its summary character may indicate the final decisive break during the tryout period of *Streetcar*.]

75. To Edwina Dakin Williams

SH: Liebling-Wood
Authors' Representatives
551 Fifth Avenue
New York 17, N.Y.
[late-November 1947]
[TLS, 1 p. HTC]

Dear Mother:

I am just in town for the day and am borrowing Audrey's office to get off a few letters. I am glad you and Dakin have decided to come up for the opening. Forewarned is forearmed so you will be prepared for a rugged evening in the theatre. Most of the ladies seem to enjoy the play a great deal and one of the Boston Cabots, a lady of great refinement, wrote me that she was "inexpressibly delighted" by the street-car ride I gave her in Boston.

I shall not listen to any moral homilies and dissertations so please leave them at home, but do bring a Spanish shawl with you, one of those that Grandfather purchased in Italy. We have been trying to get one for the play and have had no luck as they are no longer fashionable. I will see that Madame Selznick gives you several times the purchase price for it. I love to spend her money. I have been staying in luxurious suites at the best hotels on the road, as it is all out of her fifteen million dollars and I think she needs every possible assistance in reducing that all but intolerable burden.

How about the Catholic priest? Is he coming to the play, too? Wouldn't you rather stay at one of the hotels on the park such as the Plaza or the St. Moritz? I think reservations could be arranged. What do you hear from Grandfather, and is anything being done for Rose? If this play goes over I am going to establish a fund to provide for her somewhat better.

I shall be terribly busy till after opening night but I can meet your train if you let me know when you arrive on Monday.

With love, Tom.

[TW was in and out of "town" while attending the final tryout of *Streetcar* in Philadelphia (November 17-29, 1947), where it did excellent business and received the strongest notices to date. It "is bound to linger long in the memory, vividly and vitally, after most of the facile and ephemeral footlight offerings . . . have been forgotten," predicted one astute reviewer.

TW informed his grandfather at this time that Edwina and Dakin planned to attend the New York opening, although he doubted that "Mother will approve of this play: it is a little too colorful for her Presbyterian tastes. You'd like it better" (n.d., HTC). Edwina later proclaimed *Streetcar* TW's "greatest" work and added that "sons have such trouble understanding mothers!" (Edwina Dakin Williams, *Remember Me to Tom*, 1963, p. 188).]

76. To James "Jay" Laughlin

[108 East 36th Street, New York]
[December 4, 1947]
[TLS w/ enclosures, 1 p. Houghton]

Streetcar opened last night to tumultuous approval. Never witnessed such an exciting evening. So much better than New Haven you wdn't believe it; N.H. was just a reading of the play. Much more warmth, range, intelligence, interpretation, etc. - a lot of it because of better details in direction, timing. Packed house, of the usual first-night decorations, - Cecil B'ton, Valentina, D. Parker, the Selznicks, the others and so on, - and with a slow warm-up for first act, and comments like "Well, of course, it isn't a play," the second act (it's in 3 now) sent the audience zowing to mad heights, and the final one left them - and me - wilted, gasping, weak, befoozled, drained (see reviews for more words) and then an uproar of applause which went on and on. Almost no one rose from a seat till many curtains went up on whole cast, the 4 principles, then Tandy, who was greeted by a great howl of "BRavo!" from truly all over the house. Then repeat of the whole curtain schedule to Tandy again and finally .... 10 Wms crept on stage, after calls of Author! and took bows with Tandy. All was great, great, GREAT! As you can see by the reviews enclosed. Will send from evening papers tomorrow. 20th-Century Fox has already called for a copy. I want to go to play again! Bielenson is printing it this minute and shd be bound and ready next week. E says that [there] are many many orders already, and with the success, we think we shd bind all 5000. What do you? Pauper will hold type for re-print if necessary, but cdn't possibly know now.

Do you want to see the poesie I have to select, or shd I just add one or two. None are longer than 1 type (single) page. Still think you really ought to print the nurse-actor story, though. That fits with ND 10.

T. Williams

[No reviewer was more aware of the dramatic integrity of *Streetcar* than Louis Kronenberger. The play, he wrote, "carries us into the only part of the theater that really counts—not the most obviously successful part, but the part where, though people frequently blunder they seldom compromise; where imagination is seated higher than photography; and where the playwright seems to have a certain genuine interest in pleasing himself" (*PM Magazine*, December 5, 1947). James Laughlin published the book in late-December 1947, while the play went on to win the Drama Critics' Circle and the Pulitzer prizes and to amass 855 performances on Broadway. Warner Brothers would release the first film version in 1951.]

The principal Broadway cast of A Streetcar Named Desire *(1947): Karl Malden, Marlon Brando, Jessica Tandy, and Kim Hunter. "Streetcar opened last night to tumultuous approval."*

77. To John van Druten

SH: Hotel Woodrow
West 64th Street, New York
December 7, 1947
[TLS, 2 pp. BRTC]

Dear John:

Your letter is the most honest and beautiful that has come to me in connection with any of my writing. I think it is a fine "human document" and I don't want to lose it. As I shall be travelling around a good deal this year, I have given to my friend and agent Audrey Wood to keep for me. There will be times when I will want to read it again. I don't feel able, at the moment, to answer you properly but the letter has left me with a feeling of companionship. We have shared like experiences. You have weathered a great deal more success than I and I hope that I wear it as well, for your humanity is not depleted. This is amply testified in your work also by those who know you and particularly by this letter.

I think we must face the fact that there are some problems for which no perfect solution exists and popular success, the dislocation it brings, is one of those problems. However it is helped by facing it squarely. A grave illness such as you mention, anything that brings one close to fundamentals, is also a great help as I have discovered. It brings out the Chinaman in your soul and values slip back into a more natural allignment. You say that you are tempted to write a play about this problem. Why don't you? I know that "The Mermaids Sing" touched upon it, but I feel too superficially. Incidentally, "The Druid Circle" is a far, far better play and I found it more touching than "Voice of the Turtle". No one is better able than you to examine searchingly the problems of popular success in the theatre, its impact on the artist, and I think you can do it without repeating anything in your earlier work. But I, too, am faced with a problem of themes and material. There is always something but it is difficult to keep it away from stuff you have explored in the past. I don't think, for instance, I could get away with another southern play about a woman. I must try something different now. And I must not be afraid of failure. It is more a part of growth than success is.

I am hiding out temporarily in this flea-bag. Someone out of the past is making trouble. Have you ever had that? It is one of the ugly and sordid details coincident with a success. I don't want this known, but I am sailing on the 30th for Europe. If you are in town during the holidays, let us do, by all means, get together, you and Walter and I. I hope I will be back in my apartment by then and I have a basket of fine (1937) French champagne that Mme. Selznick gave me as an opening present. We will uncork one, and it will be better than that synthetic stuff I gave you at the Shelton - remember?

The best to you, John, and many, many thanks for your beautiful letter.

Ever, Tenn.

[*The Voice of the Turtle* (1943) and *I Remember Mama* (1944) illustrate the varied and successful career of the London-born playwright John van Druten (1901-1957). The plays ran for 1557 and 714 performances, respectively, the latter giving Marlon Brando his first important role on Broadway.

Van Druten wrote to applaud *Streetcar* but especially to underscore TW's recent article in the *New York Times*, "On a Streetcar Named Success" (November 30, 1947). "You have told things that I have never read in print before, yet long know to be a part of me. The turning away from people; the sense that every conversation is like a Victrola record; the mistrust of sincerity; the involuntary rudeness, cold-shouldering and neglect towards old friends; the ever-accompanying sense of a fictitious personage, bearing one's own name, who inhibits your freedom of action; and lastly, the hatred of one's own work" (December 4, 1947, BRTC). TW had used his own remarks on the "catastrophe" of success—the depression and isolation which followed the opening of *The Glass Menagerie* (1945) in New York—as a timely advertisement for *Streetcar*.

"Plush days" at the Hotel Woodrow, an old haunt of TW, were fondly recalled in a journal entry: "The portable victrola by my bed and always money enough to eat or smoke or fuck" (ca. October 20, 1941). The "someone" making "trouble" is Pancho Rodriguez.]

78. To Justin Brooks Atkinson

Liebling-Wood Inc.
551 - 5 Ave. [New York]
Monday Dec. 15, 1947.
[TLS, 1 p. BRTC]

Dear Brooks:

At last a criticism which connects directly with the essence of what I thought was the play! I mean your Sunday article which I have just read with the deepest satisfaction of any the play's success has given me. So many of the others, saying 'alcoholic', 'nymphomaniac', 'prostitute', 'boozy' and so forth seemed - though stirred by the play - to be completely off the track, or nearly so. I wanted to show that people are not definable in such terms but are things of multiple facets and all but endless complexity that they do not fit "any convenient label" and are seldom more than partially visible even to those who live just on the other side of "the portieres".

You have also touched on my main problem: expanding my material and my interests. I can't answer that question. I know it and fear it and can only make more effort to extend my "feelers" beyond what I've felt so far. Thank you, Brooks. I am leaving for Europe soon. I will get in touch with you and Orianne before I sail.

Yours, Tenn.

[Atkinson (1894-1984) shunned categorical terms and described *Streetcar* as "a work of art" which "arrives at no general moral conclusions." Instead TW has exposed a desperate woman to "an alien environment that brutally wears on her nerves." The playwright takes "no sides in the conflict" and knows how "right" it is for each character to survive the impending "disaster." The article ends with a friendly, if serious, warning that the "uniformity" shown to date in the "choice of characters and in the attitude toward life . . . may limit the range of Mr. Williams' career as a playwright" (*New York Times*, December 14, 1947).]

79. To James "Jay" Laughlin

SH: Liebling-Wood
Authors' Representatives
551 Fifth Avenue
New York 17, N.Y.
December 29, 1947
[TLS, 1 p. Houghton]

Dear Jay:

I sail for Europe tomorrow afternoon on the "America", and I will go directly to Paris where I am stopping at the hotel GEORGE V. I don't know anybody there, I just have a bunch of letters to people, so I do hope you will [be] in Paris now and then. I will probably travel around a bit, to Italy wherever it is warm and there is some swimming.

My first reaction to the book cover was adverse. I think it was the color more than the design. It's a sort of shocking pink which reminds me of a violet scented lozenge. However, everything else about the book is very fine and I have only myself to blame for not paying more attention when it was being planned. I don't need to tell you what a deep satisfaction it is to have you bring it out, so forget about the cover. The design was original and striking. I hope you will like SUMMER AND SMOKE, when it is ready to be seen well enough to bring it out too.

I'm glad you liked the article. You bet I meant every word of it, and you of all people should know that. Get in touch with me when I arrive. I will be lonesome as hell I expect. Poor Carson McCullers is over here half paralyzed due to nervous shock over a lousy dramatization of her book, but she is slowly recovering. I will arrive about January 7th. Warmest regards.

As ever, Tenn

P.S. I am nervous over the advertising on ONE ARM. I don't think the book should be publicized and sold through the usual channels. We agreed to have it sold on a subscription basis. This is mostly because of consideration for my family, and because only a few of us will understand and like it, and it is bound to be violently attacked by the rest.

TW:ew

["At the end of that December, no longer able to cope with the unremitting publicity in New York, I sailed for Europe" (*Memoirs*, p. 139).

The "shocking pink" cover of *Streetcar* depicts two abstract female forms dominated by a third, a centered male, who holds one figure in willing embrace and the other in attempted flight. James Laughlin agreed to change the background color, but he hesitated to "abandon" the cover entirely, as Audrey Wood had requested. Alvin Lustig's designs sparked controversy and sold more books "than conventional ones" (to Wood, January 17 {1948} HRC). Lustig would design the jacket of each of TW's succeeding books published by New Directions, until his death in 1955.

The "article" to which Laughlin refers is probably "On a Streetcar Named Success."

Carson McCullers socialized, drank heavily, and did little if any serious work during 1947, when she and her husband, Reeves, lived in France. She suffered paralyzing strokes and was further weakened by the stress of a collaborative relation suggested by the Theatre Guild, which had conditionally agreed to produce *The Member of the Wedding* (1946). McCullers returned to the States in December, received neurological treatment at Columbia Presbyterian Hospital, and convalesced at her mother's home in Nyack, New York. TW visited McCullers before sailing for Europe.

Laughlin reassured Wood that the forthcoming publication of *One Arm and Other Stories* (1948) would involve "no advertising" and "no review copies." "You may be sure," he added, "that I don't want any scandal any more than you do" (January 17 {1948} HRC).]

80. To Margaret "Margo" Jones

[America]
12/31/47.
[TLS w/ autograph marginalia, 2 pp. HRC]

Dearest Margo:

I am writing you on the new typewriter delivered by Monty Clift. It is an adorable little Swiss machine called Hermes Baby, is as light as a feather, almost pocket-size, and yet has everything on it the big ones have. It also has charm and humor which other machines don't have and I enjoy using it. Oddly enough I had been shopping for a new typewriter that very morning but had not found any to suit me and given up because I had so little time. Your idea was really psychic and I was deeply moved and touched by it. You will also be pleased to know that I gave my old one to Donnie. Donnie's had been stolen just a short while ago and he is still working on his novel so he needed one badly.

I am one day out on the ocean, travelling first class so that I can use the large swimming pool. That's the only agreeable feature. The first class passengers are a mess. All lousey rich and falling to pieces with age, refinement, and so forth. The assistant purser is the only one I've seen who interests me. So I am staying in my stateroom to avoid fraternization. Fortunately I have a good supply of books, mostly on physics. I have developed a great interest in atomic and cosmic science and the books on those subjects are fascinating. But I am so stupid I have to read each page twice and sometimes twice again before I absorb the content. Even so it is better than prevailing trends in fiction. I also have Dostoevsky's The Idiot, a parting gift from Donnie, my Crane and Lorca's poems.

I had a packing-bee the morning of my departure. About six people came over to pack me, as I had put it off till the last minute. Gadge brought champagne: the others drank while Joanna did all the packing, and she did a beautiful job of it. You know I always liked Joanna but the more I see of her the more I am impressed by the real beauty of her nature. She is blossoming out in New York. I think it is good for her to create her own little world as she is now doing. I think she is having many new experiences and assimilating them into new values, so it has all worked out for the best. I shall miss her in Europe, in fact I shall miss all of my friends. There are a few people I value dearly. Now that I am living alone I have felt much closer to them. Poor Pancho made such a barrier! He is now living in Miami Beach and has a job at Saks store down there. He writes me that he has a crew haircut and a deep tan and is "looking terrific"! Enclosed a snapshot to verify the statement. Also that he has met the Walter Chrysler Jr's and been entertained on their yacht: his dream factory is still working.

I had a good talk with Jo about Summer. I told him it should be designed completely away from Streetcar and Glass, using very pure colors an almost abstract design with Gothic effects and sky, sky, sky! He thinks he will have to get a really good sculptor to execute the angel: I think that is justified for we shall have to depend on the best of poetic effects. I strongly feel we should open in Chicago and play there for a couple of months, some place that hasn't seen Streetcar for the comparison will not be helpful. It takes a long out-of-town period for my stuff to catch on. Jo also thinks we should find out about Margaret Phillips availability: see what her plans are for the late summer and Fall. I think the ideal time to commence would be in August. I am thinking of giving this play to my sister so that she will have independant means if it is successful. I doubt that I could keep any money from it anyhow so it is no sacrifice.

Gadge wants to know if you would be interested in heading the Drama department at Bennington College. He was asked to take the job but he recommended you as he is too restless. It is close to New York and an important artistic center. Of course I am hoping that some day you will be at the head of ANTA when it has a real nation-wide importance. There is nothing more hopeful for the theatre than this idea of government charter and support.

I don't know whether it's the accumulated fatigue of months or the cradle rocking of the vessel but I feel sleepy all the time. My nights have been wild and wonderful in Manhattan, lasting always till five in the morning, seldom getting more than four or five hours sleep. I need this rest and I have a lot to remember.

I do hope Manning's play was a distinguished and popular success. Joanna thought it should be.

With much, much love, Tenn (at sea)

[Margo Jones directed the fall season of Theatre '47 in Dallas, including a program of one-acts by TW, and continued to plan the Broadway premiere of *Summer and Smoke* (1948). Jo Mielziner would design the set and Margaret Phillips, unavailable for the earlier production in Dallas, was signed to play Alma Winemiller.

Jones apparently rejected the offer from Bennington College. Her unhappy experience at the University of Texas in the early 1940s made her wary of another academic appointment.

Chartered by Congress in 1935, ANTA (American National Theatre and Academy) had recently launched a membership drive to achieve its goal of bringing "the best in the theatre to every State." Its programs, although far ranging and varied, were centered in New York and thus differed fundamentally from Jones's idea of a national theatre with resident companies scattered throughout "this big country of ours." Nonetheless Jones was active in ANTA and served on the board of directors. On November 30, 1947, ANTA and the National Broadcasting Company sponsored the first televised performance of a TW play, "The Last of My Solid Gold Watches" (1943).

Dallas politely received Manning Gurian's comedy, *Lemple's Old Man* (1947). Gurian was Jones's business manager and romantic interest—their intimate relationship perhaps unknown to TW.

Penned in the upper margin of page 1 is the notation "Hotel George V Paris, France (for a while)."]

81. To Paul Bigelow

SH: Hotel George V
31, Avenue George V, Paris
1/7/48
[TLS, 3 pp. Columbia U]

Dear Paul:

How I enjoyed your candy! Altogether too much, for a curvacious figure has to be watchful or it gets out of bounds. If you have seen any of my recent pictures I am sure you know what I mean. Austerity in Europe may be useful.

I arrived here yesterday after a quiet and restful crossing. I spent it mostly lying down, the accumulated fatigue of months. It was luxurious to just sleep, and sleep. I was put at the Captain's table but he was such a drip that I never showed up after the first meal. I had the others in my quarters.

Margo sent me this damned Swiss machine as a parting gift. It is about the size of a highschool geography book, but a thing of infinite complexity and caprice. Every little gadget on it seems to have a dual or triple purpose. Some day I will touch something in the wrong place and it will bite my nose off and make cocktail sausages.

This hotel is a mess, only one advantage which will please you. The bathroom has a bidet with hot and cold water! Also they serve real Brazilian coffee. But it is full of sleek women with chows. I will probably move to one of the little places in the Latin Quarter if I remain in Paris. The town has changed since I was here at sixteen. Plenty of time to do so, as you will observe. However I remember it as being so light and lively at night. Now the streets are rather dim and murky. Today and yesterday there was continual rain. However it still has charm. I will stay here a while, then probably move south to Rome and Tangiers where Paul Bowles is staying. I wonder if Gide was right about those little natives?

Pancho and I have separated, I guess you know that. He could not adjust himself to New York and the increasing involvement of my professional life. He behaved pretty badly, more than I could finally put up with, but it wasn't his fault. I am not a good person to live with. Being alone again is both a relief and a sorrow. At any rate it gives me more time with my old friends.

Paul dear, I am distressed to hear that you are still troubled with the jaw and that you must have an operation on it. I wish I could be with you during that ordeal as you were with me during the miserable times I had with my eye.

Maxwell broke his hip, gave up his job - in the opposite sequence - and is now "visiting some dear old friend" in Tampa Florida. He has a slight limp and carries a cane but is otherwise the same, quite the same, only nobody has recently mistaken him for a boy at Princeton. Donnie has finished one draft of his novel. It was turned down by Random House and he is writing it over. It needs at least another year's work but I think it has a quality that is original and striking. It is about Butch's early life in Atlanta.

Mother is finally getting a legal separation from my father. She gets the house and part of the shoe stock and he returns to Knoxville to live with his old maid sister, God help her. And God help them both. This deal was to be consummated around Christmas, in time I hope for a happy holiday. It means that my ancient grandfather, ninety years old, can return home and spend the rest of his days with Mother. I hope it may also mean that my sister can visit home, and of course that I can. So a tragic situation works itself out, a little too late, but better than never at all. As for the old man, he has probably suffered as much as anyone, possibly even more, and I am afraid it will be a lonely and bitter end to his blind and selfish life.

When you come to New York for the operation, let Audrey know. Also let me hear from you, care of her.

I am reading a lovely book that you would enjoy, "The Mysterious Universe" by Sir James Jeans - Physics!

Love - Tenn.

[TW's first night in Paris was not auspicious: "I explored the town by myself and was nearly murdered, not by Frenchmen but by a bunch of drunken GI's who 'did not like my looks'" (to Laughlin, January 7, 1948, Houghton). He soon informed Elia Kazan that all "you really need in Europe is one suit, two shirts, and a pocket full of prophylactics" (January 25, 1948, WUCA).

TW noted that reading "Miss Gide" was a "bit dry" for his own "fruity tastes," although he envied "the length and felicity of her days" (*Journal*, October 27, 1947). Several Arab boys whom André Gide met in North Africa as a young man had revealed the nature of his "propensities."

Paul Bigelow's jaw, reportedly broken in 1941 in a mugging, became chronically infected (osteomyelitis) and required surgery. At forty-three TW's friend Gilbert Maxwell was comically vain about his age and appearance and universally referred to as "Miss." Donald Windham dedicated his novel *The Dog Star* (1950) to Fred "Butch" Melton, his former companion.

Edwina traces the "legal separation" to an ultimatum that her father could no longer live with them in Clayton. "I said to Cornelius, 'I cannot allow my father to be put out on the street. You'll have to make up your mind whether you want to go or stay'" (qtd. in *Remember Me to Tom*, p. 199). Dakin Williams, who arranged his parents' separation and division of property, has reported that no divorce decree was sought and that Edwina and Cornelius never met again after nearly forty years of marriage.

The British mathematician Sir James Jeans wrote a series of popular books on astronomy including *The Mysterious Universe* (1930). When the *Saturday Review* queried TW on his "current reading" (March 6, 1948), he included Jeans's book and *The Theory of Relativity* by Albert Einstein.]

82. To Elizabeth "Tiz" Schauffler and Audrey Wood

L'Hotel Lutetia
42, Blvd. Raspail, Room 411-12
Paris, January ?, 1948
[TLS, 2 pp. HRC]

Dear Taudrey:

(THIS IS A CORPORATE FORM OF ADDRESS FOR TIZ AND AUDREY)

First of all, could you send me air-mail some cans of condensed milk? I have been having to drink black Brazilian coffee here which may (peut-etre) be good for my writing but is bad for my excitable heart!

Just three or four cans would turn the trick, as I will probably find my way eventually to the right black-marketeer who can supply me.

My impressions of Paris are mixed notices. The people seem terribly greedy, in fact avaricious, and while they like Americans, I think they like them in the way that a bird likes worms. You go to bed with fifty thousand francs and wake up with twenty-five if you are lucky! Don't ask me how you spend money in your sleep but apparently you manage it somehow. . . .

The George V was comfortable but in the bourgeois part of town. So I moved over here. When I took these two rooms the price marked on the door was about 750 francs. Next time I looked at the card it had mysterious[ly] changed to 1250 francs. Today there is no heat so I stayed in bed till about 4 PM, receiving visitors under a quilt - that is, I was! They sat in their overcoats. I probably have a stronger constitution than I usually imagine but even so if I get off this continent in better shape than Carson McCullers you will know that my good angels are still with me.

The day I sailed a bunch of people from the show came to see me off, shortly after you all departed, Gadge, Jessica, Kim, Peg, Rudy Bond and Vito Cristi - they brought me a shower of presents, a dozen fine white shirts, a cashmere sweater and a bottle of Scotch! Which proves that actors can be angels. I was really very much touched by it. I imagine it was mainly Gadge's idea but it was damned sweet of them all. Whiskey is virtually unobtainable here. I am still drinking the Scotch as a warming libation when I get out of bed and the shirts were a God send as I had practically no white ones. I wish you would mention how pleased I was with these things for I may forget to write about it.

I feel that the theatre here is 20 years behind Broadway, incredible as that may seem. This is a somewhat premature judgement as I haven't seen much. But the hamming, mugging, and the prevailingly chi-chi quality of the material, the corruption of the critics, the arrogance of the stars is really shameful. Last night I saw Louis Jouvet as Don Juan (the Moliere play). Only the decor was good. M. Jouvet preened himself like an old peacock, never spoke directly to any of the supporting cast but only to the audience or the scenery.

Mr. Rothschild intimated that I only had about 80,000 francs here. If that is so, then I think we should make other connections, for that is a sum which corresponds to something like $500. And the theatre was not a particularly good one. He seems nice but is by no means prominent. Nobody seems to have ever heard of him here. I have become acquainted with the editor of the two leading newspapers, France-Soir and L'Intransigeant through his daughter who was on the boat and he is making enquiries about Rothschild and the conduct of the production. In the meantime I am being complete[ly] non-committal. It may be entirely possible - if we think a Paris production is advisable - to function independantly without Rothschild, but that would require careful investigation on my part and talks with many people in the theatre to get a knowledge of the local conditions which are so different from ours. Here the thing of main importance is the theatre itself. The manager is really the man who owns the theatre. And the star system is infinitely more powerful than in the U.S.

Beaumont has cabled me about a London production of one-acts. I cabled back that I was taking a vacation from the theatre but would visit London in the Spring and would then be happy to discuss such a production provided the best talent was available. Badly done the one-acts would have a destructive influence on our London market. I am enclosing a rave-notice from an Englishman who is supposed to be "the George Jean Nathan of England" - I hope he deserves a better appelation. It appeared in the Evening Standard in London. Please send it on to Mother when you have read it. It would be particularly pleasing to Grandfather.

Would you mind writing Doctor Hoctor, State Hospital #4, Farmington Mo. - Enquiring why he has not answered my letter relative to getting a companion for my sister to take her out walking, Etc. And possibilities of improving her general situation. I want to keep after them till something definite is done.

I suppose you want to know how the food is! Well, it is good for my figure. You can figure that one out for yourselves. . . .

Much, much love and all thanks! Tenn

[Elizabeth Schauffler, a staff assistant at Liebling-Wood, played a minor role in efforts to improve the care of Rose Williams.

TW soon moved to the Hotel Lutétia, less staid and imposing than the George V, his first destination in Paris, but without "heat." The radiators, he informed Donald Windham, "are about as warm as Mary Hunter's left tit!" (qtd. in Windham, p. 205). He wrote a more courtly note to his grandfather, recalling their European tour of 1928: "Paris does not seem the same without you and the ladies from Mississippi" (postmarked Paris, January 17, 1948, Columbia U).

Adolf Rothschild's agency supervised the Paris production of *The Glass Menagerie* in May 1947.

Hugh "Binkie" Beaumont, managing director of H.M. Tennent Ltd., hoped to gain English rights of *The Glass Menagerie* and *Streetcar*, as well as TW's one-act plays. Wood cabled TW that she had offered the *Menagerie* to Beaumont for a spring production, with some haste, she indicated, for the Gould-Echols contract had "lapsed" and the now unwanted Louis J. Singer was planning to intervene. Beaumont, she added, was the "best producer" (January 29, 1948, HRC) in England.

Dr. Emmett Hoctor, superintendent of Missouri State Hospital No. 4, informed Wood that "there is nothing particular" which TW "could do" to improve his sister's "condition" (January 27, 1948, HRC). "What do you suggest is the next move on this?" (February 2, 1948, HRC), Wood asked in a following letter to TW.

TW wrote this letter in the week of January 11, 1948, after moving to the Hotel Lutétia on the Left Bank.]

83. To Carson McCullers

SH: Hotel Lutétia
43, Boulevard Raspail, Paris
[mid-January 1948]
[ALS, 6 pp. Duke U]

Dearest Carson -

I am laid up in bed, too! I think it is the vile food here and the absolute lack of any milk which I have depended on so much in the States. Also the noxious stuff they call coffee. I drink 3 or 4 cups and feel no stimulation, only nausea, so it is difficult to work after breakfast. Just now some mysterious Samaritan left at my door a can of <u>powdered</u> milk - no name, no message, just the can of white granules which the <u>maitre d'hotel</u>, whom I summoned to explain, says is dehydrated milk and should be mixed with hot water and he has taken it out for the mixing. Not a pleasant idea but if it turns out to be anything even remotely like milk I shall know that the anonymous donor was directly from God. Isn't it absurd how such a small comfort as a cup of milk can be so important when not accessible!

I have been here about a week, spent in getting settled, packing and unpacking. The first two hotels I tried, on the right bank, were incompatible. This one, on the left, is pleasant in every respect but heating. My two rooms are not heated at all. So I have not yet had a chance to form a good impression of the city. No place seems heavenly when you are chilled and nauseous - so I am waiting! I left all your letters of introduction in New York - <u>but</u> every one of them was sent on to me and I now have them all with me. I am so glad to have the one to Bob Myers; in case I am not better tomorrow I shall call him.

Your letter reached me today - I have read it over and over for company as I lie here in bed feeling sorry for myself.

What a relief it is to know they will not push your play into production! Believe me, Carson, it would have been disastrous. You and I cannot take such experiences without being smashed on the rocks. By next Fall the production can mature gracefully, and you can feel confident of the script being ready. Now <u>rest</u>! Let everything go like a piece of loose thread!

As for the other emotional difficulties, perhaps now is not the right time to think about them. On the other hand, whatever troubles and disturbs you deeply has to be removed because being a great artist you must save and protect yourself continually. It may seem selfish, but actually <u>not</u> to do so is finally <u>more</u> selfish. I had to act ruthlessly to save myself from Pancho. I had to lock the doors and windows of my apartment, the last time he came to New York, and hear him screaming through them and trying to hammer them down with his fists. And know that instead of helping him the two years we gave each other may have been his destruction, and not able to explain or do anything but brutally lock myself away and refuse to see or write - but otherwise I could not have survived. Now you have never wasted your love on anyone who could not understand you or it, or been forced to imitate the implacability of a stone in order to free yourself of an impossible alliance. But when such a thing is necessary - because your life and your work require it - then you must carry it out relentlessly. I am a vulnerable person, but it frightens me to see how even <u>more</u> vulnerable <u>you</u> are. Is there no way you can defend and spare yourself, learn how to live not so acutely, and still be yourself and an artist? I have been so careful of myself physically because I have to - to live - but you are quite heedless about keeping yourself physically well - when you get up again you must promise all who love you to treat yourself with all the tenderness and wisdom that your work deserves from you. Think only of restoration.

Wherever I see a bookstand here I see translations of your work, more than any other American writer.

I shall write you again when I am back on my feet - these times of "error" don't usually last long. Then I shall get to know all your friends and write you news of them.

Did Audrey give you the framed Dufy print? I did not have a chance to deliver it myself.

My love to Reeves and your wonderful Mother -

Much, much to you, Tennessee.

[One of the "letters of introduction" supplied by Carson McCullers would lead TW to Dr. Robert Myers. McCullers became infatuated with Myers after he treated her at the American Hospital in Neuilly in 1947.

Production of McCullers's play *The Member of the Wedding* had been delayed, but the Theatre Guild was "confused," as Audrey Wood informed TW, "about the next step it must take" (February 2, 1948, HRC).

McCullers wrote to TW of "intense emotional strain" and the realization that her marriage with Reeves had failed: "I can no longer be his wife and share my inner life with him. . . . He is so dependent on me in every way that he will suffer; I cannot bear to think of how he will manage. But Tenn, another year like the last one would blunt my soul. . . . It would mean that I would have to accustom myself to lies, dishonesty and that I cannot do" (January 11, 1948, HRC).

TW cites recent French translations of *The Heart Is a Lonely Hunter* (1940) and *Reflections in a Golden Eye* (1941).]

84. To Audrey Wood

[Hotel Lutétia, Paris]
1/17/48
[TLS w/ autograph marginalia,
addendum and enclosure, 3 pp. HRC]

Dear Audrey:

I have been laid up in bed two or three days with a gastric disturbance attributable mainly, I think, to the bad diet here, so as soon as I am up again, I will probably pack - God help me! - and head South, probably to Italy where I hear it is easier to obtain a bland diet of the sort I depend on. Here, for instance, only babies can get milk, and milk is essential for me despite my relatively mature age.

I am sorry to give you such an unfavorable report on Adolf Rothschild but I dislike him and I have heard nothing to indicate he is of any value to us. The earnings of the Menagerie were less than I told you originally. In fact only 62,000 francs. I don't think there is any dishonesty but just bad management and ineptitude. However I have still not succeded in obtaining this money. We have gone twice, Rothschild and I, to the authors society. The first time we found it closed. The second time Mr. Rothschild was apparently greatly surprised to learn that the money had been transferred in some way - I cannot explain how - and would not be available for about a week or more. By that time I shall probably have left France for Italy or the Mediterranean so it is unlikely that I shall get to use it. Now I have a very good and influential friend here, a Mme. Lazareff. She is editor of an enormously popular magazine named ELLE and her husband is editor of the two leading daily newspapers. Their connections are the best. She has introduced me to the actor-manager, Louis Jouvet. I have seen his screen performances in America, and you may have also. He is the top-notch manager in Paris. At Mme. Lazareff's and his request I wired for a copy of the play to submit to him. He has the best theatres at his disposal. You see it is unnecessary to use Rothschild and from what I hear, a disadvantage, for he is not known here in theatrical circles. I would like your opinion of this for you may feel that there is some commitment to Rothschild. For one thing, he gave Duhamel the translator exactly the same royalty that I received. Ordinarily the author gets ten and the translator five. We each got six percent and Bowles only got 1 percent and the leading actors were paid about six dollars a night and the director got 10,000 francs which amounts to about thirty dollars (for entire job). You can judge for yourself, from these figures, the sort of management that Rothschild was associated with and how lucky we were to get off with good notices and an "artistic success". Fortunately Claude Maritz (who has a low opinion of Rothschild) was a good and sincere director. I personally cannot forgive the man R. for dragging me twice to that damned society when I was not feeling well - and neither time accomplishing anything when he could so easily have ascertained beforehand whether or not the place was open or the money accessible. I wish you would give Mme. Tallant a full report on all this and explain my unwillingness to have any connection with Rothschild concerning Streetcar.

I don't think it fair to keep Feldman on the string any longer. It seems psychologically impossible for me to revert to that script. Especially knowing that the original conception must be weakened or distorted in some way. I cannot work without enthusiasm and I cannot feel enthusiasm over such a project. I don't think Feldman has ~~a grain of~~ enough taste and it would be better for him to sell his rights to someone who has, and let that producer hire a good writer to prepare a screen treatment that would not violate the quality and meaning of the play. The film must be honest to be any good. If I were quite well, full of vigor and there seemed an unbroken expanse of time and energy in which to do all the things I want so much to do, I would undertake the job gladly, but as it is I feel I must conserve what I have for what I have not yet done. Could Feldman understand this? I am sure that you can. If he must have his $2500 back, give it to him - but I think I did that much work on the stuff in Provincetown. I want as much as you do to see a good picture come out of it, but I can't force myself back to it now.

Hugh Beaumont has wired about doing a program of one-acts. Strikes me as an excellent idea and I have written him for further information. He mentioned the Lyric Hammerstein theatre in London.

Carson's doctor in Paris came to see me today and prescribed some powders. They are so unpalatable that I spit them right out. His report on Carson was very depressing. He doesn't think she will be able to walk again and that she has some incurable vascular disease which is likely to be progressive and result in other attacks. I don't take his word for this, however, and I hope that no one has told Carson anything of this nature. It is too awful to believe! Don't talk about it.

I will cable you when I have decided where to go in my search for better living conditions.

With love, Tenn.

P.S. Have just gotten your long letter and it has relieved my depression to hear from home which I think of your office as being. Of course I would love to have the Menagerie done in Germany and perhaps later I can accept their invitation there, when the weather is milder. Re: "nigger-peckerwood" dispute. The last time I saw Gadge he told me that numerous colored persons had assured him Walter White was all wet and that nigger in this context and from such a character was totally inoffensive. I always had a ~~profound~~ conviction that it was. Gadge wanted to revert to "nigger" so I said okay. I think old farmer is all right if you alternate it with "old peckerwood" in the next reference during the story. - I cannot at this moment recall name of the garage but it is on Royal street in the Quarter, and is the only garage along there. Why not call Dick Orme long distance, ask him name of garage and also tell him I cannot resume tenancy of the apartment? Margo removed practically all my stuff (papers) from apartment and Dick could store the rest for me. His name is Richard M. Orme, 632 St. Peter and you could best reach him about noon when he is just waking up. Assure him I would have loved to return to New Orleans but the pressure of circumstances made it impossible and would he please continue our present arrangement of subleasing the place in my name. I will enclose a note to him myself. Yes, it is better to conduct sale of car without Pancho's intervention. The less connection I maintain with him the better, since I am unable to really help him in any basic way.

Thanks for everything, and so much!

Sometimes I must seem to take all your help for granted, but that is because I have lived in such turmoil. I am infinitely obliged for everything you and Bill and Tiz did to make the trip easy for me.

T.

[Ninon Tallon, an associate of the Rothschild agency, arranged the Paris production of *La Ménagerie de Verre*. She described the play as "a sensational hit from the young intellectual point of view" and added that a majority of the French critics were also "on the positive side" (to Wood, May 10, 1947, HRC).

Audrey Wood assured TW that she could "maneuver {her} way out of the whole situation" (January 21, 1948, HRC) with Adolph Rothschild. She had also "airmailed" a copy of *Streetcar* for Louis Jouvet's consideration, warning TW not to "close any deal until advising terms and setup" (telegram, January 17, 1948, HRC). A leading figure in the French theatre, Jouvet would not have a hand in the Paris production of *Streetcar* (1949).

Charles Feldman, owner of film rights of *The Glass Menagerie*, learned in the preceding July that TW was apparently "thrilled" with the screenplay and willing to do some additional "polishing" (to Abramson, July 7, 1947, HRC), for which he would receive $5,000. Revision begun in Provincetown in August 1947 had evidently dampened TW's enthusiasm for the adaptation by Peter Berneis.

Walter White, secretary of the NAACP, criticized gratuitous use of "the word 'nigger'" (to Selznick, December 10, 1947, HRC) in Scene Three of *Streetcar*. He soon thanked TW for agreeing to substitute "'farmer'" in the off-color joke, adding that he was "sorry it took this kind of an episode to cause us to meet" (December 16, 1947, HRC). Elia Kazan's restoration of "nigger" brought "telephone complaints daily" (January 6, 1948, HRC), as Wood informed TW, who finally decided to use "peckerwood" instead. "Nigger" appeared in the first four American printings of the book (1947-1948).

As TW prepared to leave Paris after two dreary weeks, Wood sought to tie up the loose ends of his far-flung, disorderly life: an unneeded apartment in New Orleans, the everlasting sale of the Pontiac, and the threat of Pancho Rodriguez's return.

Penned in the upper margin of page 1 is the notation "via 'Air Mail.'"]

85. To Carson McCullers

[Auberge de la Colombe d'Or
St. Paul de Vence, France]
[late-January 1948]
[TLS w/ autograph marginalia, 1 p. Duke U]

Dear Carson:

This is to assure you that I am feeling a lot better and am about to set out for Rome, soon as my Italian visa is ready which will be tomorrow. I left Paris soon as I got out of the hospital where I was for two or three wretched days. Honey, I did not like that doctor of yours one bit! I don't know what was the matter with me, some kind of toxic condition. I felt like I couldn't stay awake and I couldn't eat anything. I think it was brought on by the poisonous liquor and food I had to consume in Paris and the depressing weather which never let up. Myers said I was threatened with a couple of awful sounding things like Scylla and Charybydis but I didn't like him or the hospital so I got out of bed and left town. I went down here to this little place in the Alpes Maritimes where I know a lovely girl of 18 who is a tubercular patient. It has been dull here, still raining continually and a lot of dirty white doves flopping around in the orange trees to give a quaint atmosphere, but the rest and the excellent food has done me a world of good and if I finally catch up with the sun in Rome, I shall be all right. If you know anybody there, drop me a line care of American Express in that city. I remember it as a place of misty gold light and cypresses and ruins and public fountains and some wonderful things by Michelangelo that Frankie and her new friend, Mary, would love. I shall probably remain in the South of Europe until the nasty winter is through with, and then return to Paris and take up residence at that hotel which you recommended on the right bank. Honey, they have now stabilized the franc at a wonderful figure for Americans. It is officially three hundred and something for the dollar and of course the black market has gone up even higher. I shall live like an Oriental potentate when I return from Italy! By that time you and Reeves may be ready to come back. Donald Windham is also planning to come abroad this Spring and my friend, Oliver Evans - I am sure you have heard me speak of him often, and of his prodigious energy outside academic pursuits - is going to teach English this summer at the university in Athens, so it will be like old home-week over here. I wish it were already Spring. It is silly to be in Europe in the winter, isn't it? In this place I do almost nothing but read and eat. I read a good book by Jean Paul Sartre which is called The Age of Reason. Get that. It is badly written, in a way, but there is a terrifyingly keen analysis of mental processes and emotions or lack of emotions. Do you like physics? I am reading a lot about astronomical physics and relativity and so forth as it really exercises the mind and the imagination to think about those things, such as curved space and the electrical particles that matter is made of, all of them dashing around at the rate of thousands of miles a second, and everything being made of them - fancy that! as Professor Tesman would say. Well -

You will also be pleased to hear that I have acquired a taste for Bach, out of desperation: there was nothing else to play on the victrola here. I love the Toccato and Fugue which I never could stand before.

Do you have a good victrola at home? I left a swell one in the States that I would love for you to use, an electric changer and all, if you don't have one - let Audrey Wood know. Will write from Rome - Love!

Tenn.

[A week's rest in the south of France allowed TW to slip by the medical perils of "Scylla and Charybydis"—hepatitis and mononucleosis—as diagnosed by Dr. Robert Myers, whom TW had come to regard as "a thoroughly disagreeable and cold-blooded young man" (to Bigelow, n.d., Massee Collection). McCullers later assured TW that her infatuation with Myers had ended: "I could not love anyone you do not even like" (Valentine day {February 14, 1948} Duke U).

"Frankie" dreams of traveling abroad with "her new friend, Mary," in the upbeat conclusion of *The Member of the Wedding*. With "Fancy that!" TW alludes to a second, less bracing text, *Hedda Gabler* (Ibsen, 1890), which ends with the suicide of a desperate wife—prefiguring in effect McCullers's own attempt in the following March.

Probably written in the week of January 25, 1948, this letter was forwarded to McCullers by Audrey Wood, whose apology for a "coffee stain - discourtesy Audrey Wood - " appears in the upper margin.]

86. To Oliver Evans

[Albergo Palazzo-Ambasciatori, Rome]
Jan 31, 1948.
[TLS, 2 pp. HRC]

Cher:

I have only been in Rome three days but I am already established. It is really the capitol of my heart! In Paris it rained all but continually, the food was abominable and served with disgusting flourishes, no milk except powdered, no coffee except that Brazilian stuff that blew you right out from under your beret. It all made me ill and I spent the last two days in the American hospital and a week afterwards resting at St. Paul de Vence in the Alpes Maritimes. But Rome has already made up for all the vicissitudes of the North. My first night on the Boulevard I met a young Neapolotan who is a professional lightweight boxer. How I thought of you! Thick glossy black hair and a small but imperial torso! The nightingales busted their larynx! And Miss Keats swooned in her grave! I can hardly wait for you to come over this Spring: by that time my address book will probably be running into the tricentennial edition in gold and scarlet morocco with illustrations hand-painted. I wish I could tell you more about this boxer, details, positions, amiabilities - but this pale blue paper would blush! Besides such confidences are only meant to be whispered in the bed-chamber. Orally! The tongue has inflections which the typewriter wants!

I received yesterday the copy of Voices and was delighted with the three poems, especially the one about the cow-boys. It has been so long since I have written a good poem, even a bad one, that I am humbly amazed at your lyric out-put in volume and always increasing force and quality of line, and the material, or content, is so far superior to the contrived interests of the moiety.

Well, I have much to tell you. First of all, living in Europe is inexpensive when you have learned the ropes. And in Italy there is an abundance of everything if you can afford to buy it. American cigarettes are sold on every corner for about seventy cents a package. You can live well here on $200. a month which you can't in the States. Paris - no! You can live cheaply, but bad food, lack of heat, a certain wolfish attitude in the people makes it not worth it. I doubt if I will return to Paris before late Spring when I may pass through going to England. I hear that Palermo, Sicily is the place for romance! I contemplate a visit. Write me at Rome c/o

American Express. I rub the turquoise and wish you happiness and good fortune and an early arrival on these shores! With love

Tennessee.

["As soon as I crossed the Italian border my health and life seemed to be magically restored. There was the sun and there were the smiling Italians" (*Memoirs*, p. 141). TW stayed briefly at the Ambassador on via Veneto before moving to a nearby apartment. Both were located in central Rome in a tourist area dominated by grand hotels and smart shops and cafés. TW soon bought an "old jeep" with a defective muffler in which he raced "drunk as hell" around the fountains of St. Peter's in a pre-dawn ritual of sobering up, confident that "an *Americano* could get away with a whole lot" (*Memoirs*, p. 146) in 1948.

"Rodeo," the Oliver Evans poem admired by TW, ends with a wistful appeal to the young "gladiators" of the "arena": "My lariat love lies empty at your feet" (*Voices*, January 1948).]

Tennessee Williams and Gore Vidal, Rome, 1948.
"An Americano *could get away with a whole lot"* (Memoirs).

87. To Margaret "Margo" Jones

SH: Albergo Palazzo-Ambasciatori, Roma
Feb 3, 1948
[TLS w/ autograph marginalia, 4 pp. HRC]

Dearest Margo:

I have now settled down more or less in Rome which is the first city I've been over here that I really and truly like very much. Paris was cold and wet and the people had a wolfish air about them. The food and liquor was so bad it made me ill. Then I went down to the Riviera and it was raining constantly there, too, but for the week I've been here, the city has been bathed in mellow golden light and is a dream of loveliness. I have a room with a big balcony right over Via Venuto which is the Fifth avenue of Rome and I keep it filled with fresh flowers, violets and all shades of carnations, which are sold in huge bunches on almost every street-corner. For about a hundred a week you can live the life of Tiberius in this town! Everything is available - for a little dinero! Friday I am taking a plane to Sicily for a few days to watch the making of a film down there, in which no actors, only Native Sicilians, are employed, and it is being directed by the man who directed "Zoo di Vetro" over here (Dago for Glass Menagerie). I hope to show you some of the stills from this picture, "The Earth Shall Tremble," the best most moving photography and lighting I've seen ever! I have met many people here, in fact too many. The phone is beginning to ring too much.

I have not yet gotten down seriously to work, but have been pecking away at Summer & Smoke in an effort to tighten it up and provide some sort of reliable climax. In the latter I think I am working out some improvement. You ask me why I think this play should not cover the same territory as "Streetcar" in try-outs. Honey, it is only because I am dead certain that Streetcar is a much, much better play. I know how you feel about "Summer" and how Joanna does - you are both especially equipped by nature, with sensitive hearts and responsive souls, to get things that are only half stated and to understand the unrealized intentions, but to me "Summer" was a devastating failure in comparison to what I meant it to be, and one of the bitterest I have had. I am talking about the script, you understand, and this is only for <u>you</u> to read. Since we are going to produce it we must not share my misgivings with the world at this point. In conception it was by far my <u>best</u> play but something happened to me during the work on it, I froze up or went dead on it and everything turned to powder which should have been alive and flashing. Only at scattered moments does it have the pure and tremulous candle-like glow that I meant it to have all the way through. I think it was the despair that I felt over Summer that enabled me to put such violence and passion into Streetcar in spite of my physical exhaustion at the time of writing. However I am continuing to work on it. Perhaps there will be a period of illumination, though so far there has been only an effort of will. I am concentrating on Scene 9, the one that ends with the shooting of the doctor, and I am enlarging the part of Jessie who is now a Mexican girl named Rosa. I think the Serios should be Mexican and perhaps the town should be in Texas. How does that strike you? This scene is the only one that can serve as a real climax. If I get this right, I shall attack the next weakest spot which is the scene after the doctor's death and in which John returns home a hero. That is altogether too fortuitous and adventitious. It seems to pop out of nowhere and I am afraid Yankee critics would never let us get away with it. It must be given more body and reason: somehow integrated with the line of the story. Do not be discouraged by my frank confession of failure in this play: all of my plays have been failures in some respect relative to their conceptions, for the simple reason that I have so little craftsmanship to rely on. If Milzener does a beautiful job and we get the right players we can surely create some beauty. But if we stay in the East, we will have to go over that old Hangman's Trail - New Haven, Boston, Philly. Washington is apparently still ruled out. It is a murderous routine. Each opening is a little hell to go through bare-footed! It ravages the nerves and breaks the spirit, and long before you come into New York, everyone knows whether or not you are a success or failure. The verdict is sealed already. If we opened at the Coronet in Los Angeles, say, or any good theatre in Chicago - no comparison, good or bad, could be made to "Streetcar" - we could count on three or four weeks in one-place to get the show working smoothly without everybody including Howard Rineheimer breathing down our necks. I think four weeks is long enough out of town. It proved just about right for "S.C." Well, we need not come to any decision about this for several months, in which time I will have completed my work on the script. I will certainly not discuss going to Chicago or other places with anybody: the less we talk about any of our plans the better.

It is so lovely here, it is difficult to remain indoors. I specially like riding out in the fiacres, the open horse-drawn carriages, around the

Colisseum and the Appian way. Trouble is it gets even lovelier in the Spring! The Italians are like good Mexicans. Much love -

Tenn.

[Luchino Visconti's production of *The Glass Menagerie* premiered in Rome on December 13, 1946, and was restaged in Florence and Milan the following year. Visconti regarded TW as a writer of avant-garde, if not revolutionary, tendencies and in the post-war years produced his work along with that of Erskine Caldwell, Hemingway, Cocteau, and Sartre.

TW informed Irene Selznick that he was "trying to put more iron" into *Summer and Smoke* but doubted that he would succeed "till I myself have a more metallic vibration" (January 14, 1948, Boston U). Margo Jones's unbounded enthusiasm for a faulty play did little to convince TW of her status as a major director.

TW added flair to "Scene 9" of *Summer and Smoke* by dressing Rosa Gonzales in a flamenco costume and developing her sensuality in bouts of merriment and lovemaking with John Buchanan. Poised against his dissipation and despair is Alma's chaste idealism, her attraction made evident as John is drawn mysteriously from his father's house to appear by her side in the rectory. The "enormous silence" is broken as Alma "sinks onto a love seat" and John "buries his face in her lap": "Eternity and Miss Alma have such cool hands!" (March 1948, HRC), he intones. Revision of Scene Nine was intended to add "body and reason" to the reformation of John Buchanan, which follows the murder of his father.

The New York attorney Howard E. Reinheimer represented Irene Selznick and was a financial backer—apparently overbearing—of *Streetcar*.

Penned in the upper margin of page 1 is the notation "Address = c/o American Express, Rome."]

88. To Carson McCullers

[Sicily/Naples]
2/8/48
[TLS, 2 pp. Duke U]

Dearest Carson:

First let me say you must not talk this foolishness about being wicked and punished for it. If I had never known or seen you your work alone would assure me that you are a Saintly person. It is the only modern work that gives me such an assurance of Saintliness in the writer, even more than one feels in Chekhov or Doestoevsky or in the letters of Vincent Van Gogh to his brother Theo to depart a little from the field of professional literature.

There is no evil in you at all, anywhere, so this idea is positive lunacy and is perhaps hindering your recovery so don't allow it to remain in your mind.

Then let me remind you that I decided to come to Europe because you were here and I thought would stay here and after my life with Pancho broke up in disgrace and horror, you were the only person I wanted to be with. Whenever you are strong enough you must come back here and join me. I say here in Europe for I feel that this is the place for us both, especially here in Italy, this place of soft weather and golden light and of great bunches of violets and carnations sold on every corner and the Greek ideal surviving so tangibly in the grace and beauty of the people and the antique sculpture as well. I cannot write very coherently about Rome as I love it so much! But I can see that you think of me far, far too charitably. You must remember all the bad things about me, my sensuality and license and neurotic moodiness at times - all the irregularities of my life and nature - I cannot put all of those things into a letter! - and then ask yourself if you could really endure a close association or would I perhaps add to your worries and your emotional strains. But perhaps you have already considered all these obvious defects and still believe, as I do, that being near each other would give a mutual tranquillity we both need so much. I am thinking of your work and of mine, as well, as of our lives. - Sometime will you send me "Ballad of the Sad Cafe" which I have still never read and which would perhaps make a good one-act play or two-acts - this is parenthetical indeed! - I just now thought of it.

I am glad you wrote me this about Bob Myers. He is the first doctor I have ever disliked and distrusted instinctively and I felt he was altogether lacking in common humanity. When he put me in the hospital, at my own suggestion, he did not even bother to give them any instructions about my diet or treatment. I had to instruct them myself. He told me that in a few days my skin and eyes would turn yellow and that glands under my arms would swell up, so naturally I thought I had the black plague. None of these things happened. My eyes and skin are perfectly clear and nothing is swollen. I decided to pay no attention to him and I left the hospital and went South. Incidentally, he wanted me to pay him thirty dollars instead of the (much smaller) amount in French money for his one visit to the hotel, but that is unimportant. I sent him a check and wrote a very catty letter, really quite sarcastic, praising him for his treatment and his great "human warmth which is so much more important" but probably he thought I meant it. He does not seem modest enough to suspect otherwise.

Well, Carson, as we grow older we stop blaming anybody for anything, don't we? We talk very crossly about their bad conduct but we don't really feel any bitterness against them, and that is much better. It is all so understandable, the distortions and falsities that the world creates in us all. - Audrey writes that Pancho has sold my car in New Orleans, after swearing under oath that it belonged to him and is now in California and "some mysterious person" in Hollywood has seen a number of producers and claimed to be Tennessee Williams and demanded $500. advance for certain story ideas or manuscripts, for film production! Do you suppose that could be Pancho? HA*HA!!

If you send the play to me c/o American Express in Rome I will surely receive it and give it my closest and most loving attention. Are you feeling better? Are you resting and eating properly and not worrying? I feel that we are always very close to each other: the ocean is nothing between us! I think of you each day and I pray for your happiness which I know is coming! Otherwise I would not believe in God, and I do most truly believe in Him.

With much love, Tennessee.

In my next letter I will try to tell you more about people and places. If parts of this letter seem silly, it may be because I have been travel[ling] around so much by myself that I have become a little bit touched in the head. I talk out loud to myself nearly all the time now!

[Carson McCullers began the new year by recalling their "moments at Nantucket" and anticipating "other dear times in the future" (January 11, 1948, HRC) with TW. Did he think they could "travel and have a house together" (Valentine day {February 14, 1948} Duke U), she wrote in answer to the present correspondence. Audrey Wood deemed such an arrangement "pure madness" (to TW, March 12, 1948, HRC).

McCullers's novella *The Ballad of the Sad Café* first appeared in *Harper's Bazaar* in August 1943.

Wood recently informed TW that Pancho Rodriguez had sold the Pontiac and kept the profits after swearing that he was the car's legal owner. More alarming news concerned an impostor in California who had solicited a producer for "a five hundred dollar advance" (February 5, 1948, HRC) in TW's name.

A reference in McCullers's correspondence indicates that this letter was mailed in Naples although it may have been written before TW left Sicily.]

89. To Audrey Wood

[Naples]
February 1948
[TLS w/ enclosures, 1 p. HRC]

Dear Audrey:

I have delayed writing because I do not like writing letters that sound like the outraged clucking of a wet hen, and the news that Colton had paid $30,000. income tax for last year put me into a most terrible and despondent humor - <u>You</u> know that I think of money only in terms of what it does for you. But that money could have done a whole lot, and not just for me but for several others. The productive years of an artist are pitifully few! His capital must be conserved, not only for himself but his worthy friends, dependants and beneficiaries. I am not lecturing <u>you</u> on this subject, you know that, but I think Colton ought to take his responsibilities more seriously and not arrange matters so that a big sum comes in at one time and the appalling amount of sixty thousand - thirty from me and thirty from mother! - has to be paid out as if we made that much every year of our lives on the black market! Spilt milk is spilt milk, and the government is a dreadfully implacable force for us poor mortals to mess with - However tell Colton, and very forcibly, that nothing is to be done in the future that would expose me to that sort of income tax! In other words when Streetcar is sold, it must be sold so that small amounts are paid over a period of ten years. That is <u>GOT TO BE</u>!

I was also distressed over the news that Gould-Echols contract had lapsed as just before I left New York I gave Maggie Gould my solemn promise that they could keep it. That was while Bill was in the hospital with a virus pneumonia. In the rush of departure I probably did not talk to you about this, and now I am afraid it makes me look like a bigger heel than I already actually am. Can you adjust it some way so that they will not regard it as a betrayal of trust on my part? I really would never have taken it away from them.

I am enclosing the long, long-delayed article for Leonard Lyons. It is about my trip to Sicily from which I am just returning. It is probably too long for his column. If so perhaps the TIMES would use it, or Harper's Bazaar. It is to be typed up before it goes out, and a copy sent back to me, as Visconti and Downes want to see it. Also please send me an up-to-date script or book of "Streetcar" for the Roman producers - same ones that did

Menagerie and the only progressive crowd in Italy. I am enclosing an article that came out in the Communist paper. They also had a terrifying picture of me with a caption that called me "Maggiore scrittore da Sinistra". Which means a major Communist writer! I wonder if I will be let back into the States. . . .

I am now in Naples at a hotel which is half in ruins. Will go on tomorrow, back to my room at the Ambassador in Rome. Address remains American Express in Rome. Never got the coffee and canned milk. They are probably enjoying it at the Lutetia in Paris, that horrible place where you had to stay in the bathtub all day to keep warm - I fell asleep in it and nearly drowned.

Much love, Tennessee.

[The hefty income tax paid by TW and Edwina, co-owners of *The Glass Menagerie*, reflects the sale of film rights in the preceding year. Audrey Wood quickly pacified her client with a plan to ask one million dollars for rights of *Streetcar*, with payments to be spread over ten years. She also defended the attorney Edward Colton and reminded TW that his own poor record keeping had not improved the "tax situation" (March 1, 1948, HRC), which placed him in the seventy-five percent bracket.

Wood also reminded TW that the "Gould-Echols contract" had "lapsed" after more than a year of fruitless search for funding. She advised that the last two option payments be returned to "adjust" (March 1, 1948, HRC) an awkward situation with friends. TW instructed Wood to "consummate deal with Beaumont" (telegram, February 12, 1948, HRC) to stage the *Menagerie* in London.

The enclosed "article" circulated to numerous magazines, including *The New Yorker*, whose editors considered the piece "unbelievably bad" and rejected it. "A Movie Named *La Terra Trema*" finally appeared in *'48 Magazine* (June 1948, pp.102-104, 111-113). TW admired the "tenderness toward life" which he observed in the villagers recruited by Visconti. The director himself had "a look of inflammable repose."

Fabio Coen, Wood's representative in Italy, received a copy of *Streetcar* for delivery to Campagnia Italiana di Prosa, Roman producer of *The Glass Menagerie*.

TW probably wrote this letter on February 10, 1948, the day before he returned to Rome.]

90. To Oliver Evans

[Albergo Palazzo-Ambasciatori, Rome]
2/11/48
[TLS w/ enclosure, 2 pp. HRC]

Dear Oliver:

I have just returned from a trip through southern Italy, first to Sicily where I watched the making of an Italian film using Sicilian peasants and their homes and orchards as actors and sets and directed by the man, Count Luchino Visconti, who put on "Zoo di Vetro" in Italy, a very handsome and elegant man of our tastes still in his thirties. Only trouble with Sicily is no bath-tubs which detracts from the charm of the peasants in winter when they don't swim, and I did not even have a bath-tub in my hotel for their use so it was a bit frustrating. Then I went to Naples. I think you would be disappointed in it now. Conditions are frightening, half the population or more living in destitution and bordering on violence. I got some nice little art-objects there, including a copper statue of a boy in Pompeii, which I wrote a poem about. The Galleria is not as you described it so must have changed. The idlers were too shabby and wolfish to bring into a hotel, so I hastened back to Rome, which I find most comfortable and delightful of all the places I've been in Europe. I have a room and balcony on the Via Veneto. Prokosch is also in Rome but I haven't seen him, he is staying at the swankiest hotel across the street from me. The Italians want everything you own but are generally content with what you give them. Do you remember Kimon Friar? He is in Athens, working there and has written and wired me, for permission to do "Streetcar". Has a connection with the Art Theatre in Athens. The letter was discreet - you remember how Miss Friar is! - but between the lines she is obviously having the time of her middle-aged life! Urges me to come there in Spring and go on a trip among the Aegean isles! At the same time they will be doing a revival of Menagerie along with Streetcar at the Art Theatre so I will probably go. When are you coming over? When the Spring term ends? Perhaps I will have found an apartment here in Rome by that time and you can stay with me. The climate here is a little milder than New Orleans in winter.

Audrey writes that Pancho sold my car in New Orleans after swearing under oath that it was his and apparently is now in California trying to sell some manuscripts of mine - so she thinks from a suspicious report that has reached her. Isn't that sad? Don't mention it to anybody! My life with him now seems like a fantastic dream which turned into a nightmare. Why do I have such abominable luck with romances?! I don't intend to get seriously involved with anyone ever again - life is supportable without it and loneliness is sometimes quite pleasant.

Are things any better in Lincoln?

With love, Tennessee.

[*La terra trema* (1948) was shot on location in Aci Trezza (Sicily) with the villagers serving as cast and helping Luchino Visconti to improvise a script. The slight plot involves a struggle, doomed at the outset, to free local fishermen from exploitive wholesalers and their own traditional culture. The film remains a defining example of Italian neorealism.

"Tennessee had drunk an entire bottle of Scotch and was nearly dead with fear" after a perilous flight from Rome to Sicily. Franco Zeffirelli, assistant to Visconti, went on to describe an engaging, if befuddled, visitor to the set: "When he eventually sobered up, I was charmed by him. He had a childlike naïvety which counterbalanced his rather *louche* life and which made his opinions fresh and interesting" (*The Autobiography of Zeffirelli*, 1986, p. 85). Details of the flight may be recalled in the middle section of *The Roman Spring of Mrs. Stone* (1950).

The "copper statue" led TW to write—and enclose—a lyric entitled "Testa Dell' Effebo" (*Harper's Bazaar*, August 1948).

In 1940 TW was asked to evaluate the "film possibilities" of Frederic Prokosch's novel *Night of the Poor* (1939). It seemed "phoney" to him at the time, but he and Prokosch later became friends and TW an admirer of his work.

TW had been pleased to accept Kimon Friar's invitation to read at the Poetry Center (YMHA) in New York on December 1, 1945. Friar directed the prestigious forum in the 1940s and later became a respected anthologist and translator of Greek poetry.]

91. To Paul Bowles

[45 Via Aurora, Rome]
[mid-February 1948]
[TLS w/ marginalia, 1 p. U of Delaware]

Dear Paul:

I have just moved into an apartment here in Rome. I am so delighted with the town and with the Italians that I shall probably remain here for some time. However sooner or later I shall take the trip to North Africa. I had typhoid and typhus shots before I left New York with that in mind.

There is no reason for me to return to the States before August so there is no hurry.

Paul, I was terribly disappointed that we couldn't get you to write music for Streetcar. I insisted that you should be contacted but you had already departed for Africa. However I hope that you will work with us on "Summer & Smoke" which Margo is going to produce starting about August 16th. Would you have the time or the inclination? The play has many problems. It is not as well-written as Streetcar and will need a brilliant production. Milziner will design: the set and all the plastic and atmospheric elements will be tremendously important and it really needs a musical score like Menagerie had. I would send you a script immediately except that I am still working on it. How much time do you require, that is, if you are able to undertake it? Rehearsals start August 16th but we don't open until about Sept. 5 in Buffalo and will play in Cleveland and Chicago before N.Y. If we can get together at some point on the map of Africa or Europe it would be of great advantage. This damned Swiss machine! It is light as a feather, no ballast, and plays every conceivable trick except actually kicking me in the balls and I'm sure it will eventually manage to do that!

I am very sensitive to changes of water and diet. Would Morocco be troublesome in those respects? What have you done with your house in Tangiers? Audrey showed me a lovely photo you took from a window looking over the Mediterranean.

You are fortunate to have Jane and Denby with you. I am travelling entirely alone, and have actually started talking to myself! Well, I have met a few people in Rome - many strangers! - but it would be good to encounter some old friends. In about two or three weeks I shall have completed my revisions on the script: then let me know where you're staying and I'll either mail you a copy or bring it down with me for a visit.

You remember Carson McCullers? She is paralyzed on one side as the result of a vascular disease and her condition is serious. I saw her before I left New York. We correspond now. It is a great pity! It makes no sense.

Ever - 10

[Their close friendship began in Acapulco in 1940 when a young man wearing a "floppy sombrero" and calling himself "Tennessee" met the perennial travelers, Paul (1910-1999) and Jane Bowles. Paul went on to compose incidental music for

The Glass Menagerie and would soon return to New York—from Tangier—to write the score for *Summer and Smoke*. His failure "to write music" for *Streetcar* may reflect both his absence at the time and the reported dislike of the Kazans for his exotic fiction. The visitor is Edwin Denby, American poet and former dance critic of the *New York Herald Tribune*.

TW's apartment was in a "tawny old" building near via Veneto and within a block of the Borghese Gardens—"favorite resorts for the sort of chance acquaintances that a lonely foreigner is apt to be seeking" (*Memoirs*, p. 141).

Typed in the upper margin is TW's mailing address, "American Express, Rome."]

92. *To Paul Bigelow*

[45 Via Aurora, Rome]
2/18/48
[TLS w/ autograph marginalia, 3 pp. Duke U]

Dear Paul:

This is the first nasty day we have had in Rome and I am staying in to work and write letters. I now have a two room apartment. It was an impulsive and ill-considered move. I thought it would give me more privacy but exactly the reverse has occured. The apartment is in a pensione which is operated by about six or a dozen very strange women who are never fully or even half-way dressed and their continual attentions and ministrations are nerve-wracking. I go in the bathroom to take a pee. One of them is washing my tub. I go in the bedroom. A couple of them are making my bed. I go in the front room. Three or four of them are re-arranging the furniture. Five or six times before I get up in the morning various ones of them knock to enquire if I am ready for breakfast. Their desperate concern for my comfort is about to drive me insane! But I am sure I will never have the nerve to tell them that I can't stand it and am moving out. I have been under great pains to conceal my love-life from them, waking my over-night guests at dawn and hustling them out before the ladies are stirring. But today I over-slept and so did the guest and all at once the bedroom door pops open - none of the locks work! - and a troop of the women march in serving both of us breakfast in bed and putting the top on the cold cream jar and replacing the towel and even screwing the cap back on the prophylactic tube in the bath-room! After all my secrecy. . . .

That is the charm of Italy!

As for Capri, I have not yet gone there but it is definitely on my itinerary. Old Norman Douglas is still the reigning belle of the island, though she is now in her eighties. She is living with a little boy whom radical opinion holds to be eleven years old and conservatives say is thirteen and will not go anywhere without him. I heard a marvelous story about Douglas which I wish I could repeat just as it was told me by Donald Downes, an American journalist who lives in Rome. It seems that some years ago Douglas' wife, a dope-addict, burned herself to death while smoking in bed. Douglas was expecting a house-guest that week-end. The guest phoned to offer condolences and say that of course she would postpone her visit because of the disaster. But Douglas insisted that she come ahead as planned. The guest thought she would cheer Douglas up by bringing with her an attractive young English belle of artistic pretensions. Miss Douglas received them on a chaise longue and was very laconic and they assumed that her loss had affected her more deeply than she wished to show. The belle made a great effort to be amusing, talked very eloquently about various periods of art, and got nothing out of Douglas but a few exhausted grunts. Until finally, having exhausted other topics, the belle began to talk about Italian cuisine, which was not at all to her liking, especially the way that meat was cooked in the Italian restaurants. For the first time Douglas showed a slight interest and asked the belle how she liked her meat cooked. I like it burned to a crisp on the outside, said the belle, but almost raw in the middle. Well, said Douglas, it is pity you didn't arrive here last Wednesday - You would have loved my wife. . . .

Other people who have been to Capri this season say it has not changed at all. The male population have been "kept men" for centuries and are spoiled but beautiful. The tourists are a conglomeration of faggots and fascists with Mona Williams thrown in for good measure. However I haven't heard anything about it that would keep me away when it gets warm enough for swimming, and I think it is high time that I met the other Miss Williams. For years I have been hearing elegant belles talk about "Mona". Perhaps she is now passe?

Carson and I are exchanging letters by almost every post between the continents. She says she is "unable to eat or sleep" and is in pain. Apparently a great deal of her suffering is mental. She had two unhappy loves in Europe - neither consummated, I take it - and Reeves caused her a great deal of anguish with what she says was deliberate and cunning persecution. I am relieved to learn, from her last letter, that he is now living in New York city and that she rarely sees him. One must not accept too literally Carson's account of things now. She is in a state of highly inflamed sensibilities. Reeves is also a sick person and a very pitifully maladjusted one who needs help, too. When Carson is better she hopes to join me in Europe and I am also hoping that this could be accomplished. My life is empty except for the "trapeze of flesh" as Crane called it, and it might do me good to have to devote myself to someone who needed and deserved so much care. On the other hand, I wonder if I would be good for her, or would the irregularities of my life and nature - which I know I would not give up - add to her unhappiness? I have talked this over with her in my latest letter. Of course it is very questionable whether she will be able to travel any time soon.

Margo is bound and determined to put on "summer and smoke" though I am most apprehensive about it, following "streetcar". It is by no means as well put together. Consequently I am having to devote most of my energies to re-writing it so it will not show up too badly. In the hands of Kazan - it has great plastic possibilities - it could be made very interesting but I am still skeptical about Margo's gifts as a director as I have really seen so little of her work. There is no doubt about her genius as a manager! She would have a tremendous career if she would concentrate on that end of it and use people like Kazan to do the things requiring brilliant interpretation. However I shall have to eat these words if she puts over "summer and smoke" and when she decides to do a thing nothing that heart and soul can do is left undone! She's a pretty remarkable little woman.

Well, it is time for me to take to the streets!

With love, 10.

[Later correspondence with Margo Jones saw the "pensione" become a "whorehouse" and TW a naive American tourist who belatedly learns its true nature. "At any rate," he quipped, "this is the first place I've ever stayed where I felt my private life was above suspicion and beyond reproach" (postmarked Rome, February 28, 1948, HRC).

The English writer Norman Douglas was seventy-nine and living on Capri with his friend, Kenneth Macpherson. TW's "story" catches the sardonic humor and the devotion to dining for which the author of *South Wind* (1916) was famous. Douglas was also known to speak bitterly of his former wife after their brief marriage and divorce in 1903.

Mona Harrison Williams rose above modest origins in Kentucky by marrying often and well. She was not "passe," as TW put it, but still a commanding, influential hostess who would entertain him in New York (see Vidal, *Palimpsest,* 1995, pp. 204-205). Her penchant for marriage and imperious manner may have contributed to the role of Mrs. Goforth in *The Milk Train Doesn't Stop Here Anymore* (1963).

Reeves was living in New York and trying to establish himself in a profession apart from being the husband of Carson McCullers. Discharged from the Army in 1946, he had been hampered in efforts to find a job by alcoholism, depression, and goals which surpassed his formal education.

"Yet, to the empty trapeze of your flesh, / O Magdalene, each comes back to die alone." The lines from "National Winter Garden" (1933), by Hart Crane, refer to the poet's loss of spiritual vision and the inevitable "cinch" of the flesh.

Penned in the upper margin of page 1 is the notation "A. Ex. Rome."]

93. To Carson McCullers

[45 Via Aurora, Rome]
[March 1, 1948]
[TLS w/ autograph marginalia, 1 p. Duke U]

Dearest Carson:

Sometimes the lamp burns very low indeed! For the past five or six days I have been battering my head against a wall of creative impotence. I have enough strength to do patch-work only on old scripts but I want to start new work. The scenes, the situations, the dialogue do not come to life. The characters remain half in shadow if not in total eclipse. I drink two cups of coffee. Then ring for more. At last my heart starts pounding violently and I have black spots in front of my eyes that grow larger and start to spin. I know I must stop, give up again for a while. So I take to the streets. It is the first day of March, Primavera is already here. A golden haze lies over the whole city as I look down on it from the top of the Piazza di Spagna. I feel comforted somehow. My heart stops hammering so despairingly and I go on to American Express where I find your letter and your story. Then it occurs to me that it is not necessary for me to do and say everything, that there are other writers in the world with souls of more sensibility than mine and greater power. Sometimes that thought is vexatious but today I find it soothing. Yes, individuality is an accidental thing. One being oneself does not imply as much importance and responsibility as one assumes. Perhaps it is impossible to think, feel and be through any channels other than one's own individual senses, but nevertheless all the others exist all around you. Where you fail, another succeeds. The responsibility is infinitely divided: life is multitudinous: a single wave can be thwarted but not the tide!

I am awfully, awfully glad that you are now in touch with Audrey. She has a deep understanding and a warm and sensitive heart and you will grow to love her as I have and she will have a feeling for your work that no other (merely commercial) agent could have. Joshua Logan was the man that several people wanted to direct "Streetcar". Mrs. Selznick thinks him quite marvelous. I preferred Kazan but next to him I am sure that Logan is excellent. Perhaps for your play even better as Logan used to live in the deep South and he is a man fighting to recapture an artistic position which he somewhat compromised by his work on big musicals like "Annie Get Your Gun". Don't worry anymore, I think your play is now in safe hands. And I do hope you will start on those stories, though perhaps they should wait till you are able to return abroad where we can work in adjoining trances.

Frederic Prokosch and Gore Vidal is here. I met Prokosch for the first time and found him very friendly and unpretentious. Vidal is 23 and a real beauty. His new book "The City and the Pillar" I have just read and while it is not a good book it is absorbing. There is not a really distinguished line in the book and yet a great deal of it has a curiously life-like quality. The end is trashy, alas, murder and suicide both. But you would like the boy as I do: his eyes remind me of yours!

Darling, I shall now go back to bed - the little god kept me awake all night - but I shall take "The Ballad of the Sad Cafe" to bed with me and read it before I go back to sleep. Each day is making you better! It must and it will.

All my love, 10.

[TW confirmed in later correspondence with Elia Kazan that he "started and gave up at least four plays" at this time. "The simple truth," he admitted, "is that I haven't known where to go since Streetcar." To Audrey Wood he observed that it was "frightfully hard to discover a new vein of material," having already "said so much about human relations, especially love" (February 1948, HRC).

Wood was impressed by Joshua Logan's co-writing and staging of the hit

Mister Roberts (1948) and hoped for the same happy result with *The Member of the Wedding*. She asked TW to solicit his interest when Logan visited Rome. Wood was loath, however, to formalize her "handling" (to TW, March 12, 1948, HRC) of Carson McCullers, fearing that it would eventually lead to a conflict of interest with TW.

Sir Harold Acton, observer of the expatriate community, wrote that TW, Frederic Prokosch, and Gore Vidal "created a bohemian annexe to the American Academy," while viewing "Classical and Romantic Rome" as "no more . . . than a picturesque background." He considered TW the "mildest" of the group and noted that this "moustached little man . . . wandered as a lost soul among the guests he assembled in an apartment which might have been in New York, for it contained nothing suggestive of Rome" (*More Memoirs of an Aesthete*, 1970, p. 211).

TW was unaware that McCullers had suffered a setback in late-February which alarmed her family and doctors.

Penned in the upper margin is the notation "Address 'Member' c/o American Exp."]

94. To Audrey Wood

[45 Via Aurora, Rome]
[March 1948]
[TLS, 1 p. HRC]

Dear Audrey:

Yesterday I mailed a revision of story "Night of the Iguana". I did not have a copy of the story so I am not sure exactly where this new material should be attached to the original. It replaces the long didactic speech of the writer and makes a new ending which I think is more harmonious with the rest. Please have Tiz or Creekmore, preferably Tiz, find the point at which this material connects and have the story re-typed accordingly and published this way. Tiz sent various questions from Creekmore. Please tell him the story title is not "Field of Blue Chickens". Title is "Field of Blue Children" and was published in STORY magazine sometime in 1939 or 1940. "The Important Thing" was also published in STORY. I believe in 1945. He can get both stories through Whit Burnett if you don't have them. "Something About Him" appeared in Madamoiselle a couple of springs ago. These stories must go into volume. "Bobo" is now called "The Yellow Bird". The complete and final text is the one that was published in "Town & Country." Creekmore must get copy of magazine and use their title and text for volume.

Perhaps with the new ending "Night of the Iguana" would be acceptable to "Harper's Bazaar". Please send them a copy of it in present form, which I think is shorter. Just before I left New York they wanted almost anything I had to give them - greater love hath no publisher!

Please tell Carson that I am utterly and truly entranced by her story "The Ballad of the Sad Cafe" which she recently sent me. I think it is wonderful material for a film-fantasy similar to Cocteau's film, "The Beauty and the Beast" and perhaps she and I together could work out a film treatment of it. I will write her about this idea this week.

The young (23 years old) novelist Gore Vidal is now in Rome. He and Frederic Prokosch. I see them every day. Vidal is awfully nice and his shocking new book is on the best-seller list in the States. I will see if I can get him for you! I am sure he is going to have a long and successful career.

How are you and Bill? My love to you both.

Tennessee

P.S. TIZ FORWARDED A VALENTINE GREETING FROM PANCHO IN WHICH HE SAID THAT HE WAS ENTERING "CHARITY HOSPITAL" (New Orleans) FOR A MONTH. HE GAVE NO REASON. WOULD YOU PLEASE CALL THE HOSPITAL LONG DISTANCE TO VERIFY THIS STATEMENT AND ENQUIRE ABOUT HIS CONDITION? ANONYMOUSLY IF POSSIBLE. MANY THANKS FOR YOUR LONG LETTER JUST NOW RECEIVED. I WILL HAVE TO ANSWER IT UNDER "SEPARATE COVER". CONDUCT THE GOULD-ECHOLS DEAL ACCORDING TO YOUR DISCRETION.

[Of the stories cited by TW, only "Something About Him" would not appear in *One Arm*.

Audrey Wood's cable—"Important know immediately your present attitude Jones directing" (March 11, 1948, HRC)—was prompted by Margo Jones's request that contracts for *Summer and Smoke* be drawn before her arrival in New York to cast the show. It was a final effort by Wood to deter TW from a course which she knew to be based upon personal rather than professional considerations. She was later "shocked" to learn that Jones was using her own casting agents in addition to Liebling-Wood. "This makes it a rat race as to who gets actor on phone first" (telegram, to Jones, March 25, 1948, HRC).

Pancho Rodriguez sent TW a "Valentine greeting" with news that he was entering a "charity hospital" (TW to Wood, 3/48, HRC) in New Orleans. Wood's staff could not verify the report.

TW wrote this letter, which bears a reception date of March 19, 1948, late in the week of March 7 before leaving for Amalfi, in company with Gore Vidal.]

95. To Carson McCullers

[45 Via Aurora, Rome]
[March 1948]
[TLS w/ autograph postscript, 1 p. Duke U]

Dearest Carson:

A friend of mine, Paul Moor, has just sent me a clipping of your letter about me to LIFE. Nobody has ever said such things about me and nobody but you has ever thought such things about me! Bless you for it! I am a little embarassed for the most I can ever do is approximate virtue and only that at intervals but it is deeply moving to learn that anybody could see me in such a light and perhaps it will encourage me to improve.

I have been a little worried about you as I haven't heard from you in some time, and I have not received the play that you were going to send me.

For three nights last week I read "The Ballad of the Sad Cafe" and they were the loveliest nights I have had in Europe. The story of Miss Amelia and the hunchback is in my opinion the most beautiful story in all American fiction. I wrote Audrey that I thought it would make a film. Perhaps she has called you about it. When that happy day comes when we are working together, that can be one of our projects if you like.

It is really Prima Vera here in Rome. A succession of perfectly radiant days, and I have bought a Jeep, an old one that still runs well, so that I can spend a lot of time outdoors. I finished my rewrite of "Summer and Smoke". It has been difficult for me to get started on the new play, so I am leaving it for a while and trying to improve my general condition by a lot of out-door life. Gore Vidal the young (23 year old) novelist is here. He is interesting but is infected with that awful competitive spirit and seems to be continually haunted over the successes or achievements of other writers such as Truman Capote. He is positively obsessed with poor little Truman Capote. You would think they were running neck and neck for some fabulous gold prize! I don't like that attitude and spirit in young writers. But of course it is a result of insecurity. Prokosch is also here. He is suffering from jaundice and his skin and eyes are bright yellow but his nature is healthier than Vidal's. He is sort of a hedonist, I don't like his social and political principles, but he is quite modest and friendly and has a good sense of humor. You will like him, I think, if you can ignore his social views - which are pretty reactionary and classical and all that. There is not an awful lot to choose from in the way of American society here, but that does not matter as the city and the weather and the natives are all you need.

I shall be [at] Amalfi for a few days this week (coming) to enjoy some swimming. I will write you from there. Let me hear from you as often as you feel like writing and know that my love is with you all of the time.

Tenn.

(Just got your letter, thank heavens! So happy you wrote story!)

[Carson McCullers praised author and subject of TW's profile in *Life* magazine (February 16, 1948): "Tennessee Williams is not only an extraordinarily great artist, a genius, he is also one of the wholly beautiful human beings I have ever known" (*Life*, March 8, 1948, p. 14). The author, Lincoln Barnett, closely followed the evolving Williams legend of an idyllic southern childhood, hard times in St. Louis, and long-delayed success on Broadway. Rose was cast as the "closest companion" of TW's youth, but neither her medical history nor the unhappy state of the family was mentioned in the profile.

The controversial novels of Gore Vidal and Truman Capote—*The City and the Pillar* and *Other Voices, Other Rooms*—were published within days of each other in January 1948. Capote's prose won critical honors and the notorious dust jacket the fiercely waged publicity battle. McCullers was no doubt hurt by a reviewer who ranked Capote as "a minor imitation of a very talented minor writer, Carson McCullers" (Elizabeth Hardwick, *Partisan Review*, March 1948).

TW had acquired one of the "natives," Rafaello, as discreetly named in *Memoirs*. A suggestive reference to this "'*giovane*'" in a newspaper article "launched {TW} upon a long period of personal notoriety in Rome" (*Memoirs*, p. 145), as later events would confirm.

Composition of this letter late in the week of March 7, 1948, is coincident with McCullers's reported suicide attempt. She was hospitalized in New York and by April 10 was "feeling better" (Wood to TW, April 10, 1948, HRC).]

96. To Justin Brooks Atkinson

[45 Via Aurora, Rome]
March 29, 1948
[TLS, 2 pp. BRTC]

Dear Brooks:

I have been living in Rome for two months now and would like to stay on indefinitely but, alas, it looks as if the political situation will make it most uncomfortable for foreigners, especially those from the States. Most of my American friends here are making plans to pull out before the elections which are April 18th. Frederic Prokosch has been living here and I met him for the first time and was surprised to find him quite simple and friendly, which is certainly not the impression you get from the austere pictures of him that usually appear on the back of his books. He is driving his Lincoln Continental across the French border this week. Another and more precocious American writer, Gore Vidal, is also here and he is flying to Cairo. Various others are scattering to various other places. I have not yet made any plans and the way that I drift along here, time flows almost imperceptibly although so swiftly, I doubt that I will make any move until the last moment. As I do not live at all conspicuously, and drive a second-hand Jeep, perhaps the Communists will overlook [me] completely if they come into power! Orson Welles is in Rome. I have not met him but I have seen him sitting in front of Doney's which is the fashionable sidewalk cafe in front of the fashionable hotel Excelsior where he is staying. He was reading a book called DECADENCE. I have been told that he has taken a house here for two years, so perhaps Orson is politically invulnerable. Most of the people I've talked to think that Togliatti will win. The trouble is that none of the other parties have put up candidates that appeal to the people. There is a terrific reaction here against the church particularly since Monsignor Scippio skipped off with a vast amount of money. When you mention de Gasperi to the Italian-in-the-streets he makes a wry face and says 'Prete!' Nothing at all has apparently been done by the native government, as it now exists, to relieve the really appalling social conditions. It honestly looks as if seventy percent of the Italian population are mendicants and prostitutes, families are living in the roofless shells of buildings in the bombed cities such as Naples. I feel that if we had made really sacrificial efforts to relieve the distress of Europe the Communists would have no appeal. As it is, the people in their really dire circumstances, bewildered by vacillating and make-shift puppet governments headed by weak and blandly opportunistic figures, rooted in no defined party or policy or philosophy, are a natural and easy prey to extremists. What a tragedy it is, that America, our nation, at the one great moment of destiny, suddenly lost the man, Roosevelt, who was apparently the one leader in the Western World who could see realistically and think idealistically and feel humanely enough to get us all through this interval of panic without a catastrophe which now seems to be coming. What it really took was simple human understanding which somehow seems to be lacking in the present leadership. No, of course it takes more than that, but with that as a basis I believe we might have kept the world in the hands of liberals and moderates and so kept going. - Well, a miracle may happen. - Speaking of miracles I was out at St. Peters on Good Friday and [saw] a most amusing spectacle. A dignitary of the church, in scarlet robes and cap - apparently a cardinal - was seated in a little fenced enclosure with a narrow gate at either side. There was a line of people, easily half a mile long, moving at a slow trot through one gate and out the other, for all the world like a sheep-dip, while the Cardinal sitting on his ornate throne, cracked them over the head as they went by him with a very long stick, like a black board pointer. He was apparently in a vile humor for he hit some of them so smartly that they winced with pain. One old lady was dazed by the blow he gave her and started to trot back in the opposite direction, against the current and he gave her a second crack even harder than the first which seemed to set her straight again. There was a young American priest alongside me, as irreverent as myself, and when I asked him what this ceremony was about he told me that everybody who got cracked over the head with the stick had 300 days knocked off his sentence in Purgatory!

Purgatory indeed! What most of these people needed was a bar of soap, a clean shirt and a good square meal. The Italians are a beautiful and very lovable people, I like them even better than Mexicans. I don't think Communism is really their dish but we have got to offer them a more inspiring number of alternatives if we want to keep their faith. They do not hate Americans at all, in fact the whole time I've been here I haven't had an unfriendly word or look from any of them.

I hope the theatrical season has picked up. I understand from Kazan that MR. ROBERTS is a grand play and likely to win the prizes. Joshua Logan is in Italy and has written me and I expect we will meet in Rome.

I am working pretty well here, although Primavera is even more distracting than Spring, one pure golden day after another. I sometimes suspect that I died at the American hospital in Paris and went to heaven! That is, when I think and feel selfishly which is, of course, most of the time.

My best greetings to you and to your wife,

Ever, Tennessee.

[The Christian Democrat party of Premier Alcide de Gasperi defeated the Communist-led Popular Front of Palmiro Togliatti and kept control of the government. Cold War competition of East and West had intensified the election, with the future of the Marshall Plan an issue of debate. Little violence accompanied the campaign and serious post-election disturbances did not immediately occur.

Orson Welles lived in Rome during the filming of *Black Magic* (1949). TW's remark that Welles would be "invulnerable" to a Communist government echoes charges stateside that he was "'red as a firecracker.'" He was probably reading *Decadence: A Philosophic Inquiry* (1948), by C.E.M. Joad.

Streetcar, rather than *Mister Roberts*, swept the "prizes" for the current season, winning the Drama Critics' Circle Award and the Pulitzer by wide margins. *Streetcar* was only the second play in the history of the awards to claim both—the first *The Time of Your Life* (1939) by William Saroyan.]

97. To Audrey Wood

[45 Via Aurora, Rome]
4/2/48
[TLS, 1 p. HRC]

Dear Audrey:

This must be telegraphic as I am worn out from working.

I suppose Margo will be arriving in New York this week. Do by all means put all possible (humane) pressure to assure that Summer and Smoke does not rush into New York. I think a West Coast opening would be ideal but if that is not feasible, concentrate on the subject of Chicago. If you want to (dare to) bring up the subject of Kazan directing, do so, but I doubt that you will get anywhere with it as our girl Jones unquestionably regards herself as the American Stanislavsky which it is still faintly possible that she may be however much we may doubt it. Also please make sure that no one is definitely signed before I return sometime in the middle of summer, probably not the end of July or early in August. While still on the subject, ask Eddie if it possible (legally) for me to give half of this play (Summer) to my sister, so that if it is moderately successful there will no longer be any question of there being money enough to do something for her? Also please thank Eddie for his letter which I will answer as soon as I can get around to it.

I loved your long letter and especially the part about the afternoon at McCullers! I never knew you had such a gift for graphic and lively narrative!

It is among the letters I will keep with me. I don't understand what you mean about not wanting to handle Carson, however, because of possible collision between her interests and mine. I don't see how that could happen, as she is a basically wise and sensible girl and I myself am not hysterical enough to ever want to bring out a joint volume with any other writer, let alone one who would make my work appear so pale in comparison as hers would! Frederic Prokosch has just read her "Ballad of a Sad Cafe" and pronounces it the finest piece of American (poetic) fiction. He is going to write her about it.

I am a bit worried over Windham and his friend Campbell coming over here. I don't want any unnecessary responsibilities right now and I'm afraid that is going to turn into one, especially with political crises developing all over the continent, focussing particularly on Rome. Would it be possible to get an advance, for Windham, on his novel? Otherwise I will almost certainly have to take care of him over here! - Don't mention this but please investigate the chances with the "League of Authors" Etc. His published and unpublished stories are certainly good enough to get him a fellowship or loan or advance of some kind.

I may have to leave Italy if the elections go far to the left, as probably all Americans would be in a hazardous position. I have heard from Fabio Coen, the man you mentioned, and I plan to see him. You have no idea how time flies here! The American colony is desperately gregarious and you can only work by bolting doors and shutters. Yes, some of them even climb in the window if they suspect you have a little cognac on the place!

Love - 10.

P.S. I have just met Fabio and like him extremely. We are going to collect my 30,000 lire on Friday.

[Eddie Colton advised TW that a trust fund would be the safest way "to give half" of *Summer and Smoke* to his sister Rose. He went on to pose "difficult" (April 30, 1948, HRC) legal questions which probably baffled TW.

The "afternoon at McCullers" (March 6) reminded Audrey Wood of "a Tennessee Williams story." Carson "was in bed in little boy's pink woolen pajamas" surrounded by adoring mother, sister, husband, and friends. "The only thing she could discuss over and over again was MEMBER OF THE WEDDING — and Tennessee Williams! The climax of the afternoon came when with adoration in her eyes she asked us whether we wanted to hear you recite a poem on a record. . . . It began and though I listened as hard as I ever have in my life not one word was understandable. As this monotonous noise droned on, McCullers leaned forward with great ecstasy and . . . said, 'Isn't that the most beautiful poem you have ever heard?'" (March 12, 1948, HRC).

TW would soon devise a more biting parody of McCullers in correspondence with Paul Bigelow (see letter #170).]

98. To Margaret "Margo" Jones

[45 Via Aurora, Rome]
[mid-April 1948]
[TLS, 1 p. HRC]

Dearest Girl:

I am so happy that you can really come over for a while! Also over the news that you think Margaret Phillips is available. Has the script arrived yet? I mailed it to Audrey, air mail registered, about five days ago and it certainly should have reached her by this time.

I am anxious to know Milzener's reactions. I think I have made my idea of the set, at last, quite explicit and I hope he will find it stimulating for so much depends on what he is going to give us, far more than in any other work, for this play deals with intangibles which need plastic expression far more than verbal. The knowledge that you and I and he will be working together all by ourselves is a happy one. I am sure that Audrey and Bill will also give us every possible support and altogether we should come through with colors not drooping.

Don't dismiss Todd until you're quite sure that you have someone really better. Remember the boy must be attractive! If you can get that and real ability as an actor, we will be in luck. Anyone you consider very seriously, please send me a picture air-mail. I am particularly anxious that the part of Nellie should be well-played as she has to sustain some of the weaker scenes in the play. The doctor's part has been greatly reduced with the elimination of his long scene with Alma and I think in scene eight he should not be lighted except as a silhouette, to give him an impersonal quality. The face never visible. For it is too late in the play to introduce a new character. In eight the light only on Rosa Gonzales (formerly the Serio girl). In costuming this play I think Lucinda Ballard would be marvelous.

Why don't you talk with her and see if she is willing to adapt herself to the budget? I think the period and style of the play would fit her talents which are highly interpretive as well as pictorial. Her one drawback is temperament but that is also part of her value, and she is a great person. Jo always wants her which is an excellent sign. - For God's sake get some good kids for the prologue. The play must get off to a good start. Have an understanding with everyone (except perhaps Phillips) that they are not finally cast until after the first five days of rehearsal, or rather till I have seen and heard them.

Such a sad letter from Carson McCullers. Do not mention this, but not long ago she slashed her wrist in an attempt at suicide and has recently been in a psychiatric clinic. She still has the paralytic condition of the left side and perhaps suspects that it is permanent. If I were not sure that Pancho would pounce on me, I would come back to the States. That is going to be a big problem when I do return, as he is almost certain to learn where I am and to reappear.

Helen Hayes is sailing for England early in June to do the Menagerie in London, opening I think about July fifteenth. I do hope you can stay over till then. We will spend some time here, then fly to Paris and see what is going on there, then wind up in England for the opening of Hayes. I think you should have a real vacation over here, so give yourself plenty of time. The way things look at the moment I don't think the Communists are powerful enough to make much trouble in Italy.

Love - 10.

[TW's production notes for *Summer and Smoke* were so precise and revealing, Jo Mielziner wrote, that "it would be truly difficult to design a setting for this play that was poor in concept. It might be inadequate in execution, but the extraordinarily knowledgeable and sensitive eye of the dramatist created a picture that even a mediocre designer could not spoil" (*Designing for the Theatre,* 1965, p. 153).

Tod Andrews played young John Buchanan in the Dallas and Broadway productions of *Summer and Smoke*, as well as on tour.

Lucinda Ballard designed the costumes for *Streetcar* but not for *Summer and Smoke.*

Carson McCullers was released from Payne Whitney Psychiatric Clinic in mid-April and soon began revising *The Member of the Wedding.* A draft sent to TW brought the encouraging reply, "'Script a thousand times better'" (qtd. in Carr, p. 305).]

Jo Mielziner, full set design for Summer and Smoke *(1948).*

99. To Audrey Wood

[45 Via Aurora, Rome]
4/19/48
[TLS, 2 pp. HRC]

Dear Audrey:

I have been very scatter-brained and unbusiness-like in my recent communications with the home-front and I have left undone all those things which ought to have been done. (Erred and strayed from thy ways like lost sheep! Followed too much the devices and desires of my own heart, Etc.)

It is now the day after election, a day of reckoning. I must sit down and make a few important emendations.

First off, do not send Richard Orme anymore money for that G.D. apartment of his. I can't afford (or get tax exemption) for maintaining two residences and I wrote him last January from Paris that he would have to keep the girls in the place or sublet it to someone else. I signed that lease as a friendly accomodation to him with the clear understanding that it was to be sub-let until and if I wanted it back. Now of course since I have broken up with Pancho under such distressing circumstances I could not return to New Orleans where he and his family live. Do not please state this in the letter to Orme who is a terrible and vicious gossip and a rather cruel person.

Second, please see what you can do to either stop publication of Moor's article for Harper's or see that we get final corrected proofs before it is published. It is direct contradiction of most of the known facts about me, worst of all it is terribly dull. I have written Moor to get a postponement and he has wired that is impossible. Please see, at least, that either the usual date of 1914 is given for my birth or the painful subject is altogether avoided. The article is a mass of inaccuracies and misinterpretations due to the fact that I have never really had an interview only friendly (and very laconic) meetings with Moor on three or four occasions.

Send me any good books on the frontier days (colorful anecdotal atmospheric) about the frontier days of the Texas oil-industry as that is the background of my latest attempt at a comedy. I've started three or four different plays but this is perhaps the most promising.

My masseur-gym instructor has arrived and I have to get to work. Perhaps I will think of some more jobs for you later.

With love, Tennessee.

RE: Tito Guerini. I have not yet had the heart to tell him that you think his story is bad. He refers to it as his "Seule et derniere espoir!" (We have to converse in French as my Italian remains a bit inadequate.) As a matter of fact, I think it is a good slice of Italian life, this story, but perhaps the translation is still bad. Send it to New Directions, please, if no where else - along with my account of the author. These Italians break my heart, or what's left of it. They are such lovable and pitiful people, and up against such a blank wall, politically, economically, almost every conceivable way. I hate to make friends among them - easy as that is! - because I shall feel so badly when I leave them here with the sort of future that seems to be inevitable.

If our state department could think of Europe in terms of human beings rather than parties, governments, then perhaps a world-disaster could be side-stepped.

Logan is here and also Carson's script has arrived. The script is better and I shall call Logan today. I hope he will work on it with her.

Yes, please have Tiz's father investigate Rose's circumstances. Soon as I come back [to] the States I shall find another place for her. Perhaps that could even be done before my return. She has been in that goddam place for twelve years now! I can't hardly believe it. If God has forgotten her there, we have got to remember. I have been much too preoccupied with my self.

Along with the (one good) book on Texas oil development please send me the new biography of Hart Crane, not the old one by Philip Horton which I have read. I have read, finally, Capote's book. One third of it is brilliant. The rest falls flat and is terribly derivative of Faulkner and Carson McCullers. But he has the finest writing style of any of the new novelists.

For some reason my health in Italy has been exceptionally good, absolutely no gastric disturbances since I got here, but I have not done much work. One story, one poem, and only the beginnings of several plays which have lovely conceptions but no second act complications (plots!).

Statement for Theatre Arts? Say I was pleased to get it! What more can be said about that?

[Penitential lines from *The Book of Common Prayer* were easily and accurately quoted by the grandson of an Episcopal priest.

In 1938 TW lowered his age by three years to qualify for a Group Theatre contest (see Vol. I, letter #86). Paul Moor skirted the deception by vaguely placing TW's birth "a little before the first world war" ("A Mississippian Named Tennessee," *Harper's Magazine*, July 1948).

TW's request for books about the "oil-industry" pertains to a work-in-progress entitled "The Big Time Operators." An outline tentatively identifies the "Operators" as an "Oil corporation?" (n.d., HRC) and reveals the play to be a partial study of *Sweet Bird of Youth* (1956/1959).

Tito Guerrini asked TW for help in placing a story of his, probably "My Maternal Aunt" (*New Directions Twelve*, 1949).

"Tiz" Schauffler's father, a Kansas City physician, learned that Rose Williams had shown "some improvement" following recent insulin and electric shock treatment but her prognosis was "poor" (Hoctor to Robert Schauffler, n.d., HRC). Dr. Schauffler advised that "there does not seem to be much equity in removing Miss Williams to a private hospital and physician" (to Elizabeth Schauffler, May 8, 1948, HRC).

Theatre Arts had asked TW to comment on the Drama Critics' Circle Award given to *Streetcar*.]

100. To Audrey Wood

[45 Via Aurora, Rome]
4/24/48
[TLS, 2 pp. HRC]

Dear Audrey:

I hope I remember all these things you have asked me!

First about Singer: I have no idea why he is supposed to get one percent of the London show but I hope you will do everything in your power to prevent it as you know my opinion of that [mind] and all his works. It was my understanding that we were now completely free of any legal connection with him. His influence on "Menagerie" was solely negative and came near being destructive.

Cast for London production: I do think Ross is definitely too old. His age was only acceptable when coupled with Dowling's. Also he has many other problems which make him precarious. With Hayes as the mother I think he would seem definitely too old, and I say this in spite of liking him and his performance.

Directors: Harold Clurman has just written me expressing his eagerness to direct the play in London. I have a profound respect and liking for Clurman as a director and person and would be delighted to have him if he is acceptable to Miss Hayes. Joshua Logan who is now in Rome has also told me he would like to do the show in London. My fear about him is that he goes overboard on farcical effects. I get that impression from his detailed account of Mr. Roberts as well as from the really awful job he did on Hayes show which has just closed. He seems to delight in tricks and gags of the most obvious nature. On the other hand, I find him likeable as a person. He has worked with Hayes and they seem to like each other - according to him! - I am not at all keen about Gielgud. It would quite probably be like Margaret Webster directing Battle of Angels. He is too English, too stylish, too removed from the subject and spirit of the script. I would much prefer Logan of those two - Incidentally Logan is going to England and he expressed his desire to direct "Menagerie" in a letter which reached me a few days ago in Florence, where I had gone to meet Windham, so he is obviously serious about it. I suggest that you talk to Hayes, very confidentially, about Logan and see if she thinks he can be trusted to avoid broad comedy devices - without letting her know that I personally have expressed that concern about him.

My first choice is still Clurman but I realize that I may meet with too strong opposition from all quarters on that score, which is a pity for Clurman represents the things I most value in theatre.

In any case will you please call Clurman and assure him that I have written you in recommendation of him?

I like Phil Brown for either Gentleman Caller or Tom. Awfully sorry about Monty. How about Bill Eyethe? He is supposed to be wonderful and would look good with Hayes and I like him personally.

Tell Irene I have no ideas about costumes. I can't cable replies to things like that as I cannot send cables collect and they cost enormously. I still think of myself as a poor man and I will until Colton has figured out someway to rescue me from the tax collectors. I am writing Colton this week.

On reading over Guerini's story, I still like it, but I see that it has been very awkwardly translated. I will think more about that.

I will also consider restoring scene in Summer & Smoke. I felt it did not advance the plot to any appreciable extent and that it gave the audience more time in which to get tired of Miss Alma. If Phillips is really good we can throw it back in. Windham says Clift would like to play John. What do you and Margo think about that? Originally he seemed a little lacking in vitality but perhaps he has changed in that respect. He has the looks and other qualifications for the part.

I was surprised to find that the acting edition of Menagerie contained ~~practically all~~ of the little vulgarisms which Babs and I spent practically a whole day weeding out. How did they get back in? I particularly detest that closing line * * "And this is where the play ends and your imagination begins". - Other respects show improvement.

I think the connection with Theatre Guild is regrettable because of their scandalous treatment of Guild and Equity members. Hate to seem to be sanctioning such behavior. - Carson's script is better but confidentially it is still not right. I must think of something! Logan is on the fence - very cagey about it -

Love - 10.

[*The Glass Menagerie* was set to open in London in the following July with Tennent Ltd. as managing concern. Louis J. Singer demanded one percent of TW's royalty as compensation for an option which he charged that Audrey Wood had terminated unfairly. She later advised payment to avoid lengthy arbitration.

Helen Hayes reluctantly agreed to play Amanda in London. She and Wood favored Anthony Ross, who originated the role of the Gentleman Caller, but his age and drinking worried TW.

Wood advised TW that "British labor policy" (telegram, April 21, 1948, HRC) might preclude use of an American director in staging *The Glass Menagerie*. Harold Clurman, a founder of the Group Theatre (1931-1941), would eventually direct *The Member of the Wedding* (1950). Joshua Logan received mixed rather than "awful" reviews for his direction of Hayes in *Happy Birthday* (1946). TW feared that John Gielgud would repeat the problems which Margaret Webster had brought to *Battle of Angels* (1940): both were "too English, too stylish," to direct plays "soaked in American provincialism."

Apparently Irene Selznick consulted TW about costumes for a British production of *Streetcar* which she and Hugh Beaumont were planning.

Cut in the latest version of *Summer and Smoke* was a long expository scene (Scene Two) between Alma and the elder Buchanan. The new scene opens in the rectory, rather than the doctor's office, and features a telephone call in which Alma flirtatiously reminds young John Buchanan of a promised automobile ride: "I was just reprimanding you, sir! Castigating you verbally! Ha-ha!" (March 1948, HRC). Echoes of *The Glass Menagerie* and *Streetcar* are unmistakable.

The line detested by TW—"And there my memory ends and your imagination begins"—appears in the acting edition of *The Glass Menagerie* (Dramatists Play Service, 1948), but not in the first American edition published by Random House (1945). Eddie Dowling's dissatisfaction with the final lines reportedly led to the addition.

Actors Equity recently suspended a Theatre Guild manager for harassing cast members of the musical *Allegro* (1947). TW objected in turn to the Guild's co-producing *The Glass Menagerie*, but Wood explained that it was only a "courtesy" (May 5, 1948, HRC) billing to thank the Guild for its help in casting Miss Hayes.

This letter bears a reception date of May 1, 1948.]

101. To Gore Vidal

[45 Via Aurora, Rome]
[ca. April 25, 1948]
[TLS, 2 pp. Houghton]

Bright eyes!

This is glorious news about the play! Glorious plays are not usually written in such a short time, but Saroyan did it so why not you. I imagine that you will read it over after a while and decide it is slightly less glorious than you originally supposed in the first flush of exultation. That is nearly always the unhappy case. However there is no reason why it should not be the beginning of a glorious play, anyhow. And I am hoping it is and will be. By all means do send it to me. When a thing goes that quickly it is a good sign, for it means that the impulse was vital and the vision was clear. Don't be surprised if it takes you several months more to make it as good as you first thought it was.

Windham and Sandy Campbell have come to Italy. I met them in Florence and we came down to Rome together and they are now putting up at the Inglaterra and are simply wild about Rome. Both of them think it is glorious. I hope it doesn't break up their happy marriage. We are looking at apartments this afternoon. If we find the right one we will set up housekeeping, the four of us. Yes, my mouse is still with me and swishing his little tail about as usual. Diretto! Destra! Sinistra! There has been a terrific influx of dikes. Mostly journalistic ones. Flanner (Janet) and her girl-friend came down to cover the election. Yesterday we all went to a private screening of a film called Berlin Anno Zero by the man who made Open City & Shoe Shine. When we arrived Janet said, "The ladies will sit in the front row and the gentlemen in the rear." And Esther, the biggest one of the Dikes who looks like Wallace Beery in drag, said, "Ah-ha! Sex discrimination!" They are a jolly bunch and the social life is considerably better than when there was just us girls, sunning ourselves like a bunch of lizards on the walk in front of Doney's. No word from Fritz and Russell who went off together. The French actor is still around but I haven't seen him. Poor La Traube! He has the clap now, the only one of us to be stricken, just when he was getting over the crabs. Afflictions, mortal afflictions! Especially those of love, how troublesome they are. I am glad you did not have carnal associations in Cairo, not only because it would have interfered with the glorious work but because I kept thinking, If Gore is not careful he will catch one of those things from the dirty Egyptians.

Franco Brusatti just now climbed in my window but has now climbed back out again. I told him I was working. There was no liquor, but he drank what was left of my coffee. With a threat to return. A gold filling has come out. The litany of my sorrows is now complete.

The sky is serenely blue, the light is golden. It is the sort of Roman day that we will remember all of these days being when we are back in the States.

I have one more letter to write, to Helen Hayes, who is going to do the Menagerie in London. Then to the Jeep!

I close now with an affectionate and mildly libidinous kiss on your soft under lip which I never kissed.

Ever fondly, Tennessee

Lesbia passed through Rome, heavily veiled. No sign of Willard. No word. Only a whisper of silk and a few rose leaves floating after. The scent of frangi-pangi. A few days later a gilt-edged card, saying "Sorry!" Post-marked Istanbul, dictated, unsigned. With Lesbia one is never certain, such a thin line, so easily crossed over! - Nerves . . .

[Gore Vidal (b. 1925) and TW met at a party given by the composer Samuel Barber for visiting Americans in Rome. "'I particularly like New York on hot summer nights when all the . . . uh, superfluous people are off the streets'" (qtd. in Vidal, *Palimpsest*, p. 149). So apparently began TW's first conversation with Vidal, giving a wry, conspiratorial tone to their friendship and marking the streets of Rome as erotic. "We walked—cruised—a lot in the golden age," Vidal added many years later.

TW soon pronounced the "glorious" new play "'the worst . . . he'd read in some time,'" and Vidal, for the moment, "'solemnly abandoned playwriting for good'" (qtd. in Kaplan, *Gore Vidal: A Biography*, 1999, p. 273).

Franca Danesi was Janet Flanner's liaison and assistant in reporting the recent Italian elections for *The New Yorker*. Natalia Danesi Murray, Franca's older sister, was Flanner's intimate companion. Roberto Rossellini directed *Germania, anno zero* (1947) and *Open City* (1945) but not *Shoeshine* (1946), a film by Vittorio de Sica.

Internal evidence reveals that TW wrote this letter ca. April 25, 1948.]

102. To Helen Hayes

[45 Via Aurora, Rome]
4/25/48
[TLS, 2 pp. Private Collection]

Dear Helen Hayes:

I hope that my wire conveyed something of my exultation over the tentative news, now confirmed. I did not dare to believe it was actually going to happen, but apparently it has, and I am so very happy!

Now every care must be taken to see that you have the very best direction and supporting cast that can be obtained. I have written Audrey a few suggestions, all of which are of course entirely contingent upon your approval.

I do not much like the idea of Gielgud as a director unless no American is available, and that does not seem to be the case. Joshua Logan is now in Rome. How do you feel about him? He wrote me (while I was in Florence) expressing his willingness to direct you in London if you so wished. I met him here for the first time and liked him tremendously. In complete confidence, I must say that I have a suspicion that he is inclined to lean a bit too heavily on broad comedy effects in his direction. This I gathered from his detailed account of "Mr. Roberts" which I have not seen, and the other comedies which I have. What he would do with a play requiring a delicate and finely balanced touch is a matter of faith and speculation which you are better able to judge than I am, for I have seen and known so little of him and his work, but I would unhesitatingly prefer him to Gielgud or any other Englishman.

Harold Clurman has written me saying he would love to direct the play. There is a man I would love to work with! He represents everything I most value and respect in the theatre, for his seriousness, his sensitivity, his humility and his rare intelligence. I know some people think he is too highbrow or literary but that I doubt and I think he is needing some encouragement now and deserves it certainly.

Jessica Tandy has wired me suggesting her husband Hume Cronyn. Hume I know is a good director from his work on "Portrait of a Madonna" with Jessica at the Actors' Lab in Hollywood.

My feeling against Gielgud is primarily that he is British and I think there is an inherent incapacity in the British to interpret a play that is soaked in American provincialism. The body would be there, but some indefinite but immensely important thing would be missing. Then I wonder if he is not a little bit cold and dry and too dependant on theatrical effects and devices, especially for an artist like you whose instrument is so much of the heart. Warmth and humanity is what we want above everything else and that has seemed to be lacking in the directorial work of his I have seen, however much I admire him as a technical master.

Actors? I thought Clift would be swell but now I hear he is not available. Phil Brown is about equally gifted. How about Bill Eythe who is doing a West coast production now? You and Audrey will manage all that, however.

You must satisfy yourself completely in all these matters. I am only suggesting. I do think any British actors would be a big mistake! But it would be hard to make a mistake big enough to seriously impair the effect of your Amanda which I look forward to almost as much as if it were the first time - not forgetting.

Sincerely, Tennessee.

[Audrey Wood pulled "every possible wire, string, and cobweb to lure Miss Hayes into the City of London" (to TW, April 13, 1948, HRC). Probably more telling was a promise which Laurette Taylor had secured from Hayes (1900-1993)—who regarded the older actor as her "guiding star"—to bring *The Glass Menagerie* to London if she herself could not. Hayes later wrote that meeting Edwina in London helped to explain why she felt "uneasy" playing Amanda. She realized the kind of unhappy family "memories" upon which TW had drawn and concluded that Edwina "was everything I disliked in an aging Southern belle" (*My Life in Three Acts*, 1990, p. 168).

Wood reported earlier that Hayes and Hugh Beaumont were "interested" in John Gielgud's direction of *The Glass Menagerie* and asked TW if he were "agreeable" (telegram, April 21, 1948, HRC). Gielgud was named director as TW wrote in reply or shortly thereafter. Phil Brown played the part of Tom Wingfield.]

103. To Walter Edwin Dakin

[45 Via Aurora, Rome]
May 17, 1948
[TLS, 2 pp. HTC]

Dear Grandfather:

Your letter made me feel quite sad for you. I hope you are not more than temporarily depressed, for that is not like you. I am not at all pleased with your apparent decision to stay in America. I would so much rather you came over with Mother and Dakin for I don't think there is anyone in the world who enjoys travelling as much as you do. Please think it over, reconsider, and let me <u>and</u> Audrey know. Audrey has wonderful connections with travel agencies and she can make all the arrangements for your passage by ship or by air. If you are really afraid of an ocean voyage, then why not let Audrey buy you a round-trip plane ticket which is not more expensive and which only takes about 18 hours. Mother says you are not going because you are "afraid of being buried at sea". Now that is ridiculous! In the first place you would not die. In the second place we would make sure that you were returned to Grand's side in Ohio. So put that silly idea out of your mind, and take this holiday which is due you after the long winter in Saint Louis. It will make me, personally, ever so much happier to have you there in London. I don't like the English and I am only going out of duty. It is difficult to tear myself away from Italy which is the nearest to heaven that I have ever been, the people so friendly, gentle and gracious and the days so tranquil and sunny. I have an old Jeep that I travel around in. Perhaps I shall drive it to London. Margo is flying to Rome. She will join me here on the 26th and we will go North together, either in the Jeep or by train. You and she could have some nice card-games as you did in New Orleans while I am at rehearsals. Perhaps we could all get a nice apartment together.

So if you feel you really might enjoy the trip, write Audrey a note or have Mother call her long-distance. The trip will be with my compliments, of course, and Audrey will buy the tickets and make the reservations whichever way you decide.

With much love to all of you, Tom.

[The "long winter in Saint Louis" may have led Walter Dakin to travel next to Clarksdale, Mississippi, rather than to London with his daughter and grandson.

This letter was first published in Edwina Dakin Williams's memoir, *Remember Me to Tom*, pp. 224-225.]

104. To James "Jay" Laughlin

[45 Via Aurora, Rome]
May 18, 1948.
[TLS w/ marginalia, 2 pp. Houghton]

Dear Jay:

These days the melancholy task of collecting the wildly scattered papers, letters, manuscripts begun and abandoned, sorting out, throwing away or packing: the sad and exhausting business that always puts a long-drawn period to my stay in a place: wondering if anything is worth keeping except a few letters from friends but not quite daring to obey the impulse to make a bonfire of it all. This stay in Rome has been relatively felicitous. Sunny. Peaceful. I have made some good friends here such as Frederic Prokosch and that unhappy young egotist Gore Vidal who is now in Paris and a great number of ephemeral bird-like Italians, sweet but immaterial, like cotton-candy: I shall remember all of them like one person who was very pleasant, sometimes even delightful, but like a figure met in a dream, insubstantial, not even leaving behind the memory of a conversation: the intimacies somehow less enduring than the memory of a conversation, at least seeming that way now, but possibly later invested with more reality: ghosts in the present: afterwards putting on flesh, unlike the usual way. Anyhow, Italy has been a real experience, a psychic adventure of a rather profound sort which I shall be able to define in retrospect only. I also have a feeling it is a real caesura: pause: parenthesis in my life: that it marks a division between two very different parts which I leave behind me with trepidation. The old continuity seems broken off now, by more than just travel and time. I have an insecure feeling more acute than usual. It is certainly not a good point at which to return to Broadway, but that is what I must do after a brief period in London for the Helen Hayes production of "Menagerie". Right after that, in July, I must return to New York for rehearsals of "Summer & Smoke", which is an uncertain quantity.

How right you are about the prizes! They mean nothing to me except that they make the play more profitable. Even so I shall probably not make much out of it. All I made out of "Menagerie" - after taxes and living expenses - was $30,000. If Streetcar had not been a success I would have been broke again in two years. It is evident that I have not been well-managed financially, but there is nothing that I can do about it without devoting my life to personal care of my earnings. It bothers me mostly because there are people I want to help and am not able to as much as I should. - Oh! While I'm on the subject of Streetcar - I thought the first format was infinitely preferable to the second: would it be possible to revert to it if there is another edition? All that I didn't like about the first was the color. The design was quite wonderful. The present is the worst I've ever seen on a New Directions book! I am afraid there must have been a total misunderstanding between Audrey and Creekmore. Unfortunately I was too busy at the time to make my own reactions clear to him.

About the stories: there is one very important change I want to make: the cutting of a certain passage in the story ONE ARM. Windham and I both feel that it cheapens the story, it is the #5 of my typed manuscript with the sentence: "They gave him half a tumbler of whiskey to loosen his tongue" and it ends on page seven with phrase: "assured the youth's conviction and doomed him to the chair". It was put into the story later and can be removed without affecting the continuity. Please make sure this deletion is made on the proofs. It concerns the blue-movie which was made on the broker's yacht and it really cheapens the story.

I suggest that you send me the proofs c/o Hugh Beaumont, H.M. Tennant Ltd., London. (Address is Globe Theatre, I believe.) I am afraid they might not reach me here before I start north in my Jeep with Margo who is arriving on the twenty-sixth. I may even start before she arrives and have her meet me in Paris or London. There is to be a congress of Gypsies near Arles on the 24th of May and I should like very much to see it, as well as the town where Van Gogh wrote and painted the fiercest expressions ever made of this world's terrible glory. I wish that God would allow me to write a play like one of his pictures, but that is asking too much. I am too diffuse, too "morbido" - that wonderful Italian word for soft!

You must get Carson's Ballad for your anthology, but I do not quite know how to get the manuscript for you immediately. Joshua Logan who was to direct her play borrowed it and promised to return it by mail from Florence. As yet he has not done so. Surely there are other copies! It was published twice, first in Harper's Bazaar and again in a collection of stories selected by authors as the story they would like to have written. Kay Boyle selected Carsons. If you want to use one of mine, use "Desire & The Black Masseur" which is probably the best.

Carson and I exchange letters continually and we talk about making a home together. I doubt however that we could agree upon a location. She likes places near New York: I could not live anywhere that close to Broadway and continue to function as anything loosely resembling an artist.

Windham's novel is the finest thing, in some respects, that I have read in American letters: the quality is totally original. I wish that you were in a position to make him the necessary advance: he would need about a thousand dollars: for it is a book which only New Directions should publish, no one else. It is literature of the first order, the order of angels! However Audrey is sending it around to publishers like Dodd-Mead who have no idea what it is worth artistically, now and to be. I am afraid he will settle with them simply because he needs money. I am lending him some but naturally he is reluctant to take it and anything of that sort is deleterious to a friendship. I am afraid of the book being mutilated by uncomprehending suggestions and demands from a commercial house. I have never quite understood your lack of excitement over Don as a writer. (apparent.) I do understand the difficulty of advancing money, however, when one is not a commercial publisher. That I do understand thoroughly. I am one of those who feel that New Directions has been a notably altruistic concern, the only one that exists. I also feel, however, that Windham's novel would be a sound investment financially as well as artistically if it is handled by an understanding house. Windham is now in Rome [*text obscured*] you will see him here or in Europe.

Ever - 10.

[Audrey Wood informed TW on January 21—when he was ill and in transit—that James Laughlin had agreed to change both the color and design of the *Streetcar* jacket. The second and third printings—"the worst" TW had seen—dispensed with the Lustig design and used brown lettering on a pale green background. With the fourth printing the original abstract design was reproduced on a red background, to the author's apparent satisfaction.

Canceling the passage in "One Arm" cited by TW would have removed all reference to "the blue-movie" made on the broker's yacht, as well as Oliver Winemiller's first exposure to such pornography while a sailor on leave in Marseille. Only the Marseille scene, which occurs in a brothel, and snatches of dialogue from "the blue-movie" were cut in the 1948 edition of *One Arm*—some twenty-eight lines in all.

The *New Republic* would harshly review Laughlin's forthcoming "anthology" (*New Directions Ten,* 1948), with "Desire and the Black Masseur," a story which ends in cannibalism, affording the critic a clever insult: "This little parable is delivered from a straight face, but it would be underrating Williams' showmanship to deny him the neat accomplishment here of providing an antidote to himself" (December 20, 1948).

Reviewers of *The Dog Star*, Donald Windham's first novel, were appreciative but far less enthusiastic than TW.

Typed in the upper margin of page 1 is the notation "Please bill me for 5 copies of your poems: inscribed to myself, Carson, Windham, Margo, Joanna Albus, and mail c/o Audrey Wood or Tennant Ltd in London."]

105. To Audrey Wood

Western Union
Roma
1948 May 21 PM 3 47
[Telegram, 1 p. HRC]

=HEARTILY APPROVE NEGRO COMPANY MENAGERIE TELL MARGO I WILL MEET HER AT AIRPORT LOVE=

=TENNESSEE.

[The "all Negro company" planned to visit "schools and colleges" in the South. There was "little money in this," Audrey Wood observed, but it would set a "fine precedent" (telegram, to TW, May 14, 1948, HRC) for *The Glass Menagerie* and other successful Broadway plays.

Margo Jones was due to arrive in Rome on May 26, 1948.]

106. To Carson McCullers

["on the Orient Express"]
June 8, 1948
[TLS w/ autograph marginalia, 1 p. Duke U]

Dearest Carson:

We are on the Orient Express, Margo Jones and I, travelling North to Paris, then on to London. The very thought of packing and arranging this trip had overwhelmed me but Margo with her amazing feminine competence took over and managed everything for me. All I had to do was collect my papers and letters. (That in itself was job enough for one person). Do you think people like us would ever go <u>anywhere</u> if we didn't have people like Margo pushing and pulling? I shall be in Paris for only two days but I shall finally use some of your letters of introductions which I have kept in my trunk. My first time there I was too ill for society. This time I may be too nervous. I am still as nervous as a cat! Will continue more or less in that condition until I get back to work. Until then the unused energy is a dozen wildcats under the skin. I used to think a lot of sex would release it, but somehow it doesn't at all. But I must settle somewhere to really get down to work in a satisfactory way. Trips and visitors, a continual procession, have kept me distracted and keyed up the last two months in Rome.

Honey, the news of Pancho is terrifying! He is in New York with some mysterious travelling companion staying at a very expensive hotel on Central Park, has called Audrey and everybody to inform them that he is sailing for Europe June 11th, the day I arrive in England. He lands at Liverpool and presumably will come directly to London to look me up. It gives one a feeling of inescapable doom!

How I envy your retreat to the quiet place in Florida. Only retreat is the wrong word for it. It is a wonderful progress. If I have to remain in America next year, I think Key West might be a suitable place? Do you think you would like it there? It is the least commercial of the Florida resorts and the swimming is incomparable, better even than Capri. There is a small and really nice little society of artists and many pleasant little frame houses like the one in Nantucket. Oh, I'm so glad you didn't move into that Connecticutt barn! It is much too close to Broadway for one to ever feel away.

Audrey is so proud and happy that she has secured you this contract with the New Yorker and I am crazy to read the stories. Harper's Bazaar decided not to publish mine but they took a little poem I had written in Italy, almost the only thing that I finished there.

This country is like one continual Watteau rolling past. Now and then a flash of Van Gogh, but rarely quite that intense. I guess his country was mostly in his own crazy head. To get out of one's own crazy head: wouldn't it be nice to know how?

Please be happy and well! (I feel now that you will be.)

Much love - Tenn.

["I have news for you!" Audrey Wood wrote, informing TW that "Pancho is in town!" (June 1, 1948, HRC) and planning to sail for Liverpool on June 11 with an unidentified companion. Carson McCullers also knew of his return to New York and urged TW not to worry: "You have rejected the disorder and fatigue of a Pancho existence" (n.d., Private Collection).

McCullers's plan for a Florida "retreat" did not materialize. With the exception of several brief trips, McCullers remained in Nyack through the spring and summer of 1948. She and Reeves were beginning to reconcile and spend weekends together.

Wood arranged a potentially lucrative contract for McCullers which gave *The New Yorker* "the first reading option" (to TW, May 5, 1948, HRC) on her work for one year. The "little poem" by TW is "Testa Dell' Effebo."

Penned in the upper margin is TW's interim mailing address, "American Express, London, England."]

107. To Audrey Wood

[Cumberland Hotel, London]
[June 13, 1948]
[TL, 2 pp. HRC]

Dear Audrey:

I guess England is about the most unpleasant, uncomfortable and expensive place in the world you could be right now, and this is especially true on a Sunday which seems to be regulated by the society of Scotch Protestants who made such a fuss over Princess Elizabeth's scandalous day in Paris. When I finished work, in my usual state of nerves, I went downstairs to find a bar and a drink. It was ten after two and there wasn't a drink to be had in all of London until seven. I had to take a couple of barbital tablets instead. - Binkie Beaumont is not in town, Helen has not yet arrived but I have met Gielgud and the prospective gentleman caller. He is a big fellow, about 35 I should guess, with a rather weak-looking mouth but otherwise looks okay. I thought his speech was distinctly British but the British thought it was distinctly American, so there you are. Where are you? I feel quite unnecessary here. I was not asked to hear the young man read but was told that he would rehearse with us starting Tuesday and if found unsatisfactory could be replaced. I suggested that it might be diplomatic to allow Miss Hayes to feel that she was having some part in the selection as she is accustomed to some authority of that kind and it was agreed that this might indeed be a more flattering procedure. When I arrived in town there was no word of message and there was reserved for me at the Cumberland the barest and ugliest single room that I've ever seen outside of a YMCA. There wasn't even a bed-lamp. The hotel is like a Statler except there is no laundry or valet service in less than a week's time. When Margo and I called on Gielgud he announced that Josh Logan was in town and that he was consulting him "about the original production" which he hoped not to duplicate in any way. He seemed to ignore the fact that Margo had been co-director of the original show. He seems a frightfully nervous high-handed prima donna type of person, like Guthrie, and I don't feel that I could possibly control or influence him in anyway. Perhaps Helen can. I shall stay around for the first week of rehearsal if Helen wishes, but after that I think I may as well quietly withdraw. I take it the management is not paying my expenses here. Has the advance gone to the States? I heard no more about it since signing the papers. For me it is going to be an enormously expensive trip for the exchange is unfavorable and everything high as a cat's back. - I am glad I am going to get this monthly bank statement from now on as I can keep better track of what I am spending. Please keep them informed at the bank of my address. I still have about a thousand left on my five thousand dollar letter of credit but I doubt it will last me until I leave Europe, not at the rate that money dissolves around here and I am quite incapable of learning the relative values of all these crazy coins, bobs, half crowns, ten shillings, quids, Etc. When Margo deserts me I shall be in total chaos!

What shall I do about the letter of credit when it runs out? Can I get another one from the bank? Can I draw from Tennent? What will Tennent do with my royalties when the show opens? Etc. Etc. Etc.

How much money, in the way of outright gifts to friends such as Windham, is deductible from taxes, when they are used for creative purposes? Please get Colton's statement on this, the exact or approximate amount that I can give away with exemption. I want to help my indigent friends as much as possible now while I have a lot of money coming in.

DID PANCHO SAIL ON THE MEDEA? Please cable me if he did so I can put on a fright wig and a set of whiskers. I'm afraid I would just drop dead at the sight of that character!!

Have seen Irene. She's the only one here who was really particularly pleasant to us, especially Margo.

With love,

[TW and Margo Jones arrived in London late in the week of June 6 after touring Capri and Ischia and spending several days in Paris. Audrey Wood placed TW under strict orders to attend rehearsals of *The Glass Menagerie*: "Helen Hayes is making a tremendous gesture towards you as a writer" (June 1, 1948, HRC). Following a two-week tryout in Brighton, the play was set to open in London on July 28 with a cast of three Americans and one Canadian.

Wood cabled TW on June 16 that his unsatisfactory hotel would be changed and that Pancho Rodriguez was still in New York. Unbeknown to Wood, TW had recently met an aspiring young actor who would prove a more tenacious and important friend. In *Five O'Clock Angel* (1990), her memoir cum letters, Maria Britneva (later the Lady St. Just) recalls having befriended a "little man" who "looked unassuming and vulnerable" (St. Just, p. xviii) at a party given by John Gielgud. She and TW would soon exchange letters and begin to travel together.

This letter bears a reception date of June 16, 1948.]

108. To Carson McCullers

SH: Savoy Hotel London
July 5, 1948
[TLS w/ autograph marginalia
and postscript, 7 pp. Duke U]

Dearest Carson:

Found your letter waiting for me when I returned to the hotel just now from a rainy weekend at one of the great manor-houses of England where I was guest of an immensely wealthy old member of Parliament who married into the Guinness beer fortune, got rid of the lady but kept the fortune. The place is of Georgian period and somehow I felt suddenly as if I had walked into the setting of an Isak Dinesen tale, one of the Gothic ones, probably the one about the old lady that turned into a lively monkey and scrambled up the wall in the last scene: pure enchantment! The house was built so long and it seems to have absorbed the lives of many strange and wonderful and rather secretive people. For a while, after the owning family died out, it was turned into a nunnery. Then two young nuns were found drowned in the little swan-lake. This tragedy blighted the place: everyone said it was haunted. Ghosts were certainly walking the night I was there! I had an immense chamber with a regally canopied bed in a room that had once been the chapel of the house. I locked my door but about two A.M. while I was lying in bed reading <u>Proces de Bourbons</u> - a record of Marie Antoinette's trial - I heard stealthy footsteps. My blood ran icy! They stopped right outside my door. The doorknob turned very slowly: discovered the lock: then slowly turned back again and the footsteps, even lighter than before - withdrew! In the morning I discovered it was not a ghost but the host! - bringing me a hot drink and toast. A great joke was made about this, but I was too sleepy to really enjoy it.

I seem to have met practically everyone <u>but</u> Truman Capote. I have heard from several other sources that he has met <u>me</u>. Can I have been sleep-walking? For I have not consciously had that pleasure on this side of the Atlantic. It is mistyfying extremely. Aren't you allowing yourself to judge this little boy a bit too astringently? I know you must have reasons which I don't know of. I see him as an opportunist and a careerist and a derivative writer whose tiny feet have attempted to fit the ten-league boots of Carson McCullers and succeeded only in tripping him up absurdly. But surely not one of the <u>bad</u>-boys! His little face, as photographed by Cecil

Beaton against a vast panorama of white roses, has a look of pre-natal sorrow as if he were still in the womb and already suspected how cold the world is beyond the vaginal portals.

The writers I have seen here are Christopher Isherwood, E.M. Forster and, of course, Gore Vidal. Unfortunate things happened. Cristopher is going through a sort of unhappy climacteric. The sweetness has temporarily gone out of his nature and he felt called upon to tell Gore, very obliquely and through the mouth of his intimate companion, that he did not think Gore's work of paramount importance. Gore is not able to take this kind of criticism. A real crise developed. Gore spent three sleepless nights, and then left England.

Finally I met your bushy-faced friend, Bebe Berard, and I found him awfully nice. It was at one of the big London parties so we had only a short while to talk, but only of you. I told him that you adored him. He was deeply affected, for it seems that he has the same feeling for you. I saw a ballet that he had designed and it was the most beautiful decor I have seen.

France and Italy are full of your books, prominently displayed in every bookshop, but they are not yet distributed much in England. Why is that? Have you an agent here to look after your interests? Would you like me to investigate this?

I think I have, at long last, found the right hooks for a play but it will or may take me at least a year and a half or even two years to finish it for I know that it cannot be a repetition of what I have said before and yet it has to be a southern character portrait. I must believe in the possibility of such a thing being possible.

It is a small world with Pancho in it! There is a young man here who loaned him ninety dollars to pay a hotel bill in New York and he is still trying to recover it. It seems that Pancho became involved with two very wealthy women but they are now disillusioned and Pancho, at last report, was headed back South again. He reminds me rather pathetically of a bull in the arena with his black hide full of fancy darts from the picadors, charging madly this way and that, wherever the red silk flashes until finally sometime the sword behind the red silk will put a stop to him. A brave and wonderful black bull - but I am not a bull-fighter! My veronicas were not as quick as the horns.

I now look forward, actually, to returning to the States, provided this report is accurate of the southern withdrawal. By the time I arrive the play will be in rehearsal which will keep me in New York most of the time. That is why I suggested you go to the sea now, someplace where I could join you for week-ends. But if you are comfortable and happy and at work in Nyack I understand you're wanting to stay there.

New Mown Hay and Mouchoir de Monsieur. I now have that fixed in my mind. I am tak[ing] ten days on the continent, at least passing through Paris, before the London opening and I will get the perfume for dear Cheryl as a bottled distillation of our mutual love for her.

Ever lovingly yours, Tennessee.

My week-end host was described by a catty friend as "a rose-baked sissy (city), half as old as time" which is a paraphrase of a line in some poem about Rome. funny?!!

[The manor house where TW was a guest reminded him of a "stately" old convent in Isak Dinesen's story "The Monkey" (1934).

Carson McCullers's early friendship with Truman Capote had been damaged by jealousy and a perception that *Other Voices, Other Rooms* was unduly imitative of her work, if not plagiarized. She warned TW that Capote "writes his friends (not me) that he is seeing you. What a opportunist that boy is - without any honor, or the minimum of dignity" (n.d., Private Collection).

Andrew Lyndon, a mutual friend, recalls that TW first saw Capote at a party in New York in 1947 and said admiringly, "'Baby, I think your little friend is charming! Just charming!'" (qtd. in Clarke, *Capote: A Biography*, 1988, p. 177). He and Capote would soon meet in Paris and return to the States on the *Queen Mary* amid laughter and high jinks (see *Memoirs*, pp. 150-151).

William Caskey, Christopher Isherwood's companion, thought Gore Vidal "typical American prep school." The three met in Paris in the preceding April when Vidal introduced himself and asked Isherwood "'how to manage'" (qtd. in *Diaries*, 1996) his career. E.M. Forster considered *Streetcar* a dull play to read but looked forward to "seeing it on the stage" (Forster to Isherwood, June 25, 1948, Huntington).

Christian Bébé Bérard designed sets and costumes for the London premiere of *Clock Symphony* (June 25, 1948), the ballet to which TW probably refers. His famous sets for *The Madwoman of Chaillot* (1945) were brought to New York for the 1948 production.

Pressure to diversify his theatre led TW to experiment with a biographical subject—Huey P. Long, the "Kingfish" of Louisiana politics—in "The Big Time Operators." His role as a corrupted idealist would be assumed by Chance Wayne in *Sweet Bird of Youth*. TW later noted that he did not envision the female lead as "the faded lily type of typical Williams heroine."

The perfume was intended as a gift for the producer Cheryl Crawford, a friend of McCullers who had recently advised her on staging *The Member of the Wedding*.

Penned in the upper margin of page 1 is the notation "Address me c/o H.M. Tennent Ltd., Globe Theatre, London."]

109. To Eric Bentley

SH: Royal Crescent Hotel
Brighton. [England]
July 12, 1948
[TLS, 3 pp. HRC]

Dear Mr. Bentley:

Yours is a kind of criticism that the theatre desperately needs and which is supplied by few others. However that is all the more reason why certain questionable attitudes of yours should be contested.

I think the most serious of these are two: first, a lack of respect for the extra-verbal or non-literary elements of the theatre, the various plastic elements, the purely visual things such as light and movement and color and design, which play, for example, such a tremendously important part in theatre such as Lorca's and which are as much a native part of drama as words and ideas are. I don't believe you are guilty of this, but I have read criticism in which the use of transparencies and music and subtle lighting effects, which are often as meaningful as pages of dialogue, were dismissed as "cheap tricks and devices". Actually all of these plastic things are as valid instruments of expression in the theatre as words, and needless to say, they add immeasurably to the general appeal: fortunately or unfortunately, I am not sure which, a general appeal is necessary and can and should be made for the sake of reaching more people without any vulgarization. On the other hand, it is easy for vulgarity to creep in, sometimes without the author's cognizance: there are many entrances for that sly actor!

Your other mistaken tendancy in my opinion is a curiously literal interpretation of things that have symbolic implication. I think that you were unfair to All My Sons in your Harper's Survey of the Theatre because you regarded the letter from the dead pilot son as purely and simply a letter instead of as a psychological revelation being objectified for dramatic purposes. I saw that play three times in New York and again here in London and was each time more profoundly moved by its superb structure, its continual and building tension, the boldness with which idea and meaning was translated into action and object: the memorial broken in the storm: the horoscope prepared by the superstitious neighbor: the grape drink served in the arbor: - finally, by the time the letter and the suicide came along I was prepared fully to accept these superficially melodramatic occurences as symbols or concentrations of time and discovery and fate. Likewise it appeared that in my own play you were interpreting the black-suited figures in the final scene, which could have been death or any other form of fatal consequence, a bit too literally, as I had tried to make them abstract as possible. However the leniency we always have toward our own creation when under attack by others may enter into this argument.

I have seen in London the new play by your favorite Sartre. It is a great success, moving from the suburban Lyric Hammersmith to the West End very soon. You may be shocked by some of the purely theatrical dynamics in this play. I think it is Sartre's finest piece of theatre, and the intellectual freshness and purity is really quite wonderful. I have heard that Kermit Bloomgarten has bought it for New York and I should think Montgomery Clift would be perfect for the male lead. Here it is called Crime Passionel but in Paris it had a much better title: Mains Sales.

Best wishes, Tennessee Williams

[English-born and educated at Oxford and Yale, Eric Bentley (b. 1916) reviewed theatre for *Harper's Magazine* in the late 1940s and served as drama critic for the *New Republic* from 1952 to 1956. He has also published widely as an editor, translator, anthologist, and playwright.

All My Sons (1947) and *Streetcar* were among the plays cited by Bentley in *Harper's* annual theatre review for 1947-1948. Quite ironically, he thought, Arthur Miller had solved the problem of moral responsibility in *All My Sons* by the evasive technique of "a letter in which ALL is revealed." TW avoided such "cliches" in *Streetcar* and nearly crossed "the borderline of really good drama." The last scene answered Bentley's decisive question, "how deep does the play go? The episode of the black-coated couple from the madhouse compels the answer: not very" (March 1948). Bentley and TW would clash in the mid 1950s with a threat of legal action (see letter #300).]

110. To Helen Hayes

Hotel de l'Université
Rue de l'Université, Paris
30 July, 1948
[TLS, 2 pp. Private Collection]

Dear Helen:

It is hard for me to tell from the notices sent me this morning, which are very, very English, just how things went for the play but there can be no doubt that you had a resounding reception, and that is what I most wanted. Will you forgive me for not being there? I don't think Audrey or Mother will, but I am counting on your understanding, though I must, and most shamefully, admit that I do not altogether understand myself how I happened not to manage to make it. You may put this down to my "pixy behavior" and nobody knows better than I do that I have carried it much, much, much too far! I had looked forward to it intensely for such a long time: then the last few days I became enveloped in a cloud. Overwork. Nerves. A sort of paralysis. I had bought a ticket (plane) through a travel agency and was to pick it up the day before the flight. I work hard all that day. I suddenly remember I am to pick up the ticket. I rush out and suddenly I cannot remember the name or location of the travel-agency. Only Gore Vidal knows, for it was his agent. I cannot find Gore, he is out on the town. Finally, at seven P.M., I locate him by phone. He tells me where the agency is. I rush there. The agency is shut for the night. More rushing and stewing. Finally I find another agency which happens to be still open. I say I must get to London by seven P.M. tomorrow. Only one booking is available and that is on a plane at seven the next morning. Good, marvelous! I take it. All that night I sit up in my clothes, working and drinking black coffee so I will not miss the plane. About dawn I get queer sensations, palpitations: I think I am having a heart-attack. I rush to the bathroom and swallow a handfull of barbital tablets, almost a lethal dose, to quiet this nerve-crisis. I am hardly back from the bathroom when the black-out commences and I do not come out of it until several hours after the plane has left. From two until five in the afternoon I wait at the Gare des Invalides for a possible cancellation on some plane that might still get me into London in time for the play. No luck.

All this adds up to another terrific gaucherie on the part of Tennessee, and I apologize for burdening you with an account of it. I only want you to know that I had, in Brighton, one of the truly deeply satisfying adventures of my life and to thank you for it from the bottom of a contrite heart.

Ever, Tennessee.

[A "terrific gaucherie" led TW to miss the opening of *The Glass Menagerie* on July 28. Perhaps he foresaw, as did Helen Hayes, that the Gielgud production would not repeat the success of the original. He also found London "dull" and the English "stuffy" and had discovered a more engaging situation in Paris. Gore Vidal was already in attendance and Truman Capote was expected from Italy. Sartre proved an elusive celebrity, but TW met Jean Cocteau and his companion, the actor Jean Marais.

The *Times* (London) reviewer was typical in his selective praise and invidious marking of national boundaries. Hayes had made "a great acting part out of conversational bromides," while *The Glass Menagerie* itself evolved "slow and sure in a very American way." Americans, the reviewer inferred, "must be the most patient of peoples" (July 29, 1948), if this Broadway hit were any indication. Binkie Beaumont assured TW that while the reviews were "not terribly impressive," the "general atmosphere" of the production was "one of great success" and business "excellent." The producer urged him not to "slip quietly back to America" (August 3, 1948, HRC) without making a return visit.]

111. To Walter Edwin Dakin

SH: Summer and Smoke Company
250 West 57th Street
New York 19, N.Y.
August 13, 1948.
[ALS, 4 pp. Columbia U]

Dear Grandfather -

It grieves me dreadfully to think of you spending a hot summer in Clarksdale when you could be so much more comfortable here or in some place like Monteagle.

Please take this check and remove yourself to cooler quarters. I am sure it will make you feel better and stronger. Heat can be debilitating even to a chicken, which you are not, exactly, though still the young member of the family.

The Menagerie seems to be a success in London, selling out every night. Miss Hayes is not as good as Laurette Taylor but she is as good as any living actress. Lady Sibyl Colfax gave a dinner for Miss Hayes and me the opening night but as she did not invite the other members of the cast, I did not go. In fact, I remained in Paris and only came to London a couple of days before sailing for New York. I don't see how it is possible to mix Socialism and snobbism but the English manage to do it. I don't like them much.

Mother was in Paris when I left and was planning a short trip to Switzerland. I expect she'll be back here late this month. Dakin is also travelling and that is probably why you have not heard from him. Margo and Audrey send their love and we all wish you were here - and expect you soon. Wire me your plans when you make them. My address is 235 E. 58 and my phone number is El. 5-1570.

Much, much, much love - Tom.

[Persistent doubts led TW to propose that he take over direction of *Summer and Smoke* and that Margo Jones attend to production. She refused and banished the meddlesome author from rehearsals: "'I am the director and you better know that. You get off the stage, Tennessee'" (qtd. in Sheehy, *Margo*, 1989, p. 169). Tryouts in Buffalo, Detroit, and Cleveland were critically well received and indicated a successful premiere in New York (October 6).

Monteagle, in southeastern Tennessee, is near the University of the South, where Walter Dakin studied theology as a young man.

After watching Helen Hayes in tryouts of *The Glass Menagerie*, TW accurately predicted that she will "score a big hit in London. . . . If one still remembers Laurette a bit more vividly than he sees Helen that does not mean she is not wonderful" (to Kazan, July 19, 1948, WUCA).

Although aged, ill, and financially strapped, Lady Sibyl Colefax entertained visiting celebrities in London until her death in 1950.]

112. To Justin Brooks Atkinson

235 E. 58 Street [New York]
October 10, 1948
[TLS, 2 pp. BRTC]

Dear Brooks:

Margo says she has already thanked you for coming to our rescue but I want to add mine. I doubt that there is any gratitude much greater than an author's for his one or two good notices in a storm of bad ones. Yours was not only good, it was beautiful, and not only beautiful but inspiring, for it made me feel that there was definitely some use in my continuing to try to bring poetic feeling into my work.

I do not at all agree with Maxwell Anderson's opinion that the critics have thrown a blanket over the poetic theatre but it is obvious that some of them are not doing it much intentional good and that is a pity for I think it is apparent that many theatre-goers are hungry for the difference that lyricism makes in plays. *Summer* has painful deficiencies: it often seems to me like a graceful cripple, but in a way I love it best of my plays. It is, in a way, the most affirmative: that is, spiritually affirmative, and although some reviews call it juvenile, it strikes me as the most grown-up in its thinking and feeling. The juvenile quality may be an awkwardness that ~~I am afraid always~~ goes with the handling of romantic material in such an unromantic age. And if it offered nothing else but a part for Margaret Phillips, I feel it would offer enough to make it welcome on Broadway. But with Phillips and Jo's set and Paul's music and Margo's tender direction, I do not quite see why six of the critics took such strong exception to it. Actually there was only one of the notices that made me mad. I guess you know which one I am talking about: I didn't read it but was told the contents. The others I felt were written in genuine disappointment which puzzles and troubles me but does not anger me at the writers. I wish it were possible to get some of them to go back again, for I have discovered while on the road with the show, that opinions would frequently improve at a second exposure, and if we could now get some friendlier follow-up articles I think the play might have a good chance of catching on here. Business so far has been very good, but of course they may be just rushing to see it in expectation of its imminent closing, and the audience response has been much warmer than opening night.

Rehearsals and the road-tour have made a jarring hiatus in my work, which I must now get back to. The new project is exciting but still in the woods and it will take more strength in each finger than I now have at this moment in my whole tired body!

My best regards to Orianne, as well as to you,

Ever, Tennessee.

[*Variety's* opening day headline—"Tenn. Williams' Take-Home Pay Now $7,500 WKLY" (October 6, 1948)—may have raised expectations of another smash hit, but only Atkinson found dramatic virtue in *Summer and Smoke*. The play was "charged with passion and anguish" and revealed once again TW's "almost unbearably lucid" (*New York Times*, October 7, 1948) knowledge of his characters. "Mawkish, murky, maudlin and monotonous" were the more typical descriptions of a play which seemed "juvenile" to many reviewers and compared unfavorably with *Streetcar*—still running strongly on Broadway. It was probably Robert Garland who angered TW by dubbing *Summer and Smoke* "'A Kiddy-Kar Called Conversation'" (*Journal American*, October 7, 1948). Critics praised the leads for having survived a "garrulous" script, while Margo Jones's "tender direction," as TW put it, received mixed notices.

Rehearsal of Summer and Smoke *(1948): Tennessee Williams, Margaret Phillips, Margo Jones, and Tod Andrews.*

Maxwell Anderson wrote in the aftermath of a savage attack on *Truckline Café* (1946), which closed after thirteen performances on Broadway. He protested the "enormous increase in the reviewers' power" and their virtual "censorship over the theatre" (*New York Times*, February 16, 1947).

The "exciting" new work is almost certainly "The Big Time Operators." A related script entitled "the puppets of the levantine" (n.d., HRC) was partially typed on letterhead of the "Summer and Smoke Company."]

113. To Margaret "Margo" Jones

235 East 58th Street
New York, N.Y.
October 27, 1948
[TLS, 1 p. HRC]

Dear Margo:

I drop in the play almost every night, and it seems to be holding up. Maggie says she is experimenting because she is not yet satisfied with her interpretation and feels she can do even better. Hank has taken her to task for this saying that the performance must not be allowed to vary from opening night. I think this a great mistake because the actors will remain interested if they feel some flexibility remains. They should be encouraged to work for new values as long as the established line is not altered. I have not observed any letdown whatsoever in their spirit of performance.

Now I want to take up what I suppose is a rather delicate matter. And since no delicacy is required between you and me, I will say plainly that I think you did a wrong thing in discharging and replacing Ellen James without my knowledge or consent, which, according to the Dramatists Guild contract, is one of the author's inalienable rights. You are about the only person in show business whose motives I never question. But your procedure is sometimes reminiscent of the Shuberts. How is that for plain speaking? Ha-ha. Ellen James is one of the plus qualities, and we don't have any plus qualities that we can safely throw out. I have seen the other girl and heard her read. She is a marvelous understudy for Maggie, and I heartily agree about hiring her in that capacity. The additional expense of retaining Ellen James in her present role is very slight. Liebling says she can be kept for $75.00 a week. I think we should do it. That is all I have to say about that.

I know that you are deep in the heart of Moliere. I shall soon be deep in the heart of North Africa or Italy. I have bought a new car, a Buick convertible, and I am trying to persuade grandfather to go abroad with me. Carson goes to court Friday. She is being sued for $50,000. She doesn't have $5.00. Quelle vie!

Love, Tenn.

TW/c

["Baffled and hurt," Margo Jones answered TW's rebuke by quoting a line from "The Purification" (1944): "'If men keep honor, the rest can be arranged.'" She had "tried to live up to this and if I have failed - since honor is more than a word between us - there must surely be a way to understand each other again" (November 3, 1948, Private Collection). Jones might have added that Ellen James, the actor whose firing TW disapproved, had drawn no critical attention for her brief appearance in Scene Three. A wire from TW wishing Jones "mad success" (November 6, 1948, HRC) for an opening in Dallas may have eased the tension, but it did not discharge his resentment over the critical failure of *Summer and Smoke*.

TW wrote a flurry of letters on October 27, including one to his grandfather, who had returned to the Friends Home in Waynesville, Ohio: "Perhaps after Christmas . . . I shall go gypsying about Italy and North Africa. How would you like to join me? Is your gypsy instinct still that strong?" (October 27, 1948, Columbia U).

Carson McCullers and her former collaborator, Greer Johnson, agreed to submit their disputed contract to arbitration. A finding of November 8, 1948, held the contract to be in force for one year and empowered the Theatre Guild to produce *The Member of the Wedding* during that time using the joint script (see Carr, p. 311).]

114. To James "Jay" Laughlin

235 East 58th Street
New York, N.Y.
October 27, 1948
[TLS, 1 p. Houghton]

Dear Jay:

Please remember not to let ONE ARM be displayed for sale in bookstores. When I heard that Miss Steloff had ordered 200 copies, I became alarmed with visions of you and I pinned up like our one-armed hero. I hope that the book will be distributed as we planned, entirely by subscription. Let me know how you plan to distribute it. It is the most beautiful book you have yet made, and I am crazy about it.

Call me as soon as you can.

Sincerely, T. Williams

[Publication of *One Arm* was delayed by an incorrect copyright statement which Audrey Wood immediately noticed. The printing must be recalled, she wrote, lest the error "cause the stories to fall into the public domaine" (to Laughlin, October 27, 1948, HRC). Tipped into first edition copies of *One Arm* was "A SPECIAL

REQUEST" asking that the collection be sold "by personal solicitation and subscription rather than by general display. We are particularly anxious that the book should not be displayed in windows or on open tables."

In 1943 TW worked briefly for Frances Steloff, owner of the Gotham Book Mart, proving himself an inept clerk.]

115. To Walter Dakin Williams

235 East 58th Street
New York, N.Y.
October 27, 1948
[TLS, 1 p. HTC]

Dear Grandfather:

I am dictating just a short note to let you know I am well and satisfied with the outcome of the play production although it has left me feeling rather exhausted. Margo has gone back to Texas, but I am watching over the show. I was dreadfully disappointed that you were not here when I came back.

I want you to know that I have purchased a beautiful new car, a maroon-colored Buick convertible, at a bargain price, and we are going to take some kind of trip in it as soon as the situation here permits me to leave. Perhaps after Christmas I shall return to Europe and take the car with me and go gypsying about Italy and North Africa. How would you like to join me? Is your gypsy instinct still that strong? How would you like to come back to New York after you leave Waynesville? I am sure you remember Libby Holman, whom we visited in Connecticut. She has gone on tour and says she would love for us to stay at her house while she is gone. We would have a full staff of servants at our disposal, and, of course, my car. She and her mother send you their particular love and all of your many friends here speak of you continually and ask to be remembered to you.

Devotedly, Tom

[Edward Colton later advised against a trust for Rose Williams, citing technical problems which might leave her unprotected in future years (to TW, November 30, 1948, HTC). Precisely how the legal issues were resolved is unclear.

Investigation of private care for Rose led to correspondence with the director of Stamford Hall in Connecticut, who stated weekly costs "in the range $75 to $100" (Moore to Colton, November 4, 1948, HTC). Edwina warned TW not to "do anything that will jeopardize your own financial security. I haven't laboured, and prayed, over it all these years just to see it dissipated" (November 28, 1948, Private Collection).]

116. To Jessica Tandy

[235 East 58th Street, New York]
November 2, 1948.
[TLSx, 1 p. Leavitt, p. 77]

Dear Jessica:

Many, many thanks for your letter on the Benton picture. You are so right that it really makes me ashamed of having lent my casual support to the idea. What you say about Blanche suddenly recalls to me all of my original conception of the character and what it was to me, from which you, in your delineation, have never once drifted away in spite of what I now realize must have been a continual pressure: that unwillingness of audiences to share a more intricate and special and sensitive response to things: their desire to participate more safely, familiarly, in the responses of an animal nature. I have almost forgotten (perhaps under this same pressure) that it was Blanche whom I loved and respected and whom I wished to portray, though I have never, please believe me, forgotten the exact and tender and marvelously understanding way that you brought her to life. -- I have such a divided nature! Irreconciliably divided. I look at Benton's picture and I see the strong things in it, its immediate appeal to the senses, raw, sensual, dynamic, and I forgot the play was really about those things which are opposed to that, the delicate half-approaches to something much finer. Yes, the painting is only one side of the play, and the Stanley side of it. Perhaps from the painter's point of view that was inevitable. A canvas cannot depict two worlds very easily: or the tragic division of the human spirit: at least not a painter of Benton's realistic type. Well, I am still an admirer of the painting, but, believe me, still more an admirer of yours for seeing and feeling about it more clearly than I did at first, and I should have felt the same way.

With love, Tennessee.

[The Thomas Hart Benton painting was both a Christmas present for Irene Selznick (from her estranged husband, David) and a publicity gimmick designed to launch *Streetcar* on the second year of its profitable run. *Look* magazine published the

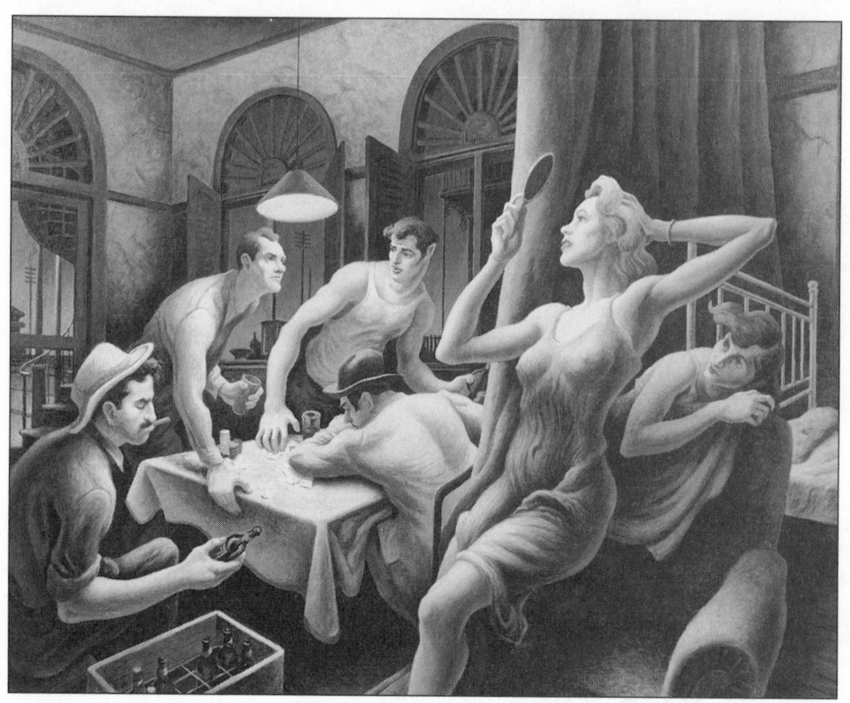

The Poker Night: *"Mr. Benton has naturally chosen to represent the brutal aspects of 'Streetcar.'"*

painting on February 1, 1949, with remarks by TW which echoed a recent controversy. Jessica Tandy (1909-1994) had declined to pose for a photographic duplication of the painting on the grounds that it would confirm Benton's unbalanced view of *Streetcar* and "lead future audiences to think that they are going to see sex in the raw." At issue was Tandy's claim that Benton's choice of the Poker Night scene emphasized the "Stanley side" (to TW, n.d., Leavitt, p. 77) of the play to the near exclusion of Blanche's more demanding role. TW's note in *Look* ends diplomatically with praise for Benton's painting and tacit approval of Tandy's objection: "Mr. Benton has naturally chosen to represent the brutal aspects of 'Streetcar' and he has done a colorful and dynamic job of it. It exists as a painting, quite apart from its connection with the play, and that is as it should be" (p. 79).]

117. To Audrey Wood

[53 Arundel Place
Clayton, Missouri]
November 18, 1948
[TLS, 2 pp. HRC]

Dear Audrey:

I came home to find Grandfather practically as well as ever, and was vastly relieved on that account.

Since I got here I have been working on the average of six or eight hours a day. This evening even working on the graveyard shift! And have accomplished, I think, a good deal. It now looks as if "The Big Time Operators", which is the present title of play, might have a fairly complete first draft sometime this Spring, and I hope it won't take more than one re-writing. The story is not at all biographical but the material is drawn mostly from Huey Long, showing the main character in a mostly sympathetic light as a man very close to the people, fantastically uninhibited, essentially honest, but shackled with a corrupt machine and machine-boss. As a good half of the play deals with him as a young man (about 29, when first elected Governor) - though actually Long was a bit older than that - I am thinking now about Marlon Brando as in every respect but age the part fits him perfectly. D'you think he could put on age in a part to be acceptable at the end of the play as a man in his late thirties? - The age when Long died, I think. The combination of Kazan and Brando would be a stimulating assurance to work with. Would it be wise to approach Brando about his commitments or plans for next Fall, so he would keep this in mind as a pregnant possibility for him? Knowing that he would be free would be an encouragement. - The girl's part is very young: something like Anne Jackson but with a bit more pathos and delicacy, though she is not at all the faded lily type of typical Williams heroine. And I think there is a good part in it for Sidney Greenstreet as the corrupt but suave boss.

I would like for Tiz to try and get me the following reference works. Two biographies which I now have from the St. Louis library. "Huey Long: A Candid Biography" published by Dodge and written by Forrest Davis. "The Kingfish - Huey P. Long, Dictator" by Thomas O. Harris, published by the Pelican Publishing company, 339 Carondelet St. in New Orleans. Also two books written by Long himself which are called "Every Man a King" and the other "My First Days in the White House". I don't know where these books are obtainable but I should think the information could be gotten from the library information desk or even Secty. of Louisiana, who might also be able to supply us with some "Memorial Volumes" which contain Long's speeches. I am going through Washington on my way back to New York and probably can pick up some material or books there. I have avoided, and will avoid reading, all fiction about Long as I don't want any unconscious coloration to creep into the play, and my character, Père Polk, will be pretty much my own creation with just as much of the Kingfish as I find theatrically enticing. For one thing he has plenty of sex-appeal, and that's what made me think of Brando for it.

This basement, or rathskeller, is a wonderful place to work! Right back of my table is Dakin's real "Seeburg" jukebox with colored lights and everything, which he bought out of a bar in one of his less judicious moments. I have played it constantly and got the mechanism all screwed up, but it still plays, however capriciously, sometimes stopping right in the middle of one record and starting another and sometimes not stopping at all. Since I threw a book at Dakin when he appeared on the stairs a few days ago I have been relatively unmolested. The jukebox, the typewriter, Grandfather and I are putting up a solid front - oh, yes, and a quart bottle of Old Taylor which I keep in reach but out of sight!

I plan to be back in New York about Thursday. Where is the Streetcar party now going to be, I wonder? - Tomorrow is my sister's birthday so we will probably drive out to the Snake Pit. The $650. a month places are out of the question. Are there no reasonable ones?

Love, Tenn.

The less said or known about my writing subject and plans the better, I think, at least till finished and copyrighted. - Want to see Sillcox soon as I return about the endowments.

[TW was free to visit Clayton now that Edwina and Cornelius were separated and the latter had departed for Knoxville.

Within a month TW's interest in "The Big Time Operators" had "dissolved," as he later informed Elia Kazan: "I couldn't convince myself that I cared enough about the character and ideas involved to put any fire into the writing" (see letter #140). Biographical subjects such as Huey Long had not proven congenial in the past, nor was TW likely to exceed the popular and critical success of *All the King's*

Men (1946), Robert Penn Warren's recent study of Long which received the Pulitzer Prize for Fiction.

Luise M. Sillcox was the executive secretary of the Authors' League and the affiliated Dramatists' Guild. TW planned to establish a fund so that grants could be made to such needy writers as Oliver Evans and Donald Windham.]

118. To Audrey Wood

[*Vulcania*]
Dec. 5, 1948.
[TLS w/ autograph postscript, 2 pp. HRC]

Dear Audrey:

I feel that I did the right thing when I got on this boat because I cannot live within phone-call of Broadway without feeling like a piece of a big machine, and a piece that doesn't fit properly. If I am to live and grow as an artist the direction of my life must be away from involvement in the frighteningly unreal realities of "The professional life". Lately I have felt drained and over-drawn. Being successful and famous makes such demands! I'm not equipped for it. I wanted it and still want it, with one part of me, but that isn't the part of me that is important or creative. I must dedicate myself, my life, to that part of me that is and make fewer, not more, concessions to the other.

You have been the greatest help to me in allowing me this necessary feeling of detachment from the business side of life, and I think that my brother can also be, as he has the legal and business sense that I lack. I hope that eventually you and he together can handle all that side of it between you so that I will not even have to think of it, as thinking of it weighs so heavily on my heart. I have asked him to come to New York, at my expense, and review my whole financial situation with you and Colton, decide about the foundation and the trust for my sister. Naturally you or he will let me know of what decisions are reached about it. Also I want him to study my tax-situation. He speaks Colton's language as he is now employed by a trust company and sits on various boards of corporations and is eminently equipped to judge in all such matters. I want him to get all my statements during my absence. I have never really been able to look at them, I just go blind when I take them out of the envelopes, and this does not make sense. All box-office and bank statements should go to him so I won't have to worry about them at all. This he should do, as I am assuming the obligation of my sister's expensive care and he is also the heir to most of my estate (hypothetical as that may be). There may be certain disagreeable or even inconvenient aspects to this arrangement, but it does or will - I hope - give me a sense of security which I know you will see is the primary consideration. It is unfortunate that I have not been able to feel any security or understanding with Colton. He simply doesn't strike me that way. I know you want me to keep him and I shall but I must have this double check that my brother can give, for while one side of my nature is trustful as a child, the paranoiac side which is full of nervous apprehensions must also be considered if I am to live in peace among the clouds. If a human life-time contained one hundred more years than are ordinarily alloted, I am sure that I could reach a state of grace in which all these impurities would be rendered to ashes.

We have been in the Gulf stream these first three days of the voyage and it is as warm as Florida. I walk on the deck in my shirtsleeves. Work about four hours each morning, getting up at nine o'clock and going to bed at midnight. My tension is already going: the whites of my eyes have turned white again and I can sleep without seconal. Who knows what Africa will do, and the Arabs?

I left two trunks in the apartment which I want to have placed in storage, and various other things such as my Italian-bound copy of Hart Crane which I am afraid is outside the trunk, on the bookshelves in the front room. Joanna said she would be glad to see that these things are all packed away. She or Donnie can take care of my phonograph and my records. The big trunk should be locked and put in storage right away as it contains my journals. I was very loath to see Maria returning to the apartment as she is not a really good friend, I've found out. Bowles says she has been talking about me to Laughlin and others, saying that I am a lost soul that only she can redeem! - Just when I was beginning to think I might be wrong about Women!

There are probably many other things I can think of later, but I shall write as soon as I know which way the blackbird and the clown and I are going. (Blackbird is English for Merlo).

With love, 10.

P.S. Please let me know how "S & S" reacts to the termination of theatre parties. I pray it will not fold up like the tents of the Arabs.

[TW's attempt to allay fears of mismanagement and still remain detached from "the business side of life" is evident in following correspondence with his brother Dakin (see letters #119 and #120). At the same time TW was "very, very anxious" to avoid any rupture with Audrey Wood, whose services were indispensable and far in excess of mere literary representation.

The preceding months in New York were enlivened by Truman Capote, Gore Vidal, and especially Maria Britneva, who arrived in mid-September as TW's guest and reportedly remained to study at the Actors Studio with Elia Kazan. Her penchant for gossip amused TW, save when he was the subject. He later chided her "vocal part" for being "astonishingly active. You seem to say all the things that discreet people only think" (qtd. in St. Just, p. 13).

Earlier in the fall TW had "a quite sudden and accidental and marvelous reencounter with Frank Philip Merlo" (*Memoirs*, p. 155). Of Sicilian descent, the twenty-six-year-old Merlo was born in Elizabeth, New Jersey, and served as a pharmacist mate in the Navy during World War II. With "the blackbird" and Paul Bowles, TW sailed on the *Vulcania* for Gibraltar and Tangier.

Summer and Smoke would not survive the "termination" of advance sales, which insured full houses on a short-term basis. Wood cabled TW at Fez, Morocco, on December 20 that the "weekly gross" was "sufficiently low" to endanger Rose's trust fund and advised a personal deposit of $3,000. On December 28 she reported a "business drop so great" that the play was "suddenly closing" (HRC) on January 1, 1949, after 102 performances—some $60,000 in debt.

The closing of *Summer and Smoke* without consultation shocked Wood, who informed Margo Jones that she could no longer represent her: "I fear you and I look at the so-called professional New York theatre from very different approaches" (January 5, 1949, HRC).]

119. To Walter Dakin Williams

"Vulcania"
Dec. 9, 1948
[TLS w/ enclosure, 1 p. Columbia U]

Dear Dakin:

Sorry I did not have a chance to get a letter off to you before I left New York. I am mailing this to you from Gibralter where we land this evening and at the same time mailing a letter to Audrey to let her know that I want you to make, at my expense, the trip to New York to confer with Colton about the trust fund for Rose (a half interest in Summer and Smoke) and also to get a clear picture of my financial situation particularly regarding taxes and the possible establishment of a foundation, a matter which

Audrey wanted me to discuss with an accountant before I left but which I did not have time to go into before sailing. Before any tax payments are made I want you to have a complete report on what these payments are to be. I, too, want to be informed of the amount of these payments before they are made, if necessary by cable, so that I will be morally and nervously prepared for my subsequent impoverishment, unlike last year when I only learned post facto. Please make every effort to exhaust all devices to save money on my taxes. I know this is asking a good deal of you, but since I am now to assume the financial responsibility for Rose I know you will see it is important, and fair, that everything be done to secure my finances so that I can continue this responsibility. I left a large envelope of various and miscellaneous business statements in the apartment with your name on it. This envelope contains all papers pertaining to my finances that I could find on the place, bank statements and box-office statements, and during my absence you will receive these statements which would otherwise be directed to me. I want you to hold them for me in Saint Louis till I get back to the States. If outside help appears necessary in tackling my tax-problem (an accountant or tax expert) I want you to call one in. Remember - or remind Colton - that all my living expenses in New York this last time should be deductible as I was there on business, the production of Summer and Smoke. Also much of my travelling expenses in Europe last year should be deductible, England for the Menagerie and France to collect royalties and arrange the future production of Streetcar. This is all I can think of at the moment. I will be very grateful to you, Dakin, for this help, and please give Audrey your cooperation and my thanks and love, also.

Tenn. / Tom

120. To Walter Dakin Williams

"Vulcania"
12/9/48
[TLS, 1 p. Columbia U]

Dear Dakin:

Writing this separately as I know you will not want to let Audrey see this part of the communication. I am very, very anxious to have you avoid betraying any sign of any distrust of her handling of my affairs as she is morbidly sensitive where I am concerned. I have no reason to think there has been any mishandling as I have not seen any evidence of it. You must handle her with great tact and diplomacy: a breach in my relations with her would be extremely dangerous and detrimental. I am asking you to watch over my interests simply because I think it is wise to have a double-check - especially when I am out of the country and may not even be accessible, at times, to the postman, as I may be travelling around a good deal in the car. So make every effort to give the trip and the conferences a friendly and non-inquisitorial atmosphere, but do keep a sharp lookout at the same time. If the statements do not seem right, if there are any important discrepancies in them, please inform me first of what they are before you take it up with Audrey and Colton. All this adds up to is one word: TACT! Hope you will drop in to Summer and Smoke while you're in New York, and give Audrey an expense account for your stay there, and enjoy yourself. Love to mother and grandfather and you -

Love - Tom.

121. To Oliver Evans

[*Vulcania*]
[December 9, 1948]
[TLS, 1 p. HRC]

Dear Oliver:

From several hints that you dropped, with the delicacy of a thunder-clap, I gathered that you might be in reduced circumstances and am hoping that the enclosed "benefaction" will be of service. Otherwise I can see you going for "Ottonte lire" in the Galleria or the Steps called Spanish, unless Maria is active enough to hustle for you both.

They have just had the fire-drill which I did not participate in. The Horse went up, so in case of fire I shall depend upon him to guide me to the proper position. I doubt however that any of the life-boats would be sufficiently Signorelli to suit me, so it is hardly worth bothering about, now, is it?

I gave up on Ford Madox Ford, but in the ship's library I came across The Aspern Papers by that original Auntie Fish, Henrietta James, and for the first time I have been really thrilled by her writing. (I had never read her before). I am now looking forward to practically everything the old girl has written. Perhaps that is the "new world" that Irene saw me playing Columbus to. Or am I a little bit late in discovering James? An odd coincidence. I once wrote a play called "Lord Byron's Love Letter" - it is in the collected one-acts - which has a startlingly similar story to it, but had never even heard of this novella.

The passenger list is so appalling that it is not even printed! All you have to do is look around to know why! Dorothy Gish we have only seen from a distance. But there is a member of the crew, seen from an equal distance, that I think you would somehow manage to establish contact with if you were aboard. The food is excellent, excellent! I am eating nothing but proteins and am having a daily work-out and massage so that I will not look quite so much like a Piggy-bank when I get to Manhattan.

We are due to arrive at Gibralter in an hour and I want to try to get this letter off there. I promised Maria I'd write but can't think of anything to say to her that I haven't said to you, especially since the Horse is getting dressed and his image in the mirror directly above my typewriter is a little distracting. I will try later.

With love, Tenn.

[The Spanish Steps in Rome and the Galleria in Naples were rendezvous of special interest to TW and Oliver Evans.

The missed "fire-drill" may have inspired a one-act play by TW entitled "Lifeboat Drill" (1979), a dark study of old age and marital unhappiness.

Henry James based *The Aspern Papers* (1888) upon the legend of Claire Clairmont, half-sister of Shelley's second wife, Mary Godwin, and briefly the lover of Lord Byron (and the mother of his daughter Allegra). As James recounts in his preface, Claire had been approached in Florence by "an ardent Shelleyite" who coveted literary papers which she presumably held. TW saw a coincidental relation between the James story and his own one-act play "Lord Byron's Love Letter" (1945). Walter Dakin's tale of an elderly woman who lived in Columbus, Mississippi, and possessed a letter written by Byron has been identified as a source for the sketch (see Leverich, p. 56).

Dorothy Gish last appeared on Broadway in *The Story of Mary Surratt* (1947). In drafting "Daughter of Revolution," an early source for *The Glass Menagerie*, TW inscribed the play "to Miss Lillian and Miss Dorothy Gish for either of whom the part of Amanda Wingfield was hopefully intended by the author" (n.d., HRC).]

PART III

1949-1950

Overleaf: Tennessee Williams and Frank Merlo.
"I seem to be buying a house in Key West."

122. To Audrey Wood

[Hotel d'Inghilterra, Rome]
Jan. 11, 1949
[TLS w/ autograph postscript, 2 pp. HRC]

Dear Audrey:

I was very grateful for your long letter and the package of Xmas cards which I picked up today, the first real contact I have had with the States. I don't think there is any reason to take the Coen-Visconti-Downes row too seriously: it is impossible for an American to fix the blame or equity in this case. Obviously the person I want to make happy is Visconti as he is the one who is important to me here: he is practically the only legitimate manager in Italy. I have seen one of his productions, LIFE WITH FATHER, which is now running here and I thought it superior in quality to the New York show. The woman to play BLANCHE is a fine actress and perfect type for it, so I am annoyed with Fabio for making so much fuss. Actually I had met Visconti (in Sicily through Downes) a week or so before I established my first reluctant contact with Fabio, and had told Visconti I hoped he would do Streetcar so actually Fabio simply forced himself into the deal and then proceeded to mess it up. It is true that Segre got credit and royalties for the translation of Menagerie, but Visconti says it had to be almost completely rewritten by Guerriri before the production. I cannot judge the right or wrong of all this, as I can only accept and compare the words of the opposite parties. Perhaps the best thing is to return the $300. to Coen and declare the agreement with him invalid: or else to pay Segre out of my royalties, as well as Guerriri. Of course I don't really care, as long as the show goes on and is well done.

The African Adventure was a mistake, as we arrived just at the start of the cold, rainy season. Our luggage was tied up in Gibralter so we could not leave Tangiers where we put up at a particularly dreadful place selected by Bowles for reasons of (his) economy. The meals cost about twenty-five cents but were scarcely worth it. There was no heat except for the fireplace in my room. Consequently the Bowles, Paul and Jane, were constant visitors which made it difficult to work. We delayed our departure for about ten days waiting for Bowles luggage to arrive - after ours finally had. His never showed up and we finally had to go on to Fez without it. Our first attempt to get across the Spanish Moroccan frontier was a fiasco. We arrived there at night in a torrential rain. Paul's twelve suitcases and our four had to be taken through customs. While this was going on (interminably) the car got away, as we had left the brakes off, and started rolling downhill backwards. Frankie chased after it, as did many Arabs, and managed by a spectacular leap to get into it soon enough to avoid a serious crash. After all this we discovered that the car keys were lost. We dared not go on without them so we had to turn around and drive back to Tangiers. The keys were later found to have fallen down in the window socket of the car, only after we had notified the American consul that they had been stolen by the Spanish Moroccan customs officers and so caused a great disturbance. The next day we started out again, in another cloudburst. That day I found that I had developed a very peculiar affliction which is still with me. Whenever I lowered my head I felt a vibration all up and down my body like a ship with its propeller out of water. Also tingling sensations in my feet and fingers. This was naturally very disturbing and was one of the reasons I left Africa as I felt I should have some competent and intelligible medical advice. I saw an English-speaking doctor at Casablanca and have seen another one here in Rome and neither seem to take a very serious view of the affliction. I myself think it is probably a circulatory disorder due to strain and fatigue and other factors, such as no swimming. Paul had told me there was wonderful swimming in Morocco, but there was none. The weather was too cold and the pools were closed. I think it is the daily swimming that keeps me functioning passably well. My blood pressure is up, 145 over 100, which is not serious enough to explain the vibrations. I still have them, but now that I am swimming again, in the pool here in Rome, they're not quite so intense. If I get working well again, that will also help. Frankie is looking for an apartment for us. At present we have two rooms at a nice hotel, the Inghilterra, but there are too many tourists, desperate for conversation, hanging about the corridors and the bar, so that sometimes you don't really know that you have gotten out of New York or the Village. Through all of these tribulations Frankie has borne up wonderfully well, though he sometimes suffers from very bad headaches. My work was seriously interrupted, but the last few days I have been getting back at it again and have a room to myself for this purpose. It is true that I am working on a movie script: it is a screen version of one of the two plays I am working on. I alternate between the stage and screen script as they seem to be mutually helpful. I wish that I had a model movie-script containing the technical language of the film:

perhaps you know of a book containing material of this kind which you could send me. However I don't know how the item about Rossolini was conceived as I don't remember ever saying anything about such a notion. I would rather work with De Sica or Kazan if the film play becomes an actuality. De Sica has produced a magnificent new one (He did Shoe Shine) which is called Ladri di Bicyclette (Bicycle Thieves).

If Summer & Smoke is revived for the road I would be very happy, but I think it would be better to replace Andrews than Phillips, and most of all, a different director, as it was that end of the production that was most deficient in my opinion. I hope Jones has no more hold over the script, now that the play has closed. This does not mean we are enemies. Just wiser friends.

What about Rose?

With love, Tenn

Please mail Grandfather a box of good candy and a $100. check as a late Xmas present from me.

Dakin likes Colton and thinks I should keep him but also feels that he himself should have a retaining fee!

Tennessee Williams and Luchino Visconti: "Obviously the person I want to make happy is Visconti."

[The "African Adventure" ended after a dismal month with TW's arrival in Rome ca. January 6. He and Frank Merlo stayed at the Inghilterra, a fashionable hotel near the Spanish Steps, before returning to the apartment on via Aurora.

Luchino Visconti rejected the first translation of *Streetcar* (1947) commissioned by Fabio Coen, Audrey Wood's agent, on the grounds that it was derived from the New York production. Coen was also expected to pay for a second ordered by Visconti. TW typically complicated matters by approving each translation at a different time. The American reporter Donald Downes introduced TW to Visconti in 1948 and had apparently entered the "row."

Paul Bowles described TW as "violently perturbed by the Moslem scene" and surmised that his vibrations occurred "whenever things were not going smoothly" (*In Touch: The Letters of Paul Bowles*, ed. Miller, 1994, p. 200).

Manuscript sources (HRC) indicate that TW was at work on narrative, dramatic, and film versions of "The Roman Spring of Mrs. Stone" (1950), as the project was first entitled. The second play-in-progress is probably *The Rose Tattoo* (1951).

News that TW planned to write a screenplay with "an African background" for Roberto Rossellini surprised Audrey Wood. "True or false?" (January 8, 1949, HRC), she inquired.

Wood informed TW that the brief run of *Summer and Smoke* (1948) made an immediate tour impractical. The Theatre Guild, she added, was considering the play for a later subscription series and had asked that Margaret Phillips be replaced by a "star" (January 8, 1949, HRC). As producer, Margo Jones would oversee the eventual tour.]

123. To Irene Mayer Selznick

[Hotel d'Inghilterra, Rome]
1/16/49
[TLS w/ autograph marginalia, 1 p. Boston U]

Dear Irene:

I am now back in Rome, wondering why I ever left there and almost determined never to make that mistake again. Incidentally a big package, containing Nescafe, cocoa, chocolate bars, and condensed milk had been waiting for me in the post-office for several months and was finally delivered into my hands. It seemed like a gesture of yours: I cannot be sure for the outer package was nearly demolished and there was no record of the donor: if it is you, my thanks once again.

They are doing Streetcar in Rome, under the title Un Tram Che Se Chiamo Desiderio. There was a row and great litigation over a superfluity of translators, exactly twice as many as needed: I arrived on the scene like the cowboy hero, just in time to halt an injunction and straighten things out to the complete happiness of all by the simple expedient of paying both translators out of my own royalties. After paying - just now according to the latest bulletin from home - $110,000. to the government, this little item was like the celebrated intercourse between the elephant and the mouse. You'll be happy to know that the Visconti production promises to be very exciting. There is no excess of restraint: in that respect it is more Italian than Dixie. Even the organist gets out of hand, at times: last night he and Blanche were closely competing in volume: she won out by a couple of pinwheel gestures but it was a photo-finish. I have a feeling it will suit the Italian public as their ordinary life is more theatrical than our theatre, for which God be praised.

We left Paul in Morocco. Everything was just exactly as he said it wasn't. It was cold, it was raining continually, there was no place to swim, the food was worse than in London - do you remember London? - and the natives might have been beautiful if they did not nearly all have scrofula or cataracts or ring-worm: anyway a visual appreciation of them was enough! I can't deny that Morocco is a mysterious and beautiful country, in spite of these things, and I am going back: not during the rainy season, however. (I still love Paul!)

I wish I could say that I am now quite well, but I'm not. I suffer from mysterious Vibrations: whenever I lower my head slightly I feel like an electric vibrator was running up and down my body! I guess it is high blood-pressure and I am going to see a doctor, recommended by the American consulate. A headline in a newspaper interview says: "Tennessee Williams Soffre Di 'Vibrazioni'!" Yes, there are reporters even in Rome. This condition interferes a bit with my work, however I don't think it is self-induced for that purpose.

Are there any picture deals at all imminent or likely for Streetcar? I hope too much money is not being demanded: if I could get, say, an assured income (after taxes) of three or four hundred a month out of it I would be very happy and I think some deal could be made on that basis. My brother, Dakin, is shocked that so far none of my earnings have been capital gain and that is why I am now broke again except for my government bonds ($60,000.). I remember we discussed this problem a bit when I had dinner in your apartment and you said some enlightening things about it: would that I could remember what they were! - Love, to you, Irene, and my warm greetings to all the passengers on the Streetcars.

Tennessee.

[*Un tram che si chiama desiderio* premiered at Rome's Theatro Eliseo on January 21, 1949, with Rina Morelli (Blanche), Vittorio Gassman (Stanley), and Marcello Mastroianni (Mitch) playing the leads. Rome was shocked by the candor of *Streetcar*, but critics deemed the production a triumph and lavished praise upon Visconti's politically inspired direction. Praise for TW was correspondingly diminished, but he admired the production nonetheless and observed that Gassman's Stanley wore "the tightest pair of dungarees" he had "ever seen on the male ass" (qtd. in Windham, pp. 229-230).

In later correspondence Audrey Wood reported a still "non-existent" market for film rights of *Streetcar*. Irene Selznick remained an alternate source of funding and seemed willing to co-produce if her father's studio—MGM—would only "open their mouth" (to TW, January 30, 1949, HRC). A fee of $750,000 and fear that Joseph Breen, Production Code administrator, would harshly censor *Streetcar* made buyers wary.

Penned in the upper margin is TW's mailing address, "c/o American Express, Rome."]

124. To Audrey Wood

[Hotel d'Inghilterra, Rome]
[January 1949]
[TLS w/ enclosure, 1 p. HRC]

Dear Audrey:

I have so far received no report on the grants which I had arranged through the Author's League. These are terribly important to the people concerned, and also to me. I cannot understand Miss Sillcox's apparent lack of courtesy in failing even to answer the applications. I know that she hasn't answered the one which I made for the Bowles for the address I gave her was care of me in Rome and it has been well over three weeks. What is the matter? Please check on it: find out whether or not she is intending to take any action. All the names that I gave her were people who deserved and needed this help very badly. I am enclosing a letter from Oliver Evans with a paragraph marked. At least a secretary might have acknowledged receipt of his application. Like all poets he is easily hurt or offended. The one thing I have accomplished this past year that I can look back on with gratification is making these grants and I want to be damned sure that they are followed through. The present treatment does not encourage me to make any further contribution through the League.

Incidentally I have also received no word about my sister, although I understood that the money I gave Mother was to be used to transfer her to the private retreat near home.

Please tell Colton I want to know the exact maximum that I am allowed to give each year in the way of gifts, endowments, Etc., so that I can give that maximum (deductible). I feel that I could probably have given a great deal more than $5,000. if I had known what was allowable. Dakin says Colton wants his fee to be doubled ($2,000.) Is this true? So far I am not convinced that Colton has affected any substantial saving for me and don't see why I should increase his fee, especially if I must also pay Dakin which he seems to expect. I actually have very little money, not even enough to live on if the two companies of Streetcar should close: that is, without selling my bonds. Dakin feels, and I feel, too, that I must be sure, hereafter - assuming I have another play to sell - to make some deal by which I get to keep some of the procedes as "capital gain". We must keep that in mind. You see I am very depressed over the news of the tax-payment. . . .

With love, Tenn.

[Luise Sillcox, executive secretary of the Authors' League, was presumably slow to acknowledge applications to a fund established by TW. He had contributed $5,000 to the League and designated Oliver Evans, Paul and Jane Bowles, Carson McCullers, and Donald Windham as recipients.

TW feared that Edwina had been persuaded by Dr. Emmitt Hoctor, the superintendent, to leave Rose in the state asylum: "So far he has opposed (or neglected to do anything about) any suggestion that has been made for her improvement" (to Dakin Williams, n.d., Columbia U).

William Liebling assured TW that *Streetcar* was still profitable: "Last week, the New York company made over $26,000, and when the Chicago company leaves for the road, it will do capacity business for a long time. . . . So for Christ's sake stop worrying!" (January 25, 1949, HRC). The Broadway show would close on December 17, 1949, having earned a profit of $500,000. The national tour continued through the following spring.

This letter, which bears a reception date of January 24, 1949, was probably written in the week of January 16.]

125. To Irene Mayer Selznick

[45 Via Aurora, Rome]
[mid-February 1949]
[TLS, 1 p. Boston U]

Dear Irene:

I am still reading and studying letters #1-4: nobody has ever said so much about so much to so few! As Margo would say, Bless you darling! (But a little more sincerely than she always does). I had a hard time composing the cable about the English production. You are very, very persuasive about Mr. Olivier and Mme. his wife. You have evidently given the matter a great deal of consideration, and I am glad to see that you have included in your consideration that Mme. Olivier has not yet given us a ghost of an idea of her latent dramatic powers. But I believe, as you do, that Mr. Olivier is a smart cookie who would not want Vivien to lay anything bigger than ostrich egg on the London stage even in a play by an American author. In my cable I was being as explicit as possible, in so short a space. I still think an American company would be far better. However if the production is put off until 1950, the chances are that interest in the play would be considerably depleted and also that I might not be able to see it or want to if I could. I hope that isn't too mysterious-sounding! The prestige of an Olivier production would certainly be enormous and every bit as intriguing to me as to anyone else. If only we could be devastatingly frank with Sir Laurence, and say, Honey, we want <u>you</u> but could do without <u>her</u>! - After the Italian production I know it is possible to have a success even without the right Blanche, for the show has been a smash-hit here in Rome in spite of the fact that practically everyone agrees that the Blanche is wrong. They have moved it to a larger theatre and it is now in its fifth week and <u>I</u> am earning (though have not yet collected) 30,000 lire a night in spite of having to pay two translators out of my royalties.

Frank has gone to Sicily to visit his relatives there. I am lonely but have more energy for my work. I now have a script with a beginning a middle and an end, but there is still not much flesh on the bones and the animation is wanting. I'll finish this one, but maybe then I'll quit and develop my voice.

I'm as happy about Art's play as I could be about any play but my own. Please send me, or have Audrey send me, the New York notices, no matter how good they are! Don't send me anymore goodies, but if you feel in a sending mood, as you often do, send something sweet to Grandpa. He is not too happy in Saint Louis. One letter says that Mother insists he is only pretending to be deaf and won't repeat anything to him so he has no idea what's going on in the house. In the next letter he says, she nags continually: "Oh, that tongue of hers!" A bit contradictory. Or maybe the electric ear is functioning better, now. One of my favorite anecdotes is of the Streetcar rehearsal when he produced the sound-effects tuning in on it.

To revert to London: I place it, like Pilate, in your hands, but please remember what a beating I took last summer in the London press and see that everything possible is done to protect us and the play, as distinct from Sir Laurence and his lady! And have it stated in the contract that no mention is to be made in the press of my figure being "short & squatty".

Love - 10.

[The Oliviers recently confirmed their availability for a London production of *Streetcar* (1949). Vivien Leigh was still primarily known for her role as Scarlett O'Hara in *Gone With the Wind* (1939)—a production of Irene Selznick's estranged husband, David—but her English stage credits were more extensive and varied than TW may have realized.

Rina Morelli's diminutive stature perhaps exaggerated her vulnerability and lessened the threat of Blanche's visitation. Nonetheless the press acclaimed both her casting and performance in *Streetcar*.

In Frank Merlo's absence TW summoned "Raffaello" and soon reported to Donald Windham—erroneously, it turned out—that he had "the clap" (qtd. in Windham, p. 231).

Death of a Salesman, by Arthur Miller, opened in New York on February 10, 1949.]

126. To Audrey Wood

[45 Via Aurora, Rome]
February 15, 1949.
[TLS w/ marginalia and
autograph postscript, 2 pp. HRC]

Dear Audrey:

I haven't meant to neglect you. In fact somewhere under all these papers is at least half a letter to you written weeks ago. But my little Secretary, or Interpreter, as the Italian press insist upon calling Frank, is visiting his parent's cousins in Sicily and my affairs are much less well-organized than usual. A forlorn postcard today says he has caught the Flu and his Aunt won't let him out of the house but is planning a big dance to celebrate his recovery, when he recovers. Otherwise life here is well-ordered. The weather has been so fine that they've had to cut down on electricity because of a water-shortage and my evenings are spent in becoming candle-light. I have red, green and white candles in honor of the Italian flag, red for the blood of Italy, white for the snow of its mountains and green for its valleys. The late afternoons I take to the streets in my "lunghissima Buick Rosso" as it is described in the papers, and it is like navigating a battleship through narrow straits getting it in and out of the tiny avenues, it goes very slowly with great pomp and everybody shouts 'Que Bella Macchina!' and only Tyrone Power cuts a more important figure here. It is nick-named "Desiderio" in honor of the "Tram" which is still playing to very good houses in its fifth week. A beautiful set of photos is being sent you. The production was extraordinarily fine except for some over-acting (rather strenuous) on the part of the Morelli who plays Blanche. Could it be arranged for me to draw my Italian royalties while I am here, instead of having them all sent to New York? It would greatly facilitate my life here, as I would not have to frequent the money-changers. I was told this afternoon that only a statement from you, directed to the Authors Society in care of Fabio Coen, could release these royalties for my use here. I will also speak to Fabio about it. I have been exchanging some lively correspondance with Irene, including cables, about the London Streetcar. She says it is not practical to organize an American company before 1950. That seems too long to wait, and in that case I should like to know if you don't think it would be wise to accept an Olivier production? The prestige of his name, and his great gifts as a showman, must certainly be considered, although I have yet to see Vivian give a striking performance. But then neither did Morelli here - or rather, hers was much too striking - and the play was still a success "clamoroso". I will leave the matter in your hands (collective). . . .

I received today five complete sets of Arthur Miller notices, more than I ever received for any play of my own. Everybody seemed most anxious that I should know how thoroughly great was his triumph. I hope that I was pleased over it. If I was not it only goes to show what dogs we can be. At least it was a play that I liked by a man I look up to. Perhaps I am being over-cautious in saying I hope I was pleased because in the incorruptible portion of my being (however small that may be) I felt an unmistakable beam of satisfaction. It is a deep, human play, warmly felt and written with a great simple dignity which comes out of Miller's own character, and the direction of it must have been a tremendous achievement for Gadge, because though I loved it, I thought the retrospective scenes would be hellishly difficult to stage. I am awfully anxious to see a picture of the set.

This is marvelous news about the imminent filming of "Menagerie". And tell Feldman that I will definitely come out as advisor anytime they want me. I can't commit myself to do any work on the script but still it might be possible for me to help with it, as it is so much to my interest (and the family's) for the picture to be done from a dignified script.

Please tell Eddie Colton for me that I am not really worried about "Capitol Gain" or anything else except my weight and my work and my occasional vibrations: those are my only real personal concerns right now. Once the tax-man has come and gone, like Santie Claus in reverse, I forget him until his next scheduled appearance. I do hope that I can manage, however, to accumulate enough money to bring me in a good monthly income, say, four or five hundred a month on which I could keep myself and a small Secretary and a big car.

Much love from your Italian client, 10.

Please kiss Luise for me, all have received their grants.

P.S. Please air mail copy of "Summer and Smoke" (the book) for Visconti.

[Tyrone Power lived in Rome while filming *Prince of Foxes* (1949). His recent marriage to Linda Christian drew hordes of unruly fans and reporters and received a papal blessing. Power's homosexual tendencies were perhaps known to TW.

Audrey Wood preferred to sell the film rights of *Streetcar* before mounting a London stage production and advised delaying the project until 1950, when an American cast and director could also be found (to TW, January 30, 1949, HRC). The critical "beating" of *The Glass Menagerie* (1945) in the preceding summer was not forgotten.

Notices for *Death of a Salesman* were uniformly positive and bore none of the reservations, moral or critical, which marked the reception of *Streetcar*. Elia Kazan, whose direction was also acclaimed, noted that Arthur Miller had learned from *Streetcar* how easily nonrealistic elements—"the retrospective scenes" to which TW refers—could be "blended with the realistic ones" (Kazan, p. 361).

Typed in the upper margin of page 1 is TW's name and mailing address, "American Express, Rome."]

127. To Irene Mayer Selznick

SH: Excelsior, Napoli
March 23, 1949.
[TLS w/ marginalia, 3 pp. Boston U]

Dear Irene:

I am travelling around with one suitcase, not large enough to contain your recent memoranda from the home-front so I am not sure that this will adequately cover the various problems brought up. But I take it, from the cable, that the most important question now pending, is who to put in Jessica's place for the summer. Of the two ladies, Deborah and Tallullah, I suspect the first is closer to the part: but isn't she also a little too much like Jessica, not enough contrast to spur a new interest, and does she have box-office draw? Tallullah certainly has the latter and certainly her interpretation would be an altogether new one and bound to stir interest. Frankly, I am ~~very~~ frightened of her, and I don't think she should be put in the play without very earnest assurance, from her, that she would play the <u>play</u> and not just Tallullah as she has been recently doing. In other words, we don't yet want the "Camp" streetcar! As I am so far away, I think I will delegate Audrey to represent my interest or voting power, in this matter. I'm perfectly sure that you and she together can weigh all the factors pro and con for each candidate, and Gadge, too, if he is still at all interested. Now as for the appeals from the London censor, I grudgingly acquiesce to his demands on every single point except the one relating to Allen Grey. Blanche's speech about her husband's homosexuality cannot be altered. There is nothing lurid or at all offensive in this speech, it is written with all requisite taste and delicacy and it is too important a thing to be deleted or changed, and if they will not accept the play with that speech, then it is clear to me that they just don't want the play produced in England and I would rather not have it done there if they don't want it. The other little textual changes demanded by the censors don't bother me much and can be done in rehearsal: I don't have either the book nor the script with me, nor even the list of the censor, so I can't refer to them now.

Grandfather is ecstatic over the candy, and over your kindness to him. He is quite in love with you, and I can think of no higher tribute that could be paid you than having won his heart so quickly and completely, for he has been a great cavalier, within the proper limits of his calling, and has known many ladies and admired only the best. A letter yesterday states that he is "busily packing". Hitting the road again, to celebrate his 93rd birthday in Mississippi! The birthday is in April.

No important news of myself: except this: I have now rough drafts of three plays. That sounds ever so much better than it actually is. When I say rough I mean like a road through the jungle! All that I want out of God is time! I also need more energy, but if I get the time, I can manage, maybe not all three, but surely one.

Truman Capote is here. That stands in a little paragraph all by itself.

And one last paragraph to say thank you! Thank you for the letters and for everything, for being such a wonderful producer and such a good friend and such a great lady!

Love, Tenn.

[Jessica Tandy, Marlon Brando, and Kim Hunter left the cast of *Streetcar* on June 1 when their contracts expired. Tandy, the most difficult to replace, was succeeded by Uta Hagen, who had relieved her in the preceding summer and toured with the national company.

Tallulah Bankhead starred in a notorious revival of *Streetcar* in 1956. Her "roustabout reputation," as a critic put it, preceded the performance and confirmed TW's fears (see letters #321 and #323).

The Lord Chamberlain's Office cited blasphemous reference in *Streetcar* to "'Christ,'" as well as Stanley's crude linking of "'kidneys'" and "'soul.'" More serious was Blanche's disclosure of Allan Grey's homosexuality in Scene Six. "The Lord Chamberlain is of opinion," wrote his assistant, "that this passage should be altered making the young husband found with a negress instead of another man" (Gwatkin, July 12, 1948, HRC). Reports of the Olivier production indicate that Blanche's telling line—"the boy I had married and an older man who had been his friend for years"—was simply omitted. John Lehmann followed suit in publishing the first English edition of *Streetcar* (1949).

The "rough drafts" cited by TW are probably *The Roman Spring of Mrs. Stone*, *The Rose Tattoo*, and "The Big Time Operators" (n.d., HRC).]

128. To Audrey Wood

SH: Excelsior, Napoli
3/23/49
[TLS w/ autograph marginalia, 2 pp. HRC]

Dear Audrey:

I have just had a reunion with my typewriter which I had left at a hotel in Florence. It is now safely back, together with the manuscript notebook I had locked in the case, but I had several very anxious and frustrating days waiting for it.

Frank and I are on our way to the sea. We travelled this far, to Naples, with Capote and Jack Dunphy, one of your writers. I got to know Jack for the first time in Rome and I like him a lot. I'm not sure, however, that the four of us will continue to Ischia where Dunphy and Capote are going. I am not sure how much Capote I can take. He is completely disarming: and then all at once, out shoots the forked tongue! And the sting is all but mortal. But there are other islands, and we, Frank and myself, will probably spend a week on one of them.

I have a feeling that I am supposed to answer an accumulation of questions: right now I can't think of them. I have just written Irene saying that I delegated my voting power in the matter of Tandy replacements to you. That I would not alter the "Allen Grey" speech for London but would make all the other little changes or deletions.

Now as to the very grave question of future producers: I would rather not take that up seriously until I have a completed play script. As long as we are closely involved with Irene I think it would be extremely dangerous, certainly on my part, to make any commitment to another producer. I think she would be not merely bitter, but dangerously vindictive in such an event. I don't want to make any secret deal behind her back, not even with Cheryl Crawford who I think the world of. There is no reason to move on this till the play is ready, and nothing is lost by refusing to decide, even in our own minds, until the issue is imminent. I have three scripts, and if I finish one of them, the chances are that I will finish all three, but the <u>if</u> is still an <u>if</u>. I am depressed and anxious over my lack of health and energy mainly on account of my work which demands so much of my physical strength and nervous power. I must be well, or relatively well, to work well. And I still have these damned vibrations. Sounds like a neurotic symptom, but it isn't. Perhaps I should leave soon for Paris, as last year I felt stimulated as soon as I went North. Now as ever I think only of how and where I can best function as a writer. Unfortunately the writer and the man are inseparable.

I would rather not sell the amateur rights to Summer & Smoke this year, which is another year in the high brackets. I would not be able to keep the money. Would much rather have it earn royalties for me over a long period as my own property. Speaking of "Summer" did you know that Margo (according to Anne Jackson according to Truman) made a speech to the cast saying that it was "the work of a dying man?" I would like to check on the authenticity of this report! Much love -

10.

[Truman Capote and his new companion, Jack Dunphy, met TW and Frank Merlo in Rome and traveled with them to Naples. TW upset a table in Capote's lap after learning of Margo Jones's "speech" to the cast of *Summer and Smoke*. Anne Jackson, who played Nellie in the Broadway production, was apparently Capote's source. Capote denied repeating the story in malice but acknowledged the "mortal" nature of his "sting": "I didn't realize that I was touching the nerve nearest Tennessee's heart. He claimed he was dying every other day. It was his favorite gambit for getting sympathy. 'You don't know it, my dear,' he would say, 'but Ah'm a dyin' man!'" (qtd. in Clarke, *Capote: A Biography*, 1988, p. 196).

Audrey Wood lost patience with Irene Selznick who refused to underwrite the film version of *Streetcar*. She reminded TW that Selznick was "hopeful of getting" his next play and that this might be used as an "emotional weapon." Cheryl Crawford, Wood's choice to succeed Selznick, had been approached informally and was "very eager to do a Tennessee Williams play" (March 1, 1949, HRC).

TW rejected Wood's advice to sell "amateur rights" of *Summer and Smoke*. Wood later prevailed after informing him that payment would be spread over several years to lower the tax rate.

Penned in the upper margin of page 1 is TW's mailing address, "American Express, Rome."]

129. To Carson McCullers

SH: Excelsior, Napoli
3/23/49
[TLS, 2 pp. Duke U]

Dearest Carson:

I just discovered among my papers, when I was packing, a letter I had written you at least a month ago. That was just after I had heard that you had moved into the city and had received a grant, and I was very happy over that news. But most of the letter, pertaining to myself, was a morbid chronicle, so it is just as well that I allowed it to remain among the discarded papers. I can't say I'm feeling a hell of a lot better now, but at least I don't feel obliged to raise such a lamentation. Rome has not done as much for me this year as it did last. For one thing, the winter seems to be everlasting. I've finally got tired of waiting for a warm sun and have set out in the Buick to find it. I may go on as far South as Sicily if I don't find any good swimming-places on the way. I am not alone, but in a way I am lonelier than if I were. Do you understand what I mean? Yes. I know you do. But that is the end of my lamentations; no more, no more! It is nobody's fault but my own. After a week or two in the sun, if I ever find it, I shall probably go up to Paris. I found it very stimulating last year, after the long stay in Rome, and I hope to God it works again this year. In a way the Buick is a burden: it is such an effort driving it around everywhere instead of just hopping on a plane.

I got copies of "Reflections" from both you and Laughlin. It seems absurd for me to write a preface to a great work by such a completely established writer and I should feel almost too embarassed to try, but I will try if you really want me to: that is, as soon as my present state of fatigue and depression has somewhat lifted, as soon as circumstances permit it to do so.

A certain young writer, I won't say his name, was in Rome for a brief while. It did not suit him and he has gone on to an island. The island is volcanic but the volcano is now extinct. In passing he managed to do a fair amount of mischief, but nothing really tangible. What is it?

I heard that you were travelling in the South. I may be back in the States, myself, sooner than I had originally planned. Let me hear from you!

Much, much love, Tenn.

[Carson McCullers wrote last to TW in the preceding January when she and Reeves, reconciled once again, shared an apartment in New York. She considered Rome "the right place" for TW and hoped that "no emotional ambivalence" involving "Frankie and Salvatore" (Raffaello) would arise to destroy his "peace." She also thanked him for the gift of a ring belonging to his sister, which she promised to treasure "always - or until the blessed time when Rose is well." The Authors' League grant, McCullers concluded, was "a rare bit of fortune": "How can I thank you?" (n.d., Duke U).

James Laughlin's plan to reprint McCullers's second novel, *Reflections in a Golden Eye* (1941), included a preface by TW.

The mischievous "young writer" to whom TW alludes is Truman Capote, as McCullers would have instantly guessed.]

130. To James "Jay" Laughlin

[45 Via Aurora, Rome]
4/10/49
[TLS w/ enclosure and autograph marginalia, 1 p. Houghton]

Dear Jay:

I had quite a hard time writing this introduction since I didn't quite know what I was supposed to do with it, that is, what purpose it should serve, since Carson and her work are already so well-known and established. I may have taken altogether the wrong slant on it, particularly in the personal anecdotes and the stuff about her influence on a writer that will certainly be recognized as Capote. Please use your own judgement in trimming this down and editing it as much as you deem necessary or discreet and it might be a good idea to let Carson see it first, since it is her book. I honestly could not think of any other way of dealing with it. It was a good hard exercise but I don't want to try it again any time soon!

I have gotten the two reprints of Menagerie and Wagons and find them stunningly well done. After a disturbing period of apathy last winter, I am plowing ahead once more and have completed a first draft of a play and of a long story so if I come home next Fall it won't be empty-handed. We, Frankie and I, are going to London the end of this month for a conference with the Oliviers, and after that we will spend some time in Paris which I found very stimulating last year, but we are keeping the little apartment in Rome to return to when it is time to relax again. The days are one long blue and gold ribbon always unwinding and giving you an illusion of permanence of at least a physical kind, which is no small bargain. Vidal has not yet returned to Europe but Capote is now on Ischia with a new red-headed lover that he dotes on. They have radioactive springs on that volcanic island which are supposed to create enormous sexual vitality so perhaps Truman will have to leave Italy with a board nailed over his ass, which is the way a red-headed sailor once said a Mardi Gras visitor would have to leave New Orleans! How is Carson? I haven't heard from her in a good while. Donnie's book is being rejected by all the big houses which is discouraging to him and mistifying to me. Maria is said to be on her way back to England in a few days and is arranging to be surprised by a big bon-voyage party and "shower".

Ever, Tenn.

Lustig covers a dream!

[James Laughlin flattered TW that his name was "very hot" and "would help to sell" the forthcoming edition of *Reflections in a Golden Eye*. He added, "Isn't it an awful commentary on our culture that a writer as great as Carson should have to have any help at all in getting her work to the public" (November 29, 1948, Houghton).

New Directions reprinted *The Glass Menagerie* and *27 Wagons Full of Cotton* (1945) in early 1949 without a copyright or a dust jacket fiasco. Laughlin also informed TW that he had earned the "tidy little sum" (April 14, 1949, Houghton) of $7,500 for sales in 1948.

TW refers to "completed" first drafts of *The Rose Tattoo* and *The Roman Spring of Mrs. Stone*.

Following the scene in Naples the parties traveled separately to the island of Ischia, where TW and Frank Merlo spent nearly two weeks. TW was reportedly jealous of Merlo's attraction to Capote, while Capote detected in Merlo "'a great crush'" (qtd. in Clarke, *Capote: A Biography*, p. 196) on Jack Dunphy.

TW described Ischia as "a dream" to Donald Windham and predicted that he would "like it best of anything in Italy" (qtd. in Windham, p. 237). He also urged Windham to "keep faith" while his novel *The Dog Star* (1950) was being circulated.

Penned in the upper margin is TW's mailing address, "American Express, Rome. (till April 20th)."]

131. To Audrey Wood

["the Neapolitan coast"]
[April 1949]
[TLS w/ autograph marginalia, 1 p. HRC]

Dear Audrey:

Frank and I are making a tour of sunny beaches along the Neapolitan coast before we face the rigors of a week in London with Irene. I have a feeling that condensed in that week will be all the harassments that you have experienced in two years of telephone conversations, and I say that still liking the woman and assuming that you still like her.

I have not known how to answer your wire about Ruth Ford Vs. Judith Evelyn. Truthfully when I saw Ruth, though I was disposed to like her, I felt that she made the whole character of Blanche seem totally phoney. I have always liked Evelyn and regarded her as an actress of remarkable power and thought she had that sort of looks that must depend on illusion that gave Blanche such physical pathos. So you see how difficult it is for me to wire an enthusiastic espousal of your side in this particular debate. When I think about the acting profession, I suspect it is about as heartbreaking as writing plays or representing playwrights!

Since I last wrote you I have been going through a relatively good period and working continually. I have finished a long story, about 35 pages, taken from one of the plays I was working on last year, The Roman Spring of Mrs. Stone, and which I now think would make a good movie script. I have discussed it slightly with De Sica, the best Italian director who made Shoe Shine and The Bicycle Thieves which has not yet been shown in the States and he is very anxious to do a film with me, is distinguished from most other big Italian directors by his simplicity and modesty and some understanding and use of English so I have a feeling that we could work together on a film if the proper arrangement could be worked out, that is, assurance of script-control for me so that I would have some creative satisfaction out of the work. It is a possible script for Garbo if she would be willing to play a woman of fifty still clinging to romance. I will have it typed in London and send you a copy.

The plays are right where they were when I last wrote but perhaps when I get North, and with the story off my hands, I will start forging ahead more rapidly on them.

While on Ischia I developed a suspicion of Truman almost equal to Carson's. How is Carson? I am worried for I haven't heard from her in quite a long while.

Love - 10.

P.S. DE SICA IS VERY ANXIOUS TO DIRECT MENAGERIE IN HOLLYWOOD IF WARNERS ARE GOING TO DO IT. HE WILL BE FREE ABOUT SEPT. OR OCT. WHAT DO YOU THINK? Have been in touch with the Dieterlie-Magnani outfit. They have a fine story and I am thinking of going down to Stromboli when I get back from London, at least for the fun of it.

[Audrey Wood later reported that Uta Hagen had been signed to replace Jessica Tandy on Broadway and Judith Evelyn to replace Hagen on tour. Ruth Ford, a client of Liebling-Wood, was no longer in contention, having demanded a salary which Irene Selznick found excessive (to TW, April 19, 1949, HRC). Wood also noted in following correspondence that Irving Rapper had been hired to direct the film version of *The Glass Menagerie* (1950) and that Jane Wyman was set to play Laura. She closed by "doubly" begging TW "not to make any commitment" on *Streetcar* or any other play while "doing London town" (April 20, 1949, HRC) in May.

TW probably wrote this letter in the week of April 17, but it was not mailed until early-May, as a notation penned in the upper margin indicates: "Later - London - Everything went fine here. We leave for Paris tomorrow (5/9/49)."]

132. To Audrey Wood

[Paris]
5/13/49
[TLS, 1 p. HRC]

Dear Audrey:

We have just arrived in Paris from London and I have not yet seen Ninon or anyone else connected with the proposed Paris production so I can't make any comments on that. Things in London seemed to be in good shape when we left.

I have gotten the movie-script for the Menagerie. I think it would be disastrous to shoot this script as it now stands. There has been a general cheapening and bastardization which I think Hollywood cannot get away with any longer, against the tide of fine new pictures being made abroad as well as the advance evident in serious films made in America. The greatest damage has been done to the character of Amanda. As depicted in this film treatment she has lost all dignity and consequently all poetry and pathos. She is cheap and brassy. Not even the remnants of a lady but just a common and vulgar shrew. You can imagine how personally embarassing I find this to be. Also Laura's pathos has been turned to bathos through sentimentalization without any real heart or poetry left in it. I make these comments with full understanding of the necessary conversion to cinema appeal. And I make it because I think that all, including cinema, appeal has been sacrificed through lack of understanding and tasteful writing. There are still some good things in the script. The rearrangement (of sequence) in the original material is not without some merits and advantages, particularly in the long scene of the gentleman caller, but I would say that practically all of the new material is so badly out of key and quality that it should be junked if the picture is to have any dignity, and I know I am right in feeling that this picture cannot succeed commercially or artistically unless that dignity is kept. Incidentally they should not put my name on the present script as author as it is obviously not my work, and a disgrace to any name that is signed to it, including ~~Arthur~~ Chas. Feldman's.

I wish that you and Eddie Colton would check on the following points: What are the percentage terms that we are given in the picture contract? In other words, the financial stake involved. Also, who is the director? I sincerely hope not Rappaport, as once mentioned, for he is known to be a just competent director and this film requires the finest, such as De Sica or Kazan or Wyler, especially since the script is now in such a mess of incomprehension. If I came out to work on it, how much artistic control would I be given? (Three questions) The last means that I would come if I were assured that I would be working with people, producer and director, that are tasteful and gifted enough to justify it. And that Mother and I have a good chance of making some money out of the picture.

As for Summer, certainly it shouldn't be revived without a fine director and a leading man better than Tod Andrews. I was shocked to hear that he had broadcast it, as he was the one person that I thought replacing might make a considerable difference, but that is characteristic of the Guild treatment, substitute for the good one and keep the lemon!

Will call Ninon this eve. -

Love - 10.

[Both Jean Anouilh and Jean Cocteau sought rights to a Paris production of *Streetcar* (1949). Audrey Wood's recommendation of Cocteau was tacitly approved when TW failed to answer correspondence. Ninon Tallon continued to represent Wood in France.

Charles Feldman reminded Wood that *The Glass Menagerie* script had not "changed fundamentally" (Wood to TW, May 18, 1949, HRC) since first read and approved by TW in July 1947. Feldman, though, had been forewarned of the present criticism. His assistant, Charles Abramson, read the script when it was first submitted and described the "conventional 'Boy Meets Girl' ending" as "too quick, too pat, and trite" (to Feldman, July 4, 1947, HRC). TW later accepted a screenwriting credit for *The Glass Menagerie*, as did the adapter, Peter Berneis.

On May 18 Wood detailed TW's "financial stake" in the film and regretted to say that the author has no legal rights over the choice of producer, director, actors, or script. She added that Irving Rapper—not H. Rappaport—was probably a more talented director than TW allowed (HRC).

In a second letter dated May 18, Wood predicted that John Shubert and the Theatre Guild, co-sponsors of the forthcoming tour of *Summer and Smoke*, would drop the play from consideration if TW demanded expensive changes in cast and direction (HRC).

The radio broadcast of *Summer and Smoke* (April 17, 1949) was co-sponsored by the United States Steel Corporation and The Theatre Guild on the Air. Robert Anderson wrote the adaptation and Dorothy McGuire and Tod Andrews spoke the leading parts.]

133. To Audrey Wood

[45 Via Aurora, Rome]
[late-May 1949]
[TLS, 2 pp. HRC]

Dear Audrey:

Today I received the best news that has come to me in a long time which is that my sister, Rose, is now out of the asylum for three days a week, in the custody of a lady in a neighboring town, that she has written home expressing her delight with the arrangement and was last seen "picking violets on her new friend's lawn". Now that I have this news, the realization of such long planning, I am very anxious to go ahead with the trust agreement giving her a half interest in "Summer & Smoke" and also to see that the play, if it goes on tour, will have every protection. I am considering coming home before the London production of Streetcar as I think my interests in America may be more pressing and important, as regards the Menagerie film and the Summer & Smoke tour. I want both of these things, so closely related to the welfare and satisfaction of my family, to be worked out as well as possible. I think the best protection (for all concerned) is to hold firm on certain points about which I have absolute conviction. I don't think a mere duplication of "S & S" will do any good. It must have the services of an imaginative director, possibly a new or young one, but one with more than stage manager's ability and license. I have always felt, very strongly, that the peculiarly dead effect created in many scenes of the play was due, unhappily, to the male lead having nothing but looks to contribute.

I like the idea of McGuire, but I am sure that someone better than Todd can be found in these post-war days when so many virile young actors with real ability can be had. See if you can't get an OK from the Shuberts to shop around both for a new male lead and a gifted young director who wouldnt demand, perhaps, any higher pay than a stage manager doing the job. I think the Oliviers would understand if I came home early to assist in the staging, as I wanted to do in the first place. Aside from Todd I would only insist on two other replacements, the Mexican Gonzales girl and the old doctor. I should prefer, of course, to replace Mrs. Winemiller and her husband as well, but I think we could get along with the same cast in all but the three parts I have mentioned, and with a new effort to inject life in the staging.

Now re: Menagerie a la Feldman. I am afraid I cannot retract anything I've said. I remember, and Feldman is perfectly right about this, that I expressed approval of the script in Hollywood but it was because I had been under the impression it would be something too awful to imagine. It wasn't that! And I certainly qualified my relief and approval. I said that I liked the way so much of the original script had been kept but I made it quite clear that I detested the new ending and that I thought all of the new material was a mere cheapening of the product, to no profitable end whatsoever. The cinema industry has shown great promise of new dignity in the last ten years or so, but this script is a most discouraging reversion to type. Mr. Feldman must remember that this play has toured the country and been very widely read. I doubt that he will find a single reviewer that will not jump down his throat for the grotesque distortion that is brought about by the phoney "Louis J. Singer ending". There are various ways of relieving the tragedy of the play if that seems necessary, but the one selected is almost the worst possible. Do you have a copy of my incomplete rewrite job on the script? I remember that it contained a suggestion for another ending, not to my entire satisfaction but certainly better than the awful Sunday-school-sentimental business that now brings the whole fabric of the play crashing down into ruins. Let us get the bull out of the china closet! If I thought the thing was hopeless I would dismiss it with a couple of sighs, but with the excellent cast that is lined up and Warners' back of it, there is still the possibility of making it into a great and successful picture. As for Rapper, I am relieved by some of his credits. The Corn Is Green was a pretty good picture, but he is still no one that I would have picked for the job. Is there anyone beside Feldman that we can work on for a dignified script?

The long story developed into a novella. It is now about finished and I am looking for a typist who can read and write English.

What was this about being black words on white paper?! I never read your wonderful letters without seeing and hearing you just as if we were talking over a martini! But I doubt that I make such good sense.

With love, Tenn.

P.S. I am glad you read Feldmann my first letter, but think we must now handle him very politely and gently to get our concessions without insulting the man's idea of himself as a producer. I shall follow this, soon, with a detailed list of what is good and bad in the screen play, and some suggestions for new work on it. How late can they start shooting? Until they see the whites of my eyes?

[TW has apparently described his sister's first release from institutional care since 1937.

Irving Rapper's direction of *The Corn Is Green* (1945) led to Academy Award nominations for the best male and female supporting roles. Bette Davis starred as a crusading teacher who brings new ideas to a Welsh mining village.

On May 23, after a hiatus of several months, TW revived his journal, writing that he had just "about finished Moon of Pause," as *The Roman Spring* was provisionally entitled, but "prefer not to have any opinion of it yet."

Wood ended her second letter of May 18 by observing that she was "tired of coming out black words on white paper." Implied was frustration with TW's lassitude and inattention to business, which she soon made explicit by asking that he "rouse" himself "to some feeling of cooperation" (July 8, 1949, HRC).

This letter, which bears a reception date of May 31, 1949, was written in the week of May 22 in reply to Wood's recent correspondence.]

134. To Charles K. Feldman and Jerry Wald

[45 Via Aurora, Rome]
5/31/49
[TLx, 2 pp. U of Delaware]

Dear Mr. Feldman and Mr. Wald:

I am writing you jointly because I understand that you are jointly concerned as producers in the filming of my play, The Glass Menagerie, and my subject is the present condition of the film-script which I have recently had the opportunity to read again.

I first saw an earlier version of this script in the summer of 1947, in Hollywood, and at that time I expressed to Mr. Feldman an agreeable surprise at the extent to which the material of the play had been kept in the screen version. I understood that this was an early, preliminary, draft of the screen-play and that it was still in a fluid state. My second reading of the screen-play, quite recently, was a good deal less agreeable for this is much closer to the date of actual shooting and I find that certain grave and important faults are still in the script and I think it is tremendously important, in every way, to everybody concerned, that these things should be eliminated before you shoot the picture and that some re-writing be done.

Let me say, before specific allusion to these defects, that I am only as concerned as I am because of my conviction, which I have always had very strongly, that this "property" has every chance of becoming a really great picture which would surpass its dimensions as a play. However the basic qualities of the play must be kept if it is going to come off successfully on the screen. The qualities that made it a successful play were primarily its true and fresh observation, its dignity, its poetry and pathos, for it had no great dramatic situations as a play nor has it any as a screen-play, and the story was slight and simple as it still is and must remain.

Now I feel that a great deal of the truth, dignity, poetry and pathos of this play has gone out the window, and this loss occurs through the insertion of certain little sequences and devices which can easily and quickly be cut out and replaced by something in keeping with the tone and quality of the play. I think you all know that I have no reputation of being "arty" or "highbrow", and that on the contrary I am known to be an exponent of sound and popular theatre which gets across to a large public, and nothing that I object to or suggest is going to hazard the popular acceptance of the screen-offering, but on the contrary, is especially intended to preserve and increase that appeal.

First of all, I specifically object to all the sequences involving "the other young man", the one who teaches art to the children and who provides "the happy ending". I object to him, first of all, because he is such a Sunday-school sissy of a character with no reality or interest, ~~a mouther of really indecently tired platitudes~~, who brings to the story nothing but tedium and incredibility. He is a most palpable "device".

Now the whole play, in mood and quality, is keyed to the original type of ending and when something like this occurs, the poetry and the pathos so carefully built up in the preceding scenes are brought crashing to earth in splinters, and the final effect is one of bathos and sentimentality.

If the play had not been widely read, and seen in many parts of the country, where several companies have taken it on tour and presented it at little theatres, this distortion of its story and quality would not be so dangerous. But it is very well known, as a play, and all who liked or admired it as such will keenly resent the loss of its basic dignity on the screen, and reviewers will be likely to attack it.

The heartening message in the character of Laura is to those thousands of girls who do not find the dream-boy who sets everything magically right in the final sequence. This heartening message can be underscored and played up in the screen version without violating the essential meaning and truth of the play, and that is what I am appealing for in this letter. It is not a difficult (although very important) change to make, and although I am deep in other work and it is naturally pretty hard for me to revert to something I worked on five years ago, I will be happy to undertake these revisions provided that I have the assurance from you, the producers, that it is equally your will to make this a really true and dignified picture. I say that with hardly any doubt that it is so, for the work of Warner Brothers has hardly ever shown any lack of interest in these matters, but on the contrary has a high reputation for making honest pictures, and my acquaintance with Mr. Feldman, and the talks I had with him two years ago, indicated that he was also interested in making this a film of power and stature that would be creditable to us all.

Cordially,

[Charles Feldman (1904-1968) was an independent producer and Jerry Wald (1911-1962) a powerful supervisor at Warner Brothers with credits for such award-winning films as *Key Largo* (1948) and *Johnny Belinda* (1948).

The "sissy" who "teaches art to the children" was perhaps first encountered by Laura in an "artists' supply store" ("Italian Conference," June 27, 1949, HRC). Both scene and character—later identified as "Sterling"—were cut in revision of *The Glass Menagerie* script.]

135. To James "Jay" Laughlin

[45 Via Aurora, Rome]
6/3/49
[TLS, 2 pp. Houghton]

Dear Jay:

Many, many thanks for your letters. I am relieved that you are satisfied with the introduction to Carson's book. I had misgivings about it, and I still hope that you will let me have a look at the proofs before it goes into print. I was afraid, for one thing, that I might have written too much of a personal nature, and of course I was also a bit worried about the unavoidable comments on "imitators". I don't want to incur the wrath of Truman, which is probably worse than the wrath of God. I have not heard directly from Carson in a long time, not for about two months, but I have heard through Audrey that she has been in the South, is well, and that her play has been sold to the producers of Medea. I can't rejoice in that last bit of news for I am afraid that it may only bring her worry and grief, unless they pay her a good-sized advance to compensate for it.

Myself I have been terribly happy over some wonderful news about my sister. She is now out of the asylum for three days a week in the custody of an elderly couple in a pleasant country town in Missouri and Mother sent me five letters she had written expressing her great joy in the liberation. The letters were quite normal except that in one of them she sent her love to her offspring, of which of course she has none, but that seems a fairly harmless and comfortable delusion compared to the ones she used to suffer.

The story I mentioned has grown to the length of a novella, about 75 pages, and is still expanding, so I have neglected the play. This may turn out to be foolish of me but I don't seem to have any choice in the matter.

I cannot make up my mind about Book Find deal of selected writings. Sounds more like something to be done in the hypothetical future, but I would love very much to have a little volume of verse brought out that is all my own, with maybe a couple of stories for ballast. Is there any way we could print "Kingdom of Earth" or get it typed up? I am afraid the only copy may get lost. Do what you like about the Lawrence play. Perhaps it could be reserved to go with the eventual selection of poems and the stories: but dispose of it exactly as you think best.

Warners have sent a very stupid, commercial director over here to discuss the filming of "Menagerie" which they are now casting and will start filming next Fall. The movie-script is a real abomination and I am raising hell about it, but perhaps quite helplessly as I have no legal control. The characters are all vulgarized, there is a ridiculous happy ending, the director has no taste or distinction, but they have rounded up a stunning array of actors, probably headed by Bette Davis and Jane Wyman, who recently won an Academy Award. Would you like to read a copy of the film-script just to see how awful they can be? Audrey could provide you with one. And do you think, since the play is really a dramatized memoir, I might sue them for libel if the characters are made too disgusting? The Mother, for instance, steals some money to bet on a race-horse! It is really worse than the proposed changes by Louis J. Singer. The director, Irving Rapper, is coming to see me for another conference at five o'clock, and the feathers will fly!

Paul and Jane Bowles are in Tangier. Lehmann in London is very happy over advance reactions to Paul's novel and I suspect it will make a real impression there. He now has the manuscript of Windham's novel which has been rejected by most of the big commercial publishers in the States.

Eyre de Lanux is a woman who was a great beauty, is now about 45 and I think she has recently had her face lifted while she was mysteriously away in Paris. She has a young Italian lover, a boy of 25, startlingly beautiful and the only real rascal that I have met in Italy. Her blind adoration of him is shocking! But quite understandable.

I have not yet located the painter (engraver?) you mentioned but I am sure I shall find him if he is still about Rome. The city is now at its loveliest, dangerously lovely for a person who should sit at home working all afternoon if he hopes to continue to get anywhere with his work.

Yours ever, 10.

Eyre's boy-friend, Paolo, recently brought her a two-year-old infant that he claims to be his bastard child and wants her to take care of it for him. It has no resemblance to him, it is obviously a trick of some kind. She has written a story about their "menage" as if it were being observed through the eyes of their cat. It is not yet good enough to send you, but perhaps the second draft will be.

[Carson McCullers later apologized for cutting a reference to a "bad-house" in TW's preface to *Reflections in a Golden Eye*. Her sister Rita Smith, fiction editor for *Mademoiselle*, had advised that it was "'too personal'" (n.d., Duke U), but McCullers invited TW to restore the passage if he wished.

Audrey Wood gave *The Member of the Wedding* (1950) to Robert Whitehead because of the producer's "taste" and "boldness" and anticipated sympathy for the author "on her first venture into playwriting" (Wood, *Represented by Audrey Wood*, 1981). Whitehead and Oliver Rea produced *Medea* in 1947.

TW would soon complete "an outline" of the "neglected" play, *The Rose Tattoo*, and seek the opinion of Wood and Elia Kazan.

James Laughlin's plan to join the Book Find Club—and its 30,000 members—in publishing an anthology of TW's writing did not materialize. Laughlin published special editions of "The Kingdom of Earth" (1954), a story which he considered "'clean dirt'" (to TW, December 18, 1948, Houghton), and "the Lawrence play" *I Rise in Flame, Cried the Phoenix* (1951).

John Lehmann issued Paul Bowles's first novel, *The Sheltering Sky* (1949), later in the fall. He was TW's English publisher and friend as well.

The painter and writer Elizabeth Eyre de Lanux was in her mid-fifties when she met TW in Rome. He later identified her as the model for Karen Stone in *The Roman Spring* and used details of her affair with the young writer Paolo Casagrande, as well as his given name. Laughlin's interest in de Lanux stems from a "charming little story" (to TW, May 25, 1949, Houghton) of hers which TW recommended for publication: "The Street of the Mouth-of-the Lion" (*New Directions Thirteen*, 1951).]

136. To Irene Mayer Selznick

[45 Via Aurora, Rome]
June 14, 1949.
[TLS, 1 p. Boston U]

Dear Irene:

I salute you with a fresh ribbon and I mean on the typewriter, not in my hair, although my curls are almost getting long enough to need one. But I believe you always liked me better when I needed a hair-cut.

We have been snowed under with American visitors. Most of them only pass through Rome and procede to Ischia where Capote and Auden are holding court, but we catch them both ways, going and coming, and are beginning to bend under the strain. Guess who is here right now? That's right! Little Maria. She arrived just as I was about to surrender the Roman field, so I am forced to remain a while longer to make some show of hospitality. Of course I like seeing her, but at night I dream of the snowy solitude of the Dolomites, and I am sure it is not like the hills of Nebraska that the missionary in "Rain" dreamed about!

Irving Rapper was here to consult with me about the film-script for "Menagerie". I took quite a liking to him and perhaps we will be able to come to some fairly dignified compromise on the script. I read it again in Paris and was terribly shocked by the ending. I don't know why, but I didn't remember its being quite that bad, and in response to my howl of dismay, which reached Mr. Feldman by way of Audrey, they dispatched Rapper to pacify me. I rashly agreed to resume work on the film-script. Hate going back to it, but I couldn't let it be filmed that way without some effort to save it. I have been busy on that for the past couple of weeks. Unfortunately the only true ending was the one in the play, and the one I have now worked out, to satisfy their demand for "an up-beat", is the lesser of various evils - at best. They want me to come to Hollywood for further consultations in July, and Audrey wants me to come to New York the first of August to re-direct "Summer and Smoke" for the proposed road-tour sponsored by John Shubert. Both undertakings are important but the thought of returning to America before I have completed my work here is very alarming. It presents a dilemma. And then of course I feel that I may be wanted in England in August. "Yes is For a Very Young Man". I am too old to be saying yes so often when my anxious heart says no!

Maria is quite broken up over Poor Tom Heggen. I don't think she realized until his death that she cared for him so deeply, but now she is pensive and tearful a great deal of the time and one is obliged to treat her very gently. She appreciated your wire so much and speaks of you with great respect and fondness, which in my presence would be necessary anyhow.

Some very happy news from home. At long last my sister is having a change. She is under the special care of an elderly woman who takes her out of the sanitarium for three days of each week, and they have forwarded letters from Rose in which she expresses her great joy at this new arrangement. The letters are quite normal except that in one of them she sends "love to her off-spring" which is a bit of a surprise as we didn't know she had any. Perhaps the world of illusion isn't so bad. - How is Judith Evelyn, or is that too indiscreet a question? Frankie joins me in sending you love.

Love! - Tennessee.

[TW last saw Irene Selznick in London in early-May as plans for the English production of *Streetcar* were nearing completion. He and Vivien Leigh reportedly became "thick as thieves," while Laurence Olivier remained aloof and ominously "asked for freedom" to cut the play, which TW "gently refused" (Selznick, *A Private View*, 1983, pp. 322-323). A limited engagement of *Streetcar* was set to open in the following October.

"Little Maria" Britneva arrived in Rome on June 9 and found TW "very detached somehow, like something that is running down." She considered Frank Merlo "possessive and destructive of every relationship Ten has, which is bad, for an artist like Ten needs some impetus—happiness or unhappiness—not just the nervous reactions of a horse" (St. Just, pp. 19, 25). TW probably told Britneva of the "ugly, violent" (*Journal*, June 7, 1949) scenes with Merlo which preceded her arrival. Should they separate, TW foresaw that he "would go on living and enduring and I suppose turn him into a poem as I've done with others" (*Journal*, May/June 1949).

In Somerset Maugham's story "Rain" (1921), the missionary dreams of a prostitute whose breasts resemble the "hills of Nebraska." Maugham's once controversial story provided the tropical setting and the theme of religious hypocrisy for TW's first-known play, "Beauty is the Word" (1930/1984).

The recent death of Tom Heggen by drowning in a bathtub was ruled a probable suicide with the contributing cause an overdose of barbiturates. TW doubted the report, believing that Heggen, the young co-author of *Mister Roberts* (1948), "simply fell asleep" after careless use of drugs. TW attributed his death to the "shock of sudden fame" (*Journal*, May/June 1949), a lethal variety of his own "catastrophe of success." Britneva supplied the final ironic detail: Heggen "never took a bath!"

Selznick recently prevailed over Audrey Wood by hiring Judith Evelyn rather than Ruth Ford—Wood's client—to play Blanche in the national tour of *Streetcar*. TW appears to have enjoyed the battle of feminine wills, although Evelyn's difficult adjustment to the role supported Wood's position.]

137. To Carson McCullers

[45 Via Aurora, Rome]
6/18/49
[TLS, 1 p. Duke U]

Dearest Carson:

I am sorry there was such a long lapse in our correspondance. I have been away most of the time, London and Paris, as well as various places in Italy. And there has been an unbroken stream of arrivals from the States. I'm almost beginning to feel like the Mayor of Rome, except that I have no golden key to offer, only an increasingly perfunctory sort of handshake and a hunted expression as I can seldom remember where I met them before, on Lexington avenue or Fire Island or Provincetown. Not that it makes much difference. One or two really good arrivals are expected, however: Oliver Evans is now crossing over and Donnie talks of coming later in the summer, and Maria Britneva is already here, a fugitive from London. Do you remember her? The little English girl who was much in evidence last Fall during the trial by "Summer". She is now here in Rome and I enjoy her company. She is full of a good kind of mischief. Most women hate her and few men know what to think of her. Last night she was arrested on suspicion of street-walking. She had strolled up into the park at two in the morning by herself. The cops fell in love with her, and bought her coffee in an all night cafe where the whores hang-out, and tried to make dates with her. Life here is full of little comedy denouements of that kind. I keep thinking how you would love it, and whenever I make a friend here I find myself wondering whether or not you would also like him or her, and I usually feel that you would. However I have a feeling that I will spend next year in the States. The Holy Year will make the town such a mess. They are already putting fig-leaves over the statues and forbidding white swimming-slips in the pools. I am thinking of Key West or San Francisco for next year, as New Orleans is still out of bounds due to the occupation by you-know-who. I have been working more lately, although the time is divided among poems and a novella and the play goes slowly. Really everything goes slowly in Rome, like old Father Tiber. Miss Buick has aged. Her rosey complexion has dimmed and her joints are creaking. She will have to be renovated, or open a tea-shop. Truman and Auden and Chester Coleman and various other of the spiteful sisterhood were all clustered on the little island of Ischia for several months but all at once there was some convulsion among them and they all came off at once. Truman and his paramour passed through town for a few days last week, Auden and Chester also at the same time. There was a great collision in the public rooms of the Inghilterra (hotel), all hissing and flapping like geese, and there are rumors that the island of Ischia has dropped back under the sea.

Frankie is sick. He has been running a high fever for several days with badly infected tonsils, has been on penicillin and sulfa and aspirin without much improvement, if any. I am worried about him, he is so quiet and pale and little-looking, all eyes and nose, like a baby sparrow, especially when he has a chill, and I have no faith in the doctor. I have to go out now to find him a book, and pick up Maria before the cops get her again. Love to your mother and Rita and Reeves, and a whole lot to you. Be well and happy! I am delighted that you and Audrey have placed the play in good hands. And even happier about the new novel.

10

[Carson McCullers's preceding letter to TW ended with a plea, "Why why don't you write????" (n.d., Duke U).

"Holy Year," a time when special indulgences may be gained by the faithful, is observed every quarter-century by the Roman Catholic Church. Pilgrimage to Rome is a familiar part of the ancient ritual.

W.H. Auden and his companion Chester Kallman spent the summer of 1949 on the island of Ischia. Truman Capote has noted that Kallman "was extremely

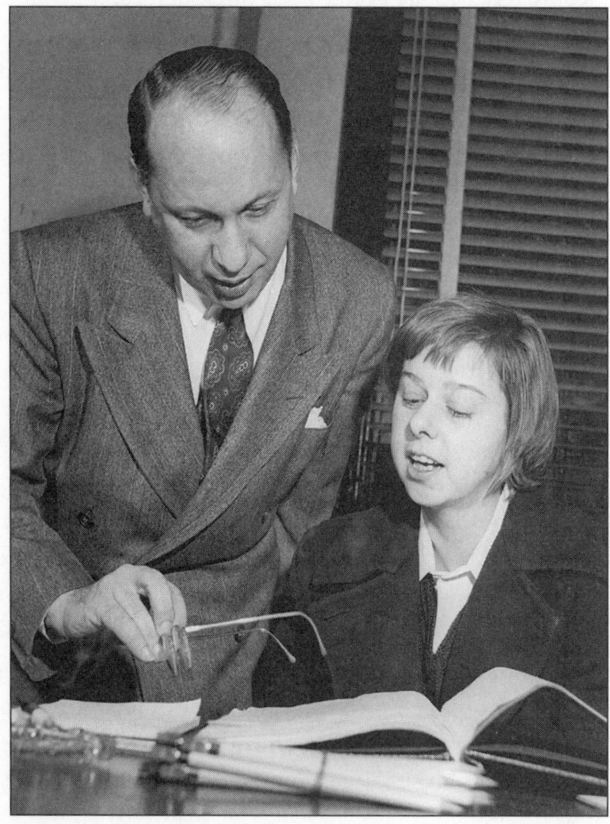

Carson McCullers and director Harold Clurman examining the script of The Member of the Wedding *(1950): "I am delighted that you and Audrey have placed the play in good hands."*

rude to Tennessee and Frankie, and he made it a point not to invite them to their house. Tennessee was very hurt" (qtd. in Clarke, *Capote: A Biography*, p. 197).

TW's report of the "spiteful sisterhood" on Ischia amused McCullers, who also wondered how "Truman" had missed being "the flowergirl" (to TW, n.d., Duke U) at the recent wedding of Rita Hayworth and Prince Aly Kahn.

McCullers's "new novel" is *Clock Without Hands* (1961).]

138. To Justin Brooks Atkinson

[45 Via Aurora, Rome]
[mid-June 1949]
[TL, 1 p. HRC]

Dear Brooks:

Yesterday I got a letter from my friend Carson McCullers sending me a recent article of yours on Uta Hagen's performance in Streetcar, and I was deeply touched, as I have been often before, by your continuing interest in this old play of mine which must be tottering into a state of senesence although you write about it as if it were born yesterday.

I wrote you a long time, sometime last winter, but I didn't mail the letter, for I fell into a ridiculous state of gloom and apathy about that time, in which I felt almost as if it were presumptuous of me to maintain any contact with the outside world. Most of that feeling has worn off now, under the benign influence of the Roman sun, and the Romans, who are almost equally warm and golden. I have been through such cycles of depression before. As I grow older they seem to stay with me longer, but I am also better able to cope with them philosophically. I guess you can imagine, better than I can, what was the matter. The misfortune of "Summer" had some connection with it. I felt like a discredited old conjurer whose bag of tricks was exhausted. I had rough drafts of a couple of plays but lacked the confidence to go on with them as soon as I left the artificial exhileration of Manhattan. When my confidence began to return a little, I worked on poems and a novella, but have only just lately gotten seriously back to work on a play, and still can't say how soon it will be completed and still am not sure it is different enough from the others to be immune from the charge that my work is repetitive. The trouble is that you can't make any real philosophical progress in a couple of years. The scope of understanding enlarges quite slowly, if it enlarges at all, and the scope of interest seems to wait upon understanding. In the meantime there is only continued observation, and variations on what you've already observed. I have noticed that painters and poets, and in fact all artists who work from the inside out, have all the same problem: they cannot make sudden, arbitrary changes of matter and treatment until the inner man is ripe for it. The blue period changes gradually to the rose, and of course there are some poets who never stop writing sonnets, and if their readers get weary of it, no one is to blame. The great challenge is keeping alive and growing as much as you can; and let the chips fall where they may!

[Brooks Atkinson declined to compare Jessica Tandy and Uta Hagen after Hagen assumed the role of Blanche on June 1. Her performance was "enlightened and exciting" and "thoroughly her own." Atkinson praised TW's "steel-like accuracy as a writer" once again and opined that *Streetcar* was still "one of the most glowing achievements of the Broadway theatre" (*New York Times*, June 12, 1949).

The unsigned typescript, unfolded and doubtless unmailed, was written in mid-June 1949 at the time of TW's preceding letter to Carson McCullers.]

139. To Audrey Wood

[45 Via Aurora, Rome]
6/21/49
[TLS w/ enclosure, 1 p. HRC]

Dear Audrey:

I am sending you herewith an outline of the long play on which I've been working off and on in Italy. I have kept a carbon of it which I may show to Gadge but would not have anybody else see it. So far I have not devoted myself to it at all consistently but I am leaving for a week or two in the northern lake country of Italy and am hoping that the change of climate will speed me up. Lack of physical energy has been a great detriment here, and if I push myself, I get hypertensive. That is one of the reasons I have been hesitant about committing myself to direct "Summer and Smoke" in New York. I seriously doubt that I would have the great physical endurance that sort of work calls for: that is, the long hours and strenuous final rehearsals. If I had a very good stage manager, of my own choice who could take over rehearsals when I was tired - then it would be feasible. Otherwise I doubt that the cost in energy would be worth while. Also I feel it would be foolish to put it on without a first rate cast. Someone better than Todd in the male part and almost as good as Maggie for the girl. Would there be any, even the remotest, chance of interesting Marlon in the boy's part for a very limited engagement? And how about asking Mary Hunter to direct?

Arthur Miller and his wife are in town. We spent last evening with them and I am taking them out to dinner tonight. They are a lovely couple: he is so warm and honest a person one can hardly believe that he was ever on Broadway or in Hollywood. I mean he still seems quite innocent. Gadge is supposed to be here, or almost here, but so far no sign of it. I ran into John Garfield at a dancing place a couple of nights ago and he is all steamed up about the Streetcar picture deal. I have not yet studied it out completely but I have an idea that a Kazan picture would be a sure thing. There is no real need to worry about censorship as rape has been handled in "Johnny Belinda" and the slight alteration of a few lines ought to take care of the other angle. Oh, well. I will read Colton's letter again. Then try to make up my mind about it all. - Could you get Feldman-Rapper to engage Windham for the "Menagerie" movie script? He needs the money and I think he'd do a fine job.

Love, 10.

[The enclosed "outline" describes the basic argument of *The Rose Tattoo*: a middle-aged widow (Pepina) who idolizes her late husband (Rosario), the disclosure of his unfaithfulness by two spiteful female "clowns," and the appearance of a lover (Umberto) to break the spell of the past. The ardent love of Pepina's daughter (Rose) for a young sailor (Jack) forms a subplot which "develops into a mighty clash between mother and daughter" (Stornello, June 21, 1949, HRC). The play is set in a fishing village on the Gulf Coast and deals primarily with characters of Sicilian descent—TW's "Terra Trema" perhaps. The outline was also mailed to Elia Kazan, as following correspondence reveals.

John Shubert was now dealing directly with Margo Jones in planning the tour of *Summer and Smoke*. Audrey Wood advised TW of this "completely Shubertian" tactic and hoped that "Jones would {not} be fool enough" (July 8, 1949, HRC) to disregard their wish to revamp the cast.

Kazan offered to produce *Streetcar* in association with an independent film company linked to his friend John Garfield. The deal would require that Garfield "play the lead." At this time Kazan considered making the film without Production Code approval in order to retain the "integrity" (Colton to TW, May 6, 1949, HRC) of the play.

TW naively assumed that the rape scene in *Streetcar* and Allan Grey's homosexuality—the "other angle"—would meet little or no resistance from the censor. A menacing score and severe lighting and shadow were used to suggest the impending rape in *Johnny Belinda*. Jane Wyman won an Academy Award for her role as a vulnerable young woman without speech or hearing who is raped and later exonerated for killing her attacker.

TW's recommendation of Donald Windham as screenwriter for *The Glass Menagerie* was belated, wishful thinking.]

140. To Molly and Elia "Gadge" Kazan

[45 Via Aurora, Rome]
7/12/49
[TLS w/ autograph marginalia, 2 pp. WUCA]

Dear Molly and Gadge:

I thank and love you both for the honesty of your letters and for the trouble you took to write them as you did when it would have been so much easier, I know, to have just been vague and nice about it. Fortunately I had already done some pretty brutal stock-taking of my self and accomplishments, or rather lack of them, on my trip through the lake country and by the time I got back to Rome, yesterday, the vapors of illusion were pretty thoroughly dispelled. So the letters were really only a confirmation, but one that was helpful. It is so good to be able to talk honestly with somebody about my dilemma as a writer! The simple truth is that I haven't known where to go since Streetcar. Everything that isn't an arbitrary, and consequently uninspired, experiment seems to be only an echo. This was true last year in Rome when I started and gave up at least four plays. When I went back to the States I seemed to be finding my way out of the predicament and I worked on a new play there, about a southern demagogue and with a social emphasis, which I thought I was seriously interested in and would push through to completion. But no sooner did I sail out of New York than my interest in it dissolved. I couldn't convince myself that I cared enough about the character and ideas involved to put any fire into the writing. Then I began to be badly frightened, and as always happens under that condition, I lost my objectivity. I wandered into work on "Stornello" simply because it seemed to demand so much less of me. It would have been more sensible to stop working, and just wait, with the hope that there would be a resurgence of energy that would allow me to continue the stronger themes that I had undertaken before I became so devitalized. But to wait is hard, when there is much uncertainty, so I began to work again without really having the power. You will be glad to hear, though, that I hadn't gone very deep into this work, not even to a point where it would be difficult to give it up, and now that the whole problem has come to a head, and there is no more possibility of delusion and evasion, I feel strangely much calmer and less anxious about it. A good deal of that came to me through your letters, the very palpable sincerity of them, the lack of any crap of a comforting nature which really would have bothered me, and at the same time the feeling that you definitely cared. I doubt that anybody else, even Audrey, could have written me in quite that way about it. I don't need to tell you that the synopsis was not a real picture of the play that I had in mind. My efforts to make it sound lively made it sound cheap, but in the character of Pepina there was a lostness which I could feel and write about with reality, and would have, if I wrote it. The trouble was that I had already written so much about the same thing. In many ways writing is the most perilous and ephemeral of the talents, and you never know whether an impasse is only temporary or final, and the only real help lies in honesty with yourself and from others and keeping alive your interest in life itself.

To divert to the somewhat less serious topic of the picture. I have a long and confusing letter from Irene and a cable that apparently has some sort of connection with it. She is thinking in terms of Lillian Hellman and a script that will pass the Hays office, and while there is no direct reference to the terms of a sale, there are indications that she feels it would be foolishly Quixotic of her not to take advantage of a declining market. God knows I see her point about that, but it increases my longing to work out some kind of deal with you for the picture to be made honestly and at the same time to assure myself a few years of security in which to try to work out the various problems with which I am beset. A cable from Audrey makes no mention of Irene's project but demands my opinion of your offer which I had already given in the cable before I saw you in Rome. Is there any way you could acquire the rights by placing in - I believe "escrow" is the word - a down payment of forty or fifty thousand to be paid in ten thousand installments over a period of four or five years? And the rest of the payment to be a speculation upon the success of the picture, which I would be very happy to make if it were placed in your hands. You see why I couldn't get the whole payment at once and why, at the same time, I need the assurance that that much money would be definitely forthcoming. All this is pure improvisation on my part, as I have not been in communication with Audrey or anyone else since the letter I showed you in Rome. I also sent Audrey a copy of the play synopsis, and perhaps that has stunned her into silence.

I have a feeling that Muni will come through with a fine performance for you, as I remember how strong he used to be in such early pictures as Scarface. You can bring him back to the surface.

With love, Tenn.

[TW's gloomy analysis of post-*Streetcar* writing includes "The Big Time Operators"—the "southern demagogue" play—as well as other works undertaken and presumably discarded.

Irene Selznick confidentially obtained a Production Code report which banned "sex perversion" in *Streetcar* and labeled the rape scene "unacceptable" because it "goes unpunished" (Breen to Paramount Pictures, June 27, 1949, Herrick). She swore TW to secrecy and explained that "in an effort to prevent a sale," the censor was often "much tougher before a property is sold" (July 1, 1949, Boston U).

Selznick also informed TW that she had hired Lillian Hellman to devise a strategy whereby *Streetcar* could "meet the Code and yet not lose substance" (July 1, 1949, Boston U). Hellman reported that omitting the "homosexual story" and the rape "need not fundamentally change" the play. The reason for Allan Grey's suicide might plausibly be obscured by Blanche's lack of knowledge or by her refusal to face the unpleasant truth. Blanche's capacity for self-deception could also be used to treat the rape as mere illusion (n.d., Irene Mayer Selznick Collection, Boston U).

Elia Kazan was apparently not involved in the production or funding of the *Streetcar* film.

Penned in the upper margin is TW's mailing address, "American Express, Rome."]

141. To Irving Rapper

[45 Via Aurora, Rome]
August 5, 1949.
[TLx, 1 p. HRC]

Dear Irving:

Here is the warehouse sequence. I am not enclosing picnic material because I hope that we may decide to eliminate it when we get together in California. It strikes me as a needless interruption of the continuity and it complicates the production without adding anything of material value to the story, since we have already agreed that it is better to reserve the announcement of the coming caller for the fire-escape scene between mother and son, as it was done on the stage. The picnic and the rainstorm could have a certain picturesque pathos, but I am wondering, now, if we don't have enough background material without it, and also enough footage, and the inclusion of a picnic would, I should think, considerably add to the budget. Think and talk this over with Jerry Wald and wire me your reaction. I think you may now have sufficiently complete material to assess a budget and prepare a preliminary shooting-script. I don't imagine a final shooting-script is possible till after our California conferences.

I have introduced Jim in the warehouse, which was something we had agreed to consider. As I worked on the script it appeared more and more desirable to me to make this introduction here, to establish him as a character before he appears for the "big scene".

Irving, I don't know what to say about the ending. It really stumped me for quite a while and that is what held up my work on the script so much longer than I had expected. Your cable indicates a dissatisfaction with the ending that I submitted, but I wish that you could comment on it more specifically so that I could tell in what direction you feel it is wrong. Is it too much, or too little? It is certainly <u>not</u> a product of great inspiration! Even so, however, I feel it is a vast improvement on "The Sterling Character". My own difficulty is that in my heart the ending as it exists in the play was the artistically inevitable ending. While I assent to a new one, my heart belongs to the old one. Now I am not welching on our agreement to look for an up-beat, and I am not going to welch on it. I would be very grateful, though, for a repeated assurance from you and Jerry that there will be no pressure to reinstate "Sterling" or that kind of fairy-tale ending which we agreed would sacrifice the play's integrity. I think it is all right to suggest the possibility of "someone else coming". And that "someone else" remaining as insubstantial as an approaching shadow in the alley which appears in conjunction with the narrative line "The long delayed but always expected something that we live for" - it strikes me as constituting a sufficiently hopeful possibility for the future, symbolically and even literally, which is about as much as the essential character of the story will admit without violation. As you say we will undoubtedly find a solution in California, but it would add to my peace of mind if you could assure me now that there has been no reversion of opinion in favor of the old type of ending. When the film comes to life I am sure we will all be surprised at how very little, how much less than we supposed, was needed to give the little anti-depressant we feel is called for.

Ever,

[Irving Rapper (1898-1999) directed Bette Davis in such notable Warner Brothers films as *Now, Voyager* (1942), *The Corn Is Green* (1945), and *Desperation* (1946). Friendship with Davis, a strong candidate to play Amanda at this time, may have influenced Rapper's appointment to direct *The Glass Menagerie*.

The "warehouse sequence" is one of several scenes written to add range and variety to the restricted setting of *The Glass Menagerie*. The "picnic material"—cut as TW advised—was also intended to diversify the film and to underscore the bleakness of the Wingfield apartment, to which the "sodden and dispirited" ("Italian Conference," June 27, 1949, HRC) family returns after the storm. The "announcement" of a gentleman caller was reserved for the "fire-escape scene" with Amanda and Tom which immediately follows.]

142. To James "Jay" Laughlin

[45 Via Aurora, Rome]
8/17/49.
[TLS w/ enclosures, 2 pp. Houghton]

Dear Jay:

Whatever decision you and Carson reach about the two prefaces is O.K. with me. My feeling was, when I read over the first version, that I appeared in that version to be talking too much about myself. If you revert to that original version I hope that you will preserve the cuts that I have made in it, particularly the long portion about "imitators". I believe that I scratched out (in the returned proofs) all but about two sentences of that material which was provoked mainly by a personal antagonism for Truman which I think should not be indulged in this place. I also wish you would compare the two versions very carefully, again, and perhaps something from the second, which I still believe had a great deal more dignity in keeping with the novel, could be appended or worked into the other.

I received yesterday a long letter from Carson, most depressing. "Health has failed steadily - can't walk more than half a block - neuritis has set in - damaged nerves constantly spastic - dreadful headache - nausea, prostration - a gland went wrong in the neck - prolonged suffering - a sort of convulsion at dawn . . ." It sounds almost fantastic! Surely she has not been given any really intelligent diagnosis or therapy. I think she should be hospitalized for several months and exhaustively examined from every angle, physiological, emotional, Etc. Of course there needs to be a special branch of medicine for the understanding and treatment of such hypersensitive artists, but since they practically never have any money, they are simply condemned. I dread the play production that she is now facing as her emotional involvement is certain to be great. Clurman is a fine director for it, but when I last saw the script it was far from being in a state to produce.

I am sailing out of Naples on the twentieth, the crossing takes ten days, and must go directly to Hollywood when I land. My work on the movie script is practically complete but they are not yet satisfied with the ending and I think I shall have a fight with them about that. They say they don't want a fairy-tale ending but there is evidence of double-talk. At least I should learn something more about the technique of film-making which I can use creatively on some other assignment perhaps over here. I am on excellent terms with Rossollini and De Sica and Visconti and would enjoy working with any one of them. Last week had supper with Ingrid Bergman and Rossolini. Their "Fuck you" attitude toward the outraged women's clubs and sob-columnists is very beautiful and should have a salutary affect on discrediting those infantile moralists that make it so hard for anyone to do honest work and live honestly in the States. If Bergman has the moral courage she appears to have, it will be a triumph.

Several weeks ago I sent you two long poems, The Soft City and Counsel, which you haven't mentioned receiving. If you hate them, for God's sake Jay, don't hesitate to say so! I depend so much on your critical opinion as there are times when my own seems to fail me. I lose objectivity about my work, as everyone does at times, but you know that I am not morbidly sensitive to adverse opinion, but on the contrary, I am grateful for it. I showed Kazan and his wife a long synopsis of the play I had been working on. They both wrote me from London of their disappointment in it quite frankly and while I felt that the synopsis had not conveyed a true idea of the play as it existed in my conception, their criticism will be helpful when I go back to work on it, if I do. Whatever I do badly (even if it is everything!) I want to know, I want to be told! Honesty about failure is the only help for it.

I am enclosing two versions, first and second draft, of another poem. I don't know which is the better or worse. Also the other ending to the Lawrence play. ~~I wonder if it would not be better to change Brett's name in the play to something like Brady, since the incident is fictitious and she might object. I don't believe Frieda would~~.

It is dreadful to leave here, but I have thrown a coin in the Fountain of Trevi.

Ever, 10

[TW recently drafted a second preface for *Reflections in a Golden Eye* and entrusted the final editing to James Laughlin. Neither personal elements nor a lengthy reference to "'imitators'" would appear in the published version, but TW probably annoyed Truman Capote by referring to "derivative talents" and Gore Vidal by ridiculing the "idea that a good novelist turns out a book once a year."

The affair of Ingrid Bergman and Roberto Rossellini during the filming of *Stromboli* (1949) caused an international scandal which forced Bergman to live and work in Europe until the mid 1950s. She divorced her Swedish husband to marry Rossellini and legitimize their unborn son.

"The Soft City" and "Counsel," poems by TW, first appeared in *New Directions Eleven* (1949).

The limited and the acting editions of *I Rise in Flame, Cried the Phoenix* (1951 and 1952, respectively) differ only in their staging of D.H. Lawrence's death—the later version briefer and less harrowing. In both editions the painter Dorothy Brett is renamed Bertha and cast as an officious disciple of Lawrence.]

143. To Frederic "Fritz" Prokosch

[*Saturnia*]
[late-August 1949]
[TLS, 1 p. Columbia U]

Dear Fritz:

Last year you gave me a copy of your book, The Asiatics, but I have only just now read it, while crossing back to the States, and I want you to know that I think it a great, an extraordinarily great, book, jewelled with wonderful images, with a wild and beautiful sort of freedom, almost anarchy, about it which I had certainly not expected, not even from your poetry, fine as that is but generally, maybe only because it is a shorter form, more subject to order. It has a feeling of freedom from usual form such as I remember finding only in Kafka or Joyce but it differs in richness of sensuosity, in pure luxury, from both of those writers. It is quite marvelous the way it surges along, breaking, foaming, and then continuing like a wave washing right over its shores, a sense of flow, continual passage, richness, excitement unlike any other piece of writing I've known. I am still reading it, have not yet finished, but wanted to let you know immediately, though this letter may not reach you for quite a while, how very much it has moved me.

Ever, Tennessee.

[TW and Frank Merlo boarded the *Saturnia* in Naples and were due to arrive in New York on August 30.

Frederic Prokosch (1906-1989) has recalled talking "about love" with his "sad-eyed friend Tennessee Williams" (Prokosch, *Voices*, 1983, p. 253), whom he met in Rome in 1948. Prokosch held a doctorate in literature from Yale, but the popular and critical success of *The Asiatics* (1935) had released him from an unwanted academic career. The book's vivid setting, which reaches from Syria to China, was surprisingly based upon written sources rather than firsthand experience.

TW cabled Margo Jones from the *Saturnia* with a gibe about the forthcoming production of *Summer and Smoke*: "Suggest change title to August Madness" (August 25, 1949, Dallas Public Library).]

144. To Walter Edwin Dakin, Edwina Dakin and Walter Dakin Williams

SH: Hotel Bel-Air
701 Stone Canyon Road
Los Angeles 24 [California]
[early-September 1949]
[TLS, 2 pp. Columbia U]

Dear Grandfather, Mother & Dakin:

I am addressing you in order of seniority this time. Am living here in great luxury at the expense of Warner Bros. They have put me in a de luxe three-room suite. Swimming pool right outside the door, and have provided me with a Buick convertible since my own is stored in New York. Our relations have been very agreeable. We seem to be in complete agreement about the script. The vulgarities have been eliminated. I have re-written the whole thing according to my own ideas and I now think it has a chance to be a very successful picture. I have not yet made any definite plans but I intend to stay in America through the winter. They are planning to go to Saint

Louis to make some locations shots for the film. I will probably visit home at that time, which may be late this month or early October. It now seems definite that Gertrude Lawrence will play Amanda. I saw her test and it was amazingly good.

Don't know yet where I shall settle for winter. But I do plan to spend some time in Key West and I want Grandfather to join me there. I can pick him up in Saint Louis and we can drive down in my car. I sent Rose a box from New York. It contained a lovely compact and Roman scarf which I had bought in Italy, and a ten dollar bill. Let me know if she received it. This Saturday the producers are giving a formal party for me, and they say practically all of Hollywood will be there! Let me hear from you, care of Audrey. Oh - I signed the trust papers for Rose. As Summer and Smoke has re-opened in Chicago. I don't know, yet, how it is doing but the notices were better than it got in New York. Love,

Tom.

[Finding an "'up-beat' for Laura at the end" (to Wood, July 29, 1949, HRC) of *The Glass Menagerie* proved TW's greatest difficulty in revising the screenplay. Before leaving Hollywood in late-September, TW completed a script which he naively thought final.

Bette Davis and Tallulah Bankhead tested for the role of Amanda, but it was the London-born Gertrude Lawrence, whose fame lay in stage musicals, who won the part. TW's endorsement of Lawrence—perhaps for benefit of family—belied his final verdict that her casting was "'a dismal error'" (qtd. in Morley, *Gertrude Lawrence*, 1981, p. 181).

The tour of *Summer and Smoke* opened in Chicago (September 5, 1949) to "better" reviews, although they were qualified and still mindful of *Streetcar*. Margo Jones's use of three actors rejected by TW led to a "big row" with Audrey Wood, who regretted that "legal technicalities" (to TW, August 22, 1949, HRC) forbade closing the show. Chicago reviewers admired the cast, including the disputed leads Tod Andrews and Katharine Balfour. TW later declared the production "a poor travesty of what it should have been" (qtd. in St. Just, p. 27).

Composition of this letter falls between TW's arrival in Los Angeles on September 5, 1949, and the "formal party" given in his honor on the 10th. The party, he observed, was "like a wet dream of Louella Parson's." He received his "first solid gold cigarette case" and saw his name "in blue letters in an illuminated block of ice!" (to Kazan, n.d., WUCA).]

145. To Irene Mayer Selznick

Western Union
New York
1949 Oct 12 PM 9 40
[Telegram, 1 p. Boston U]

PLEASE RELEASE YOUR BREATH DARLING DONT WANT YOU TO SUFFOCATE BEFORE THE SHOW STARTS MUCH MUCH LOVE AND THANKS=

=TENNESSEE=

[Irene Selznick anxiously protected *Streetcar* as it was recast and reshaped by Laurence Olivier for production in London. Olivier relieved the tension by writing a detailed letter to TW in which he attributed many of the cuts to the special needs of an English audience. "Deeply touched" by the gesture, TW cabled approval of the revised script and regretted not having worked "more closely" (October 3, 1949, HRC) with the director.

Streetcar opened at the Aldwych Theatre on October 12, 1949, drawing a large, unruly crowd and causing intense public criticism of the play's "sooty" subject matter and style. Vivien Leigh's Blanche won raves and played to full houses for 326 performances.]

146. To Paul Bowles

1431 Duncan Street
Key West [Florida]
Nov. 19, 1949
[TLS w/ autograph marginalia, 1 p. HRC]

Dear Paul:

We are very distressed to hear of your liver attacks and trust you are now entirely recovered from them. Only you would declare the food in England to be magnificent, just out of pure perversity I am sure, and because you have been eating dried goat-meat in Morocco, which is probably why you came down with a liver condition.

I wish I had some good news to give you about the Menagerie music. All I can definitely say is that we made a great effort. Played the records for Jerry Wald and gave a set of them to Ann Warner who is Jack Warner's exceedingly tiresome but good natured wife. What came of it all I have not yet discovered. My communications since leaving Hollywood have been more and more disturbing. Midnight telephones and wires, saying please give us a little more up-beat at the end. Write scene between Laura and Tom after his departure to sea. Etc. No allusion to music and I have been either too sleepy or exasperated to think of it. There was nothing more to be done and yes is the most ambiguous word that you can get out of them. I shall have Audrey investigate again. You may be sure if they don't use your music it is simply because they are too stingy and the music too good. They only like music that goes Blah-blah-blah like a Brahms symphony by Irving Berlin, and always swelling to great inspirational crescendos.

There has been great excitement over your book in New York, especially the reviews, in which I am involved. Harvey Breit of the New York Times called me up and asked if I would review it. I said, Yes, indeedy, pie! He said 600 words. I said I could not be limited to that small a notice as I felt the book required a full page. We compromised on about 900, I believe. Gore was in my room when the call was received and took a great interest and I believe he is trying to get permission to review it for one of the other papers. Had no luck with the Trib and was going to try the Sat. Lit. when I pulled out of New York. I accused him, very unkindly and/or unjustly, of bitching up my notice. The day after I turned it in, and it was received very favorably by Breit, Gore had an interview with Breit in which the notice was discussed and read and the next day Breit called me back saying the publication of the notice was dubious and that a whole page had to be cut out which was the most pertinent part of it. First I blew up and said, Send it back, don't cut a word. Then I began to suspect a nigger in the wood-pile, meaning none other than G.V., so I called back and said I was willing to make a few deletions if necessary. It seems Gore had mentioned that the Trib wouldn't let him review the book because he was a friend of yours and Breit was now worried that there might be an objection about me, also, being your friend. Well, I accused Vidal to his face, of manipulation, and he was quite hurt and I now think that I was being unfair about it and owe him an apology. Today I got the proofs of the notice and it is almost as it was originally except they cut out a very lyrical last sentence about "time". It is a very favorable notice, of course, and I hope you will like it.

Tenn.

[TW, Frank Merlo, and Walter Dakin arrived in Key West ca. November 12. Dakin had flown from St. Louis to Jacksonville, where he was met and driven to the island which TW first visited in 1941.

"For purely personal reasons" (to TW, August 30, 1949, HRC)—an inveterate poverty—Paul Bowles asked that the "Menagerie music" which he composed for Broadway be used in the forthcoming film. Max Steiner eventually wrote a new score.

Reviewing the American edition of *The Sheltering Sky* (1949) allowed TW to belittle Gore Vidal and Truman Capote once again. He contrasted their "frisky antics" (*New York Times*, December 4, 1949, sec. 7, p. 7) in the preceding literary season with Bowles's masterly first novel, issued in the writer's thirty-eighth year. Vidal later denied any influence with the *New York Times* and attributed TW's "gratuitous swipe" to jealousy caused by his own history as "a late starter" (Vidal, *Palimpsest*, 1995, pp. 185-186).

Penned in the upper margin is the notation "We, Frank, Grandfather, and I, have taken this house in Key West for the winter & early spring. A new young writer, the rage of fashionable arty circles, named Speed Lamkin is also here. They call him the 'new Capote'. I thought the old one sufficient. Love - 10. (to Janie, too)."]

147. To Audrey Wood

[1431 Duncan Street
Key West, Florida]
11/?/49
[TLS, 1 p. HRC]

Dear Audrey:

I have not written you since getting here as I have been as preoccupied with the pleasures of living as the Madwoman of Chaillot. Every day has been like one of those sentimental ballads of Irving Berlin, blue skies, cottage small, sunshine and so forth. The little house is lovely, it is what they call a Bahama type house, white frame with a white picket fence and pink shutters. There are three bedrooms, a big combination living and dining room, two baths and a kitchen. Frank and I have moved to the upstairs room as the extremely loud conversations between Grandfather and the colored maid, Charleso Marie, make sleep impossible on the same floor level. Even earlier the roosters wake us up, but after the celebration of daybreak it is possible to get back to sleep. Next door is a magnificent black goat with big yellow eyes, surely one of God's most beautiful creatures, always straining at his rope as if he had an important errand to run if he could get loose. Only one block further is Speed Lamkin whom you may know or know of, sometimes referred to as the new Truman Capote. He doesn't write as well but is more agreeable. He is dissatisfied with Kay Brown because he wants to get a Hollywood job and she had not secured one for him and wants to know if you could. Today he leaves for his home in Monroe, La., but Bigelow now occupying his New York apartment can give you all information.

President Truman and family arrived here today. Grandfather and Frank went down to see them pass along Duval street. Grandfather said that the President waved but he wasn't sure if it was at him or the crowd.

I share your concern about the King's Men. However I have not yet returned to work on the machine-boss play. Instead I rewrote the beginning of Stornello and about 40 pages of another novella. I think I will finish these items first, and in the meantime perhaps King's Men will come here or to Miami and I can see if there is too much resemblance. I am reducing Stornello to a minimal length so that it could be done on a double-bill with another longish short play like Camino Real, provided that Kazan can be coaxed into such a venture. This is not a very ambitious project but perhaps more reasonable, like placing your chips on odd or even rather than on one particular number. But the work goes much better here, so well that I have broken down the portable, now at the repair-shop, and have hired an upright machine. Did you get all the Camino revisions? There should be a new ending to Block 3, a new Block 5, and a new beginning to Block 8. Is there a chance, you think, of interesting Gene Kelly? There would also be a good part for him, as a sailor, in Stornello. Pepina and the Gypsy could be played by the same character actress. The Gypsy's daughter and Pepina's daughter could also be performed by one ingenue. Last week I also had to do a re-write on the opening narration for "Menagerie" as Jerry Wald wired me that they had changed their plans and wanted Tom on a ship. I hope they don't decide, now, to put Amanda on skates. I am very pleased over the sale to "Flair" and the amazing price received for it. You are very clever. But what has Bigelow done with poor Mrs. Stone?

Frank is going to New York, or more exactly, New Jersey, for Xmas but Grandfather and I have not yet steeled ourselves to the point of going home for the holidays. Perhaps we'll stay here. With love -

10.

[The "magnificent black goat" would soon appear in *The Rose Tattoo* as one of the play's comic effects.

A reviewer of Speed Lamkin's second novel, *The Easter Egg Hunt* (1954), mocked the "literary overtones of other writers, other books" (*New York Times*, March 7, 1954), and dispatched "the new Truman Capote."

The naval station in Key West served as a winter White House for the Truman administration. The arrival of the First Family on November 28, 1949, sets the date of this letter's composition.

The recent film premiere of *All the King's Men* (1949) raised or renewed "concern" about the originality of TW's "machine-boss" play, "The Big Time Operators."

Plans for a "double-bill" derive from TW's recent visit to the Actors Studio where Elia Kazan was rehearsing scenes from "Ten Blocks on the Camino Real" (1948): "'Oh, Kazan, we must do this. We must do this with one other play maybe, for Broadway'" (*Memoirs*, p. 165). The "Camino revisions" undertaken by TW were dated January 1950 and the project subsequently noted in the *New York Times* as set for a summer tryout. Kazan labeled the report "chatter and hopes" (to Wood, n.d., HRC) and delayed further work on the project "till spring" (to TW, n.d., HRC) when his latest film, *Panic in the Streets* (1950), would be complete.

The Glass Menagerie opens with a new prologue delivered by Arthur Kennedy—who plays Tom Wingfield—from the deck of a merchant ship.

"The Resemblance Between a Violin Case and a Coffin" (1950) appeared in the first number of *Flair* and brought the "amazing" sum of $750. So upset was Cornelius by TW's autobiographical story—in which he was termed "devilish"—that he issued a warning to Audrey Wood: "If he ever refers to my sisters or me in any of his writing I will make him regret it as long as he lives" (February 8, 1950, HRC).]

148. To Paul Bigelow

1431 Duncan
("The Annex")
[Key West, Florida]
12/4/49
[TLS w/ enclosure, autograph marginalia
and postscript, 1 p. Columbia U]

Dear Paul:

The Chief is in error. I swear by all that is holy, he give me the turquoise, he give me the goddam belt! Can I help it that Indians can't hold liquor? I took your advice about moving off the top floor. Told the Madam the tin roof made it too hot, so she put me downstairs in the basement. Much cooler. Trouble is the fucking janitor is absent-minded and locks the trap-door on me and the girls make so much noise they can't hear me holler. Tore my pink chiffon climbing out the coal-chute. But it is wonderful how the old styles are coming back, my Clara Bow hair-do, my kiss-me-quicks, and my low cut beaded gowns. And, honey, the Charleston has returned and the Black Bottom is right around the corner. I always make an entrance when they play "Five Foot Two, Eyes of blue", and it's like you always said, Honey, vivacity goes a long way even when a girl is surrounded by jealous cats!

Speed has pulled out. He says his mother ordered him home but I wonder if that is why. He had got himself on the shit-list of the local queens by snatching off the one really butch sailor at a party they gave - about 10 minutes after he got there. He was doing a lot of work but in other respects I don't think the place quite suited him, as Speed, say what he will, gets a lot of bang out of smart society, God bless him. I don't blame him a bit, as who doesn't? I got to be very fond of him and will miss him a great deal. He has invited me to Monroe at Xmas. Grandfather and I may go to New Orleans about that time so I might drop up there for a day or so. I doubt, however, that I will be ready to go all the way to New York.

Working very hard here, and I think pretty well. Did 40 pages of a new novella and several scenes of an old play that I brought back from Italy are re-written. The new novella is my first attempt at an extended piece of humor in prose. It is a fantastic satire on a southern town that has become the seat of "A Project". (military, not theatrical, but otherwise not unlike the famous "Jones Project") However I must finish a play first.

Do let me see yours soon as you get a draft of it. I have such hopes for it. Must get out, now, to the beach. A girl makes her best contacts in the afternoon when she can see what she's doing. Frank is now happy here, Grandfather even more so. Hope you will find a chance to visit us after Xmas.

Love, 10

P.S. Am enclosing letter for Speed, urgent, don't have his address.

[TW appeared as a courtesan rather than a common whore in a similar campy spoof which Paul Bigelow received from Mexico City in 1945: "I made a brief appearance at the opera last night with 2 generals and 6 duennas but in spite of most discreet behavior on my part, there has been a wave of suicides and duels and every time I go out my carriage is drawn home by students" (postcard, June 8, 1945, Massee Collection). The whorehouse with a "tin roof" recalls a similar off-stage setting in *The Rose Tattoo* named the "Square Roof."

"The Knightly Quest" was finished in 1965 and published by New Directions the following year. The fictional "southern town" is based upon Macon, Georgia, where TW and Bigelow spent the summer of 1942. Fear of spies, heightened by the

Tennessee Williams and Grandfather Dakin, Key West: "Must get out, now, to the beach."

presence of a nearby defense industry, led wary citizens to report them to the police as "'suspicious characters.'" After being detained and questioned, TW wrote presciently in the journal, "Macon swell background" (July 3, 1942). The "'Jones Project'" refers to a British scientific unit headed by the physicist R.V. Jones. He was decorated by President Truman for wartime research deemed critical in the use of radar.

Paul Bigelow's play, variously entitled "A Woman Who Came From a Boat" and "A Theme For Reason," has not been performed or published.

Penned in the lower margin is a reference to *The Rose Tattoo*, "finished first complete draft today!"]

149. To Carson McCullers

1431 Duncan
Key West [Florida]
12/6/49
[TLS w/ autograph marginalia, 1 p. Duke U]

Carson dear:

We are very, very happily situated here in a little white frame cottage, a sort of Tom Thumb house, with pink shutters and a white picket fence surrounding it. Directly across the street is a mangrove swamp extending to the sea which is about three blocks away. Last night the full moon, one of those great big yellow paper lantern moons, rose out of the mangrove swamp and over the palm tree and it was quite bewitching. But there are lots of mosquitos in the ointment and they seem peculiarly indifferent to citronella and spray-guns, evidently a strain that has developed immunity. They are only really bad when the wind blows off the swamp, and everything else is perfect.

The prodigy, Speed Lamkin, sometimes referred to as the "new Truman Capote" was here for a while, but he languished for the smart society of Manhattan and has now abandoned us. He was really a pretty nice kid and did not deserve the rather unfortunate title. Now for society we have only the White House Trumans and the sailors and our colored cook, Charleso Marie, who would make a good under-study for Bernice. Yesterday we saw a picture of Bernice, Frankie and John Henry in the Trib which somebody had on the beach. They do look perfect for the parts! Audrey is very elated over the casting, and it seems to me that the production is being handled with singular intelligence and good taste straight down the line. So far your best break was shaking off that malign combination of Guild, Collaborator and Crabtree. It seems to me that if the fates had not been in your corner you would never have managed such a favorable switch of management and director, not to mention the inspired casting. As for my coming to Philly, that is still in doubt, for I have Grandfather with me. He vehemently asserts that he will never again return to Saint Louis, you would think that he had escaped from a dungeon he is so happy to be here. We shall have to celebrate Xmas together, here in Key West it appears. But Frankie is going home for two weeks, and he will probably see you and the play while he is around New York and he will bring you good-luck as he has me. He has gone out, now, to pick up some pictures we took with our new camera and if there are any good ones, I will enclose one for you. I hope you will observe that I have lost twelve pounds! I have cut down on my liquor to a limit of five drinks a day (Ah, Spartan soul that I am!) and eat only one meal, a big supper with heroic abstention from hot-biscuits and potatoes which are my two most favorite things in the world, almost! La Vida Es Pena! But perhaps next season you will see my picture in Welch's Grape-juice Ads.

I have at long last completed a first complete draft of a play but I don't think I shall do anything with it this season. The heat of Frankie's summer (your Frankie) should keep a cautious playwright under cover! - We send you our love, all three of us.

Tenn.

[TW refers to a publicity photo of Ethel Waters, Julie Harris, and Brandon de Wilde—principals in *The Member of the Wedding*—which had recently appeared in the *New York Herald Tribune*. The "malign combination" of the Theatre Guild, collaborator Greer Johnson, and director Paul Crabtree marked the early production history of the play. Contrary to reports, TW did not attend the Philadelphia opening and apologized to Carson McCullers in later correspondence.

TW's report of happiness, productivity, and abstemious habits was stated in part in an earlier letter to Audrey Wood, which ended with an urgent postscript: "Please have Dr. Frank E. Smith send me a supply of Seconal and phenobarbital tablets" (December 5, 1949, HRC).

Penned in the lefthand margin and keyed to the Truman reference in the second paragraph is the notation "I haven't seen them so far."]

150. To William Liebling

The Lighthouse
The New York Association for the Blind
111 East 59th Street, New York 22, N.Y.
December 20, 1949
[TLS w/ enclosure, 1 p. Todd Collection]

Dear Mr. Liebling:

There is so much useless spending of time and money and emotion on selfish ends that actually, finally, gets us no where that we really want to be, that all adds up eventually to zero. It seems to me that the few dispositions of these goods that do not add up eventually to zero, that are really creative expenditures, are the ones that we make for non-selfish reasons such as the relief and the advancement and improvement of our afflicted fellow beings.

Of these none are more poignantly appealing, more deeply and touchingly needful than the ones that are blind. We all live in a good deal of darkness, but, they live in a darkness even greater than ours. Isn't it fortunate that sometimes the blind are really able to lead the blind?

Please forward your check payable to The Lighthouse in the enclosed envelope.

Sincerely yours, Tennessee Williams

[TW served as honorary chairman of the Theatrical Division of The Lighthouse, a charitable "association for the blind." In the preceding August the Lighthouse Players presented *Summer and Smoke* at the Mountain Playhouse in Jennerstown, Pennsylvania, with sightless actors in the cast. After some initial hesitation, Audrey Wood made a special release of the play to accommodate the group.]

151. To Margaret "Margo" Jones

1431 Duncan Street
Key West, Fla.
Jan. 2, 1950.
[TLS, 1 p. HRC]

Margo dear:

I am sorry to have let the holidays go by, or nearly by, without some word to you. At long last I have been completing a play, assembling a complete draft of it, which I shall take to New York for typing as soon as Frank returns from visiting his family in New Jersey for the holidays. It is a great relief but leaves me rather exhausted and I have done so little else since I got here in Key West. I have been disgracefully negligent. Most of my friends are mad at me. Particularly Donnie. He wrote me a month ago that he wanted me to make some comment for the dust-jacket of his book which Doubleday is bringing out in April, and it just slipped my mind until he wrote me a very cross letter indeed, implying that I was a faithless friend. You would think one writer would understand the preoccupations of another! As you are probably as busy and preoccupied as I am, you may understand better.

Jane and Tony Smith spent the holidays with us in Key West, and we managed to create a semblance of Xmas spirit in spite of the summer warmth and the palm trees. They are really beautiful people, and since society here has been pretty limited, it was a great joy to have them. Grandfather is having the time of his life, all 92 years of it. He was looking distressingly frail when I picked him up in Jacksonville - he flew down from St. Louis to meet me there - but he's now gained a lot of weight and walks around briskly. He's crazy about Frankie who drives him around everywhere that he takes a notion to go, and he usually has a notion to go somewhere. Keeping up with his correspondance is a problem, too, as he can't see to write anymore. He swears that he will never return to St. Louis again. He and Mother don't get along so well anymore, she refuses to repeat things to him and he says he never knows what is going on in the house. Yet he also complains of her nagging him, which is a bit contradictory, and he has never forgiven Dakin for becoming a Roman Catholic.

We have a charming little house here, white frame with pink shutters. Frank and I have the upstairs which is an ideal place for working. There is an extra bedroom downstairs if you ever feel like paying us a visit. I shall be in New York for a week out of this month and the end of the month we go to Havana for a week (it is only a half hour by air from Key West), but we shall be here from now through April and whenever you want to take a little rest in the sun from your many labors, just let us know. You must be feeling like the title of your next New York production, after the strenuous routine that you have been following. Frank and I, and possibly Grandfather also (since he won't go back to St. Louis) are planning to return to Europe in the late Spring, after our lease on the house expires; I want to see the Paris production of Streetcar with Arletty and I also want to see if Magnani can talk English and would be interested in a job here. I can't think of any American actress of her type. I have taken off 13 pounds and feel somewhat rejuvenated and moderately at peace for the first time in perhaps three years. Some interesting people are beginning to arrive for the season. The nicest is Viola Veidt who is the daughter of the late Conrad Veidt. She is a bit of a lush and we have been drunk together the past 5 nights! Love & luck!

Tennessee.

[The dust jacket "comment" which TW belatedly wired—"Windhams first novel introduces finest young talent since Carson McCullers" (qtd. in Windham, p. 248)—eclipsed author and book and promised to offend Truman Capote and Gore Vidal as well.

An Old Beat-Up Woman, Margo Jones's "next New York production," would close in Boston on January 28, 1950. In the meanwhile Jones replied with typical gusto: "'Yes, honey, I sure do feel beat up and I love it!'" (qtd. in Windham, p. 251).

Jean Cocteau's production of *Un Tramway Nommé Désir* opened at the Théâtre Edouard VII in Paris on October 19, 1949, and ran for 233 performances. Arletty added a mysterious Blanche to the canon, while Cocteau's staging eroticized the visual effects of the play. Critics and audiences were again scandalized.

Shortly before his death in 1943, Conrad Veidt played the Nazi major in *Casablanca* (1942).]

152. To Jane Lawrence and Tony Smith

1431 Duncan Street
[Key West, Florida]
Jan. 5, 1950.
[TLS w/ autograph postscript,
2 pp. Smith Collection]

Dear Jane and Tony:

The house seemed awfully empty after you left till Frank got back last night. I don't know how we should have endured the holidays without you. Janie, I have only loved one book in my life as much as the Anabasis and that is my Crane which I don't have with me. I shall have a permanent library of two books, now, in all my travels. I have taken a quote from the Anabasis for my play, the one beginning O Slinger! Crack the nut of my eye - ram's skin painted red. (beginning and end of it is all I can reproduce at the moment). And the Rousseau snake-charmer is framed above my work-table in place of that innocuous little etching that came with the house. A cut-out of Valentino as Pan is also framed close beside it, replacing a sketch of a Scotch terrier which I always thought peculiarly uninteresting. Speaking of dogs, Tony's story of the Havana Exhibition has become the great cry in smart Key West society. Everybody is barking at everybody and saying "Dogs!" It has become the usual form of greeting and provokes great hilarity, as well it might. It is particularly fitting among the crowd that has adopted it. This week two great Scandinavians showed up, one of them 6'4" tall. Donnie and I met them at the Fifth avenue palace of a exquisite East Indian prince named Dinisha. Don will remember. They told of attending a banquet given by Dinisha at which he ate only a single small nut, though there were endless courses and enormous hoopla. Grandfather was quite infatuated with the big Swede and insisted upon taking his arm and showing him the lime-tree and the two-story cactus plant. Then Frank arrived on the 9:30 bus and we had another little Christmas. He brought me several marvelous records, including Arensky's Waltz for Two Pianos which I have wanted a long time and a gold snake-ring with little diamond chips in it which is the nicest piece of jewelry I have owned and a huge bottle of Mitsouka, lest there be any doubt when I pass down Duval street. Frankie had lost weight at home and seemed glad to be back in our peaceful little world. A long wire from Audrey says they want me back on the West Coast to view the rough cut film of Menagerie but I am hoping, when I talk to Audrey long-distance after Carson's opening this evening, I can persuade them to send the film to New York so I won't have to go both places. The "stills" that Rapper sent me from Hollywood are really disgusting, the costumes and attitudes resembling Way Down East or Broken Blossoms, and I think it would be dreadful to go all the way out to the Coast just to be revolted! My collaborator, Oscar Saul, is furious with me, he says my lack of interest makes him feel insecure. All I can say is feeling insecure at $750. a week plus expenses should happen to me! Girl! as Fritzie would say. Or "Bow Wow - dogs . . . "

I guess this letter's all the writing I'll do today, as I couldn't start typing till Frank woke up which did not occur until 2 P.M. he was so exhausted, and I feel pretty stupid. But the weather at last is clear, it is a perfect beach-day. I wish I could show you my sister's latest letter: I believe it is her masterpiece. She used the word "implant" about six times, for sometime. Said she loved her new blouse and longed to implant it upon her clean, immaculate anatomy and wished that she had a brown skirt to implant with it. Finally said she was "implanting a stitch on a dish-towel, a brilliant, tragic one that she loved and hoped to bestow upon me". I guess it was the full moon. . . .

How is Buffie?

I am going to append to this letter, if possible in my stupefied condition, some additional "quotes" for Doubleday, but I hope you will use your own discretion about offering them to Donnie. The whole matter is apparently one of delicacy which I no longer know how to deal with, for Frank says

Don is still hurt over the quote, and I still don't understand how or why, except that there was the delay in getting it to him, and I have heard nothing from him since the cross letter. Is it the Flapper age that is coming back, or the age of the Prima Donna? I guess I would be equally at home in either, so have nothing to worry about! "High bosom or saucy butt, it is all the same to me! A turn, a twist, a flick of the wrist, for Mme. Tennessee!"

Much love, 10

P.S. Mailed "quotes" directly to ~~Doubleday~~ Don.

[Jane Lawrence (b. 1915) and Tony Smith (1912-1980) were married in California in 1943 with TW serving as their legal witness and informal honeymoon guest. Lawrence appeared in the original casts of *Oklahoma!* (1943) and *Where's Charley?* (1948) and later studied opera in Europe. An architect by training, Smith was associated with Frank Lloyd Wright before emerging in the 1960s as an artist who worked primarily in large-scale geometric forms. He appeared on the cover of *Time* magazine in October 1967 and was hailed as "the most dynamic, versatile and talented new sculptor" in America.

The "O Slinger!" epigraph from *Anabasis* (St.-John Perse, 1924) was used intermittently in drafts of *The Rose Tattoo*. The final line—"this world has more beauty than a ram's skin painted red!"—summarizes "the lyric as well as the Bacchantic impulse" (*Where I Live*, p. 55) which inspired the play.

"'Bow Wow - dogs'" refers to "'sex shows'" in Havana which TW was "crazy to see." A recent visitor, Smith reported that "they do every sexual act in the book and at the conclusion they get down on hands and knees, all barking like dogs, and one of the whores looks up and explains sweetly - 'Dogs!'" (TW to Kazan, January 27, 1950, WUCA).

Contrary to reports, TW did not attend the New York premiere of *The Member of the Wedding* (January 5, 1950). He planned instead to attend the opening of *Come Back, Little Sheba* on February 15 and to see *Member* at this time (to Wood, February 10, 1950, HRC).

The "disgusting" *Menagerie* "'stills'" reminded TW of D.W. Griffith's silent films *Broken Blossoms* (1919) and *Way Down East* (1920).

Charles Feldman bought film rights of *Streetcar* in the preceding October and hired Oscar Saul to write the adaptation. Saul's hope of working with TW for some four months led Frank Merlo to quip to Audrey Wood, "He does not know 'our boy' - does he?" (TW to Wood, addendum, n.d., HRC). TW's "only criticism" of Saul to date was that he "works a little too slowly" and "seems a little literal-minded in his approach, wants to explain and motivate things a little too carefully" (to Kazan, December 12, 1949, WUCA). Elia Kazan would soon agree to direct the film, while Olivia De Havilland—acclaimed for her role as a mental patient in *The Snake Pit* (1948)—was the early choice to play Blanche DuBois.

TW quotes a letter from his sister Rose dated December 28, 1949: "I miss you. Am sorry that I couldn't bestow a present upon you that isn't my love. I am implanting a stitch on a dish towel that I can allot to you. It is a brilliant tragic one that I love, hope to bestow upon you" (Columbia U).]

153. To Paul Bigelow

[1431 Duncan Street
Key West, Florida]
1/13/50
[TLS w/ autograph postscript, 1 p. Columbia U]

Paul dear:

The holidays and attendant preoccupations made a great hiatus in my contacts with the world abroad. I'm not sure I have yet thanked you for the pyjamas which are the only ones for which I have ever had a positive attachment. Frank likes them equally and it is something of a contest which of us will wear them more though there is no question who wears them better.

I am immeasurably relieved (and even a little surprised) at the great success of Carson's play. I am sure this will do a great deal for her and once more it gives me a feeling of the existence of a Providence of some kind. I have not heard much about it yet. Only a few lines from Carson came yesterday enclosing an Ad with wonderful quotes for the play. When she recuperates from the strain I am sure that great psychological benefit will be apparent and I hope that she will then return to work on her novel. If I do not say that I hope she will immediately sit down to write another play, I trust you will understand my reasoning in the matter. You have been very remiss about social reportage? What is going on in the great world nowadays? A letter from Gore says he was to sail the 9th for Italy and eventually Ceylon. I wonder if Paul Bowles knows that he is coming? I have a copy of Gore's new book and I also have the much-celebrated first novel of Frederich Buechner whose dust-jacket photo out-shines any of the literary Apollos that have yet flowered among us. Is he at large in Manhattan, and what is the scuttlebut on this item? Where is Truman going to sail to? Or will he weather the storm in a fixed position? Fortunately Speed has yet to appear and I hope he has been to the right photographer. I think this idea of cutting the photograph just at the line of the crotch (as in Buechner's) is the most provocative that has yet been devised. For Speed, however - not that I don't believe it would be equally becoming - I think a variation is indicated. The white roses, the reclining pose on the sofa, the amputated balls having already been exploited, what is there left for a girl to do on a dust-jacket this season but lick a peppermint-stick or bite her big toe?

Frankie and I (let's face it!) have fallen into virtual social oblivion here. A great old Queen Bee named Erna Shtoll or Shmole or something like that has arrived on the scene and become the center of gay society. Bedecked with yellow diamonds like 1000 watt bulbs on the marquee of a skating rink, she holds continual court on the beach and at the bars, the boys flock to her like gnats. But Erna and I took an instant aversion, one to the other. When I was introduced to her at the Bamboo Room (one evening during the holidays when I was quite drunk) she said loftily that she had met me twice before, both times in Tony's. The fact that I had no recollection even of being in Tony's more than once in my life did not improve matters any. She is a buxom widow of sixty and possibly regards me as a contender in the same weight class although I hope she acknowledges some disparity of years. I once had some modicum of social finesse in queen groups, and with queen Bees, but Frank has none whatsoever, he just looks blank and fiddles with his key-ring: so we are quite out of it. But there are still some compensating attractions. We hope that you will pay us a visit during the season. I was thinking of coming up to New York but only got as far as Miami and it seemed like far enough and came home the next day. - Is Audrey doing anything with Mrs. Stone? I <u>think</u> I have finished my play. I had it photostated in Miami and will send Audrey a copy today or tomorrow but am not yet ready for it to go out of her office except to the typist.

Much love - 10.

P.S. Gore has arrived in Key West for a week, and so has Mike James, son of <u>Times</u> editor, so the social situation has improved a bit.

[*A Long Day's Dying* (1950) was praised for craft and psychological insight and regarded as a promising first novel. The twenty-three-year-old author, Frederick Buechner, was not "at large in Manhattan" but teaching at the Lawrenceville School in New Jersey and later studying for the Presbyterian ministry, to which he was ordained in 1958. To date his fiction and theological writing have produced a large and distinguished body of work.

"The white roses, the reclining pose on the sofa," refer to provocative photographs of Truman Capote by Cecil Beaton and Harold Halma, respectively.

TW mailed "Mrs. Stone" to Audrey Wood on November 11, 1949, for typing by Paul Bigelow and delivery to James Laughlin. Enclosed was a note in which TW discounted "the literary quality" (HRC) of the novella but expressed optimism for its potential as a film.]

154. To Alfred C. Kinsey

1431 Duncan
Key West, Florida
Jan. 18, 1950
[ALS, 2 pp. Kinsey Institute]

Dear Dr. Kinsey -

I am gratified by the attention you have given "Streetcar" since I feel that your work, your research and its revelations to the ignorant and/or biased public, is of enormous social value. I hope that you will continue it and even extend its scope, for not the least desirable thing in this world is understanding, and sexual problems are especially in need of it.

I am sailing for Europe around May 28 and will probably be in New York for a couple or three weeks prior to sailing (on the Ile de France). My agents are Liebling-Wood, Inc. if you want to get in touch with me at that time, or check on my whereabouts. Their address is 551 fifth ave.

I would welcome (and enjoy) the chance to discuss my plays with you whenever you find the occasion.

Cordially, Tennessee Williams

[Alfred Kinsey (1894-1956) informed TW that he and his staff at the Institute for Sex Research (University of Indiana) were "making an extensive study of the erotic element in the arts" and had examined *Streetcar* "in some detail." Many cast members had given their "histories" to the Institute, and so it seemed possible, Kinsey thought, "to correlate their acting with their sexual backgrounds" (January 14, 1950, Kinsey Institute). The premiere of *Streetcar* in December 1947 and the publication of *Sexual Behavior in the Human Male* (a collaboration of Kinsey and his staff) in the following month formed an intense focus of public sexual candor, and furor as well. TW declined to give his own sexual history when he Kinsey met later in November.]

155. To James "Jay" Laughlin

1431 Duncan St.
Key West, Fla.
1/30/50
[TLS, 1 p. Houghton]

Dear Jay:

I am delighted that you want to publish the novella separately in the Fall and that you think I've improved it. I am still making little revisions, from time to time; it might be helpful if you would go through it, sometime, very carefully and make a note of all those points at which the writing falls down. I may be doing this myself but of course I can't altogether rely on my own perception. Since it is such a short thing it should be possible to get it completely polished. Audrey and Bigelow were displeased with my original title, MOON OF PAUSE, but I like it much better than the one they prefer, THE ROMAN SPRING OF MRS. STONE, which I think is comparatively banal and much less pertinent but I have thought of another, DEBRIS OF GIANT PALMS, which derives from a passage of Perse's "Anabasis". I think I would prefer either that or the one I had first. Which do you like?

I have completed the long play THE ROSE TATTOO and had it typed up by Audrey. She has been rather cagey about it and my own feelings about it are tentative and mixed, I am afraid to read it over. Yesterday I wired her that I must have some comment, however brief and devastating that might be, and she wired back that was "very optimistic and thought it had the making of a great commercial vehicle". I am not sure that I feel very pleased about this reaction. So far I have never aimed at a commercial vehicle and I hope that I will never be willing to settle for that. I now have $113,000. in govt. bonds which is enough to live on in Sicily or Africa for the rest of my life without bothering about making money in the theatre. What I want, of course, is to continue to write honest works with poetic feeling but am haunted by the fear that I am repeating myself, now, have totally exploited my area of sensibility and ought to retire, at least publicly, from the field. The work on this play, begun last January in Rome, has exhausted me physically and nervously. I have suffocating spells in my sleep. Sometimes they wake me up but sometimes they are woven into my dreams, such as last night when I dreamed that I was trying desperately to crawl down a long corridor of a house in the vaccuum of a tornado.

Vidal arrived here about two weeks ago and since coming has written a really excellent short story, the best thing he has ever done in my opinion. I want you to see it, and so does he. Of course I also liked his story about "the street" (Some Desperate Adventure) which you didn't care for. I thought it was not well written but that it was the most honest expression of Vidal that he has yet offered. I am encouraging him to do it as a play. It could be terrifying as a study of the modern jungle. Vidal is not likable, at least not in any familiar way, but he and Bowles are the two most honest savages I have met. Of course Bowles is still the superior artist, but I wonder if any other living writer is going to keep at it as ferociously, unremittingly as Vidal! If only he will learn that people are not going to give a hoot for his manufactured pieces like "Search for a King", Etc.! He has a mania for bringing out one book a year! They are now stacked up like planes over an airport, waiting for the runway.

Audrey suggests that I come to New York but I am waiting for news that at least one swimming-pool has reopened. Since coming here I took off fifteen pounds by diet and swimming and I don't want to put it back on in one week of Manhattan high life.

Ever - 10.

[In titling "the novella," James Laughlin shared TW's current preference for "Debris of Giant Palms," while Audrey Wood and Paul Bigelow favored the eventual selection, "The Roman Spring of Mrs. Stone." "Moon of Pause," which refers to Karen Stone's menopausal experience, appeared earlier in *Summer and Smoke* in reference to Alma Winemiller's fading youth and the "cold dead peace" (August 1946, HRC) which lay ahead. The expression made Wood "acutely uncomfortable" (to TW, January 7, 1947, Columbia U) and was cut from the play.

"Tentative and mixed" feelings are evident in TW's present description of *The Rose Tattoo*: "I call this the 'kitchen sink draft' because I have thrown into it every dramatic implement I could think of. Perhaps all of them will work. Perhaps none of them will work. Probably a few of them will work" ("Note," January 1950, HRC).

From "outline" to first draft stage, there was development rather than fundamental change in the basic elements of *The Rose Tattoo*. Rosario's mistress, originally a voice heard "sobbing over the phone," was dramatically cast as Estelle Hohengarten, a thin blonde prostitute from Texas who appears in the opening and closing scenes. At the final curtain she and Pepina kneel to gather the ashes of Rosario—an addition to the outline as well—which Pepina has long venerated but impulsively scattered after learning of her husband's betrayal ("'Kitchen Sink' Draft," January 1950, HRC).

"Three Stratagems," the "excellent" story by Gore Vidal, appeared in *New Directions Twelve* (1950). The "manufactured" work, *A Search for the King* (1950), received mixed notices.]

156. To Elia "Gadg" Kazan

[1431 Duncan Street
Key West, Florida]
2/24/50
[TLS w/ autograph marginalia, 2 pp. WUCA]

Dear Gadg:

Your letter about the play makes it possible for me to go on with it. Audrey's reaction was ambiguous and stifling. Made me feel that the script might be something to pretend had not happened like public vomiting.

I think you see the play more clearly than I did. I have this creative will tearing and fighting to get out and sometimes the violence of it makes its own block. I don't stop to analyze much. I guess I don't dare to. I am afraid it would go up in smoke. So I just attack, attack, like the goat - but with less arrogance and power! Your phrase 'comic-grotesque mass to the male force' is particularly helpful as a definition. I shall try, now, doing it with only the one man, Alvaro, and a new scene in which Pepina is a widow proud and exalted in the memory of a great fulfilled love - almost absurdly puffed up in the invidious eye of the community: brought to her knees by the double shock of Rose's precocious flight into passion and the revelation of her dead husband's infidelity. Perhaps if she alone collects the ashes it will be enough, but I must confess I was enormously intrigued by the dramatic-pictorial value of the two women doing it - and I still don't see how that is in any way incongruous to the praise of the male force. Part of the story is Pepina's reconcilement to the eternal ambivalence (and frailties) of the human animal. She is converted from an ideal to a reality and finds that it is possible to forgive it and go on loving the broken idol. The male force is in those ashes which are all that is left of it and her gathering is her forgiveness and her reconcilement and being assisted by the other woman extended the forgiveness, in a way, to the whole race of man.

You have a passion for organization, for seeing things in sharp focus, which I don't have and which makes our combination a good one. Sometimes I can make a virtue of my disorganization by keeping closer to the cloudy outlines of life which somehow gets lost when everything is too precisely stated. For instance you liked the play "Deep are the Roots" which I hated. I think you liked the orderly marshalling of forces on opposite sides, good and bad, and the message coming out in banner headlines, as it were, like the Los Angeles Examiner's announcement of Ingrid's baby. I much preferred "Death of a Salesman" where the good and bad, the pitiable and the heroic, were more cloudily intermingled in the single souls. The things that we do together will inevitably be somewhere between our two tastes in this matter. Thesis and antithesis must have a synthesis in a work of art but I don't think all of the synthesis must occur on the stage, perhaps about 40% of it can be left to occur in the minds of the audience. MYSTERY MUST BE KEPT! But I must not confuse it with sloppy writing which is probably what I have done in a good deal of Rose Tattoo.

I am terrified by the amount of work you still want to be done on "Streetcar". Why, honey, it looks like you want me to sit down and write the whole fucking thing over!!? This script is going to be the biggest patch-work quilt since the death of Aunt Dinah, and you might as well be reconciled to it. I am going to do my work on it in bits and pieces, taking little isolated segments of the Saul script and doing them over so that the replacements are made bit by bit and keeping as much of what's already done as possible, for as I explained to you the psychological block to the resumption of an old work before the satisfactory completion of a new work is a rugged thing to climb over. I think I have one exciting idea for the Stanley rape scene. No, don't have him go out to drink beer but have him suddenly smash the light-bulbs with the heel of a slipper. She cries out, 'What is that for?' - And he says, 'To see you better!' - Then dissolve as he approaches her - ("eyes blazing!")

I am going to do my version of the night-out with both the startling ideas that I had for it, the WONDER CLUB on Lake Pontchartrain with the boy singing in drag and the playing of the Varsouvianna but I will write it so that the first item can be easily eliminated from the script if you still dislike it. It appeals to me as a fresh and bold piece of screen material and a legitimate motive for Blanche's beginning to break: the dancing of the Varsouvianna - the music penetrating the powder-room where she has fled after the removal of the boy's wig - seems a marvelous springboard to the intensity of her monologue about Allan. Mitch: You mean he was like that boy in the female outfit? Blanche: No, no, no! He wasn't at all like that, there was nothing the least bit - effeminate about him - but there was - Etc."

In the last scene I am going to return almost entirely to the play as you seem to feel, as I do, that is best. I thought of having a brief shot in the hospital of Stanley, Kiefaber and Shaw sitting on a bench outside Stella's room waiting to present their testimony - their names are spoken at the door and you dissolve to Blanche huddled in Eunice's apartment and the ants crawling into the icebox. Mr. Graves (highschool superintendant) might also be among the witnesses summoned by Stanley to secure the commitment.

While I was in New York I saw the THIRD MAN and was terrifically moved by it. Greatest camera shot I have ever seen was the huge ferris wheel, even better than any pictorial effect that I can remember in Eisenstein and it had the whole lyric image of Hart Crane's poem The Bridge in it, and, Christ, what music, what music! Can't we have something equally haunting back of Streetcar? And camera effects like that?! The story itself was rambling and told in too diffuse a fashion, not concentrated enough and not enough sustained tension. Dynamics too abstruse. But it is a magic piece. Of course I had my own degenerate ideas about the relationship between Orson and Joe Cotton which made the heroine of the film a little irrelevant: but there again, the audience was supplying 40% of the synthesis!

Yes, yes, yes, there are many things to be done between dark and daylight if God gives us six months more to pursue our illogical phantoms down celluloid and paper areaways! I hope that next year we will be in Rome shooting the posthumous life of Mrs. Stone. Possibly even with Garbo.

Love - 10.

[The "kitchen sink" draft of *The Rose Tattoo* was not "ready" for staging, Elia Kazan thought, but it had greater potential than the original outline. He advised TW to stress the "UNLOCKING" of Pepina and to reconsider the static, devotional ending which blocked her movement "towards freedom." Treating Rosario as a "memory" or "legend" and beginning the action much later, perhaps with the daughter's graduation, would help to realize the play as Kazan envisioned it: "A comic Mass between what man and woman are, and what they have made of themselves" (n.d., HRC).

Deep Are the Roots (1945) ran for 477 performances and helped to establish

Kazan's reputation as a successful Broadway director. The play conventionally studies the post-war "Negro problem" in the deep South.

The "night-out" scene at the "WONDER CLUB" (Scene Six) was retained in *Streetcar*, although a swing band rather than a "boy singing in drag" provided the entertainment. The Varsouviana was not played or danced, as TW preferred, but used as spectral accompaniment to Blanche's account of Allan Grey's death. No hospital "shot" or contingent of witnesses appears in the film.

The Third Man (1949), which was filmed in post-war Vienna, won the Academy Award for black and white cinematography (Robert Krasker). The "ferris wheel" in the bombed-out Prater was used to stage the famous meeting of Orson Welles and Joseph Cotten.

The Roman Spring of Mrs. Stone was filmed by José Quintero and released in 1961. Vivien Leigh, rather than Garbo, played the lead.

Penned in the lefthand margin of page 2 is the notation "dissolve from 3 men entering Stella's room to the depredating ants crawling into icebox."

A briefer undated version of this letter is held by the HRC.]

157. To Gore Vidal

[1431 Duncan Street
Key West, Florida]
3/1/50
[TLS, 1 p. Houghton]

Fruit of Eden!

The first of your letters, the one mailed in packages, was forwarded to New York. I opened it and started to read it in the theatre when the lights went down. I never got past the first two sentences and unfortunately I left it in my program. I hope it has fallen into friendly hands and that it was not the sort of letter that would expose us to blackmail. The second I did get here. (We are back in Key West). The high point of my trip to New York was a week-end at Rhinebeck, arranged and conducted by Polly Bigelow. I became quite fond of Alice and also her husband who is not without charm. As you know, they have an indoor swimming pool and all the New York pools had been closed so it was a God send. I went to plays every night. The Cocktail Party was fascinating but nevertheless rather dull. The best was Inge's Come Back Little Sheba. Carson's was done so badly I found it difficult to appreciate, but there are standees at every performance. Lamkin was in evidence, but apparently about to leave for Hollywood. Audrey had got him a $250. week job with Charlie Feldman, like I had in

1943, but he seemed a bit wistful as though that were not quite what he had hoped to be in store for him. Truman I did not see at all: but he was purportedly present in New York. I had dinner with the Windham-Campbell menage. A very painful dinner, everyone on edge and very little to eat - the atmosphere full of a mysterious tension which I cannot understand or explain to myself and very saddening as I felt I had made every propitiatory gesture. I talked to Audrey about you. She had your letter and I assured her that she should certainly promote you with the studios if that was your wish. Hope you've heard from her. You should be able to get a better deal than Lamkin if you go after it. Polly is planning to visit us early in March but we are planning a trip to Havana first. He may occupy the house while we're away and spend a while with us after we get back. Professionally the trip was rather ambiguous. Audrey is sitting on the new script like an old hen, either because she doesn't really like it or because she doesn't want it to fall into the hands of a producer, I don't know which. I think she and Liebling hope to produce it themselves. I did show it to Kazan. He wrote a long letter about it, seemed sincerely interested and enthusiastic about most of it but wanted a different first act. So the work continues. I am tired to the point of collapse but perhaps the Havana trip will revive me. This literary life, my child, is no bed of thornless roses! Did you know that? But yesterday the social leaders of the town dropped in to see us. Grandfather was eating his rice krispies in the diningroom which, as you may remember, is continuous with the salon. I told him, Grandfather, The Newton Porters are here! He could not see the other end of the room and thought I was merely making some remark about them (it was quite early for a call) and he said, Goodness Gracious, what pests those people are! - An awkward moment ensued, as even at 92 there is a limit to what you can get away with.

Write me about Houston. I presume you're coming back to New Orleans? I may visit you there this Spring.

Love - 10.

[Paul Bigelow was a friend and companion of Alice Astor Bouverie, daughter of John Jacob Astor and mistress of Rhinebeck on the Hudson. She entertained a circle of artistic friends, including Gore Vidal, who first visited Rhinebeck in the preceding fall. The ubiquitous Speed Lamkin had introduced him to Bouverie.

T.S. Eliot's verse play *The Cocktail Party* premiered in New York on January

21, 1950, ran for a surprising 409 performances, and won the Drama Critics' Circle Award as best foreign play of the season.

A romantic interest drew Vidal to Houston.]

158. To Audrey Wood

[Hotel Inglaterra, Havana]
[early-March 1950]
[TLS, 1 p. HRC]

Dear Audrey:

I have just this moment read your very touching and very beautiful letter and it has done me a very great deal of good. Both yours and Kazan's letters have helped me immensely in getting a clarification in my own mind of what I want to do with the play, and I am going on with it. I now see the woman, the little house, the little proprieties and black dummies and parrot cage and all that as a sort of delicate, almost tissue-paper, fence built lovingly around the instinct to protect and preserve and cherish which is the meaning of WOMAN. And the goat bleating, the cries of children, the wind banging the shutters, the roar of great trucks on the highway, the fierce omni-present element of chance and destruction - as the careless universe that besieges this little woman-built cosmos or womb. I hope that all I do on the play, now, will bring this essential image and meaning out more clearly so that it will illuminate the play and lift it above an ordinary comedy or melodrama.

I am keeping the first part but with Rosario never seen, only heard behind the drawn curtains between the two rooms, which are rose-colored and bear the faint outlines of a rose. The second scene only a black silhouette so that he is never visible to the audience. The other important ideas I will discuss with you later. These only affect the PART ONE. I thought it important to keep that part, as I don't want to lose Estelle Hohengarten and the rose-colored silk shirt which are so important to the working out of the (rounded) story.

We are now running out to the beach, and thank you again with all my heart!

With my love, 10

[Elia Kazan's approach "sounds damned good," Audrey Wood wrote, but she foresaw problems in revising *The Rose Tattoo* as Kazan had directed. Could Pepina's "passion" for Rosario be retained if he were a "minor" presence in the play? And lacking such "passion," might Pepina not seem bent on pleasure, a "last fling" with Alvaro, rather than mystical union with her husband?

Wood also foresaw the difficulty of casting Pepina if Anna Magnani, for whom the part was written, should prove unavailable. Still more formidable was the "task" of following *Streetcar*. In leaving the old "southern scene" and treating a new "class of people," TW had taken a "giant step forward," but she warned that this alone would not warrant production or satisfy the critics. "In other words - don't leap - but consider all these things and know that I love you dearly as a man and admire you as much as always as a writer" (March 5, 1950, HRC).

TW began to obscure Rosario's presence in a later draft of *The Rose Tattoo* (April 1950, HRC), but he was not yet willing to "lose" Estelle Hohengarten and the "rose-colored" shirt," as Kazan's approach would entail. Before Rosario's death, Estelle employed Pepina, a seamstress, to make a silk shirt for her lover, Rosario. Pepina later gave the garment to Alvaro in the hope, or delusion, that he was her husband incarnate.

This letter bears a reception date of March 8, 1950.]

159. To Jane Lawrence Smith

1431 Duncan
[Key West, Florida]
March 8, 1950
[TLS, 1 p. Smith Collection]

Dearest Janie:

What thrilling news that you will be in Italy with us! Audrey has always secured our passages through the Westover (I believe that's the name) travel agency which operates for a small fee. They get wonderful accomodations very quickly and are certainly worth the little extra expense. Frank and I are very dubious about the possibility of your getting steamship bookings in the second or tourist class this late on any ship sailing in May or even early summer. It is always much easier to get first class space. Why don't you fly over, either directly to Paris or Rome? It is almost completely safe, now, more so than land-plane travel and I should think bookings would be easier. I shall write Audrey, or her assistant who handles our transportation for us, that you're going over and would appreciate her assistance. Suggest you call Audrey and talk to her about it. It would be so wonderful having you on the same boat with us and on the drive down to Rome, we would have such fun together!

The thing that we all dreaded but expected in Key West has finally happened. One of the New York queens was murdered in her bed last night by a sailor! The town is hot as a firecracker! Within half an hour after the news broke, the whole Erna gang had fled from the Keys in various and assorted convertibles. We were on our way to the movies when we heard. Queens could be seen scuttling in every direction like they had hornets up their asses! Five were picked up on the street and thrown into jail. You would think it was the queens that had killed the sailor, such was the panic amongst them. We made a round of the bars. Pat the drag-queen had gone into hiding. Michelle was white as a ghost. Lyle Weaver the organist at the Bamboo Room opened his program with "Nearer My God to Thee!" Shore police stood outside every bar and it was rumored that every queen in town would be locked up before daybreak. Only the night before our house-guest, Bigelow, had brought five sailors home with him - so we felt far from easy about the state of affairs and drove home by a back street. The murdered queen was an associate of the Erna gang. I am sure you remember Erna, the 60-year old nympho with all the yellow diamonds and coterie of swish. The sailor killed the guy with a copper ash-tray, splitting his head wide open. Police found them both still in bed. Details are not yet available as it happened after the paper was out. Frank is in town now, with Bigelow, getting more information. Mother arrives this evening on the 7:30 bus and we are just hoping that there will be no interviews with the police when we go into town to meet her! Thank God Frank and I had been leading a relatively quiet life. I expect it will be even quieter from now on! I am afraid it will cast a heavy shadow over Bigelow's visit.

There is really no other news at all comparable. I am still working on my play. Only Audrey and Gadge have seen it, both are very interested but felt it needed more work. I enjoy working on it as it continues to progress but wish I had the energy that I had in the old days! - the never-failing excitement.

Love to you and dear Tony - Tenn

[John Collins, 20, a sailor from the *USS Tringa*, and Atherton "Tony" Foster, 42, an artist from New York, drank heavily on the afternoon of March 7 and retired to Foster's apartment where the older man, Collins stated, made "unnatural advances." Both were found disrobed on the bed, Foster having been struck fatally with a wooden ashtray stand. Collins was convicted of manslaughter—a grand jury had reduced the charge from first degree murder—and sentenced to seven years in prison. The jury recommended mercy.

TW informed Paul Bigelow that the "only unpleasantness" he experienced at the time was "in the Patio bar on the beach when a sailor came up to me and said, 'Didn't Oscar Wilde smoke a cigarette holder like that?' I made big eyes and said, 'Who is Oscar Wilde?' Social poise <u>always</u> comes in handy" (April 11, 1950, Columbia U).

Canceled in the letterhead is the imprint of the Hotel Inglaterra, Havana, where TW and Frank Merlo spent the past few days.]

160. To Audrey Wood

[1431 Duncan Street
Key West, Florida]
March 2?, 1950.
[TLS, 1 p. HRC]

Dear Audrey:

We have had a rather disturbing time of it lately. Mother took suddenly ill in Miami, two days after she left here and was removed to a hospital with a blood-count of 19,000. They thought she had an acute appendix and would have to be operated on. Frank and I flew to Miami but by the time we got there she had improved and the blood-count gone down to 11,000. Appendicitis was apparently ruled out as a diagnosis which makes it far more disturbing. The doctors feel she can fly to St. Louis Tuesday but must undergo a series of X-ray examinations as they now suspect "a diverticulum" of the intestinal tract. We have not told grandfather anything about this, but said a party was being given for mother by The Woman's Club of Miami and he accepted the story. When we left, yesterday, Mother seemed cheerful but naturally she is apprehensive. I know, from experience, how she must feel. She is flying back to St. Louis on Tuesday and I will phone the hospital daily to check on her condition.

Bigelow is still with us. The former under-Secretary of State, Sumner Welles, was here over the week-end. We had dinner with him one night, before the call to Miami. Bigelow has dined with him twice since on Maine lobster and vintage champagne at the Casa Marina but he left this morning (Welles) and now we have only each other.

I have your two letters about "Summer and Smoke" and the "Streetcar" picture deal. I think the entire script of "Summer" should be in the acting version, including the prologue but that a note should be included saying that the prologue may be omitted and that scene two was omitted in the Broadway production. I want the third act to correspond exactly to the version printed by New Directions. I don't think my work on the "Streetcar" scenario will occupy more than three weeks but I hope you'll get a good price for my services as it is going to be very difficult for me to return to that material now. I have already done considerable work on it and I am sure the final script will be a really good one. When I get closer to Saul's script I find a lot of valuable contributions that he has made, but the end must be much closer to the play. The rape can be suggested clearly without offense.

I read "The Rose Tattoo" aloud to Paul and Frank and was terribly shocked by the poor quality of the writing in it. Words that had rung true in my mind sounded quite wrong when I read them aloud: I suspect that it is even worse than the early versions of "Summer" "You Touched Me" or "Battle". This gives me great concern. I wonder if I have not reached the point of exhaustion that lies somewhere along every writer's trail. Yet I know that I can't stop writing for the simple reason that I can think of nothing else to do between the time I get up in the morning and the time I go swimming. I don't feel ~~gloomy or~~ desperate about this at all. Perhaps because I never expected to have any success as a writer and it never really became a part of my "modus vivendi". We have had extraordinary luck with what I had to offer and no complaints are in order.

When I talked to Dakin (about Mother) over long-distance, he said that Eddie Colton had been called on the carpet about my 1947 income tax deductions and there was danger of an assessment. How is that working out?

Love - 10.

[Sumner Welles resigned his position as FDR's under-Secretary of State following allegations (*New York Times*, August 4, 1943) that he had solicited porters on a Presidential train in 1940. In early 1950 he was convalescing in Palm Beach from a catalogue of ills.

Barrett Clark omitted the prologue because of the difficulty of casting children in amateur productions. Otherwise he followed TW's directions in publishing the "acting version" of *Summer and Smoke* (Dramatists Play Service, 1950).

Audrey Wood confirmed Elia Kazan's plan to begin filming *Streetcar* in August and asked TW to specify the time needed to do "a revised version" (March 17, 1950, HRC) of the screenplay. TW informed Kazan that she "demanded three weeks at six grand per from poor old Charlie" (March 23, 1950, WUCA). TW continued to underestimate the censor's objection to the rape scene in *Streetcar*.

This letter was probably written on March 20, 1950.]

161. To Audrey Wood

SH: Key West, Florida
March 27, 1950.
[TLS, 1 p. HRC]

Dear Audrey:

For some mysterious reason I've been able to work quite well lately and the play seems to be coming out of the bushes. If I decide that I want to have this play produced next season, and I now feel pretty sure that I will, I would like to have all the plans and arrangements for it (except, of course, casting) completed before I sail for Europe, so that I can enjoy my vacation. I do sincerely hope that everybody, you and Bill and Gadg, will be happy, or at least gracefully resigned, to whatever choice I make in the matter of a producer. I am sure you all must admit that it is more important that I should feel happy and at ease in this matter than anyone else, as my relations with the producer are probably the most important to the fate of the play - always the first consideration. And since I have worked so damned hard on this script (and in a way more alone-ly than any time before) it seems pretty obvious that the decision really ought to be mine, though I shall be as grateful as ever for the help and advice of everyone else that may be involved. I have just about given up the notion of producing myself. I feel that producing is a very separate and very consequential function, that it makes a tremendous difference: first, that the producer have intelligence, taste and power and experience, second: that the author should feel at ease or at home with the producer. I think it's a real vocation, and a full-time one, to which many are called but few chosen, and I myself don't feel the calling. This, of course, and everything else, can be discussed further when I get to New York. I now speak of production as a foregone conclusion not just because I am feeling much better satisfied with the script as I think it will finally be, but because I could not simply discard it as a failure (without trial) without also discarding, by the same token and gesture, my career as a writer. As I said before, when the time comes, I can give that up, and certainly will give it up when it becomes unmistakably apparent I have nothing more to add to what I have had to say, but I doubt that what would be left of me would be much more edifying as experience or spectacle than the "posthumous life of Mrs. Stone". Another matter that I want treated with utmost confidence at the present. I am thinking of making Frankie a gift of part of The Rose Tattoo. I want him to feel some independance. His position with me now lacks the security and dignity that his character calls for. Perhaps I will give him ⅓ of it. I would like you to discuss this with Eddie and perhaps have the papers drawn up, quite secretly, so they will be ready for me to sign when I get to New York. Of course I don't want any reference made to this in our correspondance (except perhaps as "matter under discussion") until I have completely made up my mind about it in New York (before I sail) but I am interested in your opinion of it. Of course I am also hoping that a way will open for me to be of some help to Bigelow, of a more lasting nature for I am terribly fond of him and his position is such a precarious one which he has borne with touching gallantry for many years, but I want to do whatever I do without appearing to be giving alms - the alms-giver is "liked but not well-liked" and creates an uncomfortable feeling on both sides. - No other news deserving of comment except that we have acquired a white leghorn rooster and two Rhode Island red hens.

Love - Tenn.

[William Liebling once advised TW to form his own production company and to rely upon Liebling-Wood for backing. Rather than take the producer's standard fifty percent, the firm would be content with ten or fifteen and restore the remainder to the author. Such a plan, Liebling added, would help to shield TW from undue taxation (January 25, 1949, HRC). To the present letter Audrey Wood replied that "obviously all of us must resign ourselves to whatever choice you make re producer. Whatever producer is chosen however must present you with every possible financial advantage as author. Sure you will agree with me" (telegram, March 29, 1950).

"'Posthumous life'" refers to the psychological condition of "drifting" once Karen Stone's youth and beauty have faded and her stage career has ended. TW soon informed Wood that the title of the novella "is <u>definitely</u> 'The Roman Spring of Mrs. Stone'" (n.d., HRC).

Frank Merlo reportedly received ten percent of the profits from *The Rose Tattoo* (see Spoto, p. 173). The published version of the play was also dedicated "To Frank in return for Sicily."]

162. To Audrey Wood

SH: Western Union
Key West Flo
1950 Mar 28 PM 8 26
[Telegram, 1 p. HRC]

=BIRTHDAY ROSES IN ICE WATER AND ASPIRIN PERFECTLY GORGEOUS. I NEED SECCONAL TABLETS AND FRANKIE NEEDS HIS CHECK FOR THURSDAY LAST. THANKS AND LOVE=

TENNESSEE.

[TW's thirty-ninth birthday was the occasion of roses and Seconal.]

163. To Irene Mayer Selznick

1431 Duncan Street
Key West, Florida
April 5, 1950.
[TLS, 1 p. Boston U]

Dear Irene:

Your wire about Carson's award was the first to reach me. Nobody is to be congratulated but the author whose faith in the play was all but solitary. I blush to think how little faith I had in its success and that I actually thought it would be dangerous for Carson to have it produced. I am almost invariably wrong as a prophet of Broadway, for I thought that Inge's play would be the big hit, I saw no (commercial) hope for Eliot's and last year I was very dubious about the appeal of the "Salesman". Hereafter I will invest in any show that I think most likely to fail, and will probably wind up a strong rival of the Shuberts.

I have not forgotten your sailing-date. Isn't it April 15th? And I am still intending to have a script in your hands before then. Right now the second draft is at the typist's. She is a spinster with a heart condition who claims that any undue exertion might be fatal, so I cannot give her the hot-foot.

She has done 38 pages in about 3 days and it is a 130-page manuscript. She said she hoped to be through by Friday or Saturday which probably means Monday. Her typing is very beautiful - "frozen music" as a Mississippi lady once said in reference to St. Patrick's Cathedral - but a little, shall we say, - adagio? - Soon as completed I will shoot you a copy Air Mail Special in hopes it will catch your boat. For the sake of the author's nerves and vanity, and as a matter of general policy, we must not regard this as a submission for production. It's not yet time for that. I just want you to let me know what you think of it, as candidly, even brutally, as possible. I have told Audrey I am going to make up my own mind concerning everything in connection with this script which is the way it should be when one has worked on something so hard and against such odds, and she replied that she couldn't agree more completely. So I will probably decide for myself whether or not it ought to be produced and all the attendant circumstances, soon as I feel sufficiently objective about it. I do wish, while you're in Europe, you would check on Magnani for me, her command of English, her plans, Etc.? That is, if the play strikes you as being something that might appeal to her. - My feelings about the play go through continual and violent see-saws: fatuous contentment one day and despair the next. Perhaps Audrey is already consulting Bigelow and Inge about the sanitariums in Connecticutt. (for this client).

Liebling was here for one day, driving down from Coral Gables where he is recuperating from a virus infection. He looked very fit - the virus probably wishes that it had closed out of town.

There was a scandalous murder here last month, involving a middle-aged tourist and a sailor, and the town is what they call "hot". Many of our friends have been booked for vagrancy (of which there are 16 kinds in Florida law), sometimes for merely appearing on the street after dark. The overseas highway has been jammed with north-bound convertibles! - We plan to leave about the fifteenth, we hope voluntarily. Love -

10.

[*The Member of the Wedding* received seventeen of twenty-five votes in winning the Drama Critics' Circle Award for best play of the season. The Theatre Club and Donaldson prizes soon followed, while the Pulitzer went to *South Pacific* (1949).

TW described the same "violent see-saws" of emotion to Audrey Wood: "For a few days I will be in a state of euphoria, then I will suddenly hit bottom again.

No apparent reason except perhaps nervous exhaustion" (April 3, 1950, HRC). Wood replied that she felt "exactly the same way" and suggested they meet for "a nice drunken evening" (April 4, 1950, HRC).

Paul Bigelow, a production staff assistant of the Theatre Guild, kept William Inge sober and hidden from the press in a sanitarium near Greenwich, Connecticut, during rehearsals of *Come Back, Little Sheba*.]

164. To Oliver Evans

1431 Duncan Street
Key West [Florida]
7 April 1950
[TLS w/ autograph postscript, 1 p. HRC]

Dear Oliver:

The lament for your vanished youth is premature but well-fashioned. I have been lamenting mine, silently, for a long time now. What are your plans for the summer? We leave here a bit earlier than we expected. Last month a 43-year-old queen was clubbed to death by an ash-tray and a sailor, and as a reprisal for this terrible offense on the part of the queen, all the Bohemians in town are being picked up on the street and booked for vagrancy, given heavy fines and twelve hours to get off the Key. There are 16 different kinds of vagrancy in Florida law and I'm sure Frank and I, and perhaps even grandfather, would come under at least one of them! We will spend about a month in New York, then sail May 20th for Europe. I have finished my play, and the movie version of Streetcar which Kazan is going to shoot in August. I will probably come back for the shooting. Bigelow was here visiting us for a couple of weeks and I doubt that even you have ever received so many flattering attentions from the armed services. It reminded me of that bottle-capping machine they used to have in a window on Canal street! He got out just before they turned on the heat. Windham has already sailed for Europe, although his novel has not yet come off the press. Truman Capote is also reported to be considering another trip over. Paul Bowles is in India - he says Ceylon is the sexiest place he's ever been, and the natives are flirty as Mississippi maidens. Marian Vicarro was here and we renewed our friendship. She had Neal Thomas with her and Neal's lover who is a sad sack of a prissy sort of a queen. Poor Marian she doesn't seem to have found her bearings in the gay world although it is the only one she feels right in. She will have no fun playing the patsy to these temperamental girls! - That was <u>not</u> Dame Selznick in the picture you sent us. The Dame is now quite handsome with her new boyish bob, and she looks well-fucked for a change. I don't know who the lucky man is. I hope she will like my new play - I have been working like a dog on it the whole time I've been here and am still quite uncertain about its merits.

Let me hear from you soon!

Love, 10.

I have lost 23 pounds!

[TW informed Maria Britneva that Oliver Evans had "resumed his duties at Nebraska, not omitting to drop by the bus-depot at odd moments, when classes are not in session." Evans would also improve Marion Vaccaro's gay company when he visited Miami in the following summer. TW observed that Vaccaro "is as big a queen as Oliver so they must be having a wonderful time together" (qtd. in St. Just, pp. 27 and 35). Their cruising would be recast in the story "Two on a Party" (1952).]

Tennessee Williams, Irene Selznick, and the "clown," Oliver Evans.

165. To Irene Mayer Selznick

[1431 Duncan Street
Key West, Florida]
4/10/50
[TLS w/ autograph postscript, 1 p. Boston U]

Dearest Irene:

If I had not promised to send you this script before sailing I would probably not have the courage to do so, for reading it over I am still desperately dissatisfied with it, I am not even sure that it is improved since the last draft. But a promise is a promise and an excuse is just an excuse, so I am letting you read it. Will you promise me one thing? Don't show it to anyone else! I am putting you on your honor, which I believe in!

You will understand why I am so hesitant and tentative about this script when you read it, and why I am so cagey about everything concerning. Since I cannot decide that I even want it produced, it is impossible at this point to submit it to anyone for a production. The item in Sunday's Times is totally incorrect and does not emanate from any source that I know of. Cheryl has shown great interest in my work, both in Rome and when she was here recently, but I have told her, as frankly as I am telling you, that I have too grave doubts about the script to allow it to be read or considered for production at this point. I am sure you know that I am being entirely honest with you on this point, as I would always be with you on any point concerning my work. There is never any double talk or double dealing in that department of my life. Gadg and Audrey, and now you, are the only ones that have read it. I read it aloud to Frank and Bigelow. I would appreciate it very much if you would mail this copy back to me from London, soon as you arrive there, care of Audrey. In your comments you may be as devastatingly candid as you please. There is no "icon" left to be "clastic"!

With love, 10.

(this is only copy with complete revisions to date, so will need for typing in N.Y.)

[TW hastened to assure Irene Selznick that Cheryl Crawford had not been offered *The Rose Tattoo*. Lewis Funke, source of the untimely rumor, based his "deduction" (*New York Times*, April 9, 1950) upon Crawford's recent visit to Key West and her earlier contact with TW in Rome.

Preceding the visit to Key West (April 3), Crawford defended her right to produce *The Rose Tattoo*: "I imagine Irene Selznick has been inquiring too. My feeling about this is that she was handed our best playwright on a golden platter, that she has not yet earned her right to such good fortune, and that some of us who have stuck with the theatre all of our working lives, taken great chances and done the first plays of many playwrights deserve the honor of producing Tennessee Williams" (to TW, March 9, 1950, U of Houston).]

166. To Audrey Wood

[1431 Duncan Street
Key West, Florida]
April 11, 1950.
[TLS, 2 pp. HRC]

Dear Audrey:

I am very, very grateful for your frank letter about producers. Of course the big question in my mind at the moment is not who I want to produce the new play but whether or not I really want it produced. That is what I said to Cheryl when she was here and what I wrote to Irene. I must admit that at the present time I feel much closer to Irene than Cheryl. The greatest personal loyalty I have is to you. The only loyalty that takes precedence over that is to my work, but it is hard for me to conceive of a situation in which those two loyalties might conflict seriously for long, they have always been so closely bound together. What I hope you will think about is the tremendous difference it makes to an author to feel "familiar and secure" with a producer he has to work with. Now if I were not a writer and you and Bill were not heads of a tremendously complex business organization I would say that the three of us would make the ideal team for production but to be realistic, we have, all three of us, great and pressing demands beyond the production of one (So far very shaky) little play. When I think about Irene I don't even ask myself if I like her or don't like her - although I am pretty sure that I do - I just know - without thinking about it - that the woman has demonstrated one of the most extraordinary powers of will, or drive, or vitality - or whatever you call it - that I've ever seen, and that's what I lack and what the rest of us don't have time for and what is, above everything else, most needed to give a delicate play the fortification and care it must have. Dear Cheryl, she's as delicate as the play itself, for all her tailored clothes and her square-set jaw, and her very clear and honest blue eyes. I don't suppose, as a human being, I think any other producer quite measures up to her. After Irene, I suppose she's the one I'd want. But she just doesn't give the impression, somehow, of being vital or powerful enough to turn not only every stone but also some of the smaller mountains to achieve what she's after! But in conclusion I can only repeat what I said at the start. The question to decide first is whether or not the play should be produced. Then you and I can talk all this over and out about the producer. I have sent Irene a script, mailed it today, and in the letter I was very honest with her. I said it was not to be regarded as "submission for production", that I was not yet ready to talk or think in those terms - and - what is very true - I was most anxious simply to know what she thought of the script as it now stands - I am so far from being able to think or feel very clearly about it myself. I will get your copy off to you tomorrow, or Thursday - soon as I can get it assembled - I had to rush hers to catch her boat which sails Thursday midnight, and I told her to air mail the script back to you from London. As you see, I am being as prudent as ever!

Again, thanks for writing me how you felt, which always does the most good.

Love, Tenn

PS. Grandfather and I are coming up by train - we plan to leave next Tuesday - and Frank will drive the car up with an intellectual red-headed waitress as passenger. - We may never see him again! The reservations at the Sherry-N. will have to be moved forward. Frank will wire about this soon as the plans are quite final. Please alert Bigelow on swimming-pools! I have been working on film-script - hope to spend some time with Gadg preparing the ultimate draft.

P.S. (2) - Just got your wire. I have suspected right along that there was some gimmick involved in all the picture peoples' enthusiasm for "menagerie". I hope we can see it again as soon as I arrive in New York. - Reading your letter over about Irene, I must say that you are certainly not unique in your feeling about her personality problems. I was amazed, last Fall, to hear Brooks Atkinson, in Gadg's house, make something of the same observations about her. You may think it crazy of me to find these traits in her somehow endearing - pathetic - "simpatico". My own hysteria is so like it, essentially, although mine is forcibly and cautiously controlled - but it gives me an understanding of hers. I wonder if you didn't really know her, and understand her, better when you first knew her, when we first talked about her in Charleston, S.C. So often the first perception is true and the later ones a distortion brought about by the strains that exist in all associations. - Obviously if we should all work together again on a production, there would have to be a frank discussion with Irene about the things that have made it difficult in the past, that there is to be no domination, no bullying, no unfair demands of time and energy - that you, especially, cannot be subjected to that sort of pressure - that there is no reason or need for it. I have a feeling that she is wise enough to recognize this without even being told - but should be told just the same! - in the creative world, everything good seems to be involved with a certain amount of excess - of "volonte de puissance" - an over-charged person that has to be controlled, if he or she submits to that control, is usually the best bet. The Whiteheads and Reas and Bloomgartens all leave me cold - I just "dummy up" in their presence. . . .

[Audrey Wood wrote that TW had not endured Irene Selznick "head-on, the physical body day after day for three years," during the production of *Streetcar*, and so he could more easily tolerate her intrusive manner and incessant demands. A strong personality herself, Wood admitted that she did not "function well" in the "vacuum of acquiescence" created by Selznick and urged TW "not to close the door to other possibilities." By recommending a group of "new managers," she anticipated her client's aversion to "the Whiteheads and Reas" and other conventional Broadway producers. Wood suggested once again that TW produce his own work and assured him that personal gain did not enter into her "thinking" (April 10, 1950, HRC).]

167. To Carson McCullers

[1431 Duncan Street
Key West, Florida]
April 1950
[TLS, 1 p. Duke U]

Dearest Carson:

All the news I have of you is indirectly, through Bigelow, Cheryl and Audrey, but that is my fault for I don't believe I have written since I last saw you. I have been buried in work and am just now, finally, coming up to look around me a little. I have been working so hard for so long! I hope that for the next few months I will be willing and able to take it easy, relax, and get some enjoyment out of just living. I have felt driven, without even knowing why.

I gather from Bigelow that you are contemplating a trip to Ireland to visit Elizabeth Bowen. To me Ireland sounds so cold and wet somehow, I am much more drawn to Italy and France, but if you are charmed by Miss Bowen, of course that will be more important than the climate.

I do hope you are living in New York, now, instead of Nyack, for then we shall be able to see so much more of each other. Please let me know when you are sailing. That is, if it is within the next few days. We are leaving here this Sunday. Grandfather and I are going up by train and Frankie is driving up in the car with most of the luggage and with an intellectual red-headed waitress of great beauty. Perhaps we will never see him again! Our sailing date is May 20th on the Ile de France. I hope to spend some weeks in Paris. Perhaps Frank will precede me to Rome, or to Sicily, and I will follow him later by plane. My nerves must smooth out somewhere. Right now they are in a dozen frantic little knots! I shall devote the summer, not to work, but to a smoothing-out process, to making peace with myself and the world and the various phenomena of it.

The town has become pretty sad, Key West, I mean. About six weeks ago there was a murder, a middle-aged queen was beaten over the head with an ash-tray by a sailor. And as a reprisal for this ghastly offense on the part of the poor old queen, the town police have been prosecuting everyone around here who is a bit different-looking. A very ugly atmosphere has developed. Practically all the "Bohemians" have fled from the Keys. Frank and I are the sole survivors. I guess Grandfather's round collar made us appear more respectable but we have not been molested. But I stay home at night, I am actually afraid to go out on the downtown streets. A person can be arrested for sixteen different kinds of vagrancy and I'm sure I must come under at least one heading! One poor lad was picked up for having a "sissy walk"! Released on $250. bond and given a devastating lecture at court. Another poor belle known as "Tangerine" has altogether disappeared. We suspect she has committed suicide in the style of Key West. In the last ten years there have [been] 17 murders here and no convictions. When bodies are found they are nearly always called suicides, even when, in at least one notorious instance, they are found with cement sacks for ballast and with hands and feet roped together at the bottom of a lagoon! - Suicide, mind you! - But I still love this part of the country, the water, the eternal turquoise and foam of the sea and the sky. If I ever buy property, I think it will be in the Caribbean.

It is so wonderful about the award. It will mean months more duration for the play, in New York and on the road and I should certainly think a movie-sale to boot. I feel so much better about you, knowing that now, at last, you must be free of anxiety about the material quantity of living. We will be at the Sherry-Netherland. I want grandfather to have a taste of real fine living while we are together. He refuses to go to Europe with us. Much love -

10. xxxxxxxxxx

[Carson McCullers and Reeves shared a fashionable apartment in New York at this time. TW thought her plan to visit Elizabeth Bowen in Ireland a "great mistake" and informed Paul Bigelow that he would not "consider" making such a trip with McCullers. "About Sister Woman," he added, "one must remember that psychic disturbance takes the place of orgasm and she may have all of that she longs for on the Irish moors, and out of it all may come another great novel" (April 11, 1950, Columbia U).

McCullers's health was still fragile but her financial prospects robust, as TW noted in further gossip with Bigelow: "The Smiths may finally have to abandon the pose of genteel destitution and face the fact that the family includes a money-maker of no small potential. I have been reading Tom Wolfe and it astonishes me how closely his family resembles theirs. Eliza and Bebe certainly should have met!" (April 11, 1950, Columbia U)—a reference to the penurious mothers of Thomas Wolfe and Lula Carson Smith.

TW planned to write to McCullers on April 11, 1950, the probable date of this letter's composition.]

168. To Irene Mayer Selznick

Sherry-Netherland Hotel [New York]
[April 1950]
[TLS, 3 pp. Boston U]

Dearest Irene:

It was indeed quite a letter, and yesterday afternoon, when I got it, was very black, the bottom of a long, descending arc that began with the play's completion last month, broken only by the lift given by a brilliantly understanding (though highly critical) letter received from Gadg and a similar one from Molly and the enthusiasm of Bigelow when I read it aloud which had to be partly discounted as a friend's indulgence - a decline which continued by fairly gentle degrees until yesterday afternoon when your letter knocked the goddam bottom out of it and almost the top off me! For that afternoon, and the night that followed, I believed that you were right, that I had passed into madness and that power of communication was gone. Under the circumstances there [was] hardly any other conclusion to draw. Either you were "dead wrong" or I was crazy. Or that thing had happened which eventually happens to most lyric talents, the candle is burned or blown out and there's no more matches! - Then, of course, came the morning, consistent with its habit. I woke early, recognized Frank and Grandfather and even myself in the mirror - and had my coffee and sat down quietly and rationally to read over the script. Then the amazing thing came about. For the first time since this draft was completed, I liked what I had done and felt that I had done just exactly what I had meant to do in all but a few short passages, that in the play, as a whole, I had said precisely what I had wanted to say as well as it could be said, and the play existed.

Not a ballet, not a libretto, but a play with living characters and a theme of poetic truth, handled with more precision and stringency than ever before in my writing, and in a style, a medium (yes, highly plastic and visual but with those elements an integral, active and very articulate instrument of the play's total expression - not just "effects" for the sake of "effects" or symbols for the sake of being artily symbolic - but a way of saying more clearly, strongly and beautifully those things which could not have been said so well in language if they could have been said at all in language - a progress which I think very marked in the true use of theatre as distinguished from forms of verbal expression) - a medium worked out with tremendous difficulty in exact, or nearly exact, accord with the very clear and strong conception that it sprang from.

For the first time in my life I knew that I must take a solitary position of self-belief, as an artist, and that I could take it proudly because I had earned it. I had not skimped or scanted or hedged or cheated anytime, anywhere, during the year and four months in which I had struggled with the adversaries of doubt and disappointment and fatigue, the many mornings that were brick walls and the few that came open, the exhausting see-saw of exhileration and despair, the continual, unsparing drain of all I had in me to give it. That was the history of it, and this was the culmination. I had to believe. I believed.

I hope you will forgive me now for indulging myself in argument with some of your points of objection. It will do me good. You say the emotion is "felt by the characters but not shared by the reader". I wonder if emotions in a play are usually, or even ever, shared by the reader? If they were, would there be any point in the production of a play, in translating it from the cold page to the warm and living instruments of the stage? Would there be any real need for great actors and brilliant directors and for designers and technicians? I don't think a play is so different from a sheet of music, and there are not many people who can read a sheet of music and hear the music in a way that would obviate an orchestra or singer. The parallel is particularly fitting to this particular play which consists, so much, as you have observed, of signals, notations, as though to various instruments whose playing together will create the expression. Then you say: "Were I to see rather than read the play, I fear I would be at a loss to understand the sources of sustained crisis under which Pepina labors". I venture to guess that with the collaboration of someone like Magnani and someone like Gadg you would find those "sources" far easier to understand, for then the play would come out of the notes and signals and would live before you. "Sustained crisis" is true. But throughout the play (which is about a "sustained crisis") that condition is fully documented and justified. It opens, for instance, with a highly emotional woman telling her passionately loved husband that she is to bear him a child. A crisis. The death of the husband is, of course, another crisis. But how is either of these difficult to understand? In the following acts of the play - the visual and violent "knife-scene" with the daughter, the devastating revelation of the husband's betrayal, first the struggle against it and finally, gradually, the acceptance of it - this, too, is sustained crisis, but I can't for the life of me see how it would seem not motivated, not comprehendible to any of us who have loved or suffered any great loss or disillusionment in our lives, I don't expect this sustained crisis, which is the play, to be felt in reading but I cannot doubt that in performance, with skill and power, an audience could be made to feel it deeply and to enjoy its katharsis. I was well-aware, while writing the play, that the high pitch of emotion in the characters, in keeping with their race, temperament and most of all with their situation, (the crises in which they're involved) might make exhausting demands on everybody concerned. For this reason many of the scenes are deliberately low-keyed, particularly in the writing, the speeches, and the intensities are given quiet, almost submerged, forms of expression and the burden transferred as much as possible from the actor to the visual, plastic elements which you condemn as "effects". Scenes are cut-off and under-stated but always with at least some (muted) expression of the essential things, and the contrapuntal use of the children is like a modulated counter-theme or "cushion" to these intensities - (this will come out much more clearly in the final draft, for the separate play of the children developed very late in the play's composition). The great advance I have made in this play - technically, as a theatre-craftsman - is what you call its "penalizing minimum" of dialogue and the effects which you seem to think are extraneous ornamentation.

No, I feel no resentment about your letter and I do feel gratitude for your writing me what I hope was exactly what you felt, although I suspect you could have eliminated the pacifying reference to "ballet or libretto" and said, more bluntly, more <u>kindly</u> cruelly - I dislike it intensely! You're not the only one who does. I think Audrey and Bill are probably just as disappointed in it as you are. Who knows, at this point, who is right? But I would like to see it tried, produced, and I shall make an effort to see it.

Thanks and all the love as ever,

Tenn.

[Irene Selznick's letter of rejection made explicit what Elia Kazan and Audrey Wood had only implied: *The Rose Tattoo* was neither conceptually sound nor dramatically vital. The gravest problem lay with Pepina, whose motivation Selznick could neither "'know'" nor "feel." The myriad effects of the play—its "plastic medium"—were used "at the <u>expense</u> of the drama," she thought, or perhaps as compensation for the play's dramatic limitations. Selznick expressed no further interest in *The Rose Tattoo* and in closing forecast rather accurately TW's long-delayed success on Broadway: "If the 'doing' has been emotionally and artistically rewarding, I beg you to accept that return—it must lead to growth and to a more completely gratifying result in your next piece - or even the one after" (April 16, 1950, Boston U). Selznick went on to produce *Bell, Book and Candle*, a light comedy by John van Druten which opened the following November.

This letter was probably written in the week of April 16, 1950, after TW arrived in New York.]

169. To Jack Warner, Jerry Wald, and Charles K. Feldman

SH: The Sherry-Netherland
Fifth Avenue at 59th Street
New York 22, N.Y.
May 6, 1950.
[TLS, 5 pp. U of Delaware]

Dear Sirs:

I have now seen the picture three times, twice in a private screening room and finally with a regular audience in New Jersey and this letter is meant to convey as clearly as possible my own reaction to it, based on these three showings. I know and truly appreciate the tremendous enthusiasm that you have all felt and expressed for this picture, which you have made with great care. It was perhaps unfortunate that I had received nothing but highly laudatory comments on the film before I saw it, as I was not prepared to find any faults in it whatsoever. Consequently the first time I saw it, in the cold light of a private screening, my reactions were unavoidably more critical than those that you had expressed to me in your wires.

Let me begin by telling you the many things that I am grateful for and the things that I admire. First of all, the magnificent cast. I can't remember a picture in which four important actors give such uniformly fine performances and each so perfectly suited to the part. The performances of Jane Wyman and Arthur Kennedy are the best I have seen given by either of those two and have created the parts better than I have seen them in any of the stage productions of the play. Max Steiner has written a beautiful score, one that I think is really notable, which blends perfectly with the moods of the play. All of the comedy values in the picture have been brilliantly realized in Irving Rapper's direction and particularly by the playing of Lawrence and Kennedy. None of the "laughs" have been missed. I was particularly aware of this when I saw it before an audience in New Jersey. It was an audience that had come expecting to see "Cinderella", but I had the impression that the surprise on the program was generally agreeable to them. Even to my innately skeptical eye, the picture appears to have what you call "audience appeal", and being as much a showman as any of you, I think that is always a nice thing to have in any form of public entertainment.

Now I would not be willing to make any adverse comments at all if I didn't feel that certain things can still be done to protect and enhance the property as it now exists. First of all, as a premise to these criticisms, I feel that the picture runs a bit longer than it should to have its maximum effect; perhaps as much as ten minutes can be eliminated with real improvement to the film. Since the changes that I have to suggest are nearly all in the form of editing, or clipping out, this is a happy circumstance. Unfortunately Irving was not able to supply me with a copy of the final shooting script so my notes cannot have exact page-and-line references.

The things that I object to most strenuously, and very strenuously indeed, are certain changes that were made in the script after I left Hollywood and which came to me as a complete and very distressing surprise when I first heard them from the screen. I understand why you decided to dramatize Amanda's recollection-scene, but it has the unfortunate effect of making her seem not just a romanticist, which she was to some degree, but an out-and-out liar. I am thinking particularly of her statement that she had "twenty-three proposals in a single evening". Of course the background for this fanciful reminiscence is much too elaborate and somehow it seems to lack any real nostalgia or poetry, it is more like a bit of an MGM musical suddenly thrown into the middle of the picture. I understand, also, why you may not be able to take this out of the film, but I am wondering if it could not be shortened a bit, or perhaps even done in softer, mistier focus and the "twenty-three serious proposals" drowned out by the music. However, I don't want to make a particular point of this.

What I do want to make a very particular point of is the script changes that have crept into Tom's "drunk-scene". Irving Rapper is coming back with specific notes on the lines that we thought could be removed from the scene. I can only assume that they were written in by the collaborator, Mr. Berneis. Irving knows exactly what these lines are and where they occur. It seems to me that they do untold damage to the dignity of the picture as a whole, the bathos and corny philosophizing are so incongruous to the spirit of the film as a whole. I must admit that at this point in the picture, I had to retire from the projection-room for a glass of water and that they cast a shadow over the entire remainder of the film. The second scene in the warehouse could be dropped out entirely without affecting the development of the story. I originally put it in to provide an occasion for Jim's invitation to dinner, but this scene has been entirely re-written by Mr. Berneis and the invitation no longer exists: consequently the scene is pointless except that it provides some additional footage for Kirk Douglas and a few "yaks". The writing of the scene is amateurish and I believe that one of the jokes was borrowed from a well-known source. This scene, however, is not one of my really strong objections, I only feel that reducing it will result in a tighter picture.

A really strong objection concerns an insertion that has been made after Tom's final exit from the apartment. Laura follows him out into the alley and calls him back for the exchange of some more lines from the cornball department. It is the only scene in the entire picture where Miss Wyman's performance really weakens. Rapper has exact notes on this passage. The worst of these lines is "Send me your poems so I may travel with you". I would prefer the entire elimination of this little scene, which is anti-climactic and saccharine, but I particularly beseech you to eliminate the two or three utterances that Irving and I have noted upon the script. This, again, is a bit of editing that is entirely practicable and will help us immensely with the New York critics and all those who are familiar with "The Glass Menagerie" as a serious poetic play. Little touches like that, unimportant as they appear to be, can make a tremendous difference in critical attitude toward a film, to the impression of its dignity.

About the "new" gentleman-caller. In my script he was never visible on the screen. At the most, he was the sound of approaching footsteps and perhaps a shadow stretching before him as he came up the alley. This gives him a quality of poetic mystery and beauty which the picture badly needs in its final moments. Now we not only see him very plainly, his whole figure, but he is also provided with a full name, Richard Henderson. This little touch is going to stand out like a sore thumb and will gravely affect your critical reception, particularly in all those cities where the "Menagerie" has been known as a play. The light in Laura's eyes, and in her mother's, their glad "hellos" from the fire-escape were absolutely all the up-beat that the traffic could bear. As I remarked when I left my script with you, any more upbeat at this point is the straw that breaks the camel's back. I urge you most seriously to consider eliminating the shot of the actual figure coming up the alley and to remove the last name, both totally unnecessary to giving the picture its final "upbeat" and both extremely dangerous to a respect for the film's integrity among that relatively small, but terribly important, segment of the film public to which such things make a difference. (I don't think we should dismiss from our minds the possibility of an Academy Award, for instance.)

Tom's final narration is curiously lacking in real poetic feeling. We have all discussed this (Irving, Miss Wood and I) here in New York and we felt that this could be recorded again with a greater attention to the emotional quality of the lines and with the restoration of a couple of lines which Irving tells me - to my surprise and horror! - were cut out by the Breen office. The lines I think should be restored are the best, most lyric lines in the entire narration - "Then all at once my sister touches my shoulder. I turn around and look into her eyes. . . . Oh, Laura, Laura! I tried to leave you behind me. But I am more faithful than I intended to be. . . . "

Irving tells me that Breen made the disgustingly prurient charge that these lines (!!!!) contained a suggestion of INCEST! I cannot understand acquiescence to this sort of foul-minded and utterly stupid tyranny, especially in the case of a film as totally clean and pure, as remarkably devoid of anything sexual or even sensual, as the "Menagerie", both as a play and a picture. The charge is insulting to me, to my family, and an effrontery to the entire motion-picture industry! And I think you owe it to motion-pictures to defend yourselves against such prurience and tyranny by fighting it out with them. If I ever work in pictures, in America, I must know that my work is not at the mercy of the capricious whims that seem to operate in this office.

Well, boys, I have had my say! I am sure that you wanted me to have it, and I deeply appreciate your wanting me to have it and giving me the chance to have it. You have what is almost a fine picture. Don't let it remain anything less than what you are still able to make it, with only the exercise of a little scissors and paste.

Cordially and gratefully, Tennesee Williams

[Relatively few of the "changes" suggested by TW appear in the final print of *The Glass Menagerie*. Amanda's claim of "'twenty-three proposals'" was not "drowned out" by music, although the "recollection-scene" was apparently given a softer focus. The lengthy flashback was intended to create a youthful image for the fifty-one-year-old star, Gertrude Lawrence. "Otherwise," she once observed, Amanda "would have been only a character study of a middle-aged woman, and I don't want to get mother roles, and unglamorous ones at that" (qtd. in *New York Times*, October 16, 1949).

In the "'drunk-scene'" the only added, remaining, passage of "philosophizing" begins with Tom's wish that the magician's scarf cover the "whole ugly world," to which Laura replies that "the whole world is beautiful." The issuing of Jim's invitation was removed from the warehouse sequence to enhance its announcement in the following fire-escape scene. The now "pointless" scene was not "dropped," although the "borrowed" joke was cut. So too was the line which TW most deplored—"'Send me your poems'"—in Tom's new departure scene. The inserted scene was designed, and retained, to strengthen the character of Laura, who confidently bids Tom "do what you've always wanted to do. Travel, write."

The shot of the "'new' gentleman-caller" was retained and is more "actual" than the allusive "sound" or "shadow" which TW preferred. The caller's last name was deleted, though, and the deep perspective of the alley maintained. Tom's final words are indeed flat: "And that is how I remember them, my mother and my sister. And so goodbye."

Joseph Breen, Production Code administrator, stated in his first report that Tom's memory of Laura should be "carefully scrutinized and possibly rewritten, to get away from the present suggestion of an incestuous attraction toward his sister" (to J.L. Warner, March 31, 1949, Herrick). He repeated the warning in later correspondence and apparently the offending lines were cut, although restored to the final print. TW seems not to have learned of Breen's objection until late in the production.]

170. To Paul Bigelow

Paris
6/7/50
[TLS w/ autograph postscript,
2 pp. Massee Collection]

Dear Paul:

So far we have not gone to London, not because Paris is too fascinating to leave but because I don't feel morally up to the rigors of London. I knew when I left New York the strain was going to hit me like a delayed-action bomb, and it did. I arrived here in a dreadful state of nervous fatigue and depression and am just beginning to pull out of it a little.

Sister Woman returned from Ireland promptly on schedule and apparently Elizabeth Bowen got herself out of a delicate situation with amazing grace and with no offense whatsoever. Of course Carson is talking of flying to London to join her there but it is only talk so far. She and Reeves came over to our little left-bank hotel the other day and spent the entire afternoon. Jane and Paul Bowles were also present. Poor Jane Bowles was so nervous that she drank half a bottle of vodka. Sister Woman and Reeves kept the chamber-maid hopping between our rooms and the wine-shop. Right in the midst of this happy occasion the phone rang. It was long-distance, America calling Carson. It turned out to be the Martineaus. Florence was calling to inform them that Stanley had fallen "off the wagon" and pleading for advice and instructions. "Get Marty Mann!" cried Carson. Carson was then asked if Reeves had stayed, or gotten back, on the wagon. She said, Reeves is just drinking wine! And here was Reeves reeling about the room like a storm-wracked schooner. "Get Marty Mann! Tell her to get Marty Mann!" he shouted. Then both started babbling maudlinly into the phone at once, Oh, darling, oh, precious, oh, blessed, come right over here as soon as Stanley gets out of the hospital, we love you so much, we just adore you so much. Can Stanley talk? Oh, Stanley, love, how are you! Are you all right Stanley Precious? We love you so much, you know we just adore you. Honey, get Marty Mann and she'll pull you out of this thing! What, Stanley? Oh, Florence! What happened? Did he fall down? Oh, then call us back later, you precious sweet lovely thing, you! Etc. Etc. Etc. It must have been the longest and most intense transcontinental phone-call since the war ended, and the McCullers looked really happy and satisfied when they hung up and immediately sent out for another bottle of wine. Reeves called this morning, and I asked if they had had any further conversation with their producers and Reeves said, No. We just sent a cable confirming the talk on the phone!

So you see Paris is not really so far from New York, after all. I wonder if Rome will be any further? When I said we were getting an apartment in Rome (we hoped) Reeves immediately said, How many rooms? Oh, one and a half! I answered without a moment's reflection. There was a slight suggestion that Frank and I, being rather small people might be able to occupy the 'half' until I remembered that the 'half' room was really only a sort of a vestibule. Carson said, Oh, how lovely! I bet it's like Mrs. Spring's apartment in Rome, which I think was a slightly confused reference to my novel, the one that contained that extremely felicitous line about "amethyst dusk". . . .

The meeting between Reeves and Paul Bowles was not a happy one. Reeves said, Well, Son, how does it feel to be a published writer? Bowles looked like a Morrocan camel with a mouthful of the spiniest and most indigestible plant that grows on the desert. But the McCullers were so entranced over the good news about their producers that every response to their benign gestures struck them as expressing the most suitable gratitude and delight. Carson told me three times, by careful reckoning, that I did not like her play. If she had told me once more I would have agreed with her, but luckily my final response was peculiarly inspired. When have I ever not liked anything you have ever done? For this I received a tender kiss on the lips. Paul Bowles was accorded the same tribute when their hosts came to take them away. Paul is terribly squeamish about any physical contact with anything not Arab and not under fifteen and he looked more like a Camel with something suddenly impossible to get down his throat than ever.

I am sorry to devote so much space to a really American topic but nothing has yet happened of a strictly European character that is worth noting. There is a vast and dreadful crowd of tourists here and we don't [know] where, how far South or East, it will be necessary to go to feel we have really left New York. But the Bowles are a pure delight as ever and, all in all, one might say the same of the McCullers, although quite naturally in a dissimilar fashion.

Much, much love, dearest Paul, Tenn.
(from Frank, too.)

Warmest regards to Alice! And to Jordan!

[TW and Frank Merlo landed at Plymouth on May 26. The "rigors of London" probably included bad food and bad trade as well as the truncated production of *Streetcar*, which closed on August 19, 1950, apparently unseen by TW.

Elizabeth Bowen's view of Carson McCullers as "a destroyer" may reflect the marital tension which she observed during the visit of Carson and Reeves in late-July. Bowen chose not "to be closely involved" (qtd. in Carr, p. 360) with McCullers, preferring the friendship of Eudora Welty, who had visited earlier in the spring.

Summarized were thirty years of counseling and advocacy in *Marty Mann Answers Your Questions about Drinking and Alcoholism* (1970). Reeves, who had been counseled by Miss Mann, recommended that Stanley Martineau, a co-producer of *The Member of the Wedding*, find similar help.

TW refers to "the amethyst light of prima sera" in Part Three of *The Roman Spring*.

The postscript refers to Alice Bouverie and Jordan Massee.]

171. To Cheryl Crawford

[Paris]
June 9, 1950
[TLS, 1 p. BRTC]

Dear Cheryl:

Your letter which I picked up this afternoon at American Express is the first ray of light that I have had from America. Gadg's letter, which was waiting for me when I arrived, attached to the censored "Streetcar" film-script, was most depressing. He said he was sorry that "he would not be able to do my play because of his film commitments". He mentioned Zapata, which I understand, but also mentioned the unfinished film-script by Arthur Miller. I don't see how or why an unfinished film-play would take precedence over my play, since surely its schedule is far more elastic at this time. I have written him twice, once from the boat, and again after receiving this very flat and cold announcement in Paris, and I told him how thoroughly bewildered I was by his sudden reversal of attitude. Do you know what to make of it? Perhaps you can get a clearer picture than I.

I felt so badly, after receiving his letter, that I gave up the idea of going to London and plunged into the anarchistic nightlife of Paris, which made me feel even worse. Now I have given that up, too, and we are leaving for Italy tomorrow or Monday.

I worked on the play all the while I was on the boat. I have a new ending which is free-er and wilder, involving the children instead of Estelle Hohengarten, and am re-writing the whole Rosario section. It is no use describing it but I will send you and Audrey the revised material as soon as it is completed. We have the name of a new Italian actress who speaks English, Lea Padovani. She is in the English film "Christ in Concrete" and is said to be similar in style to Magnani but younger. Of course I will make every effort to see and interest Magnani in Rome. If she can read English I don't [know] how she can fail to see herself as Pepina. Still another actress is Elena Zareschi but I don't know what she has appeared in. These names were given us by the Italian screen-writer of Vive in Pace whom we met here in Paris.

If Gadg is definitely out, I think we should consider Bobby Lewis as well as Danny Mann. In many ways the play would be especially suited to Bobby with his fine sense of style and poetry. Peter Brook is another name to bear in mind, but I am still hoping that Kazan is acting upon a temporary caprice.

I did not show the script to Olivier on the boat. I simply did not feel like exposing it again while I was still working on it and while I was still recuperating from the session with Molly.

You will hear from me soon after I settle in Italy or Sicily. More thanks than I can say for your belief!

Love from us both, Tenn.

[Successful productions of *Porgy and Bess* (1942), *One Touch of Venus* (1943), and *Brigadoon* (1947) established Cheryl Crawford (1902-1986) as an astute, tasteful manager and led to the staging of four plays by TW: *The Rose Tattoo*, as well as *Camino Real* (1953), *Sweet Bird of Youth* (1959), and *Period of Adjustment* (1960). Crawford's thrift as a producer was exceeded only by her intelligence and devotion to the theatre.

Lea Padovani's ability to look both "young" and "mature" (to TW, June 28, 1950, HRC) in *Christ in Concrete* (1949) was a valuable asset, Audrey Wood thought, in playing the role of Pepina. The arresting film title refers to an exploited bricklayer who drowns in concrete.

Robert Lewis's reputation as a sensitive director led to his recommendation by TW. *Come Back, Little Sheba* was Daniel Mann's first staging of a Broadway production.]

172. To Elia "Gadg" Kazan

Am. Ex. Co., Rome.
6/16/50
[TLS w/ autograph postscript, 3 pp. WUCA]

Dear Gadg:

When I finished your letter I had tears in my eyes, which was not very manly of me, but still in character, since I have never pretended to have much hair on my chest. The moisture came from relief, for your letter removed the doubt I had felt about your continued interest in my work and myself. I have too much reserve with people, as a rule, too much doubt and suspicion, but I had thrown all that overboard in my relations with you and had been totally honest and open with you, and something in the apparently cool tone with which you told me you would not be able to do "Rose Tattoo" hurt me a great deal more than the professional set-back. Now you have dispelled that feeling and we can forget it. In this letter I am going to be a great deal more unguarded than I have ever been in the past and I am going to tell you a lot about myself and my life in the past few years because I think it may help you to understand my problems as a writer which I am now still able to hope will concern you. But that part of the letter I am going to save till the last. It is a sort of capsule-autobiography of the past five years and we should get through business matters first.

I did not see Vivien. I fell into a grim, nihilistic mood in Paris and could not go through with the planned trip to London but, plunged, instead, into the anarchistic nightlife that the city has to offer in spite of the Puritanical reforms that have lately gone on there.

I'm not worried about your not shooting the film on location as I know you will insist on getting a good studio set out of Warners. I am sorry you have changed your mind about the night-out scene which I truly liked and thought it was one place where the story was transposed into truly cinematic terms that gave it a value not in the stage version. To me Blanche's behavior in this sequence was clearly and sympathetically motivated, not hysterical but very normally human within the limits of her somewhat flighty nature. It could be toned down, if there were hysterical excesses, but basically I felt it was true and right and richly cinematic. Psychologically it couldn't be truer. She is not, at this point, madly in love with Mitch. How could she be? She is a woman desperate for understanding, affection, protection. But it isn't until the close of this scene that she comes to see that that is what he will give her, and at the point where she takes flight to the powder-room and calls up the old beau, she is hurt and clutching at straws. This could be made so very clear and poignant on the screen that I am surprised you have lost confidence in it. Don't listen to Leigh about script! The Oliviers are as bad as the Lunts in that Dept.

I don't mind the bits from scene four going back in, but I don't have a script with me, now, and can't visualize where they would go. However I am sure you must have a good place for them in mind. But do think earnestly about the night-out scene and consider whether you cannot play it down, in the heavy parts, so that the effect you fear, of a person already cracking up, can be avoided while still keeping the wonderful movement and vitality that it now has, and I am not just talking about the wind-blown flight down the stairs to the crumbling pier. In other words, I challenge your boldness.

Now let us talk about "Rose Tattoo". The fact that you have told Cheryl not to engage another director is a bit of encouragement and I am clutching at it for all it is worth. Of course I now understand about Art's picture. You should have told me more about that originally. Under the circumstances I think it should take precedence over the play in your future plans. If the Zapata thing is out, does that leave a vacancy in your schedule, and where?

I'm not really very worried about the time-element myself, but I know that Cheryl has to know about it and that I don't want the play to open on Broadway later than March at the latest. If it has to open in the Spring, could it open in Chicago and stay out of town - with a lay-off during the summer - until the early Fall? My main concern, now, is to know that you want to do it and to continue my work on it. I feel that the Rosario part is coming richly to life, and perhaps Cheryl has told you that I have a new (alternative) ending which may be better than the two women. I know what youd dislike about the two women. It represents to you a retreat for Pepina. To me it was an advance on a realistic basis. But my objection to it is that it may be just a little bit cliché, a little expected or pat. Maybe that's only because of brooding too much about it. The other ending is really wild and it involves the children. - Of course Alvaro can't take the place of Rosario. Does anybody ever take the place of the first great love? What he accomplishes is her escape from the urn of ashes and her reconcilement with life! In the new ending I may go so far as to suggest, symbolically, that she will bear a child by him. I am sure that in playing the feeling will be one of affirmative statement, not decadent melancholy, because that is how I have conceived it. But the statement will have to have pain in it too. I think of this play as a dark, blood-red translucent stone that is twisted this way and that, to give off its sombre rich light, like the ring on the crooked finger of some wise and wicked old witch of beneficent character, or perhaps some old necromancer like Bigelow. In simpler terms, I think of it as having a curious light-dark quality, a stranger and richer mystery than my other plays have had. In that way, perhaps, less human, the way that the interior of the body is less familiarly human than the hands and face. It is more about perplexity than about pain. The mystery of one to another. The baffled look, the stammered speech, the incomplete gesture, the wild rush of beings past and among each other. All of that I am trying to get in one play, with a simple, commonplace story. During the past two years I have been, for the first time in my life, happy and at home with someone and I think of this play as a monument to that happiness, a house built of images and words for that happiness to live in. But in that happiness there is the long, inescapable heritage of the painful and the perplexed like the dark corners of a big room. But the play is not at all personal, though it is dedicated to an intensely personal thing. At least I don't think it is personal, not as Menagerie or even as much as Streetcar, and the fact it is less personal (in a sense, more about a thing, a quality, than persons) may be what makes it seem inhuman to Molly. Now some of the above, especially the part about the blood-red stone, may not make much sense. I am not sure I would understand it myself, and I am talking about the play that exists in my conception and I don't know how near or far that is to the play on paper. Do you like Tchelitchew's painting "Cache-Cache" (Hide-and-Seek)? Stravinsky's Sacre du Printemps? Both of those works are masterpieces, and I have no right to compare this play to them, but they contain or suggest something of what I was trying to get and am still seeking in it which is what makes it so important to me. I hardly hope that I will be able to arrive at a full realization of this, but I think I will come close enough to make it felt as a disturbing and exciting experience in the theatre, even though it should happen to be a failure. With you, I don't think it would be. If you refuse to do it, I would still try to get it with someone like Lewis, Mann or Peter Brook, if any of them would attempt it. But of the directors I know, this is much closer to you. You have an emotional grasp of it. Not to have you would be a disaster, even before it opened. (I mean compared to what you could make it.) - One thing, very sad, I have got to face. I don't write with the effervesence that I used to. It comes harder. The peak of my virtuosity was in the one-act plays, some of which are like fire-crackers in a rope. Some of that came from sexual repression and loneliness which don't exist anymore for very good reasons, and some of it came from plain youth and freshness. As a compensation, I have a clearer, much clearer, sense of what I am doing. I have a deeper knowledge of life and people, and I think I have more sanity. As you can tell from this letter, my approach to my work is hysterical. It is infatuated and sometimes downright silly. I don't know what it is to take anything calmly although I know how to look like a fish on ice, as Maria Britneva describes me. I'll always be "a neurotic" but I don't think I am any longer in danger of becoming psychotic. But with that danger has also gone some of my uncontrolled vivacity as a writer.

Now I have written you everything but the autobiographical section, and thinking it over I know it is not necessary. For the past five years I have been (intermittently but usually) haunted by a fear, which has made it necessary for me [to] work like somebody running out of a house on fire. Make out of that what you want to!

But right now concentrate, I hope, on making a great picture which only you can in America!

With love, Tenn.

I have gotten Alvaro into the first scene as a distant cousin who comes to request a loan for his three dependants: tentative and removable. I see the value in bringing him into the first part of the play: but was fearful of the changes it would call for in the later scenes. Perhaps they are not so formidable as I had thought. Pepina does not see Alvaro clearly in the first scene for she has turned the lights out to rest her eyes after sewing all day on "First Communion" dresses.

[TW answered Elia Kazan's rejection of *The Rose Tattoo* by writing that "an uncompleted film-script {"The Hook," by Arthur Miller} can be scheduled at any time in the future. . . . It makes it appear that the real reason is somewhere between the lines, which is evasive and not like you at all" (May 30, 1950, WUCA). Kazan's subsequent letter appears to have restored TW's confidence and explained the priority of Arthur Miller's script. Kazan may also have raised TW's hopes by mentioning that another film project of his, *Viva Zapata!* (1952), had encountered political difficulties in Mexico and might not be shot after *Streetcar* was finished. The same news had reached Audrey Wood in New York and led her to hope for Kazan's final "commitment" (to TW, June 16, 1950, HRC) to *The Rose Tattoo*.

Kazan apparently feared that TW's elaboration of the "night-out scene" in *Streetcar* would be incompatible with the measured closing, as Blanche and Mitch embrace: "Sometimes—there's God—so quickly!" No hysterical "flight" to the "powder-room" or to the "crumbling pier" was filmed.

TW met the surrealist painter Pavel Tchelitchew in the mid 1940s and spoofed his gloomy metaphysical themes with the sobriquet "Chilly Death." His experimentation with "interior landscapes" of the human body—*Hide and Seek* (1940-1942) a well-known example—intrigued TW. The title served provisionally during early draft stages of *Baby Doll* (1956).

The metaphorical "house on fire" and its haunting effect upon TW refer to his operation in May 1946.

Penned in the lower margin of page 1 is the notation "Let Art have his way! Commies go brah!" TW probably refers to Arthur Miller's defiant support of liberal causes, an activity which led the State Department to withhold his passport (see letter #286) and the House Un-American Activities Committee to subpoena his testimony. The screenplay in question, "The Hook," was abandoned by Miller but proved the inspiration for Kazan's award-winning film *On the Waterfront* (1954).]

173. To Oliver Evans

[Hotel d'Inghilterra, Rome]
6/20/50
[TLS, 1 p. HRC]

Dear Oliver:

I was dreadfully shocked by the news of your accident. I do hope you've recovered from it. Isn't it strange that I always had the feeling, when you drove, that something terrible was going to happen? We are back in Rome but could not get back in our old apartment and are staying at the hotel Inhilterra while we look for a new Apt. We are seeing two this afternoon. Rome is not crowded by holy pilgrims as we had feared. In fact there seem to be fewer people than last summer. I have had two wonderful lays at the baths, one a fisherman from Capri and the other a Sicilian, blond, which are the best blonds in Europe. The last thing I did before I left America was to get Audrey hot on the problem of renewing your fellowship through the Authors' League. I don't know how much money there was left in it and unfortunately I can't make a new contribution to the fund until the money from my pictures starts coming in, sometime next winter. Right now I am just able to keep us going. I have finished a play and a novella. But the play's success is doubtful. It demands a really great actress like Magnani (the part is a Sicilian immigrant to America) and direction like Kazan's. Kazan is not entirely sold on the play and as yet I have no assurance that he will consent to do it. I am all at sixes-and-sevens, professionally. Wonder if should not quit writing. But there is only one other thing I like doing very much and you can't do that <u>all</u> the time. Or <u>can</u> you?

Our address is American Express, Rome. Let me know how things are working out. It is wonderful, wonderful news that you are transferring to City College, New York. That will make life so much easier for you, and we will see more of each other, if I am lucky next year (meaning if I am in New York for a production!)

Love, 10.

[To "the baths" of Rome TW added "the old Appian Way" as sexual rendezvous: "In the evenings, very late, after midnight, I like to drive out the old Appian Way and park the car at the side of the road and listen to the crickets among the old tombs. Sometimes a figure appears among them which is not a ghost but a Roman boy in the flesh!" (to Jane Lawrence Smith, June 29, 1950, Smith Collection).]

174. To Cheryl Crawford

[Hotel d'Inghilterra, Rome]
June 26, 1950
[TLS w/ marginalia and
autograph postscript, 2 pp. BRTC]

Dear Cheryl:

Your letters always buck me up when I am feeling down. I have not been able to rest since I left America. That is, I have not been able to quit working. I am too keyed up and things were too much "in the air" at the time of my sailing. I wanted to let everything go. Forget it. Have a good time when I arrived in Italy. But the Nemesis (feeling of incompletion, dissatisfaction, restlessness) stays with me, and every day I get up and go back to work as before, as if nothing were finished. Fortunately I seem to be working pretty well. The pity is that I am <u>not</u> resting, which would probably be more important for me right now. But as Gorki said once: "The wisdom of life is deeper and wider than the wisdom of men". So perhaps it is life that is directing me to do this.

On the boat and in Paris I worked on the Rosario section but here in Italy I am working on the idea of beginning the play after Rosario's death, with the opening scene of Act Two. (Graduation morning). This eliminates both Rosario and Estelle Hohengarten, as well as one or two minor characters. It gives the play the classic unity of time and a great deal more compactness, generally. It sacrifices some values (the red silk shirt) but I think the added values are greater. When Natalia gets back from Capri in about ten days I am going to read her this version. She will help me with the Italian. I want nearly all the first dialogue in the knife scene to be in Italian. The action is explicit enough and the emotion would make Pepina revert to her native tongue.

Eleanora Mendellsohn was also suggested by Alice Bouverie when I read her the play in New York. Certainly should be looked into. All the reports on Magnani are discouraging, particularly from Natalia, who says that she doesn't think she would consider any offer to go to America right now. I have not yet seen her but I shall continue to work on it. Today we are moving into a new apartment and I shall wait till we are settled and Natalia has returned from Capri to make a definite assault on Miss Anna. In the meantime I have gotten the names of a couple of others, Fulvia Mammi and one with a complete unspellable (from memory) second name, given me by Vittorio Gassman, who is, incidentally very interested and available for an American production. He played Stanley in the Roman Streetcar and is one of the world's (surely!) handsomest men as well as a fine actor. Perhaps is too romantic looking for the comedy values in Alvaro but he undresses like a dream, which I think is always good in a play that has some elements of sexuality in it. He speaks English, not well, but enough to master a part in that language. I will send you a picture of him presently, as we were photographed together at lunch by a Vogue photographer. Have you thought at all of Shirley Booth, or is she too "hot" right now to be approachable? There would be danger of too much similarity with her part in "Sheba". - Carson was drinking in Paris and so was Reeves, pretty heavily. Her trip to Ireland was apparently just pleasant. Not exciting. - Please keep after Gadg, and so will I, to the extent that it is possible through the mails. A cable and letter from Clurman wanting to direct. I didn't like his work in "Member", did you? It was curiously harsh and Broadwayese. I don't know what to say to him, since I like and admire him so much, intellectually and as a man.

I seem to be buying a house in Key West, according to cables from my lawyer. And Buffie has offered to rent me that apartment I loved so much in New York. It will be vacant the first of October and would be an ideal home during work on the play, whenever that may commence. I am glad you feel there is no need to rush things and that the casting of Pepina and the commitment of Kazan come first. I have a feeling that Kazan will like what I am doing in this last version of the play, as he originally said he thought Rosario was better as a memory and a legend and he felt the play broke into two parts with his death.

Frank sends his love, with mine, to both you and Ruth, and we hope you are finding rest and comfort in your Connecticutt dream-house.

Love, Tenn.

Friend saw Magnani at concert last night and said she expressed definite interest in seeing the play. An appt. is being arranged.

[TW quotes from an early story by Maxim Gorki entitled "My Fellow-Traveller" (1894).

Revision of *The Rose Tattoo* undertaken in Rome generally followed the approach suggested by Elia Kazan. Beginning the play on "Graduation morning" would cause a further obscuring of Rosario in preparation for Pepina's awakening. The elimination of Estelle Hohengarten would also require a new ending, as described in later correspondence (see letters #175 and #178). In the melodramatic "knife scene," Rose threatens suicide if Pepina will not relax her Sicilian discipline and accept the boy whom she loves, a sailor named Jack.

A native Roman, Natalia Danesi Murray married an American in the 1920s and lived thereafter in New York and Italy. She worked chiefly in broadcasting and publishing and in 1940 began an intimate relationship with the journalist Janet Flanner. She would prove a valuable liaison with Anna Magnani.

The Italian ancestry of Eleanora Mendelssohn explains her early consideration for the role of Pepina. Shirley Booth was "'hot'" after her award-winning performance in *Come Back, Little Sheba.* She played an aging romantic who lives in loneliness and reverie, as does Pepina.

Crawford and her companion Ruth Norman shared a "dream-house" named "Eastham."

Typed in the upper margin of page 1 is TW's mailing address, "American Express, Rome."]

175. To Audrey Wood

[Rome]
July ?, 1950
[TLS, 1 p. HRC]

Dear Audrey:

I really feel very deeply satisfied with the acquisition of a house, and I know that Grandfather will be equally pleased over it, for he was so happy there. It will also make a nice place for the others of the family to visit, especially my sister, when we are in New York. Incidentally Buffie Johnson has written to offer me her apartment at $400. a month. I wish I could take it for the few months I would be in New York for Tattoo as it would be an ideal refuge during that period of travail. You might contact her about it, possibly working out an exchange so that she could occupy my Key West house while I was in hers. She is now in Sag Harbor, New York with her new husband with whom she seems to be eminently satisfied. Hope he is likewise.

Tattoo is undergoing radical revisions. It now begins with the graduation morning as I finally decided that the Rosario section made it too long and unwieldy. I am building up the Pepina-Alvaro scenes as much as possible to give an effect of fullness. I think they are developing nicely. There is a new ending, without Hohengarten. I use the ancient woman ("La Fattuchiere") instead, and I have changed Pepina's name to Serafina which I think is prettier and more touching, since Serafina delle Rose means "Angel of the roses". In the end the old lady envelops her in her "grey shawl of pity" and beckons the curtain to fall. It makes a good curtain. I got the feeling that the other ending was a little pat or cliche, especially since the other woman does not, now, appear in the beginning of the play.

Magnani told a friend of mine she was eager to meet me and read the play but she does not answer her phone. She has a new villa in the country and is at present incommunicado with a new lover. Through Natalia Murray I will get in contact with other actresses such as Leah Padovani and Andreina Pagnani, a woman of 47, who is said to be the finest dramatic actress in Italy. How do you feel about Eleanora Mendolsohn? Cheryl wrote me about her. Can she play comedy well enough for the part? She is now touring in "Mad Woman" but I think she has a straight part.

What is this about the Bigelow "Sea Gull"! A marvelous idea. Is he going to produce it, or what? - My poor friend, Oliver Evans, was in a motor smash-up and is in the hospital. Is there any money for him at the Authors' League?

I don't know what to make of Gadg's behavior. I received a long letter from him, saying that the Miller picture was really very close to completion after much re-writing and that he was morally obligated to help with it. But he mentioned that the Zapata picture might fall through. I don't think we should allow him to escape us if any form of detention is availing!

Affectionate greetings to you and Bill, Tenn.

[Audrey Wood warmly approved TW's purchase of a house in Key West and assured him that he could afford the asking price of $22,500 without using his bonds (July 13, 1950, HRC). The Bahama-style cottage which TW formerly rented would see the gradual addition of a studio, guest house, pool, and the Jane Bowles Summer House, a gazebo built in memory of his friend.

Wood informed TW that he might be asked to adapt *The Sea Gull* (Chekhov, 1896) for a revival planned by Paul Bigelow. She had already listed for Bigelow "all the reasons" (to TW, July 7, 1950, HRC) why her client should avoid the project.

Further evidence of Elia Kazan's unpredictable "behavior" appeared in a *New York Times* report that Kazan had "no hesitancy" about directing *The Rose Tattoo* "if the script were held until he's available" (June 23, 1950). Wood did not "believe any of this" (HRC), as she informed TW on June 28.

The date of this letter falls between Wood's correspondence of July 7 and 13, 1950.]

176. To John Lehmann

[Rome]
10 July, 1950
[TLS, 1 p. Princeton U]

Dear John:

Rome is now the hottest it has been in 100 years, so Mrs. Stone and I are leaving Tuesday night for Vienna. If you know of any interesting public monuments we should see there, the address is American Express for about 10 days. Mrs. Stone says she wants to find "The Fourth Man" and I want to take a ride on that big ferris-wheel.

I am so glad you are going to do the novella separately. Jay has sent me a copy of his edition and the book looks fairly normal in <u>length</u> and the jacket design is superb, a fantastic bird-woman in very free style against a brilliant yellow and red.

If we sail from a northern port this time, I will make every effort, but no promise, to get over to London. I want to see you and your sisters and the Christopher Fry plays that I have heard so much about. Peter Ustinov is here doing Nero in the great MGM spectacle "Quo Vadis" which has already cost 8 million dollars and given employment to almost every street-walker in Rome: it will be a show-case of giovanni Romani if nothing else! They have a pack of lions, about 30 of them, a herd of fighting bulls, a brace of cheetas. The poveri raggazzi are quaking with terror of the scenes they have to act with this menagerie. Ustinov did not look too happy when the pair of cheetas walked on, supposedly pets of Octavia's, but perhaps he was only afraid they would steal the scene. A Vogue photographer wanted to take our picture together on Nero's throne and Ustinov said, "I don't share my throne with anybody!" - a queenly if not imperial remark!

A riverdici! Tenn.

[John Lehmann (1907-1989) lived in Vienna before the war and was coyly deemed familiar with the city's gay attractions. TW's prospective traveling companion Eyre de Lanux—"Mrs. Stone"—did not make the trip.

Lehmann originally planned to supplement the English edition of *The Roman Spring* (December 1950) with an additional story or two. Both he and James Laughlin, whose positions in British and American publishing were similar, preferred literature to commerce and encouraged adventurous new writing. By special arrangement with New Directions, Lehmann published the first English edition of TW's works before losing managerial control of his firm in 1952. Strict censorship laws apparently prohibited or discouraged an English edition of *One Arm* (1948).

Lehmann's sisters, Rosamond and Beatrix, author and actor, respectively, and the recent premiere of several verse plays by Christopher Fry were incentives for TW to visit London at this time.

Metro-Goldwyn-Mayer released *Quo Vadis?* in 1951.]

177. To Oliver Evans

[en route to Vienna]
7/13/50
[TLS, 1 p. HRC]

Dear Oliver:

I am as outraged as you by the notice in the Saturday Review. It is the most spiteful notice I've seen of a volume of poems since my own were reviewed by Randall Jarell. There is a close affinity between those two. They are both politician-poets, insanely jealous of anything genuinely lyrical. I shall write the editor of the Sat Lit but you must realize that my connection with the volume has probably done it a political disservice as I have always, for some reason, been particularly odious to the sort of professional litterateurs that write these notices. They loathe me because I have made some money out of writing and at the same time have dared to publish in avant-garde precincts. You must also remember that most of this spiteful sisterhood are thwarted queens. They usually lack the vitality or courage to have any good trade. They go to bed with each other, which puts them in a frightfully bad humor. There is something about your verse that smacks of sensual satisfaction and richness of experience and this they must deplore.

I am writing this on a train, on my way to Vienna. Rome was having the hottest summer in 100 years and I had to escape from it. I left Frank and the car and took off myself for a week or ten days. Eloi Bordelon and

William Richards, of New Orleans, were in Rome when I left. I think Eloi looks better than I have ever seen him, he has had some really miraculous skin-treatments or a marvelous new make-up for the pitted complexion was quite smooth. He told me that Frank Ford - do you remember him? - has brought out a book of poems. Frank was my best friend in New Orleans.

I have not had any response from Audrey or Sillcox about my repeated solicitations regarding the fund. It may be all gone. I bought a house in Key West, the one I occupied last winter, which I will make a permanent residence in America, and it will not be until my next play opens that I can make any fresh payments to the fund if it is now exhausted, but I am still waiting to hear. Audrey is interested in your work, for she sent me copies of both reviews, the Times and the Villa-nous one.

Suggest you read Aldington's new book on Lawrence, particularly the notices that brought about the suppression of "The Rainbow". Then you will not feel so badly or alone. Lawrence said: "I curse them all, body and soul, root, branch and leaf, to eternal damnation!" - I shall be exposed twice to the critics next year, with the short novel and the new play. I have a feeling that I shall have to buck a terrible tide of adverse criticism - the foreword to your volume is a straw in the wind. I am terribly sorry it worked against you like this, but you must rest assured that the beauty of the poems is ineluctable as this shining Alpine country that the train is now going through. I have rarely seen or heard people so moved by the reading of poems as I saw when Bigelow read yours aloud to a group in New York shortly before I left. Nobody takes Villa seriously, my dear! You will be in New York next year and there will be occasion to slit his throat, if you are after reprisal!

Love, Tenn.

[TW accused the editor of having loaded "the dice" by assigning such an "eclectic" (*Saturday Review,* August 19, 1950, p. 24) poet as José Garcia Villa to review the traditional lyrics of Oliver Evans (*Young Man With a Screwdriver*, 1950). Audrey Wood saw that Villa had "reviewed" TW's preface rather than Evans's poetry and instructed her client to think more "seriously" (July 7, 1950, HRC) about his own reputation. Villa "impressed" (to Villa, September 25, 1950, Private Collection) TW when he later offered to publish "The Kingdom of Earth" in a collection which he was editing. Villa reportedly worked for New Directions and knew of James Laughlin's reluctance to publish the story in America.

TW met Eloi Bordelon and William Richards in New Orleans in 1941. At the time he and "the Bordelon" had a "bloody matrimonial break-up," leading TW to conclude that "Marriage is not for me!"

TW cites Richard Aldington's new biography, *D.H. Lawrence, Portrait of a Genius But . . .* (1950). Lawrence's courage and endurance inspired the earlier dedication of *Battle of Angels:* "Who was while he lived the brilliant adversary of so many dark angels and who never fell, except in the treacherous flesh, the rest being flame that fought and prevailed over darkness" (November 1939, HRC).]

178. To Cheryl Crawford

[Vienna]
July 14, 1950
[TLS w/ marginalia, 2 pp. BRTC]

Dear Cheryl:

I have gone to Vienna for a few days to escape the fierce heat of Rome, the hottest summer in 100 years. It is cooler, here, but the city has a feeling of profound desolation, for the first time making me feel the psychic, as well as material, ruin of western Europe. The city was far more destroyed than I had expected. They are tearing down the ruins and a great deal of re-building is going on so that the atmosphere is filled with an odor of dust, as if you were actually breathing that quality of ruin-beyond-repair which Vienna has. There is nothing hopeful or vigorous about the re-building. I watch the workmen from my hotel window, and they seem to be working in a kind of disgust, as if they knew it was useless. They work in a sort of stupor and sometimes they kick the wheel-barrow over and sit down on it with their face in their hands. Italy is like the wonderfully wise singing clown in King Lear, sad but making songs out of it, but here you see the different melancholy of the Germanic spirit, the lightless, graceless surrender to total defeat. Whoever created the myth of Viennese gaiety!? Sausages and beer and folk-songs still go on, but without any fresh impulse. Now and then you see a young man striding mightily along the street in lederhosen as if he were marching to band-music and you can guess the reason. He has been told that the West is dead but that a new life is coming out of the East! I am afraid that our dollars, our Marshall plan, have not given them the <u>spiritual</u> transfusion which they most need, the sign of a future which is not a continuation of the past which they breathe in the dusty air of their ruined city. And I suspect that the only way we can ultimately save western Europe from what we are afraid of is by some ideological progress in ourselves beyond armaments and dollars, by transposing our democracy into a major key which is dynamic and fluid and truly representing the lightness and freedom that we know totalitarianism doesn't offer. Right now Europe is in a mood to take anything that seems altogether different from what they had in the past.

To descend to the personal level: I am still working hard on "Tattoo". As I think I told you, it now starts with the graduation morning and I have worked into the story a new element which changes the ending. It is now established in the story that Pepina received a supernatural sign when she conceived her two children, Rose and the son who died at birth the night of her husband's death. On the occasion of each conception she felt a burning pain on her left breast and saw, or imagined she saw, a stigmata, the rose tattoo of her husband appearing on it. Now in the end of the play, when she is kneeling to gather the ashes from the broken urn, the stigmata returns. She cries out. The ancient woman (La Fattuchiere) and others rush into the yard in response to her wild cries. She kneels with her breast exposed as the old woman enters the house, crying out: "The tattoo, the tattoo has come back! It means in my body another rose is growing!" The old woman, to comfort her, tells her, Yes, I see it, I see it clearly, Pepina! - and envelops her in the grey shawl of pity as the curtain comes down. - It should be felt by the audience that Pepina may be right, that she actually has received a sign that she has conceived by Alvaro. The danger is they might think she was crazy! We would have to obviate that danger by establishing the fact of the previous stigmatas - and Pepina's profound innate mysticism! - not madness! - I think that I have managed to establish these things in the revisions but of course I am very anxious to get the opinions of you and Audrey and also Gadg if he remains in the fold. So I am going to try to get a somewhat rough draft of this version of the play off to you before the end of the month. Myself, I feel very hopeful about it! - I am still hot on the elusive trail of Magnani. The day before I left Rome I was interviewed by an excellent young Italian writer and reporter for L'Europa and Il Mondo. I told him the story of the play and he was charmed by it and went immediately to the phone to call Magnani as he felt the part was very good for her. He was told that she was still out of town, at her hide-away in the country but he promised that he would be in touch with her by the time I returned from Vienna. Natalia is also going to help but she has not yet heard the play. I may read it to her when this version is completed.

I was very happy over what you said about Mrs. Stone. My object in this novella was to show the ugly and awful mutations that may occur through the obsessive pursuit of a high position, the "power-drive" as we see it so much in our society, particularly in the theatre where it seems to be thrown in particularly sharp focus. And I wanted to make the reader feel more compassion than disgust for the rapacious bird-woman. I am terribly afraid of critical reactions to the book! I am sure they will find it "rotten", "decadent", Etc. and will revive the charge that I can only deal with neurotic people. My answer to that is that, of course, when you penetrate into almost anybody you either find madness or dullness: the only way not to find them is to stay on the surface. Madness I should put in quotes. I mean what is <u>considered</u> madness or neuroticism! - which is simply the inner distortions that any sensitive, mallable nature undergoes through experience in modern society.

Going out, now, to see more of Vienna.

With love, Tenn.

[Vienna was bombed by the Allies in 1943 and further damaged two years later when Russian troops liberated the city in house-to-house fighting. Russian sector guards alarmed TW: "They snatch the passport, grunt and throw it back at you, and you say 'Thank you' in a terrified whisper! . . . I hope we don't have to fight them!" (to Wood, July 13, 1950, HRC).

The announcement of Serafina's conception and stigmata was intended to unify the sensual and mystical elements of the play in the latest revised ending. The plan to begin *The Rose Tattoo* on "graduation morning" does not appear in subsequent draft stages and may be among those revisions which TW reported "throwing out" in mid-August.

Reviews of *The Roman Spring of Mrs. Stone* were sharply mixed and generally followed the line of "'decadent'" criticism feared by TW. The *Herald Tribune* critic wrote that Karen Stone "is tracked down . . . with the same inexorableness, and submitted to the same sexual crucifixion, that awaited Blanche DuBois or the heroine of 'Summer and Smoke.'" Why does TW "arrange his dramas like inquisitions, with torture preceding the confession, and death following?" (October 22, 1950).

Typed in the upper margin of page 1 is TW's mailing address, "American Express, Rome."]

179. To Paul Bigelow

[Rome]
August 3, 1950
[TLS, 2 pp. Duke U]

Dear Paul:

The news about the Sea Gull is by far the best to reach me from New York for a long, long time. As you know, I think it's the greatest of all modern plays, and probably the first really modern poetic play as well as the greatest. I think you are divinely appointed to produce it. I can't think of anyone else who would have a finer taste for its particular aura of period and atmosphere. I shudder to think what the Lunts must have done to it, and certainly the time is peculiarly ripe, after the fearful mutilation visited on Chekhov by the Logan-Hayes combination, to introduce to Broadway the true quality of his art, which I have never seen more than suggested, and then in London by an undistinguished company from the provinces. Ina Claire is a superb choice for Arcadina provided! - and I think she is enough of a really good actress to recognize that need - she does not try to convert it into a starring vehicle as the Lunts must have tried. If you could only get Margaret Phillips for the role of Nina! But what about direction? I think the question of director is far more critical than that of a new translation. I haven't read the Stark Young one but I should think it would have grace and style. After all, it is a Victorian piece, at least temporally. A certain elegance should be the keynote of its style in every department, not a chi-chi elegance but a poetic grace of speech as well as setting, costume and performance. The Chekhov translations which I have read - mostly those by Constance Garnett - are marred mostly by a certain stiffness, a stilted quality, which I am sure the original didn't have. I would be only too proud and happy to work with you on eliminating those touches, getting a more fluent and natural style of speech, and it would be a labor of love and refreshment for which I wouldn't want any other kind of remuneration than the pleasure and satisfaction of having a chance to do it. What I would most, if I were at all capable, love to do would be to collaborate on the staging of it, either with you or someone else more acquainted than either of us with the mechanics of stage direction. It would be a thrilling experience to help bring a play like that into its difficult, very delicate sort of reality. I know it can be done, and you are the right one to do it!

I am leaving in a few hours for the northern lake region as it has become suffocatingly hot in Rome. I am stupefied. Cannot continue work here. I am hoping for some revival of energies in the north where there will be cool swimming. Frank is heading in the opposite direction, to Naples and Sicily. We'll both return here in a couple of weeks or possibly a bit less.

Oh, Paul, don't let anything deter or discourage you in this wonderful venture. I think it can be one of the few really memorable - quite unforgettable! - events in our American theatre! You can count on me for anything at all that I may be capable of doing in connection with it. I would love to see the Stark Young translation here in Europe if you or Audrey could get a copy of it to me.

Much love, Tenn.

P.S. Charlie wants me to come to Hollywood and has offered to pay our transportation and living expenses, so we will probably be returning to the States about the middle of the month, that is, starting back. They have sent me a final shooting script of "Streetcar", as assembled by Gadg, and he has done a really marvelous job on putting it together with great directness and economy of style. I think I have been unjust to Gadg about "Tattoo", that his reservations have been sincerely based on a lack of satisfaction with the script for reasons that were probably sound. It seems to me that trust in a person, if it is given after enough consideration, is practically never misplaced. Of all things it is the hardest for me to give, much harder than love, but I don't think I am ever wrong when I give it. I think about the play I will finally be guided by his decision. And Audrey's. If they still don't really and whole-heartedly like this final draft of it, I will abandon the idea of producing it, at least for this season. I have seen Magnani. She finally consented to meet me, and the meeting occured at a crowded sidewalk cafe, very carefully staged by Magnani who was in complete dominion. She looks marvelous, the sexiest looking woman on earth. She has taken off weight, and her body is quite beautiful. She has the warmth and vigor of a panther! She will not read the play till it is completely finished and she said she is far more interested in doing a film of it than on the stage in New York: that her film commitments will keep her occupied far into 1951. My guess is that she would quite definitely do the picture if it first had a success on the stage, but that it would be very difficult to ensnare her for Broadway, on exorbitant terms and with enormous power. Several people here have suggested Mata or Marta Abba. I've never seen her. I don't think any other Italian actress would do. But I have heard of an American actress named Maureen Stapleton who is said to be a sort of American Magnani. Know anything about her?

Senta, per favore! Not a word to Sister Woman about my letter describing her phone conversation with the producers! She is already inclined to list me among her persecutors, I am afraid. Hope she arrived in good condition and that Li'l Pretty's condition has also undergone noticable improvement. Is it true that George Davis was fired from "Flair"? There are rumors that Windham has gone to Florence but nothing is reported on the remainder of the explosive colony at Taormina. I guess they are busy being photographed by Cecil Beaton among the old Greek ruins. I want so much to read the completed story you mention in your letter.

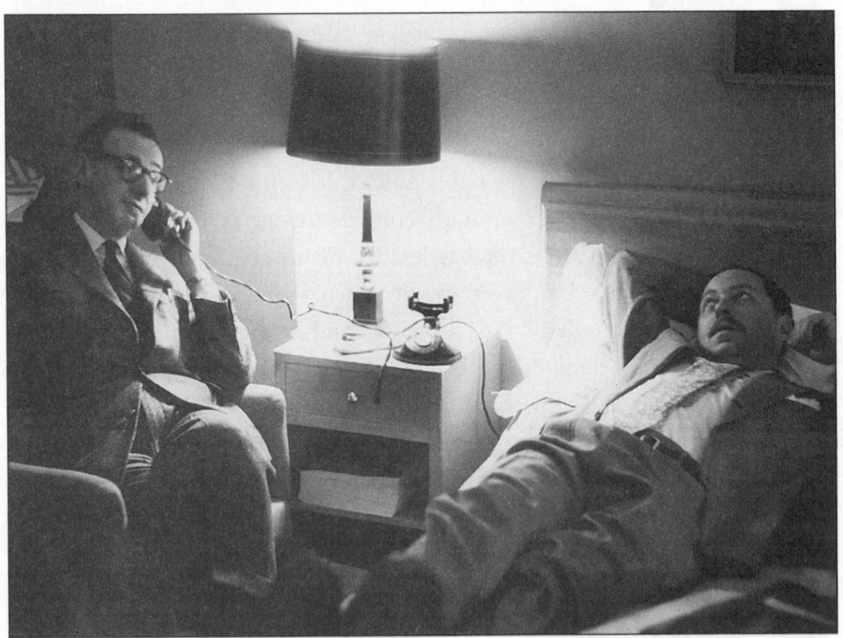

Tennessee Williams and the "legendary" Paul Bigelow.

[Plans to restage *The Sea Gull* led TW to "wonder if the present world atmosphere will not make the melancholy grace of Chekhov seem too old-fashioned?" (to Kazan, August 14, 1950, WUCA). Audrey Wood had questioned the expense of reviving the play (to TW, June 28, 1950, HRC) and in effect foretold the failure of Paul Bigelow's project.

Alfred Lunt and Lynn Fontanne starred—and Uta Hagen made her Broadway debut—in a Theatre Guild production of *The Sea Gull* in 1938. *The Wisteria Trees* (1950), loosely based upon *The Cherry Orchard* (1904), was written and produced by Joshua Logan and starred Helen Hayes. The lightly regarded adaptation of Chekhov had a modest run of 165 performances. The stage comedian Ina Claire was last seen on Broadway in *The Fatal Weakness* (1946).

In later correspondence TW restated his "dream" of directing *The Sea Gull*, with Marlon Brando and Stella Adler cast in leading roles. TW's adaptation entitled *The Notebook of Trigorin* had its world premiere at the Vancouver Playhouse in British Columbia in 1981. Allean Hale prepared the first edition (1997) for New Directions.

The summons to Hollywood led TW to reflect that "this Roman period has all the defects of the one before and very little of the occasional charm. I blame this on myself, my failure to lose myself in really satisfactory work, lack of accomplishment, disappointment in the play overshadowing the whole ambient of my present life" (*Journal*, July 26, 1950). Diminished too was "Frank's friendliness," which seemed "quite different" in Rome.

Carson McCullers and her husband "Li'l Pretty" separated once again after returning to the States in early-August.

TW began this letter in Rome shortly before he planned to leave for "the northern lake region." He went instead to Positano and then to "Naples," as indicated by a penned notation in the upper margin. The lengthy postscript may have been added in Naples and the letter mailed there.]

180. To Cheryl Crawford

[Rome]
8/11/50
[TLS, 1 p. BRTC]

Dear Cheryl:

You and Bigelow write the best letters I have ever received. I love the quotation from Whitman. What enviable serenity he had! With a spirit like that, and such assurance, it might almost be a pleasure to be a poet. I wonder if he ever had any doubts? It is odd, very odd, that not a single poem seems to express such a feeling. And yet it is not fatuous, nor is it conceited. You seem to feel that what he admires, and is confident of, in himself is himself in life: that he does not separate himself from it. And the consoling things he says to himself seem really to be addressed to other people *through* himself. He understood the *unanimity* of mankind. That is the spirit from which an *advanced democracy* should have sprung, by-passing the Stalinist crowd.

The long-awaited meeting with Magnani has finally occured. She kept me waiting ¾ of an hour, and then sent a messenger to say that she was in front of Doney's the most crowded of the sidewalk cafes at the most crowded hour, and would receive me there. She was looking quite marvelous. She has taken off at least twenty pounds. Her figure is the very meaning of sex. Her eyes and her voice and *style* are indescribably compelling. She dominated the whole street. I was overwhelmed by her. But I have serious doubts about the advisability of putting her in a play, even if she consented. She was very direct. She said immediately that picture commitments tied her up until deep into 1951, that it would take her several months to *prepare* for a stage appearance. At first she pretended not to speak English but after a while she began to speak it, with a clear accent and surprising fluency. She demanded a script. I said she could see an early draft, that the final draft was not yet finished. This she refused to do. Said she would read only the final one. I am hesitant about showing her the final script. Plagiarism is so common in Italy, particularly of foreign writers. Her picture Volcano was very close to Bergman's Stromboli, and I would hate for an Italian film to come out using ideas from "Tattoo", possibly before it opened on the stage. I had the impression that it would be very easy to get her to do the *picture*. That she would do the play only under the most extravagant terms, with almost complete control over everything. I have the telephone number of Lea Padovani and will see her this week. Several people here have mentioned Marta Abba. Do you know anything about her? Audrey does. Would Maureen Stapelton be at all right? I have never seen her but have heard she is a somewhat Magnani type.

Eli Wallach as Kilroy in Gadg's scene from "Camino Real" is the closest thing that I have seen to Alvaro so far. Quinn does not seem to have quite the flexibility, the lightness and vivacity, that the part would require, especially as it is now written, although he does have the physical appearance and sexuality. Until we know about Gadg it is almost impossible to think much about casting, for he would be so essential to the use of fresh, inexperienced actors.

They want me to come back to the States sooner than I had planned, for further negotiations with the Breen office. I sent a wire yesterday saying I could fly from London Aug. 23 and am waiting to hear if that date is early enough. I want a chance to see some of the London theatre and a few more Italian actors, and also to rest a bit before the Hollywood-New York pressure is resumed, so soon after the long spell of work.

Love - 10.

[Anna Magnani, forty-two at the time of her meeting with TW, was scheduled to film *Bellissima* (1951) in mid 1951. *Vulcano* (1950), the title of her current film, was intended to echo the central symbol of the Rossellini-Bergman film *Stromboli* (1949). By linking the rival films, which were shot on nearby islands, the producer hoped to exploit the bitter ending of Magnani's affair with her former director.

Maureen Stapleton and Eli Wallach studied together at the Actors Studio and would play the leads in *The Rose Tattoo*. TW regarded the Studio, founded in 1947 by Elia Kazan, Robert Lewis, and Cheryl Crawford, as a source of fresh talent for the play.

"Negotiations with the Breen office" concern unresolved censorship problems in filming *Streetcar*.]

181. To Cheryl Crawford and Audrey Wood

[Rome]
8/15/50
[TLS w/ marginalia, 1 p. HRC]

Dear Cheryl and Audrey:

I am terribly alarmed over the startlingly early dates mentioned in your cable and Audrey's. The only date you had suggested before was a tentative booking for New Haven sometime in January which was far more reasonable in view of the fact that nobody has yet seen the final script - not even I! - and we haven't the ghost of an idea at this point who will direct or star in it. This summer in the dead heat of Rome I have felt like a tired horse at the last high hurdle. I have driven myself to keep working, by compulsion, not inspiration, and I am afraid that most of the progress I thought I was making was wishfull thinking. I am beginning to assemble the script. A lot of the revisions I am throwing out and reverting to earlier versions. Naturally some progress has been made, but not enough. If I could have rested completely, restored my nervous reserves - then made a really fresh attack, the results would have been better. But somehow I couldn't rest and the advance can be measured in inches, instead of yards. I still believe that the flat stretches in the play will ultimately come to life, that I *will* eventually have a period of real stimulation again when I can do warm, spontaneous work that will suddenly illuminate the script where it is now like dusty glass. If Gadg were available it might be worth risking. He can do magic with fairly commonplace writing. Who else can? I feel as hurt as you must about his apparent dereliction - not resentful, but undeniably hurt! - but I still must acknowledge how badly this play needs him. - I think Mann did a good job on "Come Back, Little Sheba". But that was a far, far better play - just as a script - than Inge was given credit for writing. It almost directed itself. The texture of the writing was superb and it had a wonderful line of dramatic development, very clear and forceful, with only momentary lapses. As it now stands, this is not that good a play and not even *nearly* so easy a play to direct. This play remains what it was, the sketch for the best play that I have written, but still not *it*! - and a long way short of it. I think it would be sheer *folly to push it* into rehearsal in mid-October. I should have at least two months of rest in Key West and at least that much time should be devoted to seeking out the right people. The *absolutely* right people. Or at least, the absolutely right *Serafina*! - now that Magnani seems to be pretty definitely out. - So let's stall for time, at least keep all the dates fluid. If the play is *right*, it doesn't matter when it comes into town, really. If it *isn't* right, the time of the season is not going to help it enough to matter. - I have just about given up the idea of going to California. We will look over what I have done, all of us together, when I arrive in New York and have a completely, coldly objective round-robin discussion of it with no punches pulled. This may save us a lot of grief in the end! And I am able to take it. If it were done prematurely and failed, I am not sure that I *would* be able to take it. More later -

Much love, Tenn.

[Audrey Wood's cable ended any reasonable hope that Elia Kazan would stage *The Rose Tattoo*: "He is directing Zapata." Kazan recently informed Wood of this development and asked that she convey his regret to TW: "Tell Tennessee how badly I feel about it, which I do" (August 12, 1950, HRC). TW surveyed the damage in a separate letter to Wood and expressed a faint hope: "I don't feel badly about Gadg dropping out, I mean I don't feel *resentful* about it, although it is a terrific set-back to the play. I don't think he was ever really sold on it. I would like to talk to him in the States before I think about Lewis or Mann as substitutes. If it is only the time element that eliminates him, perhaps it would be worth-while to wait for him" (August 15, 1950, HRC). Wood's cable also implored TW to return "immediately" (August 15, 1950, HRC) for rehearsals of *The Rose Tattoo* (October 16).

Typed in the upper margin is the notation "Having no carbon, I'm sending this to Audrey so she can read it first and pass it on to you, since it concerns you equally."]

182. To Walter Edwin Dakin

SH: Hotel Algonquin
59 West 44th Street
New York 18, N.Y.
9/13/50
[TLS, 1 p. HRC]

Dear Grandfather:

I have been so busy that I can scarcely believe that I have only been back in America for a week. Three things going at once, like Ringling Brothers circus - plans and casting for my new play, press-interviews for the opening of the "Glass Menagerie" in New York, and long-distance conferences with Charlie and Mr. Kazan about "Streetcar" which is now being filmed in California. I have not even had time to see Margo, who is in town directing a new play called "Southern Exposure". Now it seems that I will have to fly out to Hollywood this week-end, but will only need to stay a few days. Then fly back here to continue preparations for "The Rose Tattoo" which is the title of my new play. Frank is spending most of his free time at the dentist, which keeps him busy as me. I am still hoping we can get down to Key West in a short while. Maybe about the first of October. If the play goes into production so soon that we have to stay in New York, would you like to come up here and join us? We are looking for an apartment. That is, friends are looking for one for us and we will make sure it has a bedroom for you. The weather is beautiful in New York now, clear and pleasantly cool, and I know you would enjoy it.

Let me know your plans care of Audrey Wood, 551 Fifth Ave., and I will advise you of any new development in mine.

Much love, Tom

["On the sea, returning to what?" (*Journal*, September 1, 1950). TW sailed on the *Queen Elizabeth* and was due to arrive in New York on September 5. Frank Merlo's flight was delayed in Newfoundland: "I suppose the Horse went out and grazed a bit on the tundra" (qtd. in St. Just, pp. 36-37), TW later quipped to Maria Britneva.

A smash hit in Dallas, *Southern Exposure* (1950) flopped in New York and closed after twenty-three performances. "It shoulda stood in Texas," the critics advised the producer-director, Margo Jones.

Walter Dakin forwarded this letter to Edwina with a note that he was "very well and happy in the Gayoso," preferring, as he did, Memphis to St. Louis.]

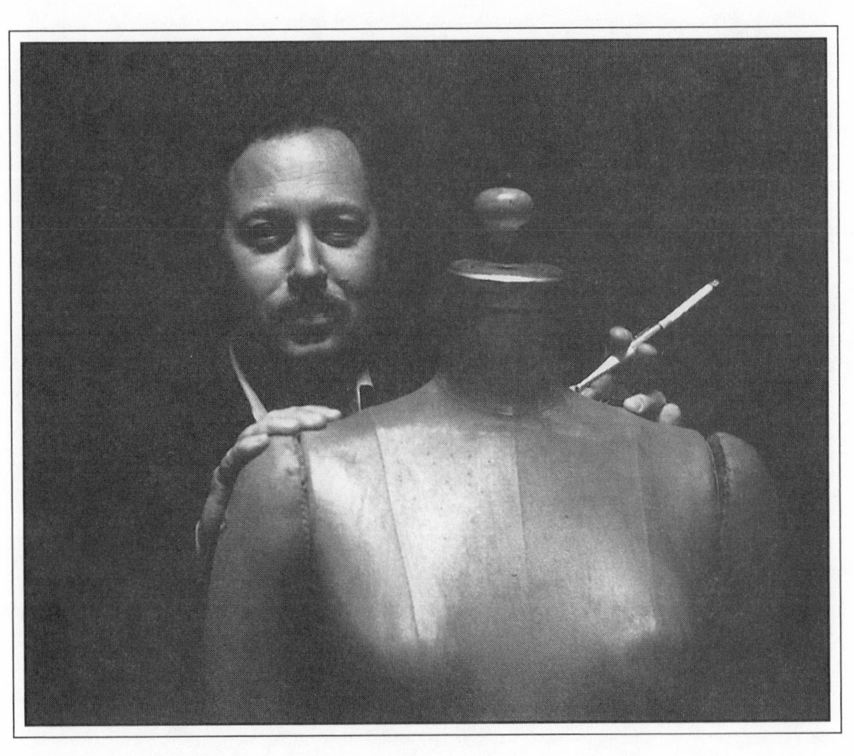

PART IV

1950-1952

*Overleaf: "Don't lean on my dummy. Sit down if you can't stand up. —What is the matter with you?" (*The Rose Tattoo*, 1951).*

183. To Irene Mayer Selznick

SH: Hotel Bel-Air
701 Stone Canyon Road
Los Angeles 24
September 26, 1950
[TLS, 1 p. Boston U]

Dearest Irene:

Thank you so much for forwarding the sweet note from Peter, and all your other good offices. You are just an irrepresibly good producer! I cannot at this moment make any move about Peter, which I will explain more thoroughly when I see you in New York. We are flying back Wednesday night, day after tomorrow. A conference this week should make it fairly plain whether or not I can offer Peter the play.

Gadg is doing a brilliant job on Streetcar, and believe it or not, Madame Olivier is nothing less than terrific! I was almost startled out of my "sissy britches" - that is a term I picked up from Marion Davies to whom I was introduced a few nights ago by one Speed Lamkin, who has left very few stones unturned in this vicinity.

We are driving out, now, to see some more "rushes". They are up to the birthday party scenes.

Love from Tenn.

[Peter Brook's interest in directing *The Rose Tattoo* (1951) would not be realized, although Brook later staged the Paris production of *Cat on a Hot Tin Roof* (1956). Acclaimed productions of Cocteau, Sartre, and Christopher Fry, as well as a budding friendship with Irene Selznick, had brought the young British director to TW's attention.

TW was called to Hollywood to deal with censorship problems related to the filming of *Streetcar* (1947). Still unresolved was Blanche's discovery speech (Scene Six), which he was asked to revise "without hurting the content" or violating the censor's presumption that Allan Grey "was not homosexual" (Feldman to TW, September 12, 1950, HRC). Treatment of the rape scene, not yet filmed, would entail lengthy negotiation with the Production Code administrator, Joseph Breen.

Vivien Leigh, a major box-office star, replaced Jessica Tandy as Blanche and joined the remaining principals of the Broadway cast. By late-September Elia Kazan had reached Scene Eight of *Streetcar*.

Marion Davies starred in a series of films in the 1920s and '30s backed by her companion, William Randolph Hearst. Renowned for philanthropy and lavish parties, she battled alcoholism and the effects of polio in later life.

Elia Kazan directing Vivien Leigh and Kim Hunter in A Streetcar Named Desire *(1951): "Madame Olivier is nothing less than terrific!"*

A composition date of September 25, 1950, is consistent with TW's plan to return to New York on "Wednesday night" after nearly ten days on the West Coast.]

184. To Walter Edwin Dakin

SH: Gladstone
East 52nd Street at Park Avenue
New York 22
[September/October 1950]
[TLS w/ enclosure and
autograph postscript, 1 p. HRC]

Dear Grandfather:

We are now back in New York and plans for the production of my new play THE ROSE TATTOO are getting under way very rapidly. It now looks like I shall have to stay in New York for the next three months and

I am wondering if you would not like to come up here for a while. Frank and I are moving back into Buffie Johnson's apartment. Do you remember the place? It was on East Fifty-Eighth street and you said it looked like a Curiosity Shop. It is where you had the picture taken, containing the reference to your Civil War uniform. If you can come up we can find a place for you either very close to our apartment or in the Royalton Hotel or some other hotel that suits you, and you might enjoy staying here, at least till the cold weather commences which should not be for quite a while as it promises to be a pleasant Fall; the weather is now bright and warm. We would love to have you up here. I would almost rather go directly to Key West and occupy the new house there, but unfortunately my work demands that I stay close to Broadway till after the play opens. I expect that will be sometime in December. This week we are going to decide about a director. Mr. Kazan's picture-duties keep him on the West Coast so it has been necessary to find someone else.

The Glass Menagerie is doing well here, and Kazan and Miss Leigh are making a really great picture of Streetcar. Please let us know if you can come up. I know you don't mind flying. Frank will have plenty of time and your presence in the city would be a great joy and comfort as well as bringing good luck. I worry a great deal about your staying by yourself in Memphis or other places. Do you think Mother and Dakin would like to use the house in Key West till we go down there this winter? Apparently it suffered no damage in the hurricane, for we have no report of any. But it is pity to leave it unoccupied all this time.

Much love, Tom

Write us at 235 E. 58th Street. We tried to find an apartment with two bedrooms but all of them wanted us to sign leases for long terms or were frightfully expensive, or had some other serious disadvantage. As you know, the apartment on 58th Street suited me perfectly when I lived there.

Enclosing a little present.

[Factors of economy and availability led Cheryl Crawford to cast *The Rose Tattoo* from the ranks of the Actors Studio. Maureen Stapleton, a twenty-five-year-old with no major Broadway roles to her credit, won the part of Serafina, while Eli Wallach, an older and more experienced actor, joined the cast as Alvaro.

Association with the Actors Studio and successful staging of *Come Back, Little Sheba* (1950) occasioned Daniel Mann's selection as director. Boris Aronson was hired to design the set. Tryouts would begin in Chicago on December 29 and run for three or four weeks.

Bosley Crowther wrote that the "poignancy" (*New York Times*, September 29, 1950) of *The Glass Menagerie* (1945) had been diminished by indulging the comedic talents of Gertrude Lawrence. A few reviewers were more positive but only one considered the film version "excellent."

A preview of *The Glass Menagerie* in April led TW to play "a scene of anguish second only to Judith Anderson's proscenium-gnawing in 'Medea'" (*New York Journal-American*, July 31, 1950). Audrey Wood deplored the untimely report in Dorothy Kilgallen's column and assured the producer, Charles Feldman, that one of TW's "henchmen" (August 14, 1950, HRC) was responsible.

TW last rented the painter Buffie Johnson's apartment on East 58th Street in 1948.]

185. To Robert "Bobbie" Lewis

SH: Gladstone
East 52nd Street at Park Avenue
New York City - 22
October 10, 1950
[TLS, 1 p. Kent State U]

Dear Bobbie:

All I can do in this letter is to give you as earnestly as possible the reasons for the abrupt decision I made about direction of "Tattoo", none of which had anything to do with any lack of faith in your unique and wonderful powers as a director. As a matter of fact, that faith had grown during our few discussions. But I suddenly felt that I just couldn't wait all that time, that I had to get moving on it right away: otherwise the tension would build to a point that it would just tear me up. Being yourself a highly keyed man with a sense of what his work can mean to an artist, you must understand about that. The long dalliance with Gadg had a great deal to do with this explosive state of nerves and the absolute need to come to quick and final decisions. It was obvious that you were not in a position to speak in terms of early and definite dates. So I just did what I felt had to be done. As it is, we now have out of town bookings beginning December 7th and are going full steam ahead. The imminence, and the impetus, will help me shape the script for production and it will be as right by that time as it could ever be. The contact with you, and your astute analysis of the play, meant a great deal to me. I am more grateful than I can easily say and I am sure that eventually we will work together on something if I am not kicked out of the theatre and if you will stay my friend.

Affectionately, 10.

[Robert Lewis (1909-1997), an original member of the Group Theatre (1931-1941), gave vital encouragement to TW when they met in New York in the early 1940s. His staging of *Brigadoon* (1947) was a critical and financial success which offset earlier "prestige failures" on Broadway. The timing of Lewis's current project was in conflict with plans to open *The Rose Tattoo* in late-December 1950.]

186. To Editor, New York Herald Tribune Book Review

235 E. 58th Street
New York, N.Y.
October 15, 1950
[TLS, 2 pp. HRC]

Dear Sir:

I am sending you a copy of the first paragraph of a letter that I have written my publisher, James Laughlin, of New Directions, as I feel that it partly concerns you.

Sincerely, Tennessee Williams

October 15, 1950

Dear Jay:

I deeply appreciate the long account you have given me of your promotion plans for "The Roman Spring". I know that this particular aspect of the publishing world is not what attracted you to it, anymore than it is the aspect of writing that is attractive to me. I must admit, though, that I am deeply concerned about the distribution of this book, and its reception, because it comes at a point in my life when I have a need for some confirmation or reassurance about my work's value. I certainly didn't get any from the notices the book has received in New York. I was startled and hurt not only by the harsh opinions but much more by the apparent lack of interest, as if the book (and my work in general) did not seem even to merit a little attention. For instance, the fact that the Herald-Tribune has ignored it completely, both in the daily and Sunday book-review sections, is the worst sort of slap in the face, not only to this one book, but also, I feel, to all the work I have done, to my whole - position is not the word I want to use! But you know what I mean. I feel that I have worked very hard and very seriously over a considerable period, that I have not done anything cheap or meretricious, that regardless of my known limitations as a writer, I have shown taste and courage and do have honesty: and, consequently, have a right to receive from journals that have literary criticism, such as The Herald-Tribune, The New Yorker, Etc., the minimal courtesy of some space within two or three weeks of the publication date, a courtesy which I am sure they have extended time and again to writers who make far less effort than I to explore the world and experience of our time with some truth and significance. If other writers such as Edith Sitwell, Cristopher Isherwood, Carson McCullers and Rosamund Lehmann have expressed an admiration for the book which I know must be sincere, surely there is something in it that merits a token of interest from the various book-page editors, even though the book may not at all accord with their personal tastes.

(FIRST PARAGRAPH OF A LETTER TO JAMES LAUGHLIN)

Tennessee Williams

[Harsh reviews of *The Roman Spring of Mrs. Stone* appeared in the *Times* and the *Saturday Review* shortly after publication on September 27, 1950. Orville Prescott dismissed the novella as "superficial, offensive and quite dull" (*New York Times*, September 29, 1950). The *Herald Tribune* notice, printed on October 22, bore the headline "Another Williams Victim" and went on to lament the author's morbidity and the "sexual crucifixion" of his "heroines." TW's complaint did not appear in the *Tribune*, although it may have hastened publication of the review.

James Laughlin described a sluggish promotional campaign for *The Roman Spring* with ads due to appear in the *New York Times* and the *Herald Tribune* on October 29 (to TW, October 12, 1950, Houghton).]

187. To Joseph Ignatius Breen

235 E. 58th Street
New York, NY
October 29, 1950
[TLx, 2 pp. HRC]

Dear Mr. Breen:

Mr. Kazan has just informed me that objections have been raised about the "rape scene" in "Streetcar" and I think perhaps it might be helpful for me to clarify the meaning and importance of this scene. As everybody must have acknowledged by now since it has been pointed out in the press by members of the clergy of all denominations, and not merely in the press but in the pulpit - "Streetcar" is an extremely and peculiarly <u>moral</u> play, in the deepest and truest sense of the term. This fact is so well known that a <u>misunderstanding</u> of it now at this late date would arouse widespread attention and indignation.

The rape of Blanche by Stanley is a pivotal, integral truth in the play, without which the play loses its meaning, which is the ravishment of the tender, the sensitive, the delicate by the savage and brutal forces in modern society. It is a poetic plea for comprehension. I did not beg the issue by making Blanche a totally "good" person, nor Stanley a totally "bad" one. But to those who have made some rational effort to understand the play, it is apparent that Blanche is neither a "dipsomaniac" nor a "nymphomaniac" but a person of intense loneliness, fallibility and a longing which is mostly spiritual for warmth and protection. I did not, of course, disavow what I think is one of the primary things of beauty and depth in human existence, which is the warmth between two people, the so-called "sensuality" in the love-relationship. If nature and God chose this to be the mean of life's continuance on earth, I see no reason to disavow it in creative work. At the same time, I know what <u>taste</u> is and what <u>vulgarity</u> is. I have drawn a very sharp and clear line between the two in all of the plays that I have had presented. I have never made an appeal to anything "low" or "cheap" in my plays and I would rather die than do so. Elia Kazan has directed "Streetcar" both on the stage and the screen, with inspired understanding of its finest values and an absolute regard for taste and propriety. I was fortunately able to see, in "rushes", all but the last three scenes of the picture before I left California. Mr. Kazan has given me a detailed description of the scenes I didn't see as they now exist on the screen. I am really amazed that any question should arise about censorship. Please remember that even in notoriously strict Boston, where the play tried out before Broadway, there was no attack on it by any responsible organ of public opinion, and on the screen the spiritual values of the play have been accentuated much more than they could be on the stage.

The poetically beautiful and touching performance of a great visiting artist, Vivien Leigh, has dominated the picture and given it a stature which surpasses that of the play. "A Streetcar Named Desire" is one of the truly great American films and one of the very few really moral films that have come out of Hollywood. To mutilate it, now, by forcing, or attempting to force, disastrous alterations in the essential truth of it would serve no good end that I can imagine.

Please remember, also, that we have already made great concessions which we felt were dangerous to attitudes which we thought were narrow. In the middle of preparations for a new play, on which I have been working for two years, I came out to Hollywood to re-write certain sequences to suit the demands of your office. No one involved in this screen production has failed in any respect to show you the cooperation, and even deference, that has been called for. But now we are fighting for what we think is the heart of the play, and when we have our backs against the wall - if we are forced into that position - none of us is going to throw in the towel! We will use every legitimate means that any of us has at his or her disposal to protect the things in this film which we think cannot be sacrificed, since we feel that it contains some very important truths about the world we live in.

Sincerely,

[Joseph Breen (1890-1965) vigorously administered the Production Code from 1934 until his retirement in the mid 1950s. The general principles of the Code—drafted in 1930 but weakly enforced by Breen's predecessor, Will Hays—forbade the production of any motion picture that would "lower the moral standard" of the audience, violate "correct standards of life," or ridicule "law, natural or human." Geoffrey Shurlock, Breen's assistant and successor, later observed that "Streetcar broke the barrier."

The troubling rape scene in *Streetcar* was "justified" by the "build-up speech" and then "left unpunished" insofar as "Stanley was concerned." Before filming began, the Production Code staff found TW and Elia Kazan uncooperative and "inclined to make speeches about the integrity of their art." A recommendation followed that the rape be "abolished" and Stanley made guilty of nothing more serious than "violently" striking Blanche. Sensing evasion, the staff later warned against any "fence-straddling" (file memoranda, May 2, July 25, October 3, 1950, Herrick) device that would allow the scene to be variously interpreted as a rape or not. Kazan's solution to the impasse was accepted by Breen in early-November. The "build-up speech" was modified but a strong indication of rape remained in the final print. TW quickly supplied the lines with which Stanley was punished by Stella and the final concern of the censor relieved: "We're not going back in there . . ." (telegram, to Kazan, November 2, 1950, Herrick).]

188. To James "Jay" Laughlin

[235 East 58th Street, New York]
November 7, 1950
[TLS, 1 p. Houghton]

Dear Jay:

Many, many thanks for your letter about the play. Please do send your copy of it to Lustig. If he comes up quickly enough with a striking design I feel sure that Cheryl would be delighted to use it for playbills, advertisements, Etc. The values of the play being less literary than usual, I feel that it will be more impressive on the stage than it is in manuscript. At least, I <u>hope</u> so. The director, Danny Mann, is no fool, in fact he is a real New York intellectual but has humor and vitality to compensate for that defect. He says that "mood" is "doom" spelt backwards which probably means that I shall have to put up a fight for the plastic-poetic elements in the production. We shall see. If casting is completed by November 15th I can take a couple of weeks in Key West to train for the contest. The girl, Maureen Stapleton, is a God-send and the rest of the cast is being slowly and very carefully put together.

I am sorry you were mistaken about the novel moving up to ninth place on the best-seller list. In fact it moved quite strongly in the other direction. I doubt that there is any hope of resuscitating sales by further advertising. Do you think so? Perhaps it would be better to contribute the sum I was planning for the "Ad" to the Authors' League to be given to the Patchens. I have gotten another letter from Miriam saying that their situation has deteriorated still further. The letter is quite touching and while I have never liked Patchen's work very much I am sure that he deserves aid and perhaps I can make a tax-deductible contribution to them through the League. Would you check on that with Luise M. Sillcox. If she approves,

I can make out a check on my book-royalties, ear-marked for Patchen.

I am enclosing a short-story by Oliver Evans which I think has a great deal of charm. He wanted you to see it for possible inclusion in the annual.

Will call you this week, if I don't hear from you, about the contribution to League. Audrey can also advise you about it.

Ever, Tenn.

[James Laughlin described *The Rose Tattoo* as "a triumph of stage writing" and guessed that it "might be even more popular than Streetcar." Nonetheless he foresaw TW developing "along another line" (to TW, November 3, 1950, Houghton), as indicated by his earlier verse play "The Purification" (1944).

On November 5 *The Roman Spring of Mrs. Stone* fell from tenth to thirteenth place on the *New York Times* bestseller list and disappeared thereafter. It fared no better in the *Herald Tribune*.

In 1950 Kenneth Patchen had the first of three operations for chronic back pain and rheumatoid arthritis. TW did contribute to his care, as Patchen's wife, Miriam, had requested. New Directions published much of Patchen's experimental prose and verse.

Laughlin found the Oliver Evans story "derivative" (to TW, November 13, 1950, Houghton) and declined to publish it.]

189. To Cheryl Crawford

[1431 Duncan Street
Key West, Florida]
November ?, 1950
[TLS w/ autograph marginalia, 1 p. BRTC]

Dear Cheryl:

The cold wave affected even the Keys so I had to stay in and work instead of taking the rest in the sun that I had planned. Yesterday I mailed Audrey a bunch of final revisions which, together with the new material that I did just before leaving New York, should be incorporated in the script before we go into rehearsal. I think we should have a script conference a day or so before the start of rehearsals, to consider this new material and the script as it now stands. We are planning to leave December 3rd. If we fly back we could have the conference the next day. If we take the train, either that evening (of the next day) or the day following. I was greatly relieved by your wire about Boris' model. Long to see it. I hope it contains the embankment stairs that Milzener suggested, which I think is the best idea that has been brought forward for the design in any of the discussions about it. Then I want to get together with David Diamond and Rose to see how their work is progressing. Perhaps they could all participate in this script-conference or general discussion as it would, then, be.

So far this season the critics have shown preposterous leniency, but it would be just my luck to have them exhaust their good-humor before we get in. If Florida were properly sunny, and I were getting enough swimming, this misanthropic state would not persist. But when one stays indoors continuing work on a script one has worked on and messed around with and fumed and fussed and fretted over for 23 almost solid months - and reads Westbrook Pegler and the tragic letters of Ezra Pound, starting off like a trumpet before the first World War and dying out to a penny-whistle in the mouth of an old man crumbling into lunacy - it is hard to keep a stout heart! Then I am depressed over grandfather. He is not as well as last year. He has a couple of skin-cancers on his face which have been treated by X-ray. The scabs are disfiguring and very distressing to him, since he has always taken such pride in his appearance. He is afraid they "look disgusting to people". I think they will clear up and Frank and I are trying hard to convince him of it.

The town has changed much for the worse, the campaign against "Bohemianism" still virulent, a spirit of suspicion making you feel uncomfortable when you go out in the evenings however innocently. Fortunately property values are thought to be increasing, and although I paid too much for this house, I may be able to get rid of it without much loss - if the present atmosphere continues, which I suppose it is bound to do, or even increase - in the event of a war. If Europe is cut off, I suppose I might try Mexico. I say "I" because I can't count on Frank remaining out of the service!

With love from "The Blue Boy" - Tenn.

[TW and Frank Merlo spent nearly two weeks in Key West, arriving ca. November 21 and returning to New York in early-December for rehearsals of *The Rose Tattoo*.

To date Boris Aronson had designed nearly forty Broadway shows, including the current hits *Season in the Sun* (1950) and *The Country Girl* (1950). In a recent interview he remarked that he was "'better known for the 'Lower Depths' than for the gayer sort of set'" (qtd. in *New York Times*, November 26, 1950). Early sketches for *The Rose Tattoo* show a path leading up the "embankment" which separates Serafina's cottage from the highway.

David Diamond, soon to begin a long residence in Italy, wrote incidental music for *The Rose Tattoo*, while Rose Bogdanoff designed the costumes.

Brooks Atkinson was one of the lenient critics who voted "raves" for *Bell, Book and Candle* (1950), the fanciful "trifle" (*New York Times*, November 15, 1950) produced by Irene Selznick and written and directed by John van Druten. The hit play had replaced *The Rose Tattoo* in Selznick's consideration and probably earned TW's disdain as a result. It was Selznick's "pretty pink and perfumed little dead pig of a baby" (TW to Kazan, November 18, 1950, WUCA).

The columnist Westbrook Pegler used a populist rhetoric to attack FDR, labor leaders, "furriners," and modern poets, whom he especially despised. TW was reading D.D. Paige's edition of *The Letters of Ezra Pound: 1907-1941* (1950).

"'Bohemianism'" was under attack in Washington as well as in Key West. A forthcoming Senate report demanded vigilance in keeping "perverts" off the "Government payroll" and strict enforcement of Civil Service rules in ousting those employed—some 3,700, it was thought, in "Washington alone" (*New York Times*, December 16, 1950).

The bungalow for which TW reportedly paid $22,500 in 1950 sold for $235,000 in 1991 and for more than a million dollars ten years later.

Penned in the upper margin is the notation "Enchanted by Boris design, just rec'd! Bigelow does not seem to know you have job for him (according to Audrey)." Paul Bigelow served as a production staff assistant to Cheryl Crawford.

Related correspondence suggests that TW wrote this letter on November 27, 1950.]

Boris Aronson, The Rose Tattoo *(1951): "Enchanted by Boris design."*

190. To Erwin Piscator

1431 Duncan
Key West, Fla.
December 1, 1950
[TLS, 1 p. Southern Illinois U]

Dear Dr. Piscator:

I am embarassed, and conscience-stricken, as I should be, by your gentle note of well-deserved reproach. I shall not say anything about my travels, or the awful concentration required by my work, but only that I am as interested as ever in what the Dramatic Workshop is doing and continually more and more impressed and admiring of its accomplishments and its endurance in the face of so much that is adverse in our present circumstances. I am not in New York or I would certainly have seen your adaptation of Kafka's great book. I hope to see it when I return in a few days. I have heard nothing but fine and exciting things about it. I feel it is one of the most significant works of our time.

Soon as the terrific strain and tension of this new play is over, I hope we can communicate more fully. I am proud to be a Board member and I hope that somehow or other I can manage to participate more than I have been able in the past.

My continual felicitations, my warm regards as ever,

Tennessee.

[Erwin Piscator (1893-1966), director of the Dramatic Workshop, scolded TW for having missed a production of *The Trial* (Kafka, April 1950) and solicited his contribution to an emergency fund-raising campaign. The need was caused by the separation of the Workshop—a liability in the conservative political climate—from its founding institution, the New School for Social Research. Neither TW's deference nor Piscator's "gentle" touch had marked earlier exchanges, when *Battle of Angels* (1940) was being considered for a Workshop production.

Membership on the Board of Trustees of the Workshop was later cited in TW's FBI file (obtained under the Freedom of Information Act) as evidence of questionable associations. An explanatory note stated that the Dramatic Workshop had been identified in 1948 "as a Communist front by the California Committee on Un-American Activities."]

191. To Edwina Dakin Williams and Walter Edwin Dakin

[235 East 58th Street, New York]
12/16/50
[TLS, 1 p. Columbia U]

Dear Mother and Grandfather:

I was tremendously relieved to learn that Grandfather's wandering trunk had been tracked down and was eventually going to reach him. Now he can make public appearances in the style that suits him, and I'm sure he felt even more relieved than I did.

Frank and I are missing the warmth and tranquillity of Key West. But I am bearing up pretty well under the strain of rehearsals. Fortunately we had all the luck in casting the play. The girl playing the lead is almost as good an actress as Laurette Taylor. In fact, she is like a young Laurette, which pleases me especially because nobody else wanted to cast her in the part, since they felt her youth and lack of experience would be too great a handicap. But she has tremendous power and honesty in her acting and I think she is going to put the show over. She is an Irish girl, not pretty in any conventional way and considerably too plump, but she has more talent than any of the leading ladies of twice her age and half her size. The Director is not as gifted as Kazan but he works twice as hard, all day and half the night. It is his big chance. The Italian women in the cast are particularly touching and wonderful. Most of them were taken off relief when they got jobs in the play. They are natural born actors, although their experience was limited mostly to the Italian radio stations around New York. Then we have an old lady who must be in her eighties who was once a star in the London music-halls. She is playing "The Strega" - Italian for "witch". She is so deaf and blind that she has to be pushed on stage when her entrances come, but she is still a terrific performer, her name is Daisy Belmore. I hope that the fact that none of these people have been seen or known before on Broadway will give a special sense of reality to the production. There is great interest and speculation around about. Kazan and Irene are going to fly to Chicago and I hope we will put on such a good show that they will wish they had stayed at home! - since neither of them had courage enough to undertake it.

Irene's new play is a big success but also a big mess.

If you have any idea what Dakin and Rose would like for Christmas, please let me know. I shall try to do some shopping next week.

Marian Vacarro has come to New York. She put the car in a Miami storage garage where we can pick it up when we come back South. I am not sure I will have a chance to visit St. Louis, I seriously doubt it, as the last days of rehearsal, around Christmas, will need my close attention. The company leaves Christmas afternoon for Chicago where I will be staying at the Hotel Sherman.

Much love, Tom

[Cheryl Crawford and associates hesitated to give the "bravura" role to a near "unknown," as Maureen Stapleton has recalled: "Obviously they'd been impressed by my reading, but they seemed to want me to *promise* them I could succeed. First Crawford, then Mann, then Miss Wood asked for some sort of guarantee. What could I guarantee? . . . I finished talking and Tennessee jumped up from his chair, declaring, 'I don't care if she turns into a dead mule on opening night. I want her for the part!'" (qtd. in Stapleton, *A Hell of a Life*, 1995, p. 84).

Daisy Belmore's seventy-six years were filled with supporting roles on stage and screen, including a bit part in the classic *Dracula* (1931) film starring Bela Lugosi.]

192. To Margaret "Margo" Jones

235 E. 58th Street, New York.
December 1950
[TLS, 2 pp. Dallas Public Library]

Dearest Margo:

Your letters are always "a beaker full of the warm South". I am more and more keenly interested, all the time, in the progress of important theatres away from New York. There is something so awful about the finality of a Broadway production under the present scheme of things. One is so dreadfully at the mercy of a handful of men who display such an alarming lack of steady, definable standards. This season has been especially frightening with the great success of things like <u>Bell, Book and Candle</u> and all the fuss made over English importations that bore the be-Jesus even out of those who like poetry as much as I do. If one happens to run against the particular current of the moment, in this particular, very regional and provincial locality called Broadway, he is boxed down like a Punch or Judy and a play which may have come arduously but truly to life after a long struggle of two years or more is pitched off the professional stage into the shadowy half-world of the non-professional little theatres here and there about the country and the limbo of the libraries. What is ANTA doing about it? It looks to me like ANTA is just another old Auntie! It is a convenient shop-window for stars to show themselves to exactly the same crowd under just about the same conditions. It is just another Broadway enterprise as far as it has demonstrated up till now. I do hope most passionately that you are serious about the national idea you were discussing when I last saw you. You are the person for it. I think you can give your personal excitement and fire to such a project and infect the whole country with it, and I think you should devote yourself to it, even though it may mean a temporary absence from Dallas or a division of your labors there. You should set up an office, probably here, get a full-time staff including the best publicity people and barn-storm about the country, presenting the idea and selling it to key people in all the cities where a theatre of this kind belongs. It would, I feel, have a profound effect on the whole cultural life of the nation which seems to be sinking into something almost worse than oblivion with the outlets of expression nearly all in the same old repressive hands. It would give the theatre a real new lease on life. Then any work of truth and vigor would have ten chances instead of one to reach the hearts of people that could respond to it.

I write this in a mood of personal anxiety about my own work but it is more than that. Do you realize that there is scarcely a newspaper, magazine, radio or TV station or cinema in the whole country that doesn't represent practically the same old tired, blind, bitter and dessicated attitude toward life? The Big Time Operators are all one guy and those are the qualities of him. So don't forget your youth and the crusading spirit of it! I would be very happy to take the stump with you when you are ready to start.

The "Tattoo" is going well, knock wood. We have all new people, new faces, mostly quite young, and a group of real Italian women who were taken off the relief rolls for this production. Most of them broke down and cried when they got their jobs! It's the most wonderful bunch of people I've ever seen collected in a show and it makes you feel a deep and frightening responsibility. If only it would make certain other people feel the same thing!

Let me hear from you again soon, and do, if you can, fly up sometime during our Chicago run. We open the 29th and may play there for four weeks at the Erlanger theatre.

With love, 10

Mother and Grandfather are occupying the house in Key West while we are away. We plan to return there in February.

[Verse plays by Christopher Fry—*The Lady's Not for Burning* and *Ring Round the Moon*—opened to acclaim in New York on November 8 and 23, 1950, respectively.

"ANTA" (American National Theatre and Academy) had recently launched a drama series in its new Playhouse on 52nd Street, formerly the Guild Theatre. The first offering—*The Tower Beyond Tragedy* (November 26, 1950), a verse play by Robinson Jeffers starring Judith Anderson as Clytemnestra—drew raves, especially from Brooks Atkinson, who deemed it "an inspired production" (*New York Times*, November 27, 1950).

TW "last saw" Margo Jones in the fall when she brought *Southern Exposure* (1950) to New York for an ill-advised production. Earlier in the summer she urged the Rockefeller Foundation to sponsor "a drive to create a national theatre" and Columbia University to "schedule a program of lectures" (Sheehy, *Margo*, 1989, p. 206) in support of the project.

This letter, which bears the imprint "Memphis, Tennessee," was probably written in mid-December 1950 in reply to Jones's latest correspondence (December 12, 1950, Dallas Public Library).]

193. To Christopher Isherwood

[235 East 58th Street, New York]
[December 1950]
[TLS, 1 p. Huntington]

Dear Chris:

I lost the long letter I wrote you on the train to Florida last month and it seems that I have also lost the advertising page from the Sunday Times book-section that Jay wanted me to enclose in this envelope, but you will doubtless see it. It contains your quote for Mrs. Stone, that poor lost lady, her epitaph in the world of letters, a very gracious and kind one for which I can't thank you enough, for she was much abused. Edith Sitwell and her brother, Osbert, also wrote me very nice things about the book but not knowing them as well as you, I didn't have the courage to ask them for permission to quote them.

"The Rose Tattoo" is in rehearsal. If for no other reason, the production will be notable for the return of Daisy Belmore, an octogenarian actress who successfully disguised the fact that was stone deaf and virtually blind when she read for the part. Fortunately she plays a Strega who has little to do but chase a black goat off and on the stage and utter witless cackles and imprecations from time to time. It may be necessary to tie a string around her ankel to get her on and off on cue. You and Bill would love her. And she would be an important addition to the ranks of "the dreaded fog-queens". How is La. by the way, is the heat still on? Has Speed recovered from his operation and returned to the Coast? Here it is very, very dull. I was in the Blue Parrot last night, the gayest bar on the bird-circuit. The queens were packed in so tight there wasn't even room to grope in. They just stood there like a wierd assortment of animals that had fled to the banks of a river from a forest fire. And blew smoke in each other's faces and sang with the juke-box. "She's a nice girl, a proper girl, but one of the roving kind!" There is a dreadful rumor that queens are going to be drafted for the next one and that the draft age is being lifted to 35. This still excludes me but it takes in Frankie. I mean the admission of queens, excludes me - not, of course, the extended age-limit! - I am still in my te-eeens . . . Frankie has not yet been summoned but is very gloomy with expectation. I am very gloomy without expectation.

Is Caskey in or out of you-know-what?!!

Love, love! 10.

[TW met Christopher Isherwood (1904-1986) in Hollywood in 1943 while working as a screenwriter at MGM. He later claimed "great friendship" (*Memoirs*, p. 77) with Isherwood, who described their sexual history shortly after TW's death: "We just found each other very sympathetic, and we went to bed together two or three times, I imagine" (qtd. in Leverich, p. 502).

Isherwood's "quote for Mrs. Stone" stated that TW "can bring tragic beauty and humor to themes which lesser writers ought never to handle" (*New York Times*, December 3, 1950).

"'We are the dreaded fog queens!'" said TW, as he, Isherwood, and Bill Caskey rode in a cab on a foggy night in London (June 1948). Isherwood recalls that they began "to elaborate on the fantasy—how the respectable citizens shudder . . . and cross themselves as the dreaded fog queens ride by" (Isherwood, *Lost Years*, 2000, p. 145).

In December 1949 Isherwood was caught in the raid of a gay bar and held for questioning by the Santa Monica police. He "denied being homosexual" but later wished that he had made "a nationwide stink" (*Diaries*, December 6, 1949). Presumably the "heat" continued.

Baron de Charlus, Proust's aging homosexual, improbably refers to the "bird-circuit" in *Camino Real* (1953): "They stand three-deep at the bar and look at themselves in the mirror and what they see is depressing." The columnist Walter Winchell later reported that "liquor authorities" in New York, alerted by TW's reference, were "scrutinizing all hooch licenses" issued to such gaily named "joynts" (*New York Daily Mirror*, April 13, 1953) as the "Blue Parrot." Guy Mitchell's recording of "The Roving Kind" reached #4 on the charts in 1951.

The recent easing of "mental standards" for recruits helped to stabilize the draft age at nineteen through twenty-five. Frank Merlo, twenty-eight, was probably not in imminent danger of being drafted for service in the Korean War.

Caskey served three months (August-October 1950) for drunk driving in San Clemente, California. His long relationship with Isherwood was strained and would soon end.]

Christopher Isherwood: "We are the dreaded fog queens!"

194. To Edwina Dakin Williams and Walter Edwin Dakin

SH: Hotel Sherman
Chicago 1, Ill.
1/6/51
[TLS, 1 p. Columbia U]

Dear Mother and Grandfather:

In the excitement of the past week we forgot to mail the household checks. Hope you have not been inconvenienced. I am including Marie's since I assume she has come back to work by now. We are anxious to keep her as we shall be back in Key West pretty soon now.

The opening was very exciting, a very warm response from a full house, the reviews were good except one who felt there was too much comedy for a serious play. He did not seem to realize that it was a serious play treated with humor. But he is coming back to see it again and will probably write a better piece. Business is improving. We have a fine theatre lined up in New York, the Martin Beck which is where you saw Cornell in Anthony and Cleopatra. I think I can get back to N.Y. the middle of this week. Chicago is so cold and unpleasant this time of year.

There was no time to do anything about Christmas but we will be able to send some little Advent remembrances later. Enjoyed Dakin's visit. He looked well and happy.

Much love, Tom.

[Sydney Harris wrote that the comedy of *The Rose Tattoo* violated the play's weighty thematics of spirit and flesh (*Chicago Daily News,* December 30, 1950). Claudia Cassidy, who had cheered for *The Glass Menagerie* during its perilous tryout in Chicago, was more positive but aware of serious lapses. *The Rose Tattoo* had not yet received "clairvoyant" direction, "mesmeric" acting, or "a luminous finale" (*Chicago Sunday Tribune*, December 31, 1950).

After the Chicago opening, Elia Kazan urged TW to examine "the last five minutes of the play" and to be sure that the ending was "fixed" (n.d., HRC). Eli Wallach has recalled the day when "Tennessee finally came in . . . and said, 'I want {Alvaro} to leave his shirt in the room when he runs up the hill. Then Serafina passes a bloodstained shirt up the hill'" (qtd. in Steen, *A Look at Tennessee Williams*, 1969, p. 292). This may be the "new ending" (to Laughlin, January 16, 1951, Houghton) to which TW referred in mid-January 1951 when the play was still in Chicago.

The season of Advent precedes Christmas in the liturgical calendar.]

195. To Justin Brooks Atkinson

[235 East 58th Street, New York]
Feb. 5, 1951
[TLS, 1 p. BRTC]

Dear Brooks:

Now that it is over, the waiting, I can tell you that I was scared out of my wits, as I knew that a sense of defeat at this point might have been altogether insurmountable. To know that you still like what I do is more reassuring than I can possibly tell you, for this play was a radical departure for me and there were many discouragements and uncertainties about it all the way along. After studying the notices, particularly yours, The News and The Trib, I feel invited to go on working for the theatre, and that is an invitation that I am only too eager to accept.

It was Orianne who let us know Saturday night that you were pleased with the play - in a telephone conversation sometime Saturday night, which made it possible to enjoy the after-opening party. So please give her my thanks, too.

Ever yours, Tennessee.

[Journal entries made before the preview and opening of *The Rose Tattoo* reveal a familiar pattern of renunciation and concern. "I mustn't ever again permit myself to care this much about any public success. It makes you little and altogether too vulnerable" (January 30, 1951). "Last night we had our first New York audience, invited - the show was down and I felt the response was not as good as Chicago" (February 1, 1951).

Atkinson found TW "in a good mood" in *The Rose Tattoo* and observed that he has written "the loveliest idyll for the stage in some time." Any fear that he might be "imprisoned within a formula" of despair was relieved by the joy and compassion of his new "comic play" (*New York Times*, February 5, 1951). Reviewers for the *Herald Tribune* and the *Daily News* were also charmed, but others faulted the play on moral or dramatic grounds, and one was "revolted" by "an unmentionable article" dropped on the stage—Alvaro's errant condom. Maureen Stapleton's Serafina was uniformly praised and *Variety* reported that *The Rose Tattoo* "Looks Hot" (February 7, 1951).]

196. To Irene Mayer Selznick

[1431 Duncan Street
Key West, Florida]
Feb. 27, 1951.
[TLS, 1 p. Boston U]

Dearest Irene:

Frank and I flew down here a week ago Friday and have had the whole family with us, Grandfather, Mother, and Dakin. I arrived with the Flu, Dakin took it and now Grandfather has it. He is a little better this morning. I think the knowledge that Mother is departing today for Saint Louis will hasten his recuperation, and I know it will be a relief to Frank and I to resume the Bohemian tenor of our ways. In the middle of April we plan to bring my sister down here with her nurse-companion for a few weeks. It will be her first long trip since she went in the sanitarium and the first time I have seen her in a long while. If it works out well, I hope it can be arranged to keep her down here most of the time. The place seems ideal for her as she adored Florida and ocean-bathing. I hope you will be here when Rose is here, for I know there would be a sympathy between you. (Frank says you were thinking of coming down. I hope so.) The production of "Tattoo" was a terrible drain on my energies. I was a wreck the last week in New York, but a satisfied wreck. If it had been a smash hit like "Streetcar" or a dismal failure like "Summer and Smoke", it would have been, either way, bad for me. As it is, I think it provides what is always most essential, a bridge to the future where I hope my best work still remains. Fortunately I had some work already under way, which it is easier to resume than it would be to start from scratch. Please thank John for the nice things he said in his Times Sunday magazine article. The wonderful and tremendously successful production of his play must be a source of great satisfaction to you, especially since he is such a fine person.

Love - Tenn.

[TW succeeded in transferring his sister Rose from Farmington State Hospital in Missouri to Stony Lodge, a private sanitarium near Ossining, New York. She lived in "her own cottage in the woods," as Dakin Williams has reported.

John van Druten called for "a new kind of playwriting" in which the "integrity of the author . . . takes precedence over all the older tricks and formulae of the theatre." Van Druten looked to TW, Arthur Miller, and Carson McCullers, a trio of young writers who held "as much promise" as any he could "remember," to "freshen our own skill and talents and deep interest" in the theatre ("A Quarter Century of the Rialto," *New York Times*, February 25, 1951).]

197. To Oliver Evans

1431 Duncan St.
Key West, Fla.
3 March 1951
[TLS w/ enclosure, 1 p. HRC]

Dear Oliver:

I am somewhat disturbed by the beautiful but enigmatic first line of a poem, sent me in the form of a wire, which is the only communication received from you since I left New York. Frank suspected it was an obscure allusion to him, since he is the only person with whom I have "entered Rome", but neither slavery nor Christianity have been involved in our relations. We entered Rome as a pair of free pagans, and that is how we left it, and how we shall go back there, if we can return this summer. I am more inclined to think the allusion was to something unpleasant in my character or manner. I am not in a good position to defend myself except by saying that for some time I have been obsessed with the will to remain alive and continue my work and that most other things, except one or two relationships, have existed in a sort of penumbra outside that central mania. But you ought to know that you are one of those few things, and show an understanding and indulgence in times of strain, the sort of understanding I once hoped for from certain old friends who now look at me with pairs of animated ice-cubes and yet are said to have said that I said that they were going blind! If you think ill of me, now, it may please you to read the enclosed letter from a young Italian who claims that the gigolo in Mrs. Stone was based on his personality. It is a poison pen letter, that much I can make out, perhaps the worst that I have received since meeting those queens in the Automat on Sixth Avenue, and I am hoping you can translate it for me and see if it contains an actual threat. Frank was unable to make it out as he doesn't read Italian much, if any, better than I. I did gather that he considers me the Empire State Building of W.C.'s!

Grandfather has been in the hospital, seriously ill with Flu and complications. He is now home but quite feeble and almost completely bed-ridden. If he is not in a critical condition, I will fly to New York next Thursday, this coming Thursday, to see the first East-coast pre-view of "Streetcar". And I will call you when I arrive in case you want to see it. Although I could not blame you for being tired of all my works, past, present or future. You have not shown me your new poems. I am jealous of them, for it has been at least five months since I have written a poem. (Some people say it's been longer!)

With love, Tenn.

[TW's failure to keep an appointment in New York offended Oliver Evans and probably led to his "enigmatic" verse: "It is with a Christian slave that one enters Rome" (TW to Healy, February 27, 1951, Columbia U). TW blamed the "'Flu'" in prior correspondence from Key West: "You know, honey boy, that I would never willingly miss an appointment with you!" (February 19, 1951, HRC).

In *The Roman Spring*, TW used the given name of Elizabeth Eyre de Lanux's young lover, Paolo Casagrande, as well as borrowed details of financial chicanery.]

198. To Cheryl Crawford

1431 Duncan
Key West, Fla.
March 3, 1951.
[TLS, 1 p. BRTC]

Dearest Cheryl:

There have been so many distractions that I really don't know whether I have written you or not since leaving New York! A seige of illness. I arrived here with the Flu. My brother, Dakin, took it, and then Grandfather. Dakin and Mother have left and poor Grandfather has just come back from the hospital in a dreadful condition, barely able to move, but thankful to be back at home with Frank and me. He will be 94 next month. I am terribly afraid that he won't last much longer. The doctor says that his lung congestion is symptomatic of a cardiac condition as much as the Flu. But he would not remain in the hospital which he said was 'a prison'. He is determined to survive! It is wonderful how even at his age the will to live can persist. We hustled Mother and Dakin back to Saint

Louis, for they depress him, and now there are just the three of us again. Frank is a wonderful nurse, and we have a negro maid who is devoted to Grandfather and gives him excellent diet and care. If he is sufficiently improved, I am flying to New York next Thursday to see the first East coast pre-view of "Streetcar". Feldmann wants to cut it, against Gadg's wishes, and I may be useful as a moral support to Gadg. I hope you can attend the pre-view with us. In spite of the Flu, and perhaps partly because of the fever, I have been unusually energetic and working hard every day. I think my happiness over "Tattoo" has been a moral support to me. I feel encouraged over the increase at the box-office. I don't suppose this is a season in which one can expect a continual sell-out. But I think if performance levels can be maintained, we should be set for a pretty good run. I hope Danny can keep in touch with the show. This has been my happiest

Cheryl Crawford, founding member of The Group Theatre and The Actors Studio

experience in the theatre so far, since it came at a crucial point when a failure might have been final, but a success seems like the opening of another door.

Much love, Tenn.

[TW returned to New York in early-March to confer with Charles Feldman and Elia Kazan on the final editing of *Streetcar*. He later urged Feldman—under intense pressure from the Roman Catholic Legion of Decency—not to "exceed cuts we all agreed upon in New York" (see letter #210).

Cheryl Crawford reported advance sales of $75,000 as well as a healthy fourth-week gross of $27,600 for *The Rose Tattoo*. "I saw it Saturday afternoon," she added, "along with thirty-odd other standees. Maureen has grown in the part and all the performances were full and rich and fine" (to TW, n.d., HTC). A campaign launched by the publicist Wolfe Kaufman led to cast appearances on the RKO Pathe newsreel and the Ed Sullivan Show.]

199. To Audrey Wood

[1431 Duncan Street
Key West, Florida]
3/14/51
[TLS w/ enclosure and
autograph postscript, 1 p. HRC]

Dear Audrey:

Here is a suggested change for the last scene of "Tattoo" which I wish you would submit to Dannie. It may help alleviate some of the "moral" antipathy and doesn't constitute a serious concession.

On reflection, it seems to me that my feeling of depression at the two performances I saw was not attributable simply to the slackening of trade. I feel that the apathy of the audience, and perhaps to a considerable extent the slump of the box-office, is due to a loss of vigor in the general performance of the play. Some scenes it is true are stronger but the general effect, particularly in the last scene is weaker than it used to be. A softening of fibre, particularly in the crowd scenes. Unfortunately strength of attack is not Danny's strong point as a director. His staging never has the precision and force that Kazan could give to group movement on the stage, and so when the actors themselves get relaxed in the parts, the whole effect becomes flaccid. On interpretation, on physically quiet scenes, his work is best and quite marvelous. I hope you will "look in" on the rehearsals of this new material, if it goes in, particularly the "telephone bit" and see that it has the necessary sharpness. I am a little vexed by Maureen's attitude toward continued work on the staging. She knows we have to put up a fight for this play and she ought to be more than willing to make a real effort. Confidentially, I think if the show goes on the road we ought to give serious consideration to the idea of getting Judith Anderson, not only for box-office draw but for professional attitude toward work. Talent is not enough, even in the young!

Love, Tenn

Grandfather much better!

[Brooks Atkinson later cited "the elimination of one lewd episode in the last act" (*New York Times*, June 3, 1951) of *The Rose Tattoo*—the still "unmentionable" condom.

Variety reported on March 14 that "some straight plays skidded," including *The Rose Tattoo*, whose weekly gross fell to $24,200.

The "'telephone bit'" used to reveal Rosario's infidelity was described as "bald" and "mechanical" in early reviews of *The Rose Tattoo*. TW's criticism of "the young" is underlined in red in the original typescript.

TW planned to return to Key West on March 12, 1951, where in all probability he wrote this letter.]

200. To Audrey Wood

Western Union
Key West Flo
1951 Mar 19 AM 4 31
[Telegram, 1 p. HRC]

AUDREY WOOD=

PLEASE SEE IF YOU HAVE DUPLICATE OF ANY DRIVERS LICENSE FOR ME ARRESTED FOR TRAFFIC VIOLATION CANNOT LOCATE MY LICENSE APPEARING IN COURT TUESDAY MORNING LOVE=

TENNESSEE=

[TW's arrest was reportedly for drunken driving. Audrey Wood mentioned only an "accident" in later correspondence and implored TW to "please drive in such a fashion that you will live to be an old man, as old I hope as Rev. Dakin" (March 20, 1951, HRC).]

201. To Max Lerner

[1431 Duncan Street
Key West, Florida]
March 21, 1951
[TLx, 2 pp. HTC]

Dear Max Lerner:

Wolfe Kaufman sent me your article before you did and I had already planned to tell you that I think that you, for the first time to my knowledge, have placed your finger directly on the most demoralizing problem that the American playwright has to face. Although it does not loom very large against the present background of world affairs, the predicament of the playwright is a very peculiar one which holds considerable interest even to those outside the profession. But it is seldom that anyone outside the profession seems to give much thought to it. You are an exception which is extremely welcome.

In technical requirements alone, the writing of plays is probably the most complex of creative forms. I think it is also by far the most physically and nervously exhausting. It literally takes the strength of an ox, if you care deeply about it, to carry a play from conception all the way through to its opening night on Broadway. There are few playwrights, I think mainly because there aren't many willing or able to stand up under the grind.

As far as I know, you are the first to reflect in print on the exorbitant demands made by critics who don't stop to consider the playwright's need for a gradual ripening or development, time in which to complete it, a degree of tolerance and patience in his mentors during this period of transition. This does not mean that messy, bad, sloppy, work should be tolerated. No self-respecting playwright, still in possession of sanity, would condone it in himself, let alone expect it from hard-boiled critics. But this should be considered. It takes ten years of a man's life, usually, to grow into a new major attitude toward existence and the world he exists in. We all know that sometimes the growth is short-circuited, falls short of fulfillment. Our literary history is studded with F. Scott Fitzgeralds! - to mention an example no less pertinent for being outside the dramatic area. Many artists have smashed themselves trying to make this transition, and painfully often their critics have collaborated in the smash-up.

Painters have it better. They are allowed to evolve new methods, new styles, by a reasonably gradual process. They are not abused for turning out creative variations on themes already stated. If a certain theme has importance, it may take a number of individual works to explore it fully. While he is evolving, growing as writer and person, the writer must go on working. Once he breaks the habit of work, his situation is most critical. He frequently becomes a lunatic or a lush or equal parts of both. The acuteness of sensibility that makes him an artist, if he is one, also makes him one of society's most vulnerable members. As for the playwright, people say: "Sure it's hard! But look at the money he makes?" -- Take it from me! No playwright who has come out since 1944 has a better than even chance of breaking even! He has a smash-hit once every five or ten years and he's in the same bracket of taxation that the industrialist is, who makes that much without fail every year!

It would help enormously if there were professional theatre centers outside of New York, so that the playwright would always be at the mercy of a single localized group. The reception of a play varies greatly wherever it goes on the road, especially if it is an experimental or controversial type of play. If only the WPA theatre had worked out! Some kind of state theatre seems to be the only eventual solution. But there are a thousand and one different messes in the world that have to be settled before people outside the theatre give a tinker's damn about the problem of the American playwright. We don't have it good right now. But does anybody? I think that most of us were born knowing that it was going to be bloody. But sometimes our critics ought to meet us half way - that is, if they want us to stand up under the unremitting strain of our profession. Some do, Brooks Atkinson, for instance, is consistently sympathetic to what he recognizes as something better than hack work. Others, such as the so-called Dean of American critics, Mr. Nathan, seems to want to blast us out of the ground at the first little sign of intransigeance, and the trouble is that they write so escruciatingly well! Do we have a chance? Whether we have one or not, the chance is that we will go on working, and usually for the love of it.

Sincerely,

[Max Lerner (1902-1992), prolific author, educator, and columnist, wrote that every successful playwright from Eugene O'Neill to TW has suffered "the critical American disease called The Recoils": "We spew up our welcoming hosannahs and ask the Genius to prove to us that he has not reverted to the bum he was before we discovered him." Consequently every play "must be a hit." TW "should be allowed a chance to deepen his talent and give shape to his outlook without fear of being hounded for his lapses" (*New York Post*, March 6, 1951). A lightly edited version of TW's reply appeared in the *New York Post* on May 16, 1951, p. 44.

"The WPA theatre" (Works Progress Administration) sponsored some 64,000 performances and employed 10,000 theatre professionals during its brief tenure (1935-1939). Conservatives in Congress cut the welfare program in opposition to FDR's New Deal politics and the perceived radicalism of its offerings.

The HRC holds a briefer signed version of the letter dated Key West, March 19, 1951.]

202. To Oliver Evans

[1431 Duncan Street
Key West, Florida]
3/31/51
[TLS, 1 p. HRC]

Dear Oliver:

I was not unaware of your inebriate condition the last evening I saw you in New York, nor, I take it, was Dame Cabot or Miss Olivia De Havilland when you cried out, during her soliloquy on the apron of the stage: "Nothing can kill the beauty of the lines!" How those ladies may feel about it I am not in a position to say. One of the very few advantages of being my friend is that the point at which I become seriously offended, or even surprised, however moderately, is hard to reach. I had a pleasant little telephone conversation with Otis the morning after the night before. He warmly reiterated his welcome to Copenhagen and other capitals of Europe, so there is apparently no lasting rancor in that quarter. I should like very much to know the sequel to your conversations with Dame Cabot. I hope they didn't appear in the obituary column of the papers next day. I am sure it is the first time she has been exposed to such vigorous language. She must have spent the rest of the night in an oxygen tent.

I saw Marian in Miami. She had not yet left for New Orleans but was leaving that afternoon. Incidentally she loaned me fifty dollars as my purse had been snatched the night before during an encounter with a baby-faced thug in Biscayne Park. Fortunately I had very little money on me and succeded in convincing him that my diamonds were worthless and he could not work the clasp on my watch. I told him that if he would just wait outside my hotel I would come out promptly with additional cash.

Needless to say I retired for the night, but the poor fool called me repeatedly on the phone, enquiring when I was coming down with the rest of his loot. Dirt is usually moronic, but this was a low-grade imbecile!

Grandfather is back on his feet, but the cook has gone on a binge and Frank has to assume her duties as well as the considerable demands already made upon him. My health? The new drugs remain intact. I tried one pill which seemed to cause a slight increase in my hypertension rather than otherwise. But the liquor supply is faithful. Now we are going out to the movies, as ever.

I love you, still and always, fratello mio!

Tenn.

[TW returned to New York in late-March to join Maureen Stapleton, Eli Wallach, and Boris Aronson in receiving "Tony" awards (March 25, 1951) for *The Rose Tattoo*. Sponsored by the American Theatre Wing, the "Tony" represented the first major prize of the season.

TW marked his fortieth birthday (March 26) by attending a lavish revival of *Romeo and Juliet*. Olivia De Havilland's Broadway debut as an aging Juliet (thirty-four) was not well received, as Oliver Evans, TW's companion, proclaimed from the audience. In *The Roman Spring*, Karen Stone was also miscast as Juliet in her final dramatic role.]

203. To James "Jay" Laughlin

[1431 Duncan Street
Key West, Florida]
4/1/51
[TLS, 1 p. Houghton]

Dear Jay:

Although I came here, ostensibly, for a rest I have been busier than usual working my way into another play. The initial stages are always the most strenuous, perhaps even worse than the final. I have been very nervous. Hypertensive. Bigelow took me to a fashionable doctor in New York who gave me some pills that are supposed to make my face flush and my ears buzz as they open the capillaries - distend the blood vessels, Etc. I took just one and felt far more hypertensive than usual so have put them on the shelf. I drink too much. About eight drinks a day at carefully spaced intervals. I am trying to work down to six. Perhaps I ought to stop working. But then I would explode from sheer ennui.

I hate to make any derogatory remarks about the Cummington boy's design. Strictly entre nous, it does look a bit like pigeon en casserole. But I sense that he feels very strongly about designing something for the book and it might be mean of us to frustrate him. The typography and paper are so beautiful. I do wish that Lustig was doing the front cover, however. I am charmed with the rose cover of the book of "Tattoo". The only other person I know who likes it is Donald Windham, but I like it very much indeed. I also love the ad, copy of which you sent me.

Thank you so much for the very detailed financial statements and I was agreeably surprised by the amount of funds. I hope sometime later in the Spring, when my own economic picture acquires more clarity, to make a new contribution to the Authors' League fund, earmarked for Oliver Evans. He is having an operation for his deafness and I would like to be able to help him with it. I may draw on my account with you for this purpose, perhaps about 1500. He is in desperate mental or nervous state, a great deal of which, I think, may be attributable to his affliction. Took eight sleeping pills one evening, fell down on the street and broke two ribs! Only quarts of black coffee saved him. On my birthday, while I was in New York, I took him to see "Romeo and Juliet" and when Miss De Havilland was delivering a soliloquy on the apron of the stage, Oliver, in the fourth row, suddenly cried out "Nothing can kill the beauty of the lines!" and tore out of the theatre. Later that night he called up an old lady who had formerly befriended him, a dowager ~~from Boston~~ who is the ranking member of the Cabot clan, and told her she was "just an old bitch and not even her heirs could stand her!" I think he deserves an endowment for life! Even if this intransigeant behavior persists.

Frank, Grandfather, and I are still in Key West. Until the end of April. We sail the middle of May for Europe, again.

Ever, Tenn.

Love to Gertrude.

[The "play" in progress may be a revision of *Battle of Angels*, reportedly underway in March 1951, as indicated by correspondence with Maureen Stapleton, whom TW had asked to play the role of Myra or Vee (see Spoto, p. 174). Talks with Stapleton continued in New York, as well as the drafting of a poem whose title—"Orpheus Descending" (1952)—would replace *Battle of Angels*.

George Crandell, TW's bibliographer, reports that the first ten copies of *I Rise in Flame, Cried the Phoenix* (1951) "were printed on Umbria paper and sold for $50.00 each." The original phoenix design gave way to a marbled pattern in shades of black and grey. TW admired the jacket of *The Rose Tattoo*—a luminous, burgeoning pink rose—and no doubt agreed with James Laughlin that "real innovators" such as the designer Alvin Lustig were "always ahead of the public taste" (to TW, April 20, 1951, Houghton).

Oliver Evans's recent call to the "dowager" Cabot punctuated an earlier outburst of candor, as reported by TW: "He told her that she had the manners of a fishwife," whereupon she forbade Evans "to enter her door" (qtd. in St. Just, p. 38).]

204. To Carson McCullers

[1431 Duncan Street]
Key West, Fla.
April 7, 1951
[TLS, 1 p. Duke U]

Dearest Carson:

It is a soft grey rustling muttering sort of a rainy afternoon with Frank gone from the house and the town and Grandfather dozing on the front room couch and me mixing a sad and lonely martini now and then and making a few ineffectual pecks at the typewriter. I decided this afternoon that I ought to stop writing and try to get close to life and people again. I feel that this obsession of work, work, work all the time has left me emotionally exhausted and only half a person. I wonder if I can quit? I wonder what I could find to take the place? Do you ever ask yourself that, and what do you think is the answer?

Last time I was in New York, about ten days ago I guess, I woke up in the night thinking about you, picked up the phone by my bed and sent you a wire. Did you get it? I was going to call you in the morning, but that morning I was very ill. Bigelow whisked me to a doctor. Then I left town with all kinds of anxieties and pills. I am a little better now, but not much.

This coming Wednesday my sister Rose arrives here with her nurse-companion to spend a week with us. It is the first long trip, or vacation, she has had since she went to the sanitarium about fifteen years ago. I sort of dread the meeting. It is bound to involve a lot of painful shocks, but we hope the change may help her, and if it does, that she will be allowed more freedom in the future.

Soon as Rose leaves I have to take Grandfather to Memphis and get him settled there for the summer. Then we return to New York, and sail May 18th for Europe. Are you planning another trip abroad? This time we go without any definite plan and will probably stay over as long as the state of the world permits.

Grandfather was so pleased with your letter. He is fully recovered, yesterday took a dip in the ocean and is walking around as more or less nimbly as ever. Give Bebe my love, and Rita, and Reeves.

Much, much to you, Tenn.

I am reading Edith Sitwell's "A Poet's Notebook" with enormous pleasure. Is she still in the States, do you see her? Please tell her how much I am enjoying that book.

[Shortly before the opening of *The Rose Tattoo*, TW wrote that "the sunshine and the stars of Key West will be good regardless of how this crucial event turns out. The sea will comfort me, and perhaps it will even restore my power to work" (*Journal*, February 1, 1951).

TW was among the poets whose reception of Edith and brother Osbert Sitwell in 1948 produced a memorable scene—photographed and published by *Life* magazine (December 6, 1948)—at the Gotham Book Mart in New York. Edith Sitwell later met and befriended Carson McCullers at a party given in the poet's honor by TW and praised her as a "'transcendental writer'" (qtd. in Carr, p. 365).

A Poet's Notebook (1943) is Edith Sitwell's collection of aphorisms describing the nature and practice of poetry.]

205. To Audrey Wood

[Paris]
6/9/51
[TLSx, 1 p. HRC]

Dear Audrey:

We are in Paris for a few days after a long stay in London. Poor Maria Britneva is in trouble, pregnant by a married man, and having to have an abortion first of next week, which is dangerous as they think she is in the fourth month of it. She was in Paris with us for a couple of days but has now gone back to prepare for the operation. Don't mention this to anyone!

Mme. Tallant has not been in town so we will not get any more francs out of the Author's League this trip. There were a lot still left in the strong-box at the Chase National Bank here, so we didn't really need them. I will get them out next time we come through Paris - the ones still held by the "League".

I am leaving tomorrow evening by train for Rome, Frank driving the new car down. We are pleased with it. We will have our original apartment in Rome, the one at 45 Via Aurora - not the one we had last summer which was so hot and uncomfortable. The telephone number there is 40779.

I do hope that "Tattoo" still survives. I expect momentarily to be informed of its demise!

Any chance of moving into the other theatre?

This week Oliver Evans will be having the operation for the recovery of his hearing - in Chicago. Could you check with Authors' League to see if he received the financial assistance I wanted them to give him? You can get his address through City College of New York, English department.

Saw a lot of Peter Brook and some of Irene in London. He seems to have replaced Binkie in her very flexible affections: hope she has better luck. The circumstances are more propitious, at least in one important respect.

With love to you and Bill, Tenn.

[TW and Frank Merlo sailed on the *Queen Mary*, due at Southampton on May 22. They spent approximately two weeks in London before leaving for Paris.

The name "Maria Britneva" has been razored from the first paragraph of the original typescript, but it remains in a signed photographic copy which serves as setting text.

After learning that royalties for *Streetcar* had been sent to the States, TW grumbled that "practically all of that will go to the government" (to Wood, September 9, 1951, HRC). Ninon Tallon continued to represent Audrey Wood in France.

The Rose Tattoo grossed $16,700 in the preceding week, down 40% from its earlier high.]

206. To Justin Brooks Atkinson

[45 Via Aurora, Rome]
June 12, 1951
[TLS, 2 pp. BRTC]

Dear Brooks:

I wrote you before on the stationary of the Queen Mary, because I gathered the impression from your new book that you had a special fondness for that ship. The letter got lost in the flurry of disembarkment at Southhamptom so I'm writing you, now, from Rome on stationary from a wonderful old hotel in London called the "Cavendish" which is the property of the only surviving mistress of Edward VII. I liked it even better than the Queen Mary.

The letter I lost was devoted mostly to praise of your book. I borrowed it from someone on the boat. It's the first time I've been almost literally unable to put down a piece of non-fiction. It's a book that comes close to the spirit of Thoreau, and I admired, and envied a little, the feeling of sensitive but tranquil adjustment to life in it, adjustment without conformity or surrender.

And I want to thank you for the recent article on my play. Cheryl just sent it to me. I am sure it has something to do with the cheering upturn of business that she mentioned. When I left New York there had been an alarming decline. About that 'unmentionable article' dropped on the floor. I would have removed it at once if it had not, somehow, failed to strike me as being at all vulgar, even though I knew it seemed that way to many people. Bohemianism seems to take such a strong hold on someone from a background so intensely Puritanical as mine was, once it is broken away from. Then I am always wanting to say and do things in a play that are not ordinarily done, to make it closer to common experience, to prove, at least to myself, that there is nothing in experience that cannot be admitted to writing. But I want to do this only <u>with taste</u>. The 'object', I thought, was a direct, bold and instant symbol of Serafina's conversion (in progress) from a non-realistic, romantic concept of the love-relation to one that was thoroughly, even somewhat grossly, down to earth! - From Rosario to a clown! And finding that life remains thrilling on either level.

I am back in Rome. I have not yet seen Mrs. Stone on the street but otherwise everything is much the same, which is good.

I wish you a pleasant summer, with birds and stars and ships, and I hope the Fall will bring an improved lot of plays.

Ever, Tenn.

[In *Once Around the Sun* (1951)—shipboard reading for TW—Atkinson recorded daily observations, including a reference to the liner upon which TW had recently sailed. The "noises" of Manhattan are "nervous, petty, sharp, impatient," he wrote, while "the voice of the *Queen Mary* is grand." Awareness of an earlier book by Atkinson, *Henry Thoreau, The Cosmic Yankee* (1927), may have prompted TW's reference to "the spirit of Thoreau."

Atkinson's "second view" of *The Rose Tattoo* was probably solicited by Cheryl Crawford to dispel the imminent box-office doldrums of summer. Atkinson still deplored TW's lapses in taste but he ended the article with quotable praise: "Behind the fury and uproar of the characters are the eyes, ears and mind of a lyric dramatist who has brought into the theatre a new freedom of style" (*New York Times*, June 3, 1951). Business did improve briefly but slumped badly in July and August.

"The streets are brilliant!" TW wrote to Oliver Evans after arriving in Rome: "The first night, a sailor from Trevisano. The next a Neapolitan at the baths. Tonight?" (June 13, 1951, HRC).]

207. To Audrey Wood

[45 Via Aurora, Rome]
June 1951
[TLS, 1 p. HRC]

Dear Audrey:

Such a great relief to learn you are mending rapidly. Frank sent the office a wire to send you three dozen red roses, the most roses I have ever sent anybody, and I do hope they got the wire and you got the roses! Isn't a sudden operation a frightening thing? To me it was sheer terror, which lasted a year afterwards, mainly because of the anesthesia, being <u>made</u> unconscious, but there is nobody else in this world quite as much a physical coward as I am, so I am sure it was not so difficult for you. Then, if I remember correctly, and I am sure that I do, I had <u>Pancho</u> with me and it was in a little hospital on a desert, filled with sinister-looking black nuns who seemed to be elderly usherettes in the lobby ~~portals~~ of the great beyond.

We are back in Rome. I am feeling well. I am writing three or four hours a day. I am nervous as a cat! - situation normal.

The new car is lovely. Frank put the first scratch on it, poor kid! But it isn't a serious scratch, and we think it's the most elegant car in Rome, all black and silver.

Rossellini wired me today that he had been calling me repeatedly but couldn't get through and gave me a number to call him, what about I don't know. Visconti wants me to re-write La Dame Aux Camellias for Anna Magnani to star in on the screen! - This - as Irene would say - I think I won't do! - I have not yet talked to Magnani, but I see her on the streets as often as I find myself there. A meeting is inevitable. Natalia Murray says that Visconti will do "Tattoo" in the Fall with an all-Sicilian cast except for the part of Serafina. I think it's a thrilling idea. Hope I can stay to see it. I have not yet talked directly to Visconti, but will this week. Right now he is directing Magnani in something for the screen, both being prima donnas there is bound to be an explosion that will make Stromboli look like a wet fire cracker.

Natalia Murray is going to America and wants to occupy our apartment, which is all right if we don't already have a tenant in it. I suppose the matter would have to be mentioned to Buffie. Natalia does not, apparently, expect to pay us anything, but that's all right. . . . . I think, however, she ought to pay for the phone and utilities while she is there, but if she doesn't offer to, perhaps we should be cavalier and say nothing about it.

We're back in our first apartment, 45 Via Aurora, phone number 460779.

Love - Tenn.

[The once energetic Audrey Wood felt "a great yearning to return to bed at all sorts of odd daylight hours" (to TW, July 2, 1951, HRC) following an appendectomy in early-June. Complications required a second procedure and a long recovery.

Luchino Visconti signed contracts in 1954 to stage *The Rose Tattoo*, but the project was vetoed by the Italian Censorship Bureau. He was currently directing Anna Magnani in *Bellissima* (1951) amid "continuous disagreements" with the star. The volcanic island on the northern coast of Sicily gave title and explosive climax to Roberto Rossellini's film *Stromboli* (1949).

The apartment on East 58th Street had been sublet and would not be available for Natalia Murray.

The numeral "25" has been penciled into the spaced, partially typed date, perhaps at Liebling-Wood.]

208. To Paul Bigelow

[45 Via Aurora, Rome]
July 3, 1951.
[TLS, 1 p. Massee Collection]

Dearest Paul:

I can't tell you how unhappy I am to hear that the jaw has been making you trouble, but I am also relieved that you are finally going to have the operation which I have always felt you should have had. This, my dear, is to be known hereafter as the "summer of operations", not merely the summer of 1951. Oliver has had his long delayed operation on his ear, and the first reports are most encouraging. The auditory nerve survived the operation, and the great danger was that it might be destroyed. Maria Britnieva, poor child, got into the immemorial trouble of warm-hearted ladies and is paying the price we never had to pay! Five days of "agonizing labor" she says and "two operations!" and the business is still going. Keep this under your Borsalino, pet! It is not supposed to be anything more exotic than ulcers. Then, Audrey! - Now, you! - Am I going to be next? - Ah, me . . . at this point you can imagine the deepest sigh of which I am capable.

I have had about 3 weeks of summer in Rome, and for the time being I think that's about enough. Lethargy has descended, work falls off, so I am planning a trip in the new Jaguar, probably to Spain, but stopping off at Perpignan to hear Pablo Cassales play his cello and to catch the end of the bull-fights at Pamplona, then on down to some good beach on the Costa Brava. I am not really, confidentially, well enough to make this trip by myself, but Frank and I have been together constantly too long and I think his present irritability means we ought to take separate trips. He may go to Vienna. As soon as Maria is able to travel, I think she will join me somewhere on the sea, for the benefit of both. I suppose it is safe to live with a lady who has just had such a severe demonstration of the consequences of uncontrolled passion. Of course I was never likely to forget them.

I will write you again when I get settled somewhere, and I hope by that time you will be all through with this distressing business.

Much, much love, 10.

[Jordan Massee described the operation on his former companion Paul Bigelow as "very serious, and not very successful."

Maria Britneva later attributed her own operation to "appendicitis" rather than "ulcers," adding that "although there were complications, their seriousness was gravely exaggerated by Tennessee" (St. Just, p. 41).]

209. To Cheryl Crawford

[45 Via Aurora, Rome]
[ca. July 9, 1951]
[TLS, 1 p. BRTC]

Dear Cheryl:

I am terribly disturbed over Paul's impending operation. I have had a long letter to him in my pocket for a number of days and I am going to get it off this afternoon when I post this one. I will be leaving here possibly tomorrow for a long auto trip, winding up on the Costa Brava, which is the Spanish Riviera north of Barcelona. The swimming is said to be marvelous there, I can see the bullfights, and I think the air will be more stimulating than it becomes here after a while.

Yesterday I met a young Porto Rican in a cafe. He had just come from New York and seen "Tattoo" and said that it was now being done completely without music. Naturally I was surprised and distressed to hear that. I don't think the composed music is essential to the play but I cannot imagine it without any music whatsoever. When we discussed it I thought it was planned to use the musicians who were sitting in the basement and have them play some simple folk tunes. Ideally, I would think a singer guitarist would be the thing! The play needs music more than any other I've had produced, partly because of the rather drastic transitions of mood that take place. Music helps the audience to follow emotionally. It softens the rough edges of which there are many, alas. I am sure the total absence of it would reduce the audience appeal far more than we can judge who have seen it so often, now, that our own reactions are mostly reminiscent. Please let me know . . .

I know, of course, the need for economy, but I would rather take lower royalties and have the music kept. For the tour, I do hope you can arrange to use a good Italian singer-guitarist. There is a man here that you heard at dinner one night in Rome - perhaps you remember him - if you don't, Natalia does! - His name is Alfredo del Pedo, he sings at the restaurant "Giorgio's" and has enormous charm at the age of sixty! I have an idea he would be delighted to go to America for the tour.

I am still working on the new "Summer". It has turned into a totally new play, even the conception of the characters is different, and it might very well be possible to present it again in the States, especially with a name like Peggy Ashcroft or Margaret Sullavan whom you mentioned. I don't think I will pick up my new scripts till Fall. I want to ruminate and gestate for a good while before I commit myself to another great trial. Note that I say 'great trial' not 'great play'! - Everybody here is very bitter over Mrs. Stone. They cross the street to tell me how much they hated it! They seem to think it was an attack on the city. - Actually I liked all the characters in that book, even the gigolo! - though I couldnt defend him. I think Mrs. Stone was superior to most of the people who tell me what a disgusting person she is.

love - 10.

[Audrey Wood later informed TW that she and Cheryl Crawford had agreed to suspend royalties when the weekly gross for *The Rose Tattoo* "hit" (August 7, 1951, HRC) a predetermined level.

TW recently asked the English producers of *Summer and Smoke* to "be patient" as he continued to revise the play: "About 80% of the brilliant progress" on the new script had "turned out to be pure illusion" (to Beaumont and Perry, June 12, 1951, HRC). Crawford soon received a more upbeat account: *Summer and Smoke* had "a straight, clean dramatic line for the first time, without the cloudy metaphysics and the melodrama that spoiled the original production" (June 14, 1951, BRTC). Alma and John were recast as near equals in sexual innocence, removing both the awkwardness of their shifting roles and the need for John's redemption. Mrs. Buchanan first appears in the "new" version as a socially ambitious mother who tries to block her son's relationship with Alma. (See "The Eccentricities of a Nightingale or The Sun That Warms the Dark," n.d., HRC.)]

210. To Charles K. Feldman

[July 1951]
[Telegram draft, 1 p. Columbia U]

Dear Charlie,

Gadg terribly disturbed over cuts made during his absence. Intends to remove his name from picture ~~unless these~~ I also feel grave mistake to exceed cuts we all agreed upon in New York. A great picture can be botched by injudicious cutting. Don't let them spoil a great picture.

Love, Tennessee.

[The penciled note—probably a telegram draft—concerns unexpected censorship of *Streetcar* by the Roman Catholic Legion of Decency, which had rejected the Production Code seal of approval. Elia Kazan was not informed of last-minute cuts made by the producers to appease the Legion, which planned to give the film a "C" rating (Condemned). He described the cuts—some four minutes of footage—in an article designed to expose the sinister influence of the Catholic Church, the corresponding weakness of the producers, and the artistic violation of "the public, the author and myself" (*New York Times*, October 21, 1951). The Legion finally granted *Streetcar* a "B" rating to indicate a film that was "objectionable in part." The banned footage, including close-ups of Kim Hunter descending the stairs in the Poker Night sequence, has been restored in a "director's version."

Streetcar premiered on September 18, 1951, received excellent notices, and won the New York Film Critics award for best picture of the year.

The Legion criticism of *Streetcar* arose in early-July 1951, suggesting that TW may have drafted the telegram in Rome before leaving for Venice.]

211. To Audrey Wood

[Hotel Excelsior, Venice]
7/22/51.
[TLS, 1 p. HRC]

Dear Audrey:

I hope this finds you convalescing smoothly, but, alas, it leaves me in a depressed condition. The last few weeks have been fraught with misadventures. First of all, I smashed up the new car, the Jaguar. I was driving North, intending to spend some weeks on the Costa Brava of Spain as the Roman summer was taking my energy and I couldn't work. About one hundred miles out of Rome I became very nervous. I took a couple - or was it three? - stiff drinks from a thermos I had with me, and the first thing I knew there was a terrific crash! The car had gone into a tree at 70 miles an hour! - It had to be towed back to Rome. One side was virtually demolished. Repairs will take a month and one thousand dollars! But they say the car will look like new. - It was amazing that I was not seriously injured. My portable typewriter flew out of the backseat and landed on my head. Only a small cut, no concussion, but the typewriter badly damaged! - Ever since, from the shock, I suppose, I have felt very tense. That is, more than usually so. I am now in Venice, on the Lido, but I don't like it here and will leave in a day or two for somewhere else. Frank did not come with me. He felt we needed a little vacation from each other. I didn't agree with him but felt it was wiser to pretend that I did. The work goes a little better out of Rome, but I am still feeling very disturbed. What a bad summer all of us are having! What have we done to deserve it?

How about Paul? Did he have his operation? One wonderful piece of news. Oliver writes me that his operation was a fabulous success, normal hearing completely restored in at least one ear. This will make a great difference for him and it gives me a sense of satisfaction to know that my money helped to accomplish it. Money does so little most of the time.

Maria also pulled through her operation, and is going back to her play. When it closes in August, she says she will join me somewhere on the sea, for a vacation.

I was shocked to learn - by chance, not by any word from Cheryl about it - that <u>all</u> of the music had been taken out of the play. I think this is a dreadful mistake. The play is built for music. It simply must not go out on tour without a singer-guitarist. I wish they would also be looking around for someone to replace the present Assunta, if it goes on tour, and that they will try to hold onto all the rest of the present cast.

Better news next time, I hope.

Love, Tenn.

P.S. Will you ask Bill what can be done about the insurance on the Jaguar? Was the Buick sold? If not perhaps I'd better hold onto it till I know the Jaguar can be successfully repaired.

[TW spent a week on the Lido in Venice bewildered and depressed by Frank Merlo's aloofness. "God knows how it is all going to work out. But I must try to be a little bit prudent, a little bit wise, and start drawing the sails of my heart back in, for the wind is against them" (*Journal*, ca. July 17, 1951).

Maria Britneva was an understudy in a London production of *The Three Sisters* (Chekhov, 1901). The present "Assunta" had a run-of-the-play contract and could not be replaced in *The Rose Tattoo*. Once the envy of Rome, TW's Buick was sold to the lyricist John Latouche, reportedly a former lover of Frank Merlo.]

212. To Theatre Musicians Union

[45 Via Aurora, Rome]
August 3, 1951.
[TLS, 2 pp. HRC]

Dear Sirs:

Let me state at the beginning, that I am second to no one that I know of in my enthusiastic endorsement of the organization or unionization of labor, which I think is essential, and I think it is also essential for artists to have protective unions. But anyone who likes unions, and what they do to protect workers and professional people and artists, is all the more deeply concerned when they appear to be operating to the detriment of the very ones they are supposed to protect through rigid and punitive rules which are not based on understanding or logic.

I am a professional worker and I belong to a union, the Dramatists' Guild.

Another union, which is yours, has committed a very damaging act against a work of mine, THE ROSE TATTOO. Incidentally, I devoted about three years to the composition of this play. It is not an opera or a musical, but it is a play in which the use of incidental music is extremely important. Music was composed for it, the sort of music suitable to its theme, setting and atmosphere, by one of our most gifted and famous American composers, David Diamond.

THE ROSE TATTOO was an artistic success but only a moderate commercial success, it has a large cast, a cast of twenty-some actors and its operating expenses are correspondingly high, not as high as they would be if "star names" were involved, but still high, and especially now, in the summer, when it has been running six months, it is necessary to practise some economies. All the while this play has been running we have had two sets of musicians, one actually playing, and one playing poker in the basement. Right on the face of it, this is a highly unreasonable situation. When business dropped off, we regretfully decided that in order to survive the summer months we would have to abandon the special musicians employed to play Mr. Diamond's music and use the ones who had been playing poker in the basement. Good Italian folk-tunes were substituted for the composed music, and the "special" musicians were released and we (at least I!) assumed that the unoccupied ones were going to take their place. No such thing! Some gimmick in your rules intervened. We still have the musicians playing poker, or Canasta, in the basement, but we don't have any music whatsoever.

Now it may very well be that I have not received a clear picture of this remarkable situation. I spend most of my time working very intensely and as squarely and fairly as possible at my own profession, also unionized, and I may not have had the time or chance to acquaint myself as fully as I should with your point of view. I wish you would clarify it for me.

Why, specifically, is it impossible, now, for us to use the card-playing musicians in the basement? Why is the play stripped of music entirely, and we still have to pay for musicians?

Incensed is a mild word for how I feel about this, and I think this whole matter of musicians in the theatre must be brought out in the open as immediately and clearly as those concerned can bring it.

Sincerely, Tennessee Williams

P.S. I am not concerned about this matter merely as it affects THE ROSE TATTOO but as it affects a whole important segment of our modern theatre. Modern creative theatre is a synthesis of all the arts, literary, plastic, musical, Etc. THE ROSE TATTOO is a notable case in point since I think it has gone further than any recent legitimate American drama to demonstrate this fact, this synthesis of various creative elements, and when music is thrown out because of a highly illogical, a downright stupid misuse of protective rulings which are <u>not</u> protective but punitive, something has to be done, at least to clarify things.

[Cheryl Crawford fired the "'special musicians,'" but her plan to replace them with idle house musicians—currently on salary—was blocked by a union rule which forbade any change in orchestration after the opening of a play. TW argued in a covering letter to Cheryl Crawford and Audrey Wood that the absence of music "makes a radical, perhaps fatal, difference in the public response" (August 3, 1951, HRC) to *The Rose Tattoo*. Irene Selznick had fought, and won, a similar battle when the union classified *Streetcar* as a "drama with music," requiring added musicians and a higher pay scale.

Apparently either Wood or Crawford removed the impolitic references to "card-playing" and sent a revised version of the letter (August 3, 1951, HRC) to Local 802 of the American Federation of Musicians. The original signed typescript is used as setting text.]

213. To Gore Vidal

[Hôtel du Pont Royal, Paris]
8/13/51.
[TLS, 1 p. Houghton]

Dear Gore:

This has been what the Chinese would call "The summer of the long knives!" No one has been spared, not even the divine bird. Some of its brightest feathers are scattered upon the floor of the cage. Practically everyone has been operated on but you and Jo Healy. How are you feeling? Oliver has had his ear operation and has recovered normal hearing in at least one ear. Something has been done about Bigelow's jaw at Manhattan General. Maria Britnieva had a surgical experience in London. And of course Audrey.

My operation occured on the Via Aurelia between Rome and Genoa in my new Jaguar. I was driving it at 70 miles an hour, fortified by a couple or three stiff martinis, when a capricious truck came out of a side road and I decided to hit a large tree instead. One side of the car was demolished. My portable typewriter flew out of the backseat and crowned me just over the hairline. I have not had a bigger or more excited audience since the opening of "Menagerie". No one could believe that the divine bird was still able to flutter! But here, I am, in Paris! Waiting for the repairs on the car, which are taking six weeks and over a thousand dollars. The Little Horse remains in Rome. Yes, it's been the summer of the long knives.

I am staying at the Hotel du Pont Royal as the Hotel de L'Universite seems to be converted into the official headquarters of something or other quite different from what it was formerly the headquarters of. It is almost deserted, the town, except for "les mouches". I had to fight with them over my lunch, and I think they got away with most of the omelette.

Prokosch is back in Rome. We became quite chummy before I left there. He is finishing a new book called "Water Music" and seems to be in better spirits than I've ever known him to be. Incidentally he mentioned having coming across the opening chapter of Truman's new book in some periodical. Have you seen it, and if so, how are you feeling? - Buechner should be fucked, not published, and I am just the little guy who would like to do it, provided his photographs on dust-jackets are at least half as honest as yours. - Rome was disappointing this summer, especially the car was kaput so early in the season, and it was fearfully hot. I also took in

Munich (good cruising and 3 very good gay bars!) and a week at the Lido of Venice. Frank did Vienna and is going to do Sicily while I'm here. But I had my best time and most exciting lay in London, of all places. . . You know, we really should have done a real season there. If it were not for Grandfather, impatiently waiting for us in Memphis, I would not come back to the States at all this year. As it is, think I will stretch the visit through October.

I have been offered a house surrounded by a large wall in New Orleans, and may live there when I return, whether or not the Mexican remains. Write me in Rome, as I have to back there for the car and shall be travelling around for the next two or three weeks.

Love - 10.

[Before leaving Rome, TW read the "'new'" *Summer and Smoke* and was dealt "a staggering blow" by its "pitiful" quality, probably "the worst job" he had "ever done" (*Journal*, August 9, 1951). Relations with Frank Merlo, who displayed "all the warmth and charm of a porcupine," were still tense. The few days which TW spent alone in Paris produced an "itchy rash," a "gassy stomach," and insomnia, which was not relieved by "secconals" (*Journal*, August 15, 1951).

Gore Vidal was living in Duchess County, New York, finishing a new novel, and helping his father to run a small factory which made plastic bread trays. Frederic Prokosch planned to spend the coming year as a Fulbright Fellow at the University of Rome. He had spotted the "opening chapter" of Truman Capote's novella *The Grass Harp* (1951) in *Botteghe Oscure* (volume 7). Frederick Buechner's only published novel to date was his first, *A Long Day's Dying* (1950).]

214. To Audrey Wood

[Cavendish Hotel, London]
August 23, 1951
[TLS w/ autograph marginalia, 1 p. HRC]

Dear Audrey:

This has been a summer of wanderings. I am now in London, in response to a wire that reached me in Paris. Maria's first cousin who had lived with her since childhood is gravely ill, complications of diabetes and nephritis, and Maria wanted me to come over, so I did. I have been here about a week, am now waiting for my typewriter to be repaired the one that hit me on the head in the smash-up. It all started falling apart. I still don't understand what my head can be made of! I have felt very odd this summer, but I'm not at all sure the typewriter can be blamed. They keep delaying the repair of the Jaguar. Now they say it won't be ready till September 8th and we are quite helpless, you can't make them do it any faster than they want to for love or money. Everything goes at a snail's pace during "the Solleone" (The lion sun) in Rome. Frank is still down there, unless he has gone to Sicily to visit his folks there. I have been travelling alone for the first time in three years, and in a way I guess it is good for me, it renews my self-reliance and possibly sharpens my wits a little, and it is a wonderful change for the Little Horse, a change which he had hinted rather broadly was about due.

I completed a first draft of the new "Summer and Smoke" (it has a different title and is almost a completely new play) but I have an idea Tennents will prefer to do the old one. This one is half an hour shorter and in its present condition it was not really ready to be read, extremely rough, but I let John Perry read it anyway, that is, I left it with him to be typed up and read if he wished to. If they do the old there is still a good deal of material in this one that can be used to improve it. I have not yet had an audience with Binkie Beaumont but I want you to know that I had lunch today with none other than Mr. T.S. Eliot the greatest living poet. He had Laughlin and I as guests to lunch at the Garrick Club, and he is the sweetest literary figure I've ever met, and fortunately I could speak with sincere admiration of his work, even of The Cocktail Party, and he seemed to be pleased. I had bought a first edition of The Cocktail Party and he inscribed it for me.

Carson is staying here in a house with a youngish and very seedy sort of mad poet, and I mean really mad, and it is really a menage. Fortunately there is one of those dedicated women there that look out for Carson, and I think she is in the bloom of a new infatuation for a middle-aged lady, the sister of John Lehmann, the one that is an actress. There is no further allusion to Edith Sitwell! I will see Carson tonight at John Lehmann's since we are both dining there. Tomorrow my repaired typewriter will return to me, and probably on Sunday I will fly back across the channel, to Paris, then on down to some "watering place" to "bathe".

I can't tell you how much I enjoyed and was relieved by your long, long letter, and the news that you are feeling like your self again.

Must leave, now, for dinner - Much love, Tenn.

[Maria Britneva's cousin lay "in a nightmarish state" during TW's present and later visit to London in October: "Shakes one's faith in the ultimate mercy even of nature" (*Journal*, October 6, 1951).

A Tennent staffer wrote that the "new" *Summer and Smoke* "amazed" everyone and "read like the first draft of a bad translation" (Kitty Black, *Upper Circle*, 1984, p. 188). In late-September Audrey Wood was still negotiating contracts with John Perry, the producer, and had "no idea which version" (to TW, September 20, 1951, HRC) of the play he would use. Perry soon clarified the situation: "Frankly, we could not have undertaken the production if Tennessee had insisted on the new version. It would be most unsuitable for this country, apart from the fact that it would have hardly played more than an hour and twenty minutes" (to Wood, September 25, 1951, HRC).

The McCullers saga took a strange turn in July when Reeves secretly left the hospital where he was being treated for alcoholism, boarded the *Queen Elizabeth* as a stowaway, and revealed himself to Carson midway through the voyage. He quickly returned to the States after the ship landed. In London McCullers lived with the "mad poet" David Gascoyne and apparently became infatuated with John Lehmann's younger sister, Beatrix (see Carr, pp. 375-381).

Penned in the upper margin is TW's mailing address, "Am. Ex. Rome."]

215. To Buffie Johnson Sykes

Cavendish Hotel, London
August 24, 1951.
[TL, 2 pp. HRC]

Dear Buffie:

I received in the mail yesterday a large and complete sheaf of correspondance between you and Audrey pertaining to the alleged damages and "theft" that occured in the apartment.

I doubt, Buffie, that you realize how preposterous your attitude and your charges are, it is charitable to have this doubt and I want to be as fair as I can under the circumstances, so I try to maintain this doubt. There is an element of (I hope) <u>unconscious</u> cruelty in your charges which is quite foreign to anything I have ever thought about you and which surprises and shocks me beyond expression. I know perfectly well that you must know, as you in fact admitted that distressing afternoon when you opened the cabinets and claimed that your jewels were stolen, that the last thing in the world that Frank and I would do or could be suspected of doing is stealing any of your belongings or even exposing them to any chance of theft. I have never in my life touched anything that did not belong to me except one grape which I remember picking off a sidewalk stand as I walked past it with my father and mother when I was seven years old and I can still feel the slap that my father gave me and his roar of indignation. We do not steal things, not Frank, and not I, fortunately we neither have to nor want to. I cannot answer for the tenants you had in the apartment before we occupied it. It seemed to be Gerald's impression, I remember, that you were only imagining these depredations, at least that was the way it seemed to turn out the afternoon when you made the extremely offensive scene about the broken jewel-box. This I attributed only - as your husband did - to an attack of nerves, perhaps consequent on your recent illness and operation, but the present renewed charges of large and systematic thefts cannot be excused in that way, they are made cold-bloodedly and with an air of calculation which is simply unspeakable as coming from someone I had regarded once as a friend, and from an artist and a person that one would expect to have a sense of equity as well as good-breeding.

As for the neglect of the apartment, you know very well that we retained the maid that you had employed in the apartment and that we had her there every morning while we were occupying it and even sometimes during our absences to water and care for the precious plants in the patio, and that in addition to this, Frank's nephew came in every day when we were necessarily out of town on the road-tour of "The Rose Tattoo" to take care of the plants and the birds, none of which suffered while we were in the apartment except perhaps from the ordinary attritions of time, for you know that plants are not immortal. You took out the great rubber plant, in fact from time to time, having free access to the apartment in spite of our tenancy, you came and removed various things, whatever you wanted to take out, and we made no objection. You took out pictures, plants, furniture. In fact we came back from a short trip to find an almost new (and very inferior) set of furniture in the studio. You also know that "hand-carved" chair you speak of was broken before we came into the apartment, for we talked about it. You also know that you never - not repeatedly and not even once - suggested that the skylight be cleaned, and God knows I would loved to have had it cleaned if you did, for I was living there and its murky condition was far more distressing to me than it could have been to you at the distance of East Hampton. If you were seriously concerned about this skylight, why didn't you speak of it to me or Frank? I have never, never, never in my life seen any of these articles you itemize as having been stolen from the apartment, and can you imagine anyone breaking into the place and sallying forth with a basket of Sevres vases, hand-painted Chinese screens, cupid-brackets and so forth? Can you seriously, for one moment, believe such a thing occured, and how or why would it!???

I do not intend to discuss this matter with you again outside of a court of law. And I assure you as earnestly as possible that I do not intend to be victimized by what it is most charitable to describe as your delusions. I don't think I have ever been quite so amazed by human behaviour in my life! Not of any individual that I have known.

Much more than incidentally, I think you should be rather ashamed of yourself for the relentless trial all this has been to Audrey during a summer when she was ill, had a severe operation and was supposed to rest. She was kind enough not to let me know about the affair till this week, as she knew how it would disturb me.

Sincerely,

[Buffie Johnson (b. 1912) complained to Audrey Wood that "serious and apparently systematic thefts" had taken place at her apartment on East 58th Street. She also charged that the property had so declined in "presentability and chic" during TW's occupancy that it would need "a complete new decoration" (July 17, 1951, Columbia U). In *Memoirs* TW described the apartment as "the loveliest" which he had occupied in New York and observed that Tony Smith had "designed" it for his—TW's—"old friend, Buffie Johnson" (pp. 151-152).

The printed version was revised by TW—a potentially libelous passage was canceled in a signed draft of the letter (August 24, 1951, HRC)—and sent to Liebling-Wood for retyping and delivery to Johnson.]

216. To Frank Merlo

SH: Cavendish Hotel
81 Jermyn Street
St. James's, S.W.1 [London]
August 29, 1951
[TLS, 2 pp. HRC]

Dear Little Horse:

We tried, Maria and I, to get you again on the telephone a couple of nights ago, from midnight until two, and the report was that you were not in, so we gave it up at last and went to our separate beds. I am leaving here this evening by plane for Paris, and all in all, it has been a good visit. I am pretty done in, pretty tired, because I have been working hard and much better than I worked in Rome or Venice I do believe. The play script was completed here and is being typed at Tennents and John Perry seems to be serious about having it done at the Lyric Hammersmith, starting rehearsals about the middle of next month, September, and opening, I suppose, toward the end of October, and I really think we ought to stay over for it. By the way, Grandfather is back with mother, so I feel better about him. I think she will be nicer to him, since Dakin has been transferred to Sacramento and she will have no one but Grandfather in the house. Isn't it sad for her? I feel terribly sorry for the poor little old lady without her one last darling left in the nest! She wrote me a sweet letter, no reproaches, no sermon. Speaking of letters, Audrey sent me a sheaf of correspondance between herself and Buffie. Madame Sykes is planning to sue me for $975., theft and damages to her apartment. Says jewels were stolen, three Sevres vases, countless other valuables, precious heirlooms, that there had been systematic thefts over a long period during our occupancy. I sat right down and wrote her the most scorching letter that I've ever written, but I think this affair will terminate in a law-court. Fortunately I don't think she has any proof of any of these alleged stolen articles having been in the apartment, since she gave us no inventory when we moved in. Audrey has put the matter in Colton's hands. Isn't Buffie a regular shit and a bitch? I just can't hardly believe it!

Carson is here, and a fish couldn't drink so much without sinking. She is brooding and mooning over John Lehmann's sister, the middle-aged one on the stage who is said to be dikish. I called on Carson last night at her lodging-house, very pleasant, in Chelsea, and found her just sitting in a stupefied way on a sofa with a cigarette and a nearly empty bottle of sherry. She is coming over for lunch. Her physical condition has not changed but this all day and half the night drinking will lead to disaster. I am hoping she will go back to the States but she is planning to come to the continent. I don't think we could stand to have her in Rome in the state she is in. She needs psychiatric treatment worse than anyone I know, even myself, and it is heartbreaking.

Maria's cousin is a bit better but the ultimate outlook is hopeless. One doctor told us a few days ago she could only live three weeks, but she has picked up since then and now is eating a little but hasn't had a bowel movement in about ten days, is too weak for an enema, and her kidneys rarely function.

Yesterday we went to see a polo match, Maria and I, with Hermione Baddeley, her 22 year old gay lover and a real Maharajah. Maria had a terrible fight with the young queen and it ended in tears. We had to get out of the car and walk a long ways before we found a taxi. The queen spit in Maria's face and called her the foulest names I've ever heard addressed to a woman by anyone but Pancho. Of course Maria provoked the quarrel by some untactful remark, called him "insufferably conceited" to his face.

I will only stay in Paris a couple of days, then I may go to St. Tropez for a little swimming, or I may even come straight on down to Rome, will let you know which the moment I've decided.

I'll be at the Pont Royal in Paris, till Thursday evening. PLEASE CHECK ON THE CAR AND MAKE SURE THEY REMEMBER THEY PROMISED TO HAVE IT COMPLETELY READY BY SEPTEMBER EIGHTH!

I've missed you an awful lot, both night and day, and Maria and I talk about you so much. But I think we needed this period away from each other.

Love, Tenn.

[*Summer and Smoke* would enter rehearsal in mid-October and have its London premiere on November 22. John Perry, an associate of Tennent Ltd., hired Peter Glenville as director.

Eddie Colton wrote that if Buffie Johnson "has any claim she had better litigate it," for "the burden of proof . . . will be upon her" (to Wood, August 22, 1951, HRC).

TW marked the death of Maria Britneva's cousin on October 11 with an elegy entitled "A Wreath for Alexandra Molostvova": "It is well to remember the chill of the vault made warm by the entrance of roses" (1956). TW wept at the Greek Orthodox service and "thought, of course, of Rose" (*Journal*, October 14, 1951).

Britneva later claimed that Hermione Baddeley's young lover, Laurence Harvey, provoked the "fight" by "extraordinarily abusive" (St. Just, p. 160) treatment of her. Baddeley hoped to play Serafina in the English production of *The Rose Tattoo* and had been introduced to TW by their mutual friend, the "Little Brit." Baddeley would not play Serafina, although she later starred as Mrs. Goforth in *The Milk Train Doesn't Stop Here Anymore* (1962/1963).

TW braced himself for the flight to Paris with "2 phenobarbs, 1 seconal, 1 martini." Their "magic," he knew, "isn't right, it isn't well, this cycle of sedation" (*Journal*, August 28, 1951).]

217. To Cheryl Crawford

SH: Hotel D'Angleterre, Copenhagen
Sept. 8, 1951.
[ALS, 4 pp. BRTC]

Dearest Cheryl -

This is a late town, but even here it is too late for me to pound a typewriter. I hope you can make out my nervous scrawl. I have been doing a tour of "Tattoo" openings in Scandinavia. There are to be eight, altogether; so far I have only seen one (very fine) in Copenhagen and another one, nearly as good, in Goteborg Sweden which has the finest stage (mechanically and in dimensions) I have ever seen.

The Danes are just as warm and lovable, in their own Northern way, as the wops. The Swedes are a little too serious and shy for a quick communication. All are fine actors, and I have never had such a warm-hearted welcome anywhere as I've had here. I needed it badly, for this has been a bad summer. I have been ill the whole time, I don't [know] whether in body or spirit or in both. I call it "The Summer of The Long Knives" - a paraphrase of a Chinese expression concerning a very difficult sort of night. I have travelled almost constantly, as if to run away from myself, and I have kept working, however badly.

Now I go back to Rome. Maybe this time the old spell will work. It didn't earlier. Then I go to London for their production of "Summer and Smoke" - I am not yet sure which version they plan to use, the new or old one. I prefer the new one, although it reflects the hysteria of my moods this summer. I want you to read it when I return to the States.

I think you have done a truly amazing job, holding the show together through the summer, keeping it going, and I make a deep bow, my forehead touching the floor, for it means a great deal to me, as you know. You are, when all is said and done, the very best of my various producers and I pray that God is willing to let me give you another play! -

Love, Tennessee.

[Frank Merlo joined TW for a "delightful" week in Copenhagen, as he cheerfully informed Walter Dakin. Tom's work, he added, was well known and admired by the Danes, including a "great gathering of university students" (September 26, 1951, HTC) which TW addressed. Lars Schmidt, Audrey Wood's agent in Scandinavia, confirmed the success of *The Rose Tattoo* and described TW as being "in the very best humour" (to Wood, September 4, 1951, HRC). Privately TW wondered "why" he had come all the "way" to Copenhagen and resolved in the future to use a "two-letter word that says 'NO!'" (*Journal*, September 9 and 11, 1951).]

218. To Audrey Wood

[45 Via Aurora, Rome]
[September 28, 1951]
[TLS, 1 p. HRC]

Dear Audrey:

No, they didn't tell me about the goat. Did he die a natural death or was he killed by economy? Will not yield an inch on his replacement. Both the goat and music are essential to the play, and the elimination of both from the cast were not reported to me by the management. Of course I feel they did a good job keeping the show going through the summer, but on the road these economies won't do. I'd rather they closed the play than not have a goat or any music in it.

I've been working, working, working all summer but some of the time it's like a man trying to run with a sprained ankle. Most of the summer I spent on "Summer and Smoke" and I completed a script but both John Perry and the director, Peter Glenville, have decided in favor of the old one. Unfortunately the new version was only 57 pages and they didn't like it anyway. They are probably right, but if I had had more time, I would have preferred the new one.

I leave here tomorrow for Paris, then directly to London, will arrive there about October 1st and the address will be the Cavendish Hotel on Jermyn Street. Frank's driving the car up. The repairs were completed and it looks like new. We have receipts for the work which Frank will send for the insurance people.

I do hope the one-acts won't go into production till after the New Year. For one thing, it would be nice to have Wallach available. Then I will need some time on Camino Real if that's to be done. I have some re-writ on one scene of it, somewhere among my papers. Will shoot it off to you soon as it turns up. Perhaps Gadg and I can spend a week together in the country when I get back and work closely on the project. ~~He is such a slippery customer!~~ Do you really think he can be pinned down? He would do a magnificent job and I think a success, with him, would be fairly certain. Can't think of anyone else who could handle those two plays.

I'm still happy over a long story I've been working on and I have a number of play scripts waiting for time and energy to be granted.

Please remember: "Goat and Guitar!" is the cry. This is the end of a long, hard day, and the end of a long, hard summer, and I suppose it is the beginning of a long, hard Fall, but what the hell, we are still with it!

MUCH LOVE, Tenn.

[*The Rose Tattoo* survived the summer and closed on October 27, 1951, after 306 performances. The tour began two days later in Montreal with Maureen Stapleton and Eli Wallach in the leads.

TW later claimed that the new script of *Summer and Smoke* had arrived "too late" to be used in the English production: "The original version of the play was already in rehearsal" (Author's Note, *The Eccentricities of a Nightingale*, 1964).

William Liebling revived an earlier project by proposing an evening of one-acts, including "Ten Blocks on the Camino Real" (1948) and "27 Wagons Full of Cotton" (1945). Elia Kazan, who was still intrigued by "Ten Blocks," had apparently agreed to direct the double bill, which Liebling would produce (Liebling to TW, September 14, 1951, HRC). TW warily observed, "Do I believe it? Well, hardly. Possible, just possible, in my cynical opinion. If {Kazan} did it would be as remarkable as if I really managed to write something good for a change" (*Journal*, September 16, 1951).

The "long story" in progress is "Three Players of a Summer Game" (1952). Drafted in Venice in July 1951, the promising story now seemed "Dull, dull!" and TW "hit the bottom!" (*Journal*, October 1, 1951).

This letter, misdated "8/28/51" by TW, has been assigned a date one month later as indicated by the sequence of events.]

219. To Audrey Wood

Cavendish [London]
October 27, 1951.
[TLS, 2 pp. HRC]

Dear Audrey:

I am very excited and a little dismayed and quite frightened over the rapid progress of plans for the short plays. I am frightened because I don't know what Gadg wants or expects of me. He talks of "work and work" (which sounds like an awful lot of it) but he doesn't say what it is to be, and I have never worked as badly in my life as I have these past few months.

Of course I don't want to express these misgivings to Gadg at this point, for it might discourage his interest in the project but I think it is necessary to let you know. Yes, we had some talks about the play but I don't remember any specific, or even general, suggestions that he made, except that he seemed to feel it needed clarification. If he is coming to England and sailing back with Frank and me on the Elizabeth, of course there will be plenty of time to investigate his views. I do hope they don't include a desire to collaborate with me on the script! That is, to take part in the actual writing. On the other hand, Gadg has a very creative mind and he might stimulate me, provided his demands are not overwhelming and his ideas compatible with mine.

Of course what intrigues me most is the vision of "Audrey Wood Presents". It will inspire me to do all I can to make the presentation something worthy of all that our association has meant to me. A sentiment pompously expressed, but felt very truly. Gadg says he understands about that, and is happy.

Two questions: is it possible to get us a little apartment in New York with room for Grandfather? And!! Is there any truth in a wild report that Carson received from her mother that Cheryl and Bigelow were going to be married?!

Speaking of Carson! Confidentially, I have never seen her in quite such nervous disorder. When we arrived in London, she was staying at sort of a nursing-home in the country where she had apparently been placed by a female hypnotist on whom she had one of her immoderate "crushes". She suddenly came to London, early one morning, and wanted us to put her up in this little room that I use for work. It was obviously impossible to combine her life and ours in such small quarters, so through the assistance of an old acquaintance from New Orleans, one Valentina Sheriff, of Russian-Chinese background, we got her into the Ritz. Then all hell busted loose! Mme. Sheriff flew into a fury, not at poor Carson, but at us! Frank lost his Sicilian temper and called the Madame a few basic things in Carson's presence. I am afraid that our friendship with Carson is at least temporarily disrupted, for she was very cold to me at parting and declined my offer to see her off on the plane to New York, to which the female hypnotist had persuaded her to return.

It is a long, long and very involved story. I only hope that Carson doesn't turn it into one of her implacable vendettas. I love her and am very distressed about it.

Glenville and Margaret Johnson are doing great work on the play. But they have put the murder back into it. In fact, all my changes practically all of them, have been discarded and they have reverted almost entirely to the original script. Not very encouraging, is it.

About the apartment: of course we will only need it if it is true that the play goes into rehearsal in December. I have a horror of hotel-life in New York or I wouldn't bring up the problem. God knows enough already exist in our lives.

With love, Tenn

[Audrey Wood may have further "dismayed" and "frightened" TW by reminding him of Elia Kazan's unpredictable behavior. "What do you want to do? Whatever it is lets do it quickly. I'm getting nervous" (October 11, 1951, HRC), she added, in reference to a production of the "short plays."

Jordan Massee dismissed "the idea" of a Crawford-Bigelow marriage as "too absurd for words." Bigelow, he observed, was "100% gay" and Crawford "exclusively Lesbian."

Carson McCullers was treated unsuccessfully with hypnosis by Dr. Katherine Cohen, a psychiatrist.

Valentine Sherriff was a Russian-born divorcee who traveled widely and had introduced McCullers to a "motley assortment of Europeans and Americans" (Carr, p. 398) in Paris. Presumably TW met Sherriff in New Orleans, where she had married a wealthy husband and kept a walled house on Burgandy Street. Earlier in October she promised to supply TW with "100 seconals" (*Journal*, October 10, 1951).

Margaret Johnston played Alma Winemiller with "distinction" in the forthcoming London production of *Summer and Smoke*. After he and the director, Peter Glenville, had conferred on the script, TW resolved that the "murder" of the elder Buchanan "must go out - one way or another" (*Journal*, October 3, 1951).

TW sailed with Kazan on the Queen Elizabeth and did indeed take up "hotel-life in New York" after disembarking on November 12.]

220. To Peter Glenville

SH: Gladstone
East 52nd Street at Park Avenue
New York City - 22
[late-November 1951]
[TL, 1 p. HRC]

Dear Peter:

The report on "S.&S." is the most gratifying thing that's happened to me in a long time. I can't tell you how enormously I admire your work on the production, not only as the director but as a person, your understanding, your patience and sweetness. It was a completely happy experience working with you, and I shall always be indebted to you for restoring my faith in the play, and this just isn't the usual sentimental testimonial after a successful opening but what I would have felt regardless of how it had turned out. You are top man on the Totem pole!

Well, things are all screwed up over here. We are having a bloody time of it. Nobody seems right for the lead in "Camino Real" except Eli Wallach and he's on tour with "Rose Tattoo". We wanted Marlon but he is being maddeningly perverse, won't say yes or no, says he is going through an "emotional crisis" and is living in an almost empty apartment with a pet raccoon who scrambles into your lap and tries to unbutton your fly soon as you enter or assume a sitting position. Then Dame Selznick, with her inimitable gallantry, her superb sense of timing, bought and submitted a new play to Gadg almost as soon as we got off the boat in New York. It is a good play and for a while I wondered if she might not succeed in snatching Kazan away. But he is sticking with us, after all, and the Dame must cool her heels, at least until we open in February or the project blows up, which is still possible.

[Peter Glenville (1913-1996) trained in the Old Vic company and made his directorial debut on Broadway in 1949 with a program of one-acts by Terence Rattigan. His staging of *Summer and Smoke* at the Lyric-Hammersmith was deemed "admirable" by the reviewers. He later directed the film version of *Summer and Smoke* (1961) and the New York production of *Out Cry* (1973).

English reviewers of *Summer and Smoke* (November 22, 1951) praised the "beguiling pen" of the author and the "genuinely moving" treatment of Alma. Kenneth Tynan, TW's sharpest critic, found an "incompleteness" in the play which he considered the mark of "a minor talent." If TW's "characters, even at their best, have a depleted look, it is probably because they start out with the disadvantage of being internally lame beyond all surgery" (*Spectator*, December 7, 1951).

Marlon Brando's "pet raccoon," Russell, reportedly slept with the star and was exercised on a leash.]

221. To Irene Mayer Selznick

SH: The Blackstone
Michigan Avenue at Balbo
Chicago 5, Illinois
December 1, 1951
[TLS, 2 pp. Boston U]

Dear Irene

Audrey says you were very disturbed over my only half serious remarks when we collided in that bar the night of Van Druten's opening. I didn't mean to disturb you, but I must say, in all honesty, that I am still wondering why you didn't mention, the night we were out together, what you were up to. Why didn't you say, Tennessee, I'm going to offer my new play to Gadge? Why did I only learn of it through Gadge, and Audrey didn't learn of it until after I had learned of it, and so forth! You can see why certain dark and ugly thoughts crept into my mind, and if you were disturbed, I can only assure you it was not half as much as I was disturbed. You know how vulnerable a writer is, sometimes even a producer! And how nervous one gets in the first stages of a production when it is still "touch and go", and you know what everything concerning my work means to me. I am glad that the only thing you were guilty of is thoughtlessness, for I don't believe, in my heart, that you would have had it in your heart to willfully injure me or my work.

Now let me congratulate you on having such a good play. I'm glad that Gadg will do it. I told him I thought he should.

Ever, Tenn.

[The casting of *Camino Real* drew TW to Chicago to scout Murray Hamilton—a potential Kilroy—in *The Moon Is Blue* (1951). The exquisitely named "Lincoln Baths" failed to enliven the trip, as TW informed Oliver Evans: They "were so dull tonight I put my clothes back on almost as soon as I took them off" (December 1, 1951, HRC).

TW apparently called Irene Selznick "'treacherous!'" (qtd. in St. Just, p. 51) for offering her "new play"—*Flight into Egypt* (1952), by George Tabori—to Elia

Kazan. She "shed a few feminine tears" and assured TW that she had "leaned over backwards" in consideration of his project, especially when Kazan said that it "was still in doubt" (December 4, 1951, Boston U). They met on November 28 at the premiere of John van Druten's latest play, *I Am a Camera* (1951).]

222. To Paul Bigelow

[Memphis, Tennessee]
PM: Memphis, December 4, 1951
[APCS, 1 p. Massee Collection]

Sol made big mistake booking me into "The Hide-Away". Mgr. says cannot use Petite Blonde type, wants dynamic red-head. I said I would take henna rinse but Mgr. very rude man. Need bus fare back to Sq. Roof. Urgent. Please advise!

Myrtle.

[The postcard extends a running joke with TW cast as "Myrtle," the Memphis prostitute in the story "The Kingdom of Earth" (1954). The impresario is probably "Sol" Hurok, while "Sq. Roof" refers to the sporting house in *The Rose Tattoo*. The razor-wielding figure in the background may allude satirically to Paul Bigelow's recent operation.]

223. To Edwina Dakin Williams

SH: Hotel Monteleone
New Orleans 12, U.S.A.
[late-December 1951]
[TLS w/ autograph postscript, 2 pp. HRC]

Dear Mother:

I feel very guilty about not visiting home for Christmas. I hope you understand how difficult it would have been. I've been operating under great pressure and had Grandfather with me. He can't take as much travel and excitement as he thinks he can. I flew to Memphis to pick him up. Kazan, his wife and I drove him down to Clarksdale, left him there while we drove about the Delta to collect background for a film that Kazan wants to make in the Delta based on my short plays. Then we picked up Grandfather again in Clarksdale and we all went back to New York, supposedly to start work on a stage production of "Camino Real". But meanwhile Liebling, who appointed himself the producer, decided it was too expensive a project to produce at this time. Nobody came forth with much money for it! So the stage production had to be postponed. I think it will be done in the early Fall, perhaps with somebody else at least as a co-producer. I am glad, now, that they came to that decision, although it was a disappointment at the time. Liebling could see nothing but the financial aspects of the plan, and was not even very efficient in handling those. I let him attempt it only because of Audrey, who is desperately anxious to give him something to do as he has become a terrible problem to her lately. So --- Grandfather and I are on our way to Key West, stopping off for a few days in New Orleans which he loves so much. He adores the restaurants here and always orders twice as much as he can eat, but he does enjoy it. We had our picture on the front page of the Times-Picayune and many old friends have been calling him.

It's lovely weather here, bright and warm. Frank will drive the car down to Key West to join us after New Year's. The car has just now arrived back in the country from England. Was shipped over at the expense of the manufacturer's, but it took a long time coming.

Grandfather says you will visit Clare in Florida so we will count on seeing you at that time. The Key West house is now vacant and waiting for us. I sent Rose a tweed coat (inter-lined) with hat and bag to match from a shop on Fifth Avenue. Did it arrive, and did it fit her allright? I'm sending you a check.

With much love and all good wishes, Tom.

1431 Duncan, Key West (after Jan 1st).

[TW and his grandfather spent nearly two weeks in New Orleans before traveling to Miami and Key West.

Precisely when the film project coalesced is unclear. Plays of interest were "This Property is Condemned" (1941), "The Last of My Solid Gold Watches" (1943), "The Unsatisfactory Supper" (1946), and especially "27 Wagons Full of Cotton" (1945). The outcome, of course, was *Baby Doll* (1956).

William Liebling "appointed himself" producer of the one-acts in the preceding September. Elia Kazan later insisted that Cheryl Crawford join the production, whereupon Liebling intended to withdraw (Wood to TW, October 11, 1951, HRC). Plans for a double bill probably gave way in November or early-December to a single production of *Camino Real*, which was shelved thereafter because of casting and financial problems and a preliminary script.

A related story in *The Times-Picayune* quoted TW as still feeling "'defensive'" about the critical reception of *Summer and Smoke*. Although praised in England, the play had not been "'given a fair break on the American stage'" (December 27, 1951, p. 1).]

224. To Amado "Pancho" Rodriguez y Gonzalez

SH: The Robert Clay
Miami, Florida
January 10, 1952
[TLS, 1 p. HRC]

Dear Pancho:

I received and put on the little gold cross just before I caught the plane to Miami and it gave me a serene and happy flight, perhaps because it was blessed by the accompanying note with its assurances of your friendship and understanding. I enjoyed my visit to New Orleans, a great deal, but nothing pleased me more than to find you well and doing well and being contented and adjusted. Of all the old crowd that I saw again, you are the one who seems to have made the most progress toward maturity of heart and mind, and I am so glad that you have.

It was a very sweet thing for you to do!

Thank you!

Always fondly, Tennessee.

[TW later reflected upon his "last" meeting with Pancho Rodriguez: "One thing for which I don't pity myself is the two years we spent together when I was not a sick thing as I am now and you were you, wild, wonderful, a poem. . . . Walk tall, walk proud through this world. When I see you again, which I hope will not be in memory only, I want you to look as I last saw you, like a Spanish Grandee, with a touch of Montezuma, who could spit out the fires of the Inquisition, or trample them out with his bare feet, and laugh at Cortez" (n.d., Private Collection). The effusive remarks may have been written in April 1952, soon after the studio in Key West, to which TW refers, was completed.]

225. To Oliver Evans

1431 Duncan
K.W. Fla.
1/18/52
[TLS, 1 p. HRC]

Dear Oliver:

I meant to wire you soon as I heard of your award. I was thrilled over it as much as you must have been. I remember the poem very distinctly, it was one of the best you have written, and I hope the award will prove a spur to you in your writing as it should be.

I think you are being sly about the cuff-links. You know very well that you did not offer them to me until after I had exclaimed over their beauty one night at Lafitte's and I didn't accept them because I presumed you were offering them because I had admired them, the way Orientals are supposed to insist that you take anything you admire in their houses. As for your going to the airport, I didn't want to seem to impose the trip on you by seeming over eager to have you along, it was a long trip and I was not sure that Valentina would make the return agreeable to you, which apparently she didn't.

I had four days in Miami waiting for Frank. My old friend Gilbert Maxwell was with me constantly and drinking heavily all the time. He is making a living there by conducting private classes in creative writing.

Really, she is such a girl! She got so drunk at one of her classes, which I attended, that she could hardly stay in her chair in a reasonably vertical position. Was reading a short story aloud in a burlesk drunken fashion. There was a cat in the apartment that started leaping about. Miss Maxwell suddenly shrieked: "Silence! Please remember that this is a study-group!" The hostess timidly explained that the cat was making that noise, and Miss Maxwell cried out: "Well, the same thing goes for your fucking cat!" I had no trade there, but a slight, tender affair with a young queen who paints and is wasting away with some mysterious blood disease.

Bud Staples was already here when we arrived in Key West. He is with a gorgeous Bill Murphy type Adonis from Southern California. I took the boy home last night. Miss Merlo arrived in a taxi just as buttons were being undone on the front-room-sofa. There was a real Gotterdamerung to pay! Screams, protestations, fury and tears, winding up with Miss Merlo in her most becoming position on the living-room carpet and me wondering if Miss Southern California would be game for a second try under more discreet circumstances! - after being denounced as the whore of Babylon. I must say that Miss Merlo, when she is in a rage, pays very little attention to inequalities of size between her and the opponent.

Much love from Tenn.

[TW and his grandfather were joined in Miami by Frank Merlo and driven to Key West.]

226. To Paul Bigelow

SH: *The* Robert Clay
Miami, Florida
PM: January 18, 1952
[TL, 1 p. Columbia U]

SAYINGS OF MISS MAXWELL, JANUARY, 1952.

"I am in a very dangerous position for any creative person. Completely surrounded by people who worship and adore me!"

"Do you realize that I am almost 42?!!"

"I am at the age that women find most attractive!"

"She is in the book department at Burdine's, and simply adores me!"

"Look! She has my book on display!"

"I am compared to Thomas Wolfe as he would have written if he had controlled his style!"

"Darling, you are losing your hair!"
"My stomach is surprisingly flat. . . ."

"I am through with love!"

"I want you to meet somebody that you will be mad about. She works in the drag-show at Leon & Eddie's but don't let that fool you. Last Saturday a sailor pulled off her wig and she knocked him across two tables!"

"Tennessee? I am downstairs!"

MORE LATER.

[TW's visit to Miami restored a friendship with Gilbert Maxwell which began in New York in 1940. He and several other transplanted southerners, including

Donald Windham and Fred Melton, formed the first gay society which TW experienced as a young man. In a later biography, *Tennessee Williams and Friends* (1965), Maxwell wrote that similar "tastes" and "unhappy" family backgrounds had secured their friendship. The reunion inspired a list of "SAYINGS" in which TW gently mocked his friend's personal vanity and literary pretension. Vanity aside, Maxwell was a productive writer with three volumes of poetry and a recent novel to his credit.

The place of mailing is obscured in the postmark.]

227. To Elia "Gadg" Kazan

1431 Duncan,
Key West, Fla.
Jan. 21, 1952
[TL, 1 p. HTC]

Dear Gadg:

HELP! HELP! SEND ME A WRITER! This is an embarassing but realistic appeal. Pick him out very carefully. First a southerner, someone such as Hubert Creekmore or Eudora Welty or even Speed Lamkin who know the Delta country. Also, preferably, someone who has done enough film-writing, or some film-writing. I will pay the financial penalty out of my advance and I may even sacrifice the screen-writing credit provided that I am given full credit for the authorship of the one-act plays it's based on.

I really did mean it, Gadg, when I wired you that I would devote myself to this film, but, Baby, you know as well as I know, that, first of all, we've got to obey the first commands of our hearts. You know that or we wouldn't be so close to each other in spirit. So send me a writer, and believe that I want one for a respectable reason.

The reason is this: I've done the stuff in those plays, not a single thing in them is left unsaid and there they are, complete, not perfect by any manner or means, but really completed. Now I feel a lot of things left unsaid, crowding my fingers on the typewriter, but they don't seem to be an essential part of these short plays, and I can't kid myself and certainly don't want to kid you that they are. SO SEND ME A WRITER.

I will work with him. I'll work with him as closely as possible and still go on with the new work that's crowding my fingers.

I think that you and Audrey and Molly will understand about this, and won't, in your hearts, blame me for it.

Under separate cover - I'm exhausted right now - I'll give you a point-by-point reaction to your outline which was a really brilliant piece of work and one that makes a good, solid basis for the script-to-be. The first two parts of it I buy without reservation. The last part gets a little bit cloudy or arbitrary - both.

Nothing but good can come out of my working with someone else on this script, provided the someone else is wisely chosen. I want this film to be almost like a documentary in its background authenticity. Let's get a writer who really knows such things as the process of ginning cotton, or who will make a quick, concentrated study of it for us, on location, the sort [*end of letter missing*]

[On January 14, 1952, Elia Kazan gave preliminary testimony before the House Un-American Activities Committee regarding past Communist activities and associations. He admitted his brief membership (mid 1930s) in the Communist Party but declined for the moment to name other members, especially those associated with the Group Theatre. Two weeks later, an anxious, depressed Kazan began rehearsals of *Flight into Egypt*, which received mixed notices and closed after forty-six performances. TW and Frank Merlo were among the unlucky investors.

Audrey Wood advised TW to use Paul Bigelow as an assistant on the *Baby Doll* project and thus forego the personal expense and shared credit of a professional collaborator. He agreed but felt it "terribly unfair to require writer to assume all liabilities on a deal so full of speculation" (telegram, January 31, 1952, HRC). TW hoped to be put on salary by Charles Feldman, the likely producer, while film rights were being negotiated and a script prepared. The film's original working title, "The Twister," was replaced by a second, "Hide and Seek."

TW admired Kazan's "outline," especially the opening sequence of the "syndicate fire," which he thought "a beautiful, thrilling, dramatic and cinematic idea" (although later cut in revision). The ending described by Kazan may have seemed flat by contrast, as Archie Lee Meighan, his arson revealed, "turns defeated and slouches off" (to Kazan, January 23, 1952, WUCA).

TW cabled the Department of Agriculture for "technical information on cotton ginning" (February 4, 1952, HRC).]

228. To Edwina Dakin Williams

[1431 Duncan Street
Key West, Florida]
1/25/52.
[TLS w/ autograph marginalia, 1 p. HTC]

Dear Daughter and Mother:

We were delighted to get your letter but still are waiting to hear what disposition is being made of Dakin, and we are glad to know that you are planning to come South. Don't put it off long. The big downstairs room is waiting for you, ready whenever you can get here.

After two most delightful weeks in New York, excepting the snow and ice, Tom and I took the train to New Orleans, and had barely registered at the Monteleone when the owner of the hotel sent a great basket of fruit to us and when we went to pay the bill, discovered that we had been his guest the entire time we were there which was about two weeks. We were interviewed and photographed and got on the radio a couple of times. Soon as the paper was out, grandfather received a number of calls by phone from old friends from Tenn. and Miss. Chiefly among them, Mrs. Flournoy who later had us over on New Year's Day for Egg-nog and a drive about Audubon Park. Grandfather wishes to add that we had fruit-cake and nuts out of their own garden. Mrs. Flournoy's son is married to a lovely woman and they have a grown daughter, soon to be married. They have a charming home. She enquired a great deal about you.

On New Years morning Mr. and Mrs. Binnings whom I married in Clarksdale about 30 years ago took me to Early Communion. We flew down from New Orleans to Miami and stayed there about four days while Frank drove the Jaguar down from New York to pick us up. The car had been delayed by the big Atlantic storms but arrived in New York without damage. We are now settled here and everything is going smoothly. We have a middle-aged white woman working for us. She cleans well but cannot cook. Frank is cooking dinner for us, and doing it very well.

We are worried about your fingers. St. Louis is noted for its medical talent and should have cured the condition by this time. As soon as you hear about Dakin let us know.

The weather here has been lovely, warm as summer. We found the house in excellent condition but are still trying to get someone to cut our grass, as we have no gardening implements.

Edwina and Tennessee Williams, Key West.

Grandfather wishes me to add that our last few days in New Orleans we were the guests of Mrs. Sheriff who gave us her entire house while she stayed at a hotel. We would have remained longer in New Orleans but didn't want to accept too much. It was a wonderful visit and we plan to stop there again on the way North this Spring.

Grandfather says we have the prospects of a brilliant social season here. Ahem!

That's all, says Grandfather. I am working on a play and a film-script, the latter at the command of Audrey and Kazan and not according to my own wishes. Do come down soon as possible. Let us know when!

Much love, Tom & Grandfather

[TW was "too shy to be pleasant" and so his mother's forthcoming visit to Key West was "sad" (*Journal*, February 1952).

Penned in the upper margin is the notation "'Summer & Smoke' has transferred to Duchess Theatre in London - has been a hit in England and should make money for Rose's trust fund. 'Tattoo' still running in Copenhagen & Norway." Despite positive reviews, *Summer and Smoke* closed after forty-four performances at the Duchess.

This letter first appeared in Edwina Dakin Williams's memoir, *Remember Me to Tom*, 1963, pp. 226-227.]

229. To Cheryl Crawford

[1431 Duncan Street
Key West, Florida]
2/10/52.
[TLS, 1 p. BRTC]

Dear Cheryl:

It is a great encouragement to me to know that you are interested in "Camino". As I told you before I left New York, there was some indication that the Lieblings would consider an associate producer. I am increasingly dubious that Liebling will want to do the play in its final form. He felt that it could be financed for less than a hundred G's, but now that it is expanded into full length the cost will be greater and I seriously doubt that he will want to attempt it. It will have to be financially treated as a musical, and my problem, now, is to give it sufficient entertainment value to justify that expense. And I do think it should be produced by someone with experience in that field. I have gotten hold of the unabridged (12 volumes) Memoirs of Casanova and DuMas novel "Camille" and the material in the play is now based on the real histories of those characters. I think the play is essentially a plastic poem on the romantic attitude toward life. One thing I wanted to ask you about: is it possible to have scenery moved by dancers? I have a couple of interior set-pieces that I want moved on and off by masked dancers, sort of grotesque mummers with gargoyle masks, and I wondered if that would violate any union rule. It's important that the movement of these set-pieces should be part of the action so that there is no interruption. They move in and out of the street-facade on wagon-stages.

The film is going great. We did about 30 pages yesterday and at least that many today so that it is now almost finished as most of the material was already present in the plays. It is such a great part for Maureen. I almost wish "Tattoo" would close on the road before the film goes into production. I mean the Mrs. Meighan part. Paul is a great help. He types as fast as I can think, and his humor stimulates mine and we laugh our heads off while working. I think it is going to be a very original and strong picture. We're using "Wagons" "Solid Gold Watches" "Property Condemned" and "The Unsatis-factory Supper" and the transitions have worked very smoothly so that it all seems to be of one piece.

Glad you're not doing any more two week stands before you hit the coast. Didn't realize you were still on subscription in St. Louie. Much love -

Tenn.

[Cheryl Crawford's "experience" with musicals was extensive and successful, although her current production, *Paint Your Wagon* (1951), would lose money after a lengthy run. A budget drafted in the preceding December listed costs of $111,000 for mounting *Camino Real* ("Tentative Budget," December 4, 1951, HRC).

To expand and authenticate *Camino Real*, TW consulted *The Memoirs of Jacques Casanova*, reprinted in twelve volumes in 1928, and the Modern Library edition of *Camille*. From the Alexandre Dumas novel (1848) he drew details of Marguerite Gautier's life as a courtesan in Paris, including her improvident love for Armand Duval. Marguerite's friend, Prudence Duvernoy, states in early drafts of the play that "you've got to be realistic on the Camino Real!"

One of the "set-pieces" to which TW refers was probably intended for a retrospective scene at the Opéra Comique, where Marguerite and Armand first meet.

Carroll Baker rather than Maureen Stapleton played the role of Mrs. Meighan in *Baby Doll*.]

230. To Oliver Evans

[1431 Duncan Street
Key West, Florida]
20 February 1952
[TLS, 1 p. HRC]

Dear Oliver:

The best news I've had in a long time, baby, is that you're writing a novel. Much as I admire your poetry, and I have sincerely remarked countless times that you're the best of the current bards, I've always felt with equal earnestness that the latitude and depth of your experience and being would find its most complete and powerful expression in prose. Take that for what it may be worth as the opinion of a friend who wishes you better than well in whatever you undertake.

I have been just a little bit more than slightly bored with Key West this year, and I guess it's fortunate that I had a lot of work to do here. Frank has found a crowd he enjoys. They do the bars all night and he rolls in about daybreak. They're composed of the "after the lost generation" guys and dolls who live on liquor and "bennies" and the fringe of lunacy. Frank dances wildly with the dolls. Possibly lays the guys. I wouldn't know. I've had a dry run of it here as far as sex is concerned. Another queen hit the dust lately. She picked up dirt and was so severely chastised that she was not recognizable. Her eye-sockets, the bone, was knocked in two inches from original position. She received 32 head-wounds anyone of which was sufficiently violent to kill her. Well, she daid! The sailor has confessed and is in the local calaboose. It struck terror to my heart, this little incident, and I do not venture far afield. Bigelow, however, cannot be discouraged and he averages about three or four tricks a night. He is the new "Florida Sweetheart." He is not staying in the house but in a place called Duke's Motel. Audrey sent him down here to apply the thumb-screws: to get me to work on the Kazan movie-script which I loathed doing but which is now done. I wonder if Bigelow's social activities will allow him time to type it up. He has given everyone around here the impression that he is my ghost-writer: somewhat annoying to me as I nearly killed myself batting the damned thing out and Miss Bigelow just sat there and put it on paper. She has just now been offered the position of chief play-reader for the Theatre Guild! About 12 grand a year.

We have a dainty little chameleon (lizard) in the house named Fairy May. She hides behind the oil paintings during the day but comes out in the evenings. Her tongue is twice as long as she is and she catches almost as many gnats and mosquitos as Bigelow does sailors.

Work hard, baby, and finish the book and get a big fat advance on it. We will do Europe this summer in the Jaguar! We will drive from Paris through Germany to Copenhagen in a blizzard of blonds. We will hit a tree at 90 miles an hour and our posthumous works will be on the Fall list.

I am impressed by Gore's new book. I cannot quarrel with your analysis of it, but I am deeply impressed by the cogency of the writing and the liquid smooth style. And I think your article proves that you can do a piece on him. Give him my love. Say that the bird gives her blessing.

Love, Tenn.

[Frank Merlo's "crowd" did not include TW: "It is 3 a.m. and Frank is still out - I've taken a sleeping tablet but I'll find it hard to sleep tonight. The same old dull tedious resentment and hurt - why do relationships have to be turned into duels. I don't want to fight - I want to trust and love and feel loved" (*Journal*, February/March 1952).

Reviews of Gore Vidal's "new" novel, *The Judgment of Paris* (1952), were mixed and the sales disappointing. John W. Aldridge wrote a condescending notice in the *New York Times*—as well as the literary study *After the Lost Generation* (1951), whose title TW applied to Merlo's "guys and dolls."]

231. To Cheryl Crawford

[1431 Duncan Street
Key West, Florida]
4/5/52
[TLS, 1 p. BRTC]

Dearest Cheryl:

I don't remember the date of your sailing but I have the impression it is soon, so Bon Voyage. Have a good time and a good rest and come back and not give a fuck, that's the only healthy attitude toward the present state of things here.

My trip to the Coast knocked me out, it was a dry run, there was really no point in going. Warners' stalled us with a lot of censorship objections and demands for revision without any signed contract. Audrey and Feldman think that Gadg's situation has a great deal to do with it. Gadg and Marlon and I were obviously screwed out of the Academy awards, and it was a hideous ordeal, sitting there with your bare face hanging out and pretending not to care. Gadg said he never saw anybody get so low in a chair, and I was afraid even to remove my flask from my pocket when Madame Clare Booth Luce got up on the platform and announced the writers awards. One part of me despises such prizes and the vulgar standards they represent, but another part of me wants to be "The Winner" of no matter what. When and how can we ever get over that, and have a dignified humility about us and a true sense of what matters?

I arrived on the Coast just too late for the L.A. stand of "Tattoo" but Audrey and Bill saw it and they said the performances were badly off, everybody was overacting and it wasn't the same show that it was in New York. Sorry to give you that report, but it was confirmed by practically everyone else, except Sheilah Graham who said it was "my best play". The San Francisco notices also seem to bear it out, one of them even complaining about Danny's staging. So "Tattoo" leaves me about where it found me, financially and morally, just as uncertain as before. That shows how demoralized I am. I should have some conviction about my own work.

If I were in good shape, "Camino" would be finished but I have only enough energy to work a couple of hours a day and the texture of the writing is very uneven, though formally it is very interesting, an extension of the free and plastic turn I undertook with "Tattoo". Nevertheless I will prepare a rough draft of the final version before I leave for Europe June 11th and I do want you to see it, although it seems unlikely to me that it will strike you as a play that could be profitably and economically produced, it is such a screwy thing and would have to be given a very dressy production. Of course Gadg will get the first look at it.

Frankie is having himself a ball. I'm just a bit cross about it, but he is like a kid at play and somebody ought to be having a good time in this sand-lot even [if] it can't be me.

Your loving Tenn.

[Warner Brothers advised TW that the principal characters in "Hide and Seek" (February 19, 1952, U of Delaware) must be punished "for their transgressions." The censor added wryly that "any suggestions of sadism, etc., such as Vacarro's whip, should be de-emphasized - and Baby Doll's bruises will need a little salve" (March 24, 1952, HRC). An early draft submitted to Joseph Breen drew an expression of "concern" regarding "the low and sordid tone of the story as a whole" (to J.L. Warner, August 1, 1952, Herrick).

Continuing investigation of Elia Kazan by the House Un-American Activities Committee apparently made "Hide and Seek" more difficult to sell to Hollywood producers.

TW attended the Academy Awards ceremony (March 20, 1952) as a nominee in the writing division for *Streetcar*. Vivien Leigh, Karl Malden, and Kim Hunter won Oscars, while Marlon Brando, Elia Kazan, and TW were "screwed," as the unhappy author put it. *An American in Paris* (1951) won Best Picture award rather than the heavily favored *Streetcar*.]

232. To Audrey Wood

[1431 Duncan Street
Key West, Florida]
4/14/52
[TLS, 1 p. HRC]

Dear Audrey:

Here is part one of a long story or novella which I started last summer in Venice and have been working on now and then since. I think it could be published separately, and I don't know when I'll have time to get back to it, with Camino to prepare and more work to be done on the screenplay, so I wish you would have this part of it typed up, and, if you approve, submit it to some magazine such as Harper's Bazaar or Madamoiselle.

I think it has the situation and characters for a play or a film, eventually. I spoke of it to Jay while he was here and he thought it would make a good title story for a collection of stories that he wants to bring out along with the selected poems. The rest of it exists in rough draft.

The Jaguar has gone from bad to worse. I think it is questionable that it could safely complete our extensive trip through the South, without drastic rehabilitation. So I was wondering if it might not be better to place it in storage and buy a new Ford, that is, if I can afford to. I'll call you about that from New Orleans. Also I would like yours or Colton's opinion about the advisability of renting the house while we're away. Frank says Colton doesn't think I should rent it, and of course I'd rather not unless the economic situation requires it. The Studio turned out well, is now completed, but the contractor exceeded his estimate by about six hundred to our painful surprise. It does enhance the property a great deal, though, is really a complete separate living-unit.

Gadg's ad in the Times is a very sad comment on our Times. Will call you from New Orleans, probably next week-end.

With love, Tenn

["Three Players of a Summer Game" appeared in *The New Yorker* on November 1, 1952, and was reprinted by New Directions in *Hard Candy: A Book of Stories* (1954). Its "situation and characters" anticipate *Cat on a Hot Tin Roof* (1955).

Elia Kazan's second appearance before the House Un-American Activities Committee (April 10, 1952) led to the naming of seven former Communist members of the Group Theatre, including the playwright Clifford Odets. Kazan's "ad" in the *Times* described his own brief membership in the Party and rationalized the disclosure of former associates as necessary "to protect ourselves from a dangerous and alien conspiracy" ("A Statement," *New York Times*, April 12, 1952).]

233. To Justin Brooks Atkinson

SH: Hotel Monteleone
New Orleans 12, U.S.A.
[early-May 1952]
[TLS, 1 p. BRTC]

Dear Brooks:

My secretary just read me your new review of the village production of "Summer & Smoke" over the phone from New York and I am so happy over it I must tell you and thank you, and at the same time, though it doesn't personally concern me, I want to commend you on the solitary stand you took for Capote's play. I didn't see it and haven't read it but I know it must have been a work of sensitivity and charm as nobody can write more delicately than that odd little boy unless it is Carson McCullers.

These times must be difficult for a critic as they are for a writer.

I have been working like a beaver, I made a long play of "Camino Real", wrote a movie script, a long story and a couple of short plays this winter and Spring. I am tired, but I feel better inside. I was worried before. I couldn't get going on anything that seemed important to me.

Affectionate regards, Tennessee.

[TW planned to spend several weeks in New Orleans before visiting Columbus, Mississippi, with his grandfather.

The revival of *Summer and Smoke* (April 24, 1952) at the Circle in the Square was directed by José Quintero and starred Geraldine Page in a role which established her career. The arena production, Atkinson wrote, revealed "a poignantly intimate play that penetrates deep into the souls of two bewildered young people" (*New York Times*, May 4, 1952). While Quintero momentarily replaced Elia Kazan as TW's "biggest hope" (*Journal*, June 10, 1952), the production ran for a year and helped to launch the off-Broadway theatre movement.

Notices for Truman Capote's play *The Grass Harp* (1952) ranged from mildly sympathetic to cruel and succeeded in closing the production after thirty-six performances. Atkinson alone found dramatic strength and timely wisdom in Capote's delicate "idyll" (*New York Times*, March 28, 1952).]

234. To Frank Merlo

SH: The Gilmer Hotel
Columbus, Mississippi
May 9, 1952.
[TLS w/ autograph marginalia, 3 pp. HTC]

Dear Petit Cheval:

As you see from the enclosed photo, we have arrived in my point of origin on this unhappy planet. Doesn't my face look spiritual and my figure a shame? I haven't weighed since I left the Key but I'm sure I must have put on six or eight pounds, eating with Grandfather in New Orleans. Oliver gained even more and is downright plump, or was when we left him there. The last time I saw him he was cruising a nine-foot giant, following him into tea-rooms to see if he was built in proportion. I thought it wise to go home as both Oliver and the giant were quite drunk. We have seen all of Columbus and met most of the prominent people. The men are nearly all like elderly editions of Peter Lindamood, that is, elegant Auntie types. The Lindamood mansion is one of the show-places of town. But it is not real anti-bellum and it looks like the administration building of a girl's college. They don't think much of Peter here, as they say he writes his widowed mother about once a year and has run through his inheritance. I am told that he invested the last of it in this property on 58th street and if that doesn't pay off he'll be broke. Also met Blanchard's twin brother who was in a dreadful condition, staggering drunk, looked about twenty years older than Blanchard. Their house is a real decayed mansion, the windowshades are hanging in shreds. Met the lady who has Lord Byron's love-letter, she is mad as a hatter, was sitting crouched in a dark corner when we arrived. And this afternoon I am to meet another maddie, a cousin of mine named Miss Sadie Lanier. She has just returned from one of her many little visits to the State Asylum. And this evening I am going out with one of the elegant Aunties, a Mr. Patty, to a big lawn party on a plantation called Sugarlock. He said the company would not be appropriate for grandfather, so grandfather is dining elsewhere. I guess it is the "gay" plantation. This old girl used to sing in the church-choir with mother and said she went an octave higher than anyone else and seemed pleased when I told her that she had now lost her voice. The homes, the interiors, are just incredibly beautiful, almost everything in them is a priceless antique. But the people's ideas are older than their furniture. I am sorry you missed this trip and hope we can take it together some other time, it is a strange part of the world and I feel as if I had always known it and I suppose I have.

The night spot, that is, the interesting one, is an old shack out on the highway called Bud & Dale's. Dale is a queen and Bud is a young lush and there are four B-girls, very pretty and all under twenty, and a great flock of boys from Mississippi State College which is 22 miles away. They all come in and hug Dale and fight over the four girls; inside liquor is forbidden, so they buy set-ups and drink outside. My Jaguar and quart of whiskey were a sensation but my popularity was excessive, there were so many around me that I couldn't get intimately acquainted with a single one, but I did get very drunk, stayed out till four A.M. and at seven grandfather was pounding my door with his cane. That was the morning this picture was taken, which may account for my expression.

If this sailor who's driving me from Memphis appears to be a good driver, I will only accompany him to the East coast, then let him drive the rest of the way alone and go ahead by train. I don't think I want to be with him long. He is one of a celebrated pair of love-birds in New Orleans, the two reigning beauties of the Quarter, and his conceit is second to none except his lover's. He shares the apartment of a poor little queen who is so unnerved by his charm that she shakes like a victim of cerebral palsy and she told me that one morning he slapped her because he woke up and found his shorts unfastened and thought she might have done him in his sleep. Both the two young lovers (not the martyred queen) are coming to New York expecting to set the town on its ears like nothing since the Rocky twins, and it will be a pleasure to see some of the bird-circuit bitches go to work on those girls and hone them down to life size.

We'll be in Memphis tomorrow night and hit the road for New York the next day or Tuesday, probably Tuesday. Anyway I'll call you before you get this letter.

Love - 10.

[The visit to Columbus, Mississippi, restored TW to his birthplace and Walter Dakin to friends and parishioners who fondly remembered his ministry at St. Paul's Episcopal Church (1905-1914). Although brief, the Columbus years formed the core of TW's southern childhood and his close relation with Rose.

Peter Lindamood was an aspiring writer who later returned to Columbus to care for his ailing mother. They were the last Lindamoods to live in the antebellum

Davis Patty, Walter Dakin, and Tennessee Williams, Columbus, Mississippi, 1952: "Doesn't my face look spiritual and my figure a shame?"

home built by the prominent merchant family. Lindamood was friendly with the poet Charles Henri Ford, who had lived in Columbus, and who is cited in present correspondence by an arrow pointing to the Gilmer imprint and the penned notation, "hotel Ch. H. Ford was thrown out of for having dark trade!"

Sadie Lanier, the mad relative to whom TW refers, is not listed in official public records of Columbus or Lowndes County, Mississippi. Social Security files indicate that several women of the same name died in Alabama and Arkansas in the 1960s.

TW visited the Harrison-Evans plantation located some forty miles south of Columbus near the former Indian village Shuqualak ("Sugarlock"). Davis Patty, who did indeed sing in the choir of St. Paul's, was TW's guide for the evening. Legend has it that the party at the so-called "'gay' plantation" supplied TW with lines spoken by Big Daddy in *Cat on a Hot Tin Roof:* "Twenty-eight thousand acres of the richest land this side of the valley Nile!" (Act Two).

A local historian has speculated that "Bud and Dale's" may be one of the so-called "home bars" which appeared during the Depression in converted houses or barns and which catered to different groups, including gay students from nearby Mississippi State University.]

235. To Walter Edwin Dakin

59 E. 54th Street [New York]
6/3/52.
[TLS, 2 pp. HRC]

Dear Grandfather:

I've been very busy since I got here. I had to do more work on the film script, then I had to prepare and give three public readings from my plays, stories and poems, then I had to get my play ready for typing, and all the social engagements, and seeing old friends, and so forth. This last week end I spent at Mrs. Bouverie's house in Rhinebeck. I'm sure you remember going there with me one time. I had a nice rest there. When I came back I had to give the third and final reading. I had packed houses for all three readings, and they say that they went off well. I was only nervous one time, the others I enjoyed doing it.

Frank's nephew Tony is being treated at the New Jersey state sanitarium. He has a mild form of dementia praecox. He and Frank are the same age and grew up as brothers so Frank is very disturbed over this and has to spend a great deal of time visiting him. The nephew is now taking insulin shock treatments.

I had to tell Liebling that he could not do my next play. So far there hasn't been any sign of resentment, but that may come out later. Kazan has left for Europe. He will meet us in Paris when we land. Then we'll have conferences on the production for next Fall, which will take place if he is pleased with the script. He hasn't seen it yet. Kazan was under great strain in New York. He had to testify before the committee and he gave the names of old friends who had been Communists when he was, fifteen years ago, and he feels quite guilty about it and left the country mainly on that account. It was a difficult thing to do, but he felt that it was a patriotic duty and so he did it.

I am feeling tired from all the activities and all the pressure since I returned to New York so the six days on the ocean will be a welcome rest.

We sail from here a week from Wednesday, June 11th is the date of the sailing. How I do wish that you were going with us this time! But I am sure you will be comfortable where you are. You must go to the mountains when it gets hot in Memphis. I imagine it's pretty warm there right now. We're not going to stay over long this time as we'll have to come back for the play if it's going to be produced in the early Fall. Frank and I will write you regularly from Europe. We'll have the old address, American Express in Rome.

I'm enclosing a check for June. Don't forget your solemn promise to me that you would spend and enjoy this money and not just put it away! You have a lot of money in your bank account and you must SPEND IT! - Audrey will mail check July & August.

Everybody enquires about you very fondly, Audrey, Bigelow, Irene, Cheryl Crawford, many others.

Do take care of yourself, and have a good time this summer.

Much, much love, Tom

[Anxious notations preceded TW's sailing on the *Liberté*: "I have been on edge for quite a while - very narrow margin indeed. Breathlessness at night, tension daily - diarrhea every A.M. F. has been pleasant enough but sort of separate. 'Camino' typed up - I havent dared read it yet" (*Journal*, June 10, 1952).

Canceled in the letterhead is the imprint of the Gladstone Hotel in New York.]

PART V
1952–1954

Overleaf: Elia Kazan examining the script of Camino Real *(1953).*
"You see form so clearly."

236. To Audrey Wood

[Hôtel du Pont Royal, Paris]
June 22, 1952
[TLS w/ autograph postscript, 3 pp. HRC]

Dear Audrey:

I must brief you very quickly on what has transpired in Paris between myself and the Turk. I was prepared for anything, but to my happy surprise he seemed to be very favorably impressed by the script and he says he wants to start rehearsals in late October. This suits me! I think it would be a mistake to put off this play till another season. Then it goes stale, I lose interest in it and so does everyone else. There isn't too much time to set up such a complicated production, but I think there's enough if we act with expedition. Gadg and I discussed everything but actors. We feel that Milzener ought to design unless a younger man appears who seems both original and safe. This should be investigated at once. Designs can be sent to me air mail special in Rome. Ballard should do the costumes. The composer: Alex North or Paul Bowles. Choreographer: Jerome Robbins or Anna Sokolov. Robbins is here in Paris and eager to see the script. All these people should start work early this summer, say, in early July. Gadg wants Cheryl to produce and I am inclined to agree with him, but I think she must forget economy in the initial expenditure and give the show a rich production, that must be thoroughly understood. Gadg says he will talk to her very frankly about it. I think her experience, her lack of other commitments or occupations, will mean a lot. The show will make great demands upon a producer, all of his or her time and capacity and experience, to organize it and keep things rolling smoothly among the various departments. This is not a show for anybody to make a debut in! I am sure, and have been sure for some while, that you and Bill would be most unwise to undertake it as your first venture into production. For one thing, I will need you to represent me versus producer. There are bound to be points of conflict where I will need protection strictly in my own corner, what with a tight producer and The Terrible Turk, although the latter has manifested, so far, only the lamb-like side of his nature. As for casting, I think Eli should have a script right away and be definitely committed. I would like for Stella Adler and perhaps Joseph Schildkraut to see the Marguerite-Jacques roles, but no commitments made yet. How about old Josephine Brown for the Gypsy? Or Old Prudence? I will return early, perhaps in August, so that there will be plenty of time for casting before rehearsals start. The important thing is to keep Gadg occupied with it. Producer must be settled immediately, I would say as soon as he and you have talked to Cheryl and she has studied the script and assessed the budget. Not later than two weeks. For the other people, designer, composer, Etc., have to be tied up soon as possible. You said in your wire that preparations should take "many months". Ideally, yes, I agree, but there are too many uncertainties to make such a postponement advisable. For one thing, my health and my nerves. I want to be around and fully competent when this play is produced, I think I have earned the price of my admission to the show, and I do want to see it. Then it is certainly wise to use Gadg when he is ready. . . .

Do you think there would be the remotest possibility of interesting Olivier and Leigh in the Jacques-Marguerite roles?

Gadg made some fine suggestions. He didn't like Marguerite's scene with the gigolo in the last block, as he said there needed to be something to clarify her change, so I have written another scene to go there which I do think is better. I have also rewritten the first Marguerite-Jacques scene (block two) to introduce more strongly the longing to escape which builds to the big funicular scene. The opera-comique scene is too long, but cutting it is going to be a delicate operation. Obviously the show is going to run too long and Gadg thinks we ought to have <u>five</u> weeks on the road. Remarkable coming from him. I should say at least four. He mentioned Chicago. I thought of Philly, Washington, and Boston. I think a total of 12 dancers, doubling in bits such as horses, dogs, streetcleaners, Etc., might be adequate but I have not yet studied the script from that angle. Costumes will be a large and important item, all the pictorial details have to be very well done, nothing skimped. That's why the production people have to get started pronto!

Maria arrives here tomorrow, with a broken heart, I suppose, and an empty purse. Rothschild surrendered 137,000 francs from his desk-drawer - for some reason we didn't go to the authors' league for the money! I wish you would get a statement directly from the Authors' League on what "Streetcar" made on its tour, which I thought was long and profitable. So far we have only gotten out of Rothschild-Tallant only about the equivalent of five or six hundred dollars, although from the Paris run, which we collected directly from the Society office, there were millions of francs, amounting to several thousands of dollars, I forget the exact figure, but there is a curious discrepancy of size in the two amounts, even granted that the road tour may have been shorter and less profitable than the run in Paris. Incidentally, I found a letter in one of my pockets containing a check for $427. from the "readings" I gave in the village. You can deduct your percentage at that end. I had not noticed the letter till we unpacked on the boat.

Talked to Carson on phone. She has moved into her country house called the "Ancienne Presbyterre" about six miles from Paris, and she sounded rather faint and wistful on the phone. We'll see her before we leave. Reeves sounded drunk, definitely not like a man on anti-buse unless he was about to go into a coma. Please send grandfather a check for $200. the first of July and again the first of August. He is expecting it! And has promised that he will not leave it to the Episcopal church but spend it lavishly on high living in Dixie. Much love -

Tenn.

P.S. I have not had time to write the "essay" they want for the recordings. Tell Miss Roney that perhaps she could use something from my introduction to the published version of "Battle of Angels." States my philosophy of art. I also told Leonard Lyons I would write a "guest column" for him. Do you think he would use, instead, a humorous poem that I will send? Please enquire. I am doing a piece for the Sunday Times magazine.

P.S. Sending revisions air mail on Monday. Only copies so please have typed and inserted in the scripts.

[TW and Frank Merlo landed at Le Havre on June 17 and spent two weeks in Paris before leaving for Rome.

Following their meeting in Paris, Elia Kazan assured TW of his willingness to stage *Camino Real* (1953) "just as is," but he urged revision and went on to draft a nine-page letter of "suggestions" (n.d., Columbia U). In "late October" TW was still trying to please "The Terrible Turk," rehearsals and production a dim prospect.

William Liebling's withdrawal as producer of *Camino Real* bore no visible "sign of resentment." Audrey Wood made the formal announcement at this time, reminding TW in later correspondence that her husband had "laid out approximately $5,000.00" (July 4, 1952, HRC) in preparation. TW planned to reimburse the expense, as a following letter indicates.

The "opera-comique scene" was designed in part to recall the legend of

Marguerite Gautier (Camille), the sentimental whore who renounces her love for a handsome youth to preserve his good name and family prospects. TW finally eliminated the scene at Kazan's request, but in preparing *Camino Real* for publication, he restored two figures—Prudence Duvernoy and Olympe—associated with Marguerite's Parisian days and her meeting of Armand Duval at the opera.

Maria Britneva joined TW in Paris and remained to play an uncredited part in the John Huston film *Moulin Rouge* (1952). She soon cabled TW in Rome: "'AT IT LIKE KNIVES. HUSTON A STEAMING HOT CUP OF TEA'" (TW to Wood, July 8, 1952, HRC). TW had been delighted to learn in the spring that she and James Laughlin planned to marry, "when he was 'free of other obligations'" (St. Just, p. 55). Laughlin's marriage with Margaret Ellen Keyser, then in the process of dissolution, and his continuing affair with Gertrude Huston, a book designer at New Directions, were the main impediments.

Carson and Reeves McCullers sailed in the preceding January, spent several months in Rome, and settled near Paris in the village of Bachvillers. Before leaving the States, Carson learned of her election to the National Institute of Arts and Letters. Elected at the same time were Eudora Welty and TW.]

237. To Cheryl Crawford

[Hôtel du Pont Royal, Paris]
6/29/52
[TLS, 1 p. BRTC]

Dear Cheryl:

I wired Audrey a couple of nights ago that I had seen Magnani and her manager and that both had assured me she wants very much to do Tattoo. Then I had lunch with her and she assured me again. She is willing to do it in America with either De Sica or Visconti. She said she would actually prefer Visconti because he is "more sensual" but she was afraid that his old association with the "C.P." might keep him out of the States, in which case De Sica would be quite acceptable. She says she won't be free of other commitments until May. I think it is essential to move on this with the utmost expedition, for La Magnani is a capricious woman, the iron is now very hot, and if papers can be drawn up and money is ready, I think she is in the bag. I am leaving this evening for Rome. Suggest you get in touch with me there right away if you are still interested in making the film yourself and can sign her up. I am supposed to see her there when I arrive.

I have prepared a revised draft of "Camino" and am sending it right away. This is the one I want you to read. Gadg seemed pleased with the first and said he wanted to go into rehearsal with it in late October and would see you as soon as he returned to the States for discussion. We both would like you to produce it, but are not sure that you will consider it a good financial risk, it will have to be budgetted very liberally to insure a full realization of its plastic values and of course it is a gamble. We both feel that you would understand it better than anyone else.

Do wish you were still in Europe, for this and the Magnani business!

Much love and also greetings to your fiance! Tenn

[Filming of The *Rose Tattoo* (1951) was delayed until late 1954 to accommodate "La Magnani," who finally agreed to play the role of Serafina. Ercole Graziadei informed Cheryl Crawford that his client's "last fee for a bilingual production" (August 1, 1952, HRC) was $90,000. Neither Vittorio de Sica nor Luchino Visconti would direct the film, nor did Crawford exercise her option to produce.

Audrey Wood warned Crawford, the eventual producer of *Camino Real*, that the play must "be done with artistic abandon and financial perfection." Crawford was enthusiastic, but she "spoke ruefully" to Wood of her "many succès d'estime" on Broadway, and of her need to have "both the esteem and the dough the next couple of times." *Camino Real* would require "further revision" (Wood to TW, July 4, 1952, HRC) to secure her interest.

TW closes with a playful allusion to Paul Bigelow, Crawford's unlikely "fiance!"]

238. To Elia "Gadg" Kazan

45 Via Aurora, Rome
7/14/52.
[TLS w/ autograph postscript, 2 pp. WUCA]

Dear Gadg:

First of all I want to say how lucky I think I am to have people like you and Audrey and Cheryl in my corner at this point. That this play should come off is of vital importance to me, and I am so happy and grateful that you are occupied with it! I received a letter from Audrey in the same mail as yours and I'm answering you both right now. I HAVE NOT YET GOTTEN YOUR NOTES! I presume they are waiting for me in Paris, at the American Express office. Perhaps it is just as well to let them rest there a few days, as I have just now, yesterday, sent my own revisions, about 22 pages of them, and perhaps you should digest those first before I take up yours. I am sure that yours will be good, as they always are, and stimulating to me, and you know how sincerely I welcome them from you. Cheryl's suggestions and criticisms will be very intelligent, and ably expressed, but I am not as sure that they will be as useful as yours, as I know she has a bias in favor of a certain element that is rarely present in my work. She expressed it best when she says she loves a "hot light" at the end of her shows. This play ends with a sort of "misty radiance" and I am not sure that will be, or can be, hot enough to suit her; if you dissolve the shimmer of mystery over this thing, you lose its fascination. It is up to me, now, to make the mystery of it appealing enough, evocative and fascinating enough, to satisfy a large and continuous audience. Of course it is also, perhaps even more at this point, up to you and the other artists who will be engaged in it. You are all correct about the problem lying in the Jacques-Marguerite story. I think I have gone quite a ways toward solving it, but there may be still further to go. What I am saying in their story is really a very clear and simple thing, that after passion, after the carneval (which means 'farewell to flesh') there <u>is</u> something else, and even something that can be more important, and we've got to believe in it. Philosophically that is about as far as I can carry their story without falsifying it, that is, without extending it beyond my own convictions. I tried to explain the play to Huston and Ferrer at lunch in Paris and I said it was a poetic search for a way to live romantically, with 'honor', in our times, royally under real conditions, and I think even as it now stands the play fulfills this aim. I want to keep away from a Maxwell Anderson sort of windiness and any sort of patness, make my points by evocation and poetic allusion. Great clarity does not come out of life, only people who die on the operating table die under a "hot light", and then it is quickly extinguished, and one is not even sure of a "misty radiance" except possibly in the recollections of one's more sentimental survivors! But perhaps I am anticipating an objection which I won't be faced with. There is very deeply and earnestly an affirmative sort of mysticism in this work, and I want that to stand, and I want it also to be a very new and enthralling piece of theatre which we can certainly make it, and that alone is a good deal.

Audrey is concerned about their losses as prospective producers which she says amount to about $5,000., including her trip to Europe. I don't want to impose this sum on the producer, whoever that may be, so I will assure her in this letter that I am willing to make it up out of my own earnings, perhaps by scaling up her percentage to the point where the loss is retrieved. I think she is right that Liebling shouldn't have to take this loss, and since it is really my responsibility, I ought to make it up. Her letter was full of good sense, honest, clear, and thoughtful.

I am very relieved that you are seeing Jo. While the other departments can wait if necessary, I think design is so important and complex on this show that it ought to be under consideration right away. Also explore Whitehead as possibility.

You can't believe the heat here in Rome unless you are sitting right in the middle of it! I have made train reservations for Hamburg on 18th. It will be easier to think and work there. Tomorrow I'm having lunch with Magnani's lawyer. She is not only willing but eager to do "Tattoo" in America in May. Do you know anybody who would like to pick up that package?

Did you see Geraldine Paige's performance in "Summer and Smoke"? Perhaps we'll get together in Bavaria if you start this summer.

I ran the Jaguar into a low concrete post but at a moderate rate of speed, so only one fender was smashed this time. I think Maria is "Shacking up" with Huston in Paris: don't breathe a word of it, dear! She wires that he is a "Steaming hot cup of tea!"

That's all the gossip at this end of the line.

With lots of mountain violets, Tenn.

Later - Audrey wired revisions haven't come worried as I mailed them July 8th air.

[Elia Kazan's "notes" reveal sharp disappointment with Marguerite Gautier's role, especially in the opera scene, which Kazan could direct only for "moment to moment effects." Kilroy was "basically excellent," he thought, but his disappearance in the "middle section" of *Camino Real* created "a big hole" and left uncertainty regarding "his story" (n.d., Columbia U).

The "bias" which TW ascribed to Cheryl Crawford is also evident in Kazan's "notes," soon to be read by TW, and in his subsequent letters of criticism, which did little to absolve the playwright of "clarity."

Jo Mielziner's anticipated collaboration on *Camino Real* would be his fourth with TW.

In later correspondence TW identified the closing imagery of "mountain violets" with the affirmative values of *Camino Real*: "tenderness" and "humanity of feeling."

The HRC holds a briefer, undated draft of this letter.]

239. To Gilbert Maxwell

[45 Via Aurora, Rome]
7/15/52.
[TLS, 1 p. HRC]

Dear Gil:

You know me too well to require an apology for my failure to function properly in any sphere of human activity. It will not surprise you to learn that I have your manuscript with me, that I take it out from time to time and peruse it privately to my great solace and joy. I did not get to give it to Laughlin, for he did not return to New York until the very evening before my sailing, and we had a five-minute session in a restaurant before I dashed off to my lawyer's to make certain arrangements in case I should perish at sea. I have been meaning, and wanting to, tell you what a great success your poems were. I only wish my own had been half so well received. "Go Looking" always got a big hand and so did "Forfeits" and "Hand To Mouth". I limited myself to three or four of them at each reading, as I also had to read from my own works, stories and plays. As you know, I read badly, but nevertheless the poems came across through their own inextinguishable merits and made a deep impression on that (Always) minority which comes with anything like a potential sensibility to lyric things. I have, as I said, the manuscript right here with me in Rome, as I thought if I had a chance to, I would start working on a short preface. However I could mail it directly to Laughlin if you prefer. I am only going to be here a few more weeks, as I have to return some time in late August for a prospective stage production in Early Fall. It would probably be better for me to keep the verse with me, and take it personally to Laughlin and give him the pitch as soon as I get back. Don't you think so? Fortunately good poetry is something that keeps, but I do feel most ashamed of not having let you know about this sooner.

Grandfather is in Monteagle, which is in the mountains of Tennessee, and Tennessee is on the plains of Rome. But leaving tomorrow for a brief visit to Germany, which I hear is both cool and gay, while Rome is just gay. Look forward to seeing you in the early Fall. Be good. Take care of yourself. Don't worry about the novel. You know you can do it, and I know you will!

Love, Tenn.

[Gilbert Maxwell (1910-1979) asked for TW's help in placing a recent selection of his poetry with New Directions.]

240. To James "Jay" Laughlin

SH: Atlantic Hotel Hamburg
7/24/52
[TLS, 1 p. Houghton]

Dear Jay:

I've had you on my mind ever since I got to Europe but I just haven't had much chance to write a letter. We spent about a week in Paris with Maria, and I have never seen her looking so well, the stay on the sea had done her a world of good, her vitality was such that I simply could not keep up with her. I left her in good hands. She had lunch with John Huston, Jose Ferrer and myself the day before I left Paris and from then on, I take it, they took up where I had left off and I think she is not quite sure which of them she prefers and gives me to understand that both are mad for her, which I do not find in the least inconceivable, do you? The Russians are mad!

I had a lot of work to do and Rome was getting too hot for it so I left there after about two weeks and came up here to Hamburg which is very cool and invigorating. I thought I would be unknown up here. Quite the contrary! Had no sooner registered than reporters were calling and I had lots of pictures taken this afternoon. Alas, for the anonymous joys of the gay cabarets! - This hotel is so swanky that one cannot bring in friends at night, so don't be surprised if my next book of poems includes a lot of bucolics and eclogues and fauns and satyrs among the moonlit trees! Just so it doesn't also include the "polizie". Hamburg is really madder than the Russians.

Gadg is giving me many notes for revisions on "Camino" so I don't know just when I will get to work on the poems, but I will as soon as possible.

Affectionate greetings to Gertrude.

Yours ever, Tenn.

[In February 1952 TW delivered fifty-odd poems to James Laughlin which were graded "A" through "E" by the author. Nearly all appeared in TW's first book of verse, *In the Winter of Cities* (1956).]

241. To Elia "Gadg" Kazan

[45 Via Aurora, Rome]
[July 29, 1952]
[TL w/ autograph postscript, 2 pp. WUCA]

Dear Gadg:

First I want to apologize for the letter I gave Frank to mail you this morning and which he has probably already mailed. I want to apologize for the cutting things I said about Jo. Not true! Comforting, momentarily, to me, but not at all true. By denigrating Jo's work, who is honest and sober and gifted, who certainly has no axe to grind in attacking my work, who has indeed on the contrary contributed more than his share to giving my work the success it has had, I am playing a shoddy game which is despicable of me, and I want, now, to face the facts about myself, which are that I have been floundering around most of the time since Streetcar, flapping my arms in the air as if they were wings. Then striking at Jo because he had the honesty to say that's what I've been doing most of the time. If you people, you, Gadg, and Cheryl and Audrey and Jo and Molly, still take me seriously as a writer it is mainly because of what I did in the past. I can't say what is the matter, why I accomplish so little. I work, God knows! But I'm not as "charged" as I was, not as loaded. I have a sort of chronic fatigue to contend with. I used to have, say, two good days out of seven. Now I have about one good day out [of] fifteen or twenty. I have to "hypo" myself into thinking that stuff is good. Otherwise I'd have even more trouble in working. I feed on delusion, beg for encouragement. In this situation the sensible thing to do would be to quit for a time, as so many writers have done, such as Rilke, and wait and pray for a new start, for a new vision, a regeneration of the tired nerve cells. But you see I committed myself completely to the life of an artist. I froze out almost everything else. I don't know how to live as anything else. Day by day existence demands that I be working at something and that I believe that it is worth while! I have not made a success of life or of love. And if my work peters out, I am a bankrupt person. The only things I really have left are the affection of certain friends like you and Audrey and Cheryl, and the little comforts of liquor and food and sex and books, and the occasional feeling that I am still able to function as an artist on a worthwhile level of competence. You won't agree with this, since it would not be kind to, but let's skip that and go on to a realistic consideration of what's to be done about the present situation regarding this play.

This play is possible because it deals precisely with my own situation. Perhaps that's why I go on with it, even though it's basically an old work, not a new one. I think it is very likely my last one. I almost hope that it is. Except for some unexpected thing that will restore my old vigor, it would be better to put writing away, after this last job, and settle for whatever I could get out of just existing. Not existing has no appeal for me whatsoever.

YOUR NOTES CAME THIS MORNING FROM PARIS. GADG, BELIEVE ME, THEY'RE BRILLIANT! Much better than the play. You see form so clearly. I am going right back to work on the J-M scenes. The most provocative notes are on the return from the Opera, the excited speculations about the "Fugitivo", or whatever we call it, going directly into the Byron scene, and then the clash between Jacques and Marguerite about the heroic gesture of going through the arch. This morning I did some work on the opera scene and on a new ending. I usually work best when I have just come to a new place. I am going to Greece with Oliver when he arrives, and will be working continually on the script while we travel. Building to the "Fugitivo" is a straight, clear line, like a rocket that explodes at the height of its trajectory.

If we keep to that line, the story will have unity & a cumulative tension & a real climax. I am terribly stimulated by these notes, fratello mio!

[After ten days in Hamburg (ca. July 18-28), TW returned to Rome with the thought that he "must be more understanding" of Frank Merlo: "What else have I got, after all, but the 'Horse' and my memories? and my work" (*Journal*, ca. July 28, 1952).

Awaiting TW in Rome were Elia Kazan's long-delayed "notes," written after the June meetings in Paris, and a subsequent letter from Kazan reporting Jo Mielziner's "'v. negative' reaction" to *Camino Real*. TW lashed out at Mielziner, decrying his lack of "enthusiasm" for the play and denigrating his recent work on "cornball musicals" (to Kazan, July 29, 1952, WUCA).

TW's latest rewrites of *Camino Real* had not, Kazan thought, solved "the problem" of Marguerite's vague motivation, nor had they "organically" integrated her "secondary" role with that of Kilroy, the presumed "emotional center" of *Camino Real*. Included with Kazan's "GENERAL POINTS" of discussion was a "SUGGESTED NEW OUTLINE" keyed to the play's "essential" story line: "How to die with dignity and honor and gallantry?" Kazan closed with a warning that Audrey Wood, Cheryl Crawford, and Jo Mielziner "all feel the confusion and lack of integration to a greater or less extent" (July 24, 1952, BRTC). TW "had hoped for too much," but he was "not crushed by this retrenchment" (*Journal*, July 29, 1952) of enthusiasm.]

242. To Carson McCullers

45 Via Aurora, Rome
8/?/52.
[TLS w/ enclosure, 1 p. Duke U]

Dearest Carson:

Your wire to Hamburg reached me just before I caught the train back to Rome. Hamburg was fascinating and I found that I liked the Germans surprisingly well in view of their reputation for bad conduct, but I got homesick after about a week, it was silly of me, but you know how one feels at times, and has to go running back where he came from even though it is actually no more home than any place else in the world.

Oliver Evans is some where in Europe but he is obviously annoyed with me and has not gotten in touch with me here. I think it is because I didn't wire him your address. He wanted to get the correct copy of that poem of yours that was badly mangled in "New Directions" as he wants to put it into the issue of Voices that he is editing and Laughlin has given permission but he doesn't have a true copy of the poem. Could you send one to "Voices" or to Oliver c/o me in Rome? I'm sure he'll turn up eventually and I can give it to him. What happened was that I didn't pick up my mail at American Express in Paris and it wasn't forwarded to me down here until just this week.

I'm enclosing still another fine notice of your book in England. Frank found this one in an English paper. It must have had a wonderful press there. Are you going to do anything about the dramatization of "Ballad"? After much initial enthusiasm, the interest in "Camino Real" seems to have subsided. Sober second thoughts, I suppose. It's awful how quickly a theatrical reputation declines on the market. A few years ago and I could have anything I wanted in the theatre, now I have to go begging. Two plays that didn't make money and, brother, you're on the skids! I wish we could spend a week or two working quietly together this summer, the way we did that wonderful summer in Nantucket, when you did "Member" and I did "Summer". The presence of someone else doing creative work is a comfort and a stimulation I think, for it is a lonely business. How is it on the estate? Is the dog having pups?

much love, 10.

[An earlier "notice" which TW sent to Carson McCullers described her as "such a mature writer that she makes most of her American contemporaries seem almost crude" (*The Observer*, July 20, 1952). Under review was an English anthology entitled *The Ballad of the Sad Café: The Novels and Stories of Carson McCullers* (1951).

In 1960 McCullers authorized Edward Albee to dramatize *The Ballad of the Sad Café* (1943). The final product disappointed her, as did the play's mixed reviews and brief run on Broadway (October 30, 1963-February 15, 1964). She later acknowledged that a lack of dialogue and action in the novella made it a poor subject for theatre.

Summer and Smoke (1948) and *The Rose Tattoo* (1951), the plays which had put TW "on the skids," lost $70,000 and $40,000, respectively, including the original Broadway show and tour.

Internal evidence suggests that TW wrote this letter on August 1 or 2, 1952, after returning to Rome.]

243. To Oliver Evans

45 Via Aurora, Rome.
8/5/52.
[TLS, 2 pp. HRC]

Dear Oliver:

What a relief to hear from you, I was afraid you might be in one of your Welsh rages because I had not responded to the cable and letter to Paris. I must explain about that. I did not call for mail at American Express in Paris, as I didn't expect any there. Consequently I missed the communications from you and also a long letter from Kazan, which led to serious misunderstandings. Finally all the Paris mail was forwarded to Rome, just last week, but you were already at sea so naturally I couldn't send you Carson's address or poem. Her address is "Ancienne Presbyterre", Bachivillers. Oise, France. She and Reeves came to Paris, both in a terrible shape. He was on liquor and sleeping tablets, she was on liquor. She said he had been threatening to kill himself and she must put him into a clinic. The next day she was threatening to kill herself and Maria was there and she didn't want me to leave the hotel with Maria because if we went out she was going to jump out of her window. It was all very upsetting. Then the next day she and Reeves went quietly back to the "Ancienne Presbyterre" but since then I have heard that they are going to sell that place and Reeves is in a clinic. I think if you can find a natural division between the two poems (they were simply run together in N.D.) that is all you need for Voices.

My dear, I was in Hamburg last week and guess who was staying in the same hotel! Miss Otis Taylor, the last of the Edwardian Aunties! We did the town together several nights, and I must say she is the most agreeable and charming company and I like her extremely much. There are three or four bars in Hamburg where the boys dance together and your sister did not miss a dance! She was the belle of the balls! Great strapping blonds whirled her about the floor to the Waltzes of Strauss, pursued her along the waterfront, kissed her among the ruins and seduced her incontinently between the cabarets. They would not allow her to rest. If they could not enter the hotel with her, which was, alas, often the case, owing to the manly roughness of their apparel, such was the heat of their passion that nothing would do but she must retire with them into the bushes. At one point she had to remain quite immobile, as if turned to marble, for about twenty minutes, in a peculiarly intimate pose with a Herculean blond who was resting his forehead on the trunk of a tree, while a policeman smoked a cigarette not ten yards away on the banks of the Alster. Eclogues and bucolics!

Why have you removed Athens from your itinerary? Miss Taylor says it is not to be believed, especially a certain park in the center of town. And aren't you coming to Rome? Please write me places and dates soon as you get this, so we can arrange to get together somewhere. I am about ready to take another trip. Rome is cool and lovely, now, and trade is abundant. You really must come here before you continue North, and Copenhagen is out of the question, completely, this summer, unless you already have your hotel reservations. The Olympic crowds. I walked and taxied all about Hamburg from midnight till five in the morning looking for a room where I could have a private conversation with one of my dancing partners. Not a room anywhere. At daybreak and after, we wound up in a whore house that rented us a bed for half an hour. You can't bring people into the good hotels after dark. And everything is booked up anyway. Better do southern Europe first, then make reservations for the northern places well in advance and don't go anywhere just expecting to find a room. Marian advised me by postcard from somewhere in Belgium that "she and Ed Birk and cousin Vac" are on the continent and going to Paris and then to Majorca. You'll probably run into them there. Let me know how that part of the continent is, I've never been there. The Jaguar is in good shape, we could take a trip.

Love, Tenn.

[Carson McCullers's threat of suicide did not detain or unduly alarm TW: "When I told her, Honey, sit tight, we'll see you later tonight, and whisked off to see Anna Magnani in preference to the big jump, I realized just what a hopelessly heartless old cynic I have become!" (qtd. in St. Just, p. 60).

Two poems by McCullers—"The Mortgaged Heart" and "When We Are Lost"—were accidentally "run together" when published in *New Directions Ten* (1948). Oliver Evans reprinted them separately in *Voices* (September-December, 1952), with a generous selection of poems by TW.]

244. To Liebling-Wood

SH: Western Union
Muenchen Via
1952 Aug 20
[Telegram, 1 p. HRC]

IN MUNICH WITH TERRIBLE TURK RETURNING ROME TOMORROW LOVE=

=TENNESSEE=

[Elia Kazan was in Munich to direct *Man on a Tightrope* (1953), a film whose timely subject matter was based upon the escape of a small, dilapidated circus from Communist Czechoslovakia. The "Terrible Turk" had invited TW to join him on location and draft "a rehearsal script" (July 24, 1952, BRTC) in accord with the new outline of *Camino Real*. TW thought it "a virtual return to the original script" and resented Kazan's intrusion: "I have fallen off remarkably in the esteem of my co-workers when they start dictating my work to me" (*Journal*, ca. August 17, 1952).]

245. To Ercole Graziadei

[45 Via Aurora, Rome]
September 6, 1952
[TL, 3 pp. Todd Collection]

Dear Dr. Graziedei:

Something happened yesterday evening which has caused me a good deal of perplexity and embarassment. A reporter from the Roman paper "Europeo" came to my apartment and asked me if I had any statement to make about the fact that my application for membership to the "Circolo de Golfo" had been turned down by the members. I was not sure that I understood him correctly, as he didn't speak English, so I asked my Secretary, Frank, to come into the room, and the reporter then explained that "some Ambassador" had told him that I had "tried to get into the club" and that the nature of my writing, particularly of my novel "The Roman Spring of Mrs. Stone" was so objectionable that the "application" could not be accepted.

I am sure you must know what a humiliating sort of experience this was, and I do hope that you can give me a little more light on the subject. The reporter had sent a photographer to take my picture. Fortunately I was not at home at the time, and of course I declined to provide him with photographs or any statement at all in this connection.

I think it should be very well known, by this time, that I am probably the greatest Italophile, and especially "Romanophile", among all the writers who come here from America. I have very truly and deeply loved the Italian people. In all the interviews that I have given to the press, to radio, to television, in all the countries that I have visited, I have never failed, and with the most sincere feeling, to express my love and my gratitude to this city and to Italy where I have spent at least a total of two out of the last five years. This comes, for that reason - if it is true! - as a most disconcerting and deeply wounding sort of a shock.

Believe me, Dr. Graziedei, I have done nothing whatsoever to offend the officials or members of the club. As you know, I go there only to swim. I have a heart condition that makes swimming essential to my health. I usually go there late in the afternoon, swim twenty lengths, dry in the sun, and leave. I have met practically no one there except some Americans such as Mr. Cushing and the Van Renssaelers. I have brought a few guests to the club, such as Noel Coward, Janet Flanner, Natalia Danesi Murray, all of whom have behaved with the most complete propriety while they were there. My own social habits are always and everywhere considerate of those around me. I am very reserved, by nature. This is the first time, in my social experience, that I have been subjected anywhere to any kind of social ostracism, and I must say that it strikes me as curiously uncalled-for.

If it is true that members have objected to my short novel, which has not been published in Italy but which has come out in several other countries and which has been warmly appreciated by excellent critics - if this is true, I suspect that they have either not read the novel or else have completely failed to understand it. The book is a serious psychological study of an unhappy

American woman. It does not deal with Rome except as a poetic background to the tragedy of a woman, whose materialistic ambition and interests in her former life had left her with no spiritual resources when her youth was gone and who consequently found herself drifting into an emotional wilderness when the sterility of her old preoccupations became apparent to her. Probably the most eminent critic in England, Cyril Connolly, the editor of the late Horizon, England's best literary review, and American critics and writers such as Cristopher Isherwood and Carson McCullers, have attested to the serious quality of this work, and I am confident that it will be seen in its true light, a book with a significant moral import, highly relevant to our times, when it is reconsidered sooner or later. It is even better known that my latest play "The Rose Tattoo" was a warmly affectionate study of those lovable traits that I have found in your people. As a matter of fact, some people have felt that I am too sentimental about Rome and Italy. I don't think so.

Of course it is true that I am not a conventional member of the "haute bourgeoisie". I was well-born and I have been well-bred, but like most artists, in America and everywhere else in the world, I have no use for money or class snobbishness. I suppose my private life is unconventional, but it is discreetly unconventional, and I have always observed the proprieties of any group that I am thrown with. I live according to fairly strict moral principles, and the predominant tone of all my work is deeply and instinctively moral.

I am not writing this as a plea for reinstatement at the club. I am sailing October 2nd and I have no present plans for a return to Italy. If the action of the club has been truly reported to me, I cannot help but regard it as a totally gratuitous "slap in the face" from a quarter where I would least expect it. Because you were kind enough to offer me the use of the pool (I have never applied for permanent membership: I paid for a 3 months guest-membership solely in order to swim there), I thought I would let you know what happened, or what this journalist told me that he had been told had happened. I would very much like to know if the report is true.

Of course I also hope to talk to you again, before I leave here, about the Anna Magnani - Tattoo situation. I have been working so hard on my new play, which has involved trips to Germany for conference with Elia Kazan, and which has left me completely exhausted, now that it is finished, that I have been more or less "out of touch" with that project lately. But I did hear recently from Miss Crawford who says that at least two important groups are very much interested in making the picture. My own interest is intense as ever, and now that the play is completed, I can give more attention to it than I have for the past month.

Please forgive me for troubling you with the other personal matter. But I'm sure you understand how something like that can hurt a person's feelings, especially when he knows it is not justified and when it casts a shadow over a place he has loved so sincerely.

Cordially

[TW was less than candid in appealing to Ercole Graziadei, who had introduced him to the private club and who was perhaps unaware of the event which now threatened disbarment: "The Mgr. called me from the pool to say 'guests had protested that Salvatore had gone in swimming without taking a shower'. Shouldn't have taken him out there. May result in loss of the pool which was my great and almost only comfort here this summer. Hate rich Italians!" (*Journal*, August 31, 1952). Salvatore Maresca, TW's former lover, reappeared during Frank Merlo's visit to Sicily (see letter # 256).

TW took revenge on the "'Circolo de Golfo'" by making it the retreat of a corrupt generalissimo in the latest draft of *Camino Real* (September 1952, HRC).]

246. To Audrey Wood

[45 Via Aurora, Rome]
9/12/52.
[TLS, 1 p. HRC]

Dear Audrey:

"To you from failing hands we throw the torch, Etc!"

Sorry about the delay but I have never felt quite so tired in my long and eventful life.

The Roman typist was terrible. It will have to be typed over, so I am sending you only one copy. Will edit and mail another copy to Gadg.

After much prompting and prodding, The Horse managed to get us bookings on the Queen Mary, sailing from South Hampton on October 2. I expect we'll be leaving here around the 20th so as to have a little time with Maria in London. She has a bit part in the Houston-Ferrer picture. We are going to store the car here, so we won't have to ship it back and forth.

Finally got a copy of Jack Dunphy's book. It is damned good. I really like his writing better than Truman's.

My own work has finally had social repercussions. I was informed that the members of the "Circolo de Golfo", a private club where I swim 20 lengths a day in a crystal-clear pool, would not accept me because of "The Roman Spring of Mrs. Stone". This news did not come directly from the club but from EUROPEO a picture-magazine. They arrived with photographers to get picture and statement from me. I gave them neither! Regret the pool but fortunately I was not kicked out till the end of the season.

With love, Tenn.

[Apropos of "failing hands," TW could find "no wings" in the revised draft of *Camino Real* which he mailed to Audrey Wood on September 15: "And such a long time on it! What a terribly tired old boy I've gotten to be" (*Journal*, September 6 or 7, 1952).

Jack Dunphy, a fiction client of Liebling-Wood, dedicated *Friends and Vague Lovers* (1952) to his companion, Truman Capote. The novel was fairly well received and reminded one critic of *The Roman Spring of Mrs. Stone* (1950) to which it bears a passing resemblance.]

247. To Jo Mielziner

[Hotel Excelsior, Naples]
[September 1952]
[TLS, 2 pp. BRTC]

Dear Jo:

Thanks for your letter and please forgive me for not replying sooner. I was in Germany when it arrived, conferring with Gadg in Munich, and after I returned there was a great deal of work to do. If the script is still not right, it isn't because of any lack of effort, I can assure you. I have virtually devoted a whole year to work on this one project. I'm not sure I should have. It never fails to excite me, but I think it is much the hardest thing I've ever tried to do. Now I've mailed a fairly definitive script to Audrey. I think this one is close enough to the final version that it should be submitted to producers, designers, Etc. as a basis for yes or no. I'm not saying it's good, I'm just saying it's just about the best that I can do with it, and I've said the same thing to Gadg. Gadg and I talked over the phone yesterday and we spoke of you and Gadg feels that you shouldn't commit yourself on the basis of "potentialities" (what the play <u>might</u> be) but how you feel about it as it now stands. He thinks you ought to feel really satisfied with it - "enthusiastic" was his word - before you undertake to design it. I think we have to have an atmosphere of enthusiasm in order to contend with this very difficult project. That doesn't mean we have to say a lot of flattering things that we don't mean about it but simply that anyone engaged in it has to feel a genuine - what's the word? - emotional alliance with it. It can't be just another job for anybody. I know you don't take "jobs" but Gadg and I were both afraid you might out of loyalty, or something like that, want to undertake it without being really keen on it, and that wouldn't do.

I think the basic scenic problem is much what we talked about before. This is an intensely romantic script, and it needs a magic background. Real visual enchantment! - both in the set and the lighting. The set no longer has much technical difficulty. Fundamentally, it is just a plaza contained by three facades and three arches, one for the alley-way-out through the "Arch of Triumph", and two "Moorish-looking" arches downstage right and left. There is <u>one</u> interior the Gypsy's which could be dropped in or pushed in from the wings. The important thing is the visual atmosphere of a romantic mystery. I can't visualize your idea of a "bear-pit" and it doesn't strike a responsive chord. It doesn't sound beautiful, and I think the plaza should have the haunting loveliness of one of those lonely-looking plazas and colonnades in a Chirico - not <u>like</u> that but being emotionally evocative and disturbing to that degree.

Audrey will give you a copy of the new script, and that has more details in it about the design. But the important point is the one of "visual enchantment", and I do think there should be a single set (aside from the Gypsy's interior) which is changed only by lighting. That, of course - the lighting! - will be terribly important. I don't need to say so. - There won't be any spatial problem as there was with "Summer and Smoke" as you have a whole plaza, a few tables on a low terrace at one side, a small fountain in the middle, as the only things to occupy the exterior space aside from the actors and dancers.

I'm sailing Oct. 2nd on the "Mary". Gadg will be in New York a week later than I get there. I do hope you will have thought this out, whether you feel enough real interest or stimulation to work well on it and what you want to do with it if you <u>do</u>, when we get there, as it will be necessary to get organized very quickly if we have a production this season.

So far no producer is set, as scripts haven't gone out. I think Lucinda will probably be sent a script at the same time.

Ever, Tennessee

[Jo Mielziner (1901-1976) "felt like an ungrateful dog" for having criticized *Camino Real*: "I suppose it was my desire to have this be your greatest script of all." He suggested a "'labyrinth'" or "bear pit" to convey Kilroy's entrapment and hoped to use "projected images and patterns and colors" (to TW, August 26, 1952, HRC) to advance the various blocks. Mielziner's sets for *The Glass Menagerie* (1945), *Streetcar* (1947), and *Summer and Smoke* (1948) had deftly realized the psychological effects of restricted space, apparently the same challenge which he foresaw in *Camino Real.*

TW wrote this letter in Naples, probably in mid-September 1952, after completing the latest revision of *Camino Real.* As planned, he and Frank Merlo sailed from Southampton on October 2 and landed in New York on the 7th.]

248. To Gilbert Maxwell

"NIX ON NIXON CLUB"
59 E. 54th Street
New York, N.Y.
October 8, 1952
[TLS, 1 p. HRC]

Dear Gil:

I think some day you should write a book in the style of your letters, perhaps a book of letters about bringing culture to Miami in the fifties! (The decade, my dear, not your age!)

I have your poems, safe and sound, but Laughlin is knocking about the Orient for the Ford foundation which is getting out a journal of which he is editor, it is to be a compedium of world letters, and he is the hatchet man in the Far East at this moment. I read the poems to myself and aloud to guests. Go Looking, October Schoolroom, The Terrapin, are probably my favorites, but so many are lovely it's hard to choose. I can't guarantee that Laughlin, with his very modern bias, will be altogether sympathetic to the traditional lyric tone of most of these poems, but if he isn't, there are other houses. I've only been back two days, and Laughlin doesn't return till late November. Miss Bigelow is here. She has a rather ambiguous sort of a sinecure at the Theatre Guild. Nobody quite knows what her position is, but I did see her literally spring up two flights of stairs to fetch Miss Helpburn a pack of Parliament cigarettes, for which gallantry she was rewarded by the sour comment that actors would smoke them up if they were left on the table. It seems that she had her name as co-producer on one of the playbills at Westport this summer. Perhaps she is really working into something there, but on the other hand she may be working out of it just as fast. She is very brisk and important, you'd hardly know Our Polly, and has put on a good deal of weight. You'd better send her the Mayo's diet. I took her to lunch. (She invited me) She had Hungarian goulash with noodles, a side order of French fries, a large salad and a butterscotch meringue pie. I had a lean lamb chop and lettuce with lemon juice, and that is the price we pay for our perennial figures! Are they worth it?!

I don't share your enthusiasm for Dick Orme. He is amusing and agreeable but can be a terrible bitch! Joel Harris I do like a great deal. Do you know Mary at Lafitte's, the former co-partner?

How long I stay here depends on whether or not the play just finished is to be produced this season, and that will not be quite definite till Kazan returns from Europe the end of this month. If it doesn't go on this season, I'll be seeing you about cranberry picking time and we can sell 'em together, with four arms. The old gentleman is enduring Saint Louis till we fetch him South again. I have been sending him an allowance of $200. a month to supplement his rather meagre pension from the Episcopal church. Yesterday Mother sent his last check back to me, saying he didn't need it since he was staying with her. I doubt very much that both of them are still alive in that house! - Love -

10.

[TW remarked earlier that Richard Nixon, the Vice-Presidential nominee, "looks like the gradeschool bully that used to wait for me behind a broken fence and twist my ear to make me say obscene things" (to Kazan, August 23, 1952, WUCA).

James Laughlin was the general editor of *Perspectives USA* (1952-1956), a publication financed by the Ford Foundation and primarily distributed abroad in foreign language editions to represent "the intellectual and artistic life of the United States" (qtd. in *New York Times*, April 7, 1952). Several stories by TW were reprinted in the quarterly, including "Three Players of a Summer Game" (1952).

Gilbert Maxwell's fourth collection, *Go Looking: Poems, 1933-1953*, was published by Bruce Humphries, Inc., in 1954. In a brief preface TW described the author as "a lyric talent of the first magnitude."

Paul Bigelow served primarily as co-director Terry Helburn's assistant at the Theatre Guild.

Richard Orme, Mary Collins, and Joel Harris were New Orleans figures associated with TW. Orme owned the property at 632 St. Peter Street which TW rented in 1946, while Collins was a co-owner of Café Lafitte in the French Quarter. Joel Harris was the grandson of Joel Chandler Harris, author of the Uncle Remus stories.]

249. To Elia "Gadg" Kazan

[59 East 54th Street, New York]
[October 1952]
[TL, 1 p. HRC]

Dear Gadg:

I do hope you are hurrying back here. Cheryl is eager to get started on the production which is quite natural since there is so much to be done, but she is making plans and decisions, I am afraid, that you ought to have a part in. I had a short letter from Jo. He says he is now "enthusiastic", but I know that Cheryl considers his fee too high and doesn't want to use him. She is also against Lucinda. She showed me a bunch of costumes sketched by some young man she's discovered. They look good to me. But all these matters should be considered by you. I don't feel that my position is at all strong without you. She says she has budgetted the show, tentatively, at $140,000. and it can break even at $19,000. These figures sound reasonable but my judgement in such matters is very incompetent, and this desire to get things at cut-rate, which is still manifest in the lady, is something that you can cope with much better than I. On the other hand, I think she is genuinely excited, now, over the project. How soon can we expect you on these shores?

This week-end I went to Philly to see the new Arthur Laurents play starring Shirley Booth. The play is thin, but pleasant and seems to appeal to the audience. Shirley magnificent in it. I was greatly impressed by Ben Edwards' set, it was practical, free, and imaginative, and he had lit it extremely well himself. I thought I'd mention this as I know you like his work, too. There's an Italian actor in it, DiLucca, who would make a fine Casanova.

Cheryl has a list of actors. Two I liked were Isa Miranda for Camille, March or Boyer for Casanova. I don't like the idea of using Merighi (the fat woman in Rose Tattoo) for the Gypsy, do you? I think the Gypsy and Old Prudence could be played by the same actress. I thought of Josephine Brown.

Still working on script, taking it to St. Louis with me for a few days visit with Mother and Grandfather.

Refrain: when do you get back?

Love,

[Added to Jo Mielziner's newfound "enthusiasm" for *Camino Real* was confidence that its "difficult production problems" could be solved with "imagination" and "ingenuity" (to TW, October 2, 1952, BRTC). Mielziner's withdrawal from the project—a "bitter disappointment" to the designer—was presumably caused by a "tight time schedule" (to TW, November 19, 1952, BRTC) rather than the producer's inflexible thrift. Lucinda Ballard designed costumes for *Streetcar* but not *Camino Real*.

The Time of the Cuckoo (1952) played in Philadelphia for two weeks (September 29-October 11) and ran for a season on Broadway. The novice producer Irene Selznick had closed the original version of the show—"Heartsong"—in Philadelphia in 1947. No actor cited by TW was cast in *Camino Real*.

TW wrote to Maria Britneva on October 25 following a brief visit to Clayton: "Dinky Dakin, sister Rose with attendant, Grandfather and Mother were all there, one big happy family! I am still alive" (qtd. in St. Just, p. 61).

When Elia Kazan returned to the States in early-November, he was singularly bent upon work and defying former friends and colleagues who had scorned his cooperation with the House Un-American Activities Committee. "Only the discerning few could see what I was saying by my behavior: 'You can't hurt me; you haven't penetrated my guard; I can beat you at any game you choose to play'" (Kazan, p. 484).

TW wrote this letter after returning from Philadelphia, perhaps early in the week of October 12, 1952.]

250. To Elia "Gadg" Kazan

[59 East 54th Street, New York]
[late-October 1952]
[TLS, 1 p. HRC]

Dear Gadg:

As Irene might phrase it: "This is to clarify my position" as stated in the cable I sent you yesterday from Audrey's office after reading her copy of your letter to Cheryl. Your letters are so portentous that they are being ~~distributed~~ passed among us like the one eye of the fatal sisters!

I am very, very disturbed by the fact that you say that you have not read the script but that it has been read by Freddie and Molly with a disfavor which I suspect you are under-stating.

I'm not going to give you any kind of a pitch for the play. Communication between you and me can be on a level where total honesty and simplicity prevail, for we are both about equally grown-up and knowing. I don't like being treated like a sensitive plant. I want to have it straight. I think I have already proved that I can take it.

I find it difficult to believe, anxiety and uncertainty notwithstanding, that there _is_ still some irreconcilable difference in what you expect of the play and what I have given it. I haven't stopped working on the script a single day since the present draft was typed up and shall doubtless continue to work on it till it opens on Broadway, but of course the possibility must be faced that you have some basic objection which I, with all the willingness in the world, might still find myself unable to satisfy. And here I am sort of hung-up in New York, you in Europe, Grandfather in Memphis, the lease running out on the apartment and a new one to be signed or not signed almost immediately and some disposition to be made of the old gentleman and ourselves, Etc! Therefore it would be enormously valuable for you to refresh yourself, temporarily, in some way, just long enough to give the script one reading and let me know the extent of your dissatisfaction with it. I am sending you a set of the changes which I have made since the script was typed up - c/o Twenty-Foxes in Paris. They mostly affect the Marguerite material - blocks 12 & 13 - and Audrey and Cheryl feel they make a real improvement. I have greatly shortened the post-Gypsy scene between Jacques and Gutman and I am thinking of changing the position of Jacques' letter-scene in Block Five as it seems to impede the flow there. Perhaps it could be worked into the very first scene of the play in a condensed form. So you see I am not stopping work on play. I know there is work to be done. I only want to know if the work you want done and the work I want done can be brought close enough together to make it possible for us to put the show on this season. Can you give me "an estimate" real soon?

Love, Tenn.

[Fredric March, who starred in *Man on a Tightrope*, and Molly Kazan, Elia's wife, were the unwelcome critics of *Camino Real*. TW described Molly as "a pain" in her husband's "derriere" and as his own "bête-noir" (qtd. in St. Just, pp. 71 and 69).

"Communication" with TW was especially close after Kazan's damaging testimony in Washington: "We both felt vulnerable to the depredations of an unsympathetic world, distrustful of the success we'd had, suspicious of those in favor, anticipating put-downs, expecting insufficient appreciation and reward. The most loyal and understanding friend I had through those black months was Tennessee Williams" (Kazan, p. 495).

"Blocks 12 & 13" (Block Ten in the published text) of *Camino Real* bring the relationship of Marguerite Gautier and Jacques Casanova to a bittersweet finale, as she rejects his offer of love and departs for an encounter with a youthful hustler.]

251. To Edwina Dakin Williams

SH: *The* Robert Clay
Miami, Florida
Nov. 9, 1952
[TLS, 2 pp. HRC]

Dear Mother:

I am here at the Robert Clay hotel in Miami for a short rest as the state of indecision about the play production had gotten on my nerves. Kazan arrives in America this Tuesday and I won't know until a day or two later whether or not he is satisfied with the play script as it now stands. I thought it was better to let him and Cheryl thrash out their difficulties alone, with me at a restful distance till the decision is made. Of course if Gadg (Kazan) is now satisfied with the script and can reconcile his views with Cheryl's, I will return in about a week to start the production with them, but if an agreement isn't reached or if Gadg wants a good deal more work done on the script, I will procede to Key West and open the house there and Frank will come on down to join me. I think it is more likely, though, that I will be called back to New York. Before I left I wired Grandfather that I was coming down here, for at least a while, and have invited him to join me if he wishes to. I had to do this as I told him in St. Louis that we would be coming South in about two weeks. Now I would like to know if you feel able to stay with him in Key West (with Susie, of course) if I do have to go back to New York for the production. I feel that Key West would be better for grandfather than New York at a time when both Frank and I will be pretty occupied with all the goings-on that are attendant on preparing a new play. If you can't make it, or Susie can't and you don't want to settle for Leona (our old maid, there) - I will take Grandfather back with me to New York. We have the bedroom for him even if we stay in the present apartment, and we've found another larger one which we will take if it's still available by the time a decision about the play has been reached, probably Wednesday or Thursday. I will be glad to pay Susie's salary ($35. a week) and transportation if you bring her down here with you and whatever other extra expenses are involved and my friend Gilbert Maxwell, who teaches here in Miami, can see about finding a place for Susie to stay here before you'd go on to Key West, or I could do that myself, since I could probably wait here till you arrive.

I sent Grandfather a special delivery letter last night explaining the situation. I hope he doesn't find it too confusing. I'm sure it will all work out, one way or another. My main consideration is making a comfortable arrangement for you and him. It would not be difficult, now, to have him in New York as I'm not likely to have much more work to do at home on the play, if the production starts now.

Incidentally our new dog has arrived, an English bull puppy only six weeks old, named "Mr. Moon". He is even cuter than Jiggs, is "paper-trained" and bursting with energy, a voracious eater, and addicted to cutting his teeth on shoes, trouser-cuffs and telephone wires. We have a little whip called a "persuader" to break him of these obnoxious habits. He gets up at daybreak and complains loudly till he is let out of the kitchen where he sleeps, but I don't suppose Grandfather would hear him and these anti-social practises will be corrected in time. Please write or wire soon as possible your plans. With love -

Tom.

[The "difficulties" faced by Elia Kazan and Cheryl Crawford were primarily financial, as TW noted in prior correspondence: "He demands an expensive production {of *Camino Real*}, she wants a modest one. I am sick of the whole thing and longing for Key West or Europe again" (qtd. in St. Just, p. 65). He warned Kazan that we may "find ourselves out of a producer unless some compromise can be effected between your prodigality and her caution" (October 21, 1952, WUCA). Crawford later reported that *Camino Real* was capitalized at $125,000, with the financial support of associates Ethel Reiner and Walter P. Chrysler, Jr.

While in Miami TW worked on a "double-volume" of poems and stories as requested by James Laughlin. In correspondence with Robert MacGregor, Laughlin's editorial assistant, TW listed eight of the nine stories which eventually appeared in the collection *Hard Candy* (1954). "Kingdom of Earth" (1954) was tentatively penned in the margin and would require special treatment when published (November 9, 1952, Houghton).

"Jiggs" was the most petted of the Williams family dogs.]

252. To Paul Bowles

[1431 Duncan Street
Key West, Florida]
[January 1953]
[TLS, 1 p. HRC]

Dear Paul:

I'm writing you from my studio in Key West and the stains on the paper, the last remaining sheet on my work-table, are from an attempt at oil-painting. This is a heavenly place to work at anything creative. The studio is only one-room but is a complete living-unit as there is a bathroom built onto it and numerous electric outlets. A sky-light and jalousies on all sides and a ventilator fan for the hot days, lots of book-shelves and cabinets. When you're in America you and Janie must visit us here. Or you could occupy the house while we are away, either or both. The social life of the island is something appaling. I have given it up. I simply go to the movies and home to bed - after supper. The sky is constantly changing, the weather is soft and lovely and at least four days out of a week the water is perfect for swimming. I wish you would tell me more about your island in the Indian ocean. Why would I love it? Are the people beautiful and friendly? The next time we go abroad, which will be in the late Spring this year, we will plan to stay much longer, perhaps for a whole year or nine months, as I will not have another play next season and also because I don't want to do much writing. I want to rest from it a while as I haven't stopped for more than a week or two in the last fifteen years and I think the brain-cells are exhausted. That is if there are any such cells left in my personality complex! I think you are wise to come back to America for a while now, even if only to see what you are missing when you're away. Frank, Audrey, and I worked very hard on Gadg to get you for "Camino" and if the show had been put off till next season, as seemed likely at one point owing to the determined resistance of Gadg's wife, we might eventually have won him over. He does like your music, but I think he and Molly Kazan have a real phobia about your writing. This comes from Molly, not Gadg. She is a dedicated person, the self-appointed scourge of Bohemia, and the year that "Sheltering Sky" came out, she sent us a carbon copy of a vitriolic review of it that she was trying unsuccessfully to market. It seemed to obsess her. I can't help thinking this attitude toward your writing has influenced Gadg against you as a composer. So far we have no composer and I doubt that there will be any original score. Probably we will just have a guitarist and selected tunes, although the play needs a score more than any other I've written. Gadg's tactical position is now very strong, and mine relatively very weak, as everything he has done has made money while my last two plays, Summer and Tattoo, have both lost money.

We saw a good deal of Janie in New York. She seems unusually well, is getting a little plump, and her play is going forward. She has a new third act. I haven't read it yet but she and Audrey both feel it is a distinct improvement. I finally got hold of "Two Serious Ladies" and it is one of my very favorite works of all time, it is altogether original and has a reality all its own, which is fearfully real. We have acquired an English-bull puppy named Mr. Moon who will be travelling with us from now on, poor creature, wherever we may go. Luckily he is blessed with an amiable nature.

Love - 10.

[TW spent the holidays with his mother and grandfather—and with Frank Merlo as well—in Key West and planned to return to New York in mid-January for rehearsals of *Camino Real*. Tryouts in New Haven (February 23-28) and Philadelphia (March 3-14) would precede the Broadway opening on March 19, 1953.

Paul Bowles composed music for *The Glass Menagerie* and *Summer and Smoke*, later for *Sweet Bird of Youth* (1959) and *The Milk Train Doesn't Stop Here Anymore* (1963). Bernardo Segall wrote the incidental score for *Camino Real*.

Correspondence between TW and the Kazans in the preceding December marked a crisis in plans for a spring production of *Camino Real*. Molly Kazan accused TW of having used his own "desperate" identification with the play as a "psychological weapon" against "friends and colleagues." She challenged him to "identify" instead with an audience and to write a first act with a climactic "carryover for Kilroy" (December 9, 1952, HRC).

Elia Kazan's "tactical" strength—occasioned by successful film work—was evident in the copious "suggestions" for revision of *Camino Real*, as repeated in recent correspondence. Kazan also urged TW to write a coherent first act—"You can forget the second act till rehearsal"—and accurately foresaw the consequences of failing to do so: "Thousand-odd people leaving their seats for the intermission not knowing what the hell we brought them to the theatre for in the first place" (December 10, 1952, HRC).

TW refers to Jane Bowles's play, *In the Summerhouse* (1953), and to her novel, *Two Serious Ladies* (1943).]

253. To Justin Brooks Atkinson

["on the train"]
March 24, 1953.
[TLS w/ marginalia, 1 p. BRTC]

Dear Brooks:

First of all, I want to thank you, as usual, for one of my most discerning and sympathetic notices, but then I want to ask you why, since you have seemingly understood so much, you have failed to understand a little bit more this time? I can't believe that you really think I have painted the world in blacker colors than it now wears, or that it is melancholia, psycopathic of me, to see it in those shades, and surely the final scenes of the play must have conveyed their true meaning which is far from negative, and which I truly believe: namely, that tenderness, humanity of feeling - "the violets in the mountains" - give the dying animal a sort of after-life, or triumph over his death. It seems to me that that point is almost too clear, too coarsely stated. I wanted no one to miss it. I think it makes this play the most affirmative one I have written. It may have been implicit in the others, I think it was, but here it is fairly shouted.

Pride tells me to keep a stoic silence about my hurt, but I don't think pride should prevail in my relations with you, the one who has most bravely, consistently stood by me in the past and for whom I have such grateful affection, in whom I feel such trust, and from whom I have no secrets as imperfect artist and person. Has this play alienated your old regard for my work? Do you feel as others that it is a "mish-mash" of muddy symbols and meaningless theatricalism, were you pulling your punches? No matter what you say, I think it would help me at this dark moment if you would level with me. All of us felt, reading your notice, that you had things to say that you were refraining from saying, perhaps out of kindness, perhaps because you weren't sure.

I wanted to talk to you before I left town. Shyness prevented me from calling you myself but Margo said she tried to reach you but couldn't. - I'm writing this on the train, going back to Key West where I hope I'll be able to pick up some other work, now that nothing more can be done to help this one. It helps me to write you this and would help me still more if you feel inclined to answer.

Ever, Tennessee.

[Invective and ridicule dominated the opening-night reviews of *Camino Real.* It was, John Chapman wrote, "an enormous jumble of five-cent philosophy, $3.98 words, ballet, music, symbolism, allegory, pretentiousness, portentousness, lackwit humor, existentialism and overall bushwah" (*New York Daily News,* March 20, 1953). Atkinson was undaunted by the complexity of the play and judged the lyrical effect to be "as eloquent and rhythmic as a piece of music." He was shocked, however, by TW's "pessimism" and revolted by the "psychopathic bitterness" of *Camino Real.* His closing would not be quoted by any publicist: "Even the people who respect Mr. Williams' courage and recognize his talent are likely to be aghast at what he has to say" (*New York Times*, March 20, 1953).

Typed in the upper margin is TW's name and Key West address.]

254. To Walter Kerr

1431 Duncan Street
Key West, Fla.
March 31, 1953
[TLS, 2 pp. SHS of Wisconsin]

Dear Mr. Kerr:

I'm feeling a little punch-drunk from the feared but not quite fully anticipated attack at your hands and a quorum of your colleagues but I would like to attempt to get a few things off my chest in reply. Your original notice was too factually inaccurate, in a seemingly cynical way, to be answerable at all, but your Sunday notice, although equally adverse to the play, does seem to indicate some serious attention.

One night out of town Kazan and I were speculating about the probable critical reception in New York and I recall saying that I thought we would only get two good notices but that one of them would be Kerr's.

I was not at all sure of getting Atkinson's, because, although he's always been my main stand-by in the past, I felt that Brooks, although he's scrupulously fair toward anything he reviews, would be appalled by the episodes of decadance and brutality, - which he was, but which, as usual, he did not allow to prejudice his estimate of the work as a whole.

What I would like to know is, Don't you see that this play - as a concentrate, a distillation of the world and time we live in - surely you don't think it is better than a night-mare!? - is a clear and honest picture?

Two: don't you also recognize it as a very earnest plea for certain fundamental, simply Christian, attributes of the human heart, through which we might still survive?

Three: have you no appreciation of the tremendous technical demands of such a work, its complexities and difficulties, and at least the technical skill with which all of us involved in the production have managed to meet them? - As far as I remember at this moment, you made no mention more than perfunctory of music or choreography or the great plastic richness contributed by the designer, Lem Ayres, and you certainly did not go a step out of your way to give due tribute to such brilliant performances as Wallach's and Barbara Baxley's. Surely they had nothing to do with whatever alienated you from the play itself and I, who am hypercritical of all performers in a work of my own, can think of no performances but Laurette Taylor's that were so luminous and touching. And how about the work of Kazan? To undertake this play took a very notable courage, since no director ever tackled a play more difficult, and there were pieces of staging in it the like of which I know, and you know, that you'll wait many and many a season to see again.

To sum up:

Mr. Kerr, I believe in your honesty! I believe you said what you honestly think and feel about this play, but I don't think you fulfilled your entire obligation as a critic, since I think you didn't try very hard to encompass intentions and attitudes that are not and should not necessarily be coincident with your own. I hope I am talking sense to you. I am almost too tired and baffled to know what I'm saying, but that is only since March 20th. I did know what I was saying and doing in "Camino Real" and that it is one of my three best plays, that I worked on it two years for no financial profit but the two thousand dollar advance. Kazan and Ayres and I all waived royalties immediately after the N.Y. opening, and were all

Lemuel Ayers, full set design for Camino Real *(1953).*

taking the minimum. (This is a rather squalid parenthetical comment, but I want you to realize that this was not a big money-making scheme, if you had any such misapprehension about it! And Cheryl Crawford lost forty thousand on Rose Tattoo and stands to lose about three times that much on this one.)

If I had not been deluged, literally, with letters and wires expressing outrage over the play's critical reception, far more than for all my other plays put together, and if so many people had not come up to me after performances, when I waited in back of the house, with such unmistakably heart-felt enthusiasm, far more than I ever got, even, from any audience at "streetcar" - I wouldn't have the nerve to question your verdict. But silence is only golden when there is nothing to say and I still think I have a great deal to say no matter how badly I say it.

Cordially, Tennessee Williams

[Walter Kerr (1913-1996) restated much of his "Sunday notice" (*New York Herald Tribune*, March 29, 1953) in reply to TW's present correspondence. Evident in *The Rose Tattoo* and *Camino Real* was a movement "toward the cerebral" which alarmed the reviewer and threatened the playwright. "Don't do it," he warned TW, for "what makes you an artist of the first rank is your intuitive gift for penetrating reality" without "junking {it} in the process" (April 13, 1953, HRC).

Kerr echoes pre-production correspondence in which Elia Kazan urged TW to integrate the "social" and "universal" aspects of *Camino Real*. Only then could he succeed in dramatizing "what is happening in the world of 1952" to those "irregulars" (November 17, 1952, HRC) with whom they both identified. The director and cast—especially Eli Wallach and Barbara Baxley, whose performances as Kilroy and Esmeralda were generally admired—survived the critical wreckage, but Kerr had little to say of their work because the production seemed "dead at the core."

Kazan later observed—and both author and producer agreed—that Lemuel Ayers had designed "a lugubrious realistic setting" (Kazan, p. 497) which lacked the "plastic richness" cited by TW. A former college friend of TW, Ayers had designed the sets for many Broadway shows, including *Oklahoma!* (1943).]

255. To Cheryl Crawford

[1431 Duncan Street
Key West, Florida]
3/31/53
[TLS, 1 p. BRTC]

Dear Cheryl:

Whenever I talk about you, I say: "Cheryl is a great fighter, she is always there when you need her." I can't possibly tell you what this experience has meant to me in the way of a reaffirmation of belief in people, and what can possibly stack up against that as a positive gain? Certainly nothing of a commercial nature!

Naturally it is not with a virginal freshness that I can continue work on the play now, but when I got back here I discovered among my old papers, left here last Spring, an introduction to play in which Quixote arrives, down an aisle of theatre, ranting and raving about the romantic quest above a loud singing wind, and it seems to me that would make a good way to begin. It involves slight changes in staging. I've also conceived a recapitulation of the Act One finale chase scene after Kilroy snatches his gold heart from the medical group. I think this gives a revival of pure physical activity which the play seemed to need after his death. The chase is now ghostly, almost all in his mind, no actual pursuers, but only sounds and voices, terminating in the box from which he leapt before. He leaps back into plaza at a point in Esmeralda's prayer. I'm working hard to get this stuff in order and it should be mailed to you before the week-end. With all this discussion and controversy, and the precedent of Logan's work on "Wish You Were Here", I think we could interest people in post-production changes of this sort. I don't doubt that they will illuminate the play and add to the final effect, but they will increase the playing time somewhat. Cuts can be made to partially compensate for them, such as the Winchell bit which obviously didn't pay off in any support from him. I'm enclosing copy of letter I just wrote Kerr. I also wrote Brooks and Hawkins, though in much different vein. I think we ought to show fight in this situation.

Much love from 10.

["Do believe that I'll always be here fighting for you," Cheryl Crawford assured TW in the aftermath of *Camino Real*. She added that the *New York Times* planned to feature the "controversy" surrounding the play and "like a panther" (April 3, 1953, U of Houston) she had arranged for Edith Sitwell to write a letter of support. "May a visiting Englishwoman say how profoundly impressed and moved she was by 'Camino Real'" (*New York Times*, April 5, 1953), began Sitwell's defense.

Regarding "gain," Crawford lost no time in persuading Audrey Wood that *Camino Real* "might have a chance to run if we pay no royalties, at least until we see if we can get out of the woods" (March 25, 1953, HRC). The second-week gross fell far below house capacity, but Crawford felt that business was "tremendously encouraging" (April 3, 1953, U of Houston), as she informed TW.

The Don Quixote "introduction" cited by TW is probably the same "first scene" to which Elia Kazan refers in correspondence. He wrote that it was added to *Camino Real* after the Broadway opening because TW "thought it necessary" (to Leighton, July 30, 1957, HRC). Publication of the book in October 1953 saw Quixote's arrival transferred to a new prologue.

Joshua Logan attended the New Haven premiere of *Camino Real* and shared with TW and Elia Kazan both his general enthusiasm for the play and his specific advice for revision: "'Work through Kilroy'" (February 26, 1953, Library of Congress).

Logan's post-production doctoring of the musical *Wish You Were Here* (1952) had turned "a crying flop" into a "sold out {hit} with standing room for two years!" (Logan, *Josh* (1976).]

256. To Justin Brooks Atkinson

1431 Duncan Street
Key West, Fla.
April 3, 1953
[TLS, 4 pp. BRTC]

Dear Brooks:

You have no idea how much less lonely your letter made me feel, even though our points of view are as disparate as you say. It was not the mandatory failure of my play that so depressed me but the feeling that I was no longer able to communicate with the arbiters of that vocation to which I have completely committed myself and my life for the past fifteen years or more. Of course your letter is not the only one that has helped to relieve this feeling of being shut out and the door barred against me. Last night I got a special delivery letter from Edith Sitwell, posted just before sailing back to Europe, which was almost in itself enough to justify the trials that I've been through, and for many days, now, ever since the play began its pilgrimage in New Haven, an unprecedented, in my experience, flood of correspondance from people, many of whom objected as you did, to certain things in the play, some aspects of it, but who nearly all repeated that same thing, that it made them "feel less lonely". When so many people, more than were moving to write me about "Streetcar" and "Menagerie" put together - even, I believe, during the whole course of their long runs - tell me that it touched and moved them deeply, I can't keep on feeling that it was all in vain. No doubt some of these letters were prompted by compassion over the play's treatment by critics, but by far the majority of them had a tone which could only come from true feeling about the work itself. For myself I am comforted, but for the others involved in the production, particularly Gadg and Cheryl and some of the young actors, I can't help feeling outraged. My work will survive in print for later consideration and probably other productions, but all the passion and power which they spent on this single production is tied up with its fate and outlives it only in memory.

I do wish you had not misunderstood the removal of the gold heart. That heart was only his physical heart. I see, now, that making it gold may have been misleading. It was only a jest upon a cliché, "heart of gold". His living, physical heart was a heart of gold, often pawned in the past, so often, in fact, that even death couldn't break the habit, but his true (spiritual) heart was not a removable or transactable thing, for he was, in spirit, the same Kilroy that he was before they cut his living heart out of him.

In writing fantasy it is terribly hard to know when you have violated the boundaries of audience acceptance. Some will allow you absolute license, others almost none, and I don't suppose there is any way of assuring a uniform disarmament, no matter how carefully or subtley you prepare them. A lot of the grotesque comedy in this work, and I think that is its dominant element, even though all of it had a serious import back of it, is tracable to the spirit of the American comic-strip and the animated cartoons, where the most outrageous absurdities give the greatest delight. I'm sure you've seen the movie cartoons where the characters are blown sky-high one moment and are skipping gaily about the next, where various members of their bodies are destroyed and restored in the flicker of the projector, and nobody seems to mind the implausibility of it. I thought that this art-form had softened up my American audiences for the manifest illogicalities of Camino! (More's the pity!) The Messrs. Chapman and Kerr - (I stopped reading the notices after those came out - except for Hawkins which a true friend read over the phone at 3 A.M. when a combination of nembutal and seconal still hadn't worked) - were obviously not willing to be budged one centimeter from the strictest of literal approaches, or at least moralistic attitudes, toward something that literally got down on its knees and begged for imaginative participation.

I know how different your world is from mine. I read the book which followed the course of a year in your life and which expressed a [philosophical] sweetness and serenity of spirit which I've [seen] expressed nowhere else in contemporary [writing] and so I know the difference in these worlds. [My] own world, Brooks, is not bitter nor brutal nor even reconciled to corruption, at least not inwardly, as it exists in me. But I must tell you that I have lived in "the lower depths", which are a large strata of society, have fought my way only partially up out of them, and my work is a record of what I have seen, heard, felt and known on the way. I have known intimately a world haunted by frustrate and dreadful longings. ("Keen for him, all maimed creatures, deformed and mutilated! His homeless ghost is your own!") I have even spent nights in southern jails - wrist handcuffed to ankle and made to crawl - and seen negro women kicked and bludgeoned up and downstairs because the circumstances of their lives had turned them to prostitution, I have lived intimately with the outcast and derelect and the desperate and found in them the longing, passionate, and bravely enduring, and, most of all, the tender. I have tried to make a record of their lives because my own has fitted me to do so. And I feel that each artist is sort of bound by honor to be the voice of that part of the world that he knows. I came out of the world that you belong to, Brooks, and descended to those under levels, passing through various levels on the way, and I have tried to keep in touch with them all. It is only the upper levels that have rejected me. I was kicked out of a Roman country-club last summer (where I swam for relief from the heat and other therapeutic measures and conducted myself with the most fastidious propriety) - because of "The Roman Spring of Mrs. Stone" and the fact that a poor young Italian painter - not of the "noblesse" - but a clean and scrupulous character - was my guest one afternoon. Some of this feeling of outrage against hypocrasy and brutishness is expressed in my work, but I don't think protest alone would ever animate that work, it is mostly the animation that comes from the finding in people of those expressions of sensibilities and longings that were in Blanche and Alma and Serafina and Kilroy and Marguerite and Jacques, and that is what my work is really about, and when it stops being about those things it will be finished. (Me, too.)

In a memorable conversation with George Jean Nathan he remarked, "A wise man is a happy man." and I said, "Well, I am a fool." but I wondered then and have wondered since if he is really happier than I am or wiser. I don't think of myself as gloomy although I am technically what Joseph Wood Krutch once called me "a romantic pessimist". But I find life so terribly engaging that I think of death with the utmost abhorrence. I could go on and on about my "world" and attitude toward it, but I am sure you don't want or need that much elucidation of it. But before I sail in June I hope to see you and give you what I think is almost the most eloquent study yet made of what goes on in the world that I try to speak for, "The Collected Letters of Hart Crane" - and maybe also his biography by Philip Horton. A tragic world but not a negative one, and his greatest work was an American anthem - "The Bridge" - whose failure was mainly one of a too intense idealism for its material. You once gave me a book which I cherish, so it will be fair return. And I will also send you a published "Camino Real". I have probably exhausted your patience, now, but I hope I have not yet forfeited your friendship!?

Yours ever, Tenn.

["Two long hand-written letters" from Brooks Atkinson asking TW to explain how he "'got that way'" (TW to Kazan, April 16, 1953, WUCA) spurred the present correspondence.

In a secondary review Atkinson described *Camino Real* as "a sensitively composed fantasy," but he observed that only Byron and Quixote escape "the jail-yard of vice" envisioned by TW. Kilroy, "'heart of gold'" notwithstanding, succumbs to "the hopelessness and degeneracy" of the Camino Real. In closing Atkinson urged TW to "find a less malignant theme" (*New York Times*, March 29, 1953).

Atkinson's "serenity of spirit" was evident in *Once Around the Sun* (1951), shipboard reading for TW in 1951. With "Keen for him, all maimed creatures," La Madrecita mourns the death of Kilroy in *Camino Real* (Block Fifteen).

George Jean Nathan, long an antagonist of TW, ridiculed *Camino Real* as an "exhausting minstrel show," whose innumerable characters "make cracks none of the others can understand, and who are presided over by an interlocutor in the person of Williams whose too many pre-performance drinks have gone to his head" (*New York Journal American*, April 5, 1953).

TW cites the Brom Weber edition of *The Letters of Hart Crane, 1916-1932* (1952), and the Philip Horton biography, *Hart Crane: The Life of an American Poet* (1937).

The right-hand margin of the fourth paragraph is partially obscured in the original typescript. Editorial insertions appear in brackets.]

Margo Jones and Brooks Atkinson, Dallas.

257. To James "Jay" Laughlin

1431 Duncan St.
Key West, Fla.
April 5, 1953
[TLS, 2 pp. Houghton]

Dear Jay:

I want to thank you for the never-failing appreciation you have for anything good in my work. Your letter meant a great deal to me, since I went through a pretty black period after those notices came out. I had suspected that we would be blasted by a quorum of the critics, ever since New Haven Gadg and I had expected or feared it pretty certainly, but even so there was a degree of militant incomprehension that seemed like an order to get out and stay out of the current theatre.

I'm glad that you felt poetry in the play. I can't agree with you about Gadg. I don't think this play was nearly as easy for him as Streetcar or Salesman, it was a much harder and more complex job, and he was working with players at least half of which were dancers and had no previous speaking experience on the stage, an inadequate budget and far from adequate time in rehearsal and try-out on the road. Gadg is not as fond of verbal values as he should be, but of all Broadway directors he has the most natural love of poetry. Not a single critic seemed to have any sense of the abstract, formal beauty of the piece. They concentrated on what each thing might mean in a literal, logical sense, and I can't help thinking that there was a general feeling of ill-will among them at what seemed new and intransigent in the work. I have had a couple of letters from Atkinson, in London, expressing moral and chauvinistic indignation over the pessimism which he says "American audiences" will not accept, that they don't like it in Anouhil and Sartre and will not accept it from me. He repeated America and American several times as if the play was a violation of national respect. Nevertheless I think he, almost alone, did make an effort to divorce his personal repugnance from his professional appraisal, and was frank about the source of that repugnance. A couple or three nights ago I got a special delivery letter from Edith Sitwell, couched in the most extravagant heart-felt terms, for which I was rightly overcome with gratitude, and there has been a flood of letters from people known and unknown, more ever than I got during the whole course of Streetcar, saying their love of the play and anger at its reception. So although it is a great, almost overpowering, professional setback for me, I don't feel altogether hopeless about it.

Your advice is good. I have nothing more to expect from Broadway and if I go on writing plays, it must be with an absolute uncompromising fidelity to myself alone, that is, quite purely from now on. They say, on good authority, that the life-expectancy of an American literary talent is about 15 years and I have already long-exceeded that mark, since I got my first pay-check for writing at sixteen and have written every day since that I was able to punch the type-writer keys and very few days when I wasn't can be remembered. But I think the pressure of things to say is as great as ever, if not greater, but a lot of the native energy is depleted and the time has come to let up a little, shift gears, work under less steam. It would be a good thing if I could stop altogether for a while, but I find my daily existence almost unbearably tedious without beginning it at the typewriter. Frank and I plan to go abroad, this year, for a really extended stay, in fact we are planning to go all the way around the world, beginning in Italy, then Spain, then North Africa, then Greece and Istanbul, then Helsinki for a festival production of some plays of mine, then on from the near East to the Orient, to Ceylon and India and Japan. Thence back to America, when it will be necessary to start trying to "make a living" again, as I will have nothing left but my bonds by that time. Early next month I'm going to try my hand at directing a play. The play is Donald Windham's family-portrait called "The Starless Air", structurally inept but very true and poetic, and there is a chance, if this Houston try-out goes well, I might return to the States to stage it for Broadway about Xmas time: it's about a family Christmas dinner in Georgia.

May I start sending you short-stories for the proposed collection? I have them with me and am getting them in shape. They will have to be typed at your end of the line, and I think they ought to be sold by subscription only, since I want to include some, such as "Two On A Party" that might precipitate an awful row in the present time of reaction.

Ever, Tenn.

[Reviews of the New Haven tryout accurately forecast trouble for *Camino Real*. *Variety* predicted that "the ultimate reception will be governed by the ratio of playgoers who look for stimulation rather than straight entertainment in their theatrical fare." The preliminary verdict was that *Camino Real* presented "a severe mental challenge to an audience" (February 25, 1953) and seemed an unlikely hit.

Following the New York opening of *Camino Real,* James Laughlin commiserated with TW and criticized Elia Kazan's direction for having obscured the play's "philosophical depth and tragic beauty" (March 26, 1953, Houghton). TW's defense of Kazan brought a harsh reply from Laughlin: "Nobody who really had a 'natural love of poetry' could have behaved the way he did over his former Communist friends. There are limits. Gadge loves money and fame. I hope they make him miserable" (April 11, 1953, Houghton).

Laughlin proposed that the "bulk" of the stories intended for *Hard Candy* be issued in "a public volume" and the more controversial ones—"Two on a Party" (1952), "Hard Candy" (1954), "The Kingdom of Earth" (1954)—held for "a separate limited edition" (to TW, April 11, 1953, Houghton).]

258. To Justin Brooks Atkinson

1431 Duncan
Key West [Florida]
[early-April 1953]
[TLS, 2 pp. HRC]

Dear Brooks:

My heart is very light this evening, your letters and a continual flood of others have very effectively stemmed the gravitation it felt when I packed my bags in Manhattan a couple of weeks ago, when I first poured out my woes to you. Although Camino has built steadily since it opened and Audrey Wood says it may do over 20 grand this week, none of us are receiving or expect to receive a penny royalty from it, but the work was done for exactly what it has gained, a communion with people. I wish, only, that it could continue longer, of course it can't very long. Preserving it on paper isn't enough, a published play is only the shadow of one and not even a clear shadow. The colors, the music, the grace, the levitation, the quick inter-play of live beings suspended like fitful lightning in a cloud, those things are the play, not words, certainly not words on paper and certainly not any thoughts or ideas of an author, those shabby things snatched off basement counters at Gimbel's. The clearest thing ever said about a living work, for theatre or any medium, was said in a speech of Shaw's in "The Doctor's Dilemma" but I don't remember a single line of it now, I only remember that when I heard it I thought, Yes, that's what it is, not words, not thoughts or ideas, but those abstract things such as form and light and color that living things are made of. But I do, as I say, feel up-lifted and so does Kazan, who wrote me a long letter the other day when he returned from the country. Not the least of the spiritual benefits that both of us are so keenly aware of is something rare and fine that we found in the long work together, and even more in its failure than we could have found in its success: the fact that never once in the two years it took to plan and execute this job, and the tortuous aftermath of it, did either of us once disappoint or betray the other's faith. This may sound like not such a remarkable thing, but believe me, in theatre as I have known it, it <u>is</u>! It's almost incredible! At one point or another, when things begin to go badly, when the fighting gets thick, somebody almost always "chickens out" or covers up or turns "bitchy", but in this out-fit, not a single one did - so what's a failure? Gadg and I are going to work together, next on a film, of which I've already written the first draft, maybe even another play after that. Meanwhile I'm going to try my hand at directing, a play of Donald Windham's, in the Houston Playhouse, end of this month. I've never tried staging before and I hope I find that I am able to do it.

I'll be in New York about ten days before my sailing-date which is June 5th. Don't worry about being in the town or the country, I'll get in touch with you. I have a car and my Secretary, Frank Merlo, has a license to drive, if you happen to be in the country. We can drive out, and though I am even less able to express myself in talk than I am in writing, which is little enough, it will be a pleasure to try. It would not be inconvenient as I have four or five different friends in Connecticutt and up the Hudson, whose places we always make a tour of before sailing.

If Windham's play works out well (there still are problems) I will ask him to send you a copy. Both the Houston Playhouse and the Theatre Guild are considering it for Fall production on Broadway. It is a very true and simple play, potentially as lovely as "Member of the Wedding", and I hope that the try-out in the "round" in Houston will make Windham able to see and master the structural problems before a major production.

Ever, Tenn.

[*Camino Real* peaked at $19,600 in the fourth week of production. TW later amused Maria Britneva with a wry account of finances, noting that "Mother Crawford" took nearly everyone "off royalties" when the bad notices "came out" and that she hoped "to scrape along by such economies as lighting the stage by fire-flies and a smokey old kerosene lamp" (qtd. in St. Just, p. 75).

TW's reference to the "levitation" of performance reappears in the "Afterword" to the first and subsequent editions of *Camino Real.* Also reprinted there is the speech of the dying painter in *The Doctor's Dilemma* (Shaw, 1906): "I believe in Michelangelo, Velasquez and Rembrandt; in the might of design, the mystery of color, the redemption of all things by beauty everlasting and the message of art that has made these hands blessed. Amen" (Act IV).

TW completed a revised "first draft" of *Baby Doll* (1956)—"Hide and Seek," February 19, 1952, U of Delaware—at Key West in early 1952. His collaboration with Elia Kazan on the film project would be prolonged and at times contentious.

This letter, misdated "June 7 or 8, 1953" by TW, was written two months earlier in the week of April 5. The Houston Playhouse production of Donald Windham's play, *The Starless Air*, opened on May 13, 1953.]

259. To Walter Edwin Dakin

SH: Playhouse
Houston 2, Texas
5/3/53
[TLS w/ enclosure, 1 p. Columbia U]

Dear Grandfather

I'm here in Houston directing Don's play. It is a much harder job than I'd anticipated and I think I should have stuck to writing plays. But it's too late now to back out, I just have to struggle through with it as best I can. There is so much talk in the play and so little action. I have to wrack my brain inventing things for the actors to do while delivering their long speeches. Well, we open in about twelve days and I'll be leaving immediately afterwards, the quicker the better, as Houston is the dullest city I've ever been in. Joanna is wonderful to work with, patient, sympathetic and understanding. Don is pretty irritable, but I suppose any playwright would be under the circumstances. I'll be awfully tired when I get through this! A few quiet days in the mountains would be wonderful or even just at the Hotel Gayoso.

I'm glad you're comfortably situated. I should have mailed your raincoat and this check days ago, but it's been one continual "hassle" since I got here. Take care of yourself, but do have a good time with your old friends.

Give Alice and Nalle and Mrs. Rhodes my particular fond regards.

Much love, Tom.

My address is Hotel Shamrock or The Playhouse. Got your letter this morning so I guess you already knew it.

[TW spent approximately three weeks in Houston casting and rehearsing *The Starless Air*. The lead was played by Margaret Phillips, who starred in the original Broadway production of *Summer and Smoke*. Joanna Albus, formerly associated with Margo Jones in Dallas, founded the Playhouse in 1952.

Alice and Nalle and Mrs. Rhodes are friends of Walter Dakin.]

260. To James "Jay" Laughlin

SH: The Shamrock
Houston 5, Texas
[May 9, 1953]
[TLS w/ enclosure, 2 pp. Houghton]

Dear Jay:

I just got your letter and I thank you for your patience and understanding about this problem of getting the script ready for publication. Here is the introduction to the book. I had meant to devote this A.M., Saturday, to getting the book together, but last night a "crise" occured between myself and Windham. He accused me of "completely re-writing" his play while he was keeping "TV" and interview appointments, and having accordingly ruined it. It threw me into such a despondancy I couldn't sleep and this whole day I have been immobilized except for sitting and taking notes on an afternoon run-through. But tomorrow, Sunday, I really will buckle down to the script. I'm sorry to say the "Bigelow script" was hopeless. It was just a typed up copy of the prompt book and simply couldn't be published, as I say in this introduction. If I weren't involved in this directing job I could turn in a much smoother script for publication. However this one that I will mail to you on Monday will only need a little brushing up which I could do from proofs when I get back to New York about the end of next week. Affectly.

10.

[The enclosed "introduction" first appeared in the *New York Times* on March 15, 1953, shortly before the opening of *Camino Real*. The copy which TW revised for book publication is nearly the same as the original.

The "'crise'" occurred when Donald Windham, banned from rehearsals by the director, found that TW "was writing and inserting speeches about mendacity that belonged in a play of his and not of mine. (They turn up, almost word for word, in *Cat on a Hot Tin Roof.*) Foreseeing the same fate for this play as for *You Touched Me* if I remained silent, I spoke out. A compromise was reached that allowed the script to be improved but kept it in my control" (Windham, p. 278).

In prior correspondence with Windham, TW cited the "*horrible mendacity*" of male characters in *The Starless Air* and described the "central theme" of the play as "revolt against lying!" (qtd. in Windham, pp. 275-276). His tactic for prompting authorial revision was vintage Kazan.]

Tennessee Williams and Donald Windham, Houston, 1953: "Last night a 'crise' occured between myself and Windham."

261. To Cheryl Crawford

SH: Hotel Gayoso
Memphis 1, Tenn.
May 17, 1953
[TLS, 1 p. BRTC]

Cheryl dear:

I'm spending a few days with Grandpa on my way back to New York. Bigelow and I flew here yesterday but he went on this morning in response to an urgent call from Terry.

Windham's play had a pretty good reception, though better for me than the play. We only had twelve days' rehearsal, so the work was intensive. I was amazed at how easily it went, the 8-hour sessions seemed to pass like an hour and there was a feeling of real creative activity and outlet in it for me. Of course I would prefer to stage the works of dead authors, or at least not the works of old friends, but if I can't write another play, and God knows whether I can or can't, I do believe I might be able to make a living as a director.

Phyllis Anderson and Audrey, as well as Bigelow and Langner, flew down for the occasion. What a very sweet person Phyllis is! I had never gotten to know her before. She is so gentle and reasonable and did a great deal to smooth over a very tense and disagreeable situation which had developed about the Playhouse which professional ethics forbid me to go further into.

I see by a movie fan-magazine that Brando would like to do a play for Cheryl Crawford. Is there anything specific in this?

See you soon!

Affectionately, Tenn.

[Donald Windham and his untried play were nearly eclipsed by the celebrity director, whose staging, one critic wrote, showed "exceptional insight into human nature." TW's prominence was further enhanced by a concurrent production of *The Rose Tattoo* at the Alley Theatre in Houston.

Reviewers found occasional brilliance in Windham's study of a declining southern family, but they doubted that *The Starless Air* had "enough power, sharpness and compulsion to interest an audience not especially susceptible to its Southern manners" (*Houston Post*, May 14, 1953).

Prominent visitors to Houston included Lawrence Langner, co-director of the Theatre Guild, who had taken an option on *The Starless Air* for a summer production and a possible transfer of the play to Broadway—neither of which occurred.

Phyllis Anderson, wife of the playwright Robert Anderson, was Windham's agent at this time. She died in 1956, remembered by many on Broadway for having "led a whole new generation of playwrights into the theatre," as John Gassner wrote.]

262. To Edith Sitwell

SH: Hotel Gayoso
Memphis 1, Tenn.
May 17, 1953
[TLS, 2 pp. HRC]

Dear Dr. Sitwell:

I meant to write you much sooner but have been in the slough of despondancy which I only got out of by undertaking the staging of a friend's play in Houston, Texas, which was my first essay at direction. It turned out well and the forced activity was good for me and lifted the state of my spirit.

Immediately upon receiving your wire about "Camino" I wired you at the Hotel St. Regis in New York. I hope it reached you before you sailed. I'm sure that none of the messages of appreciation that I got about the play meant even half so much to me as yours, and without it the play's failure would have been far more crushing. I hope you understand this and how much I do thank you. Of course I knew already how warm and generous your attitude is toward works of others. I have read Denton Welch's journal which gives such touching testimony to this rare thing which distinguishes Edith Sitwell the woman as much as your work distinguishes you as a poet, or rather, which complements that work in the only suitable way.

"Camino" closed last Saturday. I don't think it needed to, for the last week's business was nearly double the week before and indicated that there was still a lot of interest in the play. But it was expensive to operate and the producer had not planned wisely. Like most brave people she had only made provisions against success. Not being brave, I always think in terms of possible failure, and yet when it comes it never fails to depress me. Nevertheless I am prepared for it and able to take suitable measures to cope with it.

I'm sailing June 5th but my boat lands at Havre and I shall make the quickest possible retreat to Rome. I shall be abroad until early November and it may turn out that I'll be in London sometime during that period, and if I do, I will surely get in touch with you.

Please believe that you have done a great deal to help me over a very difficult event in my life.

With "devoir", Tennessee.

[Edith Sitwell (1887-1964) wrote later in May to commiserate with TW over the closing of *Camino Real* and to declare the critics "fools!" for having rejected the play "out of sheer obstinacy." She consoled her friend with the thought that "when one can no longer raise" in the "stupid" an "absolute frenzy of hatred and anger - it means that one is dead" (May 24, 1953, Massee Collection).

Sitwell championed many young writers, including the novelist Denton Welch, who found it "so winey, so toxic, always to be hearing fine things about one's attempts from someone famous" (*The Journals of Denton Welch*, ed. De-la-Noy, 1984).

Camino Real closed on May 9, 1953, after sixty performances and a loss of $115,000. The final week's gross of $22,000 followed a sharp decline in business and was no doubt a reaction to the play's closing notice.]

263. To Edwina Dakin Williams

SH: Hotel Gayoso
Memphis 1, Tenn.
[ca. May 17, 1953]
[TLS, 2 pp. HRC]

Dear Mother:

I am spending a couple of days here with Grandfather enroute to New York, after a very strenuous three weeks in Houston, putting on Windham's play. It was my first attempt at direction and the results were gratifying, at least all the notices praised the direction but they were not so kind to the play. Actually the play was not quite ready to be produced, and what made it most unfortunate was that Windham, far from being grateful for my services, sat next to me while I was working with the actors, objecting to everything and giving them contrary directions. I finally had to ask him to stay out of the theatre till the initial staging was finished, which he took in very poor grace. Lawrence Langner of the Theatre Guild came down for the opening, as did Bigelow and Audrey and some other Broadway figures. Langner wants me to stage the play in New York if it is done there, but I would be reluctant to involve myself again in a work of Windham's.

I am terribly, terribly concerned over the changes you are contemplating for Rose. Surely she won't be put back in the asylum! That, I am sure, would be the final blow, as she would almost certainly give up all hope if her limited freedom that she has with Mrs. Turner is taken away. I am convinced, from all evidence, that these state institutions are perfect nightmares - "Snake-pits". If Mrs. Turner won't keep her, someone else must. Please let me know about this before I sail for Europe June 5th.

Grandfather is about as well as when you last saw him and is having plenty of society here - too much for me! He is spending one more week here before he goes to Clarksdale where he intends to spend June. In July, about the first, he's planning to go to Tuckaway Inn. Are you going to join him there?

"Camino" closed last Saturday in spite of the fact that the final week did almost twice the business of the week before. Cheryl Crawford managed it very badly. She did not even put advertisements in The New Yorker or show-cards in the ticket-agency windows.

Of course this branded the play as a failure at the outset. I think it would be a mistake to trust her with another. Excitement and interest in the play was very high and if it had been properly exploited, it could have turned the tide. I am now busy preparing the manuscript for publication and Audrey has made contracts for its presentation here and there in Europe. "Rose Tattoo" has had a very successful opening in Paris and I will see it when I get there in June.

Grandfather says to give you his love and also the Widow Brown. I'm glad I stopped off to see him here as I was afraid he might not be comfortably settled. He is. If you could send Grandfather his "straw hat" he would be happy but says it is not necessary - a Knox panama, he says. He has the light grey one so it should not be essential.

Send Dakin my love. I do hope he gets the promotion, though it would be nice for you to have him back in Saint Louis, I suppose.

Much love, Tom.

[The precise date and circumstances of Rose Williams's departure from Stony Lodge in New York are unclear. An indication of her current status may be found in TW's correspondence with Elia Kazan: "I don't know who told you that my sister was worse. She is the same as ever but yours truly is just about ready to join her on that chicken-farm in Missouri. Her letters indicate that she thinks I am already there. She wrote me recently that the yard was full of 'tragic fowls' and she listed them by all our family names and said they were 'holding prayers' for me" (postmarked Le Havre, France, June 10, 1953, WUCA).]

264. To Paul Bowles

[11 Via Firenzie, Rome]
June 22, 1953.
[TLS, 2 pp. HRC]

Dear Paul:

We are back in Rome and have taken an apartment, a 4-floor walk-up which one cannot climb more than once a day and survive it, but it has two lovely terraces that catch the morning and afternoon sun and the portiere disappears after ten PM. So all in all it's a good deal.

Frank and the dog may remain here most of the summer but I am taking off for Spain and Tanger in a couple of weeks. I want to see some bull-fights and then I want to settle down near the beach in Tanger and get back in shape. I've been pretty seedy.

Today Luchino Visconti came to see us. He wanted me to do English dialogue for a film he is making with several American stars late this summer. I am simply not in condition, nervously, to undertake a job of this sort but I told him that you would be a perfect choice for it if you would be interested. He wanted me to write you at once and see if you'd like to. I dare say there would be a sizable increment. This he did not go into but there is American backing with stars such as Farley Granger involved. It might be worth your while if you are looking for "loot". He does not know your work as he cannot speak nor read English but I spoke of your books. He wants me to act in a "supervisory" capacity, which means that I would lend advice and assistance if needed. He wants to pay both of us but since I would not be doing any of the actual work I would - confidentially - turn over whatever I received to you. Visconti made the latest Anna Magnani film, "Bellissima", which is a great success now in America, and also a much greater film, "Terra Trema". He also has directed "Streetcar" and

"Menagerie" in the Italian theatre, and is by far the greatest stage director in Italy as well as a "grand Seigneur", the Viscontis being one of the three oldest families in the country - this is irrelevant but interesting, I think, since he is also very "leftish". I like him and I think his dealings would be completely equitable - this is relevant.

Has Ahmed come back? I hope so, for I sense your loneliness without him and it seemed a very good and workable relationship. I think what happened was a very temporary thing, a sort of "coup de feu" or derangement that came from the sudden collision of two very different cultures at a critical time. It is nothing that could not be understood by a man of your philosophical latitude. Of course I know very little about it all. Somehow I feel it is very sad for Libby . . . not for you.

I will let you know when I start for Spain, probably by air. I don't trust myself in a car, too many smash-ups, and the Jaguar is permanently off balance as a result. Besides there is more fluidity without one, and I have almost entirely gotten over my dread of the air. Is there a good hotel, not the Rif, near the beach in Tanger? Perhaps even the Rif would be tolerable in good weather. It was agreeable to hear of the bull-ring. I have a passion for corridas. I expect Frank and "Mr. Moon" would join me later. If you come to Rome we have an extra room for you here. We have this place for four months. You could work on one terrazza and me on the other. It is right over the opera house and we could hear them rehearsing as we worked! Tra la la! LAAAAAAAAAA! - very stimulating.

Love, Tenn.

[TW sailed on June 5 with little hope of serenity. "A neurosis," he wrote, "is worrying the ragged edges of my nerves and I was disturbed by a tearful scene put on by F's friend Ellen in front of others." The old "blue-devils" of fear and depression returned on the second day, TW still "running hard" (*Journal*, June 5 and 6, 1953) to elude them. He and Frank Merlo settled in Rome near the Teatro dell'Opera: "Tra la la! LAAAAAAAAAA!"

Senso (1954), the Luchino Visconti film to which TW refers, is set in Venice in the 1860s against the historical background of the Austrian occupation. Farley Granger played the role of Franz Mahler, an officer who is exposed as a traitor by his Venetian lover and executed by the Austrians for desertion.

Paul Bowles sailed unhappily for Tangier, while his companion Ahmed Yacoubi, a painter who had been adopted by smart society in New York, remained to enjoy a brief notoriety. He was currently "living in sin," Bowles remarked, at Libby Holman's estate in Connecticut. A famous torch singer,

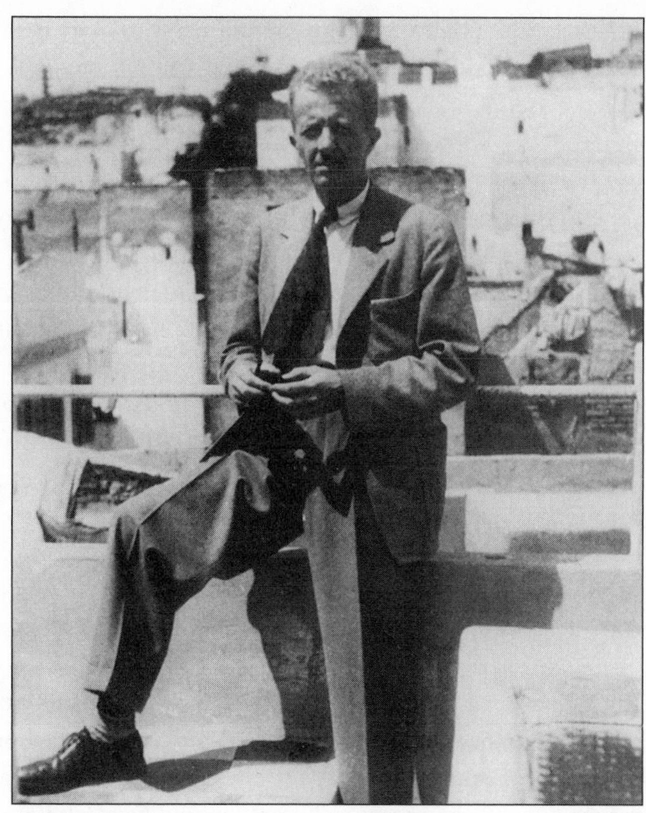

Paul Bowles, Tangier.

Holman lived under a shadow of suspicion after being charged in 1932 (although not prosecuted) with the murder of her husband, Smith Reynolds, a principal heir of the Reynolds tobacco fortune. Holman was a mutual friend of TW and Paul and Jane Bowles.]

265. To Justin Brooks Atkinson

11 Via Firenze, Rome
June 25, 1953
[TLS, 3 pp. BRTC]

Dear Brooks:

I had certainly meant to get in touch with you before I sailed this month but the long-delayed reckoning with my burned up nerves which I knew was coming but which I had skillfully evaded by keeping very busy, plunging into new work in Key West, and directing Windham's play in

Houston, did finally overtake me during that short period in New York. Practically every morning was like climbing out of a grave, and each one I asked myself, Can I call Brooks today? I did want very much to talk to you. But each day I obviously wasn't in a suitable state to see anybody but a few old friends who are accustomed to these recessive periods of mine. At such times, in company, I sit with a fixed, anxious smile and say nothing. I go to Rome each summer almost as a therapeutic measure. It is hard, even for me, to remain continually tense and anxious in this serene golden city, so now, as usual, I am coming out of it a little and by the time I return to the States I'll be ready to pick up and go on, perhaps with a new work of my own, if I work rapidly enough, perhaps to do Windham's play on Broadway for the Theatre Guild. I enjoyed directing. I was surprised to discover how satisfactory a creative outlet it was, and certainly it was good for me to change positions, to get a first-hand impression of what a director goes through with. I have a brand new appreciation of Gadg. I always loved and admired him, but when I consider how many times I "blew my top" at poor Windham and how often Gadg must have wanted to scream at me, but never did, I feel a real awe of his composure or control. Still I think that I can be a director at times when I have no work of my own to offer. The eight-hour periods seem to pass like a single hour and at the end of the day I would feel more refreshed than fatigued. And I felt the same satisfaction, when it went well, that I would have felt if it had been my own work. But direction is an art that has to be learned, like all arts, slowly, and while writing is a good preparation, it doesn't completely prepare you in place of experience. My dream is some day to direct "The Sea Gull" which is my favorite of all plays. I would like to have Brando as Constantine, Stella Adler as Mme. Arcadina, Geraldine Page as Nina, and maybe David Stewart could play Trigorin.

I have found an apartment here with two terraces, one that catches the morning sun and one for the afternoon, and yesterday I went to Magnani's. She wants to do two things, a film of Rose Tattoo which was written for her originally and she wants me to write her a modern de-sentimentalized version of "Camille". Censors have forbidden the showing of "Tattoo" on the Italian stage and also the release of the film of "Streetcar", but the best Italian stage director, Luchino Visconti, is keen to present "Camino" next season and I wonder if the church and/or government will permit it. Book-burning and banning and so forth is having a fearful ascendancy these days, and that's why I think a single honest and courageously outspoken critic is more important to us right now than writers are, since the latter cannot function at all without the support of the first. What I value so highly in your criticism is that even when a work is personally distasteful to you, you are able to separate that subjective reaction to a remarkable degree from your objective evaluation of the thing itself. I hate works that are rooted in bitterness and hatred and disgust, such as Celline's and Malaparte's and Henry Miller's. These are black works and revolt me. But I catch flashes of a "tortured sensibility" in the best of Sartre. I don't mind a work being dark if it is rooted in compassion. In a notebook I once copied the following bit from Sartre's "Age of Reason": - "Various well-bred moralities had already discreetly offered him their services: disillusioned epicureanism, smiling tolerance, resignation, common sense, stoicism - all the aids whereby a man may savor, minute by minute, like a connoisseur, the failure of a life." - The sadness in this reflection is a genuine thing, truthful and therefore moving. Of course there must be more comfort in his existence than in his "existentialism" or he couldn't endure it, I agree with you about that. I'm sure he is comforted by the esteem of his followers, for instance, and by the excellent French wines and restaurants and the civilized freedom of thought that still prevails and is the great tradition in his country. Apparently he has no use for me. In the summer of 1948 I gave a cocktail party for theatrical friends in Paris and sent him a long wire, inviting him, to which he didn't respond, and during the party I heard he was in a bar nearby and dispatched a French writer to bring him over. He assured the writer he would come, but a short while later he strolled by my hotel without even looking up. Cocteau did not come, either, but he came early in the morning to explain why he couldn't come in the evening. As for Anouhil, all I know of his work is Antigone which seemed quite meaningless to me. If the sorrow and confusion and longing in a man's heart is eloquently expressed through art, I think it gives comfort and even exaltation to his audience, by making them feel less lonely. I had that experience lately at a play. It was Jane Bowles' In A Summerhouse which I saw in Ann Arbor shortly before I sailed. Although it was written before Carson's Member of the Wedding and bears no resemblance to it otherwise, it has a similar theme of spiritual isolation, it is one of the funniest and saddest and most original plays ever written. The feeling of loneliness in it was almost unbearably poignant but the effect was heart-warming, it made me feel not alone. In fact, after seeing it three times, consecutively, I felt genuinely uplifted and peaceful for the first time in several months. The notices gave it no quarter but the audiences, although I'm not sure they knew what to make of it, were held fascinated and the producers are going to bring it into New York next Fall. Well, that's about all, right now - except for a funny remark that George Kaufmann made on the ship coming over about Eric Bentley's new book. He said the full title is "In Search Of A Theatre, and God Help It If I Find One!"

Yours ever, Tennessee.

[By late-June TW had "just about run through" the annual therapy of Rome. The work was "petering out" and things began to seem "a little too familiar": "I think I need the shock of something new to keep me from sinking into the old summer lethargy and stupefaction" (*Journal*, June 29, 1953). A trip to Spain followed in mid-July.

TW did not pursue Anna Magnani's request, or a similar bid by *Studio One*, a popular television showcase, to modernize the story of "Camille." A Visconti production of *Camino Real* also failed to materialize.

TW quotes the final lines of *The Age of Reason* (1945) by Jean-Paul Sartre.

A tryout cast featuring Miriam Hopkins and Mildred Dunnock could not save the new Jane Bowles play from harsh "notices" in Ann Arbor, Michigan. *In the Summerhouse* was panned by the critics as "pretentious, wordy nonsense" (*Detroit News*, May 20, 1953).

The Broadway producer-director George S. Kaufman mocked the title and pretention of Eric Bentley's collection of essays and reviews, *In Search of Theater* (1953).]

266. To Audrey Wood

11 Via Firenze
Rome
June 29, 1953
[TLS, 2 pp. HRC]

Dearest Audrey:

I always feel that there is a sort of telepathic communication between us across the Atlantic and I don't have to write you in order to let you know the general condition of things. So far things are okay. In Paris I saw the last two performances of "Rose Tattoo" before it shut down for the summer. They say it will re-open in September. I am happy to report they did a fine job on it. Maria came over and it turned out that the Serafina, Leila Kedrova, was an old Russian friend of her mother's, and so they hit it off like a house afire, to the tune of thousands of francs at Russian night-clubs at my expense. But Kedrova is really superb, and I do wish they would use her in London. Her grunts alone are worth the admission price. She has great comedy and sexuality and her husband directed it well. It was really the first time I have seen the play truly performed, and this in spite of the stage being not much larger than a room at the "Y". Kedrova speaks some English and is eager to play in London and could pick up the language well enough to play it in a month or two. The truck-driver, also Russian, was equally good in his part. Do you suppose Binkie would be interested in having me direct the play, with Kedrova, for the Lyric-Hammersmith?

I have seen Magnani here in Rome. She invited me to her apartment and says she wants to make the film in Sicily with Brando, and that she thinks Mangiacavallo should be an American GI of Sicilian descent stationed there during the occupation. It sounds feasible enough, but is Brando interested and is an American film company prepared to produce it? She also wants me to write her a modern de-sentimentalized version of "Camille" to do on the stage in America, her idea is to do a reportory of three works, a musical revue, Rose Tattoo, and a "new Camille". A lady of limitless energy!

I had accumulated some francs from "Tattoo" but Ninon said she couldn't get them out on such short notice so the last day of my stay in Paris she came over with a check for $500. in francs, I believe it was 175,000 francs, which she said was an advance on "Summer and Smoke", which is now being translated by the lady who translated "Tattoo" and will be done at a still tinier theatre in the Fall. I signed two receipts (not carbons) for the francs, since she said one was to be sent to you and one for her to keep. Maria was highly skeptical about all this and I must say I think the handling of French royalties is something we had better keep an eye on, now that American earnings are at such an ebb.

We have taken an apartment at 11 Via Firenze. It has a terrace that catches the afternoon sun, and Frank and Mr. Moon are quite satisfied here, but since I can't use that wonderful swimming-pool at the country-club I was kicked out of, I feel restless in Rome and I think I'll fly to Barcelona in a short time, and maybe wire Maria to join me in Madrid for a couple of weeks, as it is cheap there and I think I need the stimulation of a new background.

I talked to Carson on the phone in Paris and she was in great distress over Reeves. He has never stopped drinking and was then in the American hospital and she said she desperately wanted to talk to me about things and that I could drive out in their car which was at the hospital. I went to the hospital the next day with Maria but Reeves had checked out and the car was not there. I myself was feeling pretty seedy and did not attempt the trip to Bachivilliers by bus. The Carson-Reeves situation is apparently insoluble, I don't think there is anything anyone can do about it. Short of devoting your life to Carson, I don't see how you can help her, though she certainly needs help. Of course I feel guilty about it. I should have gone out there, somehow. But we left the next day for Rome. She had a French woman with her who answered the phone so at least her physical needs are being cared for.

How is Inge? Liquor seems to be the particular Nemesis of American writers. Says I, about to go inside for a Scotch on the rocks . . .

I've done some work on the film script and am also working on "Battle" and "Kingdom of Earth". Something should be finished by the time I get back to the States. Me or the cold war or something! Love to Liebling and to Bigelow, may God bless them, and Ida, may God bless her, and Grandfather and "Neesie" and Gadg - may God bless them and keep them in good health and spirits this summer as I hope he will try to keep me. May he do the same for Margo Jones and Joanna Albus and Alice Bouverie but may he be less concerned with the welfare of Geo. Jean Nathan than he is with that of the rat that bit off the nose of the little boy they call "Pig Face" in the slums of Chicago, because he has no nose, or even the rat that devoured the nine-months old baby, in the room that the Chicago News reporter mistook for an empty coal-bin. And God bless you and me, too!

Love, Tenn.

[Ninon Tallon sent an article in which TW had raved about Lila Kedrova, who played Serafina in the Paris production of *The Rose Tattoo* (1953). "Were you this happy," Audrey Wood asked her capricious client, for "I have known you to make speeches publicly and then confidentially tell me you were miserable!" (June 25, 1953, HRC).

"Binkie" Beaumont, managing director of Tennent Ltd., assumed that Peter Brook was TW's first choice to stage *The Rose Tattoo* in London. Beaumont's fear that censorship rulings would hinder the project had been confirmed in February when the Lord Chamberlain's office issued a list of mandatory "alterations." Before leaving Key West in April, TW approved the changes, including the removal of a vulgar reference to "the sex of a parrot" (February 17, 1953, HRC).

The prospect of Marlon Brando starring in *The Rose Tattoo* had unwelcome consequences, as Wood later informed TW (July 3, 1953, HRC). Hal Wallis, the producer with whom she was negotiating film rights, reasoned that signing Brando would make Anna Magnani expendable. He was unwilling to pay the $150,000 fee which she now asked.

William Inge's latest hit, *Picnic*, opened to strong notices on February 19, 1953, and won both the Pulitzer Prize and the Drama Critics' Circle Award—a feat last accomplished by Arthur Miller with *Death of a Salesman* (1949).

"Must soon decide whether to work on 'Battle of Angels' - 'Kingdom of Earth' or the film script," TW wrote concurrently in the journal. "Perhaps the wisest decision," he opined, "would be no work at all, but Spain would have to be awfully fascinating to make that tolerable" (June 29, 1953). Precisely when he began a dramatic adaptation of "The Kingdom of Earth" is unclear. The play was staged unsuccessfully in 1968 as *The Seven Descents of Myrtle*.]

267. To Carson McCullers

[Hotel Colón, Barcelona]
7/15/53
[TLS, 1 p. HRC]

Dearest Carson:

I've been having a rough time of it this summer. I was sick in Paris and haven't been well since. Right now I'm in Barcelona, resting on the beach, and Frank is in Rome. I have worried ever since I talked to you on the phone in Paris. I went out to the American hospital that Sunday to pick up your car and drive out to see you but Reeves had already checked out and we left that night for Rome. I do hope that both of you are better now, bad seasons are usually followed by relatively good ones. I've had a couple in a row but that's exceptional and I'm sure some relief is due. I don't know just how long I'll stay here. Relations with Frank had been strained and they reached the point where communication had ceased. After a couple of weeks of that I thought I'd better take off regardless of how little I felt like travelling. It's cool here and the beach is delightful. I have lunch on it every day with a bottle of wine which is the world's most agreeable soporific and rest on the beach several hours. Paul Bowles is in Madrid and we'll probably get together in a few days. I got him a job writing dialogue in English for an Italian film. I didn't feel able to undertake the job myself and so persuaded Visconti to engage Paul. I guess we'll fly back to Rome together and perhaps the presence of another party we both like will relieve the tension with Frank which is probably the consequence of being together too constantly too long, and the fact he has never found a personal life for himself, that is any independant sort of activity. I understand it but I can't cope with it right now.

I understand that Miss Capote is in Europe, in Italy, but we have not collided. She is now reported to be at the fashionable resort of Portofino, which is much smarter than Capri. Did I tell you we have a dog? An English bull named Mr. Moon. I'm afraid the poor thing will perish on the streets of Rome as bulls don't stand heat well and Frank will not move without him, they are inseparable, Frank trots and he waddles after as rapidly as he can with that great jowly head of his barely clearing the sidewalk. Maria Britneva calls him "The Froggy Footman".

Our Roman address is 11 Via Firenze or American Express,

LOVE, 10.

[Carson and Reeves McCullers—still living at Bachvillers—entered the final dark months of their marriage in mid 1953 when Reeves attempted suicide. Carson quickly returned to the States once his plan for a double suicide became clear.

While Frank Merlo consorted with a "whore" named Alvaro, TW depended upon trade which was "brought in two or three times a week" (*Journal*, June 27 or 28, 1953). He soon grew "tired of begging for crumbs." The forthcoming trip to Spain was "the only answer," TW thought, to Merlo's behavior, "and maybe that only half one" (*Journal*, July 1 and 10, 1953).

"I spent 6 hours on the San Sebastian beach and had an affair in my cabana with someone procured by Franz" (*Journal*, July 11, 1953). *Suddenly Last Summer* (1958) would evolve from the Barcelona trip (July 10-20), as would the themes of sexual procurement and predation. TW also saw a band of "black-plucked-sparrow children shrilling about for bread and making percussive serenades with flattened out tin cans" (to Kazan, n.d., WUCA) who would reappear in the play as unwitting agents of retribution.

In Portofino "there was a gabble of voices, a cascade of laughter, a buzz of gossip" (Clarke, *Capote: A Biography*, 1988) to which TW and Merlo added their voices while visiting Truman Capote in August. Mr. Moon, however, was not invited, since Capote had received as a gift a female bulldog. TW observed to Maria Britneva that "more than one bitch" (qtd. in St. Just, p. 77) now lived in Capote's house.]

268. To Audrey Wood

[Positano, Italy]
August 2?, 1953.
[TLS w/ autograph marginalia
and postscript, 2 pp. HRC]

Dear Audrey:

A supplement to the hasty letter we scribbled while checking out of the Excelsior in Naples, Maria and I. We are now in Positano, working on the Visconti film script. I know that I should have gotten in touch with you about this sooner but everything came up very rapidly. I got Bowles the job but his work on it, for a number of reasons, was disappointing, and so I felt obligated to do what I could to pull it together, since Visconti had taken him on my recommendation. Paul is not at all well, he has liver trouble and has fallen off to 112 pounds, and the Arab boy who travels with him has been driving him nearly insane. He was not in a condition to undertake this work but he desperately needed the money. I am doing all I can with the script but only accepting one week's salary, $500., the same as Paul was getting a week. Paul is still drawing salary and finishing his version of the script in Rome. Maria is helping me here and Visconti has employed her. Her position is somewhat vague but she gets $250 a month and is drawing $6. a day for expenses on this trip and afterwards when she is with the company in Verona and Venice where the film will be shot. Visconti is already shooting the battle scenes in Verona and Maria will join him soon as her work with me is finished. She will be employed about four months and she is terribly happy as it's the first decently paid job she's ever had. She's a great help to me in this week's work on the script. Fortunately I only have to re-write the three love scenes. The picture is "Urgano d'estate" and the stars are Alida Valli and Farley Granger. It is a big technicolor production with an English version as well as Italian. Maria thinks my work on it is good.

I haven't spoken of the "dossier" business. There didn't seem to be anything to say, it was almost too ridiculous to take seriously except that its implications are so unspeakable. I really didn't know whether to laugh or cry! Of course the worst offense was the reference to you. I trust you have humor enough, now that the first shock is over, to see the funny side. I do. No use regarding it except as something out of Jonathan Swift. . . .

I found my letter of credit in the trunk of the car. Maria and I believe it was stolen from my luggage and put there after they found it couldn't be cashed without identifications.

As I said in last letter, I'm still working on my new version of "Battle". I think I can mail you the script before the end of August. The three principals are radically different. Myra is now the daughter of an Italian immigrant and the part might be fine for Isa Mirande. The part of Cassandra might be right for Julie Harris. The play itself is much less realistic and even wilder than before. I can't judge it, I only know it excites me to work on it, so I depend on you to read and decide about it, and I know you will tell me frankly what you think. Love -

Tennessee.

Please control those spasms!

[The long week that TW spent in Positano (August 25-September 2) was "productive and peaceful and, on the whole, quite pleasant" (*Journal*, August 31, 1953). He continued to revise *Battle of Angels* (1940) and began a promising new story entitled "Man Bring This Up Road" (1959). Mrs. Flora Goforth, the principal character, was "a composite of various vampires" (*Journal*, August 29, 1953) whom TW had known. She would be recast in *The Milk Train Doesn't Stop Here Anymore* (1962/1963).

Ahmed was traveling again with Paul Bowles but "not sleeping with him." Libby Holman, TW reported, said that "such relations were very evil and the opinions of a lady with thirty million dollars cannot be taken lightly by a young Arab whose family live in one room" (qtd. in Windham, p. 282).

Audrey Wood "frankly" evaluated the "new" *Battle of Angels* in late-September.

Penned in the upper margin of p. 1 is the notation "Write me c/o Am. Ex. Co., Rome."]

269. To Cheryl Crawford

SH: Harry's Bar, Venezia
PM: Venice, September 8, 1953
[APCS, 1 p. U of Houston]

Dearest Cheryl -

This is where good queens and bad go when they die in Europe. A few living ones also get here. Just saw the Aga Khan go staggering out followed by an impatient looking Begum. Maria is here. We are both working on a new film for Visconti which is to be a sort of wop "Gone With the Wind" in technicolor. Paul Bowles worked on it, too, and I think it may be beautiful if they don't f--- it up! Also writing on plays and film for Gadg. F. and Moon in Rome.

Good luck & Love - Tenn.

[The Visconti film in progress is *Senso*.]

Tennessee Williams and Maria Britneva on the Lido, 1953: "Maria calls me 'Forty Winks' because in the evenings I have a tendency to nod like the Dormouse in Alice."

Dearest Cheryl – This is where good queens and bad go when they die in Europe. A few living ones also get here. Just saw the Aga Khan go staggering out followed by an impotent looking Begum. Maria is here. We are both working on a new film for Visconti which is to be a sort of wop "Gone with the Wind" in Technicolor. Paul Bowles worked on it, too, and I think it may be beautiful if they don't f--- it up! Also writing on plays and film for Gadg. F. and moon in Rome. Good luck & Love – Tenn.

HARRY'S BAR * VENEZIA * PHONE 23-819

POSTE ITALIANE 35 LIRE

VENEZIA 8-9 1953

Cheryl Crawford
49 W. 45th Street
New York, N.Y.
U.S.A.

Via aerea

Edizione Zanetti

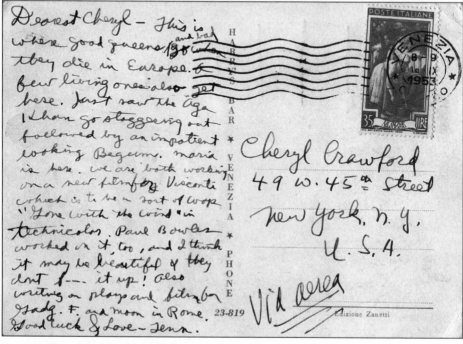

270. To Edwina Dakin Williams and Walter Edwin Dakin

[11 Via Firenze, Rome]
Sept. 19, 1953.
[TLS, 1 p. HRC]

Dear Mother & Grandfather:

I hope and presume that you are back together in Clayton. This has been the busiest summer that I've had in Europe. Working on two films and two plays and also doing a lot of travelling around.

The big news is that Anna Magnani, the Italian star, has finally come to terms with Paramount and the "Rose Tattoo" film deal is apparently all set. It will probably be filmed in America, on the Gulf coast, next summer. I called Anna and she is ecstatic about it and full of plans and suggestions and I will probably have to write the film-story, I hope for a good price. The exact terms of the movie-sale have not yet been told me by Audrey but I suspect she got a hundred thousand and a percentage of the distributor's gross.

Maria Britneva has been here most of the summer and I got her a job working on an Italian film, as well as Paul Bowles. He and I collaborated on the English dialogue, both getting $500. a week which is a good salary for Italy, though only one tenth of what I would get in America. But Visconti is the producer of my plays here and I felt obligated to him. Jane Lawrence and Tony Smith, Grandfather will remember them very well, just arrived in Rome and we will all get together for dinner tonight at a restaurant in the most beautiful plaza in Rome. The weather has turned cool but still bright.

I go to Helsinki for the Finnish premiere of "Tattoo" and to address the university there on the 28th October, and will sail for America immediately afterwards, arriving New York about November 8th.

Both of you take good care of yourselves. Much love,

Tom.

[Audrey Wood's threat "to push toward other producing bodies" (June 24, 1953, HRC) apparently convinced Hal Wallis to sign Anna Magnani for *The Rose Tattoo*.

The Finnish American Society informed TW of plans by the National Theatre to stage *The Rose Tattoo* in May and *The Glass Menagerie* in October. The productions would run concurrently during TW's forthcoming visit to Helsinki (March 2, 1953, HRC).]

271. To Audrey Wood

[11 Via Firenze, Rome]
September 19, 1953
[TLS w/ autograph postscript, 2 pp. HRC]

Dear Audrey:

I've worked harder this summer than any that I can remember but the quantity of work is much clearer than the quality. I know I ought to lay off it, to freshen up, but time seems short, and fewer and fewer things, as I grow older, seem to be interesting enough to fill a day with. This may be because I am tired. Maria calls me "Forty Winks" because in the evenings I have a tendancy to nod like the Dormouse in Alice.

I'm afraid I have been rather foolish about this picture and you may be cross about it, I mean the Visconti film work. When Bowles didn't do a satisfactory job, I felt obliged to take over since Visconti hired him at my recommendation, and this film is a crucial job for Visconti. He may never get another if it doesn't come off, and as you know, I have a very profound admiration for him and affection. Then also he gave Maria her first good job she's ever had in the theatre, at least from a money point of view, she's getting six dollars a day in living expenses and $250 a month salary. I have gotten only one thousand for two weeks work and of course I know I should have demanded more, especially since they are going to use my name, with Bowles, as English dialogue writer. But Visconti was "on the spot" and it seemed an occasion on which one ought to be self-forgetful. Do you agree?

Irene (Dame Selznick) is here and she says that you will be cross about it, so I am briefing you on all the circumstances.

Now I wish you would brief me on the "Tattoo" film deal. I don't know a thing about it. I called Magnani and she seemed ecstatic and was full of suggestions. We must go to Paris together to track down Brando - obviously she is mad for him! - the script must be half in English and half in Italian so that in the violent scenes she will not be reaching for words. And so forth and so forth. But she is genuinely delighted. What troubles me most is the suspicion that Dannie Mann will direct. I did so hope that it could be offered to Gadg for whom it was written along with Magnani, and who told me he would like to make a film of it, and I know he would if he could fit it into his schedule. Of course it might conflict with "27 Wagons", I don't know, but it seems to me the schedules could be juggled around to arrange it. I can't see the intellectual Mr. Mann and the fiery Signora Magnani hitting it off together, nor can I see Dannie getting the poetry and wildness out of the script that it calls for. Please don't let Dannie know I have these reservations about him, I do think he is much superior to Irving Rapper, and I like him well enough personally despite the lack of any rapport between us. I would like to work on the script for Magnani with a director that would stimulate me as she does. With a fine director, "Tattoo" and Magnani would out-shine "Streetcar" and out-gross it, I do believe, but the director should be a plus value as well as the star.

I am still committed to appear in Helsinki October 28th so I'm afraid I'll have to make that trip, little as I like it. Then we couldn't sail till the first week in November. For a while I thought of calling it off and returning in early October but importunate wires and letters from the Finnish American society came in, and I succumbed.

Jane Lawrence and Tony Smith have just arrived,* seeing them tonight, and Paul Bowles and his Arabs have just got back from Istanbul where he went to do a travel piece for Holiday magazine.

I'm working on a play which I might possibly finish, in first draft, before I get back to the States and will now resume work on Gadg's film. How was "Tea & Sympathy" received? I hope well, although the theme struck me as rather improbable, not the circumstances but their solution.

With love, Tenn

*Jane is having a baby in January!

[TW and Paul Bowles shared the English dialogue credit for *Senso*. When finally shown in New York, the film was panned for being "closer to soap opera than Mr. Visconti imagined" (*New York Times*, July 9, 1968).

Audrey Wood last reported negotiating a "film deal" with Hal Wallis that would pay "$75,000 and 5% of the distributor's gross over $1,000,000" (to TW, July 3, 1953, HRC) for rights of *The Rose Tattoo*. Reservations aside, TW had approved Daniel Mann as director when he and Wood conferred in the preceding May.

Signs of the new play—*Cat on a Hot Tin Roof* (1955)—appear in the journal perhaps as early as February 1953. Donald Windham suggested as much in his complaint that lines written for *Cat* were appearing in his own play, *The Starless Air*, during rehearsals in May. TW further specified the origins of *Cat* with reference to "a short-long play based on the characters in 'Three Players'" which he drafted in Rome in summer 1953. He also ascribed his "terrible state of depression" to the new play, which he could not seem to "grip" at this time (see letters #283 and #284).

Tea and Sympathy (1953), Robert Anderson's study of a naive schoolboy accused of homosexual tendencies, was directed by Elia Kazan and ran for 712 performances on Broadway. The play ended improbably, TW thought, with the restoration of the boy's masculinity by the wife of a teacher who was the main persecutor. Laura, speaking to Tom, delivers the closing line: "Years from now—when you talk about this—and you will—be kind."]

272. To Oliver Evans

[Granada, Spain]
10/7/53
[TLS 1 p. HRC]

Dear Oliver:

I am so sorry that you didn't come to Europe, as I kept hoping, for then you could be taking this trip with us and I'm sure you would enjoy it much more than I am. As you know, I'm the world's most fatiguable sight-seer, and here we are in Granada and I'm not even sure that I shall go to see the Alhambra, all I can think of is where they may be holding the bull-fights tomorrow and how quickly can we get to Tangier and have a little rest before sailing back to the States. We are travelling in two Jaguars, Paul's and mine. Paul with his Arab lover Ahmed and his chauffeur Mohammed in their Jaguar and Frank and I and Mr. Moon in ours. They have terrible rubber on their car, probably a result of so many trips through the Sahara and Spain, and we stop every few hours, sometimes less, to change the tires. Luckily I don't know how to do a thing so I just sit restlessly along the road and watch. The country, of course, is very beautiful, much like parts of Mexico, the mountains like the Sierra Madres. But the men are very disappointing to look at, after Italy, I have seen no one like Sebastian, even remotely, the food does not agree with me and I feel slightly ill all the time. However I dread going back to the States. I feel that the country is simply galloping into totalitarianism, now, what I see in the papers and magazines strikes terror in me. I wouldn't go back if it weren't for Grandfather waiting for me in St. Louis. I have been thinking we might go to New Orleans instead of Key West this time, it would be much more agreeable for the old man. Would you have an apartment for us to rent in your house? I've been happier those short times in New Orleans than anywhere else these last few years. Please forgive me for the long delay in writing, it's been a terribly active summer for me, much moving around and Maria with us nearly the whole time. Now I've got her a job with Luchino Visconti who is making a big technicolor film that Bowles and I wrote the English dialogue for. They are shooting it near Vicenza, in Northern Italy, and later in Venice which will keep Maria busy till late December. She's loads of fun to be with and I do miss her. Will you please let me hear from you, where you are, what you're up to, c/o Paul Bowles, British Post Office, Tangier (Box #137). We'll probably be sailing in about three weeks. I haven't completed any new play and have no plans after we get back.

With love, Tenn.

[Evidence of "totalitarianism," as TW put it, was to be found in daily news reports of McCarthyism, loyalty boards, Smith Act trials (anti-sedition law), and other provisions against the Red scare. Earlier in June, Vincent Hartnett labeled Broadway "the last stronghold of show-business Marxists and their supporters" and placed TW in the second category by virtue of his "on-again, off-again flirtation with the Communist-front movement" ("New York's Great Red Way," *American Mercury*, June 1953). When challenged by TW's attorney, the editor of the *Mercury* defended Hartnett and threatened a full-scale exposé of the playwright's questionable associations. Hartnett was a primary contributor to *Red Channels* (1950), a pamphlet listing entertainment figures with alleged Communist ties or sympathies that was distributed to employers.]

273. To Audrey Wood

Hotel Rembrandt, Tangier
10/14/53
[TLS, 3 pp. HRC]

Dear Audrey:

We have arrived in Tangier with Paul Bowles after a ten day trip through Italy and Spain in the two Jaguars, Paul's and ours, and many vicissitudes and adventures along the way. Frank is now out investigating sailings out of Gibralter, the earliest likely prospect is the Andrea Doree on the 27th. Soon as we're booked onto something, we'll cable you, maybe before you get this letter. I want to get back soon as possible, now, as I'm worried about Grandfather.

Your long letter contained no mention of "Tattoo". Was the deal completed? A little good news about that would lift my spirit which was somewhat downcast by your reaction to "the new Battle". I'm glad you wrote me so candidly about it. Your reaction to a script means much more to me than anyone else's, including the critics. Just before I sailed for Europe this time, Bill Inge said to me, Tenn, don't you feel that you are blocked as a writer? I told him that I had always been blocked as a writer but that my desire to write had always been so strong that it broke through the block. But this summer I'm afraid the block has been stronger than I am and the break-through hasn't occured. The situation is much plainer than the solution. There is a mysterious weakness and fatigue in my work now, the morning energy expires in about half an hour or an hour. I pick it up, artificially, with a stiff drink or two but this sort of "forced" energy is reflected in forced writing, which is often off-key and leaves me each day a little more depleted than the day before. I can't help thinking that there is something physiological at the root of this, some organic trouble that is sapping the physical vitality that I need for good work. I feel so "fagged out" in the evenings that I can hardly stay awake through a good movie and have lost all interest in any evening society but Frank's and Mr. Moon's.

Since the script simply doesn't "come off", I don't know if there is much point in telling you what I was aiming at but I will try to. What always bothered me in it was the juvenile poetics, the inflated style of the writing, so I tried to "bring it down to earth", to give the characters a tougher, more realistic treatment. Also I wanted to simplify the story-line, to make it cleaner and straighter, by eliminating such things as "The woman from Waco", Val's literary pretensions, the great load of background and atmospheric detail, and the hi-faluting style of Cassandra's speeches such as "Behold Cassandra, shouting doom at the gates!" and all that sort of crap which seemed so lovely to me in 1940. Unfortunately in 1940 I was a younger and stronger and - curiously! - more confident writer than I am in the Fall of 1953. Now I am a maturer and more knowledgeable craftsman of the theatre, my experience inside and outside the profession is vastly wider, but still the exchange appears to be to my loss. I don't need to tell you how hard I have worked to compensate for that loss, devotion to work is something we have in common.

However I still believe, although I don't have a copy of the script, that what I have done with it is defensible and that if, as a director, I had to choose among all the existing versions, this is the one I would want to put on the stage. It's true that my conception of the characters is radically different, but I have re-written all of their speeches since this change of conception, and I think the disparity between the lyrical passages and the ordinary speech is justified by the heightened emotion at those times. It's only on rare occasions that our hearts are uncovered and their voices released and that's when poetry comes and the deepest emotion, and expression, of Val and Lady is no different from that of Val and Myra, both the new and the old conceptions of them would speak as they do at such moments. Lady is a woman coarsened, even brutalized, by her "marriage with death" as Val has been brutalized by the places and circumstances of his wanderings but at moments their true hearts and the true speech of their hearts break through and those are the lyrical passages of the play and I think they should have this contrast to the coarse common speech. The coarseness is deliberate and serves a creative purpose which is not sensational. Things like "perfect control of functions" are doubtless written too broadly and would have to be toned down in production but they are in character since Val has the sort of primitive innocense that would express such things freely without embarassment, he is outside of a world of conventional evasions and that is his meaning. I agree with you that the "Junior" bit might be offensive but that's of no importance. I think "sugar in the urine" is legitimate, it's just the sort of phrase that lower middle-class southern women use. As for the ending, I suspect that by the time you came to that, your interest had already been alienated because, unless there have been omissions in typing, what happens to Val is made completely clear, both in the speeches of the mob in the store and in the final bit when the conjure man gives his snakeskin jacket to Cassandra. When she is shot, Lady is covering Val. She falls and then she climbs up "his motionless body" - whence she staggers into the confectionery and dies out of sight, as she has always done in all the various versions. I think Cassandra's presence at that demise is "de trop" and should be removed. I also think it should be established that the doctor's office is right across the street from the store and that "there is a light in his window" so Lady's rushing out to confirm her pregnancy will seem more plausible.

Despite the coarse touches in the dialogue, I think the total effect of the play would be one of tragic purity, that is, when I have refined its texture a bit. Why did I make Lady the daughter of "a dago bootlegger"? I think it was just because the story of the burning of her father's wine garden

(I once called it "The Wine Garden of My Father") and her marriage to the man who burned it was poetically moving and significant, and because it fits the theme of the play, the destruction of the wild and lovely by "the dismembering Furies" that our civilized world produces.

Here the defense rests.

We have a room here with a great window that looks over two continents and the sea between them and all the ships that pass East and West, and it's a wonderful place in which to contemplate the end of the world and other grand and awful things that I wish I were able to get back into my writing.

Looking forward to that brass bed and red carpet which you say I have feathered my nest with in Manhattan.

Love, 10.

[Tangier held "no beauty" for TW, who left after a painful visit of two weeks. "It is just like Miami Beach thrown in the middle of some ghastly slums. The Arabs are inscrutable, you could never get to know them if you lived here a hundred years and they dislike and despise all Christians" (qtd. in St. Just, p. 80).

The "new" *Battle of Angels* was not merely "cleaner and straighter," as TW claimed, but it now lacked the "tragic love story" of Myra and Val which Audrey Wood associated with the original play. She also noted inconsistencies in characterization and dialogue and advised TW to "reconsider" who his "characters are in themselves and in relationship to each other" (September 28, 1953, HRC). In effect Wood confirmed TW's suspicion that his recent work had been "off-key, forced, hysterical," that the revised *Battle of Angels* was indeed "a fiasco" (*Journal*, August 13 and 23, 1953). The HRC holds a composite typescript of *Orpheus Descending* (September 1953) which is based upon the text mailed to Wood in September.

TW did not visit Helsinki as planned but returned directly to New York on the Andrea Doria, arriving November 2.]

274. To Friend

The Dylan Thomas Fund
November 10, 1953
[*Partisan Review*, January-February 1954, p. 128]

Dear Friend,

I am sure you have read in the press of the sudden and tragic death of the great poet Dylan Thomas. Thomas died of encephalopathy at St. Vincent's Hospital in New York on November 9th, after an illness of four days. He was only 39 years old. He was attended by one of the finest brain surgeons in New York and everything possible was done to save him.

Thomas' death is an incalculable loss to literature. His work was growing in stature with every year. But there is also a personal tragedy—he leaves a widow without means of support and three children—which gravely concerns his friends and admirers.

As spokesmen for a committee of his friends we are making this urgent appeal to you for a contribution to The Dylan Thomas Fund, which we have hastily organized, which will be used to meet his medical bills and funeral expenses and, if the response is as generous as we hope, to tide his family over the next difficult months.

Please send your check to The Dylan Thomas Fund, care of Philip Wittenberg, Treasurer, 70 West 40th Street, New York City. An accounting of disbursements from the Fund will be sent to the contributors at a later date.

For the DYLAN THOMAS FUND COMMITTEE

W.H. Auden
E.E. Cummings
Arthur Miller
Marianne Moore
Wallace Stevens
Thornton Wilder
Tennessee Williams

[Dylan Thomas arrived in New York in mid-October to direct the American premiere of his play *Under Milk Wood* (1953) and to collaborate with Igor Stravinsky on a new operatic work. His fatal illness was diagnosed as "a severe insult to the brain" caused by "alcoholic toxicity." James Laughlin, Thomas's American publisher, was instrumental in establishing the memorial fund.

TW chose lines from Thomas's poem "Do not go gentle into that good night" (1951) as epigraph for *Cat on a Hot Tin Roof*.]

275. To Oliver Evans

[323 East 58th Street, New York]
[late-November 1953]
[TLS, 1 p. HRC]

Dear Oliver -

I'm still lingering in New York, furnishing a two-room apartment on 58th Street, above Nicholson's cafe, which we will hold as a permanent pied-a-terre in New York, sub-leasing when we are abroad. I'm going through some of what you've been through. Just furnishing the two rooms has cost me $1600. But fortunately the rent is low, only $150. a month, and we can probably rent it for fifty more than we're paying. The rooms are charming, in a late Victorian style with a big glittering brass bed, a carpet sprinkled with garlands of roses, and much brass and colored glass in the decor. Frank will stay on here for at least a month after I go South. I will spend a few days in Saint Louis and bring Grandfather on down with me if I find him in condition to leave. I'm pretty sure he will be. Of course I would prefer to have a small furnished apartment for a month in New Orleans but will probably have to put up at the Monteleone or Saint Charles. However if you know of something that would be suitable for us (ground floor, with two bedrooms, or up a short flight of stairs), I wish you'd let me know. Do you think I could have the use of the Athletic Club pool? We have moved in Saint Louis, that is, Mother has bought a new house there, the address is 6360 Wydown Blvd. and I should be there about the end of this week or by early the next. I have someone, Mike Steen whom you may remember from New Orleans (a sailor at the time) to drive me down as he is going to Louisiana for the holidays. I'll come in the Ford convertible if Frank will ever bring it back from New Jersey where it was stored in his family garage. Have a lot to tell you but it will keep till we meet and I am momently expecting the arrival of someone Gore says I would love. I must get into a becoming peignoir and arrange the pillows on the chaise longue and see that the lights are subtle and the ice-cubes frozen. One bit of news: Carson McCullers' husband committed suicide last week in Paris. He had been planning it for more than a year and so terrorized her that she had fled from Europe to escape him. She is terribly disturbed because I don't think she had really expected him to do it. Love -

Tennessee.

[TW spent a pleasant month in New York visiting James Laughlin, Bob MacGregor, Gore Vidal, and Paul Bigelow. They "were all remarkably nice," including Frank Merlo, who was "on his rare best behavior" (*Journal*, December 4, 1953).

Mike Steen later interviewed friends and colleagues of TW and published their remarks in a collection entitled *A Look at Tennessee Williams* (1969).

Reeves McCullers died in Paris on November 19, 1953, from a probable overdose of barbiturates and alcohol. TW commented in 1972 that "'Reeves died, ultimately, out of great love for Carson. His was a desperate loneliness. Without her, he was an empty shell'" (qtd. in Carr, p. 403).

TW wrote this letter in the week of November 22, 1953, before visiting his family in Clayton.]

276. To Audrey Wood

SH: Hotel Monteleone
New Orleans 12, U.S.A.
12/23/53
[TLS, 3 pp. HRC]

Dear Audrey:

Just finished a good day's work on the film-script "Hide & Seek" or "Whipmaster". A couple of more equally good days should finish the job. I hated to quit work on the new "Battle" for this job but I sure can use the money if you can get it for me, and I hope you can! Now that I'm into it the work is interesting to me and I am pushing it fast and hard as I can, did 15 pages today and about 10 yesterday. As I told you, I'm only re-writing the beginning and end of the play and the sequences that formerly included the old salesman. I think the major problem is reconciling, artistically, the hilarious comedy which is the keynote of the film, and the very heavy "punishment for sins" ending of it demanded by the censors, but maybe that can be cheated a little the way we did the "moral ending" in Streetcar.

Are you getting any concrete concessions from Wallis? If he doesn't phrase the contract so that I am assured of script approval and choice of directors (if Danny should not do it) then I think the cash payments should be upped to at least one hundred thousand. I'm sure that was the figure he was prepared and able to pay if he had to pay it, and he has got to pay it unless he can give me an absolutely reliable check on the story and so forth.

I received a sweet letter from Danny Mann and will enclose an answer, as I don't know his address and perhaps you do.

A funny thing happened a couple of days ago, somebody called me and identified himself as a nephew of Hal Wallis' wife, Louise Fazenda, and asked me how he could get in touch with Wallis, said he'd heard that he was going to do "Rose Tattoo" and that he had never been able to get in touch with him! I said it was much too early in the morning for me to solve such a weighty problem and to call me back later in the afternoon or evening, but he didn't.

Oliver Evans has completed his renovations on his French Quarter house, but his tenants moved out yesterday while he was giving a party for the officers on a French naval vessel which is paying a good-will visit to New Orleans. He wants Grandfather and I to occupy the vacated premises till the Key West house is ready. I don't know when that will be. I'm trying to get in touch with the realty company but they don't answer the phone this morning. Another possibility is Havana, but I think the sooner I get Grandfather settled down somewhere the better. He fell flat on his face in the Monteleone lobby night before last. He's very unsteady this year and I'm in constant dread that he'll break his hip-bone or something. Please make train or plane reservations for Frank right away! I can't manage alone in Key West. And Frank is likely to put if off unless the bookings are made for him. Please ask your travel agent to book him and Moon on something to Miami on or about Jan. 1st!

I'll manage to get there somehow in the car.

Now I must go downstairs and see if I can get the old man off his sofa in the lobby and into Gluck's restaurant next door for his creole gumbo and hot mince pie. Since that fall in the lobby, he has cut out the Manhattan cocktails.

We both send our love to you and Bill, Tenn.

[TW mailed the latest draft of "Hide & Seek" (n.d., HRC) to Audrey Wood with an admission that he had lost interest in the screenplay and hoped that "a southern writer" (January 15, 1954, HRC) could be found to complete it.

The "old salesman," Mister Charlie, derives from a one-act entitled "The Last of My Solid Gold Watches" (1943). Early drafts of *Baby Doll* begin with his arrival in the Mississippi Delta on the Yellow Dog train, but the role was cut in revision and the opening scene replaced by a more dramatic beginning.

Joseph Breen warned that Baby Doll's seduction in "Hide and Seek" represented a grave censorship problem, especially if treated as "a weapon of retribution against Meighan" (to J.L. Warner, August 1, 1952, Herrick). The warning, issued in 1952, had apparently stimulated thoughts about a "'moral ending'" for the film.

Hospitalization and the prospect of surgery for hemorrhoids would extend the New Orleans visit into the new year. Frank Merlo's arrival from New York led a distraught TW to proclaim that "my 'Horse' is my little world" (*Journal*, December 30, 1953). Oliver Evans added to his friend's abiding fear of cancer by repeating a doctor's warning that hemorrhoids "could become malignant" (*Journal*, January 1, 1954) without surgery.]

277. To Justin Brooks Atkinson

1431 Duncan St.
Key West, Fla.
Jan. 14, 1954
[TLS, 3 pp. BRTC]

Dear Brooks:

I'm so glad that Orianne was able to assemble that tricky little contraption for you and that you are pleased with it. A poet friend of mine, Oliver Evans, presented me with one in New Orleans and I was charmed by it and found out where he got it and thought that a critic who liked Miss Alma and Blanche would share my pleasure and theirs in this small and lyric adaptation of the great natural forces of heat and motion. I agree with you that it's a pity, to put it mildly, that these natural forces can't all be put to such innocent and charming uses or big ones that are equally benign. I went to a cocktail party in New Orleans that was completely still-born, dead and dull as ditch-water, until the lights were turned out and the angel chimes were set in motion, and then a mysterious softening and lightening of the atmosphere occured, and people started talking and being together in a warm and intimate way as if by magic, all through the influence of "The Angel Chimes", so I think they are more important than they look and worth the trouble of putting them together.

I read your Sunday piece on Jane Bowles' play and I blushed with that rather shameful satisfaction that you get from being favorably mentioned in print. I haven't had that satisfaction much lately and I am ashamed to admit that I was languishing for it. I hope you don't mind, or rather, I'm sure you don't, my taking exception to your assessment of the "Summerhouse". I wrote you about it early last summer and told you how much it had thrilled me at the try-out in Ann Arbor, which I saw just before I sailed for Europe. When I saw it again, just before I left for the South, this

Fall, it had undergone some alterations which were not for the good. Poor little Janie had succumbed, in the last act, to those well-meaning influences that surround the author of a play regarded as "special", and the efforts to motivate and clarify and justify the happenings in the play seemed to me to be at the expense of its purity and its "magic". Fortunately these efforts to make things clear were confined to the last act, and the two earlier acts were virtually the same as when I first saw them. But I don't think "The Queen of Tragedy" was a wise choice for the part of Mrs. Eastman-Cuevas. At least she wasn't at the Hartford opening which I attended. Miriam Hopkins, though not so powerful an actress, was much better in the part. She gave the greatest performance I've ever seen her give and was somehow exactly right for it. She had an off-beat humor and zany sort of extravagance that was both heartbreaking and hilarious, she was really Gertrude Eastman-Cuevas in the flesh. I think that this part is the subtlest part and the writing of the first two acts is the subtlest and most original theatre-writing of our times. I would have great, impossible, difficulty in writing a review of the play, so I thoroughly sympathize with your divided reactions. I mean I understand them. I wish, however, that critics could somehow devise a means of supporting plays which they can't approve or recommend as pieces of fine theatrical craftsmanship but which they recognize as having qualities much rarer than craftsmanship, a degree of sensibility and revelation which make them more important (don't they?) than all the hits of the season. Of course it would be wonderful, in fact, ideal, if a writer like Jane Bowles could also possess the professional know-how of a George Axelrod, but there is a jealous quarrel among the Muses which prevents this from being. I think, in other words, we need two separate and clearly defined standards of dramatic criticism, one for the George Axelrods and one for the Jane B's. They should not have to compete on the same terms in the same arena. In view of the fact that these two separate standards don't exist, or have never been openly defined in a way that's intelligible to the theatre public, the critics are probably being as fair as they can be, without favoring what they must feel are "special" interests.

As for myself, this is not a good time for me, I have been going through one of those long periods that have to be borne with patience because there is no other way to bear them. I have kept on working but my vitality is at a low ebb. I don't think this is discouragement, I think it is simply fatigue, which I hope will be passing. There are certainly lots of things I still want to do.

Yours ever, Tennessee.

P.S. I believe the biography I promised to give you was Phillip Horton's biography of the American poet Hart Crane which I think is the most illuminating picture yet drawn of a poet's difficulties in our modern world. I'll send you my own copy, autographed by the author, but when I get back to New York in the Spring I will give you another copy in exchange for that one. If you find it interesting, you should also read Hart Crane's Collected Letters which came out last Spring and which will fill out the picture and relieve the gloom, as Crane himself was much brighter and livelier than his life. The letters were published by "Hermitage" and edited by Brom Weber, and I think they rank with the letters of D.H. Lawrence.

[TW "blushed" to be called "a consummate artist" whose lyricism had become "an eloquent medium of theatrical expression." Such familiar praise by Atkinson formed the core of his objection to *In the Summerhouse*, which premiered in New York on December 29, 1953, and closed after fifty-five performances. "Scene by scene," the Jane Bowles play was "original, exotic and adventuresome," but it left the reviewer "in a muddle about the characters and with a feeling of flatness" (*New York Times*, January 10, 1954) for the overall production. The clarifications reportedly imposed upon the script were not evident to Atkinson, nor did he share TW's distaste for Judith Anderson, who replaced Miriam Hopkins as the imperious Mrs. Eastman-Cuevas.

TW cites George Axelrod, author of the long-running comedy *The Seven Year Itch* (1952), as a shrewd writer of popular Broadway fare. During the 1960s he worked primarily in Hollywood, writing screenplays for *Breakfast at Tiffany's* (1961) and *The Manchurian Candidate* (1962).]

278. To Cheryl Crawford

1431 Duncan St.,
Key West [Florida]
Jan. 22, 1954
[TLS, 2 pp. BRTC]

Dearest Cheryl:

Everybody who writes me from New York says, Isn't it wonderful, Cheryl has a "big hit", and each one says it with true satisfaction as if it was a personal success. I don't think anyone has ever had a hit that was enjoyed by so many people without a touch of the invidious in their reaction, and I can understand why. I feel the same way about it. I knew in Philadelphia that it would probably be a hit and it really did give me a wonderful feeling. Especially since the play is admirable. It is warm and witty and civilized and creditable to everybody in it, and I don't think I've ever seen better casting in the theatre. Of course you are justly famous for your casting. You have the greatest instinct for right actors in the theatre. I think this is the beginning of a new period for you. You needed just this little reassurance of luck to get you going again in full stride. Of course I have never seen you when you appeared disheartened. I don't think I ever will. It's hard to see how a person can be as strong as you are and still remain a presumably vulnerable thing of flesh and blood. We have forgotten about the Yankee spirit and you are a living reminder of what it was and apparently still can be.

I also like you for being honest and kind. . . .

So much for you!

I have the letters of Byron and I browse among them every night. It is impossible to get a book here which is a pity as there is no TV and the movies are old ones and bad ones and Frank and I are trying to stay away from the bars which are full of navy and navy intelligence, as they call it, and when we leave this island we don't want it to be on the famous "lavender bus" as they call it when you are told to get out. The weather is heavenly and all of us are feeling better. I was in the hospital for about a week in New Orleans. I had an attack of hemorrhoids, thrombosed, which is a complaint that is common among gentlemen of middle and late years and which is exquisitely painful. They were going to operate but at the last moment, observing my anxiety, they decided not to, and to see if the condition would not subside automatically, which it did and has now apparently disappeared. But they warned me that the hemmorrhoid veins should be removed if I want to avoid a possible recurrence. I may have this done in the Spring. I had to sleep under morphine several nights and I didn't enjoy it. I always felt like I was dying and didn't want to! Soon as I got out of the hospital, the same day, Grandfather and I took a plane for Miami. It took six hours, stopping at every cow-pasture! For several days afterwards I was so light-headed I couldn't walk a straight line but now I am feeling about as well as ever. I am working again, not easily, but with persistence and I hope I'll have something to show you in the Spring.

Devotedly, Tenn.

[Critics deemed *Oh, Men! Oh, Women!*, Cheryl Crawford's new production, "the funniest, wackiest, cockeyedest comedy to hit the Main Stem in a long time" (*New York Daily Mirror*, December 18, 1953). The story of a psychoanalyst who accidentally discovers his fiancée's sexual history premiered on December 17, 1953, and ran for 382 performances.

TW was probably reading a new selection of Byron letters edited by Jacques Barzun and published in 1953.

TW had good reason to shun "navy intelligence" in Key West. His FBI file indicates that the "Office of Naval Intelligence" has "secured statements from individuals who admitted participating in homosexual acts with Williams." Neither the date of the investigation nor the content of the "statements" is revealed in the file.]

279. To Gore Vidal

1431 Duncan Street
Key West, Fla.
January 27, 1954
[TLS, 2 pp. Houghton]

Dear Gore:

It seems that we just missed you here, which is regrettable as I had looked forward to the company of a bird in this place where the song bird is a very rare avis. There is a rumor that you may be coming back. Are you? The weather is divine here, the days blue and gold in continual succession, and those of our sisters who get around freely at night have reported sensational fortune. Little Arthur Williams is here, you may have crossed paths with him in Europe, he was on the Rome-Paris circuit for five or six years while we were on it. Frank can't stand him but I find him charming. He is very rich and utterly self-centered but he has a complete candor which is something that Latins cannot understand or tolerate, confusing it with bad taste, of which it is actually the opposite in my opinion. He is small and blond with a sort of gentle dry wit, small, perfect features, he looks rather like a much younger Lillian Gish or a gay little nephew of hers, he makes me think of that title of Elinor Wylies', "The Venetian Glass Nephew". But he has to have some dental work done and he is leaving today or tomorrow which is a pity as I shall then be a very solitary land bird among the gulls at South Beach. I do not go around at night. The bird was not well: plummetted to earth in New Orleans with a very dull thud and was confined to "Tuoro Infirmary" with an hideous affliction called "thrombosed hemmorrhoids", which attacked the tail of the bird and brought it to earth like a good hunter's shot-gun. They were going to operate but decided, at zero hour, that the bird's anxiety made it a bad surgical risk and gave a reprieve on condition that the swelling, large as a hen's egg, subsided, which it gradually did, in the course of ten days. The bird's tail is now back to normal but they say that the hemmorrhoid veins should be cut in the Spring in order to prevent a recurrence. The pain was exquisite and the bird was pumped full of various drugs and morphine which had an upsetting affect on the circulatory system and the nerves. You know the repugnance with which the bird regards the prospect of its eventual demise. . . .

What I wanted to write you about today was your story in "New World Writing" which I finally read last night and which I must say is quite the best thing of yours I have seen to date. Unfortunately the first two pages are fairly routine, which threw me off it, when I first started to read it in New York, but it develops richly, in a new vein of yours that bodes very well for the future. The style is superbly smooth and polished and there are flashes of poetry in it that took me by surprise as I hadn't found them so much in your prose-writing before. It is written with impressive control and restraint, in fact it's one fault is an excessive diffidence about making its points. I thought the women in the library, "The Fatal Sisters" could have been pointed up just a bit more before he woke from his sun-nap to hear them plotting his destruction. And the scenes with the boy were cut just a tiny bit short of the point at which they would have been clearly comprehensible perhaps because you were afraid of evoking some echo of "Death in Venice", which I don't think should have bothered you, as all works of art that I can think of strike echos of others and the story is completely your own. This shade too much of diffidence is a fault on the side of the angel's, though it may prevent some people from getting as much from the story as there is there. I think it would make a fine play and I wish you had chosen it as the theme for the play you are working on. The people and background are very much at home with you and the fact that there is so much room for expansion in the story makes it a good play prospect.

Do write me some bulletins on New York if you're not coming back here soon. What happened to Paul and Janie? I talked to them over long-distance after the play opened but Janie was incoherent and Paul was very cool and non-committal. He talked as if he thought the wires were tapped by the FBI. I only gathered that he was leaving this month for Tangier and that Ahmed would never be able to leave there, for Ceylon or anywhere else, because of trouble with passport. But Paul always takes the blackest possible view of a situation, a queer sort of defense against the jealous gods. I am trying to complete all manuscripts that are close enough to completion, so that I can leave for Ceylon or somewhere with a clean slate, that is, with nothing hanging over my head except the future which is quite enough to hang over any bird's head in these times.

Heard that Truman's mother died. Have you seen him? I saw Speed in Monroe but he was headed almost immediately for New York so must be there now. Oliver is living a very disordered life in New Orleans, cruising feverishly night and day and doing no work, but looks and seems to feel well.

Love, Tenn.

[Gore Vidal returned to New York at this time to develop a successful career in television writing.

The title of Elinor Wylie's novel *The Venetian Glass Nephew* (1925) refers to a creature made of glass who is brought to life by a necromancer's art.

"The Ladies in the Library" (1953), the Vidal story admired by TW, was dedicated to Alice Bouverie, whose estate on the Hudson may have provided setting and locale. The "Ladies," an incarnation of the mythological Fates, are overheard by a visiting writer as they plot his imminent death by a massive heart attack.

Truman Capote's mother Nina died on January 4, 1954, from an overdose of barbiturates and alcohol.]

280. To Jane Lawrence and Tony Smith

1431 Duncan
Key West [Florida]
Feb 8, 1954
[TLS, 1 p. Smith Collection]

Dear Jane & Tony:

I'm not able to write you a good letter right now, I'm not able to write anything good right now, but I don't want to let another day pass without telling you how happy I am over the birth of Clare Lanier. My middle name is also Lanier so I think of her as a relative.

In many ways you are the two most wonderful people that I have ever known. I have always suspected that you actually are, it would not surprise me if I am right about that.

The child will be as wonderful as you both put together.

There's nothing I would like as well tonight as hearing Jane singing "My Bill" or Tosca or Carmen but all I hear is the palms scraping together and a distant radio.

Grandfather and Frank and I are back in Key West. The days are lovely but the nights are dull. But you remember how Key West is. We will be sailing back to Europe sometime in May by way of Gibralter and then up through Europe, with some stops in Spain and a long stay in Rome. Maybe after that we'll even take a boat to Ceylon with Paul Bowles and Ahmed, if Ahmed is permitted to leave Tangier by the French immigration authorities.

Grandfather says to give Clare Lanier his love and "apostolic blessing".

Mine to all three of you, Tennessee.

Town is dull this year, result of various acts of violence against queens in the past few seasons. One poor girl, a night auditor at the Casa Marina, was dispatched with twenty-two knife wounds by a party unknown. Blood was all over the apartment as if she had run till exhausted from room to room, probably defending herself as best she could with her manicure set and tweezers. Neighbors reported no out-cry. She probably had on her long-playing opera records, and didn't have time to turn them off as she flew!

281. To Lilla Van Saher

[1431 Duncan Street
Key West, Florida]
Feb 16, 1954
[TLS, 1 p. HRC]

Dear Lilla:

Sorry we just missed you in Key West, Regina St. Paul told us you'd been here. I trust we'll have better luck in the Spring. We plan to sail around the middle of May and will spend at least a month in New York before sailing. Our new address there is the floor above Cafe Nicholson on East Fifty-eighth street, phone is Murry Hill 8-6744. Gore will know when we get back or possibly when we're expected, and I do hope you'll be around.

The town is dead, no interesting society, almost no one to talk to. But the days are lovely. I get up at daybreak, work all morning and rest on the beach all afternoon, so the absence of any night-life is unimportant.

I'll fly over to Havana when some excitement becomes imperative.

Grandfather's still with us, and Frank and Mr. Moon.

It's kind of you to see my influence, favorably, in the current theatre season, but actually the only good play of the lot, "In The Summerhouse" was written long before any influence of mine existed. You'd love Jane Bowles: you might call her, she stays with Oliver Smith, the designer-producer, 28 W. 10th Street, A 1. 4-2085. She may be feeling depressed about the commercial failure of her play and you would be good for her, you have such a warm heart for other writers.

Ever yours, Tennessee.

[Lilla Van Saher (1912-1968), one of TW's "vampire" women, wrote *The Echo* (1947), a psychiatric novel, and *Macamba* (1949), a florid romance set in the Caribbean. TW described her as "a dominatrix" and dubbed her "the crepe de Chine Gypsy" (*Conversations*, p. 357).]

282. To Audrey Wood

SH: Hotel Nacional de Cuba, Havana
March 6, 1954
[TLS w/ autograph postscript, 2 pp. HRC]

Dear Audrey:

As you see I have removed to Cuba. Danny and I had three meetings and heart-to-heart talks before I left and everything was understood. I didn't think it wise to sign the contracts until we had gotten through to Hal Wallis, directly, about the matter of authorship. I don't know whether or not you read the "approach" that was submitted to us, but as Frankie remarked, it is actually a "retreat" and a very disastrous one. I suggest that you read it right away. You will agree with me about it. Remove the poetry from "Tattoo" and you have the cheapest kind of a grade B picture. There was no hint of poetry in this treatment. "Tattoo" is admirably suited to the screen. It will blossom out as a picture, even without Magnani, and with Magnani, it will have a stunning impact, IF-IF-IF! - it is not destroyed by the writer. Consequently I feel that I am obligated, not only to the play and myself, but equally to Magnani, and all of us concerned, to make sure that the lyrical values, the plastic values, and so forth, are kept in it and given a chance to flower as Magnani will make them. ~~I don't believe that Wallis either appreciates Magnani or the play itself. Or he wouldn't even permit this~~.

I think that you can persuade Hal Wallis, not only of my good and honest and rational intentions, but of my taste and my capability to see that he has a script worthy of Anna Magnani, whether I have to do it alone, or with a ~~suitable~~ collaborator who will be willing to work under my direction, since I think it is reasonable to assume that I, who created the play and the characters in it, am best able to judge whether or not they are being re-created for the screen. Danny agrees with me about this a hundred percent and I know that you will. Perhaps Wallis does not want "Tattoo" but another film very loosely related to it. But he must remember that Magnani agreed to do "Tattoo" and that that is the play we are giving him. If he doesn't really like it, if he wants something else, then there is no point in continuing to deal with him. It would be another "Menagerie" or worse, for the episodes in "Tattoo" will be grotesque and Serafina a ridiculous slob unless it exists in the poetic atmosphere of the original ~~play~~.

I have already written the opening sequences of the film, up to the death of Rosario. I am satisfied with the elimination of all censorable material. But I am going to keep the boy kneeling before the shrine to promise that he will respect the daughter's innocense. This was disgustingly treated in the "approach", he promised that he would "honor his father and mother" and "punctured his finger with a needle" to make some sort of blood oath. This gives you an idea of the "approach". The kneeling to the shrine could never offend anybody, it never did, and on the screen it could be handled still more scrupulously, with absolute purity and touching devoutness.

I like the suggestion of Serafina actually going to the Square Roof to confront Estelle Hohengarten instead of calling her on the phone. That's good. (Maybe) I also like every opportunity of taking the picture outside the house. There is nothing I like better than freedom and movement, and Wallis should not be worried on that score.

Please try to sell him on three points: my taste, my professional capability and the humble objectivity that I think I now have developed in regard to my work.

I want to write you separately about Inge. I was terribly disturbed by the one-acts he gave me to read and which he demanded right back to show to Danny. I think he is going through what I went through after "Streetcar", post-success ~~trauma~~ "shock", but he is over-compensating in the wrong way. To exhibit this work is extremely damaging. I think you must deal with him as candidly as you do with me when I send you "crap". It's the only way to help a panicky writer. If I hadn't been leaving immediately for Cuba, I would have talked to him about this problem. Perhaps I will have a chance to before he returns to New York.

Love - 10.

How can I "make friends" with Wallis? I want to.

[TW expressed "fury over the 'Tattoo' script" developed by his collaborator, who "couldn't write 'I see the cat.'" He wished that he could "shut a door on all that dreary buy and sell side of writing and work purely again for myself alone. I am sick of being peddled. Perhaps if I could have escaped being peddled I might have become a major artist" (*Journal*, April 17, 1954). Joe Hazen, one of the film's co-producers, later informed TW that Hal Kanter was "off the script" (July 9, 1954, HRC). Daniel Mann was set to direct the film.

Censorship problems occasioned by *The Rose Tattoo* were last summarized in a Production Code report dated May 5, 1953. Joseph Breen advised that "romance rather than lust" guide the "big scene" between Alvaro and Serafina, and that Alvaro conveniently "pass out" from too much "wine" to avert any sexual intimacy. The advice, which was taken, would allow Serafina's daughter Rosa to "misconstrue" (to Wallis, May 5, 1953, Herrick) the suggestive events of the night. Restored to the film was the boy's promise to respect the "innocense" of Rosa, a distasteful reference which the censor preferred to delete. No Sicilian "blood oath" remained in the final print.]

283. To Audrey Wood

[1431 Duncan Street
Key West, Florida]
March 21, 1954
[TLS, 2 pp. HRC]

Dear Audrey:

Although I understand your letter about "Kingdom of Earth" and the practicality of your objections to the story's publication, I am distressed over its omission from the book and have very little interest left in publishing these stories. I think "Kingdom" is by far my best and strongest piece of prose-writing. Without it the little book will be thin and pale as a leaf of under-nourished cabbage, and I would almost, perhaps quite, prefer not to have it brought out. It will not compare favorably to One Arm, people will say it's a "come down". With "Kingdom" they couldn't say that, even though that story might offend or disgust them. I wish that New Directions was willing to bring the book out much more privately and keep "Kingdom" in it, bring it out the way they did "I Rise in Flame", very de luxe and expensive and a small edition, not distributed by mail or through commercial book-stores but done strictly as an art venture and sold slowly without immediate profit. If it is a really exciting book, as it would be with Kingdom, it would have a much more permanent interest and eventually a bigger and more profitable sale. I don't mind at all if the sales are postponed till after these films are released if you really think it would hurt them. I don't think it would. On the contrary, I think the artistry of the story is defensible and that even if it is attacked by censors, it will not be damaging to my other projects.

MacGregor and I discussed, tentatively, a compromise arrangement, by which "Kingdom of Earth" would be "tipped into" a hundred or hundred and fifty "special" copies and held on reserve, for much more private distribution, at a higher price than the "trade edition". But I really don't think there should be a trade edition. It would suit me far better if there was only the special, private edition, distributed by hand directly by the publishers, to avoid legal trouble. I wouldn't suggest such a thing if I didn't think in the long run it would pay off at least as well. Actually the "queer" stories in the book will be more damaging than "Kingdom" which is merely sensual, if that is to be considered.

I hope I'll get a typed copy of "the new Battle" in a few days before we leave Key West. I'm eager to see how it reads. I think Act Two Scene one is particularly improved, but perhaps Carol should appear first at the store-entrance, perhaps during the altercation between Lady and Val, before she starts honking at the service-station, --- the store door could be locked and Val or Lady could shout, 'Not open!' --- I think it's much better not having Lady rush out to the doctor after the nurse charges her with pregnancy. Of course I know the play is pitched in an almost hysterical key, but if a non-realistic tone is established in staging right from the start, - also in design, lighting, Etc. - it might be acceptable at least as "the work of a mad man". I'd like to show it to Gadg and Jose Quintero. Send me a couple of copies, one for notes.

I think I've done all the important scenes for "Tattoo" already. It is surprisingly easy, it takes to the screen by instinct.

I'm also pulling together a short-long play based on the characters in "Three Players" which I started last summer in Rome but don't expect that till you see it, as I might not like it when I read it aloud.

My feet still feel like I'm walking on two sponges! I am taking massive shots of Vitamin B12, in alternate cheeks, every other day, which is energizing but has no effect on the pedal extremities. I don't for one moment believe the doctor's opinion that it is "peripheral neuritis", it is something, all right, but not that! I want to have a medical check-up soon as I get back to New York to determine the true cause of the trouble: I think it is circulatory.

Jimmie Elliot wrote me a long, long letter about his plan to produce Raffaelo de Banfield's opera based on "Lord Byron's Love Letter". How do you feel about this? He said you approved. I think a production by Jimmie would need careful supervision as he has had nothing but flops and is still pretty young. I like the kid, though, and his enthusiasm is important. I guess there's not much to lose.

Bigelow's two-day visit has stretched and stretched, it's like the famous girdle called the Two-way stretch! But I love having him around, he livens things up considerably. It will be expensive, this pleasure, but I always feel that Bigelow is worth every cent he may cost you. IF - you can afford him . . .

Gertrude Houston was also here for a couple of days with a girl-friend. No allusions were made on either side to the Jay-Maria situation and she and her friend were rushing to meet a yacht in Miami and planning to join some oil-millionaire in Houston. Jay is definitely in India. I haven't heard a word from Maria! - the suspense is intolerable almost.

Love, Tenn

[Audrey Wood feared that publishing "The Kingdom of Earth" would cause publicity "detrimental" (to TW, March 18, 1954, HRC) to current and forthcoming film projects. The "sensual" story, drafted in 1942 and entitled "Spiritchel Gates" (HRC), is set in the Mississippi Delta and narrated by Chicken: "It's earth I'm after and now I am honest about it and don't pretend I'm nothing but what I am, a lustful creature determined on satisfaction and likely as not to get my full share of it" (*Collected Stories*, p. 378). Chicken's determination leads indirectly to the death of Lot, his consumptive half-brother, and to the appropriation of Lot's prostitute-bride, Myrtle.

A "compromise" led New Directions to publish both a trade edition entitled *Hard Candy: A Book of Stories* (1954), and a limited edition entitled *The Kingdom of Earth with Hard Candy* (1954). TW demanded once again that his most controversial work not be openly sold or displayed in St. Louis.

The "short-long play" in preparation is *Cat on a Hot Tin Roof*.

Raffaello de Banfield wrote the music and TW the libretto for *Lord Byron's Love Letter: Opera in One Act*, which premiered in New Orleans on January 17, 1955. James Elliott produced the new opera on a bill which included the one-act "27 Wagons Full of Cotton."

TW informed Wood in early-February that the Laughlin-Britneva affair had been revived and that they planned to marry soon. TW, one of those chosen "'to hold the crown'" in the Russian Orthodox ceremony, quipped that "if this comes off, I'll be willing to wear the crown or even sit on it!" (February 1, 1954, HRC). Laughlin's untimely travel abroad only added to the mystery of his intentions. Gertrude Huston, formerly an intimate companion of the publisher, was visiting Key West with a friend.]

284. To Elia "Gadg" Kazan

[1431 Duncan Street
Key West, Florida]
March 31, 1954
[TLS, 2 pp. WUCA]

Dear Gadg:

You should never put off doing a play or a picture because when you do, somebody works on you, or you work on yourself, and the blood of art runs out through the mortal wound of excessive cogitation! Do you mind me telling you this? I am not afraid to say anything I want to say to you because I regard you as so close and true a friend that no dissimulation is necessary between us.

If you had hopped over here for a couple of days, we could have accomplished much more, batting ideas back and forth in talk than we can by exchanging letters about them in which each of us is determined to explain and defend his views and position.

The frog-gigging was your idea, I embraced it immediately as I do most of your ideas which are so startling, so brilliantly apposite, so direct to the core of the story. A modern version of the medieval tournament with frog-sticks instead of lances and a panicky dyed blond as the lady fair and the mossy swamps of the deep South as the field of honor was a divinely apposite idea and one to which I made an immediate, humble obeisance. Now you have succumbed to the weakness of Hamlet. You have brooded and chewed over it for a year and a half, or more, and you have talked yourself out of it. Well, I still say it was a GREAT, GREAT IDEA! And you haven't talked me out of it. . . .

Sure, you could do a scene with a big party, but it wouldn't have anything like the dramatic poetry, the visual and symbolic richness of the men with the frog-sticks making human frogs of each other, rival phalluses - excuse me, phalli - I see what you mean when you say it comes out of a cocked hat, a magician's topper, but I don't agree with you, I don't think it does, I think it is an exactly parallel situation, and anyhow, it can easily be predicated or announced in one of the earlier scenes, Ruby can say they're going frog-sticking tonight and ball it up in the bayou! "What's fun about sticking frogs?" - "nothing, honey, if there was nothin' but frogs. . ." --- If we see the two men walking off side by side, after the very funny Gaston and Alfonso bit, one raging, grim, frustrate, the other, confident, smiling - the story is told. <u>We</u> know damned well that Vacarro isn't the frog! - that Meighan is already the stuck frog! - the story was completed, the whole thing actually resolved, when Vacarro put the horns on him, and after that all we want to do is hit hard and get out fast. The phone-bit is overdone. I don't think she should speak to God on the phone. After her conversation to the chief of police, she should drop the receiver exhaustedly into her lap and speak the words to God as if to herself in prayer, just holding the phone in her hand. I love the last line it gives us. "Scared in this big empty house". IT describes, or sums up, the whole individual human situation, alone and scared in a big empty house of a universe, so much too big for any single soul in it.

I had to pitch in and write the "Tattoo" script as the studio writer Wallis put on it did a shockingly bad job on it, worse than that other writer did on "Streetcar". Now Magnani and Lancaster are squabbling over top-billing, the gentleman wants to go in front of the lady and vice versa, and maybe she won't even do it, show-business is hell! - real frog-sticking!

Ask Audrey to let you read the re-write I did on "Battle of Angels".

I did it last summer in Rome and Spain. Audrey didn't like it and I did it over again here. Maybe she still doesn't like it, but I think it is an exciting and different piece of theatre and I would love to have your reaction to it. I also would like you to read a short-long play, originally a long one, called "A Cat on a Hot Tin Roof". It would require a curtain-raiser to make a full evening and the story is grim. I will show it to you before I sail for Europe May 15th. When are you leaving New York? I get there about the tenth of April, after delivering grandfather to the Gayoso lobby in Memphis.

Play it cool, baby!

Love, Tenn.

Skipper was here and should have had him a ball. For some reason this year the Island is over-run by beautiful nymphos, really attractive ones, who almost rape the men in public, let alone what they may do in private. They grope you at the bar and literally howl to be fucked. Won't take no for an answer if they can possibly get any other. I think Skipper was scared. He left mighty quick. But not as quick as Bigelow! - a cop named Buster walked into Logun's patio one night and took Bigelow by the seat of his pants and turkey-trotted him out to the paddy-wagon at the door. (I wasn't there but heard a vivid account) - It cost me five hundred bucks to get him off the keys the next morning. . . .

I thought this would give you a laugh, but please forget that I told you about it, please! You and I both love gossip. At heart I'm a back-fence biddy. . . .

[At first TW mildly resisted the "frog-sticking" conclusion of "Hide and Seek" because he had "never gigged frogs. Do you suppose the research dept. at Warners' could provide me with a graphic account of one?" (April 16, 1953, WUCA), he asked Elia Kazan. A draft of "Hide and Seek" dated March 25, 1954, includes a "Gaston and Alfonso bit" played by Archie Lee and Silva, who carry sharp gigs but tramp comically toward the bayou "side by side like a pair of sweethearts!" Violence is averted for the moment, as the scene dissolves to Baby Doll on the back porch of the Meighan residence calling the chief of police: "I'm all alone, I'm scared, in this - big - empty - house" (HTC). The present ending, Kazan may have felt, lacked a dramatic denouement and the necessary punishment of vice.]

285. To Audrey Wood

[1431 Duncan Street
Key West, Florida]
[ca. April 1, 1954]
[TLS w/ enclosure, 1 p. HRC]

Dear Audrey:

Here's a sort of rough draft of the play that threw me into such a terrible state of depression last summer in Europe, I couldn't seem to get a grip on it. I haven't done much with it since then, but I would like to have this draft typed up, so that I will at least be able to read it with less confusion. Although it is very wordy it is still too short and would need a curtain-raiser to make a full evening. But I do think it has a terrible sort of truthfulness about it, and the tightest structure of anything I have done. And a terrifyingly strong final curtain.

I am sending it to you a little prematurely since I am hitting the air-lanes with Grandfather this afternoon. Yesterday I sent you my work on "Rose Tattoo". I hope you will at least get the impression that I am still a hard-worker. . . .

A discouraging letter from Gadg. He wants a completely different ending to "Hide & Seek", although it was he who wanted me to end it with the frog-sticking party. I think that's an excellent ending and am not at all in sympathy with his new notions about it. I wrote him so. Is it true that he is going to do a play in the Fall by Robert Anderson? How can he do both? Is this the play you said you had for him? - I am getting jealous. . . .

With love, Tenn.

The news that Arthur Miller lost his passport is shocking and disgusting. It is also frightening to me, since I have not yet had any news of mine. Do you think they'll refuse it? I didn't send my old passport along with the application. Is that necessary? I am enclosing a letter of protest to the State Dept. but I will let you decide whether or not to send it. This is cowardly, but if I lost my passport, I would just curl up and die! - I have to get out of this country at least once a year, the way things are now. . . . Please make a copy of the letter and send the original to the State Dept, if you think this advisable. The other copy you might send to Arthur or to "The Times".

[The "rough draft" with a "strong final curtain" is *Cat on a Hot Tin Roof*. TW later reported some "messy" work on the play and worried that "the intrusion of the homosexual theme may be fucking it up again" (*Journal*, April 3, 1954).

Robert Anderson's new play *All Summer Long* opened on September 23, 1954, with direction by Alan Schneider rather than Elia Kazan. It closed after 60 performances on Broadway.

The enclosure regarding Arthur Miller's "lost" passport is printed as a separate letter.]

286. The State Department Washington, D.C.

[1431 Duncan Street
Key West, Florida]
April 1, 1954
[TL, 1 p. HRC]

Dear Sirs:

I feel obliged to tell you how shocked I am by the news that Arthur Miller, a fellow playwright, has been refused a passport to attend the opening of a play of his in Brussels.

I know only the circumstances of the case that have been reported in the papers, but since I have been spending summers abroad since 1948, I am in a position to tell you that Mr. Miller and his work occupy the very highest critical and popular position in the esteem of Western Europe, and this action can only serve to implement the Communist propaganda, which holds that our country is persecuting its finest artists and renouncing the principles of freedom on which our ancestors founded it.

I would like to add that there is nothing in Arthur Miller's work, or my personal acquaintance with him, that suggests to me the possibility that he is helpful or sympathetic to the Communist or any other subversive cause. I have seen all his theatrical works. Not one of them contains anything but the most profound human sympathy and nobility of spirit that the American theatre has shown in our time and perhaps in any time before. He is one man that I could never suspect of telling a lie, and he has categorically stated that he has <u>not</u> supported Communism or been a Communist.

I don't think you have properly estimated the enormous injury that an action of this kind can do our country, even in the minds of those who are still prejudiced in our favor in Western Europe.

Yours respectfully,

[A spokesman for the State Department noted that Arthur Miller's application had been "rejected under regulations denying passports to persons believed to be supporting the Communist movement, whether or not they are members of the Communist party." Miller replied that he was not "'supporting any Communist movement,'" adding that "his plays would make more friends for American culture than the State Department" (*New York Times*, March 31, 1954). Miller planned to visit Brussels to attend the premiere of his play *The Crucible* (1953), a thinly veiled indictment of McCarthyism.

TW did not mail the letter of protest, fearing that his own passport would not be renewed for a sailing date of May 15 (see letter #294). Citation of a similar gesture of support for the "Hollywood Ten," screenwriters and directors investigated by the House Un-American Activities Committee in 1947, appears in TW's FBI file and was reported to the United States Information Agency in July 1954. At issue was TW's participation in a radio broadcast planned in 1950 which did not materialize.]

PART VI

1954–1957

Overleaf: Tennessee Williams and Anna Magnani.
"The sexiest looking woman on earth."

287. To Robert MacGregor

SH: Rembrandt Hotel, Tanger
5/29/54.
[TLS, 3 pp. Houghton]

Dear Bob:

Frank says he mailed the proofs to you yesterday. I'm sorry about the delay, I didn't realize you were in a hurry for them. I only came across one serious error, the omission of a phrase in "Hard Candy" which made a sentence meaningless, and I wrote the omitted phrase in the margin. Two or three stories are still here as I haven't yet read them. Mattress, 3 Players, Violin Case, The Vine and Widow Holly. As you have correct Mss. on these 4, it will be easy to check the proofs at your end. That is, if there is need for haste. I felt so fatigued, so run down, when I got on the boat that I knew I would loathe the stories if I read them. So I put it off till the last day of the voyage, when I was beginning to feel recovered. I liked most of them, especially "Two on a Party" which I almost wish were the title story of the book. Frank is disturbed over having both "Hard Candy" and "Mysteries of the Joy Rio" in the book. I think there should be a note stating that the latter is actually a first draft of the title story but that we felt there was enough difference to justify printing both. I think it might obviate some criticism, and criticism should certainly be obviated wherever possible, don't you think? I wonder if obviated is the right word. . . .

Now please do me this favor. Don't distribute the book anywhere that my mother would be likely to get her hands on it. That is, around Saint Louis. It must not be displayed in windows or on counters anywhere. Don't you agree? Or do you? My mother's reaction is the only one that concerns me. I think she would be shocked to death by "Two on a Party" - although it seems that she did get hold of "One Arm" somehow or other. It still makes me shudder to think of her reaction! She has aged greatly since. . .

Isn't it awful to have conventional blood ties? You just can't break them.

Soon as we landed in Tangier we found ourselves involved in the turbulent lives of the Bowles'. Jane is hopeless enamored of an Arab woman in the grain-market, a courtship which has continued without success for six years, and Paul's Arab, Ahmed, has moved out of his house, at least for "Rhamadan", a religious period of abstinence like our Lent, which is now going on here. A cannon which shakes the whole city is fired at 3 A.M.

announcing that eating, drinking, fucking must stop. It is fired again at 7 P.M. to signal the resumption of these practises, but Ahmed says that total abstinence is necessary in the third practise. Paul is languishing, liver trouble and paratyphoid came on him with Rhamadan.

It appears that we have inherited Maria for the summer. A letter was waiting for me at Gibralter in which she declared that she was brutally jilted and cannot stay in London, as everybody is sending her wedding presents and congratulatory messages. She is on a Mediterranean cruise to escape this humiliation. But she proposes to get off the boat at Corsica and come to Rome as she can't face London again under the circumstances. Funny as it does sound, I do feel sorry for her. Why did Jay propose to her if he wasn't prepared to go through with it? I wanted to have a quiet summer. . . . Of course when she arrives I will be happy to have her with us as she really does brighten a scene with her unquenchable spirits and love of fun. Jay says he was frightened of her vitality. Perhaps someone should have held his nose and made him swallow it for his own good, I can't see how, unless he is going to marry Gertrude after all, he will ever find anybody that will give him the lively companionship he seems to want and need.

Ever & truly, Tenn.

[Robert MacGregor (1911-1974) increasingly took over editorial tasks handled by James Laughlin at New Directions.

"Hard Candy" and "The Mysteries of the Joy Rio" are set in a "third-rate cinema" whose "galleries" have witnessed "every device and fashion of carnality" (*Collected Stories*, p. 103). So marked was their difference "in result" ("Editor's Note") that both stories would be published in *Hard Candy* (1954). TW preferred "Joy Rio," the early version, because of its greater compassion and unity (to MacGregor, March 1, 1954, Houghton).

MacGregor promised TW that relatively few copies of *Hard Candy* would be sent to St. Louis and that local book sellers had agreed to accommodate only preferred customers who "cannot be alienated" (August 24, 1954, Houghton).

TW was "shocked," if not surprised, by Laughlin's jilting of Maria Britneva. "Most of all," he wrote to her, "it seems so foolish, so pitiably foolish, of J. because you would have made him a perfect wife and would have given him a faith in himself, as a poet and as a person" (qtd. in St. Just, pp. 91-92). Audrey Wood reported a later conversation in which Laughlin expressed fear of Britneva's "'great will'" (to TW, July 19, 1954, HRC) and of her many social activities, both of which would interfere with his preferred manner of life.

Britneva's invitation to join TW in Rome came with an understanding that "we won't be wearing black chiffon or broken hearts on our sleeves, but enjoy the golden city in the golden summer" (qtd. in St. Just, p. 92).]

288. To Justin Brooks Atkinson

[Rome]
[early-June 1954]
[TLS, 2 pp. BRTC]

DEAR BROOKS:

Audrey Wood just stuck under my hotel door, here in Rome, your notice of "Purification" in Dallas and I can't even wait to get some decent paper on which to write you. Encouragement works in mysterious ways. I immediately sat down and conquered a scene in a play which had totally eluded and almost maddened and unmanned me for weeks past. Now my nerves are calm, my fingers don't shake, I look appreciatively out into the fine blue and gold morning that almost never fails to appear in Roman summer. Why are you so good to me? I certainly don't deserve it, although I do try to.

Did Margo really do a beautiful production? I think she sometimes can. She did a beautiful production of "You Touched Me" in Pasadena. Perhaps she failed to, with Summer & Smoke in New York because we were fighting. I am terribly attached to her, she has the quickest sympathies and warmest affections of any one I've ever known in my life, except my grandmother. And the deepest passion for the theatre. The tragedy is that her performance rarely lives up to her passion. Like a lover so anxious, so frightened of his desire, that he can't carry it through. . . . I have not been very good to her, have been cool and reserved since the clash over "Summer" but she has never seemed to resent it or hold it against me. She has true gallantry of spirit and ENORMOUS courage. I think what most annoyed me about "Summer" was not so much her refusal to let me work directly with the actors as the story, that came to me "round about", that she had made a speech to the actors saying that it was the work of "a dying playwright". I had been ~~terribly~~ ill at the time, but "dying" was the furthest thing from my intention, then or any time since, and anyway it struck me as an irrelevant or false and certainly not helpful sort of "appeal". Actors always do their best, and the real or imaginary sickness of an author doesn't and shouldn't, couldn't, alter their contribution to the production.

Rome has never looked lovelier, than it does now, after the sick atmosphere of Tangier, which was only relieved by the beach and charm of Jane and Paul Bowles who make their home there, mostly because it's about the most economical place to live in the western half of the world.

Yours ever and truly and fondly, Tennessee.

[TW was "completely shattered by the 2 plane flights" from Tangier to Rome and reported "panic Panic!" in correspondence with Jane and Paul Bowles (6/?/54, HRC), whom he invited to visit the new ménage: "It is wonderful being all together in 1 place 'en famille' even when the horse sleeps with the chauffeur (??!)."

Margo Jones's staging of "The Purification" and "The Apollo of Bellac" (Jean Giraudoux, 1947) reassured Brooks Atkinson, who had come to regard the Dallas theatre project as "stock company merchandising." The plays, he wrote, "complement each other perfectly" and were "singularly beautiful" (*New York Times*, May 29, 1954) in their presentation. Jones had proven a sympathetic director of TW's early works, including "The Purification" in 1944.

In *Memoirs* TW recalled Jones's "speech" to the cast of *Summer and Smoke* (1948) and observed that "I did not like to be reminded that my apparent good health was so profoundly suspect" (p. 153).]

289. To Cheryl Crawford

[Rome]
[June 1954]
[TLS, 3 pp. BRTC]

Cheryl dear:

I hope you are not thinking badly of me because of my silence. I have been passing through, and still not out of, the worst nervous crisis of my nervous existence and I thought for a while I'd crack up. I've been approaching it for more than a year, evading with liquor and sedatives and distractions. But when it became imperative to stop work for a while, to take the rest I'd promised myself so long, I really fell apart at the seams. When I got up in the morning, there was nothing to do but draw deep, sighing breaths and exhale them and stare stupidly this way and that. What do people do with themselves when they don't work? Frank fusses over the dog for a couple of hours but I can't get interested in this new dog. I came to love Moon and he died and this new dog seems stupid and bad-tempered to me, although he has the touching pathos of all small beings. (That is, except insects!) - I feel, now, that I should have remained in the States and possibly sought out some good psychiatrist or nerve-doctor this summer, regardless of my loathing of that sort of surrender or admission of helplessness. But the point has come when I can't rely on myself. The present "syndrome" is temporary at best. I go as far through the day as I can without a sleeping tablet. Then - sometimes before noon, rarely much after - I wash one down with a stiff drink. Five hours later the tension builds up again and I need another. So far I haven't exceeded three in the course of a day. But this is no good, it can't go on, you know, it is just temporizing. As Miss Alma said to the old doctor, "I don't see how I'm going to get through the summer." It has gotten so bad, Cheryl, that I don't dare to turn down a street unless I can sight a bar not more than a block and a half down it. Sometimes I have to stop and lean against a wall and ask somebody with me to run ahead and bring me a glass of cognac from the bar. . . . I don't understand what is back of these crises, panics. It could be simply a physical thing. Or it could be a physical expression of some deep mental crisis that's going on. I am telling you these embarassingly personal things because I think we have a relationship that permits confession and understanding. I could also tell Audrey, but unless she guesses, I am somehow too shy with her (always have been) to tell her things like that. - Now I do think that I can get through the summer but when I get back I want to tackle this dilemma in a radical way, even if it means submitting to analysis. Dr. Kinsey, after a four and a half hour talk in 1949 or 50, told me that I needed analysis and that he would recommend a good man for me. He seemed to realize that I was facing an eventual impasse, at which I am now arriving. I've put it off because of work and the need to travel. But now the sustained crisis has exhausted the working apparatus, so something has to be done to get at the root of it, even if it means facing something that I'm afraid to face. Lawrence said: "Face the facts and live beyond them". I've tried to live beyond them by not facing them and come to the logical pay-off that entails. I'll probably return earlier than usual this summer, perhaps in August, and if, in the meanwhile, you can get the name of some good man in the psychiatric field (perhaps through Kinsey), I think that I will be ready to give him a try. I don't want Inge's man, I don't like what he has done with Inge who seems to be living in a state of false complacense, peaceful on the surface, but with an apparent suspension of his critical faculties at least regarding his own work, an "afflatus" that only makes him pompously self-satisfied and showing bad scripts around like fresh-plucked flowers. There is probably not more than one man who would be any good for me but I want to find him and find out, one way or the other, if I am susceptible to outside help. Without illusions. . . .

So much for the screaming "ME-mies"!

In spite of the state in which I worked on it, I still think "Orpheus" may have some, and possibly even enough, of the lyric beauty and intensity which I tried to put into it, to justify its production. Of course it was bound to suffer from its author's suffering to some extent. A line from Rabindranath Tagore: "With the shadow of my passion have I darkened your eyes." There is torment in this play, violence and horror - it is the under kingdom, all right! - that reflects what I was going through, or approaching, as I wrote it, but I think I may have managed, finally, at this point of stopping work on it, to keep the music over the thunder of disintegration. Perhaps if I had not been so tormented myself it would have been less authentic. Because I could not work with the old vitality, I had to find new ways and may have found some.

But I trust that our talks in New York made it clear that I want nothing but your usual absolute honesty from you, about this and anything between us, professionally or personally, something one can ask from very few people one knows in the course of a life-time. I certainly [don't] want the production of a play doomed to failure. So regard this work objectively as you can.

I'm enclosing the new third act and a new part of the second. I believe you got a script from Audrey, the one submitted just before I sailed, and you can insert these re-writes at the proper points. Then read it over, please, and let Gadg read it. I am keeping carbons of the new material for my own script.

I let Audrey read "Cat on a Tin Roof" while she was here and to my surprise she seemed to take a great liking to it, said the material excited her more than anything I've done since "Streetcar". But she doesn't find it complete in its present form and wants me to add another act to it. So far I don't agree with her. I think it tells a full story, though it is under conventional length, and that as soon, or if, I get back my creative breath, I can fill out these two acts (or 3 long scenes as they actually are) to a full evening without extending the story as I see it.

We have found an apartment, a pent-house with a terrace, looking over the Tiber and level with the evening flight of the "rondinelli", I have a club to swim at, Maria is expected, having been jilted by Laughlin, and so the external circumstances are not so bad. How are things in Glocamara? What of Bigelow? Surely he is back by now! If not, "attention must be paid to this man!"

With love, Tenn.

[Amid the "crisis" TW lamented his "heartbroken home. Mother. The sad distance come between us. My desperate old father. And the fate of Rose. And my soul, if I have one still, sighs and shudders and sickens" (*Journal*, June 6, 1954).

TW continued to revise *Orpheus Descending* (1957) in Tangier and Rome. A rewrite of Act III, scene 2, was "put in" the script on June 12 to further characterize Vee Talbott and intensify her blinding vision of Christ. The ending was also focused more sharply on Lady and Val with the removal of Carol Cutrere from the early part of the scene (n.d., HRC).

Audrey Wood recalls that she "stayed up until four in the morning" reading the untidy "'work script'" of *Cat on a Hot Tin Roof* (1955). She was "terribly excited" by the new play but demanded a "'third act,'" warning TW that "'it can't end with Big Daddy's speech, as it does. You've got to work on the story by sticking with Brick and Maggie'" (qtd. in Wood, *Represented by Audrey Wood*, 1981, pp. 165-166).

The "'rondinelli'" are the tiny birds of Rome which TW mentioned in *The Roman Spring of Mrs. Stone* (1950) and repeated in *Orpheus Descending*—as a symbol of escape from the corrupting influence of earth, citing the legend that they never touched earth until they died.

Linda vows that "attention must be paid" to her husband, Willy Loman, in light of his betrayal by a harsh economic order—in Act I of *Death of a Salesman* (Miller, 1949). TW would later use the same passage in poignant reference to Frank Merlo.

TW wrote this letter in June 1945, after moving on the 11th to the new apartment overlooking the Tiber.]

290. To Audrey Wood

Barcelona
8/5/54
[TLS w/ enclosure, 2 pp. HRC]

Dear Audrey:

Maria and I have been hopping around Europe like a pair of fleas, to escape the heat and lethargy of Rome. That little apartment turned out to be a regular oven. You don't need a stove, you just have to leave things out of the ice-box to cook them! Work was impossible. So Maria and I took off for Vienna, then to Venice where I saw Joe Mankiewicz, then back to Rome to see if it was cooler. It was hotter. So then we took off again to Barcelona. I am sorry that I will not meet Colton in Rome but maybe it's just as well to avoid any action on that "Summer and Smoke" deal till I am slightly more certain of how I am going to get along with Wallis. We talked about this in Rome and you agreed with me that it would be wise to delay. Of course I am greatly relieved by the news that Kanter is off the script but I feel that some additional assurances are necessary before making further commitments. I feel that the "Summer" deal should wait till I get back in the States, the end of September. (We're sailing with Magnani on the 22nd). Then you and I can discuss it in detail and make sure that we have the most protection obtainable. Films are more lasting than play productions and I'm afraid that my plays will be remembered mostly by the films made of them, and for that reason it is terribly important to me that I should get as much artistic control as possible in all film contracts. "Summer" could be done like a soap-opera, if it lacked this protection, and the reviews of "Mrs Leslie" make it clear that the critics, at least, are not buying that sort of thing anymore. Financially it looks like a good deal. But please let's wait till there's a final, really trustworthy, agreement on the "Tattoo" script, say, a week or two before they start shooting it, or at least till we can talk in New York the end of September. Do you agree? I sent the new ending from Rome. I am enclosing another version of Serafina's first scene, in the Ideal Grocery. It includes a meeting with Father de Leo which they seemed to desire. Magnani has received a script from Wallis and is having it translated into Italian. She is rightly very concerned over the script, as concerned as I am. I went through her script, scratching out the scenes which I am re-writing. (It was the yellow version they sent her.) If I am allowed to replace Kanter's stuff with my own, I think we will be in good shape. Neither Danny's nor

Hal's letters dealt at all specifically with our list of objections, the phrasing was disturbingly vague.

Their reaction to the new ending will be very significant.

I think it's very important that we maintain a completely friendly atmosphere, I don't want to seem unduly suspicious or "difficult" at this point, not till I am quite sure that a fight will be necessary. I am very hopeful that it can be avoided. In confidence: Mankiewicz described Wallis as "a cruel man". But I never accept other's opinions of people. Rarely agree with them. And the fact that Wallis wants to buy my plays is a great deal in his favor.

I enjoyed the meeting with Joe and we got along wonderfully in Venice. His ideas about "Orpheus" were interesting and showed a genuine concern, but I feel that his ideas are a bit too literal or realistic for a poetic play of this sort. He wants it too black and white. I'd prefer Gadg, if Gadg is at all interested. Meanwhile I am working steadily so that I'll have complete rough drafts of both "Cat" and "Kingdom of Earth" and my own final version of "Tattoo" when I return.

Oliver Evans is in Barcelona. He and Maria have gone off together to visit a young fisherman friend of Oliver's somewhere down the Coast but I expect them back this afternoon for the bull-fights. We'll probably fly to Madrid late this week but you'll get a wire if we do. I'll keep you informed of any moves that I make, never fear!

With love, Tenn

[Audrey Wood cabled producers Joe Hazen and Hal Wallis that Edward Colton had been sent to Rome to pacify TW on *The Rose Tattoo* script. To keep "peace on earth" (July 19, 1954, HRC), she advised that they not yet inform TW of their plan to retain "artistic control" of *Summer and Smoke*. Wallis produced the film in 1961.

About Mrs. Leslie (1954) was panned in the *New York Times* and *Variety* as a "saccharine saga" which is "only occasionally interesting." Daniel Mann directed and Shirley Booth played the lead in Wallis's current film.

The "Ideal Grocery" scene would expand the original setting of *The Rose Tattoo* and reveal Serafina's haughty pride in her unfaithful husband. The "new ending" to which TW refers, if the same as in the filmed version, involves a flagpole serenade by Alvaro, Serafina's return of the emblematic silk shirt, and the implied consummation of their "conversation."

On July 20 Wood asked Elia Kazan for his "very honest opinion" (July 20,

1954, HRC) of *Orpheus Descending*. Molly Kazan read the script first, deemed it "quite magical" though "not yet masterful," and warned that her husband was extremely "TIRED" (to Wood, July 30, 1954, HRC).

TW informed Wood of a recent exchange with "Poor little Maria": "I said she must forget Jay and go back to her old life. She said, What life? I have none. I said, Well, you've got to make one. Nobody can be that Russian this long!" (n.d., HRC).]

291. To Cheryl Crawford

"Amexco" Rome
August 23, 1954
[TLS, 1 p. HRC]

Dear Cheryl:

I am sorry about my last letter to you, I was a little bit drunk and feeling sorry for myself, I suppose. That's over now. I have been hopping all over Europe by plane with little Maria Britneva, like a pair of fleas, Vienna for a week, then ten days in Venice, Zurich, Rome again. Then off to Spain where we joined my poet friend Oliver Evans and took a trip by car along the Costa Brava, two weeks in Barcelona in which we saw seven bull-fights. "Mother's Ruin" is still a good friend of mine but I've cut down on it. Also rarely exceed one, and sometimes none of the "pinkies" in a day. And if I keep busy next Fall, and it looks like I'll have lots to do, I think I can keep off the analyst's couch a while longer, attractive tho it does seem in your current offering.

Cheryl, stop worrying about Orpheus, it is obviously not for you, that was apparent from our first phone talk about it last Spring. When I talk to you about it, it is only because I like to talk to you about my work, not because I am trying to sell it to you like a persistent huckster in the Medina. When you asked me, last Spring, why I didn't write a comedy - as if you didn't know that I only write for self-expression and that what I have to express is not, alas, a highly risible concept of the mysteries we live in - then I knew that on the conscious level you probably still want to do difficult, disturbing and challenging plays but that you now have a strong unconscious resistance to them, a circumstance that grew out of the terrible failure of Camino and the great success of "oh, Men, oh, Women!" and which is altogether understandable. But when you talk to Gadg about Orpheus -

Audrey wired me he likes it and may be able to do it in December - please don't low-rate it to him. Because I do honestly think you are wrong. Only one of the characters, Carol, is self-explanatory, and she is meant to be for she is a sort of sibyl or visionary, and I think the dynamics of the play are very powerful and that either Gadg or Mankiewicz, whichever does it, or even I, if neither of them will, could make it wildly exciting on the stage. That doesn't mean the critics would adore it, or it would be a big box-office hit, but I don't think either of those boys is afraid to reckon with chances, otherwise they wouldn't have done "Julius Caesar" and "Waterfront", even with Gielgud and Brando. "Out of this nettle, danger, Etc." - truest words the Bard ever lisped!

See you in Manhattan end of September. Fondly,

[TW returned to Rome after three weeks in Barcelona with "nothing" to show for his money but "boredom" and "irritation" (*Journal*, August 20, 1954). Maria Britneva's commanding behavior had removed any doubt of her possessive intentions. Oliver Evans would soon be offended by his portrait in *Hard Candy* and retaliate with a scurrilous postcard (see letter #312). In Rome the work went "not badly" but the "blue devils" returned after a brief respite. A claustrophobic attack in a cinema sent TW staggering "into the nearest bar. How disgusting! I must rise above it. I will" (*Journal*, August 23, 1954). Britneva recorded the episode and described "the terror of claustrophobia" which increasingly beset TW: "His heart pounds and pounds and he feels as though he were suffocating and panics, and so has to have a drink to relax" (St. Just, p. 97).

Cheryl Crawford's "offering" was probably Dr. Robert Laidlaw, a psychiatrist recommended to her by Alfred Kinsey, to whom she had relayed TW's earlier request.

TW recently learned of Crawford's opinion that production of "a fresh, new play" should ideally precede *Orpheus Descending*. Audrey Wood agreed and restated her wish that *Cat on a Hot Tin Roof* be developed into "a full evening" of theatre (Wood to TW, July 19, 1954, HRC).

Awaiting TW in Rome was a cable from Wood reporting Elia Kazan's preliminary interest in staging *Orpheus Descending*, "if you would do serious work" (August 16, 1954, HRC) on the script.

Julius Caesar (1953) and *On the Waterfront* (1954) were praised for imaginative direction by Joseph Mankiewicz and Elia Kazan, respectively. Marlon Brando played Mark Antony and the longshoreman Terry Malloy.

TW closes with a quotation from Shakespeare: "Out of this nettle, danger, we pluck this flower, safety" (*I Henry IV*, Act II.]

292. To Edwina Dakin Williams and Walter Edwin Dakin

[Rome]
[ca. August 23, 1954]
[TLS, 2 pp. HRC]

Dear Mother & Grandfather:

I've had to keep travelling about Europe this summer to escape the heat in Rome which was unusually bad this year and the attractive little apartment I described to you earlier turned out to be rather badly ventilated as it is divided into so many small rooms with windows opening mostly on a courtyard. Maria Britneva came to Rome and we flew to Zurich, then to Vienna, then to Venice, then back to Rome and then to Barcelona for two weeks where I met my friend Oliver Evans who was visiting there. We took an auto trip up the Mediterranean coast, called the Costa Brava, Oliver was searching for a place where he could live comfortably on the rent from his house in New Orleans, as he wants to spend a year in Spain and devote himself to writing instead of teaching in the States. Everywhere life was extremely cheap, you could live on fifty dollars a month, but we all agreed that the villages would be very tiresome after the first few days. So Oliver has now returned to the States, via Tangier, and will probably remain in New Orleans after all. We stayed in Spain about two weeks and when we got back here in Rome, the heat had broken. It is now delightfully cool and I'm enjoying the apartment again. We'll stay on here till September 22nd when we sail back to the States on the Andrea Doria with Anna Magnani.

I shall have to go out to Hollywood soon after I get back but can go through Saint Louis and spend some time with you. They want me to be on hand when they start shooting "Tattoo". They've finally decided to use a little town on the West Coast, close to the studio, instead of Mississippi or Florida. Which I think is sensible, as it is much less expensive and the less the picture costs the more I am likely to make out of it as my percentage comes after they recover the cost of the production. Kazan will be in Hollywood at the same time and Audrey cabled me that he is very interested in one of my new plays and might be able to do it on Broadway in December. Joe Mankiewicz is also interested in the same play and we have had talks about it in Venice and Rome. He's the man who made the recent film of Julius Caesar with Brando and Gielgud in the cast. Anyway it looks like I'll have a busy year ahead of me and I hope it will be profitable. Maybe Frank and Grandfather will have to open the house in Key West before I get there.

I bought Mother a lovely black lace mantilla, all sewn by hand, in Barcelona and will mail it from here. I thought it would look nice with her pearls and big tortoise shell comb for gala evenings. I think the Spanish ladies wear them to give them height as they are the tiniest women I've seen, few of them more than five feet. Much love to you all,

Tom.

[Exteriors for *The Rose Tattoo* were filmed in Key West on a lot adjacent to TW's bungalow.

This letter is written on stationery of the Hotel Colón in Barcelona.]

293. To Audrey Wood

[Rome]
[early-September 1954]
[TLS, 2 pp. HRC]

Dear Audrey:

I agree in principle with what you say in your letter (August 25) but I feel there are circumstances to consider carefully in this instance. For one thing, I gathered that your enthusiasm for the "Cat" play is more or less contingent on my adding another act to it. To me the story is complete in its present form, it says all that I had to say about these characters and their situation, it was conceived as a short full-length play: there are three acts in it. First, Brick and his wife. Second, Brick and Big Daddy. Third, The family conference. They are short acts but complete, and I thought at least structurally the play was just right, I liked there being no time lapse between the acts, one flowing directly into the others, and it all taking place in the exact time that it occupies in the theatre. I would hate to lose that tightness, that simplicity, by somehow forcing it into a more extended form simply to satisfy a convention of theatre, would much rather risk the prejudice that might be incurred by bringing down a curtain at 10:30 or 10:45 and possibly raising it a little later to compensate. Or even using a good one act play as a curtain-raiser. It seems to me that all those one-act plays may have been just sitting there for this particular occasion to come along! Why not use one?

On the other hand, "Orpheus" is as ready as it will ever be. I will read it over when I get the manuscript but I doubt that there is much more I can do to it, except maybe do a little more with the Carol bit in Act Three. I think it is nothing short of miraculous that two great directors want to do it, even with reservations. Now I think it is only fair that Gadg should let me know, at once, what he demands in the way of a re-write so that I can compare it with what Joe wants and decide which I can best satisfy, which is closer to my own point of view. The only way to deal with this situation is frankly and directly. Gadg wants to help me, I know. Why not tell him very frankly that I have this other offer, from Joe? In fact, I already wrote him about it a week or so ago, making it clear, however, that if he is willing to commit himself definitely to produce it, at a stated time this season, he should have it. Since Gadg has not written me, or approached me directly about this play or clearly stated what work he thinks it requires, and since Joe has, it appears likely to me that his interest is more nebulous or tentative of the two. I think he must be fair about this and put himself, imaginatively, in my uncomfortable but hopeful shoes. And make some definite move while there is still another "mighty director" somehow dangling on the same delicate line. Have I made myself clear? If not, I will send you a singing Western Union boy. On second thought, No, I might have to write the lyric.

Somehow I feel that you will work all this out with your usual unparallelled tact and perception, all I have to say, really, basically, is don't lose Joe unless you know you have Gadg, and when! Don't you think Mitchum is a great idea for Val? There's a wonderful piece on Mitchum in the August or September issue of Modern Screen which is almost Val's life story without Hollywood. Everyone here says Miranda is "N.G." Anyway Joe wouldn't use her and I doubt that Gadg would. I can't remember seeing Cortesi either, we'd better both have a look at her in something.

[Maria] is still here, and our domestic situation has deteriorated to a point where I am about to fly down to Sicily alone. I've been working only on "Kingdom of Earth" the last few weeks so that I'll have both of these new plays in complete first drafts when I get back to the States. Still sailing Sept. 22nd on the Doria with Magnani. Wallis leaves today. We got along well, I hope.

Love, Tenn.

["No one wants a Williams' play in New York this season more than I do," Audrey Wood assured her client, but she wished to observe the "order that is best for Tennessee Williams' career" rather than a "mighty" director. *Cat* seemed the more desirable property, assuming that TW could submit a full draft when he returned to New York in late-September (to TW, August 25, 1954, HRC). Unacceptable to Wood was TW's earlier suggestion—restated in essence—that *Cat* be done with "Kingdom of Earth" on a double bill: "Although totally different in background, the plays are complementary in theme and would go well together" (TW to Wood, July 10, 1954, HRC).

Isa Miranda starred as Lady in the London production of *Orpheus Descending* (1959). Robert Mitchum did not appear in any work by TW.

The name "Maria" has been razored from the last paragraph in the original typescript. It is supplied in bracketed form.

This letter bears a reception date of September 7, 1954. The receiving office, however, was not Liebling-Wood but MCA (Music Corporation of America) to which the small firm founded in 1937 had recently been sold. Wood continued to represent her clients while her husband and business partner, William Liebling, partially retired.]

294. To Justin Brooks Atkinson

Sicily
Sept 4 1954
[TLS, 1 p. BRTC]

Dear Brooks:

Audrey Wood sent me a clipping from The Times bearing a letter from you to the editor about our recent decline of democratic freedom in the States. Her note said "I am deeply impressed by this". I am sure many people were. I certainly was. All the more deeply because I lacked the courage to write such a letter myself. When Art Miller lost his passport, I got as far as writing a letter to the State Department but only that far (didn't post it). I remembered that I had not yet received my own passport and I was afraid to antagonize the department and risk losing my own. That shows what an atmosphere of intimidation has come to exist among us. For a man in your position to speak up so boldly and clearly is not only brave but consequential. For courage is just as infectious as cowardice. I trust that now more and more of our writers and theatre people and so forth will dare to protest publicly against this creeping, sometimes galloping, decay of freedom. At least it has made us realize what a great and beautiful nation we belonged to, a few years back. Of course I don't believe our people will ever surrender as abjectly to these influences as, say, the Germans, Italians, and Russians, for we have never been serfs, peasants and slaves. Here in

Sicily, for instance, a sort of feudal serfdom still exists, also in much of Italy, and I'm afraid, to counter Communism, we should have shown more interest in propogating democracy among those countries that we were liberating from Fascism. We didn't make it sufficiently apparent to these people that democracy is something truly different from what they'd had before: so they got the idea that the only truly different thing would be communism. Same sort of blindness, inside and outside, when vision is most necessary. I wonder what pretty Mrs. Luce really thinks and says about things over here? I would love to hear her report to Mr. Dulles. De Gasperi's death was unfortunate for I believe he tried sincerely to check intemperate forces. He needed more inspiring fellowship on our side. I'll be leaving here soon. Each time more doubtful that I can get back again. And they are such beautiful people and there are so many cold eyes and hard faces elsewhere on earth! Yours ever,

10.

["Totalitarian attitudes and practices" cited by Atkinson include the refusal of passports and visas, domestic spying and the use of informers, the summoning of citizens before official committees "to answer for their personal ideas," the firing of civil servants "who do not parrot the party line," and various other restraints of traditional American freedom. The chief offender was Senator Joseph McCarthy, whom the "Government" had implicitly supported as "public prosecutor." "I wonder," Atkinson concluded, "if Americans really want it this way" (*New York Times*, August 16, 1954). Later he ruefully observed that Soviet induced "hysteria and fear" had made "most Americans McCarthyites in one degree or another" (to TW, September 23, 1954, BRTC).

Clare Boothe Luce, United States Ambassador to Italy, stirred controversy in early 1954 when off-the-record remarks critical of Italian politics—especially the Communist presence in labor and government—were reported in the press. John Foster Dulles, Secretary of State, was one of TW's favorite villains in international relations.

The death of former Italian Premier Alcide de Gasperi from a heart attack unnerved TW and revived his own "cardiac neurosis, in prodigious flower" (*Journal*, August 23, 1954).]

295. To Audrey Wood

[Rome]
Sept. [1954]
[TLSx, 2 pp. HRC]

Dearest Audrey:

All hell has broke loose here. Maria has denounced Frank as "common, ill-bred, Etc." and, at least for the past night, has removed herself from the premises. The trouble is that she wants to be treated constantly as a guest although, since she has been with us all summer, we can only treat her as a member of the family without giving up our agreeable pattern of life. Another trouble is that she is without any personal funds, to speak of, and is embarassingly dependant on us. She will not be realistic about this but wants us to entertain her titled friends at expensive restaurants, Etc., and when she leaves in the mornings, there is usually a message on the table giving us instructions of what to do. I tolerate this because I am very fond of her and am keenly aware of her emotional upset over being jilted by Jay, Etc. But Frank is naturally less inclined to put up with it and so it is "ending in tears". I do hope there can be some pacification before we separate next week.

Right now: Valentina Cortesi is here and reading script of new "Battle" with which she expresses great delight. I think she appears too young and beautiful for the part, she is really exquisite looking, but of course if she is a really fine actress that needn't rule her out. She had the idea, which doesn't seem bad to me, that her husband Richard Basehart might play opposite her as VAL. I just saw him do a great performance in an Italian film "La Strada" which got a prize at Venice, he seems a good type for it and is a fine actor. Please speak to Joe about this.

The news of Kazan is still ambiguous to me. I do wish he would write me about the script if he is truly interested in it. It would be a pity to lose Joe and then discover that Kazan wanted a sort of re-write that I could not attempt or agree with, which is always possible. Now that I've completed a very rough first draft, but a complete one, of "Kingdom of Earth" (or "The Seven Descents of Myrtle") I am working again on the new "Battle", doing over the Carol-Lady bit in the last act and I think that's the most critical point in the play and that I am making progress toward a solution of it.

"Big Nat" (Murray) is here. We're having dinner tonight with her and La Magnani, at 11 o'clock, if I don't die of hunger first. That's the hour when La Magnani is willing to take to the streets, not sooner. A wire today from

Wallis. "Ask Tennessee can he airmail rewrite Rosario scenes Plaza New York Mann meeting me there." The only thing wrong with that is that I really can't see any reason to re-write those scenes as they will play beautifully and they say exactly what they are meant to say. Mann said he thought Rosario should show more devotion to Magnani but it seems to me that the point is that she is the one that has the devotion, he has a mistress. Naturally he cares for her, maybe a lot, but in the stress of the situation it seems a little much to ask me to dramatize a great love on his part. I will attempt this, if it is really necessary, but can't we wait till I have talked with Mann in New York? It would not involve much re-writing but it is necessary to be quite clear, and agreed, about how to do this. Also there is the point that I am not on salary and have already far exceeded the three-weeks period of my employment as script-writer. How about that? And how about my expenses in California? I would be happy to settle for that, as a recompense for my continued services, but I don't think I should have to, or can afford, to go to California and stay there at my own expense, though I think my presence is essential, both for Magnani's security and the protection of the script. I am willing to live on a relatively modest level, of course. Can you work that out, you think? I am worried about money! - for the first time in ten years. . . .

Love, Tenn.

[Shortly before the blowup, Maria Britneva described Frank Merlo as "intelligent and good, but unfortunately very coarse." His "understanding," for which she was "grateful" (St. Just, p. 97), had apparently been exhausted.

Neither Valentina Cortese, twenty-nine at the time of her reading, nor her husband, Richard Basehart, appeared in *Orpheus Descending*.

Elia Kazan restated his wife's warning—"I'm quite exhausted. Out of gas. (petrol) No gissum left"—and offered to step aside if Joe Mankiewicz were "hot" to direct *Orpheus Descending*. Perhaps he should "wait for one of the new plays" (to TW, n.d., HRC), Kazan opined, signaling in effect his preference for *Cat on a Hot Tin Roof*.

Natalia Danesi Murray served as a personal assistant to Anna Magnani on the set of *The Rose Tattoo*. TW's reluctance to domesticate Rosario apparently prevailed. As filmed, he remains a shadowy character who ignores Serafina's announcement of "new life" in her body.

The names "Maria" and "Jay" have been razored from the first paragraph of the original typescript. They remain, however, in a photographic copy which serves as published text, and which bears a reception date of September 20, 1954.]

296. To Elia "Gadg" Kazan

[323 East 58th Street, New York]
[October 1954]
[TLS, 1 p. HTC]

Dear Gadg:

There is certainly no use in my trying to disguise or dissimulate the fact that I passionately long for you to do this play. But I can understand why you are afraid of its failure although I am not. I don't mean I think it couldn't fail. I think it not only could fail but has a fifty-fifty chance of failure, and know how much I have to lose from such a failure, but still I do passionately long for its production and for you to ~~produce~~ stage it because I think it does that thing which is the pure aim of art, the highest pure aim of art, which is to catch and illuminate truly and passionately the true, true quality of human existence. It so happens that the second act has the highest degree of dramatic tension. That has happened before in very fine plays and they have survived it. It has to be compensated, not by a trick or distortion but by charging the final scene with something <u>plus</u>, underlining and dramatizing as powerfully as possible the sheer <u>truth</u> of the material, it's very <u>lack</u> of shrewd showmanship, because I think critics and real theatre lovers will respect it all the more for not making some facile, easy, obvious concession to the things which a lot of people have complained about in us, both, a too professional, showy, sock-finish to theatre. Am I rationalizing again? Maybe, but on the other hand, I may be simply trying to articulate to you my side of the case.

You say that I didn't have faith in this play till you and Audrey liked it. Surely you understand <u>why</u>! I never had any confidence in my work, in fact I couldn't believe my ears when Audrey first told me that "Streetcar" was a good play because ever since 1946, the spring of it, I didn't see how I could do good things anymore. But God has been with me, and you and Audrey and a bunch of people who like truth stated with passion on the stage, no matter how cruel or black and often <u>bungling</u>, have noted and appreciated the fact that I continued to do it in spite of not thinking I could.

Even if "Cat" is not a good play, it's a goddam fiercely <u>true</u> play, and what other play this season is going to be <u>that</u>?

I resumed work this morning, at 8 A.M. after not much sleep, on Act Three, determined to get what you want without losing what I want.

(Assuming they are essentially the same thing, just conceived of in different fashions) I dare to believe that I can work this out, but it would help me immeasurably if you and some producer would give me a vote of confidence by committing yourselves to a date of production with the work still on the bench. I don't think that I would fail you. Of course I will be disappointed if you refuse, perhaps even angry at you - I was angry with you last night, too angry to sleep! - but I will not hate you for it, and we would still do something together again. I know that you are my friend.

Ever, Tennessee.

P.S. Hope this doesn't sound like "a pitch"?

[With "great tensions and contentions," the decision to stage *Cat* was made after TW arrived in New York on September 30. He informed Maria Britneva in late-October that Elia Kazan was "genuinely enthusiastic about the script" and had "verbally" committed himself to direct the new play, with rehearsals set to begin on "February 1st" (qtd. in St. Just, pp. 101, 103).]

297. To Elia "Gadg" Kazan

[1431 Duncan Street
Key West, Florida]
Nov. 3, 1954
[TLS, 2 pp. WUCA]

Dear Gadg:

We arrived back here to find our whole property transformed into the Strega's house (next door to Serafina's), trees planted to hide our house and a dilapidated false front with tin roof built over my studio in the backyard. I hit the ceiling, that is, I would have hit it if there had been a ceiling to hit! I thought they had wrecked my studio and I charged out of the car like the strega's goat, shouting, "Who the blankety blank sonofabitches gave them permission to ruin my little house!" All the pent up emotion of the past week exploded, Grandfather's illness, my rage at mother and at life, all broke loose on the Paramount art department and production manager and assistants. I was not pacified till told that both houses would be completely repainted and that the hideous facade of my precious little studio could be removed without a scar on the original. But you should see the yard!

Practically all the junk and refuse in town has been heaped and scattered over it, and tomorrow comes the goat! Our next door nieghbor is getting twenty-five bucks a day for the use of his yard and porch but I guess all we're getting is free paint job when it's over. They start shooting daybreak tomorrow. I've never been this close to a movie production before and I must say that it's just too massive, too huge and implacable a machine, to be interesting. It no longer seems to have any relation to me or my own world, it's like some great Frankenstein that suddenly came clomping up to the door and took everything over. I am already bored with the whole thing, before it has started, and am interested only in plans for "Cat on a Tin Roof" and the return of sanity and quiet when the monster goes clomping back where it came from. I have just finished reading a ~~great~~ book "The Producer" by Richard Brooks which is an inside, almost documentary, account of how pictures are made. Incidentally, you are mentioned in it. Have you read it? Published by Cardinal reprints, originally by Simon & Schuster. Get it if you haven't. I think I'd rather read about making pictures than make them, it's too big, it involves too much money, it's a miracle when anything simple, true or creative manages to slip through, I suppose unnoticed by the boys on top, production heads, bankers and stockholders. That something like "Waterfront" or "Streetcar" can come out of it - man alive! <u>How</u>?! - Magnani, even Anna, looks shaken by the mass and weight of the mechanism. Wallis and Mann look like gleeful little boys who have just reached into their Xmas stockings! Are they kidding?

I suppose you have heard the sad news about Grandfather. He had a slight stroke just a couple of days before we arrived to pick him up for the winter. His left side is partially paralyzed and he is now in a nursing home in Saint Louis. We spent a week with him, he was improving a little when we left, but he says he is on his deathbed and since he would be 98 in April, it is not easy to argue him, or myself, out of it. It was so badly timed, however, as all this to-do in Key West would have been more thrilling to him than anyone else involved in it.

I am glad that in "Cat" we are getting off the chest some of the terrible things that we have to say about human fate. I want to keep the core of the play very hard, because I detest plays that are built around something mushy such as I feel under the surface of many sentimental successes in the theatre. I want the core of the play to be as hard and fierce as Big Daddy. I think he strikes the keynote of the play. A terrible black anger and ferocity, a rock-bottom honesty. Only against this background can his moments of tenderness, of longing, move us deeply. This is a play about good bastards and good bitches. I mean it exposes the startling co-existence of good and evil, the shocking duality of the single heart. I am as happy as you are that our discussions have led to a way of high-lighting the good in Maggie, the indestructible spirit of Big Daddy, so that the final effect of the play is not negative, this is a forward step, a step toward a larger truth which will add immeasurably to the play's power of communication or scope of communication. More later. Anna, looking pale and scared, has just arrived at the door.

Next day: - whole town is on the street in front of the house and overflowing the whole premises except my studio which hides inviolate behind its false front. Three hours have been consumed in shooting about three minutes of the picture. Wallis made Marisa Pavan cry, which killed another half hour, by blowing his stack because she fluffed a line, the same one, in five takes. He is a hard customer!, that one. I wish he didn't want to buy my plays, or, rather, I wish somebody else did want to buy them, he is not hard in the right way, I am afraid. Danny is gentle. I am happy to say that he showed his annoyance to Wallis in the girl's defense. He and I will never have a true rapport but I respect and like him: he will never do anything great, I fear, without the collaboration of a Magnani, but he will always bring heart and - heart! - to his work, unless the Frankenstein takes it out of him.

Have just seen Magnani tear into the part! Forget that bit about her being nervous. That dame is nervous in a way that's terrific! She takes over like Grant did Richmond! And I must say that Danny has the good grace to be grateful for it, as he well should be, and even Hal Wallis began to grin a little. I was so shaken that on the way back from location, I had a "crise de nerfs" and had to stop a police car, yes, mind you, a police car! - to drive me home. I was shaking all over and the policeman was sympathetic . . . . An attack like the one I read you about from my journal. "Ten miles from no where and uphill all the way!"

(This letter is crazy because my nerves are shot right now.)

To get back to "Cat". I will not insult you by saying, "Don't ask me to sweeten it up." I know what you want. You don't want me to take the cliché route into tiresome old defeatism or romantic melancholy, you want me to make it hard, even savage, but with a respect for the quality of truth, and the truth that there is: in the individual rising above himself, herself, at moments, under extreme pressure, to say or do something absolutely, uncompromisingly, true. And not self-loving only or self-pitying only.

This thing is going to come right, and I think soon enough for this season. I'm going to send off the new material sooner than I ought to, because we are late and have to work fast. Sometimes it's better that way. Work can die from delay and cogitation. Surprisingly, most of Maggie's stuff still fits our new conception of her. I was already unconsciously her friend when I wrote it. Please don't ask me to write over her part, I couldn't do it nearly as well, and all it really needs is bits of add and subtract. (Since we don't want to deny that she has the desperation and savagery of a cat on a tin roof).

Wired to ask if you could come down here when the film is finished here. I do hope you can, you'd like this place, and we could get the script right.

Love, 10.

[Hal Wallis has recalled the search for a shooting location in Key West: "We drove all over town looking for a wood frame house that would best fit the requirements as Serafina's home. Finally, I saw one . . . {that} looked perfect but there was a fence too close to it which enclosed a goat yard belonging to the house next door" (qtd. in Steen, *A Look at Tennessee Williams*, 1969). Wallis was surprised to learn that the owner was none other than the volatile author of *The Rose Tattoo*.

In *The Producer* (1951) Elia Kazan is mentioned as a socially conscious director. The author, Richard Brooks, later directed and wrote the screenplays for *Cat on a Hot Tin Roof* (1958) and *Sweet Bird of Youth* (1962).

The character of Maggie evolved from a sinister, domineering figure in "Three Players of a Summer Game" (1952). Her "more charming" development in *Cat*, as TW later put it, was consistent with the ending used for the Broadway production.]

298. To Audrey Wood

[1431 Duncan Street
Key West, Florida]
Nov 23, 1954
[TLS w/ enclosure, 1 p. HRC]

Dear Audrey:

I'm shooting this off to you before I've had a chance to consider it myself at all properly. I'm also sending, to save time, a copy to Gadg. I agree with you that time must be considered now. I think Gadg must let us know right away if he is or isn't willing to make a definite commitment at a specific time, and soon enough for us to make other plans if he isn't. I am not at all sure that this new ending is what I want. Do you think it contains an echo of "Tea and Sympathy"? The other, harder, ending of it didn't. Here is another case of a woman giving a man back his manhood, while in the original conception it was about a vital, strong woman dominating a weak man and achieving her will. Also: does Big Daddy's reappearance really and truly add anything that's important to the story besides making it softer or sweeter or easier to take?

Christopher Isherwood strengthened my faith in the original play. I read him the first typed draft and he loved it, said he thought it in many ways my best play. He felt only that the story of Maggie-Brick-Skipper needed to be developed more fully to make it more clearly understood, what had actually happened, as that was the heart of the story. I've tried to do that in a re-write of the scene between Brick and Maggie about Skipper. I'm also now doing a re-write of the scene between Big Daddy and Brick about Skipper.

Should I go out to the Coast, to watch over the "Tattoo" shooting and at the same time confer with Kazan? Isherwood will be there and possibly the three of us could arrive at an agreement about the "Cat" script that would satisfy both Gadg and me. If Gadg wants "out", how about Jose Quintero? He is someone that I could work with and I think he would have sympathy and understanding of this script. Clurman is also a possibility but I think Jose is a better, fresher and more vital, director, and particularly one that I would find it easier to communicate with. Is Ben Gazzara still available? I am also interested in your suggestion of Dorothy McGuire. If I go to the coast, and Gadg remains interested, perhaps some casting could be done out there. . . .

Cast of "Tattoo" left last night, I am worn out and glad to resume the quiet life.

Don't you think it is important to get a producer lined up for "Cat" if it is really going to be produced this season? I don't want to produce it myself, I am not ready for that, I need the support of a top-flight management of experience and prestige to get it organized and provide the calm, workman-like atmosphere that such a delicate undertaking will need behind it.

My love, Tenn

[The enclosed revision of *Cat* led Elia Kazan to wire his approval and TW to write—as he flew nervously to Los Angeles—that "things look bright" (*Journal*, November 27, 1954).

The unwanted "echo of 'Tea and Sympathy'" (1953) refers to the ending of Robert Anderson's play, in which a schoolboy wrongly accused of homosexual tendencies is reassured by a sympathetic woman.

Reference to "the original conception" of *Cat* foreshadows TW's decision to publish both versions of the third act. At issue, as TW would state in a controversial "Note of Explanation," were Kazan's preference for the return of Big Daddy in Act Three, the development of Brick following his disclosure in Act Two, and the humanization of Maggie the Cat. These debated issues would guide the final stages of revision and give a theatrical shape to the so-called "Broadway Version" of Act Three.

Although both were reportedly "hot" for the play, neither Cheryl Crawford nor Irene Selznick would produce *Cat on a Hot Tin Roof*. With reference to experienced "management," TW doubtless intended to preempt consideration of William Liebling. Audrey Wood finally selected the Playwrights' Company.]

299. To Elia "Gadg" Kazan

[Beverly Hills Hotel
Beverly Hills, California]
November 31, 1954
[TLS w/ autograph postscript, 3 pp. WUCA]

Dear Gadg,

I've got to use a very light touch as I'm writing this at 4:30 AM in the Beverly Hills branch of Utter McKinley. This will also force me to be concise as opposed to abstruse in my statements.

I "buy" a lot of your letter but of course not all: possibly I "buy" more than half, and after a couple of nights studying it out, I think I understand it.

To be brief: the part I buy is that there has to be a reason for Brick's impasse (his drinking is only an expression of it) that will "hold water".

Why does a man drink: in quotes "drink". There's two reasons, separate or together. 1. He's scared shitless of something. 2. He can't face the truth about something. - Then of course there's the natural degenerates that just fall into any weak, indulgent habit that comes along but we are not dealing with that sad but unimportant category in Brick. - Here's the conclusion I've come to. Brick did love Skipper, "the one great good thing in his life which was true". He identified Skipper with sports, the romantic world of adolesence which he couldn't go past. Further: to reverse my original (somewhat tentative) premise,

I now believe that, in the deeper sense, not the literal sense, Brick is homosexual with a heterosexual adjustment: a thing I've suspected of several others, such as Brando, for instance. (He hasn't cracked up but I think he bears watching. He strikes me as being a compulsive eccentric). I think these people are often undersexed, prefer pet raccoons or sports or something to sex with either gender. They have deep attachments, idealistic, romantic: sublimated loves! They are terrible Puritans. (Marlon dislikes me. Why? I'm "corrupt") These people may have a glandular set-up which will keep them "banked", at low-pressure, enough to get by without the eventual crack-up. Take Brando again: he's smoldering with something and I don't think it's Josanne! Sorry to make him my guinea pig in this analysis (Please give this letter back to me!) but he's the nearest thing to Brick that we both know. Their innocense, their blindness, makes them very, very touching, very beautiful and sad. Often they make fine artists, having to sublimate so much of their love, and believe me, homosexual love is something that also requires more than a physical expression. But if a mask is ripped off, suddenly, roughly, that's quite enough to blast the whole Mechanism, the whole adjustment, knock the world out from under their feet, and leave them no alternative but - owning up to the truth or retreat into something like liquor. . . .

Maggie: What happened in here tonight between you and Big Daddy?

Brick: We - - - had a - - - talk. . . .

Maggie: About what? What about?

Brick: We - had a - talk! (Count 10: dead silence, Maggie the cat drawing a bead on him with her eyes, him at the proscenium, looking out into the house) - He says that I loved Skipper!

Maggie: Did you hit him with your crutch?

Brick: (Somewhat lifelessly) No, I didn't. - I mean - Yes, I did. . .

~~Maggie: (Abruptly) Thank you.~~

(X's quickly to liquor cabinet)

~~Brick: For what~~?

~~Maggie: (Count five in which she decides not to probe the topic above any further just now) It was gallant of you to save my face when I lied~~.

Then the "click" bit?

Also, in Act Two:

(Right after Brick has told "B.D." his Skipper story)

Brick: Now are you satisfied?

Big Daddy: - Are <u>you</u> satisfied?

Brick: What with?

Big Daddy: That half-ass story?

Brick: 'Half ass'?

Big: I'm not satisfied with it, you left something out, something is missing from it.

(Phone rings in hall: the sound reminds Brick of something)

Brick: Yes. A telephone call in which Skipper made a, a, a! - "dictated confession" to me: and on which I hung up! - last time we spoke to each other. . .

Big Daddy: Who was it dictated by?

Brick: It was fed him by Maggie. - "The Cat".

Big Daddy: (After a pause) Anyhow now! - I think we've located the lie you're disgusted with. Your own to yourself! - You dug the grave of your friend and kicked him in it because you couldn't face the truth about something?

Brick: (Violent and sudden) Who the hell can, can YOU?! How about these birthday congratulations, these many happy returns when everybody but you knows there won't be any?

(You notice a transposition has occured: "Young and believing" is now before Skipper story)

- Don't you feel this does it? There's your plain and simple and believable reason: he had the problem I referred to above.

In a way, this is progress for Brick. He's faced the truth, I think, under Big Daddy's pressure, and maybe the block is broken. I just said maybe. I don't really think so. I think that Brick is doomed by the falsities and cruel prejudices of the world he comes out of, belongs to, the world of Big Daddy and Big Mama. Sucking a dick or two or fucking a reasonable facsimile of Skipper some day won't solve it for him, if he ever does such "dirty things"! He's the living sacrifice, the victim, of the play, and I don't want to part with that "Tragic elegance" about him. You know, paralysis in a character can be just as significant and just as dramatic as progress, and is also less shop-worn. How about Chekhov?

Now business. The above is just about as far as I can go with you. You've got to tell me, now, whether or not you will do this play this season. If not, I must go at once to New York and start setting up another production for it. I will not, I'm afraid, want to do it next season. You sort of said why in Anna's room Monday night. This play is too important to me, too much a synthesis of all my life, to leave it in hands that aren't mine, and I'm longing to see it!

Let's be brave. Now what do you have to lose?

My love, Tenn.

Must have this letter back to copy the dialogue in it.

[Elia Kazan's reassuring telegram (received November 27, 1954) was followed by "a 5 page letter" in which Kazan stated "his remaining objection" to *Cat*, apparently focused upon the character of Brick. "I do get his point," TW wrote, "but I am afraid he doesn't quite get mine. Things are not always explained. Situations are not always resolved. Characters don't always 'progress'. But I shall, of course, try to arrive at another compromise with him" (*Journal*, November 29, 1954).

Marlon Brando later wrote that he had been "afraid" for TW "because success sings a deadly lullaby to most people. Success is a real and subtle whore who would like nothing better that to catch you sleeping and bite your cock off. You have been as brave as any body I've known and its comforting to think about" (to TW, n.d., Columbia U).

The new Act Two dialogue was intended to offer "a reason" for Brick's "impasse" that would "'hold water,'" as Kazan had recently put it. Presumably the explanatory lines—published with little change in the first and later editions of *Cat*—do not violate the mystery of Brick's character, which TW further defended in a manuscript fragment held by the HRC: "The poetic mystery of BRICK is the poem of the play, not its story but the poem of the story, and must not be dispelled by any dishonestly oracular conclusions about him: I don't know him any better than I know my closest relative or dearest friend which isn't well at all: the only people we think we know well are those who mean little to us" (n.d.).

Rehearsals of *Cat* began on February 9, 1955, followed by a two-week tryout in Philadelphia (March 7-19).]

*Ben Gazzara and Burl Ives: "I can hop on one foot, and if I fall, I can crawl!" (*Cat on a Hot Tin Roof*, 1955).*

300. To the Drama Editor

[Beverly Hills Hotel
Beverly Hills, California]
[December 1954]
[TLS, 1 p. HRC]

To the Drama Editor:

I would like a little space to say simply that Mr. Eric Bentley has told an out-and-out lie, without the excuse of any possible misunderstanding, in his recently book-published claim that "A Streetcar Named Desire" (and "Death of a Salesman") were virtually co-authored by their director. Mr. Kazan who was the director of both my play and Mr. Miller's, was just as indignant as I am over this preposterous charge. At the time it first appeared, a strangely parenthetical supplement to Bentley's review of Camino Real, Mr. Kazan immediately wrote a note of protest about it, utterly disclaiming and denying any such thing. But it doesn't seem that Mr. Bentley's aim is to get at the truth. Consequently I feel obliged to point out, for whatever my word may be worth, that there isn't a line in "Streetcar" I didn't write, and that the interpretation of the play couldn't have been more exactly what the author had in mind when he wrote it. When I acknowledge the greatness of Kazan's direction (and Thank God for it) I think I do it more honestly than Bentley and I think Gadg appreciates it more from me. Into a play like "Streetcar" or "Salesman", the playwright has invested too much that is deeply personal, involving all his existence, to tolerate such a claim as Bentley has had the disgusting mischief and mendacity to publish.

Sincerely, Tennessee Williams

[Of grave concern to TW was Eric Bentley's claim that *Streetcar* (1947) had been "virtually" co-authored by Elia Kazan. TW's attorney threatened a suit if the publisher failed to "recall all outstanding copies" of *The Dramatic Event* (1954) and to "have the statement in question deleted" (Colton to Bentley and Horizon Press, December 2, 1954, HRC). Later printings retain the disputed passage, along with a prominently displayed note—formerly an addendum—in which Kazan is quoted as not having written "one line" of *Streetcar.* Bentley claimed nonetheless that his staging had profoundly altered the characterization, "without recourse to new dialogue." Bentley cited no correspondence from TW.

The printed letter represents a four-stage drafting process, as sources held by the HRC indicate. Related correspondence suggests that the letter—probably intended for publication in the *New York Times*—was written in the first two weeks of December 1954, before TW left California.]

301. To Walter Edwin Dakin

SH: Beverly Hills Hotel
Beverly Hills · California
[mid-December 1954]
[TLS, 1 p. HRC]

Dearest Grandfather:

I have fallen a little behind in my letters lately as I have been going through the busiest period in recent years, what with casting a play with Kazan and watching over the shooting of "Rose Tattoo". I don't even know precisely how long I've been out here, but I have to fly back tonight as Kazan is casting the new play in New York and I have to pass judgement tomorrow on Barbara Bel Geddes for the female lead. She is a fine actress who has appeared in a number of hits on Broadway but I am not sure she is right for this part so I have to return at once to take a look at her.

Anna Magnani and Burt Lancaster had their first fight on the set yesterday, as she was directing the scene and he didn't like it. So he walked off and there was a long and heated consultation before things could be resumed. Both are temperamental. I wish I could remain here as a referee is needed, but I shall just have to hope and pray that Danny Mann, the director, can keep peace between them long enough to finish the picture. So far the picture looks great. There's about two more weeks of work on it, at least.

Frank and the dog are flying to New York from Key West tomorrow so we'll all arrive there about the same time. I haven't gotten much rest or much sun this year, but so far I'm holding up pretty well under the pressure. The fact that I will have Kazan on the play is reassuring and takes a lot of anxiety off me. I just heard today that the Playwrights Company will be the producers, which is good, since they are much more generous with money than Cheryl Crawford who is a penny-pincher.

I talked to Dakin and Margo over long-distance a few days ago, he was visiting her in Dallas. He says he is "sweating out" his promotion which is a slang expression for waiting and hoping that he will get it. I hope so, too, and that if he does, he'll stay in the air-force till economic conditions in the country are more settled.

If I didn't have to put this play on now I would be in Saint Louis with you. I think about you every day. You must get out of bed as often as you can. I know it takes patience and effort, but we are depending on you to be ready and able to return to Key West with us when we go back in the early Spring. That's the nicest time of year there, you remember.

Much love from Tom

[TW rejoined Elia Kazan in New York in mid-December after spending two "ghastly" (*Journal*, December 3, 1954) weeks in California bereft of friends and sexual partners.

Kazan apparently told Barbara Bel Geddes, whom he directed in *Deep Are the Roots* (1945), that she was the "joint choice" of author and director to play Maggie the Cat. Audrey Wood's telegram (December 14, 1954, HRC) to that effect led TW to examine her casting more closely after a hasty return to New York. Kazan later admitted that Bel Geddes was his "kind of actress" (Kazan, p. 540), although not TW's. Her work in *Cat* would lead to nomination for a Tony Award.

Filming of *The Rose Tattoo*—shifted to California for interior scenes—ended in early-January 1955. Natalia Murray wrote at the time that the Production Code office "gave praise to the film as well as to Anna's acting" (to Wood, January 9, 1955, HRC).

Walter Dakin, ninety-seven years of age, would not return to Key West following his recent stroke. He died on February 14, 1955. TW probably learned of the sad event from Audrey Wood, who had been cabled by Edwina: "Please tell Tom that Grandfather passed away at 630 this morning" (February 14, 1955, HRC). According to Paul Bigelow, he "'left two small bequests, one hundred dollars for Frankie Merlo, and one hundred dollars for me. It was all the old gentleman had in the world'" (qtd. in Spoto, p. 200).

This letter was first printed in Edwina Dakin Williams's memoir, *Remember Me to Tom*, 1963, pp. 229-230.]

302. To the Book Review Editor, Time

[323 East 58th Street, New York]
[January 1955]
[TL, 1 p. HRC]

Dear Sir or Miss or Madam:

I would like to suggest to you, without expressed rancor, that your review of my six-year-old book of stories, ONE ARM, is a piece of critical McCarthyism. I am a constant and constantly admiring reader and fan of TIME, because it's the best news-coverage we have, and is especially valuable to me in Europe in the summers when I can't get American papers, and the quality of the reportorial writing is always good and often brilliant, and because I was particularly impressed by your forthright and highly effective stand against the threat of McCarthy to our American principles. But now and again you shock me terribly by a corresponding (to McCarthy) type of intolerance, bordering on persecution, in your attitude toward the arts, theatre and literary. It is totally unworthy of everything else that you represent! "Human garbage" is a curiously un-Christian term to apply to those unfortunates that I (very admittedly!) have somehow been inclined to deal with more than with so-called "healthy and normal" individuals. If I went into the reasons for this, it would be unnecessarily apologetic. An artist must portray, as honestly as he can, what he knows. I have always done so. When you say I have raided "psycophathis sexualis for TV skits", are you being quite honest? What is there in any of these stories, either in content or style, that might conceivably be adaptable to TV as we now have it? These stories stretch all the way back, in time, to my adolescence, and God Knows, and I know, too, that they represent various degrees of writing skill, but you know as well as I know that they do not pander ever, in any way, to what is cheap or sensational anymore than my plays do.

[*One Arm and Other Stories* (1948)—reissued by New Directions in December 1954—"wears the scent of human garbage as if it were the latest Parisian perfume." The *Time* reviewer also surmised that TW had "raided" *Psychopathia Sexualis* (1886), Krafft-Ebing's study of sexual deviation, for his own case studies of "male and female prostitutes, harridans, and homosexuals." Only "Portrait of a Girl in Glass," which shone with "a luminous pity" (January 3, 1955, p. 76), escaped the harsh criticism. TW's letter did not appear in *Time* magazine.]

303. To Justin Brooks Atkinson

SH: Hollywood Roosevelt Hotel
Hollywood 28, California
1/25/55
[TLS w/ enclosure, 1 p. BRTC]

Dear Brooks:

We flew out here from New Orleans to see the rough-cut of "Rose Tattoo", which is still very rough but has promise of being a beautiful and moving film because of Magnani's great performance and Lancaster's surprisingly good one. Maureen and I, the night before I left New Orleans, had someone read us your notice of the double-bill over the "blower", as Maria calls phones, and I want to thank you for us both, Maureen and I, for your kindness to the play and players. I agree with all you said, though I feel sorry about de Banfield. I think he keyed his score to the remembered romance rather than to the tawdry present existence of the old ladies, but this pantomime in the background was too clumsily handled to justify the soaring music. I think it ought to have another try somewhere, under better conditions. There was a chance to bring Maureen into the Bijou on a bill with "Trouble in Tahiti", the Leonard Bernstein musical, but all my advisors in New York were dead set against it, so the project collapsed. I hope it can be revived later, after my new long play has opened, perhaps in the late Spring.

Anyway I thought the enclosed account of what happened between play and opera on opening night might amuse you and Orianne. It is a very mild account of what actually took place, since it doesn't include the banshee cries and imprecations that paled even the most barbaric possible interpretation that might have been given to those bloody wagons that had passed before!

Thanks again, Brooks, as so often before, Tennessee.

[The New Orleans project was a "blunder," Atkinson wrote, despite "the good will" of the local sponsors. His "kindness to the play and players," especially to Maureen Stapleton who starred in "27 Wagons Full of Cotton" (1945), did not include the direction, which Atkinson deemed "soft and maundering." The companion piece, "Lord Byron's Love Letter" (1945), was "demolished by a powerful score and an orchestra of fifty instrumentalists" (*New York Times*, January 19, 1955). TW wrote the libretto and Raffaello de Banfield the excessive accompaniment. Publication of the book (*Lord Byron's Love Letter: Opera in One Act*, Ricordi, 1955) coincided with the premiere on January 17, 1955. TW may have enclosed an article published in the *Times-Picayune* on January 16 which reported "madness" in the company as opening night approached.

Atkinson would soon review Maria Britneva's performance as Blanche DuBois in an off-Broadway production of *Streetcar* (March 3, 1955). She failed, he wrote, "to express the inner tensions of that haunted gentlewoman" (*New York Times*, March 4, 1955). A preliminary search of the *Times* has failed to locate the positive review by Atkinson which Britneva quotes in *Five O'Clock Angel* (p. 112).]

304. To Elia "Gadg" Kazan

Tues, midnight at the St. James.
[March 1, 1955]
[Philadelphia, Pennsylvania]
[TLS w/ cover letter, 3 pp. WUCA]

Dear Gadg

Some notes and reflections on last run through in New York

The bare stage background in New York may have been partly responsible but it seemed to me that the last act of the play, the first part of Act III, suffers from an undue portentousness as if we were trying to cover up some lack of significant content by giving it a "tricky" or inflated style of performance.

In manuscript, in style of writing, this is almost the most realistic scene that I have ever written. I gave ~~enormous~~ care to restricting all the speeches to just precisely what I thought the person would say in precisely such a situation, I tried to give it the quality of an exact transcription of such a scene except for the removal of any worthless irrelevancies. I assumed, and still believe, that the emotional essence of the situation was strong enough to hold interest, and that <u>the exact quality of experience</u>, if captured truly, would give it theatrical distinction. Learning that someone deeply loved and long lived with is dying strikes me as being a material for strong drama, especially when played by Millie Dunnock, but to me, at least, I was continually distracted from the basically moving scene by details of staging and playing which seemed like a kind of legerdemain, as if it were necessary to conceal the actual scene rather than perform it. (Of course I am over-stating this, as usual, to make my point more vividly). There is a "poetry of the macabre" which I was creating in all the silly, trivial speeches that precede and surround the announcement to Big Mama, the fuss over what he ate at dinner, the observations about Keeley cure, anti-buse, vitamin B12, the southern gush and playfulness, these all contribute to a shocking comment upon the false, heartless, grotesquely undignified way that such events are treated in our society with its resolute concentration on the trivia of life. Practically all these values disappeared, for me at least, in a distractingly formalistic treatment of the situation. THE BASIC IDEA back of this formalism IS EXCELLENT! - Big Mama a victim in a pit or arena with her mockingly sympathetic, pitiless executioners gradually tightening a circle about her - this is a creative conception which does not distort or violate in any way the original. But somehow the execution of the idea gets in the way of it. It would be much more effective if it were done more simply and naturally, almost precisely as it would be done in life, Big Mama seated with the others ranged at various positions about her, not in a pair of tight little groups whispering dummy-lines to each other. I don't think dummy-lines should ever be used in a play since they distract the actors from the truth of the scene they're playing: also faked whispers do the same thing. If the scene is really and truly too long, I will cut it, but first I would like to see it played more naturally and audibly, I would like to catch every line of the script in this scene except where there is a natural over-lapping. I think we ought to have a line-reading of this scene before you go back to work on it, which I hope you will do, so that we can re-evaluate the dialogue about which you and I have always had our greatest difference of opinion in the play.

I'm not happy over the interpretation of Doc Baugh whom I had conceived as a sort of gently ironical figure who had seen so much life and death and participated actively in so much of it that he had a sort of sad, sometimes slightly saturnine, detachment from the scene, a calm and kindly detachment, but he plays like a member of the family, in the same over-charged manner, like a fellow conspirator, especially at the moment when he starts abruptly forward as if about to deliver a speech and says the Keely cure bit at stage-center with such startling emphasis. It is off-beat, off-key little details like this which give the beginning of Act Three its curiously unreal look-for-the-rabbit-out-of-the-silk-hat air. . . I think this seriously impairs the effect of the more intense scene that follows and the play as a whole suffers from it. It can be very simply and easily corrected as the basic idea, as I said, is sound and good, it is simply a damaging over-elaboration and formalization. . . .

(Like a person apologizing profusely for something completely unnoticed by anyone but him.)

ATMOSPHERIC DETAILS, outbreak of storm and fireworks.

I think it is right to treat these unconventionally, non-realistically, as we do, but still they ought to be prepared for in a way that will make them <u>recognizable</u> as what they are. It is not natural or believable that there is only the single burst of fire-works and that it occasions such a suddenly started and ended hullaballoo. Can't we have it preceded by some flashes of light in the sky as if from Roman candles, with some muted cries, before all hell breaks loose with the pyrotechnics that are so precisely cued, in a rather cornily symbolic way, by the Brick telling Big Daddy he is dying of cancer bit?

Same is true of the storm. I would like to hear every one of the very few lines in the script about the storm and I would like the storm to approach less abruptly. Otherwise it can only be a tornado or an atom-bomb going off as close as Clarksdale. . .

I love the noise of the storm fading into the lovely negro lullabye: that's a true and beautiful bit of non-realistic staging which comes at the right moment and isn't the least bit exaggerated, in fact I would like to hear the singing better.

You know, of course, that the first view of the setting gave me a horrible, almost death-dealing, blow this afternoon, so I won't go into that subject! I have never had a play that had to get by without visual atmosphere which fitted it, and I am terrified that this may be the first and last time! I have no one to blame but myself as I saw the sketches, but somehow I had always thought, well, Jo is a genius, and Gadg is a genius, and they know what they are doing and who am I to open my ass-hole about it. . .

Tomorrow I will try to think of some more things to squeal about. But now I am going downstairs for a drink and will leave this in your box without reading it over lest I get chicken and afraid to offend you.

I am being utterly sincere when I say that, on the whole, you have done one of your greatest jobs. I just want all of it to measure up to the truest and best of it, and to make it plain to everybody that this play is maybe not a great play, maybe not even a very good play, but a terribly, terribly, terribly true play about truth, human truth.

Devotedly, 10.

[TW warned in a brief cover letter that the depressing effect of the set, installed at the Forrest Theatre in Philadelphia, may have "influenced" his criticism of the final run through of *Cat* in New York.

Mildred Dunnock, an experienced, versatile actor, was last directed by Elia Kazan in *Death of a Salesman*. Her performance as Big Mama was admired in Philadelphia and New York.

Jo Mielziner's enthusiasm for *Cat* was unmistakable: "You have no idea, Tennessee, how exciting this is to work on. This makes up for months and months of slaving over trivia." He also acknowledged, and presumably shared, TW's "concern" that the setting "not turn into a coldly classical abstraction" (January 27, 1955, BRTC). Later correspondence (Wood to TW, April 12, 1955, HRC) confirmed TW's displeasure with Mielziner's set design and his wish not to represent it in the first edition of *Cat*. Kazan, by contrast, not only approved the setting but had also encouraged Mielziner to execute a design that would insure a non-realistic staging of the play (see Kazan, pp. 542-543).

The Philadelphia notices were glowing. *Cat* was a "powerful, free-swinging play" in which TW had "surpassed even the fire and quality" of *Streetcar.* Its "symphonic" construction, brilliantly orchestrated by Kazan, held the audience "in thrall." Act Three played well, especially the conclusion, in which Maggie entices Brick to "the marital bed" with a "hopeful hint for the future." *Variety* reported that the box office was "torrid" after the first week of performance.]

Jo Mielziner, full set design for Cat on a Hot Tin Roof *(1955).*

305. To Justin Brooks Atkinson

[323 East 58th Street, New York]
March 25, 1955
[TLS w/ autograph marginalia, 1 p. BRTC]

Dear Brooks:

Now that you've written your lovely notice I can tell you that I would have just died if you hadn't liked and praised "Cat", I would have literally just died! I can't explain to you or myself or anybody why the reception of this play meant so damnably much to me, why I was so disgustingly craven about it, why the wait for the morning notices to come out was the most unendurable interval of my life. Of course it's always been like that, every time since it started with that little theatre in Saint Louis in 1938, but it gets worse instead of better, and before I go through it again, I've got to sit down with myself long and privately and try to figure out what makes it and what I can do about it besides not writing more plays. It must stem from some really fearful lack of security, some abysmal self-doubt. Also it takes such ugly, odious tangential forms, such as my invidious resentment of Inge's great success despite my friendly attitude toward Bill and his toward me. I was consumed with envy of his play's success and could hardly discuss it with you when we met in the Village a week or so ago. Hideous competitiveness which I never had in me before! But after "Camino" I was plunged into such depths, I thought I would never rise from. I love writing too much, and to love anything too much is to feel a terror of loss: it's a kind of madness. Enough of this, since all I wanted to say was my heartfelt thanks. That's just a phrase when it appears on paper, but believe me I mean it!

Fondly, Tenn.

Some time I would like you to read the original (first) version of Cat before I re-wrote Act III for production purposes. Both versions will be published and, confidentially, I do mean confidentially, I still much prefer the original. It was harder and purer: a blacker play but one that cut closer to the bone of the truth I believe. I doubt that it would have had the chance of success that the present version has and since I had so desperate a need of success, and reassurance about my work, I think all in all Kazan was quite right in persuading me to shape Act III about the return of Big Daddy - in the original the family conference was interrupted not by a storm but by his off-stage cry when pain struck.

[So "limpid and effortless" was *Cat on a Hot Tin Roof* (March 24, 1955) that it seemed "not to have been written. It is the quintessence of life." While Atkinson ranked *Cat* as TW's "finest drama" (*New York Times*, March 25, 1955), his peers were less convinced of its unqualified merit. Walter Kerr cited a lack of candor; Robert Coleman found the characters "repulsive"; John Chapman slighted TW's "command," observing that the action seemed "pointless" at times. *Streetcar* did not, however, arise to judge *Cat* inferior, nor did the "unnatural relationship" of Brick and Skipper unduly concern the critics. Elia Kazan's direction and the work of the principal actors—Barbara Bel Geddes (Maggie), Burl Ives (Big Daddy), Ben Gazzara (Brick)—were uniformly admired. Presumed faults aside, *Cat* had immense theatrical power and would run for nearly 700 performances.

Only Richard Watts was troubled by the ending of *Cat* and perhaps intuitively shared TW's preference for the original version. The "apparent reconciliation" of Brick and Maggie seemed "almost a happy conclusion, yet the final impression is one of doom" (*New York Post*, March 25, 1955).

Atkinson hoped "to read the original version" of *Cat*, as he later informed TW. He was amazed, however, by TW's self-doubt: "I should think your popular success, if nothing else, would give you a feeling of command, for you, Arthur Miller and Bill Inge are the only contemporary playwrights who have been everywhere accepted as theatre artists of first rank" (March 30, 1955, HRC). Inge's latest success was *Bus Stop* (1955).

Penned in the upper margin is a note by Carson McCullers addressed to Atkinson: "I am so thankful you are in the theatre." The dating of the letter is also in her uncertain hand.]

306. To Walter Kerr

[323 East 58th Street, New York]
April 9, 1955
[TLS w/ enclosure, 1 p. SHS of Wisconsin]

Dear Mr. Kerr:

I liked your notices of "Cat" but I thought you brought up an arguable point about "evasions" so I have done the enclosed piece as a reply. Of course I would like to have it published. I feel it would interest everyone who is interested in the play and the various criticisms of it.

I'm now off to Key West or I would like very much to have a less formal discussion with you, but maybe we can have lunch or cocktails when I return in May.

Thank you for the keen intelligence and perception your notices of the play showed. I know that my ambiguities need examination of this kind.

Cordially, Tennessee.

["'Cat on a Hot Tin Roof' is a beautifully written, perfectly directed, stunningly acted play of evasion: evasion on the part of its principal character, evasion perhaps on the part of its playwright." At fault, Walter Kerr argued, was TW's "tantalizing reluctance" to dramatize Brick's "precise feelings" (*New York Herald Tribune*, March 25, 1955) for his friend Skipper. TW answered that ambiguity was a defense against "'pat' conclusions" and "facile definitions" and concluded that theatregoers should expect "views" rather than "certainties" (*New York Herald Tribune*, April 17, 1955; rpt. in *Where I Live*, pp. 70-74).]

307. To Players

SH: Western Union
Key West Flo
1955 May 2 PM 8 32
[Telegram, 1 p. HRC]

DEAR PLAYERS: I WANT YOU TO KNOW THAT I KNOW THAT YOU ALL GAVE ME THE PRIZES ALL MY LOVE=

=TENNESSEE=

[After *Cat* received the Pulitzer and the Drama Critics' Award, TW observed to Elia Kazan that prizes "do disturb one a little as they have so little, or so fantastically remote, a connection with the period and circumstances of work, the lonely, sometimes desperate, mornings of work and the doubts and so forth." Nonetheless "to have them gives you a deep down, slow-burning satisfaction. As if God had given a sign of being with you" (May 3, 1955, WUCA). Satisfying too was the financial performance of *Cat*, which played to standing room and was projected to return the original investment of $102,000 by late-May.]

308. To Cheryl Crawford

SH: Comodoro Hotel
Oceanfront at 72nd Street
Havana, Cuba
5/7/55
[TLS w/ autograph marginalia, 1 p. BRTC]

Dearest Cheryl:

Frank and I suddenly realized last night that your play had opened by this time and we hadn't heard, or said, a word about it. Excuses? A continual stream of guests, beginning with Carson and continuing through

Francoise Sagan and three other "froggies" and my publisher trying to unravel the devious threads of several scripts for publication of "Cat". And then just plain exhaustion, the most valid excuse of all. I don't need to tell you that we hope the "Honey" was a success. We'll be back in New York early next week, well, about the middle anyhow, so don't bother to write us a report down here. Hal Wallis got me on "the blower" as Maria calls phones, about an hour ago and is going to show us "Tattoo" in New York soon as we return. That will be an evening when we can all get together, us four, at least and have a quiet dinner together and then see what Vista-Vision has done to our play. And our Magnani. . .

I wish I could say something definite about Cheri but I've got too many things stacked up right now, a film to finish for Gadg, a couple of unfinished play scripts and a volume of verse to prepare for the printer. Besides it appears that Anna is keen on doing "Orpheus" right now and I don't want to distract her from that. I've been thinking, why not Jane Bowles for "Cheri"? We'll talk about it next week. Meanwhile, much love from your wandering brother Tom. . . .

T.

[Carson McCullers's visit to Key West consisted of "swilling" TW's liquor and "gobbling" his "pinkies" until the host "reeled with apprehension" (qtd. in St. Just, p. 113). Françoise Sagan was the nineteen-year-old author of *Bonjour Tristesse* (1954), a *succès de scandale* recently translated and published in the States. TW had interrupted her tour with an invitation to visit Key West, where she spent a "riotous two weeks" (Sagan, *With Fondest Regards*, 1985).

Cheryl Crawford's latest production, *The Honeys* (1955), was not "a success." Hume Cronyn and Jessica Tandy starred in the Roald Dahl comedy which closed after thirty-six performances. Crawford's interest in *Chéri* did not materialize. The Playwrights' Company unsuccessfully staged the Colette adaptation in 1959.

TW's complaint of "too many things" included making final revisions for a forthcoming book of poetry, planning a production of *Orpheus Descending*, in which Anna Magnani had recently shown interest, and finishing the "unfinished" script of *Baby Doll* (1956).

Penned in the upper margin with an arrow pointing to the Comodoro imprint is the notation "Don't forget this hotel, its a dream!"]

309. To Audrey Wood

SH: Hotel Excelsior, Roma
[early-June 1955]
[TLS, 1 p. HRC]

Dear Audrey:

I was thrilled to get a cable from Gadg last night which said "Brando Available". How authentic is this? Being available does not mean committed or signed, and I am from Missouri and my first name is Thomas! I got a letter from Brando, saying he was very seriously interested in Orpheus. . . . Anyhow it was most exciting, and if it is true that Brando is doing the film, it will be much easier for me to continue work on it. I am going through a bad time with work right now, it is difficult and slow. The events of the year have drained my nervous reserves, I guess. And I have to have a room to myself, and so far that has been impossible, travelling with Frank in a stateroom and a single hotel-room, and he is a late riser, you know. I will mail as much of the new material on the film as I think is fairly presentable on Saturday, as I wired you just now, with notes on further plans for it. The fact, or possibility, of having Brando should be a spur. I know how to write for that boy.

Had lunch with Gloria Swanson, just by chance, but have not yet seen Anna. I'm waiting till Frank catches up with me as conversation is much easier when he's about. He should arrive this evening. We have a huge bathroom, and I plan to work in there till we get an apartment. Tell Gadg to be patient, and I won't let him down.

The Olivetti just broke, the spacer came loose so I shall have to cut this short. I'll get it fixed bright and early tomorrow.

Lefkowitz cabled that the artistic control on "Summer" was all that could be "reasonably expected". How about the money? Was there any improvement in that? And what about the film sale of Cat? There is no reason to expect the bidding to get any hotter or the property to increase in value, so if I were you, dearie, I would dispose of it while that roof is still sizzling, and the cat jumping thereon, at whatever offer is highest. Otherwise - remember "Menagerie"?

Forgive my jaundiced eye.

Love, Tennessee.

[In correspondence Marlon Brando ranked *Orpheus Descending* as TW's "best play" and asked "exactly" when it would be staged. Magnani, he added, "doesn't frighten me. . . . She yearns to be subjigated in a way that is natural to all women but she can't find anybody with enough fire to "burn her down." Brando welcomed the chance to act with her, providing their roles were "equally volital." TW had apparently invited Brando to direct *Orpheus*, a prospect which both "thrilled" and "scared" the actor and led him to return the compliment: "You wrote your funky ass off in that play!" (n.d., Columbia U). Brando's reported interest in *Baby Doll* did not materialize.

TW recently hired Julius Lefkowitz as a business manager. The accountant's first letter (June 2, 1955, HRC) promised cogent advice with a dash and humor and literary taste.

Audrey Wood soon presented TW with a handsome offer for film rights of *Cat*. He wrote earlier to Elia Kazan that she "has 'folie de grandeur' about what she can get for the property" and asked that he talk "realistically" (n.d., WUCA) to her about the market.

TW wrote this letter in the week of June 5. The reception date of 5/13/55 is in error.]

310. To Audrey Wood

[Hotel Colón, Barcelona]
7/11/55
[TLS w/ autograph marginalia, 1 p. HRC]

Dear Audrey:

I'm afraid your patience, and Gadge's, will be sorely tried with me this summer, I am running away from something, but don't know what I am running away from. Each new place disappoints me, after a couple of days it seems like an awful mistake to have gone there. But when I return to Rome, that's no good either. Frank seems put out by my unexpectedly early return and the old routine is lifeless. Magnani is out-spokenly puzzled by my behavior, and I'm afraid we may lose her simply because I act like a Zombie whenever I am with her, despite my true affection for her and great desire to have her do the play. If only Brando would commit himself, this would set things going! Her romantic interest in him is luckily over but being a very sensible, as well as great, artist, she wants very much to work with him and is unwilling to make any definite commitment till he has made one, as she feels that his power and "draw" would give her the confidence to attempt an American play. Her English really has improved, though she hasn't been studying as much as she should.

Frank read me your long wire over the phone. The connection was so bad that I could only get bits of it, and I didn't know whether you were talking about "Orpheus" or "Cat" when you spoke of "ten year payments", Etc. "Rose Dakin Productions" is all right. I would prefer Williams-Wood, unless you feel it is necessary to disguise the identities of the producers. Also I think we ought to be in association with a name producer or one that has lots of the hard stuff. (The hard stuff I am talking about is money). - It's a phrase of Maria's.

I may go down to Tangier and talk to Bowles about doing background music for the play, I think we ought to use him since he wrote the music for the ballads to be used in the play, and I think this one does need music. Also I don't think we ought to delay about a director, Lewis or Clurman or Quintero, if Kazan is definitely unwilling, which I think is the case.

Unless my nervous problems work themselves out in the course of this "summer of the long knives", I am definitely going to start psychiatric treatment when I return in the Fall. Please send me right away to Rome the very first version of "Summer and Smoke", or maybe it was the second, anyway - the one that had film-sequences in it, so I can start immediately on the screen-play. I sent you this version from New Orleans in the winter of 1946, when I had the lunatic notion of using stage and screen in combo to tell the story. It has some good screen material that will be enormously useful to me now.

I am quite well, otherwise, except that I have a cold, from swimming in various unsanitary pools about Europe. Please try to get a payment to Rose's trust fund the earliest possible as Mother is waiting for this to make some better provisions for her comfort and care. If the payments must be delayed, then I think I should advance money to the fund if that can be worked out tax-wise by Lefkowitz. Have you heard that Louella Parsons had a stroke in Rome? One side of her face is twisted up very oddly, according to Jean Stein, who called on her there. I sent her roses and phoned several times, as I've always rather liked that old girl despite her silliness and prejudices.

With love, Tennessee.

[TW spent the better part of July in Barcelona. He thought Frank Merlo "put out" by his "unexpectedly early return" to Rome in June following a trip to Athens and Istanbul.

"Figures stagger imagination approve get the loot" (telegram, TW to Wood, July 2, 1955, HRC). MGM offered $500,000 for film rights of *Cat* with payments to be spread over ten years. Studio executives were also confident, Wood had noted, that they could "solve" (telegram, to TW, June 30, 1955, HRC) the censorship problems which filming *Cat* would entail.

Wood later thanked TW for suggesting that their production company be named "Williams-Wood" (August 3, 1955, HRC) rather than "RoseDakin," as she had proposed. *Orpheus Descending* was to be the first venture.

Julius Lefkowitz advised TW in prior correspondence to write the screenplay for *Summer and Smoke* as a way of protecting the "artistic integrity" (June 2, 1955, HRC) of the original work.

Penned in the upper margin is the notation "(will wire next address)".]

311. To Elia "Gadge" Kazan

[Hotel Colón, Barcelona]
[July 1955]
[TL, 3 pp. WUCA]

Gadge Baby:

My imagination, weary, jaded ole thing which it is this summer, was not exactly fired by your outline (which reached me yesterday, not till then, because of a bad-phone-connection between here and Rome so that Frank thought I meant to hold my mail there, until I called him again). On the contrary: it (my imagination) was somewhat chilled and dampened, and I will try to tell you why, without being unnecessarily expository. We get each other's points too readily, when there's one to be gotten, without a lot of wearisome palaver.

I feel that my own original conception of the film-story as a grotesque folk-comedy of the modern South, with some serious over-tones, carefully kept within the atmospheric frame of the story, is still the only right one. The course which you indicate for the ending is far too heavy, at least for a work that is to have any sort of artistic unity. You are talking about HEAVY DRAMA! - that winds up with a genteel woman's FULFILLMENT, Death for one man, prison for the other. I know that I have not been very fair with you because there was a point where I appeared to accept this sort of an ending, Meighan killing Silva, dragged off in chains, Etc. But that was before I became really "engaged" in this material, I had a couple of plays and play productions on my mind so I gave it all too little serious consideration. If I had thought about it, I would have realized that to have tragedy on stage or screen you have to build up to it, everything has to be conceived and done in a way that establishes a premise for a tragic ending, mood and style of writing have got to prepare it. Otherwise, one thing defeats the other, the result is nowhere! So even before this summer, I discarded the idea of a heavy ending. I can't go back to it now, like a dog to his vomit, I would just puke it right back up again, because it is really indigestible, it will not sit on my critical stomach, nor would it sit on yours if you were sitting down here trying to lap it up yourself, because it is not only vomit, it is cold vomit, and vomit can only be lapped back up and successfully returned to the belly while it is hot. (I am trying to make you laugh but am probably just making you angry.) When Frank gets angry at me he sometimes shouts, 'What you want is a yes-man and I am nobody's yes-man!' I am saying, more quietly, the same thing to you, that is, if you persist in this folly . . . Baby Doll Meighan cannot be turned into a starring role for Grace Kelly or Deborah Kerr, it's a part for a sexy little comedienne, and as such, could be delightful and fresh and a great popular hit on the screen. Baby Doll is about as genteel as Paddy's Pig. Have you ever noticed her grammar, the cultural, intellectual and spiritual content of her speech and behavior? She is touchingly comic, a grotesquely witless creature, about as deep as kitty-cat's pee. Who the fuck gives a shit if she is, was, or ever will be "FULFILLED AS A WOMAN"? Besides, though I would be the last to denigrate the value of a good fuck, I don't think people are transformed, redeemed, fulfilled in this fashion, any more than you learn piano in ten easy lessons by mail. She gets laid, she gets laid good, maybe, and she will doubtless be having the most satisfactory summer of her life, but a person's fulfillment, if such a thing exists, can only occur through self-integration, a slow process, demanding, in the first place a degree of intelligence and maturity, at least enough to enable the person to see and know his own self. I am afraid this kind of fulfillment, the only kind that much matters, is not for the Baby Doll Meighans of this world. She can have a vaginal fulfillment and a fulfillment of the womb, but I can't see it going past that, and my knees ache with boredom at the thought of trying to take her, or make an audience take her, seriously as a "Fulfilled Woman"? You mention Pagnol. I am not sure I have seen a Pagnol film but the name suggests a lightness, a delicacy, a playfulness, in which case the film is now on the right track, though still a long way from its destination.

But I don't think a Pagnol atmosphere, if I am interpreting it rightly, can have an early Eugene O'Neill finish tacked onto it without the most serious disagreement between the two, each impaling the other upon a frog-gig!

And I said I was not going to be "Expository"!

Now here, in the crudest sort of a sketchy cornball fashion, is how I think the film might end. (Incidentally, I disagree with you entirely about the end of the play being the important or exciting part. I think the main dynamic lies in Silva's relentless, step-by-step sensual ravishment of this sexy little virgin-wife for revenge and for proof of the arson.)

After the chop-sticks bit, SILVA goes to kitchen for ice-water. Back there he takes a stub pencil, hanging from a nail on kitchen wall, and scribbles the note of confession on the back of a receipt for milk or ice or something, folds it into his pocket and returns to parlor, finds whip which Baby Doll had childishly concealed in the piano-bench. Goes out, grinning, with ice-water to join her on porch. (I've sent Audrey a pretty good re-write on that bit). Step-by-step she is isolated with Vacarro, her panic-attraction-panic steadily building up, with or without the trip to Clarksdale, which I still like. (Why does it break the unity anymore than your idea of them going to the Brite Spot that night? We have created a geographic unity out of the whole community, I mean the early part of the film has already included the town in the frame or canvas.) - When the big chase scene culminates, serio-comically in the falling plaster in attic, Baby Doll's ankle caught between cracking lathes, he hands her the confession to sign before extricating her. This done, he gets her out. Then what does he do, to her astonishment, but go calmly downstairs and out of the house. She is amazed, disappointed. Defended virginity turns to frustrated libido. She calls down the stairs, and across the lawn, as he goes, 'Where you going?' - 'Home, for a nap, I didn't sleep good last night.' - 'Hey! - We got a bed left here.' - 'Where?' - 'The nursery!' - - - HE stops under the big pecan tree, leaps into it, suddenly, and springs down with a pecan in his mouth, cracks it between his teeth, and casually hands her the two nut-meats. This time she accepts without fastidious comment. He whistles reflectively for a moment: then says: "I'm sleepy, it's a long hot walk to my place . . . I'm five feet ten and one half. How long is the crib?' - 'The bars let down!' - 'Aw, you let down the bars, huh? Well - ' . . . . . He starts toward the house. We dissolve to the nursery, seeing it for the first time, the pathos of a child's room in a house without children. Perhaps he winds up a musical top as she lowers the slats of the crib. He sighs and lies down. She remains standing over him. He looks up at her with one eye, winks slightly, and curls up with his back to her. SHE crouches beside the crib, which rocks, and rocks it very gently, beginning to sing 'Rock-A-Bye-Baby' - stopping at his first snore. The (phallic) whip slips from his fingers. She picks it up tenderly and replaces it in his loose, sleeping hand. So we fade out without proving, or disproving, that he laid her or not. The audience is free to think what it will. Anyhow something humanly touching has occured, or been stated, the child in man that meets and plays with and loves the child in woman.

Eli Wallach and Carroll Baker: "I'm five feet ten and one half. How long is the crib?" (Baby Doll, *1956).*

As for the frog-gigging party: you can carry it on to the point where Meighan's nerve deserts him, he gives way before Silva, takes flight, slips and flounders in muddy water, falls sobbing to his knees among cypress-knees. . . .

Silva to Rock: 'Get him up. I'm goin' back for dry clothes.'

We close on Silva re-entering the old plantation house. It lights up!

- Meighan limping like a lame old dog back along the now deserted bayou.

- I still like the ending we have already, however.

- Do we go on with this thing, now, or deduct it from taxes as a human error? Write me in Rome. I'll be going back there in a few more days.

Love,

[Preserved in early drafts of *Baby Doll* is the "discarded" frog-gigging scene cited by TW: "We see a tall Negro bearing a man's body. . . . Baby Doll screams, the figures divide. Vacarro lies smiling mysteriously, eyes open, a gig through his bare belly. . . . Dissolve to Big Shot {Archie Lee Meighan} wading out of the water . . . the sheriff behind him" (n.d., HRC).

Elia Kazan's "outline" of *Baby Doll* was an older conception which had been delayed in delivery and superseded by a script that TW would eagerly approve (see letter #315). Kazan agreed nonetheless that the "HEAVY" ending which he had devised violated "the first nine-tenths of the picture." Wrong too, he thought, was the coy "Lady and the Tiger" ending which TW now proposed: it failed to satisfy "the interest in all three" characters. To soften the frog-gigging scene, Kazan suggested that Vacarro and Meighan be reconciled. Perhaps Meighan, bitten by a snake, could be tended by Vacarro "in some fantastic kind of brotherhood." It was, he admitted, a "weird idea," but it might restore the "grotesque style" (to TW, n.d., HRC) of the film.

Kazan apparently mentioned the French playwright and film director Marcel Pagnol. His Marseille trilogy had recently been adapted as a musical—*Fanny* (1954)—and staged successfully on Broadway.

As filmed, the "attic" and the "crib" scenes closely follow TW's direction. TW was no less variable than Kazan regarding the end of *Baby Doll*. In May he restated his preference for a final dissolve to a forlorn Baby Doll sitting on the back porch of the Meighan residence phoning the police—an ending which he boasted was almost "perfect!" and "practically censor-proof" (to Kazan, May 3, 1955, WUCA).

In June he described the present "crib" scene, with a final dissolve to Aunt Rose in the County Hospital, as a more suitable closing (to Kazan, n.d., WUCA).

A briefer signed version of this letter, dated July 23, 1955, is held by the HRC. The printed version bears a reception date of July 28, 1955.]

312. To Frank Merlo

[Hotel Colón, Barcelona]
[July 22, 1955]
[TLS, 2 pp. HTC]

Dearest Horse:

I am working on Red Cross to send you a "gift package" containing one dozen rolls finest Swan's down toilet tissue, one quart blood plasma, and a bottle of spirits of ammonia. (Ha ha, this is a joke!) More seriously, I am worried over the persistence of the complaint. I never had it that bad, even in Mexico when I first had it, and I hope you are being careful and seeing Anna's doctor. You really mustn't go to Sicily! You remember you had a bad attack of dysentery when you went there the first time, and also the summer heat there would be awfully hard on Buffo. If you want to take a trip, and I can understand why you might, I think you should try Capri or Positano or Amalfi. I could join you in Naples, when I leave here, sailing out of some Spanish port. I find the bathing, regularly, and the sun, does so much for me, physically. One does get run down in Rome. I've been remarkably well since I started spending my days on the beach. However Miss Egleston is back on the trail, now, she calls every day, almost, to announce she is waiting downstairs in the bar. I'm glad the fiesta Brava starts in Valencia this Sunday so I have a reason to cut out. Tynan is here with an English queen who has just done 18 months in Worms Scrubwood or Scrubwood Worms for the hideous offense of buggery! His victim was an RAF boy, his lover for three years. He tells me Tynan is a sadist, gets his kicks having girls put on little school-girl costumes and caning them about the legs till they dance and howl. Very pretty, I must say! Claude Marchand, the colored dancer, is also in Barcelona, with his English lover, and they are good company. Society snow-balls here. More and more, till you scarcely have a moment to yourself. It takes real strategy to contrive some precious hours of solitude. A wire from Audrey confirmed sale of Cat to Metro for half million, which means we don't have to worry about "the hard stuff" for another ten years, I guess. We'll be old girls, by then, and can get our social security when it runs out, and by such little economies as saving old tea-bags and turning collars and cuffs, we can eke out a comfortable elderly existence in some quaint little cold-water walk-up in the west nineties, with an occasional splurge at the YMHA when a surviving Sitwell gives a reading there. I'm afraid my eyesight will be getting rather dim, by that time, but my hearing may hold up. I hope you will have stopped having diarrhea. Perhaps Miss Butterfly or Ladybird will have provided us with a warm-hearted, short-winded companion for our excursions to the corner delicatessen and to (as far as) Bloomingdale's on their 99¢ sales-days. Queens have settled for less in ten years' time. . .

Does this sound like Leslie Eggleston? No wonder. I've had him in my ears going in and coming out for the past six hours, without interval or respite. The poor thing has hepatitis, which is the only noticeable improvement, an improvement because he orders fewer drinks. One more bull-fight, tomorrow, and I am off for Valencia. Marian Vacarro sent me clippings about the death of poor Valentina Sheriff. ("How dare you talk to me like this in the Ritz!" - remember?) She was found dead in her negligee in a New Orleans hotel among various empty and half empty pill-bottles which are being analyzed by chemists to see which snuffed out her existence. Poor Valentina, as Marian said! - And then went blithely on about the gay crew on the banana boat to Venezuala that she was on lately. Letter from Paul Bowles said Oliver Evans had been there, very nervous, going to doctor daily for terrible head-aches. It is not a good year for us Bohemian type people, is it, ducks? Gadg sent me his outline for the film. Baby Doll must be a "Fulfilled woman", Silva dead, and Archie Lee in prison in the last reel. I had to write him a rather sharp reply. I told him that when you get mad at me you shout: 'What you want is a yes-man and I am nobody's yes-man' and I said that this was exactly how I felt about his fucking outline. . . .

If the paper was softer, I would send it to you, as a supplement to supplies in the bathroom.

I am being careful, as careful as I can be, and I hope that you are, too. Horazio could be worse, let him wash the car when you feel up to it again. He is a nice, honest boy, and you are safe with him, if you don't forget the "mother's aid" in the tube.

Audrey wired, also, that Brando is willing to play "Orpheus" in the Fall of '56, provided some changes were made in his part. I think he's another one to be told to fuck off. Don't you? You'd better let Anna know about this. Also that Clurman is available in December. (This year.) I think we can do without the great ones in the male department if we can get her to learn English.

I bought Anna a very fine leather bag with her initials in gold-plate and I'm getting her a wide belt to go with it. I'm trying to find the right sort of comb and mantilla for <u>you</u>, something suitable for the bathroom at midnight.

Don't forget to wire me if you take a trip anywhere, Baby. You know how awful it would be for me to pop back to Rome, unexpectedly, and no Horse and no car! Just a few old blood-stains on the bathroom floor. . . .

I wouldn't know whether it was murder or mementos of chronic colitis! - No more cracks on that subject, I promise.

All my love to you, Tenn

[Frank Merlo was "so cross" that TW thought it wise "to stay on the hoof; besides, I am restless this summer" (qtd. in St. Just, p. 121).

TW reported an "icy" (qtd. in St. Just, p. 125) meeting with Oliver Evans in Barcelona. His friend had recognized himself as the vain, aging homosexual in "Two on a Party," reprinted in *Hard Candy* (1954). He answered at the time with a taunting postcard and a threatening note: "You are so ugly, how could you

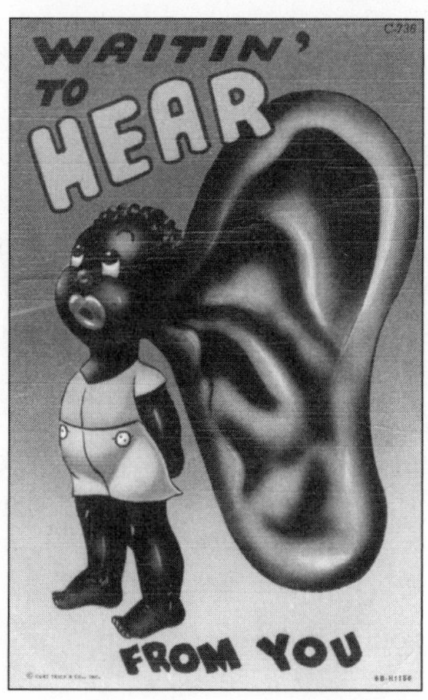

possibly interest anyone you didn't pay? Just read your new book & don't think you should return to New Orleans. A number of people join me in thinking it's very unhealthy for you - Love (not really) Oliver." (TW enclosed postcard and note in a letter to Elia Kazan dated September 16, 1954, WUCA.) The estrangement of friends ended in 1958, when Evans expressed new understanding of his portrait in *Hard Candy* and TW replied that his fondness for him had "never faltered" (November 15, 1958, HRC).]

313. To Robert MacGregor

SH: Hotel Colón, Barcelona
7/22/55
[TLS, 1 p. Houghton]

Dear Bob:

At last I got your letters, they were much delayed by a telephone misunderstand[ing], Frank thought I said to hold mail and I had told him to send it to me here, and this was not corrected till I called him again a week later, after waiting here all that time for the mail to come.

I do wish you could hold the book back, now, until I return to the States. It will doubtless be the only book of poems I will ever have published and I would like to be in closer touch with its preparation, there have already been misunderstandings. You haven't gotten all the poems on the list and you are not yet clear about the ones I want omitted. "The Angels of Fructification" should definitely go in, as it is one of the better ones. This is because I didn't have enough time to go over the collection with you before I sailed, but when I return, there'll be much more leisure and less pressure. I would like to confer with you about the cover design, and the type, for instance. Also I don't want any of the dates and places of composition at the ends of poems as they were in the "Five Poets" book. This is pretentiously silly so let's omit it, as an error of one's lyric youth corrected by prose reflection in middle years. Who gives a shit where and when I wrote these undistinguished verses? Only I. And I can remember. Also I still hope that somehow and sometime or other a better, more provocative, title will occur to me. I am enclosing a re-write of "Those Who Ignore the Appropriate Time Of Their Going". Does this strike you as a good title for the book, or is it too long and fancy? If you reflect upon it, it does describe or suggest a great deal about most of us. People expect me to provide good titles, and I haven't this time, have I? - This re-write is only of the poem's last section. I would also like to change the beginning slightly, to:

> Those who ignore the appropriate time of their going
> are the most valiant explorers,
> going into a country that no one is meant to go into.

Could you send me the old version of the poem so I can fit it together with the revision?

I'm flying to Valencia tomorrow to attend a week of bull-fights with the English critic, Kenneth Tynan, who's doing a piece about me for Harper's Bazaar and is getting altogether too much confidential material here in Spain, though I am also getting a lot on him! Frank's in Rome. I will be returning there after the bull-fights, so you'd better address any mail to me there, #12 Via Corsini or c/o American Express.

Ever - Tennessee

[*In the Winter of Cities* was not published until June 1956, nor would it be TW's "only book of poems."

"Valentine to Tennessee Williams" appeared in *Mademoiselle* (February 1956) and was reprinted by the author, Kenneth Tynan, in *Curtains* (1961). In light of his harsh review of *Summer and Smoke*, Tynan wrote a surprisingly mild, conventional profile of TW. He cast him as a nomad, a hypochondriac, a solitary writer who "longs for intimacy, but shrinks from its responsibilities." Tynan's biographical summary followed the familiar outline of TW's painful departure from the South and prolonged exile in St. Louis. Unmentioned were personal and family matters including the illness of Rose. Tynan saved his aggression for Elia Kazan, who was accused of interfering with the composition of *Cat*. Tynan, drama critic for *The Observer* (London), drew from an autobiographical statement prepared by TW and dated July 26, 1955 (rpt. in Windham, pp. 301-307).]

314. To Audrey Wood

[Hotel Colón, Barcelona]
7/28/55
[TLS, 1 p. HRC]

Dear Audrey:

I still don't believe that you actually sold "Cat" for half a million. It's just fantastic. What a doll you are! I haven't adequately thanked you, and I'm afraid my importunities before the sale was consummated were inconsiderate of me. This is a down-beat summer, I just can't seem to get the work going, and that always throws me into a negative and unpleasant state of mind. Oh, well, you understand that, as you do most things. . .

I had to tell Gadg off, not rudely but firmly. He sent me a five-page outline for the film play which would have meant starting over from scratch even if I thought it was right, and it was corny as hell and old-fashioned melodrama that just wouldn't come off. I've stopped trying to work on it, at least until further word from him. If he's got any sense, he'll come to his senses, and leave me alone with the script to work it out my own way. I think he cheapened Cat, still think so, despite the prizes. That doesn't mean I doubt his good intentions, or don't like him, now, it's just that I don't want to work with him again on a basis in which [he] will tell me what to do and I will be so intimidated, and so anxious to please him, that I will be gutlessly willing to go against my own taste and convictions.

I'm still in Barcelona. The beach is wonderful, I swim a lot and it has picked up my physical condition, and there's the bull-fights. Frank's been sick all summer, first the hang-over from the hepatitis and then a fierce attack of colitis which went on for weeks. I don't think my company made him feel any better so it's just as well that I went away. Next year I'm going to insist that the boy go to a good analyst, he can afford it now and I can if he can't. I think these illnesses are a good part psychosomatic. He is haunted continually by the feeling of insufficiency, that he is dependant on me, and yet doesn't seem to be able to bring himself to the point of taking any positive action to change this state. We never joke and laugh together, which is bad, as jokes and laughter do so much to relieve the human dilemma, but he touches me deeply, and while I doubt that I have ever deeply loved him, according to my extremely romantic conception of what love should be - as distinguished from the pleasures of bed - still, he's given me an awful lot in a period when it was needed. So I want to do all I can to help him find himself now, not just keep going over and over the same beaten track, following me, North, South, East and West, and making little abortive efforts, however violently shouted, to "say it isn't so". He's a true person, honest, intelligent, warm. "Attention must be paid to this man" before it's too late. His humility alone is great beauty.

I must, must get Brando's demands for his part soon, soon! If the demands are practicable, and Anna is willing to wait, then I wouldn't mind the delay till next the 1956 Fall. But if they are like most actors and directors demands, I'd rather forget him and try to find someone else. Anna suggested Jimmie Dean. I don't think that's a bad choice, except he's younger than Val ought to be. Clift is another possibility. Who else? I'm happy about Clurman, and I know that Anna would break through his tendancy to make a play a bit static or "fixed". Please tell him I am delighted that he may do it, and ask him to start thinking, planning for a mid-winter production. Anna is ready at that time. I think she would be so terrific, so true, in the role, that Brando is dispensable if difficult to please.

I will be back in Rome in about four days.

With love - 10.

PS. Please ask Bob MacGregor not to send poetry book to printers till he hears from me. I have further revisions and probably a different title. Would prefer holding it back till I return States late September. There is no hurry about it.

[Audrey Wood urged TW to spare himself and follow her own don't "ask" (August 3, 1955, HRC) policy regarding studio plans to censor *Cat on a Hot Tin Roof*. Such plans were already evident in an outline prepared by MGM and discussed with the Production Code staff before the sale of film rights. The proposed treatment would "stress the father-son relationship" and "omit any inference of homo-sexuality" between Skipper and Brick. Skipper would callously seduce Maggie, which Brick refuses to acknowledge until Big Daddy convinces him that his friend was "a rotter" (Production Code memorandum, June 23, 1955, Herrick).

Wood informed TW that Marlon Brando was still considering the lead in *Orpheus*, although he would not be available until fall 1956 and his commitment would entail difficult revision of the play. As written, the part of Val Xavier did not carry "enough weight," Brando thought, while the "blow torch ending" in which Val is emasculated was "tough to take" (August 4, 1955, HRC).

TW had not yet learned of Margo Jones's death on July 24, 1955, from exposure to a toxic cleaning agent. He later doubted the accidental nature of her death and surmised that Jones "may have had an abortion. That frequently results in uremic poisoning, if it goes wrong." It hurt TW "to think how often we laughed at dear Margo for her little silliness and paid too little attention to her great heart" (qtd. in St. Just, p. 124). His cable of condolence arrived after the funeral on July 26.]

315. To Elia "Gadg" Kazan

[12 Via Corsini, Rome]
[August 1955]
[TLx, 1 p. Private Collection]

Dear Gadg:

Frankie the Horse has just trotted in with the repaired Olivetti and I'm back on it, Baby. He also brought the script and your letter. I'm going to write you about it after only reading the first few pages and the last few pages. Later I'll write you a more dispassionate and qualified appraisal, but let me say right off, you're a better man than I am, Gunga Din! The end sounds great, it's great film-writing, perhaps it's even great writing. It doesn't sound like corn, it sounds like dynamite. (Remember! - I've only read about six pages, divided between the beginning and the end.) Of course you realize that if I use your stuff I will have to use your name as co-author, I couldn't honorably do otherwise. I would be happy to do this, and believe me I mean it. Owing people is shit. That is, owing a friend is shit. But nevertheless, the fact stays that I owe you what makes it possible for me to get through this summer, to live. A success when I had given up thought of anything but failure, and a sort of vague whimpering end to life. No, maybe not whimpering. Give the devil his due, I might not whimper. On the other hand, I might.

BELIEVE ME! - I've only read your letter and three pages at the beginning and about three at the end, but the shouting to the men on the bank with Archie Lee at the end of the gig, is great, great, great, great THEATRE! - What we live for, what we try to be in these silly makeshift existences of ours, and I pay you homage for it.

This is all for right now, Baby. But I hope that I will discover some way to persuade you to keep in "Chopsticks" and "Charm-bracelet" bits just as a sort of identification mark of my own that says, "Here lies Tennessee." -

You take the big guns, the heavy artillery, but let me have a little of my old little flute-playing here and there in the script to signify that I was your partner in it.

True love,

[TW's refers to a shooting script of *Baby Doll* assembled by Elia Kazan which post-dates the rejected "five-page outline." In the new opening sequence Meighan leers at his sleeping virgin-bride through a peephole in the plaster. Staged in the conclusion is an epic battle between Vacarro and Meighan which ends with Meighan "shouting to the men on the bank" that he burned the syndicate gin: "I did it. I did it" (July 29, 1955, HTC). One of the silent witnesses, goaded by Vacarro to acknowledge the confession, kills the outsider with a rifle shot. This climactic scene was not filmed, nor would there be more than a trace of the original frog-gigging party—recast as a fishing expedition—in the final print. The present script ends with a close shot of Aunt Rose humming a lullaby to Baby Doll.

Audrey Wood received a copy of this letter from Kazan and instructed TW not to offer him co-authorship of *Baby Doll*: "All of this should be handled by AW and not TW. You are a writer and not a business man. Stop making your own deals - I am much better as a dealer than you - Remember Metro Goldwyn Mayer!" (August 16, 1955, HRC).]

316. To the Editor, Theatre Arts

[12 Via Corsini, Rome]
[August/September 1955]
[*Theatre Arts*, October 1955, p. 3]

Dear Sir:

Due to my travels in Europe I was late in getting the July issue of your magazine containing the alleged interview with me ["Tennessee Williams: Ten Years Later"]. It is true that the interview took place; it took place very dimly, almost unconsciously, during the dreadful last week before the New York opening of my play *Cat*. But even considering the conditions under which I had this interview, I am not able to believe that I actually said the things that I am directly quoted as having said . . . I would certainly never be so unfaithful to the greatest lady of my life, Blanche Du Bois, to describe her as "weak," "pitiful," almost "a mental case." This, I know, I did *not!* In some respects Blanche, who went to the madhouse, was the most rational of all the characters I've created, and in almost all ways, she was the strongest. She certainly fought on a much more desperate field than Maggie the Cat fights on, she fought with all odds against her and with unfailing valor, with gallantry that persisted and even reached its peak at the final curtain. It must be obvious to anyone that I prefer her to Maggie the Cat, though I have great admiration for both ladies. For very different reasons. It should also be obvious that I could never have denigrated *Camino Real* as something for which I can only ask for indulgence, granted after. I am not at all sure that it isn't the one I love most of my plays, though I know it commits the huge structural error of deviating from a straight narrative line. [Elia] Kazan and I both are very proud of this "failure" and talk of another production. My article in the [New York] *Herald Tribune* deals accurately with my attitude toward Brick's sexual nature, not the one given in quotes in this interview. I don't doubt that Arthur Waters was conscientious but I think it is necessary to be much more attentive to exact words and exact meanings when you use quotation marks in interviews, especially when you are interviewing someone who, under the circumstances, wants only to sit and wait as quietly as possible for the stroke of doom or deliverance. Finally, it is quite true that Kazan is my favorite director, but it was inaccurate and unkind, equally both, to suggest that I blamed *Rose Tattoo's* relative lack of success on its direction. Daniel Mann did a beautiful job on the stage version of *Tattoo* and a still more beautiful job on the film. Gadg would have demanded a stronger, tighter script from me: Danny was willing to take a chance on the script submitted.

Tennessee Williams
Rome, Italy

[Quotations attributed to TW—accurately or not—fail to convey his well-known preference for the ambiguity of character. Far too explicit were statements that "'Brick is definitely not a homosexual'" and that his drinking may be attributed to attacks on Skipper rather than his own "'personal involvement.'" Uncontested by TW were his reported opinions that the theatre was holding "its own" and that artistic standards for American films have "improved" (*Theatre Arts*, October 1955, p. 3; rpt. in *Conversations*, pp. 34-37).

The brackets and ellipsis were inserted by *Theatre Arts*.]

317. To Audrey Wood

[Rome/Paris]
[August/September 1955]
[TLS w/ enclosure, 2 pp. HRC]

Dearest Audrey:

The reaper is not only grim but active and rapid this season. It was Mel Ferrer that told me about Lem's death and it gave me a shock for Lem was my closest male friend at Iowa and I'd always been particularly fond of him. He was not only very gifted but also very kind and understanding. Mel said he died of leukemia after a three years' illness in which he carried on his work even when bed-ridden.

Wallis is here and we were at the Ferrers for dinner last night because Hal wants to sign Audrey Hepburn for Summer and Smoke. I think it's an excellent choice. Kurt Frings and his wife went along. Both of them struck me as having a merely surface geniality. Masking a lot of malice. I believe Hal is intending to get Ketti Frings to write the screen play for Summer and Smoke. I hope you will block this idea, she strikes me as having a basically vulgar mind. I'd rather work on it, if I find that I need a collaborator, with a male writer. I can handle the feminine side of the story but a good, sensitive male writer of quality could help me a lot with the action stuff, such as the fever epidemic and the melodramatic death of the old doctor. Also she would take the lion's share of the screenwriter's pay, no doubt, with Mr. Frings in her corner. I spoke of you and he said, 'I have never known such a domineering woman.' This did not please me at all as I feel you are quite the contrary.

Audrey Hepburn is fabulous! Truly! She was Miss Alma in the flesh! I can't think of better casting for this part. She has long thin arms, a long thin neck, long thin body and long thin legs - and eyes that break your heart with their youth and sweetness. No accent: exquisite grace. I almost found myself admiring Hal Wallis for thinking of her for it. Her price is $350,000 and he is willing to pay it! The deal is not yet completed but I had a distinct feeling that both she and Mel were very favorable to it. We discussed directors. Do you think the man who directed "Marty" would be right for it? Another one mentioned was William Wyler who directed her in "Roman Holiday".

I am flying to Stockholm on Wednesday where I will be the guest of the very rich Mrs. Lilla Van Saher Riwkin at the Castle Hotel. You can reach me there.

LATER - Found this unfinished letter among my papers when I got back here in Paris. This is my vague summer! - have been through everything but a flash flood at Inge's summer palace in Buck's County, PA. Seems to be good for me, never felt better in my life! - except that I don't write well. Now waiting here for Frank and Magnani to show. No word about when. But patience is a virtue in late summer or early Fall that one must respect. And practise. Saw Toby Roland (in London) about Tattoo. I like that man very much, and the director that he has in mind for Tattoo is the best in Europe, a young guy (23) named Peter Hall who put on "Waiting for Godot" now playing in London which I am not sure is not the greatest play of our time. Directed with absolute genius! - I'm trying to sell Roland on Stapleton as the lead. He has in mind a night-club performer that I never heard of. Lars Schmidt is coming here to confer with me about Tattoo for London and Cat for Paris. So things are jumping! I still have the new power-of-attorney. Haven't gotten around to notarizing it yet, but I will soon as I get back in the States where it can be done so much more easily. I'm sure there's no immediate crisis. Or is there? If there is, wire me. You're the only person that I trust in this world. You know that, don't you? But still I would prefer to go over the document with you prior to signing.

The matter of Orpheus is settled as far as I am concerned. We are going to produce it together. No playwrights! - in my heart it is hard for me to like any playwright who is still writing plays. Miller, yes! Inge, sometimes . . . . an ugly effect of the competitive system. They have to stun me with splendor that drives vanity out! Or I wish they'd quit writing as I have nearly this summer.

At this point, I'm afraid there is nothing to do about "Hide And Seek" but try very hard to like everything that Kazan suggests. I'm going out now (my first morning in Paris) to pick up his latest draft of it. Got a long-distance call from Jack Warner (from Cannes) praising the new script to the skies! Kazan probably writes better than it reads. However the script so far seems to be about 90% my stuff and I think he ought to be content with credit as the adaptor for screen. We'll talk about that in New York.

Is it possible that poor Rose is still in the State Asylum? If so, would you wire Mother that I want her to be transferred at once to Saint Vincent's in Saint Louis at my expense? I also have an old maid Aunt on my hands now. Dad has cut off her fifty-dollar-a-month allowance and I have to take it on. Please tell Lefkowitz. She can be deductible as a dependant. She is

Miss Ella Williams at 1633 West Clinch Ave., Knoxville, Tennessee. A wonderful old lady, very brave and proud, eighty years old. I have already sent her a check for $500. to tide her over the next few months but I think the monthly payments ought to be started to give her a feeling of security. I enclose her letter thanking me for the check so you can see her character.

With love, Tenn.

[The stage designer Lemuel Ayers died on August 14, 1955, at the age of forty.

Audrey Hepburn and her husband, Mel Ferrer, were evidently less "favorable" to *Summer and Smoke* than TW imagined. He later urged Hepburn not to consider the play a "downbeat" story: "It concerns victory of spirit over a circumstantial defeat which is only possible victory in life" (telegram, August 26, 1955, Herrick). Geraldine Page would play Alma in the 1961 film. The screenwriter Ketti Frings (*Come Back, Little Sheba*, 1952) had no hand in the production.

The trip to Scandinavia (ca. August 31-September 3) for the European premiere of *Cat* was "a mess!" as TW informed Maria Britneva. Lilla Van Saher apparently created a public relations fiasco in Stockholm by exploiting TW's presence. TW later implied that she had ruined his impending nomination for the Nobel Prize (see *Conversations*, p. 357). The play, if not the author, was "a huge success" (qtd. in St. Just, p. 127).

Casting, production, and censorship problems delayed the London premiere of *The Rose Tattoo* until 1959. Lea Padovani rather than Maureen Stapleton played the lead.

Audrey Wood recently criticized the Playwrights' Company for sloppy production of *Cat*. Presumably she hoped to moderate TW's high regard for the producing group and to strengthen the new corporation of Williams-Wood (Wood to TW, August 22, 1955, HRC).

No formal credit was given for the adaptation of *Baby Doll*. TW claimed the full screenwriting credit.

"Poor Rose" Williams was soon transferred to St. Vincent's Sanitarium in St. Louis County, where her custodial care began in 1937.

TW wrote the first part of this letter in Rome in the week of August 21, 1955. He added the "Later" part in Paris, probably in mid-September, after visiting Scandinavia, Hamburg, and London. The letter bears a reception date of September 19, 1955, three days before he and Frank Merlo sailed for the States.]

318. To Audrey Wood

[Comodoro Hotel, Havana]
Nov. 18 (or 20), '55
[TLS w/ autograph postscript
and enclosure, 2 pp. HRC]

Dear Audrey:

Frank told me over the phone yesterday that Otis Guernsey of the Trib wanted me to contribute a piece about Anna. Here it is. Will you please have it typed up and send copies to him and to me. I'm afraid it's a bit diffuse and over-length but I think the portrait is true and sympathetic. If the Trib doesn't take it, it might be submitted elsewhere.

Don't you think we are moving too slow on "Orpheus"? I think the dead-line for decisions from both Brando and Kazan should be the end of December, after Anna has arrived in the States. I also think it's imperative that she come over at that time, so we can sign her, and get the production under way. Until we know we have HER, it is hard to cast the others. I read the script over and I can't dispute Marlon's view that his part is weaker than hers. Nor can I see any way to expand it very appreciably without changing, adulterating, the truth of the play, and on this occasion, I am determined to express just me, not a director or actors. Almost everybody of taste that I have talked to about "Cat" are disturbed and thrown off somewhat by a sense of falsity, in the ending, and I don't want this to ever happen again, even if it means giving up the top-rank names as co-workers.

I have developed a sore gut and some fever, so I'm cutting my stay here short and flying back to Miami, this afternoon, unless I feel a lot better in the next few hours.

With love, Tenn.

P.S. Rose has been transferred to St. Louis hospital.

[TW spent the fall in New York and Key West before visiting Havana in mid-November. Staging *Orpheus* was uppermost in mind, but other projects vied for attention, especially the filming of *Baby Doll* and plans for European productions of *The Rose Tattoo* and *Cat*. A new play, *Sweet Bird of Youth* (1956/1959), was also underway at this time.

Publication of "Anna Magnani, Tigress of the Tiber," was timed to coincide with the release of *The Rose Tattoo* on December 12, 1955. TW wrote that the art of Anna Magnani and Laurette Taylor was "closely related. Both owned that same uncanny sense of truth and measure and justice" (*New York Herald Tribune*, December 11, 1955, sec. 4, p. 3).

Casting *Orpheus* would be tedious and prolonged. Her son's hospitalization in Rome (the debilitating effects of polio) led Magnani to cancel plans for a late-December arrival in the States. Presumably she retained a strong interest in the play, although her financial terms—deemed "unconscionably exorbitant" by Audrey Wood—and demand for a brief engagement were inhibiting factors. Wood informed TW in the new year that signing Marlon Brando appeared "almost hopeless" (January 16, 1956, HRC), but as later correspondence reveals, his "final word" was still awaited in the following August.]

319. To Hodding and Betty Carter

[6360 Wydown Boulevard
Clayton, Missouri]
12/6/55
[TLS, 1 p. HRC]

Dear Hodding and Betty:

I had to cut my stay in Greenville a bit short in order to be back in New York for the premiere of Rose Tattoo and also get in a brief visit with what remains of the family here in Saint Louis. I am trying to write this letter on a machine that has probably not been used in the last twenty years, and is reluctant to return to active duty.

The boat trip

Interruption! Went downstairs to unpack my Olivetti. This is better. I was about to mention the boat-trip, the only, very delightful social event of my stay in Greenville. I would come back before the film's finished but I must admit that I had a feeling of being on the slopes of a very lively volcano. Saw and heard some things, nights out in the county, that made my hair stand on end. I think you're very, very brave! I pay you homage! (From my safe distance, physical courage not being one of my virtues.) I hear that Faulkner is going through the same thing as you. The script that I wrote for Kazan was not a "social comment" but if I know Kazan, I doubt that some rumbles of the tense and turbulent background will fail to make themselves heard in the completed work. I never believe in pointing the finger of shame or blame. I think Mississippi is handling this problem as well as Massachusetts would handle the same problem if it existed up there. People are the same the world over. But ignoring the facts is totally unuseful. There are people like you in Mississippi, a lot of them I trust, and I think the present situation is a challenge to the innate nobility and sense of justice which I believe is part of the southern tradition.

Thanks to you, and good luck, with my fond regards,

Tennessee.

[Hodding Carter (1907-1972) won the Pulitzer Prize in 1946 for editorials opposing racial bigotry and segregation. He was the publisher-editor of the Greenville, Miss., *Delta Democrat-Times* for nearly four decades.

Elia Kazan cast TW as a wary visitor to the set of *Baby Doll* in Benoit, Mississippi. He attributed TW's abrupt departure to his feeling of banishment from the South for his sexual difference and his present fear of being "'insulted'" (qtd. in *Kazan on Kazan*, ed. Ciment, 1974, p. 74). TW was joined in Greenville by Lilla Van Saher.

Anna Magnani had "a triumphant field day," wrote Bosley Crowther in review of *The Rose Tattoo*. Although one might question the "validity" of Serafina's character and the "logic" of her "conversion to a natural life," the critic preferred not to quibble: Magnani "overwhelms all objectivity with the rush of her subjective force" (*New York Times*, December 13, 1955). She also overcame stiff competition from Susan Hayward, Katharine Hepburn, and Jennifer Jones to win the Oscar in her first American film.]

Elia Kazan (in sweater) and Tennessee Williams (on Kazan's left) on the Baby Doll *(1956) set in Benoit, Mississippi, 1955.*

320. To Elia "Gadg" Kazan

SH: *The* Robert Clay
Miami, Florida
[ca. early-January 1956]
[TLS, 2 pp. WUCA]

Dear Gadg:

I know you are always interested in my first reaction, which is always stronger and often better than my more considered reaction, so I wired you immediately after reading the "continuity" for the proposed ending, and this morning I am going to try to amplify or clarify that telegraphic out-cry of protest. No one knows better than I that in the heat of creation, which heat you are now enjoying in Greenville, cold as it is down there, you have an irresistible urge to expand, to blow up and burst the frame, of the work in progress. Maybe I have misinterpreted your continuity, despite prefatory comment that you always shoot more than you use, but! - You say that whenever I am in trouble I go poetic. I say whenever you are in trouble, you start building up a "SMASH!" finish. - As if you didn't really trust the story that goes before. It is only this final burst of excess that mars your film-masterpieces such as "East of Eden", and it is in these final fireworks that you descend (only then) to something expected or banal which all the preceding artistry and sense of measure and poetry - yes, you are a poet, too! no matter how much you hate it! - leads one not to expect. I simply can't believe that you have been shooting a film that demands a finish like this outline. I sense that you have been creating all of the values, and more, that we had in mind for a poignantly true, human, grotesquely humorous and touching, truly original piece of comedie humaine! It's all right, in fact it's wonderful, for Archie Lee to go berserk and shoot up the place, but when he kills a negro, somehow a false note is struck. Not false to the country. The hell with the Delta! But false to the key and mood of the story, because! - I don't think either you or I can accept a killing of a negro, whom we love, as just an ironical twist, just a final wry comment, as a tag to a tale which is endearingly close to universal human behavior till then. And killing a negro is not a part of universal human behavior, witness all the universal Archie Lees in this world who never killed a negro and never quite would! They would commit arson, yes, they would lie and cheat and jerk off back of a peep-hole, but they wouldn't be likely to kill a negro and slam the car door on his dying body and go on shooting and shouting, now, would they?! Or if they do, and we are giving their portrait, everything in the picture has to be changed to meet this new comment, which is naturally more important than any preceding comment the picture has made. The wounding of a negro is more in scale. That might happen. Or maybe the shot goes wild and you add a very funny touch by Archie blasting the interior of the Pierce, opening the door and saying, 'Oh, you! Excuse me. . .' - And the colored boy gives a low whistle and looks up at God! - this is in the mood and the key, inside the frame, of the story. A killing is not so much a moral discrepancy as it is an artistic outrage of the film-play's natural limits. I think that ending I sent you, with the addition of the Baby Doll-Silva dialogue under the tree, comprises a very complete and satisfying finish to the story and stays inside the frame of it. Don't panic! And shoot wild as Archie Lee Meighan! I actually think you've got all the material from me that you need but I will supply more anyhow. But please have Jean Stein copy all the dialogue that belongs to the ending which I have so far sent you. When I unpacked my papers I found that I had left all of that stuff in New York. I am going to write out some speeches between Silva and the Marshall right now in case you decide to have an audible conference between them. I hope you don't. I think you have finished your story very, very powerfully and successfully before you come to the final bit and all you have to do is keep it in key, and in measure.

Love, Tenn.

[The *Baby Doll* company—including Eli Wallach (Silva Vacarro), Carroll Baker (Baby Doll), Karl Malden (Archie Lee Meighan), and Mildred Dunnock (Aunt Rose)—spent ten weeks on location in the Delta (November 1955-January 1956). Elia Kazan deplored the racial mores of the region and twice shielded Negroes from the police. Nonetheless he found the locals to be charmingly European in their rural culture and to have "great affection for each other" (qtd. in *Kazan on Kazan*, ed. Ciment, p. 75). With a single exception, they played all of the roles save the four principals.

As filmed, the finale of *Baby Doll* completes the "hide and seek" motif which originally entitled the script. Meighan, drunk and enraged by his wife's apparent seduction, goes "berserk" with a shotgun while Vacarro and Baby Doll crouch in a tree. The accidental killing of a Negro—the "false note" to which TW refers—does not occur in the film. Instead Meighan pulls open the door of an abandoned car only to find a Negro, to whom he politely says "excuse me."

Additional dialogue—typed on Hotel Greenville letterhead—stresses Vacarro's callous treatment of Baby Doll after Meighan's arrest has completed the theme of revenge. "What about ME!?!" she cries, as Vacarro prepares to leave. "Happy birthday to you!" he replies. Baby Doll's unsureness regarding the future leads Aunt Rose to speak the closing line, "We'll find out tomorrow" (TW, "Sketch for possible new end of film," n.d., HRC).

TW's presence in Miami in early-January 1956 may support the speculative dating of this letter.]

321. To Audrey Wood

[1431 Duncan Street
Key West, Florida]
1/20/56.
[TLS, 1 p. HRC]

Dearest Audrey:

I have been too preoccupied with Tallulah and Streetcar to properly consider the problems of the next play. I agree that we should move at once to Paul Newman. Gore Vidal is here, and he says Paul is very eager to do the play. He has just come from Hollywood and saw Paul frequently there. It is possible that Newman will be better in the part than Brando, and will certainly cost less and play longer. The great problem, now, is to sell Magnani on him. Gore says she ought to see a print of his picture "The Rack". He thinks if she sees it, she will be convinced that he is an acceptable replacement for Brando. I think it may even be worth our while to fly together to Rome to show her this film and make an all-out effort to get her signed up.

This morning I did another re-write on the Val-Lady scene in Act Three. If it still seems right tomorrow, I will mail it to you.

Had a terrible fight with Tallulah. She screamed at me and I screamed back even louder, and she shut up! I flew to Key West and last night she called me and peace appears to be restored between us. Her first night was dreadful but her following performance, the next night, was legitimate and brilliant. She has it in her to play this part better than it has ever been played, the problem is to keep Tallulah inside the role of Blanche. Machiz understands, but is weak. After opening night, Jean Dalrymple and I discussed the possibility of replacing him with Jed Harris, and in which event I would forego my royalties. But the second night performance was so much better that I think this drastic (and cruel) step may not be necessary. Even when she is bad, (Tallulah, not Blanche) the audience seems to adore her and we have played, so far, to packed houses, and Machiz phoned last night (collect!) to say that there were standees at both matinee and evening.

Maria is with us. Tallulah calls her 'That Cruikshank cartoon', 'that black-mailing bitch', and so forth. That was what precipitated the row. Also her sycophantic attendants had told her that I had deplored her opening performance in characteristically incontinent terms. . .

I think we must now make an all-out campaign to get Magnani signed up without Brando.

Love, 10

[In *The Rack* (1956) Paul Newman plays an Army captain accused of collaborating with the enemy while a prisoner in the Korean War. His performance was greatly admired, although Newman's looks would not please Anna Magnani.

The "fight" with Tallulah Bankhead began with TW's banishment from rehearsals of the *Streetcar* revival for making both star and director feel "self-conscious." The opening night performance, as reviewed by TW, was a disaster: "There were all these faggots in the house. Tallulah began to play to them. There was hardly anything else she could do. They insisted on it. And I got very drunk and at the conclusion of the evening I was sulking around and somebody said: 'Come over and speak to Tallulah.' And I said: 'I don't want to. She pissed on my play'" (qtd. in Brian, *Tallulah, Darling*, 1972, p. 204). *Streetcar* ran for three weeks (January 16-February 4, 1956) at the Coconut Grove Playhouse in Miami before transferring to City Center in New York.

Jean Dalrymple, executive director of the City Center Theatre Company, supervised the *Streetcar* revival. Herbert Machiz, thirty-three at the time, directed and brought the play to New York for a two-week engagement.

TW had apparently recommended that Maria Britneva play Stella in the forthcoming revival. Bankhead dismissed the idea after meeting her in New York: "How DARE you bring that Cruikshank cartoon to my apartment and tell me that she looks like my sister" (qtd. in Brian, *Tallulah, Darling*, p. 204). George Cruikshank was a Victorian illustrator with a talent for biting satire. Britneva was "rather impressed" that Bankhead knew of his work.]

322. To Cheryl Crawford

SH: Western Union
Key West Flo
1956 Feb 27 PM 1 55
[Telegram, 1 p. BRTC]

DEAREST CHERYL,

THANKS SO MUCH FOR YOUR WIRE. AM PLANNING TO TRY OUT BRAND NEW PLAY DISCRETELY AS POSSIBLE AT SMALL THEATER STUDIO M CORAL GABLES AM TRYING TO GET MAUREEN TO CONTRIBUTE HER SERVICES WITH PROMISE OF BROADWAY WHEN AND IF. WOULD LOVE FOR YOU TO SEE IT AND CONSIDER IT ALSO. YOU ARE STILL MY FAVORITE PRODUCER BY TEN COUNTRY MILES ESPECIALLY WHEN AUDREY WISHES. WILL CALL YOU SOON ABOUT DATES AND FURTHER DEVELOPMENTS MUCH LOVE

TENNESSEE=

[The "brand new play" evolved in part from "The Big Time Operators" (n.d., HRC), the Huey Long project which TW had shelved in late 1948. The premiere at Studio M Playhouse, Coral Gables, Florida, was set for April 16, 1956, with direction by George Keathley. Maureen Stapleton would not "contribute her services" to this or to any other production of *Sweet Bird of Youth*, as the work-in-progress was now entitled.]

323. To the Drama Editor, New York Times

"Drama Mailbag," *New York Times*
March 4, 1956, section 2, p. 3

To the Drama Editor:

To the considerable and lively controversy about Tallulah Bankhead as Blanche DuBois, in the recent City Center revival of my play, "A Streetcar Named Desire," I would like, "just for the record," as they say, to add my personal acknowledgment, praise and thanksgiving for what I think is probably the most heroic accomplishment in acting since Laurette Taylor returned, in the Chicago winter of 1944-45, to stand all her admirers and her doubters on their ears in "The Glass Menagerie."

I have loved all the Blanches I've seen, and I think the question of which was the best is irrelevant to the recent revival. Several weeks ago, on the morning after the opening in Coconut Grove, Miami, Fla., the director and I called on Miss Bankhead in her boudoir where this small, mighty woman was crouched in bed, looking like the ghost of Tallulah and as quiet as a mouse. I sat there gravely and talked to her with the most unsparing honesty that I've ever used in my life, not cruelly, on purpose, but with an utter candor. It seemed the only thing that could save the situation.

If you know and love Tallulah as I do, you will not find it reprehensible that she asked me meekly if she had played Blanche better than anyone else had played her. I hope you will forgive me for having answered, "No, your performance was the worst I have seen." The remarkable thing is that she looked at me and nodded in sad acquiescence to this opinion.

Contrary to rumor, I never stated publicly, to my sober recollection, that she had ruined my play. What I said was phrased in barroom lingo. I was talking to myself, not to all who would listen, though certainly into my cups. But that morning, after the opening, Tallulah and I talked quietly and gently together in a totally truthful vein.

She kept listening and nodding, which may have been an unprecedented behavior in her career. The director and I gave her notes. I went back that night, and every note she was given was taken and brilliantly followed in performance. I left town, then, because I knew that I had hurt her deeply (though for her good) and that she would feel more comfortable without me watching her work.

I doubt that any actress has ever worked harder, for Miss Bankhead is a great "pro," as true as they make them. I think she knew, all at once, that her legend, the audience which her legend had drawn about her, presented an obstacle which her deepest instinct as an artist demanded that she conquer, and for those next three weeks she set about this conquest with a dedication that was one of those things that make faith in the human potential, the human spirit, seem far from sentimental: that give it justification. Think for a moment of the manifold disadvantages which I won't name that beset her in this awful effort! She had only two weeks rehearsal.

When the play opened at the City Center, this small, mighty woman had met and conquered the challenge. Of course, there were few people there who had my peculiar advantage of knowing what she'd been through, and only a few of her critics appeared to sense it. To me she brought to mind the return of some great matador to the bull ring in Madrid, for the first time after having been almost fatally gored, and facing his most dangerous bull with his finest valor, a bullfighter such as Belmonte or Manolete, conquering himself and his spectators and his bull, all at once and together, with brilliant cape-work and no standing back from the "terrain of the bull." I'm not ashamed to say that I shed tears almost all the way through and that when the play was finished I rushed up to her and fell to my knees at her feet.

The human drama, the play of a woman's great valor and an artist's truth, her own, far superseded, and even eclipsed, to my eye, the performance of my own play. Such an experience in the life of a playwright demands some tribute from him, and this late, awkward confession is my effort to give it.

Tennessee Williams.

[Notices for the New York opening of *Streetcar* (February 15, 1956) were tempered by the inherent challenge of playing Blanche DuBois and by the unique complications which Tallulah Bankhead brought to the role. The "adoring saboteurs" who came to laugh on cue were disappointed by a performance which transcended the campy Bankhead legend. Brooks Atkinson was not alone, however, in thinking Bankhead miscast. Hers, he wrote, "is a personality that . . . is worldly and sophisticated, decisive and self-sufficient: it is fundamentally comic" (*New York Times*, February 16, 1956). TW later dismissed Bankhead's claim that he had written "every good role for her" but saluted the courage with which she had played "against the faggots" (1970; qtd. in *Conversations*, p. 154) in New York. Bankhead quipped in reply to the present tribute that "Mr. Williams' talents as a playwright are considerable, but in his manifesto he forever scuttled the ancient legend, *in vino veritas*'" (*New York Times*, March 11, 1956).

A draft version of this letter is held by the UCLA Research Library.]

324. To John Bernard Myers

[1431 Duncan Street
Key West, Florida]
3/15/56
[TLS, 2 pp. Columbia U]

Dear John

This is not a 'dear John' letter, believe me. . .

I did not talk to Jay Laughlin about Playbook preface but to Bob MacGregor. I talked to him one day before the opening at the Center and without having seen Herbert's work on the play since Miami. I talked to both you and Herbert about my injured feelings and my feeling of betrayal in my personal relationship with Herbert during the play's preparation. That I felt he should have told me <u>not</u> to go away when Tallulah told me to <u>go</u>, that he should at least have called me to say that he was sorry I'd gone. Actually - being as wise as an old shit-house rat! - I could have done a great deal to benefit the production, both for Tallulah's sake and for Herbert's. But being much prouder than an old shit-house rat, I could not insist upon that privelege of remaining when I was dismissed by the star with the very clear acquiesence of the director.

That's all it amounts to, Baby, just that, and nothing more.

As for my regard for Herbert's work as a director, I think he came through a very severe test with colors that were not drooping. I have seen him do much better: I have seen "name directors" do worse!

My decision not to attempt a preface to the playbook was not because of any disappointment in Herbert professionally - in fact, the disappointment of a personal nature is now a thing of the past, among <u>un</u>-harbored resentments. I don't know all that went on in Herbert's mind during that period which prevented him from keeping in contact with me as he should have. That's all over! Done with! However you may think of me, I think of you as still being friends I am fond of. As for the preface, I couldn't possibly do it, now, simply because I have only two weeks in which to complete film script for "Summer and Smoke" and am, at the same time, producing the first draft of a new play at the Studio M in Coral Gables and am having to break my balls to steer it clear of disaster. Just an adventure, but the dynamics of a big play, which will some day emerge.

The saddest thing that could possibly come out of the Tallulah-Streetcar thing is that Herbert and I, through a complex of misunderstandings, should lose our love for each other, which was quite real, on my part, or otherwise I could never have felt such outrage when he seemed to dismiss me.

The whole thing had the elements of a poetic tragedy in modern terms, don't you think? I think everyone involved has grown through the experience. At least I am sure that I have. I was deeply grateful to Tallulah - having heard that she loathed my letter to the Times - for limiting her response to a couple of sentences merely saying that I was driven to drink. To which I was not unfamiliar beforehand. I have written to thank her. I want to write a play for her. She is quite possibly "the greatest demented artist of our time", as you called her. At any rate, she's an artist.

Love to you both, Tenn

Considering the personal elements which were involved, it is very likely that I am unable to properly assess Herbert's professional contribution, that it was much, much greater than I was able to judge. (I was not there.)

[John Myers (1919-1987), a contemporary art dealer, joined Herbert Machiz to present experimental plays at the Artists' Theatre in New York. Myers served as producer and artistic adviser while Machiz directed. At issue was a request that TW write a preface for *Playbook* (1956), a New Directions anthology to be dedicated to Myers and Machiz.

His Broadway debut with *Streetcar* drew little attention, but Machiz went on to direct three later plays by TW: *Garden District* (1958), *The Milk Train Doesn't Stop Here Anymore* (1962/1963), and *In the Bar of a Tokyo Hotel* (1969).

This letter is written on stationery of the Robert Clay in Miami.]

325. To Audrey Wood

Key West [Florida]
3/16/56
[TLS, 2 pp. HRC]

Dearest Audrey:

I am dividing my time about equally between the play and film-script which is unfortunate for the latter, but this is the first time in years that I have been able to work with unflagging interest on a play script for six and eight hours a day and though it will be a first draft that's exposed at Coral Gables, it has the dynamics of what I think may very well turn out to be the strongest play I have written. I've had to impose a terribly difficult task on the young director-producer George Keathley, since I have to keep shooting him revisions while he is in rehearsal with actors who are fairly inexperienced except for the one, Margaret Wyler, whom we brought down from New York. I've watched his work over a period of years, and, believe me, this is not another Herbert Machiz. He is crazy about the play. As fast as I send a new bit, he has it mimeographed in triplicates and shoots copies back to me. I am waiting till I feel I've done all I can, at this point, to send you a fairly definite acting version, to have copyrighted. A good deal of the writing is still rough and corny but it will have a great impact as theatre. We cast it very carefully, with the best talent that was available in the Miami area, and George is giving it every protection. On the marquee it says only: Play in Rehearsal, Watch for Opening date. There have been no press-releases and won't be, if I can help it. I'm flying back to Miami this coming Monday to see how it's getting along.

Now about "Summer and Smoke": I have it all in my head! It's going to be amazingly easy to knock it out in full, soon as this immediate project, which surely deserves to take precedence, being a brand new creation and one that stirs me deeply, is squared away, in a few days now. Of course I feel regretful, if not guilty, about not giving film my full attention right now. But after all, you yourself admitted that it was a lousey deal and nothing much has been done to make it better. Honestly if they decided to drop it entirely, I would be happy. It would mean that I could have all of next summer to turn out the best film play I've done. And then make better terms for its sale later. The little that I have worked on the film play so far has convinced me that it can be as big as "Gone With The Wind" if I am permitted to work on it as a serious writer should work, not with a strict dead-line but with some sense of how a serious writer functions: not on a belt-conveyor, but with a reasonable adjustment to his best working-methods, involving contemplation and delicate revisions. "Rose Tattoo" was nominated for almost every reward *but* for script. I don't want that repeated. Craven submission to censorship, which films such as "Man With the Golden Arm" bucked with singular success, a deep-rooted fear of risking off-beat distinction, playing it dully safe, all conspired to turn a very hastily written but ~~highly~~ original and moving script into the closest possible approximation of a regular Hollywood property, raised above its level by one artist, Magnani, who simply couldn't be reduced to it. When people mention the picture, nobody praises the film itself, they just say: "God, that Magnani!" Well, for "Summer and Smoke" there won't be any Magnani. I ask that I be permitted to give them the only thing that they must know that they need, a really distinguished script on a play which is too peculiarly my own to be successfully handled by anyone else. I know and understand their problems, and I don't blame them for wanting to get this script as soon as they can. Reciprocally, they should know and understand *my* problems and speculate on the likelihood of my serving them best if I am not crowded now. If they *do* insist on a script on April Fool's day: I will give them one which will not be an April Fool's trick: but it will just be a pretty detailed sketch, along with those few scenes which depart most radically from the play done on Broadway, such as the doctor's killing, (the casino scene in which the old doctor smashes up the gaming tables with his cane and is shot by Gonzales), the fever epidemic and the reformation of young Dr. John. All the rest fits so naturally into a film scenario that all I have to do is transcribe it with those cuts and plastic and mobile freedoms that the screen gives. A work that only requires about two or three weeks of undistracted attention. (At least for a 1st reading draft)

But you know that my salvation, truly, depends on my being able to go on turning out new works, and even though faith may falter in my power to do so, we should cling to it still.

Tell Bill I'll be in Miami Monday evening and can see Cloris Leachman any time thereafter. Frank says she's a fine actress. I don't know her work. If necessary, I can fly up to New York to participate in solving these replacement problems for "Cat". Hope you liked Sidney Blackmer.

Love, Tenn.

PS. I have decided to remove the suggestion of a castration from Orpheus. I don't think it is necessary and since the new play ends in a similar act of violence which is much more necessary and organic, to theme and development of story, am willing to sacrifice it in Orpheus. What do you think? I think it was one of things that disturbed Marlon, and that such an incident should only be used in a play when it is organically essential to the play's meaning, Etc.

[*Sweet Bird of Youth* claimed TW's "full attention" in advance of the premiere. Work on the *Summer and Smoke* film script was delayed accordingly.

The Rose Tattoo was nominated for eight Academy Awards, including Best Actress (won) and Best Picture. Nominations for art direction, cinematography, costume, editing, and music accentuate the lack of any recognition for screenwriting.

Otto Preminger "bucked" the Production Code by treating the forbidden subject of drug addiction in *The Man with the Golden Arm* (1955). The film was released without Code approval.]

326. To Edwina Dakin Williams

[1431 Duncan Street
Key West, Florida]
PM: Key West, March 18, 1956
[ALS, 3 pp. HTC]

Dear Mother -

I'm so sick of the typewriter I'm using a pen, have been working 6 or 8 hours a day and that studio is beginning to get pretty hot. It's warm as mid-summer, now, in Key West, and only one room is air-conditioned, but there's a breeze at night. Our faithful old "retainer" Leoncie is back with us, she comes and goes on my bicycle in a snow white, severely starched linen dress, yelling and waving to all the neighbors as she approaches or makes her departure. Our house has become a regular stop for the sight-seeing buses and cars in Key West. They all want to see where "Rose Tattoo" was shot. So Leoncie and Mr. Anderson (old Charlie) are having a lot of public attention. Frank does practically all the cooking, has bought an out-door charcoal grill for chicken, steak, Etc. We eat "mighty good".

I am trying out the first draft of a new play very secretly at a tiny theatre in Coral Gables just to size it up for myself. Most of my present work is on this. I'm afraid Paramount will have to wait a while longer for the "Summer & Smoke" film script. I wish they would just let it go, as I am not at all pleased with the terms of the contract, and think I could have gotten much more for it, elsewhere. But Harold Clurman has been signed to direct it, and he is a brilliant director.

I had to cancel flight to St. Thomas due to work here.

I hope to go North by way of New Orleans and St. Louis next month.

Nice letter today from Dakin. He seems to expect to return to St. Louis before next Xmas.

Much love - Tom.

[Edwina noted that her son's "Key West ménage is made up of Frank, Leoncie, a Bahama maid, two bulldogs and a parrot." She was seventy-one at this time and would soon be hospitalized in St. Louis with an emotional disorder.

This letter first appeared in Edwina Dakin Williams's memoir, *Remember Me to Tom*, 1963, p. 219.]

327. To Joseph H. Hazen and Hal B. Wallis

1431 Duncan St.
Key West [Florida]
March 28, 1956
[TLS, 1 p. Herrick]

Dear Joe: and Hal:

When an actress in Hollywood gets pregnant I believe you call it an act of God and make allowances for it and the schedule is adjusted to this unavoidable circumstance. A parallel thing has happened to me, quite unexpectedly: I was knocked up with an idea for a play. Plays are what I live for! You know that. I had to push everything else aside till 'the delivery'. I did some work on the screen play but it is not nearly finished. Only a few scenes are done. It was not a matter of choice. I do have a sense of responsibility, but I feel that my first responsibility is always to new work. Enough defense of this thing which I know you will understand.

The play is now finished. It's already in rehearsal and will open (sort of a sneak try-out) at Studio M, Coral Gables, about the middle of April. Obviously this means that I am not going to give you a finished film-script on the first. Also, obviously, you will be justified, from a contractual point of view, in cancelling the deal or in consigning the film-script to another writer. For your sake, as well as my own, if the delay is inexcusable, I would rather have you call the whole deal off than have someone else do a script which only I could transpose to the screen successfully. It is so completely my own material and my own style, and of all my plays, this is the one that already existed most clearly in my mind as a screen-play. It can be completed faster than I did "Rose Tattoo", all the material for it is in my head and in the various versions of it that I have on my work table. However the fact remains that we had agreed on a dead-line which I can't meet. I will be back in New York by the end of April and after the play opens, or sooner, I can give my undivided attention to the film. I would guess, sincerely, that I could complete a good script for you before I sail for Europe late in May. The question is, are you willing to give me that much extension? I am not worried about the money for the film-script. If you feel that you can't wait, and want to put someone else on it right away, you certainly have that privelege. I doubt that it would turn out satisfactorily, but if it doesn't, you can always engage me for revision with shared credit at whatever weekly pay Audrey thinks right for it. I will accept 'shared credit' provided that I don't finally have to write it all myself. I was very, very happy about the choice of Harold Clurman to direct the script, and I know that Harold and I can work together to give you a picture that will win more awards than "Tattoo": that is, if you feel that you can grant this temporal allowance. Time is of the essence, I know, but the right screen-play is more so.

I know I thanked you verbally for the tape-recorder but I'm afraid I haven't yet written you what a valuable acquisition it is. I still work mostly on the typewriter, but in revisions it is very helpful to read the stuff to the recorder and hear the lines spoken back to me on it.

I wish you would forward this letter to Hal: it is written to you both, naturally. This bad start is my fault and I do want a chance to compensate for it.

Ever yours, Tenn.

[Hal Wallis (1899-1986) and Joe Hazen (1898-1994) purchased film rights of *Summer and Smoke* in the preceding July. The contract specified that TW deliver a first draft of the script by April 1, 1956. Peter Glenville rather than Harold Clurman eventually directed the film.]

328. To Joyce Croft Williams

1431 Duncan St.
Key West, Fla.
4/20/56.
[TLS, 1 p. HRC]

Dear Joyce:

Dake must have told you what a bad letter-writer I am. I wanted to write you at once how much I appreciated your letter about "Tattoo" but I was immersed in a try-out production of a new play here in Miami (Coral Gables, to be specific) and it's taken all my time and energy lately. It was well-received here and will probably go on Broadway sometime next season.

I'm so glad Dakin is returning from the Far East, I think he's had enough military life. I wish he would get started in law-practise and work into politics which is in the Williams (Tennessee) tradition. I think our father was the first Williams who never held a political office since colonial days.

If you'll forgive the impropriety of the suggestion, I hope you'll make me an uncle. I'd love a nephew or niece as much as a child of my own. Right now I'm going out to look for a new puppy. The bull-dog, Buffo, died suddenly a few weeks ago and left an awful void. A friend is driving me over to "The Beach" to look at a little Boxer.

I'm going to join Mother in New Orleans late this month, spend a week with her there. She hasn't been at all well this year and I don't want to leave the States, for my summer trip abroad, without a visit with her. We'll call you from there in case you might be able to drive over for a week-end with us.

Love, Tom

[Dakin Williams and Joyce Croft (b. 1921) married in October 1955 before Dakin was dispatched to Taiwan as a legal affairs officer. Prior assignments in California and Texas followed his recall to active duty in 1951 as a captain in the Air Force. Dakin later served as an Assistant United States Attorney in Eastern Illinois and ran unsuccessfully for several statewide offices. He and Joyce did indeed make an "uncle" of TW by adopting two daughters.

This letter is written on stationery of the Towers in Miami.]

329. To Cheryl Crawford

SH: *The* Towers
Miami, Florida
5/?/56.
[TLS, 1 p. BRTC]

Dearest Cheryl:

I'm late writing you because of a flood of visitors, Mother, Maria, and Bigelow all at once, and Kazan and yesterday Audrey again, and also continual re-writing on the play. A big new piece went in last night, replacing the church and hospital bits which are now handled as exposition at Boss Finley's house. Yesterday was the first performance of this new material and it was not as much improvement as I had hoped, due partly, perhaps, to its newness, but also I'm afraid to an over load of exposition. It leaned heavily on the ingenue who is the weakest member of the cast. Audrey kept a tight mouth about it. I could not gather at all clearly from her manner or anything she said whether or not she felt an important advance had been made. I guess I have to work this thing out alone. And stop seeking confirmation from others in the profession. Kazan saw it before the changes and promised to come back to catch it again after the changes went in, but he is still in Sarasota with Budd Schulberg, working on their film, and has not set a definite date for his return if he makes one. I'll wait a few more days to see if he does. Meanwhile we continue to turn away patrons every night and put up folding chairs for special ones.

Keathley is coming to New York right after we close here, May 20th, because of Margrit Wyler's return to Europe. I do hope we can devise something for him. I think he is gifted, and that contact with the New York theatre would provide him with the technical skill which is his one serious deficiency. I do admire and like him, and I know that you do.

Your letter meant much more to me than any other reaction I've had. It's too early to discuss a New York production more than tentatively. Everything rests on me, now, and on my ability to solve the play's problems this summer. I shall devote myself [to] it, even if it means turning over my film-committment, Summer and Smoke, to another writer. I really would have no choice, unless this thing works out very quickly. I want to talk to you soon as I get back to New York, and show you the changes.

Much love, Tenn.

P.S. I have been drinking too much because of tensions. Do you think I ought to stay in New York and try to lick that problem, or let it ride for the summer, with whatever control I can manage on my own hook, till I have finished a satisfactory draft of this work? I don't think I could do both at the same time.

[TW invited Elia Kazan and Jo Mielziner to "look at" the Studio M production of *Sweet Bird of Youth*. Both were sufficiently impressed, it appears, to collaborate on the later Broadway version (March 10, 1959).

Boss Finley appears in "The Big Time Operators" as a shady political figure who blocks the affair of his daughter Rose and Phil Beam (Heavenly and Chance Wayne on Broadway). Their plot line was complicated in later drafts by the redefined and expanded role of the Princess—originally conceived as Artemis Pazmezoglu, a male exile from Vienna. Dropped in the evolution of *Sweet Bird* was Pere, the Huey Long figure who defies Boss Finley after being raised to the governorship by his machine.

The "church and hospital bits" refer to Rose Finley's exalted experience on

Easter morning that the "power to bear life" has been restored following her abortion and hysterectomy. After the church service, she demands that x-rays be taken at the hospital to confirm the restoration. The so-called "'miracle pictures'" show only the effect of "a well-performed operation" (*Sweet Bird of Youth*, May 1956, HRC), as the surgeon, Dr. Scudder, concludes. Reviews of *Sweet Bird* in the Miami press were positive, if brief and amateurish.

George Keathley considered the Playhouse a steppingstone to New York, but he feared that "the 'means' might strangle the possible 'end'" (to Wood, April 27, 1956, HRC). He directed at least two additional plays by TW: a Broadway revival of *The Glass Menagerie* (1965) and the Chicago production of *Out Cry* (1971).

Cheryl Crawford reminded Audrey Wood that producing *The Rose Tattoo* (1951) and especially *Camino Real* (1953) had entailed creative risk without "financial advantage" to herself. She also attributed her unlucky refusal of *Cat* to such losses but hoped "desperately to be involved" (April 24, 1956, HRC) with the production of *Sweet Bird of Youth*.

Crawford cited problems of scenic arrangement and continuity in *Sweet Bird* but assured TW that she was moved by its power. "I hope, hope, hope" (April 25, 1956, U of Houston) was her closing plea for consideration.]

330. To Christopher Isherwood and Don Bachardy

[*The* Towers, Miami]
May 12/ '56
[TLS, 1 p. Huntington]

Dearest Cris and Don:

Those sweet people the Masslinks gave me your address which I had carefully stashed away in my Key West studio. I am totally benumbed by throwing on a play, like a fit, in Coral Gables. Reached the point of exhaustion from which there is no return, or so it appears to me now, living on Milltowns, seconals and double shots of vodka with a splash of orange juice. Frankie couldn't take it and has gone to New York: a purely geographic separation. We are supposed to sail May 31st for Europe on a Greek boat I'd never heard of, the Queen Frederica, because Jane Bowles will be on it and it puts in at Gibralter where we can see Paul. However I just might, at the last moment, switch plans and go West instead. That is, East by way of West. I feel that I've had Europe and would like to see places like Japan and Ceylon and China. Also I have had Key West for reasons too multiple and complex to go into, though maybe they could be described as simple boredom. Do you think we would be happy on the West Coast? I thought maybe we could buy a little ranch and collect animals and have a swimming pool on it. I'm going to New York in a few days. Let me hear from you, will you? The address is 323 E. 58th Street.

With my love, Tenn.

[Don Bachardy (b. 1934), a well-known portraitist, was Christopher Isherwood's new companion.

George Keathley visited Key West in the preceding March and found tensions between TW and Frank Merlo to be raw. He witnessed a blowup which led Merlo to pack and leave with a familiar parting shot, "'I'm not your goddamned yes-man!'" Keathley surmised that he had missed the "'prelude'" to this quarrel but not the aftermath in which "'they separated more and more'" (qtd. in Spoto, p. 205).

TW and Merlo sailed on the *Queen Frederica* (May 31, 1956) with Jane Bowles and Lilla Van Saher. They were scheduled to arrive at Gibraltar on June 7.]

Lilla Van Saher, Jane Bowles, and Tennessee Williams aboard the Queen Frederica, *1956.*

331. To Audrey Wood

[51 Via Del Babuino, Rome]
June 29, 1956
[TLS, 2 pp. HRC]

Dear Audrey:

I am very relieved by the news that Jimmie McGhee has the job. It would have been quite impossible for me to tackle it this summer, alone. Jimmie has taste, as well as theatre sense and a certain amount of experience behind him, and what is most important in this instance, we have, I believe, a similar kind of "sensibility". I know how little that term implies to big Hollywood studios, but nevertheless it is the important element in dealing with this film. A typical Hollywood writer would not succeed in turning it into a commercial picture, as the studio would conceive it, but oddly enough I think that Jimmie and I, working together with mutual understanding, can do just that, as well as keeping its artistic worth. Jimmie will do most of the actual new writing, and of course should have equal screen credit. I will give him all of my old material on the play to work with and will keep a constant eye on his progress without being a Simon Legree.

Of course I would love to have done this all by myself, but I can't tell you how tired, how totally exhausted, I feel this summer! I knew this feeling was coming, and it has come, and I hope that, like most things that come it will also go! All that I am fit for, at the moment, is bits and pieces of patchwork on "Orpheus" and "Bird", if "Bird" ever flies here. About next year's production, I think the situation ought to be kept "fluid".

Anna unmistakably is very anxious to do "Orpheus", but she feels that even four months is too long a run in a play! She hopes to whittle it down. Maybe to two months! I find it difficult to believe that Paramount would be willing to absorb such a big loss as a two months run of a hundred thousand dollar production would call for. What's your opinion? I think they would hedge on the production and it would be second rate if not third or fourth. I don't think, even with Anna, as complex and challenging a play as "Orpheus" could make a good impression without all the best talents that the theatre can offer involved in its production, do you?

Harold Clurman is here, and he thinks that Stella Adler would be great in the part, and that with her, Brando might be available. Again: what do you think? Stella is not necessarily too old for the part, but she has become such a special sort of figure, such an overwhelmingly glamorous great lady that I wonder if she could give the part the necessary sort of earthiness and pathos. I think of her more as Mrs. Stone in a Roman Spring, or summer . . . What do you think, again?

Anna was not pleased with the pictures of Newman. She said his face was coarse, unpoetic. She wants to see pictures of Franciosa. - It occurs to me that she may be bluffing about the two-months run and that if she really liked a certain player opposite her, she might be willing to play four. After all, time passes quickly, and I feel that Frank and I could keep her amused in Manhattan if we stayed in constant attendance on her and there was Mr. X to take over "after hours", not necessarily her co-star. Here she has a new lover: he is 23 years old. I don't take it seriously, even if she does, she orders the boy around [like] a flunkey and I don't [think] she notices all of his facial expressions as he receives these orders! - How about Ben Gazzara? He was too fat when I last saw him but if he could shed a few pounds, he might look right, and I think his quality is intense and poetic. Also he is not married, now, is he?

Anna has lost a lot of weight but I am not sure that her English has improved much if any. Her ego surpasses mine but is more excusable.

We have moved into a charming apartment at #51 Via Della, Babuino but Frank smashed up the MG on the road to Rome. We are using a rented car. When the MG is repaired, I think I will drive down to Sicily so I can have the daily swims that are so important to my well-being, relative as that is under all circumstances.

Happy to hear that Marjorie opened well. What are the other replacements going to be like?

With love, Tenn.

[James Poe and Meade Roberts shared the screenwriting credit for *Summer and Smoke* when the film was released in 1961.

Resumed at this time, the journal records "an almost unbroken decline in health and spirits" as well as "unprecedented weakness" (ca. July 28, 1956) in TW's writing. He later observed that "some people think I like pain, suffering. That's bull! There is nothing more painful than pain and I long to escape it but my nature and the circumstances of my life imposed it on me, and I could find no escape." Adding to the desolation of TW's ninth summer in Rome was "another big row with F, who's now quit the house" (August 6, 1956).

Stella Adler, fifty-five and married to Harold Clurman, eventual director of *Orpheus*, would not play Lady in the stage production. She was revered by Marlon Brando as a teacher and mentor.

TW surmised that Gabriel, Anna Magnani's new lover, "blows the horn satisfactorily." He added in wry correspondence with Maria Britneva that "Anna still has the disconcerting habit of pounding her abdomen, so I guess you would call it a two-piece band!" (qtd. in St. Just, p. 135).]

332. To William Liebling

SH: Hotel Colón, Barcelona
July 21, 1956
[TLS, 1 p. HRC]

Dear Bill:

I loved and appreciated your letter but I think you are being unduly concerned over an unimportant matter. I mean you know how I am inclined to speak out tactlessly but honestly about things, especially when I am under great nervous tension. Isn't there a little bit of justice on both sides? There usually is in all matters of disagreement. Surely if you were not representing the actor you would have felt, as strongly as the management felt and as I did, that maybe his demanded increase in salary was a little bit bigger than ought to be demanded so late in the run of a show that was falling off at the box-office? You see, Bill, you can't avoid being in a "divided position" when you are representing the actors in the show and also representing the show. I value all that you said in your letter, especially your devoted watch over the production and the excellent choices you have suggested in the re-casting such as that marvelous actress now playing Big Mama and I know you would never sell the play down the river for the sake of larger commissions, but, Bill, at the same time, you are simply OBLIGED to try to get as large a price for an actor as he wants, and usually actors ask for more than a play, late in its run, with falling box-office, can afford to pay them without cutting down on their stay. That's all I meant. I only meant that you were in a difficult position. I am astonished and full of admiration that you are able to handle it so well, with such fairness, but I wish that you were not placed in such a position for it creates this kind of tension between us.

Honest speech is bound to hurt feelings. In Florida, for instance, you suggested that I give up "Orpheus Descending" as a play and liquidate it as a financial asset by selling outright to the movies. This is a play that will be destroyed by the movies at least as an honest and passionate work of art. I will have no interest in it as a film unless Magnani plays it and even then I will probably only be interested and satisfied by her performance as I was in the case of "Rose Tattoo". I worked, God, what a long, long time on that script as a play. As a PLAY! It stung me terribly to have it proposed that I send it to the glue-factory.

You see? You didn't mean to hurt me and I didn't mean to hurt you. We are BOTH kind people and we are both sincerely fond of each other, but sometimes there is a divergent point of view, and when those times occur, frank speech is preferable to hypocritical silence. Do you agree with me about this?

Love, 10.

[At issue, TW thought, was Bill Liebling's "'divided position'" in supervising *Cat on a Hot Tin Roof* and representing Alex Nicol, who replaced Ben Gazzara as Brick. Liebling denied TW's "intimation" of conniving and self-interest, claiming that Nicol's recent salary demand, while high, had been met to protect the "welfare" of the play. *Cat's* profit to date of $425,000, he added, bore out the wisdom of hiring topflight actors. Liebling later apologized for having offended TW with the advice to film *Orpheus Descending* and dispense with a Broadway production. He had hoped to relax a burdened writer by shedding a play which always seemed "out in the cold" (to TW, July 6 and August 6, 1956, HRC).]

333. To Jim Adams

SH: Hotel Colón, Barcelona
July 21, 1956.
[TLS, 1 p. Rendell]

Dear Jim:

I have also been going through a sort of nervous crisis, which has kept me from answering your letter earlier. I knew it was coming, as I was terribly worn out when I left New York, I nearly always go to pieces for a while in the summer as a way of recovering from the strains of the other seasons. After you've been through a few of these periods you know that they come and go and you just "sweat it out". Of course you have to do certain things, mostly things of a physical nature to improve your general condition, such as spending as much time as possible in the sun and also, preferably, by the sea. I tried Rome for a few weeks but got feeling worse all the time, I flew to Barcelona where there is a good beach only five minutes from this hotel and after a week of sun-bathing and swimming I feel much better and I think I can get thru the summer without much further disturbance. Of course New York is more difficult, but there are some good pools and you can even get to the sea now and then if you don't mind a long subway ride. I enjoyed my first few years in New York. I think you may too when you have found your bearings. Do you see or hear from Bigelow? I think he's a genuinely warm and good person, at least he has always been in his relations with me which have lasted for 16 years now. What are you doing about studying for theatre, or have you really given that up? I thought, sincerely, that your reading showed talent, but unless you yourself are convinced that you want to be an actor, and are willing to buck the long, or fairly long, period of preparation, of waiting for a "break", well, it may not be worth the struggle. Or anguish! But, finally, we always do what we want or <u>need</u> to do, there isn't much conscious choice.

We are flying back to New York about the middle of September, yes, flying this time, for the first time, that is, across the ocean. I have seen three bull-fights this week and now I am going to another which is a double-header with twelve bulls and six matadors, twice the usual number of each. It is a great theatre, and pageantry. Let me hear from you soon, Jim.

Fondly, Tom.

Write me at 51 Via Babuino, Rome, or c/o American Express there, Rome.

[Jim Adams and TW, distant cousins, were probably related through the Otte branch of the family which settled in Tennessee in the 1880s. Adams wrote first to TW, who replied in March 1956 that his relative seemed to be "struggling" with himself and searching for "a 'different' life" following his graduation from college. TW enclosed a small check: "Lets say it's from Aunt Rose" (March 5, 1956, Rendell). To Maria Britneva he recommended Adams as "a very nice, naive kid" (qtd. in St. Just, p. 134).]

334. To Audrey Wood

SH: Hotel Colón, Barcelona
[ca. July 21, 1956]
[TLS, 4 pp. HRC]

Dear Audrey:

I think it is a highly Quixotic gesture for a major Hollywood studio to offer a half million dollars for a play that hasn't yet been completed, which is still in first draft, but that is too large a sum for me to regard with frivolity so if they really want to negotiate on the basis of a brief synopsis, I will try to provide one.

I would say that "Sweet Bird of Youth" has the biggest and clearest theme of any work I have done to this point. It is almost a synthesis of the ideas in the other plays, come to a needle-point of clarity, and directness.

It is about: the betrayal of people's hearts by the subtle progress of a corruption which is both personal and social, the two influences, the native power-drive of the individual and the false values with their accent on being "top-dog", on fierce competition for a superior position, that defeat the possible true and pure and compassionately loving relations between people.

The two principal protagonists are a boy who almost "made the grade" but was always blocked by something just short of what he longed for, and a middle-aged woman who was a great star in films, who had a career like Garbo's, and quit when she felt that her youth and beauty were failing: retired to places abroad and to various easy distractions and bought pleasures and finally to the illusory, brief comfort of drugs.

She was importuned by old friends and business associates to attempt a "come-back picture". She made it. She returned to America to attend the premiere. When she saw her face on the screen, bearing the history of her long and erratic departure from the vocation which she had lived for, she fled in panic from the theatre, fled from the city without any communication with anybody she knew, and landed in a Florida hotel where she registered under the name she acquired by her fourth marriage as Princess Pazmezoglu, in a rather naive and inefficient attempt at obscurity, and there plunged deeper, continually, in the drugged state of semi-oblivion which is what an artist has left when he abandons his art, because, for some mysterious reason related to the passage of time and the accent on false values and youth's loss, its moral and physical process of degeneration, -

well, there seemed to be nothing else left for her to do. She acquired a hard and cynical kind of wisdom in this world to which she had retreated. But in the Florida hotel, she met a boy, Phil Beam, who was employed there as a beach-boy. He, too, had arrived at a breaking point in his life. He had started out with enormous promise and every apparent gift. He was exceptionally goodlooking and had exceptional charm. He seemed the boy most likely to succeed. He almost did, countless times, but something always held him just short of what he aimed at. He recognized "The Princess" as the retired star, Ariadne Del Lago, and, being used by this time, he is now thirty, to prostituting what is left of his youth, looks, and charm for the "chance to make good" he still hopes for, he makes himself valuable to her as a sort of "caretaker-lover" from whom she has no secrets, including her use of drugs, but "holds out for something", keeps the relation between them a little bit short of satisfaction to "hold her interest".

The Princess is asked to leave the Florida hotel when the odor of the smoked drugs (hashish) drifts into the corridor, and the boy drives her off, along the old Spanish trail of the conquistadors, toward a Texas town where she has oil-wells that she wants to sell at a huge profit (She is already very rich) and then on to the West Coast, where she will launch the boy on his passionately longed-for career in films, she being a major stock-holder in a sort of third rate Hollywood studio. A contract exists between them. But the boy has stopped at the town of Saint Cloud on the Gulf Coast.

He has stopped there because it is where he started. He was born in this town and he has kept coming back to it because his life-long sweetheart lives there, the daughter of a local political boss whose power and influence are much greater than local and who is now about to enter "the national arena".

The boy cannot resist the chance to be seen driving about Saint Cloud in the magnificent Mercedez-Benz of the Princess, and blowing the long silver trumpets at the street-crossings and being seen by the townspeople who had come to regard him as a failure, in such apparent splendor. But the main objective of his return is to re-claim the girl: the two of them used to be the handsomest and most glamorous young pair in Saint Cloud.

He has hit upon a shrewd and vicious device to enslave his travelling-companion, the Princess Pazmezoglu. In the first act of the play, when they wake up together in the Hotel Belvedere of Saint Cloud, she has suffered an eclipse of memory, an attack of amnesia, perhaps mostly voluntary, and he has concealed under the bed a tape-recorder, and he leads her to make admissions, while they take the drug together, that would disgrace her. Her memory clears up. She recalls the come-back picture and the shock of anticipated fiasco that she had fled from. She turns to the boy, passionately, for the necessary distraction, love-making: then he discloses the trick. However the Princess trumps his ace. She laughs at his threat of blackmail and easily secures the upper hand again and forces him to serve her as a "kept lover": then signs some traveller's checks for him as a "token of some satisfaction". He goes. He leaves her alone in the hotel room, with her drugs, her oxygen mask for her attacks of panicky "air-shortage" and her recollection of a blasted dream of coming back as an artist.

The play, then, shifts to the sweetheart of Phil Beam and to her father, Boss Finley, and brother, Boss Finley, Junior. This scene establishes the fact that the girl, Valerie has become an object of scandal that threatens the Boss's political career. She had an illegal operation done on her after Phil's last visit to Saint Cloud. We have already heard about this in the first scene of the play, when the doctor, George Scudder, who had performed the operation on her, calls on Phil in the hotel room, before the Princess has wakened from her drugged sleep, and warns him to get out of town and without disclosing all that had happened to Valerie, implies that Phil will "be cut, too" if he doesn't leave town at once.

Boss Finley demands that his daughter appear on the platform with him, that night, at a meeting of "The Youth for Tom Finley Club" - to "scotch the rumors" about her, dressed all in white like a virgin with lilies of the valley pinned on her. The Boss is running for office on the issue of white supremacy. He is a comical but foully hypocritical character, who has had a mistress of twenty years, Miss Lucy, whom he keeps in great luxury at the Hotel Belvedere.

When Valerie defies her father and refuses to appear on the platform with him, he discloses that Phil Beam has returned to Saint Cloud and says that if she doesn't comply with his demand, that Phil Beam will suffer an operation, performed by Dr. Scudder, under force, that will correspond to the one that she has suffered, which has deprived her of her life-bearing organs.

That is the basic situation of the play.

The following scenes include a scene in the cocktail lounge of the hotel, where Miss Lucy finally makes it clear to Phil Beam what has happened to

Valerie, as a result of his last stay in Saint Cloud, a scene between Phil and Valerie's maiden Aunt in which he begs to see her but is turned away from the house and almost caught by the police car that arrives to take Valerie to the "rally". A scene between Phil and the Princess in which he tries to force her to call a famous columnist who has been her faithful friend, all the years, to launch a publicity campaign about the "two young stars of tomorrow", himself and Valerie. The Princess makes the call and is informed by the columnist that the defeat she fled from was not, after all, a defeat but that, on the contrary, the picture has scored an enormous success and that the industry is gasping for her. The "rally" of the "Youth for Tom Finley Club" at which Valerie Finley stands on one side of her father and Tom Junior on the other while the Boss sounds the tocsin for the white supremacy battle. A heckler in the crowd shouts a question about the "mysterious operation" performed on Boss Finley's daughter at the Thomas J. Finley hospital and this incites a riot, the heckler being dragged into the palm garden and pistol-whipped there.

After the Princess has learned of her unsuspected triumph in her "come-back" she turns on Phil with righteous outrage and laughs at his attempt to use her to advance himself and the wild dream of co-starring with Valerie and the Princess in a picture. She exposes him as a "pitiful monster". She admits: "I am a monster, too" but points out that she has created "out of the passion and torment of her life" something that won her an inextinguishable light of acclaim, while all that he has is "a crown of laurel, put on his head too early, and already withered". That he has gone past something he couldn't afford to go past, the meridian of his youth.

Phil rushes once more to the girl's house. She has returned there from the disastrous rally which she had attended to protect him. She is alone in the house. The police car has rushed back to the riot, after returning her home. He speaks to her, pleads with her, through a latched screen door to forget everything that's happened and to come away with him in the car of the Princess. She refuses to see, refuses to come to the door, they talk without facing each other, she in the parlor, he on the porch, by the locked screen door under the relentlessly turning light from Point Lookout. Finally, his exhortation failing, he attempts to force entrance. She runs to the phone and calls a panicky warning. Phil still refuses to leave. She warns him of her father's threat to castrate him as she was "cut" after he had last come back to Saint Cloud. Still he stays on the porch. He waits for the telephone warning to bring the doctor, The Boss, and Tom Junior to the house. He speaks the tragic import of the play as a soliloquy. Then the three men arrive and he is removed without protest.

Valerie remains. She comes out on the porch. A car is heard driving up. The Princess in a taxicab has spotted her car and approaches the porch, calling for Phil Beam. Valerie stares at her mutely. There is a far away cry. Valerie turns away in horror. The Princess is frightened, we hear the lament in the air, a sound-effect which has occured off-and-on in the play. The Princess, panicky, tells the cab driver to remove her luggage to her own car and directs him to drive her out of the town, leave his cab there - she'll pay whatever he asks for. . . .

Valerie turns back to the audience and calls out: "Oh, Lady, wrap me in your starry blue robe, make my heart your perpetual novena!" - So the play ends.

This is a terribly bad, ragged, dislocated synopsis of it, but I don't think I can ever give a synopsis of my plays, this one especially not.

If you can get half a million for it, I will eat my Olivetti!

Love, 10

P.S. Dearest Audrey: It was awfully hard, for some reason, for me to write this synopsis. I suggest that you have it done over by Bigelow, using this as a base, and tell him I will give him five grand if it results in a half million dollar film sale! I have left out such important plot points as the scene between Scudder and Phil in the first act and Phil's effort to discover what exactly has happened to the girl. Bigelow knows the play well enough to rectify these omissions and give a more complete and organized synopsis. In the next few days I will send you some important re-writes on "Orpheus". Much love, Tenn.

[Audrey Wood cabled TW on July 2 that she had "just ended extremely encouraging meeting with Metro re financing and preproduction deal Sweet Bird Hope to have definite proposition before end this week" (July 2, 1956, HRC). Albert S. Rogell (Roxbury Productions) and Metro-Goldwyn-Mayer were the eventual producers of *Sweet Bird of Youth*.

This letter, received on July 23, 1956, was probably written at the time of TW's preceding correspondence with William Liebling.]

335. To Audrey Wood

[51 Via Del Babuino, Rome]
8/1/56
[TLS w/ autograph marginalia, 1 p. HRC]

Dearest Audrey:

I hope you're back from a refreshing vacation. I wish that I was. This is the worst summer I have spent in Europe. For some reason which I can't account for I haven't been able to sleep, on an average, more than 2 1/2 or 3 hours a night and have been depressed most of the time. We are in a very unfortunate apartment. Everybody comes out and screams in the court-yard at about Seven A.M. and goes on screaming till long after dark. I go to the window and shout: 'Sta Zit, sta zit!' like Serafina in her most violent moments but the Wops just ignore me. The dog barks sympathetically in protest but Frank goes on snoring, sleeping the sleep of the just, being Italian, immune to loud voices, as a disturbance.

Anna plans to sail for the States about September 26 on the sister ship of the ill-fated Andrea Doria and wants us to go with her, in fact insists on it. I wanted to fly over this time. At least I wanted to get back earlier since there is so much to be arranged for the "Orpheus Production". To answer your questions, relayed through Lefkowitz by wire this morning, I think we ought to start rehearsals soon after arrival in States. Maybe two weeks after. And plan on a month out of town and book a New York theatre for some date in December. Jean Dalrymple has offered the City Center and I think it might be a good place for a two-months run to occur. I stood at the back of the house when Streetcar played there and it didn't seem to be distractingly big, and the weekly gross at capacity would almost pay off the production. Of course I assume we would do capacity business with a fine production even if we got mixed notices on the play. The notices on Anna will inevitably be raves.

I'm having my final re-writes on the play typed up and will mail copies this week-end. They only affect third act, the difficult section with Carol.

"Sweet Bird" was so appallingly mixed up, despite my directions to typist, that I have not been able to read it this summer, let alone work on it. I shall try to tackle it again when I return to Stateside.

Not a single word from Mother since I left, and no report on whether or not Rose has been transferred to the Institute for Living, as her Saint Louis doctor suggested and to which I consented.

What's to become of Bigelow without Bouverie? Did you know Maria is married? She married Peter Saint Juste, an old beau of hers in London, and I believe the title of 'Lady' goes with it. She's on her honeymoon, on the continent, and will probably descend to Rome before long. Is she still on my pay-roll? I think we might drop her, now, and the funds can be diverted to my old maid Aunt in Knoxville if that venerable spinster survives, she has been living on fifty a month, and is at least 80, and not at all well.

You haven't written me this summer. Am I in the dog-house, for any number of imaginable reasons?

Love, Tenn.

Essential get SCENE DESIGNER!

[TW inferred that the previous lodger left the noisy premises "to escape from his eighty-five-year-old termagant and shrew of a mother who has a *connecting* apartment. . . . When she falls silent for more than twenty minutes we can only suspect that {the servants} have brained her" (qtd. in St. Just, p. 135).

Carol Cutrere's entrance in Act Three of *Orpheus* is probably the "difficult section" to which TW refers. In a draft fragment she alludes to the myth of Orpheus and charges Lady with Val's earthly corruption (n.d., HRC). The passage was replaced with an impersonal reference to the modern wasteland, "sick with neon."

Alice Astor Bouverie died on July 19, 1956. Her friend and frequent companion Paul Bigelow was not a legatee of the will.

Maria Britneva acquired a title and a classic Palladian house in Wiltshire when she married Peter St. Just on July 25, 1956.

Penned in the upper margin is TW's mailing address, "Amexco, Rome."]

336. To Audrey Wood

[51 Via Del Babuino] Rome.
8/25/56
[TLS, 1 p. HRC]

Dear Audrey:

I've been out of touch with the world these past ten days which I spent at Ravello and Positano on the sea. I came back to find Magnani in a stew. I gather from Frank that she wants me to give her a cut of the picture-sale money. It seems that she doesn't feel she is being adequately recompensed for her stage-appearance, that her expenses in New York will run higher than her pay. Frank says this is my fault because I let her know that you had worked out a very good contract for me with Wallis which gave me a hundred thousand more in tax-savings. Perhaps Frank understands Magnani better than I do, since they have the same sort of blood in their veins, but I cling romantically to the feeling that she just wants another demonstration of devotion to her, as right now, being in love with an Italian boy young enough to play her son on the screen, she must be a lonely woman. Of course I don't think I should have to pay Magnani, but I am willing to make some gesture of that sort if getting her on the stage depends on it. Sometimes I wonder if it would not have been better to use an American actress in the stage production and let Anna do just the film. Then again I think how thrilling she will be in some of the scenes, and feel, again, that all the hassle will justify itself in the end.

LATER.

- - - I've talked to you on phone since above paragraph and also had another meeting with Anna. I am still willing to give her a share of my profits on the screen-play, if that will make her satisfied. What I am much more concerned about is her willingness to adapt herself to our theatre system. She has to accept our casting and our director, and the script that she's given, and I think she should perform at least one matinee a week. Her chief concern about the director is whether or not he will give her "freedom to create in her own way". I have assured her that Clurman would do that, within all reasonable limits, that he is profoundly sympathetic to creativity in the people he works with. The main difficulty, here, is that in Italy the theatre is not regarded seriously. And it is the one thing that I do regard very seriously in my work. I think Jurow and Graziedei must make it very plain to her that she will have her creative freedom but that she must not trespass upon ours, author's, director's and producer's, which is for her protection as well as ours, as she would be working in a theatre system that she doesn't know. I am also concerned over her English. She has not been studying the language. She apparently expects to master it in the one or two months in New York before she goes into rehearsal. Especially if we are playing in a large house, like The Palace, it's essential that she deliver her lines with clarity and assurance.

I think I understand and I know that I love Anna, but I don't want to make this play, on which I have worked long and hard, just a show-piece for Magnani. Since the final revisions I have made this summer (some of which you've received) I am confident that it can stand on its own legs and though another actress would be a compromise, I feel that with very careful casting and a fine production, it could get the sort of notices and popular support that would insure a long run. To sacrifice the long run is an important concession which I have already made to her, much more important than giving up any sum of money to her. These things have to be made clear to Anna, by Jurow, through Graziedei since she is frighteningly inclined to concentrate on her own interests, result of working so long in the Italian film-industry where it's every man for himself, with a vengeance!

I think you might have a preliminary talk with Jurow about these matters and set up a conference with him for the evening of the day I get to New York or as soon thereafter as possible. With love

Tenn.

[A play script of *Orpheus* submitted to the Production Code staff by Hal Wallis drew criticism for "excessive emphasis upon sex" and the absence of a "'voice for morality'" (Shurlock to Wallis, July 30, 1956, Herrick). Audrey Wood was negotiating film rights with Wallis, although they would eventually be purchased by Martin Jurow and Richard Shepherd.]

337. To Anna Magnani

[51 Via Del Babuino, Rome]
August 26, 1956.
[TLS, 1 p. HTC]

Dearest Anna:

I will be going to see Ercole in about an hour but I would like to point out to you, directly and beforehand, my own side of the situation. I am not sure that you realize that I am also making a large financial sacrifice. I am limiting the Broadway run of what I truly believe is my most important play, on which I have written very long and very hard, over a period of many years, to a two-months run, as if I thought that its only value rested in the fact that it would be played by Anna Magnani. My established royalties are ten percent of the weekly box-office gross plus about ten percent of the profits of the play or even fifteen. This means that I am going to lose about two hundred and fifty thousand dollars if the play has the success that I believe it would have. Then I am also losing another hundred and fifty thousand on the picture sale, since a long-run success, such as "Cat on a Hot Tin Roof", has a picture sale of half a million dollars and a percentage, while I am taking for "Orpheus" only $350,000. plus percentage.

The idea of sharing my picture-profits with you is not very distressing or disturbing to me, as I am not so much interested in money right now. My great concern is whether or not you really and truly <u>want</u> to do the stage-play. Perhaps you would rather not. Perhaps you would rather confine yourself to the film, in which case the stage part could be taken by an American actress who would doubtless be inferior to you in the part but would play it for the usual run of a successful play and make it possible for us to have a profitable stage production, seen by a great many people, playing to large audiences for a long time, in New York and on the road.

I am mentioning this alternative possibility so that you will not feel that you are trapped or compelled to do something that you would rather avoid, because you may feel that the language barrier presents you with too great a risk on the stage. I cannot honestly attempt to minimize the fact that this particular risk does exist. At the present time, your English is certainly not adequate for a New York stage appearance and there is the question of whether or not you can make it ready in time for the start of the production this coming winter.

Needless to say, since you know how deeply I feel about this dream of ours, it would be a grave disappointment to see another actress create the part of Lady on the stage. My primary motive in writing this professional letter to you is so that you will not feel <u>obliged</u> to do something which you may regard as a great risk and sacrifice and feel reluctant to do it.

Meanwhile, my love as always, Tennessee.

[TW assumed that a two-month run of *Orpheus Descending* would be compatible with the proposed sale of film rights to Hal Wallis. He was later advised of the contractual terms which made such a brief engagement impossible, as he informed Anna Magnani (1908-1973). Ercole Graziadei, Magnani's agent, would attempt to maintain high salary terms for his client, which TW emphatically dismissed as a cause for his reluctance to cast Magnani on Broadway.]

338. To Edwina Dakin Williams

[323 East 58th Street, New York]
Sept. 24, 1956
[TLS, 1 p. Columbia U]

Dearest Mother:

It was a great shock to me to find a telegram saying you were in the hospital when I got back from visiting Rose in Hartford. However my phone conversations with Dr. Alexander and Dr. Gildea have been reassuring, as they say that you are only suffering from a nervous upset caused by worry and tension, and they feel that a short hospital rest is all that you need. I asked them if I should come to Saint Louis and they did not advise me to. However if you want me to come, I'll be glad to. I have had a very tiring summer myself and there has been a great deal of tension and strain connected with the preparations for a new play production this winter. I was planning, and had made arrangements, to fly down to the Virgin Islands and spend a couple of weeks resting completely on the beach, which is my kind of hospital. Of course I would give this up if you feel you need me in Saint Louis right now, but neither of the doctors thought that you had any serious or organic trouble and that you would be all right by the time I came back. I will arrange to come back through Saint Louis and by that time I'm sure you will be quite recovered: at least, so I gathered from the doctors' reports. Also I will be in a much better condition. I have been as nervous as a "cat on a hot tin roof" myself, lately. A writer's life is no bed of roses! And it [is] a bed of thorns when he is writing for the stage. As Amanda said in "Menagerie": "It calls for Spartan endurance".

I think that I straightened out things at Rose's hospital in Hartford. I was very unhappy over her appearance. She had on a shabby house-dress and a cheap cotton sweater that clashed with it in color and her hair looked greasy and was cut too short. I told them she must be encouraged to keep herself dressed nicely and must go to the beauty parlor twice a week, as I feel that pride in appearance is an excellent therapy, especially for women. The second time I saw her, (I went on Friday and again on Saturday) - she was dressed better and in better spirits. She does not complain about the staff at the Institute, she just says she would like to be back in Saint Louis and practise on the grand piano at home. I brought her a pretty little inexpensive wrist-watch, but they put it away for her. She <u>does</u> need one of her coats. All she seems to have now, is a short woolen jacket, and of course it is going to be quite chilly in Connecticutt in a short time now. She asked for her "Spring coat", but did not seem to want the fur one right now. She gave me a list of other things she wanted which I passed on to her doctor who said he would check on whether or not she actually needed them or just imagined she did. When I get back here I will pay her another visit, and will see her every two or three weeks while I am in the North this winter. If I am not satisfied with things there, I think we should try something else, but we ought to give the place a fair chance first.

Do take a good rest in the hospital. You can write me c/o Audrey and it will be forwarded to me at once. Her address is 598 Madison Ave., c/o MCA.

Much love, Tom.

[TW returned to New York in early-September and reportedly sublet an apartment on East 36th Street, where he worked apart from Frank Merlo.

TW informed Maria Britneva that his mother "had been put in a psychiatric ward, suffering from paranoia. She thought her colored maid was trying to poison her and the colored chauffeur to murder her, result of her disturbance over the anti-segregation violence in the South, and had not eaten for days and was in a state of hallucination" (qtd. in St. Just, p. 139).

For several months Rose Williams was an unhappy patient at the renowned Institute of Living in Hartford, Connecticut, apparently her fifth residence in as many years. She soon returned to Stony Lodge in Ossining, New York. A visit by Frank Merlo produced an "encouraging report," which TW conveyed to Edwina: Rose "looked lovely" and "talked completely normally" (n.d., HRC).]

339. To Kermit Bloomgarden

SH: The New Flamboyant Hotel
St. Thomas, Virgin Islands
September 28, 1956
[TLS, 1 p. SHS of Wisconsin]

Dear Kermit:

I am deeply touched by your wire, believe me. If I had known earlier that you wanted to produce a play for me perhaps we would have worked it out but now it's too late. It wasn't till the day before I left New York that I finally gave up the idea of producing with Audrey. Then I began to see that the emphasis was being put on things that were not my true concern, and we broke up the corporation. I asked Audrey and Clurman to offer the play to some good, experienced producer who could guarantee a house for us. As it was already so late, I think that the matter of booking a house took priority in their choice. Also my demand for immediate action. The Stevens-Whitehead group were immediately accessible and seemed to offer us the assurance of a house. I've had Roger Stevens as a producer before and the relationship was excellent. However I do sincerely hope that some time you and I can get together as I respect so highly your values in the theatre, your dedication to plays that have something to say of value in our time.

Again, many thanks, and all my best wishes,

Sincerely, Tennessee.

[Apparently the break-up of the Williams-Wood corporation left no public trace of hard feelings, nor is there any indication of the "things" which alarmed TW. Kermit Bloomgarden (1904-1976) advised TW that his name "will get a theatre faster than Bloomgarden, or Stevens or Whitehead. Don't let it interfere with your choice again" (October 15, 1956, SHS of Wisconsin). Robert Whitehead and Roger L. Stevens, associates of the Producers Theatre, formally agreed in early-October to stage *Orpheus Descending*.]

340. To the Editors of Time

[The New Flamboyant Hotel
St. Thomas, Virgin Islands]
September 28, 1956
[TLS, 1 p. *Time* Inc. Archives]

Dear Sirs:

Much as I am flattered by your reference to me, in the book section, as "the high priest" of something, even something called "Merde", I must put in my two cents worth of protest. I feel that scatology is notably absent from my work. However if I did make references of that nature, I would not exercise the subterfuge of a foreign word for it.

The gentleman quoted, Dean Fitch, may have gone to "Cat On A Hot Tin Roof" but he went to it with a pair of tin ears and came out of it with a tin horn to blow. "Cat" is the most highly, intensely moral work that I have produced, and that is what gives it power. It is an out-cry of fury, from start to finish, against those falsities in life that provide a good fertilizer for corruption. What it says, in essence, through the character of Big Daddy, is this: when your time comes to die, do you want to die in a hot-bed of lies or on a cold stone of truth?

Mr. Fitch takes dangerous exception to "honesty". Is that, now, to be put down as a dirty word like the word "intellectual"? If so, then all American artists must beware. We are in for a revival of cultural Fascism. Of course there are such things as false "intellectuals" and false "honesty", but the damage to us all that may derive from attaching odium to these words by slick sophistries about them, such as purveyed by Dean Fitch, talking about "stars over the dump heap" in feeble paraphrase of Oscar Wilde, is much more important than the virtue of pointing out their occasional misappropriations.

I propose that writers concerned with honesty are more likely to be honest than those who are <u>not</u> concerned with it, and I would like to see a list of those works that Dean Fitch approves along with those he condemns, it would be more fully instructive.

Sincerely, Tennessee Williams

[Robert Elliot Fitch, dean of the Pacific School of Religion (Berkeley, California), claimed that a "'cult'" of talented contemporary writers was intent upon deifying "'dirt.'" Hemingway, O'Neill, Norman Mailer, and James Jones were "merde mystics," whose "special ethic of honesty" was designed to replace Christian values with a debased secular morality. TW, current "high priest of the cult," epitomized the "*mystique* of obscenity," especially in *Cat*, whose "final merit" was "'to describe the town dump so that we smell the garbage'" ("Mystique de la Merde," *Time*, October 1, 1956).

Printed in *Time* (October 22, 1956, pp. 11-12) was a heavily edited version of TW's original letter, the last two paragraphs cut entirely.]

341. To Cheryl Crawford

SH: The New Flamboyant Hotel
St. Thomas, Virgin Islands
[early-October 1956]
[TLS, 2 pp. BRTC]

Dear Cheryl:

You shouldn't have listened to anything I said, at least not with such a critical ear, after that nightmare trip to Hartford. I was outraged by the world and the human situation and myself, myself mostly, and anybody that was mentioned, Terry or Jesus Christ or anybody, would have seemed monstrous to me. I have no real hard feelings against Terry. It makes me smile now to remember calling her "A BEAST OF THE APOCALYPSE!" As a matter of fact, Terry has always seemed oddly likable to me despite the fact that she's even more selfish than I am and even less able to be helpfully engaged in other's concerns. But of course I know her very little. I don't know why I should [have] harked back to an incident of sixteen years ago and something she blurted out to cover up her embarassment and the sense of shame that she couldn't admit herself without feeling obliged to do something for someone in whom she was disappointed and whose catastrophe she wasn't able or willing to cope with.

I was also very angry at you because you said such a cruel thing about my ravaged sister, that she was "just a body". It doesn't jive, that remark, with the sentimental side of your nature. She isn't any more just a body than you and I are, and if you looked at her, at her tortured face and observed her desperate effort to meet the terrible moment of facing the person she loved most as a girl, and to whom she was closest, and knew that she was a lunatic being visited by him in a bug-house, a plush-lined snake-pit, I don't see how you could call her just a body. Madness doesn't mean the cease of personality, it simply means that the personality has lost touch with what we call reality, and I think, myself, that their mental and emotional world is much more vivid than ours is.

I regret that instant of anger which simply struck out, conveniently, at your friend Terry. We're all inclined to project our own guilt into others, and strike at them in order to spare ourselves.

It's lovely here, lonely, but very therapeutic. I'm stretching out the stay as long as I can.

About Orpheus: Don't you remember telling me that it would only impress you as the work of an unproduced young playwright, a work of promise but not a play for production? I showed it to you first.

I think the best thing Bigelow's friends can do for him is to draw him back into the theatre where he seemed to be at home and to function with real creative interest. He's had too much dependance on people for someone with his basic strength of character and originality of mind. And they've all let him down. Alice's failure to put him in her will is a shocking thing, but it jives with my observations of the very rich ones. Bigelow has had that jaw condition since 1941, he has learned to live with it, and since he's had it and lived with it that long, I don't think there's any imminent gravity about it, and that the minor operation will probably relieve or remove the pain, and he must pick up his life as it was before the rupture with Jordan and the affair with Alice. I hope that Boris will need him, as he did in "Tattoo", to assist in the setting, if that will be a temporary assistance to Paul, and I always feel that his connection with a production is enormously valuable.

I'm working again on "Sweet Bird of Youth" and the work's going better with the improvement in physical condition.

See you sometime this month. My love to Ruth, and to you.

Tenn.

[The "incident" to which TW refers followed the disastrous premiere of *Battle of Angels* in 1940. Terry Helburn, co-director of the Theatre Guild, consoled the crest-fallen playwright with an unforgettable line: "'Well, at least you're not out of pocket'" (qtd. in Leverich, p. 395).

Boris Aronson—rather than Jo Mielziner, who was strongly drawn to the project—designed the set for *Orpheus Descending*. There is no indication that Paul Bigelow served as a production assistant.]

Boris Aronson, full set design for Orpheus Descending *(1957)*

342. To Anna Magnani

[*The* Towers, Miami]
[ca. early-October 1956]
[TLS, 2 pp. HTC]

Dearest Anna:

Here is what has happened. When I arrived in New York I received the first complete and clear picture of the proposed deal with Wallis. It contained a clause of which I had no knowledge before, namely, that the $125,000. production would be paid out of my money for the film and would be about half of it. This total amount could be lost if, for some reason, the play either closed out of town, before coming into New York, or if it received bad notices and failed in New York. If we were coming into New York for a reasonable run, say a run of six months, it might be worth the gamble, but coming in for only two months it is the sort of wild speculation which I am not in a position to make. You know that I am taxed 87 or 90 percent of my earnings each year so that I have not been able to accumulate much money for a very uncertain future which also involves the care of my sister ($800. a month), a spinster Aunt, partial support of my mother, Frank, and the maintenance, off and on, of the present Lady St. Just who has been deserted by her new husband with a five pound note.

All of my advisors, here, think that the idea of doing "Orpheus" for two months on Broadway is fantastic. They think it would be a great injustice to the play, in which they all believe strongly, and feel that it would [be] a slap in the face of the American theatre which has conferred on me its highest awards. They also feel that it creates a bad impression for you. Also it would be necessary to put the play in a theatre much too large for it, a huge barn of a theatre, the Palace on Broadway or the Globe. The whole production would have the atmosphere of a stunt, it would antagonize the press and create hostility throughout the American theatre.

Now I know that you would make every effort to bring the play into New York, once you'd started upon it, but many unforeseen things might come up. For instance, I am not sure that you know what it is like to try out a new play on the road. Almost every evening changes are made in the script, new speeches are put in, old speeches are cut out. I must tell you, with all love and honesty in my heart, that I am not of the opinion that your command of the English language is adequate to this sort of thing. It would drive you crazy, it might make you collapse. Because I could not possibly sacrifice my play by failing to make those adjustments which are always necessary in the preparation of a new play for a Broadway opening.

Of course the terms demanded for you are extremely high, but please believe me when I say to you that it is not my unwillingness to meet your salary terms that have brought me to the conclusion that either we must persuade you to play for six months on Broadway, or release you from this "act of homage" to me which would certainly be an almost unbearable strain upon your nerves, emotions, and physical power. I doubt that you will feel yourself able to play for six months. That being the case, wouldn't it be better, dear Anna, for you to just come to make the picture? The picture will not be given to any other actress you can count on that. Then after you've made the picture and become very familiar with the part and mastered the English language, then you could have a short, triumphant run in the play on Broadway, perhaps at the City Center. I think this could be worked out.

You know my plays usually run, if successful for a year and a half or two years. I receive over a thousand dollars a week, on the average, over this period. Eighty-seven or ninety percent of this goes to the government but I have deductible expenses and am able to live well and travel and meet my sentimental and moral obligations to others while a successful play is running. Therefore I would be suffering an enormous loss by putting on a play for such a short period that it would be unlikely even to recover the initial cost of the production, not to mention the loss of my share of its profits and the loss of half its film-sale value through the necessity of having to finance it by borrowing from a film studio with a pre-production deal which is unfavorable to me.

Audrey will write you about this matter more knowingly than I can, and I'm sure you will also hear from Jurow. But please do let me hear from you as soon as possible, whether or not you feel able to play on Broadway long enough to do the play justice and to spare me a financial loss which I am not able to bear.

All my love as ever, Tennessee

Still haven't mailed this letter because I wasn't sure, yet, that I had said to you precisely what was most important to say. I think you will believe me when I say that money doesn't come first but that what I am committed to, first, is the service of the theatre. I could give the theatre an exciting starring vehicle with you in the role of Lady but the play itself would be bound to suffer through something as simple as your difficulty with the English language. I will have to make continual changes in the script of this play all through its month of try-outs before coming into New York. You know, as well as I know, that it would be impossible for you to change speeches nightly. Probably no one could play this part better than you, even with perfect command of English, but the play itself would have to be denied the fluid, quick-changing, condition which is necessary to bring it into New York successfully. You would make a desperate effort to cope with this necessity. It would exhaust you. It would almost kill you. I don't think it is the right time to ask you to go through such an ordeal which might, after all, turn out to be a failure, damaging to your prestige.

[A partial draft, typed on stationery of the Towers in Miami, refers to the "long letter" (n.d., HTC) printed above. It was probably written in Miami in early-October 1956 after TW returned from a lonely trip to St. Thomas. Precisely when Anna Magnani and Marlon Brando withdrew from the *Orpheus* production is unclear, but the roles were assumed on Broadway by Maureen Stapleton and Cliff Robertson. Magnani and Brando appeared in the film version *The Fugitive Kind* (1959).]

343. To Harold Clurman and Robert Whitehead

[323 East 58th Street, New York]
[ca. late-October 1956]
[TLS, 1 p. HTC]

Dear Harold & Bob:

Before we get into this thing too deep, I think we ought to face and cope with, or decide not to cope with, certain conditions of this play production. To begin with, I have lived with this play and these characters for sixteen years, with great concentration and love, and you have made a recent acquaintance with them. By the time this production has opened, if it does open, you may know them as well or better than I do, but at the present moment my familiarity with them and understanding of them is much, much greater than yours. You will find me absolutely adamant in casting the parts. I will demand to have precisely the actor that I think most suitable for each part because I respect the work, despite all its fault, I respect it as much as any play I have written and I am determined, for your sake as well as mine, to give it the protection of my so much longer and deeper understanding of it than yours. Yesterday, I felt sort of isolated, as if I stood in one corner, and you two in another. This sort of situation predicates the possibility of a play-production full of contention and dissention and so forth, with the author an embattled minority faced by a pair who see eye to eye but not as clearly as he naturally sees it. However I can't stand the strain of such a situation. You noticed that I drank more than usual yesterday and it was because I suddenly felt that I was being backed into a corner as a minority of one. I respect the function of a producer but I feel that before he undertakes to produce a play he must accept the author's conception of the important characters and meaning of the play as a whole and not seek to adjust them to his own personal point-of-view, which is too recent to be penetrating. That doesn't mean that he shouldn't express his point-of-view or that it might not prove valuable. What it means, primarily, is that he SHOULD express it. Emphatically and clearly as possible to director and author so that the disparities among the different points-of-view can be aired and settled in the very beginning, before a destructive opposition develops. But it must be understood that <u>my</u> conception prevails. Not that it is fixed and frozen, but that it must necessarily be adhered to ----- I think it's imperative that the three of us, and Audrey, have a conference before we go any further in which there must be a totally candid comparison of our possibly variant points-of-view about the play's characters and meaning, and I think this should occur before we continue the readings on Monday. I am sending this special delivery to the office. I don't have any carbon paper on hand so I am mailing this one copy to Bob. We can begin by reading it - this letter - aloud and go on from there. Among the things I want to discuss is my very strong feeling that $75,000. is much too modest a capital investment in a play of this kind, which simply must be supported by the highest production values. No compromises! I don't approve of any unnecessary expenditures but I think that stinting on this production indicates a lack of faith in it, and we can't start on that premise with any safety. I don't myself see how it could be capitalized at less than a hundred grand with a twenty percent over-call. I notice in <u>Variety</u> that "Light A Penny Candle" is capitalized at $85,000. with the same over-call of twenty percent and I cannot accept the idea that this play can get by with less. We have a large cast and I want a truly shining production. . . . or <u>none</u>!

Sincerely, Tennessee.

[Harold Clurman (1901-1980), principal founder of the Group Theatre (1931-1941), and Robert Whitehead (1916-2002), former director of ANTA, brought exceptional taste and experience to the production of *Orpheus Descending*. TW's defensiveness was doubtless inspired by the bittersweet experience of *Cat*.

Earlier in the fall TW opposed the casting of Cliff Robertson as Val Xavier. Audrey Wood instructed her client to listen to her "with both ears" (telegram, October 3, 1956, HRC) and rethink his position. Robertson replaced Robert Loggia during the Philadelphia tryout and opened on Broadway.

TW drafted an "Imaginary Interview" in which he stated the "theme" of *Orpheus Descending*: "More tolerance and respect for the wild and lyric impulses that the human heart feels and so often is forced to repress, in order to avoid social censure and worse" (n.d., HTC). Precisely how the director and producer had violated this conception is unclear. Maureen Stapleton, who played Lady, has stated that rehearsals were tense and that use of the prologue (finally removed) caused sharp disagreement (see Spoto, p. 212).

TW briefly visited St. Louis and returned to New York in mid-October with Edwina. The closing reference to an article in *Variety*, dated October 24, 1956, suggests that he wrote to Clurman and Whitehead toward the end of the month.]

344. To Cheryl Crawford

[1431 Duncan Street
Key West, Florida]
December '56
[TLS, 2 pp. U of Houston]

Dearest Cheryl:

A note in Winchell's column a few days ago said that "Girls of Summer" had risen from 16 grand to 28 grand in one week, and I do hope this is an accurate report, for it pained me to find such a depressed note in a letter from someone who, to me at least, if not to us all, is synonomous with "semper invictus" as it applies to the spirit.

I find it dismaying as you do that you have this run of bad luck. But that's how it goes, rough as a cob sometimes, and sometimes smooth as silk. I have had a remarkably good time lately, feeling well and relaxed (for me!), and with a renewal of energy which made it possible for me to complete rough sketches of two plays in a few weeks time, but now I'm exhausted again, the spurt of energy has subsided. Tonight my stomach is swollen up like a basketball and hot as fire. I can't even take a drink. I am not at all sure it is not the presence of mother. Mom is here. She could not stay in Saint Louis. She said 'That outfit would put her back in the bug-house', so she descended to Florida. I don't know why she affects me like this, but I feel that everything she says and everything she looks is an implied criticism. Guilt, I suppose. I love her and feel sorry for her, but she drives me somewhat crazy.

Poor Miss Brinda is in heat. We took her to the Vet this afternoon and the vet said he had never seen a worse specimen of any breed of a dog than she is and he would not recommend the perpetuation of her line by breeding her. Funny, but I think she's the most charming animal I've ever known. Maybe because both of us are equally wall-eyed, and would be equally bad bets for perpetuation of our lines.

Ivan Oblolensky (no less!) called me long-distance from New York a few days ago about Paul. They want to go ahead with the operation right away and Ivan wanted me to go fifty-fifty on the cost of it which is $1500. I asked him: "Didn't your mother leave Paul any money?" Answer: "Unfortunately not." - Me: — "What a pity. . ." - Then I assured him that I would guarantee a fifty percent of the cost but that with two members of my family very expensively not well, I did hope he could raise the money through other channels, but that if he didn't, I would certainly under-write the project. Paul says a wonderful thing about rich people, the very rich ones: "They have a phenomenal faith in the efficacy of small sums!"

Anyway, it is good to do something for such a rare person as Paul even if you can't, at the moment, afford to.

For your own sake, honey, I am glad you are not doing "Orpheus". I think it is a beautiful and true play that says something very clearly but I don't think many people are going to like what it says. I was frightened by Brooks write-up of "Menagerie". He indicated that he thought I had become harsh and cruel, since then, and this may mean that I will lose my only consistently good critic, the next time around. You must not do anything risky, the next time, and "Orpheus" is a big risk.

We will have to break camp soon, but we will be coming back in the Spring. It would be nice if you and Ruth could visit us then and of course you could use the house anytime we are away. It's a sweet little place and the air and the sky and the water are the best I have found in the States with the possible exception of Taos, but that doesn't have the water.

Will be seeing you soon.

Love, 10.

[Cheryl Crawford's run of "bad luck" included *The Honeys* (1955), *Mister Johnson* (1956), and *Girls of Summer* (1956), none of which reached sixty performances on Broadway.

Miss Brinda was the ungainly successor of Signor Buffo, who died from heat exhaustion.

The publisher-financier Ivan Obolensky is the son of Alice Astor and her first husband, Prince Serge Obolensky. Her large estate was whittled down by debt, taxes, and legal fees, leaving fewer than two million dollars for the legatees.

A City Center revival of *The Glass Menagerie* (November 21, 1956)—starring Helen Hayes, formerly a reluctant Amanda—led Brooks Atkinson to contrast this "delicate and moving" early work with TW's later plays: "There is a streak of savagery in his work now. The humor is bitter. The ugliness is shocking" (*New York Times*, November 22, 1956).

TW broke "camp" in Key West to attend the New York premiere of *Baby Doll* on December 18, 1956. The film was condemned by the Roman Catholic Legion of Decency and denounced from the pulpit by Francis Cardinal Spellman, who forbade the faithful to see it under pain of sin. *Time* magazine declared *Baby Doll* "just possibly the dirtiest American-made motion picture that has ever been legally exhibited" (December 27, 1956).

Spending Christmas with Rose—"quite pretty again"—reassured TW that her "sweetness, patience, and poise" had survived the "snake-pits." She remains, he wrote to Maria St. Just, "an unmistakable lady" (qtd. in St. Just, p. 141).]

345. To Edwina and Walter Dakin Williams

[323 East 58th Street, New York]
[February 1957]
[TLS, 2 pp. HTC]

Dear Mother and Dakin:

The Chicago production of "Orpheus" has been called off due to "an act of God". The tent collapses in a cloud-burst, slightly injuring 43 people. I'm sorry about the casualties but somewhat relieved that we don't have to open the play in a tent in Chicago, and so are the actors. Since I won't be going to Chicago, Mother perhaps you would like to visit New York. We could drive out to see Rose. I visited her last Sunday and was distressed by the fact that she has lost so much weight, eighteen pounds, and was refusing to wear her new teeth. She claims they upset her stomach. Also she had been picking at her face again and made a sore on her forehead. The head doctor, Dr. Bernard, feels it may be necessary to give her a few mild shock treatments to bring her out of this present phase of disturbance. At the advice of my analyst, I got in touch with a specialist in Lobotomy cases who will go out and take a look at her before a decision is reached about the shock treatments. She was doing quite well at Stony Lodge till lately. I guess we have to expect these recurrent lapses, and I feel she is in the best possible hands. However she is still longing for St. Louis and after she gets through this present disturbed condition, we might discuss the question of transferring her to the place Dakin mentioned near his air-base so that he could keep an eye on her and she could have an occasional visit at home. Aside from the lost weight, she seemed physically well and did not complain of anything. We took her in town and she bought twelve bars of soap, although I had seen about twice that many in her room at the Lodge. SHE had laid them out on the window sill, each on its own little nest of tissue paper like a bunch of holy candles. She also wanted a box of candy. She consulted the "Doctor in her ears" about which box to select and he advised her to pick out the biggest. It seems that milk and candy are the only things she wants to eat right now, but they are giving her vitamin injections to keep up her strength.

I will let you know what the specialist decides in the next few days.

Anna Magnani is here in New York and Audrey is negotiating with Hal Wallis who wants to buy "Orpheus" for her. Sam Spiegel, producer of "Waterfront" is also bidding for it as a vehicle for Ingrid Bergmann, so with interest from two competitive quarters, we may realize a good movie sale after all.

Love, Tom

[Reviews of *Orpheus Descending* in Washington (February 21-March 2) and Philadelphia (March 5-16) were mixed and business only fair. The *Variety* reviewer considered *Orpheus* a potential hit but stressed both the "reminiscent" nature of the play—"a murky tale of inbred, hard-eyed people in a Mississippi village"—and its structural limitations. A more negative critic in Washington described TW as his "own prisoner" and concluded that *Orpheus* is "murky, ineffective and sometimes tasteless" (*Washington Post and Times Herald*, February 22, 1957). The Philadelphia notices were stronger on the whole, but the play was viewed unfavorably in relation to TW's earlier hits and the box office remained fairly soft.]

346. To Justin Brooks Atkinson

[323 East 58th Street, New York]
3/24/57
[TLS, 1 p. BRTC]

Dear Brooks:

I believe I've always written you a letter of thanks for an appreciative review after openings of my plays and I see no reason to discontinue the practise on this occasion even though the appreciation, on this occasion, was more qualified than usual. It seems to me that several of the critics failed to regard the play in its true light, as a dramatic poem. I remember when I went to Copenhagen when "Rose Tattoo" opened there, the leading drama critic remarked to me, 'This isn't a play, it's a poem.' I think the same remark holds true of 'Orpheus Descending' but it was apparently regarded as a melodrama, and naturally I don't know for sure if I am right or the critics are right. But I do know that critics are more objective about a playwright's work, as a rule, than he is. Anyway I would love to see you again, after all this time, and have a frank talk with you. I've always felt a silly embarassment about having social contact with theatre critics because I feared it might seem like an attempt to disarm them in their attitude toward my work. But I've reached a certain stop, or point of departure, in my professional life, now, and I think it would help to discuss things with you, if you are not disinclined. I want to present my side of the argument that seems to have come up between us. And I want, even more, to hear yours expressed with a more private frankness, and I think I can take it. After the past few weeks, I think I can take anything at all. And since I know that you do care seriously about my work, I think you might also welcome the occasion to take the kid gloves off and put the verbal boxing gloves on with me. I think it would help me. So will you call me, anytime early this week? I'm at my typewriter for about three hours every day, from about ten to one P.M. with a phone by me, so unless you feel that I am past all redemption, please do call me.

Ever affectionately yours, Tenn.

Phone number: Plaza 5-9741

[Praise for *Orpheus Descending* was tepid at best and forecast an unsuccessful run on Broadway (March 21-May 18, 1957). Occasional "streaks" of poetry failed to compensate for a dramatic structure that was "loosely woven," unsure in its "progressions," and "not soundly motivated," as Atkinson observed. He did not find "savagery" in the work, as TW feared, but oddly thought *Orpheus* one of TW's "pleasantest plays" (*New York Times*, March 22, 1957). Walter Kerr found "essential artifice" rather than unsureness at the core of the work and concluded that its "passions" were mere "excuses for handsome big scenes" (*New York Herald Tribune*, March 22, 1957). Maureen Stapleton and Cliff Robertson gave strong performances, but attendance steadily declined and the show closed after sixty-eight performances, some $65,000 in the red.]

347. To Elia "Gadg" Kazan:

SH: *The* Towers
Miami, Florida
April 3, 1957.
[TLS, 2 pp. WUCA]

Dear Gadg:

Frank read me your letter over the phone and I am truly grateful for your frankness about the play. I have had to absorb a great deal of very frank criticism of my work on this time around, and I can't see that it has done me any harm. I feel a little bit better than usual, as a matter of fact. Of course it could be the "anesthesia of shock". But I have been living for years with an always partially and sometimes completely "blocked" talent, which was only quite free in "Streetcar" and for the very special reason that I thought I was dying, and that thought eclipsed the anxiety which had always blocked my talent. Of course I was ten years younger, then, too. We know what youth is, don't we? However I came back with "Cat" and it could happen again. I still hope that it will. I know that of all the people I've known and worked with, you are probably the one that most shares that hope with me. When Budd Schulberg said to me, opening night of "Orpheus", at intermission in a bar, that you were hurt because I hadn't invited you to the opening, I said, That's impossible. He knows me too well. He knows me better than anyone in the world. - I meant that. I think you do. I think we know each other, despite the huge differences in our natures, so well that we can't hurt each other. Maybe the correspondances in our natures are bigger than the differences, after all. We are both obsessed by the same thing. Work. Saying. Speaking out our hearts, and though we both bear in our different ways a great burden of guilt, I believe we have atoned for most of it in our devotion to honest creative work.

Am I wrong in thinking that if you had directed "Orpheus" it would have been one of our great successes? I don't think so. I think your appreciation of its basic truth would have inspired me to lift it above its theatricalism, such as the boy entering on the dead cue of the Choctaw cry, and you could have made the "prologue speech" work so that the story could have risen out of an eloquent premise. You could have staged the ending so it would play and score. You would have found the "key" in which the play is written, not just intellectually but with an artist's and poet's vision, and gotten a stunning performance from Maureen all the way through.

Here is my program: have a complete change this summer, go to Japan and Hong Kong and so forth. In the Fall, take up residence again in New Orleans, and start analysis there if I still feel I need it and there is a good analyst there. Try to kick the liquor habit or cut down on it. I'm not an alcoholic, I almost never get drunk, but I do drink too much and my working hours in the morning are affected by resulting hang-overs and depression. Cultivate a cooler, more objective attitude toward my work, and recapture some of my earlier warmth and openness in relation to people, which began to go when I began to be famous.

Love, Tenn.

INDEX OF RECIPIENTS

Letters are cited by reference number in the Index of Recipients.

GENERAL INDEX

WORKS INDEX